Alternative Investments and Fixed Income

CFA® PROGRAM CURRICULUM • VOLUME 5

LEVEL II
2012

PEARSON

Cover photograph courtesy of Hector Emanuel.

2 3 4 5 6 7 8 9 10 V313 16 15 14 13 12 11

000200010270652637

AG/JW

Please visit our website at *www.pearsoned.com*

ISBN 10: 0-558-92511-1
ISBN 13: 978-0-558-92511-6

CONTENTS

⊗ indicates an optional segment

READING 46

indicates an optional segment

$4\frac{5}{8}$ $4\frac{11}{16}$ $-\frac{3}{8}$

$5\frac{1}{2}$ $5\frac{1}{2}$ $-\frac{3}{8}$

$5\frac{1}{2}$ $20\frac{5}{8}$ $21\frac{3}{16}$ $-\frac{1}{4}$

$17\frac{3}{8}$ $18\frac{1}{8}$ $+\frac{7}{8}$

$13\frac{1}{2}$ $6\frac{1}{2}$ $6\frac{1}{2}$ $-\frac{1}{2}$

$7\frac{1}{4}$ $\frac{15}{16}$ $\frac{31}{32}$ $-\frac{1}{8}$

$\frac{9}{16}$ $\frac{9}{8}$

$1\frac{9}{32}$ $7\frac{13}{16}$ $7\frac{15}{8}$

$7\frac{5}{16}$ $2\frac{11}{32}$ $2\frac{1}{2}$ $+$

$2\frac{5}{8}$ $2\frac{1}{4}$ $2\frac{1}{4}$

$2\frac{3}{4}$ $2\frac{1}{4}$ $1\frac{3}{8}$ $+$

$12\frac{1}{16}$ $11\frac{3}{8}$ $11\frac{3}{4}$ $+$

$33\frac{3}{4}$ 33 $33\frac{1}{16}$ $-$

$25\frac{5}{8}$ $24\frac{9}{16}$ $25\frac{3}{8}$ $+$

12 $11\frac{5}{8}$ $11\frac{7}{8}$ $+$

16 $10\frac{1}{2}$ $10\frac{1}{2}$ $10\frac{1}{2}$

$15\frac{7}{8}$ $15\frac{13}{16}$ $15\frac{7}{8}$ $-$

$9\frac{1}{16}$ $8\frac{1}{4}$ $8\frac{7}{8}$ $+$

$11\frac{1}{4}$ $10\frac{3}{8}$

HOW TO USE THE CFA PROGRAM CURRICULUM

Congratulations on passing Level I of the Chartered Financial Analyst (CFA®) Program. This exciting and rewarding program of study reflects your desire to become a serious investment professional. You are embarking on a program noted for its high ethical standards and the breadth of knowledge, skills, and abilities it develops. Your commitment to the CFA Program should be educationally and professionally rewarding.

The credential you seek is respected around the world as a mark of accomplishment and dedication. Each level of the program represents a distinct achievement in professional development. Successful completion of the program is rewarded with membership in a prestigious global community of investment professionals. CFA charterholders are dedicated to life-long learning and maintaining currency with the ever-changing dynamics of a challenging profession. The CFA Program represents the first step towards a career-long commitment to professional education.

The CFA examination measures your degree of mastery of the assigned CFA Program curriculum. Therefore, the key to your success on the examination is to master the Candidate Body of Knowledge (CBOK™), which can be accomplished by reading and studying the CFA Program curriculum. The CBOK contains the core knowledge, skills, and abilities (competencies) that are generally accepted and applied by investment professionals. These competencies are used in practice in a generalist context and are expected to be demonstrated by a recently qualified CFA charterholder. The remaining sections provide background on the CBOK, the organization of the curriculum, and tips for developing an effective study program.

Curriculum Development

The CFA Program curriculum is grounded in the practice of the investment profession. Utilizing the Global Body of Investment Knowledge (GBIK) collaborative website, CFA Institute performs a continuous practice analysis with investment professionals around the world to determine the knowledge, skills, and abilities that are relevant to the profession. Regional expert panels and targeted surveys are conducted annually to verify and reinforce the continuous feedback from the GBIK collaborative website. The practice analysis process ultimately defines the CBOK. The CBOK consists of four components:

▶ A broad topic outline that lists the major top-level topic areas (CBOK Topic Outline)

▶ Topic area weights that indicate the relative exam weightings of the top-level topic areas

▶ Learning Outcome Statements (LOS) that advise candidates about the specific knowledge, skills, and abilities they should acquire from readings covering a topic area (LOS are provided in online study sessions and at the beginning of each reading)

▶ The curriculum of material (readings and end-of-reading questions) that candidates receive upon exam registration and are expected to master

A committee consisting of practicing charterholders, in conjunction with CFA Institute staff, designs the CFA Program curriculum to deliver the CBOK to candidates. The examinations, also written by practicing charterholders, are designed to allow you to demonstrate your mastery of the CBOK as set forth in the CFA Program curriculum. As you structure your personal study program, you should emphasize mastery of the CBOK and the practical application of that knowledge. For more information on the practice analysis, CBOK, and development of the CFA Program curriculum, please visit www.cfainstitute.org.

Organization of the Curriculum

The Level II CFA Program curriculum is organized into 10 topic areas. Each topic area begins with a brief statement of the material and the depth of knowledge expected.

Each topic area is then divided into one or more study sessions. These study sessions—18 sessions in the Level II curriculum—should form the basic structure of your reading and preparation.

Each study session includes a statement of its structure and objective, and is further divided into specific reading assignments. The outline on the inside front cover of each volume illustrates the organization of these 18 study sessions.

The reading assignments are the basis for all examination questions, and are selected or developed specifically to teach the knowledge, skills, and abilities reflected in the CBOK. These readings are drawn from CFA Program-commissioned content, textbook chapters, professional journal articles, research analyst reports, and cases. All readings include problems and solutions as well as appendices to help you understand and master the topic areas.

Reading-specific Learning Outcome Statements (LOS) are listed at the beginning of each reading. These LOS indicate what you should be able to accomplish after studying the reading. The LOS, the reading, and the end-of-reading questions are dependent on each other, with the reading and questions providing context for understanding the scope of the LOS.

You should use the LOS to guide and focus your study, as each examination question is based on an assigned reading and one or more LOS. The readings provide context for the LOS and enable you to apply a principle or concept in a variety of scenarios. The candidate is responsible for the entirety of all of the required material in a study session, the assigned readings as well as the end-of-reading questions and problems.

We encourage you to review the material on LOS, including the descriptions of LOS "command words," at www.cfainstitute.org.

Features of the Curriculum

▶ **Required vs. Optional Segments** - You should read all of an assigned reading. In some cases, however, we have reprinted an entire chapter or article and marked certain parts as "optional." The CFA examination is based only on the required segments, and the optional segments are included only when they might help you to better understand the required segments (by seeing the required material in its full context). When an optional segment begins, you will see an icon and a solid vertical bar in the outside margin that will continue until the optional segment ends, accompanied by another icon. *Unless the material is specifically marked as optional, you should assume it is required.* You should rely on the required segments and the reading-specific LOS in preparing for the examination.

▶ **Problems/Solutions** - *All questions and problems in the readings as well as their solutions (which are provided directly following the problems) are part of the curriculum and required material for the exam.* When appropriate, we have included problems within and after the readings to demonstrate practical application and reinforce your understanding of the concepts presented.

The questions and problems are designed to help you learn these concepts and may serve as a basis for exam questions. Many of these questions are adapted from past CFA examinations.

▶ **Margins** - The wide margins in each volume provide space for your note-taking.

▶ **Six-volume Structure** - For portability of the curriculum, the material is spread over six volumes.

▶ **Glossary and Index** - For your convenience, we have printed a comprehensive glossary and volume-specific index in each volume. Throughout the curriculum, a **bolded blue** word in a reading denotes a term defined in the glossary.

▶ **Source Material** - The authorship, publisher, and copyright owners are given for each reading for your reference. We recommend that you use this CFA Institute curriculum rather than the original source materials because the curriculum may include only selected pages from outside readings, updated sections within the readings, and contains problems and solutions tailored to the CFA Program.

▶ **LOS Self-check** - We have inserted checkboxes next to each LOS that you can use to track your progress in mastering the concepts in each reading.

Designing Your Personal Study Program

Create a Schedule - An orderly, systematic approach to examination preparation is critical. You should dedicate a consistent block of time every week to reading and studying. Complete all reading assignments and the associated problems and solutions in each study session. Review the LOS both before and after you study each reading to ensure that you have mastered the applicable content and can demonstrate the knowledge, skill, or ability described by the LOS and the assigned reading. Use the LOS self-check to track your progress and highlight areas of weakness for later review.

You will receive periodic e-mail communications that contain important study tips and preparation strategies. Be sure to read these carefully. Curriculum errata are periodically updated and posted on the study session page at www.cfainstitute.org. You may also sign up for an RSS feed to alert you to the latest errata update.

Successful candidates report an average of 300 hours preparing for each exam. Your preparation time will vary based on your prior education and experience. For each level of the curriculum, there are 18 study sessions, so a good plan is to devote 15–20 hours per week, for 18 weeks, to studying the material. Use the final four to six weeks before the exam to review what you've learned and practice with sample and mock exams. This recommendation, however, may substantially underestimate the hours needed for appropriate examination preparation depending on your individual circumstances, relevant experience, and academic background. You will undoubtedly adjust your study time to conform to your own strengths and weaknesses, and your educational and professional background.

You will probably spend more time on some study sessions than on others, but on average you should plan on devoting 15 hours per study session. You should allow ample time for both in-depth study of all topic areas and additional concentration on those topic areas for which you feel least prepared.

Online Sample Examinations - CFA Institute online sample examinations are intended to assess your exam preparation as you progress toward the end of your study. After each question, you will receive immediate feedback noting the correct response and indicating the relevant assigned reading, so you'll be able to identify areas of weakness for further study. The 120-minute sample examinations reflect the question formats, topics, and level of difficulty of the actual CFA examinations. Aggregate data indicate that the CFA examination pass rate was higher among candidates who took one or more online sample examinations than among candidates who did not take the online sample examinations. For more information on the online sample examinations, please visit www.cfainstitute.org.

Online Mock Examinations - In response to candidate requests, CFA Institute has developed mock examinations that mimic the actual CFA examinations not only in question format and level of difficulty, but also in length. The three-hour online mock exams simulate the morning and afternoon sessions of the actual CFA exam, and are intended to be taken after you complete your study of the full curriculum, so you can test your understanding of the CBOK and your readiness for the exam. To further differentiate, the mock exams are available in a printable PDF format with feedback provided at the end of the exam, rather than after each question as with the sample exams. CFA Institute recommends that you take these mock exams at the final stage of your preparation toward the actual CFA examination. For more information on the online mock examinations, please visit www.cfainstitute.org.

Preparatory Providers - After you enroll in the CFA Program, you may receive numerous solicitations for preparatory courses and review materials. When considering a prep course, make sure the provider is in compliance with the CFA Institute Prep Provider Guidelines Program (www.cfainstitute .org/partners/examprep/pages/cfa_prep_provider_prog_participants.aspx). Just remember, there are no shortcuts to success on the CFA examinations; reading and studying the CFA curriculum is the key to success on the examination. The CFA examinations reference only the CFA Institute assigned curriculum—no preparatory course or review course materials are consulted or referenced.

SUMMARY

Every question on the CFA examination is based on specific pages in the required readings and on one or more LOS. Frequently, an examination question is also tied to a specific example highlighted within a reading or to a specific end-of-reading question and/or problem and its solution. To make effective use of the curriculum, please remember these key points:

1. All pages printed in the Custom Curriculum are required reading for the examination except for occasional sections marked as optional. You may read optional pages as background, but you will not be tested on them.

2. All questions, problems, and their solutions - printed at the end of readings - are part of the curriculum and required study material for the examination.

3. You should make appropriate use of the online sample/mock examinations and other resources available at www.cfainstitute.org.

4. You should schedule and commit sufficient study time to cover the 18 study sessions, review the materials, and take sample/mock examinations.

5. **Note:** Some of the concepts in the study sessions may be superseded by updated rulings and/or pronouncements issued after a reading was published. Candidates are expected to be familiar with the overall analytical framework contained in the assigned readings. Candidates are not responsible for changes that occur after the material was written.

Feedback

At CFA Institute, we are committed to delivering a comprehensive and rigorous curriculum for the development of competent, ethically grounded investment professionals. We rely on candidate and member feedback as we work to incorporate content, design, and packaging improvements. You can be assured that we will continue to listen to your suggestions. Please send any comments or feedback to curriculum@cfainstitute.org. Ongoing improvements in the curriculum will help you prepare for success on the upcoming examinations, and for a lifetime of learning as a serious investment professional.

$4^{5}/_{8}$ $4^{11}/_{16}$ ... $3/_{8}$

$5^{1}/_{2}$ $5^{1}/_{2}$ − $3/_{8}$

$5^{1}/_{2}$ $2^{13}/_{16}$ − $1/_{8}$

$20^{5}/_{8}$ $21^{3}/_{16}$ − $1/_{8}$

$17^{3}/_{8}$ $18^{1}/_{8}$ + $7/_{8}$

$6^{1}/_{2}$ $6^{1}/_{2}$ − $1/_{2}$

$6^{1}/_{2}$ $31/_{32}$ − $1/_{8}$

$7^{1}/_{4}$

$15/_{16}$ $9/_{16}$

$9/_{16}$

$7/_{32}$ $7^{13}/_{16}$ $7^{15}/_{16}$

$7^{15}/_{16}$

$2^{5}/_{8}$ $2^{11}/_{32}$ $2^{1}/_{2}$ +

$2^{3}/_{4}$ $2^{1}/_{4}$ $2^{1}/_{4}$

$5^{7}/_{8}$ $12^{1}/_{16}$ $11^{3}/_{8}$ $11^{3}/_{4}$ +

87 $33^{3}/_{4}$ 33 $33^{1}/_{4}$ −

602 $25^{5}/_{8}$ $24^{9}/_{16}$ $25^{3}/_{8}$ +

833 12 $11^{5}/_{8}$ $11^{5}/_{8}$ +

16 $10^{1}/_{2}$ $10^{1}/_{2}$ $10^{7}/_{8}$ −

78 $15^{7}/_{8}$ $15^{13}/_{16}$ $15^{7}/_{8}$ −

$9^{1}/_{16}$ $8^{1}/_{4}$ $8^{7}/_{8}$ +

430 $11^{1}/_{4}$ $10^{7}/_{8}$

ALTERNATIVE INVESTMENTS

STUDY SESSION

Study Session 13   Alternative Investments

TOPIC LEVEL LEARNING OUTCOME

The candidate should be able to analyze and evaluate commodities, real estate, and private equity using appropriate valuation concepts and techniques.

$4\frac{5}{8}$ $4\frac{7}{16}$ — $\frac{3}{8}$

$5\frac{1}{2}$ $5\frac{1}{2}$ — $\frac{1}{16}$

$20\frac{5}{8}$ $21\frac{3}{16}$ — $\frac{7}{8}$

$17\frac{3}{8}$ $18\frac{1}{8}$ + $\frac{7}{8}$

$6\frac{1}{2}$ $6\frac{1}{2}$ — $\frac{1}{2}$

$7\frac{1}{4}$ $6\frac{1}{2}$ $3\frac{1}{32}$ — $\frac{1}{8}$

$\frac{15}{16}$

$9\frac{16}{}$ $\frac{9}{8}$

$\frac{1}{32}$ $7\frac{13}{16}$ $7\frac{15}{8}$

$7\frac{15}{16}$ $7\frac{13}{16}$ $2\frac{1}{2}$ +

$2\frac{5}{8}$ $2\frac{11}{32}$

$2\frac{3}{4}$ $2\frac{1}{4}$ $2\frac{1}{4}$

$12\frac{1}{16}$ $11\frac{3}{8}$ $11\frac{3}{4}$ +

87 $33\frac{3}{4}$ 33 $33\frac{1}{8}$ —

$25\frac{5}{8}$ $24\frac{9}{16}$ $25\frac{5}{8}$ +

602 12 $11\frac{5}{8}$ $11\frac{7}{8}$ +

833 16 $10\frac{1}{2}$ $10\frac{1}{2}$ $10\frac{1}{2}$ —

78 $15\frac{7}{8}$ $15\frac{13}{16}$ $15\frac{7}{8}$ —

$9\frac{1}{16}$ $8\frac{1}{4}$ $8\frac{1}{8}$ +

330 $11\frac{1}{4}$ $10\frac{5}{8}$

$4\frac{5}{8}$

STUDY SESSION 13
ALTERNATIVE INVESTMENTS

The major asset categories included in alternative investments are real estate, private equity, commodities, and hedge funds. Private equity, including venture capital and leveraged buyouts, is examined from the perspective of a private equity firm evaluating equity investments for its portfolio and an investor evaluating participation in a private equity fund. The characteristics of commodity markets are described along with the inflation hedging benefits of commodities investment. Finally, the unique challenges in evaluating hedge funds are presented.

READING ASSIGNMENTS

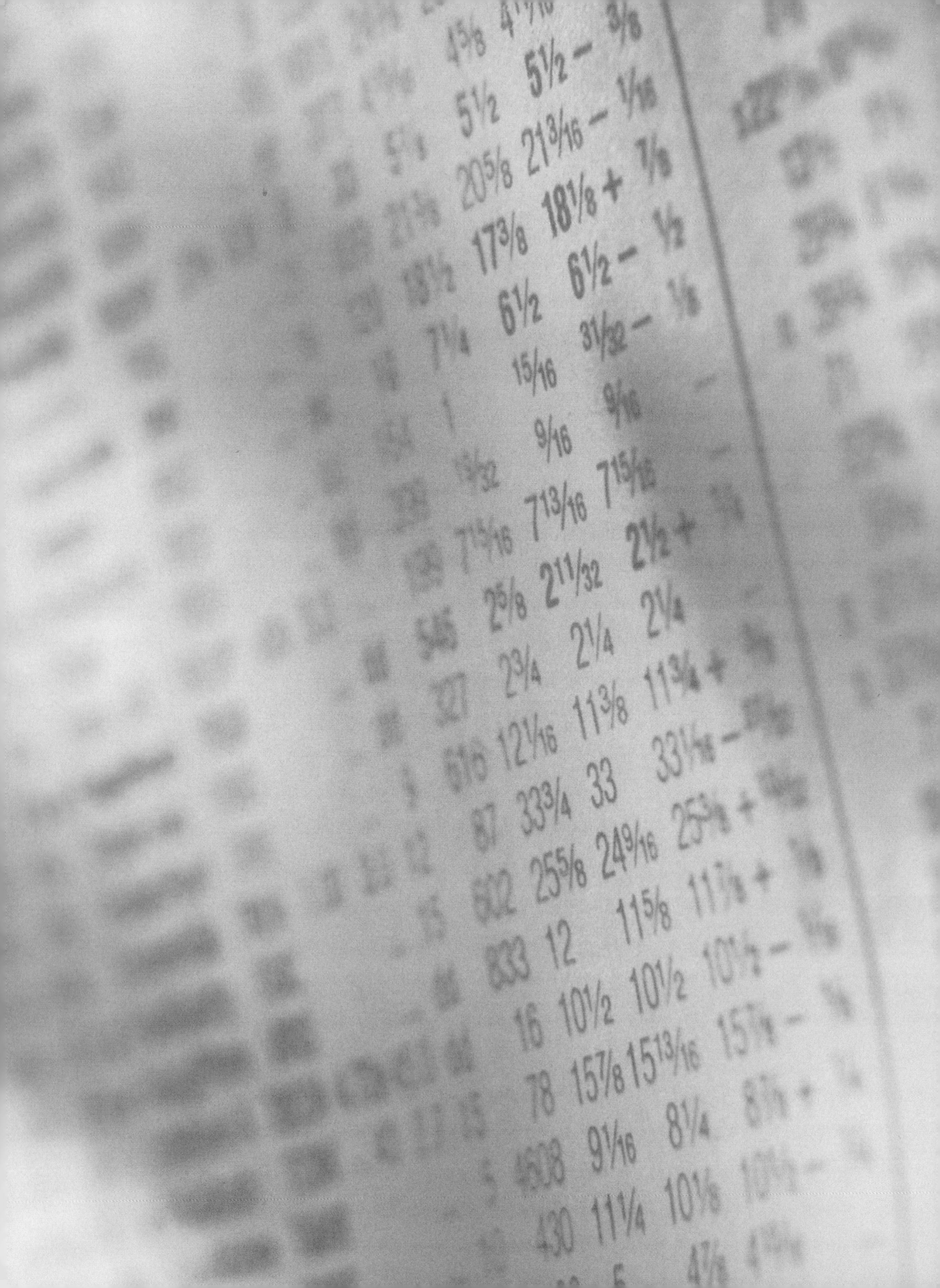

INVESTMENT ANALYSIS
by James D. Shilling

LEARNING OUTCOMES

The candidate should be able to:	Mastery
a. explain, for each type of real property investment, the main value determinants, investment characteristics, principal risks, and most likely investors;	☐
b. evaluate a real estate investment using net present value (NPV) and internal rate of return (IRR) from the perspective of an equity investor;	☐
c. calculate the after-tax cash flow and the after-tax equity reversion from real estate properties;	☐
d. explain potential problems associated with using IRR as a measurement tool in real estate investments.	☐

Buy land. They ain't making any more of the stuff.

—*Will Rogers, American humorist*

Investors have varying goals depending on their available resources (mainly money), age, and decision-making horizon. A recent college graduate with $5,000 to invest differs from an established family with investment experience and $100,000 to invest. An elderly person with $500,000 looking for an investment opportunity would be in still another class.

Some investors may want the comfort and convenience of owning a personal residence free-and-clear of any debt. Others may seek to own real estate as protection against inflation. Still others may enter real estate as a way of building prestige and maximizing wealth.

Real Estate, Thirteenth Edition, by James D. Shilling. Copyright © 2002 by Cengage South-Western. Reprinted with permission of South-Western, a division of Cengage Learning.

Investors also operate subject to constraints or limitations. Age, analytical ability, executive ability, energy level, work preferences, and time availability all act as constraints on an investor. A young person can afford a longer time horizon than can an elderly person. A person with limited time or energy is probably best advised to invest in a medium requiring little effort. Likewise, a person with limited ability to analyze and administer investments is better off avoiding active investments, meaning most real estate investments. Locational preferences as personal constraints are self-explanatory.

Note that we make simple, everyday decisions about what to eat or wear or do, about whom to see or where to go, by feel, habit, hunch, or intuition. Actions generally flow out of the decisions in a very natural manner. As situations become more complex, it becomes worthwhile to devote more time to identifying alternatives and their implications prior to making a decision and taking action. It also becomes worthwhile to devote more time to administering or implementing the decision. The benefits of a good decision or the costs of a bad decision become great enough at some point to warrant spending extra time, money, and effort to reach the best choice.

Real estate decisions clearly warrant spending extra time, money, and effort to reach the best choice. On a long-term basis, the investment must be reviewed periodically to determine if past choices and actions are working out. Often this means comparing the risks and rates of return from stocks and bonds with the risks and rates of return from real estate; it is a portfolio management concern. Additional or larger real estate investments may eventually be desirable. Investment in different types of properties may also become advantageous.

In this reading we devote considerable attention to identifying real estate investment opportunities and making investment decisions. Here we will assume that the property to be acquired is 100 percent equity-financed, meaning that the property is purchased for all cash.

1   WHY INVEST IN REAL ESTATE?

Many of the advantages of real estate as an investment are in its surrounding traditions and institutions.

Leverage   *Leverage* is the use of borrowed money to increase the rate of return earned from an equity real estate investment. Traditionally, real estate investors have been able to borrow up to 90 percent of the value of any property owned or acquired. Nowadays, because of the tightening of the credit markets for any new development, even the best financiers of real estate are rarely able to borrow more than 60 to 75 percent of the value of the property acquired. Nonetheless, leverage can be advantageous when the investment earns a higher rate of return than the interest on the borrowed money.

Leverage also enables an investor to control more property with a given amount of money. An investor can leverage by stretching out the repayment schedule or by refinancing. By maintaining high leverage, an investor may pyramid investments more quickly. **Pyramiding** is controlling additional property through reinvestment, refinancing, and exchanging. The objective is to control the maximum value in property with the least resources. Needless to say, pyramiding carries a high risk of a total wipe-out during a recession.

Tax Shelter   Tax depreciation, installment sales, and tax-deferred exchanges all enable a real estate investor to minimize or defer income taxes.

Purchasing Power Protection   Real estate usually offers protection against inflation. Whereas most capital assets tend to lose value in terms of purchasing power or constant dollars in inflationary periods, adequately improved realty, especially apartments, shopping centers, and selected commercial properties, tend to gain value as measured in constant dollars. In the absence of rent and price controls, real property, like a ship upon ocean waters, floats above its purchasing power-constant dollar line irrespective of depth or rise in the level of prices. For this real-value holding power to be true of a specific parcel of income real estate, the property must be well located, have rentals that can be adjusted periodically, and not be subject to sudden sharp increases in operating costs.

Pride of Ownership   Many real estate investors gain identity by being "in the game" or by being "shrewd operators." Some investors also realize great satisfaction from owning something tangible that can be touched, felt, and shown to friends and relatives.

Control   The immediate and direct control of an owner over realty enables the owner or an agent to make continuing decisions about the property as a financial asset and as a productive property. This control enables the investor to manage property to meet personal goals, whether they are to maintain the property as a showpiece for pride of ownership or to operate the property for maximum rate of return. Many owners experience a great sense of power and independence in this control.

Entrepreneurial Profit   A last important advantage is that added value may be realized by building or rehabilitating a property, and the added value is immediately invested in the property without being taxed. Thus, many investors also develop property. Other investors combine real estate investing with brokerage or property management.

RATIONAL INVESTOR VERSUS ECONOMIC-BEING ASSUMPTION

2

The person making the real estate investment decision is assumed to be a rational investor. The assumptions about this rational investor are generally consistent with the *economic person* theory commonly found in economics. Each acts in self-interest. Each is strongly influenced by the institutional environment. But there are differences.

An economic person is defined in economic literature as a primary decision-maker motivated to maximize his or her economic return. The economic person has an uncanny knowledge of the alternatives and of what to expect under varying production, cost, and pricing strategies. In this sense, the economic person looks at the use of land resources from the viewpoint of the typical investor.

A *rational investor* operates under slightly different assumptions than does the economic person. Knowledge is less than total, which means that risk and uncertainty are present. Also, institutional considerations (laws and taxes, mainly) affect investors individually and specifically. These differences are the major reasons why the viewpoint of an individual, rational investor is preferred in making decisions about real estate as a financial asset.

The goal of maximizing self-interest (wealth) is an important assumption for our rational investor. The concept of a rational investor was developed shortly after World War II by Herbert Simon, who won a Nobel Prize for his work in economic and decision theory in 1978. Acting in self-interest, a rational investor always selects the choice or alternative within his or her range of knowledge that gives the greatest personal advantage. A rational investor will also anticipate the future and incorporate any expected changes into the current market price of real estate.

Note that self-interest is neither good nor bad, desirable nor undesirable, per se. In a sense, self-interest is to people as gravity is to the earth. Gravity may keep us from flying at will and require us to exert energy to conquer distance or elevation, but gravity also works to our advantage. It causes rain to fall and rivers to flow downhill. We turn gravity to our advantage in our work and play when we irrigate gardens, ski, skydive, or play ball.

Self-interest is a force or motivation that causes us to try to maximize our satisfactions in life. We seek leisure, self-expression, travel, company of loved ones, thrills from skydiving, or social changes out of self-interest. Most of us seek money only as an intermediate goal. In our complex society, an investor seeking profits may be making a contribution to society as great as or even greater than a doctor seeking fees or a politician seeking power.

Self-interest acts to push real estate to its highest-and-best use. *Highest-and-best use* is that legal and possible land use that gives it its greatest present value while preserving its utility. A *land use* is that activity by which a parcel of real estate is made productive—that is, it generates services of value—as a residential, commercial, or industrial property.

Highest-and-best use of a parcel to one investor in the market may well differ from the highest-and-best use of another investor because of differences in what each is seeking to maximize. This difference is the major reason why a financial approach rather than an economic approach to real estate investment is needed. Using a financial approach provides us with a highly useful model for numerous investment decisions about real estate as an asset.

3   HOW DO DIFFERENT PROPERTY TYPES STACK UP?

Differing property types offer distinct advantages to specific investors. Figure 1 summarizes these comments.

Vacant or Raw Land

Land is only one of several alternatives open to an investor. Supply is limited; demand is growing; therefore, investing in land is a sure thing. While generally valid, this argument is also limited.

The return from land must be realized through value appreciation, which depends on supply and demand. The supply of land is limited. But the supply of urban land may be increased simply by extending roads, water and sewer lines, and electrical services.

Demand for land depends on expansion of demand in the specific community. Location relative to local road and travel patterns goes far to determine the demand for a specific parcel of realty. Finally, planning, zoning, and probable highest-and-best use greatly determine chances for value enhancement.

Land is passive and illiquid as an investment medium. Low loan-to-value ratios make it difficult to leverage land highly. Owning land gives no tax depreciation, and carrying costs must be capitalized. In that land earns little or no income, an investor must pay carrying costs from other income. Such an investment is sometimes called an "alligator" because it has to be fed. If the owner suffers reduced income, a distress sale may be necessary. The rate and amount of value appreciation likely to occur over a period adds additional uncertainty to investment in land.

The most likely investors in land are speculators for short-term gains and developers for long-term operating needs. Estates and others seeking a store of value and an easily managed hedge against inflation are also likely investor types for land.

Apartments

The number of households and income levels are the primary determinants of value for residential real estate. Some apartment buildings also realize value based on prestige considerations. Location, convenience, and environment also greatly influence value.

Apartments require moderately active attention as an investment. Apartments are more liquid than most realty investments because investors are more knowledgeable about residential properties than other types of property. Thus, with more investors, the market is broader. Also, high leverage is possible; up to 90 percent, and sometimes higher, loan-to-value ratios are possible. The rate of return may be enhanced both by periodic receipt of income and increase in value.

Apartments offer a good inflation hedge because apartment leases are adjusted annually (compared to three-to-ten-year terms common on other property types). Apartment performance has been less volatile than most other property types. Occupancy levels over the long term have rarely dropped below 90 percent. The commodity nature of apartments tends to produce a more efficient market.

The major risks in apartment investment are during the start-up period of new properties and in obtaining or providing quality management on a continuing basis. For large complexes, professional management is almost a must because of the considerable know-how required and the need to avoid harassment from tenants and others. Smaller properties, roughly 12 units or less, may be managed and maintained by an owner with adequate time. Personal management gives the owner closer control, in addition to "psychological payment" for the services rendered.

The competition from single family homes as an alternative to renting is often cited as a main deterrent to apartment investment. Apartment construction has declined steadily since 1985. Multifamily starts peaked in 1985 at 576,000 units. Multifamily starts dropped to a 35-year low of 138,000 units in 1991 (see Figure 2). In many communities, current construction has not kept pace with demolition and conversion.

FIGURE 1   Generalized Characteristics of Real Property Investment Types

Property Type	Main Value Determinants	Investment Characteristics	Principal Risks	Most Likely Investor Type
Vacant or raw land	Expansion of demand Convenient location Travel patterns Planning/zoning/ highest-and-best use	Passive Illiquid Limited leverage Rate of return by value appreciation No tax depreciation Capital gains taxation Expenses capitalized	Carrying costs: "alligator" Value appreciation uncertain	Speculator Developer Estate as store of value
Residential rentals (apartments)	Expanding population	Moderately liquid	Start up when new	
	Rising incomes	High leverage (loan-to-value ratio)	Management: probably necessary to hire professional for larger projects	High income: benefiting from tax shelter
	Location: convenience, favorable exposure	Rate of return by periodic income and value appreciation		Suitable for anyone but must be able to put up equity investment
	Prestige, sometimes important	Tax depreciation		
		Ordinary and capital gains taxation		
Office buildings	Expanding local economy	Active, unless leased to one firm	Start up when new	High income: needing tax shelter
	Location linkages	Moderately liquid	Management: high level of service provided	Suitable for anyone if professional management hired and able to put up initial equity investment
	Prestige/status sometimes important Tenant mix compatibility	Rate of return by periodic income and value appreciation Tax depreciation Ordinary and capital gains taxation	Competitive facilities Obsolescence Shift in location of business activity	
Warehouses	Commercial/industrial activity	Most passive: often on long-term lease	Obsolescence due to changes in material handling equipment and technology	Retired: desiring both cash flow and limited management

Property Type	Main Value Determinants	Investment Characteristics	Principal Risks	Most Likely Investor Type
	Location for ease of movement Structural design to endure change	Moderately liquid Moderate leverage Rate of return mainly by periodic income Tax depreciation Ordinary and capital gains taxation		Anyone desiring tax shelter who has adequate initial equity capital
Neighborhood shopping centers	Community growth Effective demand: population and income Convenient location relative to competition Adequate parking Tenant mix relative to spending patterns Effective lease negotiation	Moderately active Liquidity limited Moderate leverage Rate of return by periodic income and value appreciation Tax depreciation Ordinary and capital gains taxation	Start up: getting proper tenant mix Management: need to provide adequate level of service Vacancies Competitive facilities Obsolescence	Reasonably wealthy: need to make large equity investment Anyone able to use tax shelter plus other benefits
Hotels/motels	Location: linkages and convenience Demand: conference, tourist, resort, business Mix of facilities and services	Active Moderately liquid Moderate to poor leverage Rate of return periodic income and value appreciation Tax depreciation Ordinary and capital gains taxation	Management: high tenant turnover (professional management almost a necessity) Competing facilities	Anyone able to use tax shelter and with adequate initial equity capital Smaller properties suitable for investors also willing to manage and maintain

FIGURE 2   Multifamily Housing

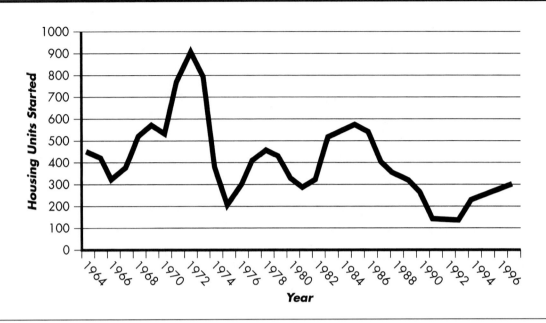

Source: www.census.gov/ftp/pub/const/www/c20index.html.

Development of multifamily units tends to be somewhat difficult. Land zoned for multifamily use in most communities is scarce. Moreover, government regulations for new apartment development are becoming more stringent, increasing the cost of new construction. In-fill properties in strong markets where single family alternatives are relatively expensive are where you can often find monopolistic opportunities.

The assisted living rental housing market is one of the fastest growing markets in the United States today. Assisted living residences are housing environments that provide individualized health and personal care assistance in a home-like setting. The level of care provided is between that provided in congregate housing (housing with meal services) and a skilled nursing home. Most assisted living residences are targeted toward individuals needing help preparing meals, bathing, and dressing. Assisted living residences also are targeted toward individuals requiring some health care assistance or monitoring, or individuals needing transportation to doctors, shopping, and personal business. Demand for assisted living housing is extraordinary. Supply is somewhat limited, however. Most attempts to build assisted living facilities divide nearby residents and advocates of affordable housing for the elderly.

Office Buildings

The value of office buildings depends heavily on the business health of the area. A convenient location, a compatible tenant mix, and a prestigious image also add to value. Office buildings generally require active participation of an owner unless leased to a single party, because tenant demands must be dealt with. Liquidity and leverage are generally moderate. The rate of return is produced both by periodic receipt of income and value appreciation.

The main risks with an office property are during start-up, maintaining high-quality management, and obsolescence, most of which are within the control of the owner. Shifts in location of business activity and development of competitive facilities are risks outside the direct influence of the owner.

Likely owners of large office buildings are wealthy or high-income investors who are likely to have the high initial equity investment required, as is implied by the moderate leverage. Public and private business organizations are often formed to own office buildings, thereby opening the investment opportunity to persons of more moderate means.

For most office buildings, it is difficult to say which comes first, the building or the lease. Lenders normally want leases first. They want these leases to provide security for their loans. Leases with AAA tenants provide better collateral than leases to local tenants.

New York City has the highest rents per square foot in downtown office markets in the United States, while Shreveport, Louisiana has the lowest. Not only does New York City lead the way in terms of rents per square feet in a downtown office market, it also has the highest expenses (including cleaning expenses, repairs/maintenance, utilities, roads/grounds, security, and administration).

Lease terms in most office buildings are staggered—not all tenants can move at the same time. Moreover, a long-term tenant may want room to expand in the future, therefore planning that his or her immediate neighbors will be given short-term leases. Having long-term office leases that run for five or 10 years and carry options to renew for 10 or 20 years more means that it will normally take a few years to obtain a rent structure that will be quite close to the final stable one. In a recovering office market, then, increases in net operating income will tend to lag behind increases in asking rents.

Vacancies have a big impact on office rents. Office vacancy rates currently are as low as they have been since the early 1980s. The consequence has been steadily rising office rents and prices, often at a double-digit pace (see Figure 3). Of course, whether this trend continues is the most significant long-term risk to

FIGURE 3   Prices and Rents per Square Foot of Office Space

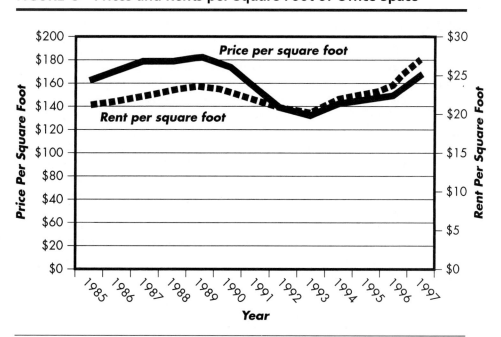

Source: National Real Estate Index, National CBD Office Market.

the office market. If the supply of new office space once again were to outstrip the absorption of new space, vacancy rates would rise, and rents and prices could easily fall.

Warehouses

Warehouses obviously depend heavily on the level of commercial and industrial activity for value. To maintain value, warehouses must be designed and built to accommodate changes in the methods of handling materials. Ceilings too low and aisles too narrow to accommodate forklift trucks caused many warehouses to become obsolete in the 1950s and 1960s, for example. Warehouse value also depends on a location that allows easy movement through a community.

A warehouse on long-term lease to one firm tends to be a passive investment. Leverage and liquidity are moderate. Cash flow tends to be somewhat higher as a proportion of value than with some other improved properties because less value appreciation is expected. In turn, people desiring high cash flow and limited management requirements find warehouses an excellent investment. In most other respects, warehouses are similar to apartment and office buildings.

REITs and institutional investors tend to favor larger and more modern facilities. For these properties, debt financing is readily available. The most active industrial warehouse markets appear to be the Southeast. Industrial warehouse space is relatively inexpensive to build, which makes the warehouse market prone to conditions of oversupply.

Another advantage of an industrial warehouse building is its low lease rollover cost. When one tenant moves out and another tenant moves in, there is very little that an industrial warehouse landlord needs to do with that space in order to make it reuseable. It also is an area that can grow on its own, especially given the shift that is taking place in the United States from an economy dealing with hard goods to an economy dealing with information, entertainment, and communications.

Shopping Centers

The value of shopping centers depends heavily on adequate purchasing power, meaning people and incomes, in their tributary area. The location must be convenient for the population and parking must be plentiful. Finally, the tenant mix must be suited to the demands of the population in the tributary area. Supermarkets, small variety and discount stores, restaurants, and gasoline stations are typical tenants.

Active management is required to establish and maintain a center. Effective lease negotiation is important. Liquidity is limited because few investors have the broad knowledge needed to manage a center; also, leverage is moderate. The tax treatment of shopping center investment is similar to that of other commercial properties. Vacancies and lease negotiation, obsolescence, and development of competitive facilities are the main risks of shopping center ownership. Also, as with office buildings, a reasonably large equity investment is required. In other respects, any investor seeking periodic income and capital gains would find shopping center investment inviting.

Figure 4 shows the number of centers in six size categories, together with the average gross leaseable area for each category and the average sales per square foot for each category. As can be seen, most shopping centers are fairly small, less than 100,001 square feet. Total annual sales in shopping centers are around $980 billion, representing 55 percent of all non-automotive retail sales in the nation.

FIGURE 4　Shopping Center Census

Average Center Size (in Square Feet)	Number of Centers	Percent of Total	Total Sales (in Billion $)	Average Gross Leaseable Area per Center	Sales per Square Foot
Less than 100,001	26,928	62.69%	$285	48,951	215.9
100,001–200,000	10,400	24.21%	$249	137,594	173.98
200,001–400,000	3,595	8.37%	$150	266,902	155.99
400,001–800,000	1,324	3.08%	$127	556,178	172.39
800,001–1,000,000	316	0.74%	$62	901,206	219.38
More than 1,000,000	390	0.91%	$107	1,281,277	214.90
Total	42,953	100.00%	$980	121,749	187.4

One drawback of shopping centers is that most anchor tenants require substantial inducement to become part of the center. These inducements have included: free land for the store site, with the anchor tenant erecting its own store, or tenancy in a store custom built to the anchor tenant's requirements at a rental rate that produces no economic return to the developer. In some cases, major tenants also are able to negotiate large signing bonuses—dollars that tenants have used to buy inventory with. To offset these low rental tenancies and inducements, it is necessary for shopping center developers to include in the center a large amount of space rented to small chains and independent retailers paying a high rental rate. These stores are often relegated to inferior locations in the center. They also tend to be higher risk tenants.

Financing for a shopping center generally cannot be obtained until leases with the anchor tenants are finalized. Shopping center financing also tends to be contingent on receiving a minimum or base rental. Without this minimum or base rental, most permanent lenders are unwilling to make a mortgage on a shopping center.

Hotels and Motels

Hotels and motels depend primarily on tourist and business travelers for their demand. In recent years it has been in vogue to hold business conferences in large hotels. Having a location and the facilities to satisfy this demand with ease is a large determinant of value.

Hotels and motels are active investments with limited liquidity and offer moderate-to-poor leverage. They receive tax treatment as business property.

Major risks in hotel and motel investment are maintaining adequate size and competent management. Economies of scale apply. And high tenant turnover means that management must be effective. Obsolescence and the development of more adequate competing facilities are also major risks.

Large hotels and motels require considerable equity investment and, therefore, are limited to REITs and wealthy investors. Smaller properties are suitable for less affluent investors who are also willing to manage and maintain the property.

There are three types of hotels: limited service hotels, mid-priced limited service hotels, and traditional full service hotels. Limited service hotels offer guests the amenities that they need while omitting those amenities not wanted. Mid-priced

FIGURE 5   Hotel Room Occupancy and Room Rental Rates

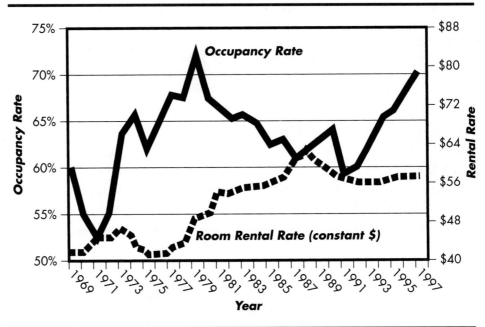

Source: William C. Wheaton and Lawrence Rossoff, "The Cyclic Behavior of the U.S. Lodging Industry," *Real Estate Economics*, 26: 1988, 67–82.

limited service hotels provide guests with a slightly higher level of amenities at a higher price. Traditional full service hotels offer a full range of guest services.

Demand for hotel night stays—the measure of lodging demand—moves very closely with the level of economic activity. This is because most overnight stays are business related. The desire to maximize profits leads most hotels to not fully book up space with (low-rate) plan-in-advance business travel. Most hotels, instead, prefer to hold some inventory for the more variable (high-rate) walk-in traveler.

Hotel room occupancy rates and room rental rates (constant dollars) are shown in Figure 5. As can be seen, occupancy rates can be quite cyclic. One reason for the cycles seems to be the slow adjustment of room rates and the long delivery lags with supply. Part of the long delivery lags with supply reflects considerable planning and/or site assembly times.

4   HOW SPECIFIC INVESTMENTS ARE ANALYZED

Why are buildings like the Bank of America building in San Francisco or New York's Rockefeller Center eagerly sought by investors? The answer seems clear: they are the best in their markets. They are the most attractive, rentable, and efficient. Also, they generally yield a handsome rate of return.

By way of contrast, why are no-frills older buildings, with mixed or low tenant prestige, poor design, inferior locations, and below-average workmanship and materials often sought by investors? The answer: even the worst properties in a market can yield an attractive rate of return if priced appropriately.

The point to note is that, after all things are considered, most decisions to invest in real estate are undertaken to earn a profit. One widely used criterion for measuring whether a specific project is likely to earn a profit over and above a normal required rate of return is known as the net present value rule.

Let us look more closely at the net present value (NPV) criterion. **Net present value** is simply the difference between the present value of benefits and the market value or cost of the investment. If we define $ATCF_t$ as the expected *after-tax cash flow* generated by the property in period t and $ATER$ as the *after-tax equity reversion* due on sale, we may write:

NPV = Present worth of cash flows − Equity investment

$$NPV = \frac{ATCF_1}{(1 + r_a)^1} + \frac{ATCF_2}{(1 + r_a)^2} + \cdots + \frac{ATCF_n}{(1 + r_a)^n} + \frac{ATER}{(1 + r_a)^n} - I$$

where r_a denotes the required after-tax rate of return on the property and I is the equity cost of the investment.[1]

The NPV formula tells us if $NPV > 0$ or if $NPV = 0$, then buy. The rationale is as follows: a positive NPV means that the present worth of the property is greater than the equity cost of the investment; hence, the position of the equity investor is improved by undertaking the investment. A zero NPV means that the wealth of the equity investor is unaffected. Projects with zero NPV are a matter of indifference and, consequently, should be undertaken. In either of these circumstances, the buyer's investment goals will be realized or exceeded.

If $NPV < 0$, then don't invest. A negative NPV means that the investment is worth less than it costs. In this situation, the investor would not invest since the investment is not expected to earn the required rate of return if purchased at the market value.

NET PRESENT VALUE ANALYSIS FOR DOUGLAS MANOR APARTMENTS—AN EXAMPLE

5

Our case property, Douglas Manor Apartments, will be used to illustrate the elements and techniques of NPV analysis, with cash flows on an after-tax basis. The viewpoint is that of the equity investor.

The data or information needed to determine investment value, plus any additional assumptions or inputs for Douglas Manor Apartments, are stated here in summary form for easy reference. Figure 6 provides a summary of projected cash flows and market value levels for the Douglas Manor Apartments. What follows is summary data:

1. Net operating income is $64,000.

2. The purchase price of Douglas Manor Apartments is taken to be $525,000 (rounded).

3. Improvements are assumed to make up 85.9 percent of the $525,000 purchase price, or $451,000. Using a 27.5-year life, with straight-line cost recovery as required by the Tax Reform Act of 1986, gives $16,399 per year of tax depreciation.

4. Equity contribution: $131,250.

---

[1] For ease of exposition, we have assumed that the project's discount rate, r_a, is a constant across all periods. It is a simple matter, however, to allow r_a to vary from period to period.

FIGURE 6   Douglas Manor Apartments: Projected Cash Flows and Market Value Levels

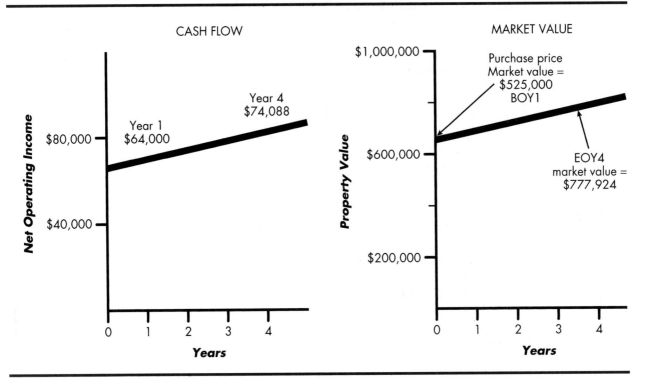

5. Debt contribution: a fixed-rate mortgage is obtained for $393,750 at 8 percent per annum (compounded monthly) for 30 years. The monthly payment to amortize this loan is $2,889.20. The loan-to-value ratio is 75 percent.

6. The investors are assumed to have a 36 percent marginal income tax rate. The investor's capital gains tax rate is 20 percent. Recaptured depreciation will be taxed at the rate of 25 percent.

7. The investors have a minimum of 12 percent per year after-tax required rate of return on any equity investment.

8. The property is assumed to be held for only four years, during which time its net operating income is expected to increase at 5 percent per year. The end-of-year 4 market value, which is also the disposition price, is expected to be $777,924. Disposition or selling costs at the end of year 4 are assumed to be 7 percent of the sales price. The outstanding loan balance at the end of year 4 is $378,862 (rounded).

9. Annual compounding is used for the equity time-value-of-money calculations.

We begin by calculating the investment value of Douglas Manor Apartments. Investment value equals the present value of the cash flow from operations, plus the present value of the reversion upon sale at the end of the holding period, discounted at the investor's required rate of return.

Note that with circumstances unique to an individual investor, such as being in a favorable tax position or having access to available financing at a below-market interest rate, the investment value of the property can conceivably exceed the market value of the property. This can also happen when individual investors are motivated by reasons other than wealth maximization for investing in a specific real estate project. In many instances real estate investors are willing to accept a lower rate of return on their investment in return for certain other intangible or subjective benefits, which are often difficult to quantify.

PROCESS USED TO DETERMINE AFTER-TAX CASH FLOW AND AFTER-TAX EQUITY REVERSION

6

The process used to calculate the **after-tax cash flow (ATCF)** from operations and the **after-tax equity reversion (ATER)** is illustrated below and in Figure 7.

Step 1: Determining Tax Payable

Generally speaking, taxable income from real estate equals net operating income less the depreciation expense and less interest paid on money borrowed to finance the property.

Depreciation expense, you may recall, is a tax-deductible allowance to account for the decline in value or useful life of the real estate resulting from wear, tear, obsolescence, or actions of the elements. Depreciation expense can be taken regardless of whether the equity investor is leveraged. Interest expense, on the other hand, can be taken only if you borrow money to finance the purchase. Annual interest expense can be calculated as the year's total debt service payments less the change in principal balance over this same period. Multiplying the taxable income by the marginal income tax rate gives the tax payable on income from the property.

Figures 8 and 9 give a detailed cash-flow projection for the Douglas Manor Apartments, including the calculation of the income tax payable by an owner in a 36 percent tax bracket.

FIGURE 7 Process for Calculating Tax Payable and After-Tax Cash Flow

Calculation of Tax Payable		Calculation of After-Tax Cash Flow	
Potential gross income	$		
Less: Vacancy and collection losses	_____		
Effective gross income	$		
Less: Operating expenses	_____		
Net operating income	$	Net operating income	$ _____
Less: Tax depreciation		Less: Annual debt service	_____
Less: Interest on loan	_____		
Taxable income	$	Before-tax cash flow	$
Multiplied by tax rate		Less: Tax payable	_____
Tax payable	$ _____	After-tax cash flow	$ _____

FIGURE 8   Douglas Manor Apartments: Calculation of Annual Tax on Income for an Equity Owner in 36 Percent Tax Bracket

	Year			
	1	2	3	4
Net operating income	$64,000	$67,200	$70,560	$74,088
Less: Straight-line tax depreciation	−16,399	−16,399	−16,399	−16,399
Less: Interest paid	−31,381	−31,108	−30,812	−30,492
Taxable income	$16,220	$19,693	$23,349	$27,197
Times: Tax rate	×36%	×36%	×36%	×36%
Income tax payable	$5,839	$7,089	$8,406	$9,791

For year 1, taxable income is $16,220 and income tax payable is $5,839:

Net operating income	$64,000
Less: Depreciation	$16,399
Less: Interest paid	$31,381
Taxable income	$16,220
Times: Income tax rate	× 0.36
Income tax payable (tax savings)	$5,839

By year 4 in Figure 8, *NOI* has increased so that the Douglas Manor Apartments has taxes payable of $9,791.

Step 2: Determining After-Tax Cash Flow

The next step in the analysis is to determine *ATCF* from the property for each year of ownership. Generally speaking, **before-tax cash flow (BTCF)** equals *NOI* less annual debt service. Subtracting the tax payable on income from operations yields the *ATCF* that can be pocketed.

Having financed 75 percent of the purchase price with debt, the *BTCF* will equal *NOI* less the required annual debt service payment to the lender.

FIGURE 9   Douglas Manor Apartments: Calculation of After-Tax Cash Flows from Operations

	Year			
	1	2	3	4
Net operating income	$64,000	$67,200	$70,560	$74,088
Less: Annual debt service	−34,670	−34,670	−34,670	−34,670
Before-tax cash flow	$29,330	$32,530	$35,890	$39,418
Less: Tax payable	($5,839)	($7,089)	($8,406)	($9,791)
After-tax cash flow	$23,491	$25,441	$27,484	$29,627

For year 1, annual debt service payments of $34,670 are deducted from a *NOI* of $64,000 resulting in a *BTCF*-to-equity of $29,330. Deducting the income tax payable from *BTCF* gives an *ATCF* of $23,491:

Net operating income	$64,000
Less: Annual debt service	$34,670
Before-tax cash flow	$29,330
Less: Income tax payable	$5,839
After-tax cash flow	$23,491

By year 4, *ATCF* has increased to $29,627.

Step 3: After-Tax Equity Reversion

After-tax equity reversion equals sale price less disposition costs, less the amortized mortgage balance, if any, and less capital gains taxes.

Let us look now at the projected disposition or sale of Douglas Manor Apartments. The calculations are summarized in Figure 10. Douglas Manor Apartments is projected to have increased in value by more than 48 percent, so a disposition sale price of $777,924 is realized. This figure is arrived at by taking the expected *NOI* for year 5, $77,792, and dividing by a 10 percent overall capitalization rate.

FIGURE 10 Douglas Manor Apartments: Calculation of End of Year 4 Taxes Due on Sale and After-Tax Equity Reversion

Sales price, end-of-year 4		$777,924
Less: Selling expenses @ 7.0%		54,455
Net sales price		$723,469
Less: Adjusted basis		
Purchase price	$525,000	
Less: Accumulated depreciation	65,596	$459,404
Gain realized on sale		$264,065
Gain realized on sale		$264,065
Less: Depreciation recaptured		$65,596
Gain recognized on sale		$198,469
Tax on depreciation recapture	$65,596 × 25% =	$16,399
Tax on capital gain	$198,469 × 20% =	39,694
Taxes due on sale		$56,093
Sales price, end-of-year 4		$777,924
Less: Selling expenses @ 7.0%		54,455
Net sales price		$723,469
Less: Mortgage balance outstanding		378,862
Before-tax equity reversion		$344,607
Less: Taxes due on sale		56,093
After-tax equity reversion		$288,514

The mortgage balance at the end of four years is $378,862. The long-term capital gain realized on the sale is $264,065. Of this gain, $65,596 is subject to depreciation recapture and the remaining $198,469 is a long-term capital gain. Total taxes payable are $56,093. Total payments deducted from the sales price amount to $110,548 (selling expense of $54,455 plus taxes payable of $56,093), which leaves a net after-tax equity reversion of $288,514.

7   NET PRESENT VALUE

At a 12 percent required rate of return, the net present value of Douglas Manor Apartments is $131,752:

$$NPV = \frac{\$23{,}491}{(1 + .12)^1} + \frac{\$25{,}441}{(1 + .12)^2} + \frac{\$27{,}484}{(1 + .12)^3}$$

$$+ \frac{\$29{,}627}{(1 + .12)^4} + \frac{\$288{,}514}{(1 + .12)^4} - \$131{,}250 = \$131{,}752$$

For decision purposes, the rule is that NPV must be zero or positive for a go decision to invest. Thus, in this case, the decision rule says invest.

At a 38 percent required rate of return, we get a present value for the cash flows of $128,560. In turn, NPV of the investment is a negative $2,690:

$$NPV = \frac{\$23{,}491}{(1 + .38)^1} + \frac{\$25{,}441}{(1 + .38)^2} + \frac{\$27{,}484}{(1 + .38)^3} + \frac{\$29{,}627}{(1 + .38)^4}$$

$$+ \frac{\$288{,}514}{(1 + .38)^4} - \$131{,}250 = (\$2{,}690)$$

In this case, the decision rule says "do not invest."

8   INTERNAL RATE OF RETURN

The internal rate of return is sometimes used as an alternative to NPV in making financial decisions. The **internal rate of return (IRR)** is that rate of return that discounts future cash flows to the exact amount of the investment. Stated another way, if used in NPV analysis, IRR would result in NPV of zero.

Let us calculate IRR for Douglas Manor Apartments. We already have enough information to approximate it. The present value of the cash flows at 12 percent is $263,002, and at 38 percent it is $128,560. The equity investment cash outlay is $131,250; therefore, NPV of the cash flows at 12 percent is $131,752, and it is ($2,690) at 38 percent. Thus, we know that IRR is somewhere between 12 and 38 percent. By trial and error, we find that IRR is:

$$NPV = \frac{\$23{,}491}{(1 + .3714)^1} + \frac{\$25{,}441}{(1 + .3714)^2} + \frac{\$27{,}484}{(1 + .3714)^3}$$

$$+ \frac{\$29{,}627}{(1 + .3714)^4} + \frac{\$288{,}514}{(1 + .3714)^4} - \$131{,}250 = 0$$

or 37.14 percent after tax. The same result could be obtained either through the use of a financial calculator or by interpolation.[2]

The decision rule for *IRR* is that if *IRR* is greater than or equal to the required rate of return, the investment should be made. Since the *IRR* of 37.14 percent exceeds 12 percent, the investment should be made.

NEGOTIATION AND RATE OF RETURN   9

What options are available when *IRR* is less than the investor's required rate of return? The decision rule for *IRR* would say "do not invest." Possible alternatives are to renegotiate a lower purchase price or shift some of the risk.

Frequent negotiation between the buyer and seller is likely when the *IRR* is less than the investor's required rate of return. It is a fair assumption that the owner will want to sell for as much as possible and is unlikely to accept less than market value. In turn, the investor will want to buy for as little as possible.

Successful negotiating involves the following four steps:

1. An investor must understand his or her personal goals and negotiating style. What are the relative priorities of the goals? What negotiating style best achieves the goals?

2. The property must be understood. What is its highest investment value to me as a buyer-investor? What is the lowest price at which as an owner, I will sell (market value, unless in distress)? What influence will terms have on these prices?

3. The investor must know the opponent and his or her goals. When buying, look in the public records to find out how much the seller paid for the property and how long it has been owned. Is the owner's tax depreciation about used up? Also, estimate the owner's mortgage balance and terms, if not included in the listing. Are there other liens against the property? Under how much pressure to sell is the owner?

4. Don't buy real estate, buy a set of financial assumptions. Some real estate locations are better than other locations. Likewise, some buildings are more attractive than other buildings. Yet, no matter how good the site or attractive the building, unless you are able to earn a suitable return on investment, you should not invest in real estate. This statement is true regardless of whether this is your first investment in real estate or your

---

[2] The target *NPV* value equals \$131,752 at 12 percent and (\$2,690) at 38 percent. By interpolation, then, the approximate *IRR* is calculated as follows: the difference between *NPV* at 12 percent and 38 percent is:

Difference between *NPV* @ 12% and 38% = \$131,752 − (\$2,690) = \$134,442

Likewise, the difference between *NPV* at 12 percent and IRR% (by definition) is

Difference between *NPV* @ 12% and *IRR*% = \$131,752 − 0 = \$131,752

This implies an approximate *IRR* of:

$$\text{Approximate } IRR\% = 12\% + (38\% - 12\%)\frac{\$131,752}{\$134,442} = 37.48\%$$

By calculator, the *IRR* is 37.14% after tax.

twentieth investment in real estate, or whether you are investing U.S. capital in the United States, French capital in France, or German capital in Germany, or some combination thereof. You never should buy real estate unless the property has a return that is higher than the cost of debt, and has a high or a higher value to you than it does to the seller. Also recognize that a lot of assumptions go into forecasting the value of a property, and that it is unrealistic to expect every one of these forecasts to be achieved. Thus, if you cannot buy the assumptions as presented, you cannot afford the real estate about which those assumptions were made. Of course, once a bargain is struck, you should look for ways in which to improve upon the exchange by modifying terms. Cooperative negotiations are better for both parties in the long run.

Clearly, undue pressure on a buyer or seller, differences in negotiating ability, or lack of adequate information might result in an agreed price being above or below market value.

10   A CAUTION ABOUT BEING TOO OPTIMISTIC

Being overly optimistic in your forecasts can lead to artificially inflated *NPV*s. Thus, when in doubt, always look first to the marketplace for objective information about market rents and expenses, and a market-derived discount rate. A positive *NPV* may simply be an indication that either something has been left out of normal operating expenses, like reserves and replacements for a new roof or new fixtures, or market rents have been overstated. Of course, a positive *NPV* may be indicative of monopoly profits, but don't expect these monopoly profits to last forever. Whenever there are positive excess profits to be made, supply will usually increase, thereby exerting downward pressure on market rents and profit levels.

If your development project is large enough, you will also have to worry about how the increased supply of new space will affect market rents. In such circumstances it will not be good enough simply to look at market rents in forecasting expected revenues; instead, one must estimate *ex post market rents*—that is, market rents after the new supply has been added to the market. Only in instances where you are reasonably protected by local zoning, or in the case of a regional shopping center, by a natural monopoly, do you not have to worry about increased competition exerting downward pressure on rents and profit levels.

11   A CAUTION ABOUT RELYING TOO HEAVILY ON INTERNAL RATE OF RETURN ANALYSIS

IRR analysis is fraught with potential problems when the cash flows from investment start out positive and then become negative. In this case *IRR* may have multiple roots—one positive and one negative. *IRR* analysis may also be misleading when comparing investments of different size or varying durations. Some examples follow.

Multiple Solutions

Most real estate projects will have a unique rate of return, which implies the *NPV* function crosses the horizontal axis once, and only once. To illustrate, consider the following real estate project:

Project A: $2 Million Office Building		
Year	ATCF ($000's)	ATER ($000's)
0	($2,000)	
1	$400	
2	$400	$2,000

If the required rate of return is 10 percent after tax, what is *NPV?* The calculation of *NPV* is:

$$NPV = \frac{\$400,000}{(1 + .10)} + \frac{\$400,000}{(1 + .10)^2} + \frac{\$2,000,000}{(1 + .10)^2} - \$2,000,000 = \$347,000$$

If you plot a graph like Figure 11, you will find that *NPV* decreases as the discount rate increases. You can also see in Figure 11 that *IRR* is 20 percent after tax.

FIGURE 11   Relationship between *NPV* and Required Rate of Return for $2 Million Office Building

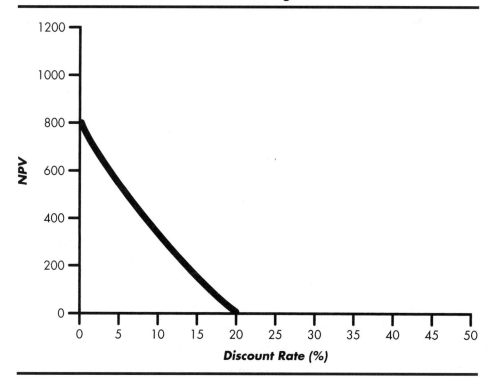

Now compare this investment to a $2 million coal mine, with the following cash flows:

Project B: $2 Million Coal Mine		
Year	ATCF ($000's)	ATER ($000's)
0	($2,000)	
1	$12,000	
2	$0	($11,000)

This project has an *IRR* of both 13 and 387 percent (see Figure 12). The two *IRR*s come about because the project generates $12 million in year 1 and then requires the investor to pay out $11 million in year 2.

Different Scales of Investment

NPV and *IRR* analysis will rank mutually exclusive projects differently when the scale of investment is different. To illustrate, consider the following mutually exclusive real estate investments:

FIGURE 12   Relationship between *NPV* and Required Rate of Return for $2 Million Coal Mine

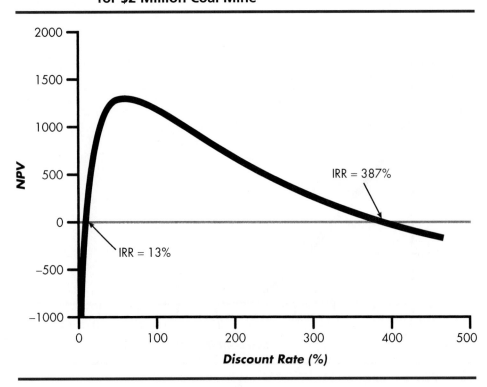

SUMMARY

Investment analysis attempts to ascertain the *NPV* of a property to a specific investor, based on available financing, desired rate of return, tax position, and other assumptions unique to the investor. *NPV* is the difference between the equity cost of an investment and the present value of the cash flows from the investment, discounted at the investor's required rate of return:

$$NPV = \frac{ATCF_1}{(1 + r_a)^1} + \frac{ATCF_2}{(1 + r_a)^2} + \cdots + \frac{ATCF_n}{(1 + r_a)^n} + \frac{ATER}{(1 + r_a)^n} - I$$

The decision rule is that *NPV* must be zero or positive in order for the investment to be undertaken; otherwise, the investment should be rejected.

IRR is sometimes used as an alternative to *NPV* analysis. The *IRR* of an investment is that rate of return that discounts future cash flows to the exact amount of the investment or, stated another way, it is the return on the property. The decision rule for *IRR* is that if *IRR* is greater than or equal to the required rate of return, the investment should be made; otherwise, the investment should be rejected.

4⅝ 4?

5½ − ⅜

5½

20⅝ 21³⁄₁₆ − ⅛

17⅜ 18⅛ + ⅞

6½ 6½ − ½

7¼ 6½ 3½₃₂ −

15/16

1 9⅝

9/16

7¹⁵⁄₁₆

7⁹⁄₁₆ 7¹³⁄₁₆

2⅝ 2¹¹⁄₃₂ 2½ +

2¾ 2¼ 2¼

12¹⁄₁₆ 11⅜ 11¾ +

87 33¾ 33 33⅛ −

255⅝ 24⁹⁄₁₆ 25⅝ +

12 11⅝ 11⅞ +

16 10½ 10½ 10½ −

78 15⅞ 15¹³⁄₁₆ 15⅞ −

9⁹⁄₁₆ 8¼ 8⅛ +

430 11¼ 10⅝

INCOME PROPERTY ANALYSIS AND APPRAISAL

by James D. Shilling

LEARNING OUTCOMES

The candidate should be able to:	Mastery
a. explain the relation between a real estate capitalization rate and a discount rate;	☐
b. estimate the capitalization rate by the market-extraction method, band-of-investment method, and built-up method, and justify each method's use in capitalization rate determination;	☐
c. estimate the market value of a real estate investment using the direct income capitalization approach and the gross income multiplier technique;	☐
d. contrast limitations of the direct capitalization approach to those of the gross income multiplier technique.	☐

There are few sorrows, however poignant, in which a good income is of no avail.

—*Logan Pearsall Smith*

In this reading, our attention is directed to the estimation of market value for income-producing property. Income-producing real estate is generally owned as an investment. In turn, the value of any income property is a direct result of the quality, amount, and duration of the income it generates. That is, the higher the earning power of a property, the greater its value.

Valuing income properties involves estimating both market value and investment value. *Investment value* is the value to a specific investor and is akin to subjective value, or value in use. Market value is the most probable selling price and is equivalent to objective value or value in exchange. Market value is based on impersonal, detached, market-oriented data and assumptions;

investment value, on the other hand, depends on data and assumptions that are personal and subjective. Market and investment value may coincide if the data and assumptions of the specific investor are the same as those of the typical investor in the market.

Market value is clearly the focal point of almost any real estate decision. Whether buying, selling, investing, developing, lending, exchanging, renting, assessing, or acquiring property for public use, market value needs to be known for the decision and action to be sound.

1   HOW INCOME PROPERTIES ARE VALUED

The market value of an income-producing property is the present value of an expected cash flow stream. This is usually written as:

$$MV_0 = \sum_{t=1}^{n} \frac{NOI_t}{(1 + r)^t} + \frac{MV_n}{(1 + r)^n}$$

where MV_0 is the current market value of the property, NOI_t is the property's net operating income at time t, MV_n is the expected sales price of the property at the end of n period, and n is some finite holding period. Here we ignore the effects of selling expenses on the net sales proceeds at disposition. The term Σ is a short-hand notation for the word *summation*. Therefore, the equation above could also be written as:

$$MV_0 = \frac{NOI_1}{(1 + r)^1} + \frac{NOI_2}{(1 + r)^2} + \cdots + \frac{NOI_n}{(1 + r)^n} + \frac{MV_n}{(1 + r)^n}$$

Notice that if this price formula holds, then investors n periods from now will also determine MV_n by looking at the property's net operating income and its expected sales proceeds over the m-period holding period from $t = n + 1$ to $t = n + m$. This means that we can express MV_n in terms of NOI_t and $MV_{n + m}$:

$$MV_n = \sum_{t=n+1}^{n+m} \frac{NOI_t}{(1 + r)^{t-n}} + \frac{MV_{n+m}}{(1 + r)^m}$$

The same is true for the value of the property when it is resold at time $n + m$:

$$MV_{n+m} = \sum_{t=n+m+1}^{n+m+k} \frac{NOI_t}{(1 + r)^{t-n-m}} + \frac{MV_{n+m+k}}{(1 + r)^k}$$

In this case we assume that the property will be held for k periods; that is, from time $n + m + 1$ to time $n + m + k$.

In principle, with an infinite horizon and an infinite chain of investors succeeding each other, the market value of the property is:

$$MV_0 = \sum_{t=1}^{\infty} \frac{NOI_t}{(1 + r)^t}$$

where the sign ∞ is used to indicate infinity.

FIGURE 1　Steps in the Direct Capitalization Approach to Estimating Market Value

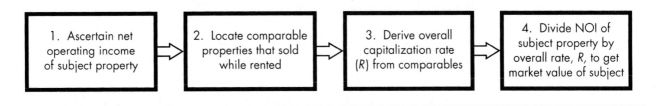

This discounted cash flow formula for the market value of real estate reduces to:

$$MV_0 = \frac{NOI}{r - g} = \frac{NOI}{R_0}$$

assuming *NOI* is growing at a constant rate, *g*, and $g < r$. In valuation terminology, the above expression is known as the **direct income capitalization approach** and $R_0 = r - g$ is known as the *capitalization rate* or *going-in rate*. The idea of direct income capitalization is to convert a stream of expected future income payments into a lump sum, or capital, value. See Figure 1 for the steps involved.

RELATIONSHIP BETWEEN DISCOUNT RATES AND CAPITALIZATION RATES

2

It is extremely important to distinguish between discount rates and capitalization rates. Discount rates represent the required rate of return, or yield, on real estate. For a retail shopping center, for example, pretax yields might range from 11 to 15 percent, depending on the risk involved. On a high-rise suburban office building, pretax yields might range from 12 to 17 percent.

Capitalization rates, on the other hand, are net of value appreciation or depreciation. In times of rapid inflation, a very low capitalization rate is likely. Also, experience has shown that capitalization rates vary over time with the fluctuation in interest rates. To illustrate, consider the recent acquisition of South Hills Village Mall, one of Pittsburgh's oldest enclosed malls, by the New York-based O'Connor Group. The O'Connor Group purchased the 24-year-old mall on behalf of Shopping Center Associates, an investment group, and an unidentified investor.

Suppose the O'Connor Group expects to earn an 11 percent pretax return on the investment. Further suppose that South Hills Village Mall is expected to appreciate by 3.5 percent per annum. This means:

$$
\begin{aligned}
R_0 &= r - g \\
&= 11\% - 3.5\% = 7.5\%
\end{aligned}
$$

The R_0 in this example is 7.5 percent. But the expected pretax rate of return on investment is 11 percent. The lower R_0 gives a higher value, reflecting favorable future income and/or capital gains expectations.

Notice that we could have just as easily dealt with the situation in which South Hills Village Mall was expected to depreciate by 3.5 percent per annum. In this case the overall capitalization rate is:

$$R_0 = r - g$$
$$= 11\% - (-3.5\%) = 14.5\%$$

The effect of this assumption is to raise, rather than lower, the overall capitalization rate and to lower appraised value for a given *NOI*. The negative 3.5 percent premium in this case represents a **recapture premium**—that is, an amortization of the building component. This is as it should be; absent inflation, *NOI* must also provide for a return *of* the invested capital. Otherwise there would be no mechanism by which investors could recapture the building's future depreciation.

There is also the possibility that with a 25-year remaining economic life, South Hills Village Mall could depreciate in real terms by 1.5 percent per annum, while appreciating in nominal terms by 3.5 percent per annum. The net (of depreciation) recapture rate in this case is 2 percent and the overall capitalization rate applicable to the building is:

$$R_0 = r - g$$
$$= 11\% - 2\% = 9\%$$

Appropriate capitalization rates are clearly influenced by the conditions under which the particular investment is being operated. Capitalization rates are also affected by prevailing interest rates, availability of funds, and risk.

3   DERIVING THE CAPITALIZATION RATE

Market-Extraction Method

Direct income capitalization is most meaningful when the capitalization rate is derived from the market. This is called the **market-extraction method**.

Assuming comparable income properties can be found, the only information required about each property is its net operating income and its sale price. Dividing the sale price into the net operating income yields:

$$R_0 = r - g = \frac{NOI}{MV_0}$$

This is really only a reversal of the process of estimating MV_0. With three comparable office buildings, the calculations might be as follows:

$$\text{For comparable 1} \quad R_0 = \frac{\$594,000}{\$6,000,000} = 0.0990, \text{ or } 9.9\%$$

$$\text{For comparable 2} \quad R_0 = \frac{\$748,000}{\$7,400,000} = 0.1011, \text{ or } 10.01\%$$

$$\text{For comparable 3} \quad R_0 = \frac{\$465,000}{\$4,680,000} = 0.0994, \text{ or } 9.94\%$$

On the basis of these three ratios, an overall capitalization rate of 10 percent would seem to be a reasonable reflection of what the market is actually doing.

Given an estimate of R_0, finding the indicated market value of an income-producing property is straightforward. The *NOI* of the subject property is divided by the market-derived overall capitalization rate, R_0.

The proper calculation is:

$$MV_0 = \frac{NOI}{.1000} = \frac{\$780,000}{.1000} = \$7,800,000$$

assuming that *NOI* in a stabilized year of operation for the subject property is $780,000. With R_0 equal to 10 percent, we obtain an indicated market value of $7,800,000.

Band-of-Investment Method

Under the **band-of-investment method**, individual rates of interest applicable to properties that use both debt and equity financing are weighted to arrive at the market rate of capitalization. To illustrate: assuming that first mortgage loans are made for up to 65 percent of property value at 8 percent interest for 20 years (monthly compounding), and that the equity balance requires a return of 12 percent—after provision for appreciation or depreciation—to be financially attractive to owners or investors, then the market rate would be as follows:

1. We know that the lender will require an 8 percent return on all funds advanced. We also know that the lender requires that the first mortgage loan be amortized over 20 years, with monthly compounding. Thus, we must set aside an annuity each month to pay off the mortgage at the end of 20 years. The amount of the annuity at 8 percent interest for 20 years is:

$$\text{Return of capital to lender} = \frac{i}{(1 + i)^n - 1}$$

$$= \frac{.08/12}{(1 + .08/12)^{240} - 1}$$

$$= .0017 \text{ per month}$$

$$= .0017 \times 12 = .0204 \text{ per annum}$$

This fraction is known as a **sinking fund factor**—that is, it is the amount that must be set aside each period to have $1 at the end of 20 years if we are paying an 8 percent rate. This fraction can also be computed using a financial calculator. Simply enter $1 for future value, 8% ÷ 12 for interest rate, 20 × 12 = 240 for the number of periods, and solve for the annuity payment. Then multiply by 12 to convert to an annual interest rate factor.

The total required payment to the lender is thus:

$$\text{Mortgage constant} = \text{Return on funds} + \text{Return of capital to lender}$$
$$= .08 + .0204$$
$$= 10.04\%$$

2. We know that the equity investor requires a return of 12 percent after provision for appreciation or depreciation. Thus, the weighted average rate is:

Split Interest	Percent of Value		Split Rate	Weighted Rate
First mortgage	65%	×	10.04%	= 6.53%
Equity	35%	×	12.00%	= 4.20%
Total	1.00			10.73%

If the net income of a property were $800,000 per annum, then the capitalized value of that income at 10.73 percent would be $800,000 divided by .1073, or $7,455,732. The income of $800,000 would be distributed as follows:

Split Interest	Value		Rate of Earning	Dollar Earnings
First mortgage	$4,846,226	×	10.04%	= $487,000
Equity	$2,609,506	×	12.00%	= $313,000
Total	$7,455,732			$800,000

It is to be emphasized that the weighted average rate (10.73 percent in this example) represents an **overall capitalization rate** for the property. It applies to any property that is 65 percent debt-financed that is priced to yield a total required payment to the lender of 10.04 percent and a cash-on-cash return to the equity investor of 12 percent. This 12 percent cash-on-cash return to the equity investor is known as the **equity dividend rate**.

Built-Up Method

Under the **built-up method**, the rate of capitalization would be a composite of the following: 1) pure interest, e.g., interest that can be secured on government bonds (adjusted for the tax savings associated with real estate); 2) rate for nonliquidity, e.g., rate necessary to compensate for relative inability to cash in the investment; 3) a recapture premium, e.g., a return of investment or an adjustment for appreciation; and 4) rate of risk. The risk rate varies with the type of investment.

To illustrate, the rate applicable to an equity property may be composed as follows:

Pure interest	6.50 percent
Nonliquidity	1.00 percent
Recapture premium	2.00 percent
Risk (of loss)	2.00 percent
Total	11.50 percent

The recapture premium in this case provides for a 2 percent return of investment, net of appreciation. This adjustment to the pure interest rate accounts for the fact that improvements have limited lives. It also supposedly accounts for the value of the land 10, 30, 50, or more years in the future, when its availability, free from present structural improvements, may be counted on, and it also accounts for any appreciation or depreciation in the value of the improvements.

Here is a simple example: we will make the following assumptions to demonstrate the application of the built-up method of capitalization.

Net operating income	$130,000
Anticipated economic life of structure	50 years
Pure interest rate	6.50%
Nonliquidity premium	2.00%
Recapture premium	2.00%
Risk premium	1.50%

The built-up rate is thus:

$$R_0 = 6.50\% + 2.00\% + 2.00\% + 1.50\% = 12.00\%$$

which provides for an amortization rate of 2 percent per year (under the assumption that the property is expected to last fifty years).

The capitalized value of net income is:

$$MV = \frac{NOI}{R_0}$$
$$= \frac{\$130,000}{.12}$$
$$= \$1,083,333$$

The higher the built-up rate of capitalization when applied to a given income, the lower the resultant value. To illustrate, suppose the built-up rate of capitalization were equal to 18 percent. With no change in net income, the capitalized value would be:

$$MV = \frac{NOI}{R_0}$$
$$= \frac{\$130,000}{.18}$$
$$= \$722,222$$

To be conservative, therefore, many appraisers use a high built-up rate for capitalization of net income.

LIMITATIONS OF DIRECT CAPITALIZATION 4

The chief difficulty in the direct capitalization approach to value lies in the selection of a capitalization rate. In order to make the maximum use of the capitalization approach, the capitalization rate must accurately reflect the behavior of investors in the marketplace. This difficulty might explain why appraisers typically regard the capitalization rate as a ratio that is derived from the market. Recall that the ratio of net operating income to value is a direct measure of the capitalization rate on a specific property. Where such data are available and of sufficient quality, viewing the capitalization rate as a ratio provides the most compelling evidence of the equity yields necessary to attract potential investors. Where the data on net operating income or value are lacking, or are not clear, as frequently happens, the appraiser must select a capitalization rate by considering the equity yield rates and financing conditions available, plus the possibility of increased rentals and capital appreciation. In selecting a capitalization rate, certainty of the returns, the relative ease of liquidation of the investment, the relative burden of managing the investment, and the possibility of producing tax-sheltered cash flow must also be considered.

Also note that the income approach to value, as a rule, is limited to property that is used primarily for income or investment purposes. It does not provide an accurate valuation of owner-occupied homes because the benefits or amenities derived by owners are difficult to measure in terms of dollars, or even as hypothetical rental income. For apartment houses, commercial, or industrial properties, however, the income approach is applicable.

5   GROSS INCOME MULTIPLIER TECHNIQUE

The gross income multiplier technique is also used primarily for income-producing properties. A **gross income multiplier (GIM)** relates total annual income to market value. The basic steps in the GIM technique are: 1) ascertain the gross annual market income of the subject property, 2) derive a GIM from the market, and 3) apply the GIM to the subject property to estimate its market value. For small, one- to four-family residential properties, monthly rental is commonly used instead of gross annual market income.

Derivation of the market GIM is equivalent to extracting the market capitalization rate. That is, sales prices of comparable properties are divided by their respective gross annual incomes to get a range of GIMs. Sample calculations follow.

Suppose we collected a sample of three comparable brownstone rental dwelling units. The term *brownstone* is used as a generic word to denote small, urban, multiple dwellings (up to 10 units) that either are rented or sold as condominiums. These buildings may also be called *graystones* or *townhouses*. Dividing sales price by the gross annual market income gives a GIM. The calculations are:

$$\text{GIM for a property} = \frac{\text{Sales price}}{\text{Gross annual income}}$$

$$\text{GIM, comparable 1} = \frac{\$610,000}{\$101,400} = 6.02$$

$$\text{GIM, comparable 2} = \frac{\$745,760}{\$124,500} = 5.99$$

$$\text{GIM, comparable 3} = \frac{\$680,000}{\$113,200} = 6.01$$

On the basis of these calculations, a market GIM of 6.00 seems reasonable for brownstone units in this particular neighborhood at this time.

Applying the market GIM to the gross annual income of the subject property, $108,000, gives an indicated market value of:

$$\text{Indicated market value} = \text{Gross income} \times \text{Market-derived GIM}$$
$$= \$108,000 \times 6.00 = \$648,000$$

LIMITATIONS OF THE GIM TECHNIQUE 6

One of the major limitations of the gross income multiplier approach is that sales of some types of income properties occur infrequently; thus, the derivation of a market GIM must be based on limited information. In addition, rental data are not always available for deriving the multiplier. Another limitation is that gross rents are used instead of net operating income; if the building-to-land ratios differ, or if the buildings are different ages, the results may be distorted. Further, the GIM is subject to some distortion because adverse zoning, lack of maintenance, or heavy property taxes will negatively influence sale price with little effect on rental levels. Thus, unless the comparables are similar in all respects, a distorted GIM may be derived from the market. Finally, the technique is not useful for properties that are unique or that generate income in the form of amenities.

SUMMARY

The procedure whereby the market value of income-producing property is calculated by capitalizing the annual net income generated by the property at an overall capitalization rate is known as direct capitalization. The process can be summarized as follows:

$$MV_0 = \frac{NOI}{R_0}$$

where MV_0 is market value, NOI is annual net income, and R_0 is the capitalization rate necessary to attract investors.

The capitalization rate represents the required rate of return, or yield, on real estate, less the possibility of capital appreciation. Also considered by investors in selecting a capitalization rate are the certainty of the returns, the relative ease of liquidation of the investment, the relative burden of managing the investment, and the possibility of producing tax-sheltered cash flow. In order to make maximum use of the direct capitalization approach, the capitalization rate must accurately reflect the behavior of investors in the marketplace.

An alternative income approach to value is the gross income multiplier (GIM) technique. The GIM approach to value relates total annual income to market value. The basic formula is:

Indicated market value = Gross income × Market-derived GIM

The GIM multiplier is derived by looking at the sales prices of comparable properties, divided by their respective gross annual incomes.

PRACTICE PROBLEMS FOR READING 45

The following information relates to Questions 1–6

Kristen Kratky, CFA, is a real estate investment analyst who is evaluating real estate properties before making a recommendation to Rudy Salazar, CFA, a portfolio manager at her firm. Kratky has compiled data for four alternative properties, of which two are apartment complexes, one is a warehouse, and one is a hotel. Selected characteristics for the four income properties are presented in Exhibit 1.

EXHIBIT 1	Selected Information on Income Properties			
	Property 1 Apartment Complex	Property 2 Warehouse	Property 3 Hotel	Property 4 Apartment Complex
Desirability of location	High	Medium	Medium	High
Annual gross income	$1,112,000	$984,000	$1,297,000	$962,000
Annual net operating income	$594,000	$706,000	$485,000	$536,000
Discount rate	13.1%	11.8%	14.1%	12.8%
Capitalization rate	9.1%	13.2%	10.8%	8.9%
Risk premium	1.4%	1.5%	2.2%	1.5%

Kratky believes that Property 4, which sold for $6.25 million earlier in the week, is a comparable for Property 1.

Salazar states: "Property 3 has higher property taxes than the properties that are considered its comparables. As a result, the value estimated from the gross income multiplier approach is likely to be higher than both the quoted market value of the property and the value estimated from the direct capitalization approach."

Salazar requests that Kratky evaluate the properties using a capitalization rate that explicitly recognizes the use of leverage in financing a project.

Kratky decides to gather more information about capitalization rates, so she consults with Timur Gok, a senior analyst at her firm. Gok indicates that he prefers to use the market-extraction method to derive a capitalization rate. He states that "calculation of a capitalization rate by the market-extraction method requires the sales price and the gross income for a comparable property."

1. Based on Exhibit 1, which of the properties is expected to depreciate in value?

   A. Property 1.

   B. Property 2.

   C. Property 3.

2. Based on Exhibit 1 and using the direct income capitalization approach, the estimated value of Property 2 is *closest* to:

   A. $5.3 million.

   B. $6.0 million.

   C. $7.5 million.

3. Based on Kratky's analysis of comparable properties, the estimated market value of Property 1 from the gross income multiplier approach is *closest* to:

   A. $5.4 million.

   B. $6.5 million.

   C. $7.2 million.

4. Is Salazar's statement regarding Property 3's value estimated from the gross income multiplier approach correct with respect to the quoted market value and the value estimated from the direct capitalization approach?

   A. Yes.

   B. Only with respect to the quoted market value.

   C. Only with respect to the value estimated from the direct capitalization approach.

5. Which method should Kratky use to satisfy Salazar's request regarding the use of the capitalization rate?

   A. Built-up.

   B. Market extraction.

   C. Band-of-investment.

6. Is Gok's statement regarding the calculation of capitalization rates by the market extraction method correct with respect to sales price and gross income?

   A. Yes.

   B. Only with respect to sales price.

   C. Only with respect to gross income.

SOLUTIONS FOR READING 45

1. B is correct. The capitalization rate is greater than the discount rate, which means g is negative, $11.8 - 13.2 = -1.4$.

Capitalization rate = Discount rate − Growth rate (g); thus,

g = Discount rate − Capitalization rate. Therefore, a negative value for g implies a depreciating property value.

2. A is correct. Market value = $NOI \div$ Capitalization rate = $706,000 \div 0.132 =$ 5,348K. NOI = Net operating income.

3. C is correct. Market value = Gross income $\times$ GIM = 1,112k $\times$ 6.4969 = 7,224.5K.

GIM = Gross income multiplier = Comparable property sales price $\div$ Gross income = $6,250,000 \div 962,000 = 6.4969$.

4. A is correct. The gross income multiplier (GIM) approach considers only rental income, not costs; thus, in this case, GIM will yield an estimate that is upwardly biased, and it will likely exceed the property's market value and the estimate from the direct capitalization (DC) approach, which does consider costs. Therefore, Salazar's claim that the GIM derived value is likely to exceed both the market value and the DC approach value is correct.

5. C is correct. The band-of-investment method is the only method of capitalization rate determination that considers the financing mix used in a real estate transaction.

6. B is correct. The market extraction method requires only two inputs, a comparable property's sales price and its "net operating income."

	4⅝	4⅞	⅜
	5½	5½ −	⅜
5½	2¹³⁄₁₆ −	1⁄16	
20⅝	2¹³⁄₁₆ +	⅞	
17⅜	18⅛ +	½	
9½	6½	6½ −	⅛
7¼	31⁄32 −		
	15⁄16		
	9⁄16	9⁄16	
7⁄32			
7¹⁵⁄₁₆	7¹³⁄₁₆	7¹⁵⁄₁₆	
2⅝	2¹¹⁄₃₂	2½ +	
	2¾	2¼	2⅛
121⁄16	11⅜	11¾ +	
87	33¾	33	33¼ −
622	25⅝	24⁹⁄₁₆	25⅜ +
833	12	11⅝	11⅞ +
16	10½	10½	10½ −
78	15⅞	15¹³⁄₁₆	15⅞ −
			8⅜ +
5 4508	9¹⁄₁₆	8¼	
430	11¼	10⅛	
			4⅜

PRIVATE EQUITY VALUATION

by Yves Courtois, CFA and Tim Jenkinson

LEARNING OUTCOMES

The candidate should be able to:	Mastery
a. explain sources of value creation in private equity;	☐
b. explain how private equity firms align their interests with those of the managers of portfolio companies;	☐
c. distinguish between the characteristics of buyout and venture capital investments;	☐
d. describe valuation issues in buyout and venture capital transactions;	☐
e. explain alternative exit routes in private equity and their impact on value;	☐
f. explain private equity fund structures, terms, valuation, and due diligence in the context of an analysis of private equity fund returns;	☐
g. explain risks and costs of investing in private equity;	☐
h. interpret and compare financial performance of private equity funds from the perspective of an investor;	☐
i. calculate management fees, carried interest, net asset value, distributed to paid in (DPI), residual value to paid in (RVPI), and total value to paid in (TVPI) of a private equity fund;	☐

A Note on Valuation of Venture Capital Deals: (Appendix 46)

j. calculate pre-money valuation, post-money valuation, ownership fraction, and price per share applying the venture capital method 1) with single and multiple financing rounds and 2) in terms of IRR;	☐
k. demonstrate alternative methods to account for risk in venture capital.	☐

1

INTRODUCTION

Private equity is playing an increasing role in the global economy. In the last decade, private equity has grown from a small, niche activity to a critical component of the financial system. One manifestation of this has been the huge amount of money that investors have committed to private equity, estimated at around $1.5 trillion globally between 1998 and 2006. And this is just the equity portion of total financing. As will be explained later, many private equity deals employ significant amounts of debt, and so the value of the transactions involving private equity funds is often 2 or 3 times the actual equity raised. Until recently, few people even knew the names of the main private equity players. But now such organizations as Blackstone, Carlyle, KKR, Texas Pacific Group, and Permira are recognized as major forces in the global financial system. Fund sizes have grown—to over $20 billion at their largest—as have the size and complexity of the transactions that private equity funds are able to undertake, such as the $45 billion acquisition of the U.S. energy company TXU. In 2006, it was estimated that private equity funds were involved in approximately one-quarter of all merger and acquisition activities.

There can be two perspectives on private equity valuation. In Section 2, we primarily take the perspective of the private equity firm that is evaluating potential investments. When a private equity firm is performing valuations of potential acquisitions, this effort is particularly complex because in most cases, except for public-to-private transactions, there will be no market prices to refer to. Private equity firms can face considerable challenges in valuing these companies, and this reading discusses the main ways in which valuation is approached. In Section 3, we take the perspective of an outside investor who is looking at the costs and risks of investing in a fund sponsored by the private equity firm.

Definitions of private equity differ, but in this reading we include the entire asset class of equity investments that are not quoted on stock markets. The private equity class stretches from venture capital (VC)—working with early stage companies that in many cases have no revenues but have potentially good ideas or technology—all the way through to large buyouts (leveraged buyout, or LBO) in which the private equity firm buys the entire company. In some cases, these companies might themselves be quoted on the stock market, and the private equity fund performs a public-to-private transaction thereby removing the entire company from the stock market. But in the majority of cases, buyout transactions will involve privately owned companies and, very often, a particular division of an existing company. There are many other forms of later-stage financing, such as providing capital to back the expansion of existing businesses, but for this reading we will refer simply to *venture capital* and *buyouts* as the two main forms of private equity.

Many classifications of private equity are available. Exhibit 1 provides a set of classifications proposed by the European Venture Capital Association (EVCA).

EXHIBIT 1	Classification of Private Equity in Terms of Stage and Type of Financing of Portfolio Companies	
Broad Category	**Subcategory**	**Brief Description**
Venture capital	Seed stage	Financing provided to research business ideas, develop prototype products, or conduct market research.
	Start-up stage	Financing to recently created companies with well articulated business and marketing plans.
	Expansion stage	Financing to companies that have started their selling effort and may be already breaking even. Financing may serve to expand production capacity, product development, or provide working capital.
	Replacement capital	Financing provided to purchase shares from other existing venture capital investors or to reduce financial leverage.
Buyout	Acquisition capital	Financing in the form of debt, equity, or quasi-equity provided to a company to acquire another company.
	Leverage buyout	Financing provided by a LBO firm to acquire a company.
	Management buyout	Financing provided to the management to acquire a company, specific product line, or division (carve-out).
Special situations	Mezzanine finance	Financing generally provided in the form of subordinated debt and an equity kicker (warrants, equity, etc.) frequently in the context of LBO transactions.
	Distressed securities	Financing of companies in need of restructuring or facing financial distress.
	One-time opportunities	Financing in relation to changing industry trends and new government regulations.
	Others	Other forms of private equity financing are also possible (i.e., activist investing, etc.).

Source: www.evca.com.

These classifications are not exhaustive. Private equity funds may also be classified depending on their geographical (national, regional, or global) and/or sector focus (e.g., diversified industrials, telecommunications, biotechnologies, healthcare, industrials, etc.).

How is the invested money split between venture capital and buyout deals? In broad terms, around four-fifths of the money has been flowing into buyouts in recent years in both the United States and Europe. In part this is because of the sheer scale of buyouts in which an individual deal can absorb several billion dollars of capital. In contrast, venture capital deals tend to drip feed money into companies as they develop. But investors also have been increasingly focusing on buyout funds, in which, in recent years at least, the average returns earned have tended to be higher.

Where does the money come from and how are the private equity funds organized? Most of the money comes from institutional investors, such as pension funds, endowments, and insurance companies, although many high-net-worth individuals also invest directly or through fund-of-funds intermediaries who provide their investors with a more diversified portfolio of investments. At present, the proportion of assets allocated by investors to private equity is considerably higher in the United States than in Europe, although surveys of European investors find that the fund managers plan to increase their allocation to private equity. So the flow of money into private equity is likely to continue and indeed grow, depending, of course, on market conditions.

One distinctive characteristic of private equity investment is a buy-to-sell orientation. Private equity fund investors typically expect their money returned, with a handsome profit, within 10 years of committing their funds. The economic incentives of the funds are aligned with this goal, as is explained later. In the next section we discuss this buy-to-sell approach and how funds are typically organized.

2   INTRODUCTION TO VALUATION TECHNIQUES IN PRIVATE EQUITY TRANSACTIONS

This reading is not intended to be a comprehensive review of valuation techniques applicable to private equity transactions. Instead, we highlight some essential considerations specific to private equity. As you might expect, private equity firms are a rich laboratory for applying the principles of asset and equity valuation. The case study on venture capital valuation that follows this reading demonstrates how a specific valuation technique can be applied.

First and foremost, we must distinguish between the price paid for a private equity stake and the valuation of such private equity stake. The price paid for a private equity stake is the outcome of a negotiation process between two or more parties with each possibly assigning a different value to that same private equity stake. Unlike shares of public companies that are traded regularly on a regulated market, buyers and sellers of private equity interests generally employ more efforts to uncover their value. Private equity valuation is thus time bound and dependent on the respective motives and interests of buyers and sellers.

The selection of the appropriate valuation methodologies depends largely on the stage of development of a private equity portfolio company. Exhibit 2 provides an overview of some of the main methodologies employed in private equity valuation and an indication of the stage of company development for which they may apply.

EXHIBIT 2	Overview of Selected Valuation Methodologies and Their Possible Application in Private Equity	
Valuation Technique	**Brief Description**	**Application**
Income approach: Discounted cash flows (DCF)	Value is obtained by discounting expected future cash flows at an appropriate cost of capital.	Generally applies across the broad spectrum of company stages. Given the emphasis on expected cash flows, this methodology provides the most relevant results when applied to companies with a sufficient operating history. Therefore, most applicable to companies operating from the expansion up to the maturity phase.
Relative value: Earnings multiples	Application of an earnings multiple to the earnings of a portfolio company. The earnings multiple is frequently obtained from the average of a group of public companies operating in a similar business and of comparable size. Commonly used multiples include: Price/Earnings (P/E), Enterprise Value/EBITDA, Enterprise Value/Sales.	Generally applies to companies with a significant operating history and predictable stream of cash flows. May also apply with caution to companies operating at the expansion stage. Rarely applies to early stage or start-up companies.
Real option	The right to undertake a business decision (call or put option). Requires judgmental assumptions about key option parameters.	Generally applies to situations in which the management or shareholders have significant flexibility in making radically different strategic decisions (i.e., option to undertake or abandon a high risk, high return project). Therefore, generally applies to some companies operating at the seed or start-up phase.

(Exhibit continued on next page . . .)

EXHIBIT 2	(continued)	
Valuation Technique	**Brief Description**	**Application**
Replacement cost	Estimated cost to recreate the business as it stands as of the valuation date.	Generally applies to early (seed and start-up) stage companies or companies operating at the development stage and generating negative cash flows.
		Rarely applies to mature companies as it is difficult to estimate the cost to recreate a company with a long operating history. For example, it would be difficult to estimate the cost to recreate a long established brand like Coca-Cola, whereas the replacement cost methodology may be used to estimate the brand value for a recently launched beverage (R&D expenses, marketing costs, etc.).

One other methodology, the venture capital method, is discussed more fully as part of the case study that follows this reading.

Note that in a vibrant and booming private equity market, there is a natural tendency among participants to focus primarily on the earnings approach to determine value. This approach is perceived as providing a benchmark value corresponding best to the state of the current private equity market. Because of the lack of liquidity of private equity investments, the concurrent use of other valuation metrics is strongly recommended.

Thus, valuation does not involve simply performing a net present value calculation on a static set of future profit projections. The forecasts of the existing management or vendors are, of course, a natural place to start, but one of the key ways private equity firms add value is by challenging the way businesses are run. The business would have additional value if the private equity firm improves the business's financing, operations, management, and marketing.

In most transactions, private equity investors are faced with a set of investment decisions that are based on an assessment of prospective returns and associated probabilities. Private equity firms are confronted generally with a large flow of information arising from detailed due diligence investigations and from complex financial models. It is essential to understand the extent of the upside and downside potential of internal and external factors affecting the business and their resulting effect on net income and free cash flows. Any possible scenario must pass the judgmental test of how realistic it is. The defined scenarios should be based not only on the analysis of past events, but on what future events may realistically happen, given knowledge of the present. The interplay between exogenous factors (such as favorable and unfavorable macroeconomic conditions, interest rates, and exchange rates) and value drivers for the business (such as sales margins and required investments) should also be considered carefully. For example, what will be the sales growth if competition increases or if competing new technologies are introduced?

When building the financial forecasts, all variables in the financial projections should be linked to key fundamental factors influencing the business with assigned subjective probabilities. The use of Monte Carlo simulation, often using a spreadsheet add-in such as Crystal Ball™ or @RISK, further enhances the quality of the analysis and may be instrumental in identifying significant financial upsides and downsides to the business. In a Monte Carlo simulation, the analyst must model the fundamental value drivers of the portfolio company, which are in turn linked to a valuation model. Base case, worst case, and best case scenarios (sometimes called a triangular approach) and associated probabilities should be discussed with line managers for each value driver with the objective being to ensure that the simulation is as close as possible to the realities of the business and encompasses the range of possible outcomes.

Other key considerations when evaluating a private equity transaction include the value of control, the impact of illiquidity, and the extent of any country risk. Estimating the discount for illiquidity and marketability and a premium for control are among the most subjective decisions in private equity valuation. The control premium is an incremental value associated with a bloc of shares that will be instrumental in gaining control of a company. In most buyouts, the entire equity capital is acquired by the private equity purchasers. But in venture capital deals, investors often acquire minority positions. In this case the control premium (if any) largely depends on the relative strength and alignment of interest of shareholders willing to gain control. For example, in a situation with only a limited number of investors able to acquire control, the control premium is likely to be much more significant relative to a situation with a dominant controlling shareholder invested along with a large number of much smaller shareholders.

The distinction between marketability and liquidity is more subtle. The cost of illiquidity may be defined as the cost of finding prospective buyers and represents the speed of conversion of the assets to cash, whereas the cost of marketability is closely related to the right to sell the assets. In practice, the marketability and liquidity discounts are frequently lumped together.

The cost for illiquidity and premium for control may be closely related because illiquidity may be more acute when there is a fierce battle for control. But there are many dimensions to illiquidity. The size of the illiquidity discount may be influenced by such factors as the shareholding structure, the level of profitability and its expected sustainability, the possibility of an initial public offering (IPO) in the near future, and the size of the private company. Because determining the relative importance of each factor may be difficult, the illiquidity discount is frequently assessed overall on a judgmental basis. In practice, the discount for illiquidity and premium for control are both adjustments to the preliminary value estimate instead of being factored into the cost of capital.

When valuing private equity portfolio companies in emerging markets, country risk may also represent a significant additional source of risk frequently added to a modified version of the standard CAPM. Estimating the appropriate country risk premium represents another significant challenge in emerging markets private equity valuation. These technical hurdles relate not only to private equity investments in emerging markets but also increasingly to global private equity transactions conducted "en-bloc" in multiple countries. More than 15 approaches exist for the estimation of the country risk premium.[1]

---

[1] The modified country spread model, also called the modified Goldman model, is frequently used in practice. The Erb, Harvey, and Viskanta model, also called the country risk rating model, is gaining increasing popularity among valuation practitioners, partly because of its ease of use and theoretical appeal. For a comprehensive analysis of this topic, see *Estimating cost of capital in emerging markets*, Yves Courtois, CFA Institute webcasts, www.cfawebcasts.org.

Valuation in private equity transactions is, therefore, very challenging. Whereas traditional valuation methodologies, such as discounted cash flow analysis, adjusted present value, and techniques based on comparisons from the public market of precedent transactions, are used frequently by investment and valuation professionals, they are applied to private equity situations with care, taking into consideration stress tests and a range of possible future scenarios for the business. Given the challenges of private equity valuation, value estimates based on a combination of several valuation methodologies will provide the strongest support for the estimated value. Private equity valuation is a process that starts as a support for decision making at the transaction phase but should also serve as a monitoring tool to capture new opportunities, or protect from losses, with the objective to continuously create value until the investment is exited. It also serves as a performance reporting tool to investors while the company remains in the fund portfolio. These ongoing valuation and reporting issues are discussed in Section 3.

2.1 How Is Value Created in Private Equity?

The question of how private equity funds actually create value has been much debated inside and outside the private equity industry. The survival of the private equity governance model depends on some economic advantages it may have over the public equity governance model. These potential advantages, described more fully below, include 1) the ability to re-engineer the private firm to generate superior returns, 2) the ability to access credit markets on favorable terms, and 3) a better alignment of interests between private equity firm owners and the managers of the firms they control.

Do private equity houses have superior ability to re-engineer companies and, therefore, generate superior returns? Some of the largest private equity organizations, such as Kohlberg Kravis Roberts (KKR), The Carlyle Group, Texas Pacific Group (TPG), or Blackstone Group, have developed in-house high-end consulting capabilities supported frequently by seasoned industry veterans (former CEOs, CFOs, senior advisers), and have a proven ability to execute deals on a global basis. Irrespective of their size, some of the very best private equity firms have developed effective re-engineering capabilities to add value to their investments. But it is hard to believe that this factor, all else being equal, is the main driver of value added in private equity. Assuming that private equity houses have a superior ability to re-engineer companies, this would mean that public companies have inherently less ability to conduct re-engineering or organizational changes relative to corporations held by private equity organizations. Many public companies, like General Electric or Toyota, have established a long track record of creating value. Thus, only a part of value added created by private equity houses may be explained by superior reorganization and re-engineering capabilities. The answer must also come from other factors.

Is financial leverage the main driver of private equity returns in buyouts? Ample availability of credit at favorable terms (such as low credit spreads and few covenants) led in 2006 and the first half of 2007 to a significant increase in leverage available to buyout transactions. Borrowing 6 to 8 times EBITDA (earnings before interest, taxes, depreciation, and amortization) has been frequent for large transactions conducted during this period. Note that in private equity, leverage is typically measured as a multiple of EBITDA instead of equity. Relative to comparable publicly quoted companies, there is a much greater use of debt in a typical buyout transaction.

When considering the impact of leverage on value, we should naturally turn to one of the foundations of modern finance: the Modigliani–Miller theorem.[2] This theorem, in its basic form, states that, in the absence of taxes, asymmetric information, bankruptcy costs, and assuming efficient markets, the value of a firm is not affected by how the firm is financed. In other words, it should not matter if the firm is financed by equity or debt. The relaxing of the "no taxes assumption" raises interesting questions in leveraged buyouts as the tax shield on the acquisition debt creates value as a result of tax deductibility of interest. One would also expect that the financial leverage of a firm would be set at a level where bankruptcy costs do not outweigh these tax benefits. Unlike public companies, private equity firms may have a better ability to raise higher levels of debt as a result of a better control over management but also as a result of their reputation for having raised, and repaid, such high levels of debt in previous transactions.

Such debt financing is raised initially from the syndicated loan market, but then is frequently repackaged via sophisticated structured products, such as collateralized loan obligations (CLOs), which consist of a portfolio of leveraged loans. In some cases the private equity funds issue high-yield bonds as a way of financing the portfolio company, and these often are sold to funds that create collateralized debt obligations (CDOs). This raises the question of whether a massive transfer of risks to the credit markets is taking place in private equity. If the answer to this last question is positive, then one would expect that it will self-correct during the next economic downturn. Note that at the time of this writing (early 2008), the CDO and CLO markets were undergoing a significant slowdown as a result of the credit market turmoil that started in the summer of 2007, triggered by the subprime mortgage crisis. The CDO and CLO markets are (at this time) inactive. As a result, the LBO market for very large transactions ("mega buyouts") was affected by a lack of financing. Additional leverage is also gained by means of equity-like instruments at the acquisition vehicle level, which are frequently located in a favorable jurisdiction such as Luxembourg, the Channel Islands, Cayman Islands, or the British Virgin Islands. Note that acquisitions by large buyout private equity firms are generally held by a top holding company in a favorable tax jurisdiction. The top holding company's share capital and equity-like instruments are held in turn by investment funds run by a general partner who is controlled by the private equity buyout firm. These instruments are treated as debt for tax purposes within the limits of thin capitalization rules in certain jurisdictions. In Luxembourg, such equity-like instruments are called convertible preferred equity certificates, or CPECs.

The effect of leverage may also be analyzed through Jensen's free cash flow hypothesis.[3] According to Jensen, low growth companies generating high free cash flows tend to invest in projects destroying value (i.e., with a negative net present value) instead of distributing excess cash to shareholders. This argument is a possible explanation[4] as to why a LBO transaction may generate value as excess cash is used to repay the senior debt tranche, effectively removing the management's discretionary use of cash. Part of the value added in private equity may thus be explained by the level of financial leverage.

What other factors may then significantly explain the returns earned by private equity funds? One important factor is the alignment of economic interests between private equity owners and the managers of the companies they control,

---

[2] F. Modigliani and M. Miller, "The Cost of Capital, Corporation Finance and the Theory of Investment." *American Economic Review* (June 1958).

[3] Jensen, M., "Agency Costs of Free Cash Flow, Corporate Finance and Takeovers," *American Economic Review*, vol. 76 no. 2 (1986).

[4] Jensen, M., "Eclipse of the Public Corporation," *Harvard Business Review*, 67 (1989).

which can crystallize management efforts to achieve ambitious milestones set by the private equity owners. Results-driven management pay packages, along with various contractual clauses, ensure that managers receive proper incentives to reach their targets, and that they will not be left behind after the private equity house exits their investment. Examples of such contract terms include tag-along, drag-along rights, which are contractual provisions in share purchase agreements that ensure any potential future acquirer of the company may not acquire control without extending an acquisition offer to all shareholders, including the management of the company.

Empirical evidence also shows that managers from public companies subsequently acquired by private equity groups tend to acknowledge an increased level of directness and intensity of input enabling them to conduct higher value-added projects over a longer time frame after the buyout, as opposed to the "short-termism" prevailing during their public market period. This short-termism is mostly driven by shareholders' expectations, the analyst community, and the broad market participants who place a significant emphasis on management to meet quarterly earnings targets. As private equity firms have a longer time horizon in managing their equity investments, they are able to attract talented managers having the ability to implement sometimes profound restructuring plans in isolation of short-term market consequences. Note however, that private equity firms are not the sole catalysts of change at large companies. Some large organizations, for example General Electric, have a proven ability to stir entrepreneurship at all levels within the company and generate substantial value over a long time horizon.

Effective structuring of investments terms (called the "term sheet") results in a balance of rights and obligations between the private equity firm and the management team. In addition to the clauses discussed above, the following contractual clauses are important illustrations of how private equity firms ensure that the management team is focused on achieving the business plan and that if the objectives are not met, the control and equity allocation held by the private equity firm will increase:

▶ *Corporate board seats*: ensures private equity control in case of major corporate events such as company sale, takeover, restructuring, IPO, bankruptcy, or liquidation.

▶ *Noncompete clause*: generally imposed on founders and prevents them from restarting the same activity during a predefined period of time.

▶ *Preferred dividends and liquidation preference*: private equity firms generally come first when distributions take place, and may be guaranteed a minimum multiple of their original investment before other shareholders receive their returns.

▶ *Reserved matters*: some domains of strategic importance (such as changes in the business plan, acquisitions, or divestitures) are subject to approval or veto by the private equity firm.

▶ *Earn-outs (mostly in venture capital)*: mechanism linking the acquisition price paid by the private equity firm to the company's future financial performance over a predetermined time horizon, generally not exceeding 2 to 3 years.

Effective contractual structuring of the investment can thus be a significant source of return to private equity firms. In particular, it may allow venture capital firms, which invest in companies with considerable uncertainties over their future, to significantly increase their level of control over time and even seize control in case the company fails to achieve the agreed goals.

2.2 Using Market Data in Valuation

In most private equity transactions—with the exception of public-to-privates—there is no direct market evidence on the valuation of the company being acquired. But virtually all valuation techniques employ evidence from the market at differing stages in the calculation, rather than relying entirely on accounting data and management forecasts.

The two most important ways in which market data are used to infer the value of the entity being acquired are by analyzing comparison companies that are quoted on public markets and valuations implied by recent transactions involving similar entities. Typically, these techniques focus on the trading or acquisition multiples that exist in the public markets or in recent transactions. For instance, suppose a valuation is sought in the food sector for a retail chain, which is currently a privately owned company. The comparison company approach would look at the trading multiples—such as enterprise value to EBITDA—of comparable public companies, and use this multiple to value the target. Similarly, if there are recent M&A transactions in the food retail sector, the transactions multiples paid could be used to inform the current market value of the target. Of course, it is very important to make sure that the comparisons are appropriate, and this is not always possible, especially for certain businesses that operate in niche sectors or that are pioneering in terms of their products or services.

The use of market data is also important in the DCF approaches, in particular in estimating an appropriate discount rate. Cost of capital for private companies is estimated generally using the same weighted average cost of capital (WACC) formula[5] used for public companies. A serious challenge, however, in assessing the cost of equity in private equity settings is the lack of public historical data on share prices and returns. Therefore, beta (β), which represents the relative exposure of company shares to the market, must be estimated by means of a proxy. This is performed typically by estimating the beta for comparable companies, and then adjusting for financial and operating leverage. When conducting this benchmark exercise, several issues that may depend on analyst judgment should be considered: To what extent are the selected comparable public firms genuinely comparable to the target firm? Should outlying companies be excluded? What is the target debt-to-equity ratio of the target firm vs. industry average? What group of comparable public companies should be selected if the target firm operates in several business segments?

Finally, in DCF valuation techniques, forecasts of future financial performance usually are only available for a few years ahead. Therefore, it is almost always necessary to estimate the terminal value of the company beyond this forecasting horizon. In order to do this, it is possible to apply a perpetual growth rate assumption, although small changes in the assumed growth rate, which are very difficult to predict, can have a significant impact on the resulting valuation. An alternative is to use an assumption about the trading multiple that exists (or is predicted to exist) in public markets, and apply this to the last years' forecast values. For instance, if over the economic cycle the average enterprise value to EBITDA ratio for the publicly quoted companies in an industry is 10, then this might be applied to the final forecast value for EBITDA for the private target as a way of estimating the terminal value.

---

[5] WACC $= [E/(E + D)] \times$ (Cost of equity) $+ [D/(E + D)] \times$ (Cost of debt) $(1 - $ Tax rate), where E is the market value of equity and D is the market value of debt.

2.3 Contrasting Valuation in Venture Capital and Buyout Settings

Buyout and venture capital funds are the two main categories of private equity investments both in terms of number of funds and invested amounts. Whereas a venture capital firm may have a specialized industry focus—looking for the next rising star in technology, in life sciences, or another industry—LBO firms generally invest in a portfolio of firms with more predictable cash flow patterns. Venture capital firms (investing in new firms and new technologies) seek revenue growth, whereas buyout firms (investing in larger, established firms) focus more on EBIT or EBITDA growth. The approach to company valuation is thus fundamentally different, and Exhibit 3 presents some of the key distinctions.

EXHIBIT 3	Characteristics of Buyout and Venture Capital Investments

Buyout Investments:	Venture Capital Investments:
▶ Steady and predictable cash flows	▶ Low cash flow predictability, cash flow projections may not be realistic
▶ Excellent market position (can be a niche player)	▶ Lack of market history, new market and possibly unproven future market (early stage venture)
▶ Significant asset base (may serve as basis for collateral lending)	▶ Weak asset base
▶ Strong and experienced management team	▶ Newly formed management team with strong individual track record as entrepreneurs
▶ Extensive use of leverage consisting of a large proportion of senior debt and significant layer of junior and/or mezzanine debt	▶ Primarily equity funded. Use of leverage is rare and very limited
▶ Risk is measurable (mature businesses, long operating history)	▶ Assessment of risk is difficult because of new technologies, new markets, lack of operating history
▶ Predictable exit (secondary buyout, sale to a strategic buyer, IPO)	▶ Exit difficult to anticipate (IPO, trade sale, secondary venture sale)
▶ Established products	▶ Technological breakthrough but route to market yet to be proven
▶ Potential for restructuring and cost reduction	▶ Significant cash burn rate required to ensure company development and commercial viability
▶ Low working capital requirement	▶ Expanding capital requirement if in the growth phase
▶ Buyout firm typically conducts full blown due diligence approach before investing in the target firm (financial, strategic, commercial, legal, tax, environmental)	▶ Venture capital firm tends to conduct primarily a technology and commercial due diligence before investing; financial due diligence is limited as portfolio companies have no or very little operating history
▶ Buyout firm monitors cash flow management, strategic, and business planning	▶ Venture capital firm monitors achievement of milestones defined in business plan and growth management

(Exhibit continued on next page . . .)

EXHIBIT 3	(continued)

Buyout Investments:	**Venture Capital Investments:**
▶ Returns of investment portfolios are generally characterized by lower variance across returns from underlying investments; bankruptcies are rare events	▶ Returns of investment portfolios are generally characterized by very high returns from a limited number of highly successful investments and a significant number of write-offs from low performing investments or failures
▶ Large buyout firms are generally significant players in capital markets	▶ Venture capital firms tend to be much less active in capital markets
▶ Most transactions are auctions, involving multiple potential acquirers	▶ Many transactions are "proprietary," being the result of relationships between venture capitalists and entrepreneurs
▶ Strong performing buyout firms tend to have a better ability to raise larger funds after they have successfully raised their first funds[6]	▶ Venture capital firms tend to be less scalable relative to buyout firms; the increase in size of subsequent funds tend to be less significant[7]
▶ Variable revenue to the general partner (GP) at buyout firms generally comprise the following three sources: carried interest, transaction fees, and monitoring fees[8]	▶ Carried interest (participation in profits) is generally the main source of variable revenue to the general partner at venture capital firms; transaction and monitoring fees are rare in practice[9]

2.4 Valuation Issues in Buyout Transactions

A buyout is a form of private equity transaction in which the buyer acquires from the seller a controlling stake in the equity capital of a target company. The generic term "buyout" thus refers explicitly to the notion of acquiring control. It comprises a wide range of techniques, including but not limited to, management buyouts (MBOs), leveraged buyouts (LBOs), or takeovers. Our focus in this reading will be on LBOs, which consist in the acquisition of a company using borrowed money to finance a significant portion of the acquisition price.

Typically, the structuring of LBO transactions involves a negotiation between the providers of equity capital, senior debt, high yield bonds, and mezzanine finance. Mezzanine finance[10] is a hybrid form of financing that may be perceived as a bridge between equity and debt. It is generally structured flexibly and tailored to fit the specific requirements of every transaction.

2.4.1 The LBO Model

The LBO model is not a separate valuation technique, but rather a way of determining the impact of the capital structure, purchase price, and various other parameters on the returns expected by the private equity fund from the deal.

---

[6] Andrew Metrick and Ayako Yasuda, "The Economics of Private Equity Funds." University of Pennsylvania, The Wharton School (September 9, 2007).

[7] Ibid.

[8] Ibid.

[9] Ibid.

[10] For a more comprehensive discussion of mezzanine finance, refer to "Mezzanine finance—a hybrid instrument with a future," *Economic Briefing No 42*, Credit Suisse (2006).

The LBO model has three main input parameters: the cash flow forecasts of the target company, the expected return from the providers of financing (equity, senior debt, high yield bonds, mezzanine), and the amount of financing available for the transaction. The free cash flow forecasts of the target company are generally prepared by the management of the target company and are subject to an extensive due diligence process (strategic, commercial, financial, legal, and environmental) to determine the reliability of such forecasts. These forecasts are prepared on the basis of an explicit forecast horizon that generally corresponds to the expected holding horizon of the private equity firm in the equity capital of the target company.

The exit year is typically considered as a variable with the objective to determine the expected IRR sensitivity on the equity capital around the anticipated exit date. The exit value is determined most frequently by reference to an expected range of exit multiples determined on the basis of a peer group of comparable companies (Enterprise Value-to-EBITDA).

On the basis of the input parameters, the LBO model provides the maximum price that can be paid to the seller while satisfying the target returns for the providers of financing. This is why the LBO model is not a valuation methodology per se. It is a negotiation tool that helps develop a range of acceptable prices to conclude the transaction.

EXHIBIT 4	Typical Leveraged Buyout Value Creation Chart

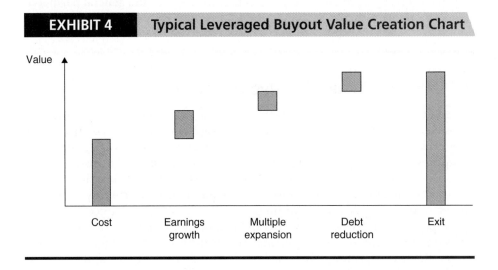

Exhibit 4 is a "value creation chart," summarizing the sources of the additional value between the exit value and the original cost. Value creation comes from a combination of factors: earnings growth arising from operational improvements and enhanced corporate governance; multiple expansion depending on pre-identified potential exits; and optimal financial leverage and repayment of part of the debt with operational cash flows before the exit. Each component of the value creation chart should be carefully considered and backed by supporting analyses, frequently coming from the lengthy due diligence process (especially commercial, tax, and financial) and also from a strategic review with the objective to quantify the range of plausible value creation.

Exhibit 5 provides an example of a €5,000 (amounts in millions) investment in a private equity transaction. The transaction is financed with 50 percent debt and 50 percent equity. The €2,500 equity investment is further broken into €2,400 of preference shares owned by the private equity fund, €95 of equity owned by the private equity fund, and €5 of management equity. The preference

EXHIBIT 5	Stakeholder Payoffs

	Invested	Proceeds	Multiple	IRR
Management	€5m	€109m	21.8x	85%
PE fund	€2,495m	€6,291m	2.5x	20%

€5,000m enterprise value
12% rolled up dividend to preference shares
Management contribute €5m of equity
PE fund €95m equity and all the preference shares
Lenders fund the debt

€8,000m

€5,000m

2008	2013
Management Equity 5 / PE Equity 95	Management 109
Preference Shares 2,400	PE Fund's Equity 2,061
Debt 2,500	Preference Shares 4,230
	Debt 1,600

shares are promised a 12 percent annual return (paid at exit). The private equity firm equity is promised 95 percent of the residual value of the firm after creditors and preference shares are paid, and management equity holders are promised the remaining 5 percent.

Assume that the exit value, five years after investment, is 1.6 times the original cost. The initial investment of €5,000 has an exit value of €8,000. The specific payoffs for the four claimants are as follows:

▶ Senior debt has been partially retired with operational cash flows, reducing debt from €2,500 to €1,600. So debtholders get €1,600.

▶ Preference shares are paid a 12 percent return for 5 years, so they receive €2,400$(1.12)^5$ = €4,230.

▶ PE Fund equity receives 95 percent of the terminal equity value, or 0.95[8000 − (4230 + 1600)] = €2,061.

▶ Management equity receives 5 percent of the terminal equity value, or 0.05[8000 − (4230 + 1600)] = €109.

As you can see, preference shares increase in value over time as a result of their preferred dividend being capitalized, and the equity held by the PE fund and by the management is expected to increase significantly depending on the total enterprise value upon exit. Both the equity sold to managers, frequently known as the management equity program (MEP), and the equity held by the private equity firm are most sensitive to the level of the exit. The larger the exit multiple, the larger the upside potential for both the MEP and the equity held by the private equity firm. In the example, assuming that an exit of 1.6 times cash may be achieved at the anticipated exit date (2013), the management would realize an IRR of 85 percent per annum on its investment and the private equity fund equity holders an IRR of 20 percent per annum. The private equity firm also earns 12 percent per annum on its preference shares.

This chart also demonstrates the critical importance of leverage in buyout transactions. A reduction in financial leverage over time is instrumental in magnifying returns available to shareholders. Note that the bulk of financial leverage in LBOs consists of senior debt, much of which will be amortizing. Therefore, the reduction in financial leverage gradually increases over time as a proportion of principal is paid back to senior lenders on an annual or semi-annual basis depending on the terms of senior debt. As a result of senior debt gradual repayment over time, a larger proportion of operating cash flows becomes available to equity holders. Of course, this mechanism works well as long as no significant adverse economic factors negatively impact the business of the target LBO company and also provided that a successful exit can be handled in the foreseeable future. It should be remembered, however, that these high levels of debt increase significantly the risks borne by the equity investors, and such increased risk should be taken into account when comparing the realized returns with alternative investment classes (such as investments in the stock market).

Typically, a series of scenarios with varying levels of cash exits, growth assumptions, and debt levels are engineered with the use of an LBO model, using as inputs the required rate of return from each stakeholder (equity, mezzanine, senior debt holders), to gain a sound understanding of the buyout firm's flexibility in conducting the deal.

2.5 Valuation Issues in Venture Capital Transactions

In venture capital, pre-money valuation and post-money valuation are two fundamental concepts. Pre-money valuation (PRE) refers to the agreed value of a company prior to a round of financing or investment (I). Post-money valuation (POST) is the value of a company after the financing or investing round. Therefore:

$$POST = PRE + I$$

The proportionate ownership of the venture capital investor is determined by I/POST.

EXAMPLE 1

Investment and Ownership Interest of a VC Firm

A venture capital firm invests £1 million on a £1.5 million pre-money valuation and the VC firm obtains 40 percent of shares. In this case, PRE is £1.5 million, POST is £2.5 million, and the proportion financed by venture capital is £1 million/£2.5 million. The parties agreed that the VC firm would retain 40 percent of the shares and have that proportion of the rights of shareholders should dividends be paid or the firm sold.

Typically, both pre-money valuation and the level of the venture capital investment are subject to intense negotiations between the founders and the venture capital firm, bearing in mind the fundamental issue of dilution of ownership. Dilution of ownership is the reduction in the proportional ownership of a shareholder in the capital of a company resulting from the issuance of additional shares and/or of securities convertible into shares at some stage in the future. Additional financing rounds and the issuance of stock options to the management of a company are examples of dilution of ownership.

In VC transactions, there is typically significant uncertainty surrounding the projected future cash flows. Consequently, the discounted cash flow methodology is rarely used as the first method to determine value. Similarly, there are challenges applying the comparable companies approach as start-ups generally have unique features and it may be extremely difficult to find comparable quoted companies operating in the same field. Alternative valuation methodologies including the venture capital approach[11] or the real option methodology are also used to determine value. Traditional valuation methodologies typically comprise the income approach (discounted cash flow valuation), the relative value or market approach (information relative to a group of comparable companies is gathered and normalized relative to the EBITDA, EBIT, and revenue of the company being valued), and the cost approach (cost to recreate or replace the asset or company). Generally speaking, the appraisal of intangible assets, comprising the founder's know-how, experience, licenses, patents, and in progress research and development (IPRD), along with an assessment of the expected market potential of the company's product or products in development form the basis for assessing a pre-money valuation. Because of the significant level of uncertainty surrounding the business, it is not infrequent to observe a cap on the pre-money valuation (i.e., €3 million, €5 million, etc.).

In buyouts, given the significant predictability of cash flows, the income-based approach (discounted cash flows, adjusted present value, LBO model, target IRR) is frequently used as a primary method to determine the value of equity, considering the expected change in leverage until the time of exit of the investment. The initial high and declining financial leverage is the main technical valuation issue that needs to be adequately factored into the income approach when applied to a buyout valuation. The value is also frequently corroborated by an analysis of the peer group of comparable publicly traded companies.

2.6 Exit Routes: Returning Cash to Investors

The exit is among the most critical mechanisms to unlock value in private equity. Most private equity firms consider their exit options prior to investing and factor their assessment of the exit outcome into their analysis of target and expected internal rate of return.

Private equity investors generally have access to the following four exit routes for their investments:

▶ *Initial Public Offering (IPO)*: going public offers significant advantages including higher valuation multiples as a result of an enhanced liquidity, access to large amounts of capital, and the possibility to attract higher caliber managers. But an IPO comes at the expense of a cumbersome process, less flexibility, and significant costs. Therefore, an IPO is an appropriate exit route for private companies with an established operating history, excellent growth prospects, and having a sufficient size. Timing of the IPO is also an important consideration. After the internet bubble collapse in March 2000, the number of successful IPOs plummeted in the

---

[11] Discussed in "A Note on Valuation of Venture Capital Deals."

subsequent years, forcing venture capital firms to change their exit plans for many of their investments.

▶ *Secondary Market*: sale of stake held by a financial investor to other financial investors or to strategic investors (companies operating or willing to establish in the same sector or market of the portfolio company). With the increased segmentation of private equity, secondary market transactions tend to occur within each segment, i.e., buyout firms tend to sell to other buyout firms (secondary buyouts) and venture firms to other venture firms (secondary venture capital transactions). These secondary market transactions are very common in practice and currently account for a significant proportion of exits, especially in the buyout segment. Venture capital exits by means of a buyout are also possible but rare in practice as buyout firms are reluctant to finance development stage companies with a significant amount of leverage. The two main advantages of secondary market transactions are 1) the possibility to achieve the highest valuation multiples in the absence of an IPO, and 2) with the segmentation of private equity firms, specialized firms have the skill to bring their portfolio companies to the next level (restructuring, merger, new market) and sell either to a strategic investor seeking to exploit synergies or to another private equity firm having another set of skills and the ability to further add value to the portfolio company.

▶ *Management Buyout (MBO)*: takeover by the management group using significant amounts of leverage to finance the acquisition of the company. Alignment of interest is optimal under this exit scenario but may come at the expense of an excessive leverage that may significantly reduce the company's flexibility.

▶ *Liquidation*: controlling shareholders have the power to liquidate the company if the company is no longer viable. This exit mechanism generally results in a floor value for the portfolio company but may come at a cost of very negative publicity for the private equity firm if the portfolio company is large and the employee count is significant.

Timing the exit and determining the optimal exit route are important investment management decisions to be made by private equity firms. Although the exit may be carefully planned, the unexpected can cause changes to the exit plan. This may mean that the exit could be delayed or accelerated depending on the market or purely opportunistic circumstances. Suppose, for example, that an LBO firm is planning an exit of one of its portfolio companies but the public market and economic conditions have collapsed, rendering any exit via a trade sale or an IPO unprofitable. The LBO firm may instead conduct another acquisition at depressed prices, merge this acquisition with the portfolio company with the objective to strengthen its market position or product range, and wait for better market conditions before conducting the sale. Flexibility is thus critical in private equity during harder times and underlines the importance for a private equity firm to have sufficient financial strength.

There seems to be no boundaries to the size of the largest buyout transactions as expectations have been consistently exceeded over the past few years and the $50 billion threshold appears now to be in sight for the largest buyout firms. The three largest buyout transactions in history, HCA Inc., Equity Office, and TXU Corporation, were all undertaken over the eighteen months before this reading was written. Private equity firms appear to be moving into uncharted territory in regards to managing exits at that level. The central question about these mega buyout transactions is how the exit will take place given that the extent of the exit possibilities is much more limited relative to smaller deals. IPOs, for example, raise significantly more challenges, such as the need for a gradual exit over time because only a single block of shares can be sold initially, and may prove excessively risky if market conditions are suboptimal. Some large companies may be viewed as holding companies of a portfolio of real assets. Such companies may be sold in tranches to prospective buyers. The real challenge will be for unified companies for which an exit will need to take place for the entire entity.

Understanding the anticipated exit provides clues as to what valuation methodologies or IRR models to employ. Timing of the exit will influence the way stress testing is conducted on the expected exit multiple. When the exit is anticipated in the near future (one to two years), the prevailing valuation multiples extracted from comparable quoted firms provide good guidance on the expected exit multiple. Stress tests on that value may be conducted for small incremental changes and on the basis of market knowledge. If the exit is anticipated in a much longer time horizon, the current valuation multiples are less relevant and stress tests may need to be conducted on a wider range of values to determine the anticipated exit multiple. Stress testing in this context consists of simulating incremental changes in the input variables of the valuation model (such as components of the discount factor, terminal growth rates, etc.) and to financial forecasts (sales growth, assumed future operating margins, etc.) in order to determine the range of value outcomes and to assess the stability of the valuation methodology.

2.7 Summary

Valuation is the most critical aspect of private equity transactions. The investment decision-making process typically flows from the screening of investment opportunities to preparing a proposal, appraising the investment, structuring the deal, and finally to the negotiating phase. Because of the difficulties in valuing private companies, a variety of alternative valuation methods are typically used to provide guidance on the appropriate range. Along with the various due diligence investigations (commercial or strategic, financial, legal, tax, environmental) generally conducted on private equity investment opportunities, valuation serves a dual purpose: assessing a company's ability to generate superior cash flows from a distinctive competitive advantage and serving as a benchmark for negotiations with the seller. After all, although seeing opportunities for adding value is important, it is also essential—for the investors in the private equity fund—that the seller does not appropriate all the potential gains by extracting a high price during the transaction.

Post-investment, valuation of private equity investments is also very important, as investors expect to be fully informed about the performance of the portfolio companies. This raises a separate set of issues, which are considered in the next section.

PRIVATE EQUITY FUND STRUCTURES AND VALUATION

3

When analyzing and evaluating financial performance of a private equity fund from the perspective of an investor, a solid grasp of private equity fund structures, terms of investment, private equity fund valuation, and due diligence are an absolute prerequisite. The distinctive characteristics of private equity relative to public equities raise many more challenges when interpreting financial performance. Two of the main differentiating characteristics of private equity, in addition to the structure and terms, relate to the nature of subscriptions made by investors in private equity structures and to the "J" curve effect. Investors commit initially a certain amount to the private equity fund that is subsequently drawn by the fund as the fund's capital is deployed in target portfolio companies. This contrasts with public market investing in which investment orders typically are disbursed fully at the time the orders are settled on the markets. The "J-curve" effect refers to the typical time profile of reported returns by private equity funds, whereby low or negative returns are reported in the early years of a private equity fund (in large part as a result of the fees' impact on net returns), followed by increased returns thereafter as the private equity firm manages portfolio companies toward the exit.

3.1 Understanding Private Equity Fund Structures

The limited partnership has emerged as the dominant form for private equity structures in most jurisdictions. Funds that are structured as limited partnerships are governed by a limited partnership agreement between the fund manager, called the general partner (GP), and the fund's investors, called limited partners (LPs). Whereas the GP has management control over the fund and is jointly liable for all debts, LPs have limited liability, i.e., they do not risk more than the amount of their investment in the fund. The other main alternative to the limited partnership is a corporate structure, called company limited by shares, which mirrors in its functioning the limited partnership but offers a better legal protection to the GP and to some extent the LPs, depending on the jurisdictions. Some fund structures, especially the Luxembourg-based private equity fund vehicle SICAR (société d'investissement en capital à risque), are subject to a light regulatory oversight offering enhanced protection to LPs. The vast majority of these private equity fund structures are "closed end," which restricts existing investors from redeeming their shares over the lifetime of the fund and limiting new investors to entering the fund only at predefined time periods, at the discretion of the GP.

Private equity firms operate effectively in two businesses: the business of managing private equity investments and the business of raising funds. Therefore, private equity firms tend to plan their marketing efforts well in advance of the launch of their funds to ensure that the announced target fund size will be met successfully once the fund is effectively started. The premarketing phase of a private equity fund, depending on whether it is a first fund or a following fund, may take between one to two years. Once investors effectively commit their investments in the fund, private equity managers draw on investors' commitments as the fund is being deployed and invested in portfolio companies. Private equity funds tend to have a duration of 10–12 years, generally extendable to an additional 2–3 years. Exhibit 6 illustrates the funding stages for a private equity fund.

Fund terms are contractually defined in a fund prospectus or limited partnership agreement available to qualified prospective investors. The definition of qualified investors depends on the jurisdiction. Typically, wealth criteria (exceeding US$1 million, for example) and/or a minimum subscription threshold (minimum €125,000, for example) apply. The nature of the terms are frequently the result of the balance of negotiation power between GPs and LPs. Although the balance of negotiation power used to be in favor of LPs, it has now

---

EXHIBIT 6   **Funding Stages for a Private Equity Fund**

How are private equity funds structured?

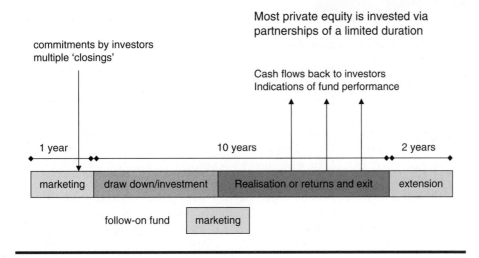

---

turned in favor of GPs, at least among the oversubscribed funds. Any significant downturn in private equity may change the balance of power in favor of LPs. Negotiation of terms has the objective to ensure alignment of interests between the GP and LPs and defining the GP's incentives (transaction fees, profit shares, etc.) The most significant terms may be categorized into economic and corporate governance terms.

Economic Terms

▶ *Management fees* represent a percentage of committed capital paid annually to the GP during the lifetime of the fund. Fees in the region of 1.5 percent to 2.5 percent are fairly common. Although less frequent, management fees may also be calculated on the basis of the net asset value or on invested capital.

▶ *Transaction fees* are fees paid to GPs in their advisory capacity when they provide investment banking services for a transaction (mergers and acquisitions, IPOs) benefiting the fund. These fees may be subject to sharing agreements with LPs, typically according to a 50/50 split between the GP and LPs. When such fee-sharing agreements apply, they generally come as a deduction to the management fees.

▶ *Carried interest* represents the general partner's share of profits generated by a private equity fund. Carried interest is frequently in the region of 20 percent of the fund's profits (after management fees).

▶ *Ratchet* is a mechanism that determines the allocation of equity between shareholders and the management team of the private equity controlled company. A ratchet enables the management team to increase its equity allocation depending on the company's actual performance and the return achieved by the private equity firm.

▶ *Hurdle rate* is the internal rate of return that a private equity fund must achieve before the GP receives any carried interest. The hurdle rate is typically in the range of 7 percent to 10 percent. The objective is to align the interests of the GP with those of LPs by giving additional incentives to the GP to outperform traditional investment benchmarks.

EXAMPLE 2

Calculation of Carried Interest

Suppose that a LBO fund has committed capital of US$100 million, carried interest of 20 percent, and a hurdle rate of 8 percent. The fund called 75 percent of its commitments from investors at the beginning of year 1, which was invested at the beginning of year 1 in target company A for $40 million and target company B for $35 million. Suppose that at the end of year 2, a profit of $5 million has been realized by the GP upon exit of the investment in company A, and the value of the investment in company B has remained unchanged. Suppose also that the GP is entitled to carried interest on a deal-by-deal basis, i.e., the IRR used to calculate carried interest is calculated for each investment upon exit. A theoretical carried interest of $1 million (20 percent of $5 million) could be granted to the GP, but the IRR upon exit of investment in company A is only 6.1 percent. Until the IRR exceeds the hurdle rate, no carried interest may be paid to the GP.

▶ *Target fund size* is expressed as an absolute amount in the fund prospectus or information memorandum. This information is critical as it provides a signal both about the GP's capacity to manage a portfolio of a predefined size and also in terms of fund raising. A fund that closed with a significantly lower size relative to the target size would raise questions about the GP's ability to raise funds on the market and would be perceived as a negative signal.

▶ *Vintage year* is the year the private equity fund was launched. Reference to vintage year allows performance comparison of funds of the same stage and industry focus.

▶ *Term of the fund* is typically 10 years, extendable for additional shorter periods (by agreement with the investors). Although infrequently observed, funds can also be of unlimited duration, and in this case are often quoted on stock markets (such as investment trusts).

Corporate Governance Terms

▶ *Key man clause.* Under the key man clause, a certain number of key named executives are expected to play an active role in the management of the fund. In case of the departure of such a key executive or insufficient time spent in the management of the fund, the "key man" clause provides that the GP may be prohibited from making any new investments until a new key executive is appointed.

▶ *Disclosure and confidentiality.* Private equity firms have no obligations to disclose publicly their financial performance. A court ruling[12] requiring

---

[12] S. Chaplinsky and S. Perry, "CalPERS vs. Mercury News: Disclosure comes to private equity," Darden Business Publishing.

California Public Employees Retirement System (CalPERS) to report publicly its returns on private equity investments, the Freedom of Information Act (FOIA) in the United States, and similar legislation in other European countries have led public pension funds to report information about their private equity investments. Disclosable information relates to financial performance of the underlying funds but does not extend to information on the companies in which the funds invest. This latter information is not typically disclosed. The reporting by CalPERS is a prominent example of the application of this clause.[13] Some private equity fund terms may be more restrictive on confidentiality and information disclosure and effectively limit information available to investors subject to FOIA.

▶ *Clawback provision.* A clawback provision requires the GP to return capital to LPs in excess of the agreed profit split between the GP and LPs. This provision ensures that, when a private equity firm exits from a highly profitable investment early in the fund's life but subsequent exits are less profitable, the GP pays back capital contributions, fees, and expenses to LPs to ensure that the profit split is in line with the fund's prospectus. The clawback is normally due on termination of the fund but may be subject to an annual reconciliation (or "true-up").

▶ *Distribution waterfall.* A distribution waterfall is a mechanism providing an order of distributions to LPs first before the GP receives carried interest. Two distinct distribution mechanisms are predominant: deal-by-deal waterfalls allowing earlier distribution of carried interest to the GP after each individual deal (mostly employed in the United States) and total return waterfalls resulting in earlier distributions to LPs as carried interest is calculated on the profits of the entire portfolio (mostly employed in Europe and for funds-of-funds). Under the total return method, two alternatives are possible to calculate carried interest. In the first alternative, the GP receives carried interest only after the fund has returned the entire committed capital to LPs. In the second alternative, the GP receives carried interest on any distribution as long as the value of the investment portfolio exceeds a certain threshold (usually 20 percent) above invested capital.

EXAMPLE 3

Distribution Waterfalls

Suppose a private equity fund has a committed capital totaling £300 million and a carried interest of 20 percent. After a first investment of £30 million, the fund exits the investment 9 months later with a £15 million profit. Under the deal-by-deal method, the GP would be entitled to 20 percent of the deal profit, i.e., £3 million. In the first alternative of the total return method, the entire proceeds of the sale, i.e., £45 million, are entitled to the LPs and nothing (yet) to the GP. In the second alternative, the exit value of £45 million exceeds by more than 20 percent the invested value of £30 million. The GP would thus be entitled to £3 million.

Continuing the above example with a clawback provision with an annual true-up, suppose that the deal-by-deal method applies and that a

[13] Information about CalPERS' private equity holdings is available from the company's website, www.calpers.gov.

> second investment of £25 million is concluded with a loss of £5 million 1 year later. Therefore, at the annual true-up, the GP would have to pay back £1 million to LPs. In practice, an escrow account is used to regulate these fluctuations until termination of the fund.

▶ *Tag-along, drag along rights* are contractual provisions in share purchase agreements that ensure any potential future acquirer of the company may not acquire control without extending an acquisition offer to all shareholders, including the management of the company.

▶ *No-fault divorce.* A GP may be removed without cause, provided that a super majority (generally above 75 percent) of LPs approve that removal.

▶ *Removal for "cause"* is a clause that allows either a removal of the GP or an earlier termination of the fund for "cause." Such "cause" may include gross negligence of the GP, a "key person" event, a felony conviction of a key management person, bankruptcy of the GP, or a material breach of the fund prospectus.

▶ *Investment restrictions* generally impose a minimum level of diversification of the fund's investments, a geographic and/or sector focus, or limits on borrowing.

▶ *Co-investment.* LPs generally have a first right of co-investing along with the GP. This can be advantageous for the LPs as fees and profit share are likely to be lower (or zero) on co-invested capital. The GP and affiliated parties are also typically restricted in their co-investments to prevent conflicts of interest with their LPs. Crossover co-investments are a classic example of a conflict of interest. A crossover co-investment occurs when a subsequent fund launched by the same GP invests in a portfolio company that has received funding from a previous fund.

3.2 What Are the Risks and Costs of Investing in Private Equity?

Private equity investing is typically restricted by laws and regulations in most jurisdictions to "qualified investors" comprising institutions and high-net-worth individuals meeting certain wealth criteria. These restrictions are motivated by the high levels of risks incurred in private equity investing, and are generally subject to disclosure in the private equity fund prospectus. Such risks may be categorized as general private equity risk factors, investment strategy specific risk factors (buyout, venture capital, mezzanine), industry specific risk factors, risk factors specific to the investment vehicle, and sometimes regional or emerging market risks when applicable.

Following are some general private equity risk factors:

▶ *Illiquidity of investments*: Because private equity investments are generally not traded on any securities market, the exit of investments may not be conducted on a timely basis.

▶ *Unquoted investments*: Investing in unquoted securities may be risky relative to investing in securities quoted on a regulated securities exchange.

▶ *Competition for attractive investment opportunities*: Competition for finding investment opportunities on attractive terms may be high.

▶ *Reliance on the management of investee companies (agency risk)*: There is no assurance that the management of the investee companies will run the company in the best interests of the private equity firm, particularly in earlier stage deals in which the management may retain a controlling stake in the company and enjoy certain private benefits of control.

▶ *Loss of capital*: High business and financial risks may result in substantial loss of capital.

▶ *Government regulations*: Investee companies' product and services may be subject to changes in government regulations that adversely impact their business model.

▶ *Taxation risk*: Tax treatment of capital gains, dividends, or limited partnerships may change over time.

▶ *Valuation of investments*: Valuation of private equity investments is subject to significant judgment. When valuations are not conducted by an independent party, they may be subject to biases.

▶ *Lack of investment capital*: Investee companies may require additional future financing that may not be available.

▶ *Lack of diversification*: Investment portfolios may be highly concentrated and may, therefore, be exposed to significant losses. Investors generally want to invest in a mix of private equity funds of different vintages, different stages of developments for underlying investments in portfolio companies, and achieve a certain level of diversification across various private equity strategies (large and mid-market buyout, venture capital, mezzanine, restructuring).

▶ *Market risk*: Changes in general market conditions (interest rates, currency exchange rates) may adversely affect private equity investments. The impact of market risk is, however, long term in nature given the long-term horizon of private equity firms. Temporary short-term market fluctuations are generally irrelevant.

Costs associated with private equity investing are substantially more significant relative to public market investing. These costs may be broken down as follows:

▶ *Transaction fees*: Corresponding to due diligence, bank financing costs, legal fees for arranging acquisition, and sale transactions in investee companies.

▶ *Investment vehicle fund setup costs*: Comprises mainly legal costs for the setup of the investment vehicle. Such costs are typically amortized over the life of the investment vehicle.

▶ *Administrative costs*: Custodian, transfer agent, and accounting costs generally charged yearly as a fraction of the investment vehicle's net asset value.

▶ *Audit costs*: A fixed annual fee.

▶ *Management and performance fees*: These are generally more significant relative to plain investment funds. A 2 percent management fee and a 20 percent performance fee are common in the private equity industry.

▶ *Dilution*: A more subtle source of cost, dilution may come from stock option plans granted to the management and to the private equity firm and from additional rounds of financing.

▶ *Placement fees*: Fundraising fees may be charged up front or by means of a trailer fee by the fund raiser. A trailer fee is generally charged annually, corresponding to a fraction of the amount invested by limited partners as long as these amounts remain invested in the investment vehicle. An up front placement fee of 2 percent is not uncommon in private equity.

3.3 Due Diligence Investigations by Potential Investors

Prior to investing in a private equity fund, prospective investors generally conduct a thorough due diligence on the fund. Several fundamental characteristics of private equity funds underline the importance of the due diligence process.

▶ Private equity funds tend to exhibit a strong persistence of returns over time. This means that top performing funds tend to continue to outperform and poor performing funds also tend to continue to perform poorly or disappear.

▶ The performance range between funds is extremely large. For example, the difference between top quartile and third quartile fund IRRs can be about 20 percentage points.

▶ Liquidity in private equity is typically very limited and thus LPs are locked for the long term. On the other hand, when private equity funds exit an investment, they return the cash to the investors immediately. Therefore, the "duration" of an investment in private equity is typically shorter than the maximum life of the fund.

The European Venture Capital association (EVCA) has issued an "Illustrative due diligence questionnaire—Venture capital funds," that may serve as a guide, but not as a substitute, for the due diligence process conducted by LPs before investing in a venture capital or private equity fund.

3.4 Private Equity Fund Valuation

The description of private equity valuation[14] in a fund prospectus is generally associated with the fund's calculation of net asset value (NAV). The NAV is generally defined as the value of the fund assets less liabilities corresponding to the accrued fund expenses. The fund's assets are frequently valued by GPs, depending on their valuation policies, in the following ways:[15]

1. at cost with significant adjustments for subsequent financing events or deterioration

2. at lower of cost or market value

3. by a revaluation of a portfolio company whenever a new financing round involving new investors takes place

4. at cost with no interim adjustment until the exit

5. with a discount for restricted securities[16]

6. more rarely, marked to market by reference to a peer group of public comparables and applying illiquidity discounts.

---

[14] For a comprehensive discussion of this topic, refer to Thomas Meyer and Pierre-Yves Mathonet, *Beyond the J Curve: Managing a Portfolio of Venture Capital and Private Equity Funds*, Wiley, (2004).

[15] Foster Center for Entrepreneurship and Private Equity, Dartmouth College.

[16] Example: Reg. 144 securities.

Private equity industry valuation standards, such as those originally produced by the British, French, and European industry associations (latest revisions can be found at www.privateequityvaluation.com), have increasingly been adopted by funds operating in many jurisdictions.

Industry practices suggest that because a valuation is adjusted with a new round of financing, the NAV may be more stale in down markets when there is a long gap between funding rounds. This mechanism is similar to the valuation of investment funds of publicly quoted securities. There is thus a fundamental implicit break-up assumption whereby the fund may be broken up at any time, the funds underlying investments may be liquidated individually and immediately, and the proceeds returned to LPs. Whereas this fundamental break-up assumption may hold for publicly traded securities, which are marked to market, this assumption may be more questionable for private equity investment portfolios typically held over a long period of time. The fundamental question facing investors is: At what value should investments in portfolio companies be reported, prior to the private equity fund exiting the investment and returning the proceeds to the LPs? There is no straight answer to that question as there is no market for securities issued by private equity companies.

Undrawn LP commitments raise additional challenges for private equity fund valuation. Although undrawn commitments represent a LP's legal obligations to meet capital calls in the future, they are not accounted for in the NAV calculation. The value of such undrawn commitments largely depends on the expected cash flows that will be generated by future investments made by the GP. Although undrawn commitments are not part of the NAV, they should be viewed as unfunded liabilities. McGrady[17] suggested to "gauge the reaction to the unfunded portion, a seller may consider the ease with which a general partnership could raise another fund in the current market."

Comparisons between private equity funds following different investment strategies require a careful analysis of their respective valuation policies in order to avoid biases. Whereas, for example, an early stage venture capital fund may keep its investments at cost, a late stage development capital fund may mark its portfolio companies by reference to public market comparables. At times when a market bubble is forming in certain sectors, such as the technology bubble in 2000, such reference to public market comparables may distort the valuation of portfolio companies and thus reported fund returns.

Another important aspect of private equity valuations is that they are mostly performed by GPs. Under the pressure from LPs, an increasing number of annual or semi-annual valuations are performed by independent valuers that are mandated by GPs.

The above discussion on private equity valuation emphasizes both the qualitative and quantitative issues that need to be taken into consideration.

3.5 Evaluating Fund Performance

Because each private equity fund is unique, the assessment of financial performance needs to be made with a good knowledge of the specific fund structure, terms, valuation policies, and the outcome of the due diligence. Typically, an analysis of a private equity fund's financial performance includes the following.

---

[17] C. McGrady, Pricing private equity secondary transactions, Dallas, TX, Cogent Partners (2002).

3.5.1 Analysis of IRR and Multiples Gross and Net of Fees since Inception

Here, net of fees means net of management fees, carried interest, or of any other financial arrangements that accrue to the GP. The IRR, a cash-flow-weighted rate of return, is deemed the most appropriate measure of private equity performance by the Global Investment Performance Standards (GIPS), Venture Capital and Private Equity Valuation Principles, and by other venture capital and private equity standards. The interpretation of IRR in private equity should, however, be subject to caution because an implicit assumption behind the IRR calculation is that the fund is fully liquid, whereas a significant portion of the NAV is illiquid during a substantial part of a private equity fund's life. Therefore, valuation of portfolio companies according to industry standards is important to ensure the quality of the IRR figures.

The distinction between gross and net IRR is also important. Gross IRR relates cash flows between the private equity fund and its portfolio companies and is often considered a good measure of the investment management team's track record in creating value. Net IRR relates cash flows between the private equity fund and LPs, and so captures the returns enjoyed by investors. Fees and profit shares create significant deviations between gross and net IRRs. IRR analysis is often combined with a benchmark IRR analysis, i.e., the median IRR for the relevant peer group of comparable private equity funds operating with a similar investment strategy and vintage year. This is particularly important because there are clear trends over time in private equity returns, with some vintage years producing much higher returns than others.

In addition to IRR, multiples are used frequently as a measure of performance. Multiples simply measure the total return to investors relative to the total sum invested. Although multiples ignore the time value of money, their ease of calculation and their ability to differentiate between "realized" actual proceeds from divestments and "unrealized" portfolio subject to GP valuation make these ratios very popular among LPs. The multiples used most frequently by LPs and also defined by GIPS that provide additional information about private equity funds performance are as follows:

▶ PIC (paid in capital): the ratio of paid in capital to date divided by committed capital. This ratio provides information about the proportion of capital called by a GP.

▶ DPI (distributed to paid in): cumulative distributions paid out to LPs as a proportion of the cumulative invested capital. This ratio is often called "cash-on-cash return." It provides an indication of the private equity fund's realized return on investment. DPI is presented net of management fees and carried interest.

▶ RVPI (residual value to paid in): value of LPs' shareholding held with the private equity fund as a proportion of the cumulative invested capital. The numerator is measured as the remaining portfolio companies as valued by the GP. This ratio is a measure of the private equity fund's unrealized return on investment. RVPI is presented net of management fees and carried interest.

▶ TVPI (total value to paid in): the portfolio companies' distributed and undistributed value as a proportion of the cumulative invested capital. TVPI is the sum of DPI and RVPI. TVPI is presented net of management fees and carried interest.

In addition to quantitative measures of return, an analysis of a private equity fund financial performance also includes:

▶ an analysis of realized investments since inception, commenting on all successes and failures;

▶ an analysis of unrealized investments, highlighting all red flags in the portfolio and the expected time to exit per portfolio company;

▶ a cash flow forecast at the portfolio company level and for the aggregate portfolio; and

▶ an analysis of portfolio valuation, audited financial statements, and the NAV.

EXAMPLE 4

Calculating and Interpreting a Private Equity Fund Performance

Suppose that a private equity fund has a DPI of 0.07 and a RVPI of 0.62 after 5 years. IRR is –17 percent. The fund follows a venture capital strategy in high technology, has a vintage year of 1999, and a term of 10 years. A DPI of 7 percent indicates that few successful exits were made. A RVPI of 62 percent points to an extended J-curve effect for the fund as TVPI amounts to 69 percent at the midlife of the fund. A vintage year of 1999 provides hints that the fund was actually started before the technology market crash of 2000 and that the routes to exit for portfolio companies have been dramatically changed. During the technology market crash, the investment portfolio probably suffered a number of complete write-offs. In this situation, an LP should thus consider the state of the existing portfolio to examine the number of write-offs and other signals of ailing companies in the fund portfolio. The risk of not recovering the invested amount at termination of the fund is significant. Compliance with valuation policies by the GP should also be closely monitored by LPs to ensure that the GP's expectations are not excessive given the current state of the portfolio.

Note that with the increased allocations to private equity, performance comparisons across asset classes are often misinterpreted. IRR, the standard measure of private equity returns, is cash-flow-weighted, whereas performance of most other asset classes is measured in terms of time-weighted rate of return. In an attempt to solve these performance comparison issues, new performance measurement techniques have been developed. One of them, called the Public Market Equivalent (PME), was proposed by Austin Long and Craig Nickles in the mid-1990s. It provides a solution to this benchmarking issue, but its reliability poses, at times, serious problems.[18] Put simply, PME is the cash-flow-weighted rate of return of an index (S&P 500 or any other index) assuming the same cash flow pattern as a private equity fund. It is thus an index return measure.

---

[18] Christophe Rouvinez, "Private Equity Benchmarking with PME+," *Venture Capital Journal* (August 2003).

4 CONCEPT IN ACTION: EVALUATING A PRIVATE EQUITY FUND

This section illustrates the use of many of the concepts above to evaluate the performance of a private equity fund.

Michael Hornsby, CFA, is a Senior Investment Officer at Icarus, a U.K.-based institutional investor in private equity. He is contemplating an investment in Europa Venture Partners III, a new late stage technology venture capital fund, after a thorough due diligence performed on the fund and an updated due diligence on the GP. Icarus has been an investor in Europa Venture Partners' (EVP) previous two funds, EVP I and EVP II. Icarus has been satisfied with the performance of EVP so far and is seeking to further expand its relationship with this GP because Icarus considers it a niche venture capital firm operating in a less crowded segment of the pan-European technology markets. As a result of its success, EVP decided to increase its carried interest for the third fund to 25 percent from 20 percent for the previous two funds. Hornsby has received the information about the fund's financial performance and is seeking assistance in calculating and interpreting financial performance for a number of specific queries as outlined below.

Europa Venture Partners (EVP)

General Partner Europa Venture Partners (EVP) was established to provide equity financing to later stage technology companies in need of development capital across Europe. The GP seeks to provide strategic support to seasoned entrepreneurial teams and bring proven new technologies to the market. The GP targets investment in portfolio companies between €2 million and €10 million.

		Established in 1999		Type: Development Capital				
Fund	Vintage	Actual Fund Size (€ Millions)	Capital Called (%)	Mgmt Fees (%)	Carried Interest (%)	Hurdle Rate (%)	Term	Report Date
EVP I	2001	125	92	2	20	8	2009	31 Dec 2006
EVP II	2003	360	48	2	20	8	2012	31 Dec 2006

Financial performance for investments by Icarus in EVP funds

Fund	Committed Capital (€ Millions)	Capital Called Down	Gross IRR (%)	Net IRR (%)	DPI (X)	RVPI (X)	TVPI (X)	Quartile
EVP I	10	9.2	16.1	11.3	1.26	1.29	2.55	1
EVP II	25	12.0	1.6	(0.4)	0.35	1.13	1.48	2

Hornsby also is interested in verifying management fees, carried interest, and the NAV of EVP I. He has the following information about yearly capital calls, operating results, and distributions.

Calls, Operating Results, and Distributions (€ Million)						
	2001	2002	2003	2004	2005	2006
Called-down	50	15	10	25	10	5
Realized results	0	0	10	35	40	80
Unrealized results	−5	−15	15	10	15	25
Distributions	—	—		25	45	75

Operating results correspond to the sum of realized results from exits of portfolio companies and of unrealized results from the revaluation of investments held in portfolio companies. In addition to the information available on EVP I, Hornsby also knows from the fund prospectus that the distribution waterfall is calculated according to the total return method following the first alternative, i.e., the GP receives carried interest only after the fund has returned the entire committed capital to LPs. Management fees are calculated on the basis of the paid-in capital. Hornsby also wants to calculate DPI, RVPI, and TVPI of EVP I for 2006 and is interested in understanding how to calculate gross and net IRRs.

1. Interpret and compare the financial performance of EVP I and EVP II.

2. Based on the information given, calculate the management fees, carried interest, and the NAV of EVP I. Also calculate DPI, RVPI, and TVPI of EVP I for 2006. Explain on the basis of EVP I how gross and net IRRs are calculated, and calculate the gross and net IRRs.

Solution to 1: In the table above, the first venture capital fund (EVP I) made its first capital call in 2001 and returned €1.26 (all amounts in millions) for every €1 that had been drawn down to LPs two years ahead of the termination of the fund. EVP I residual value remains high at 1.29 times capital drawn down, which is a good signal about the profitability of the fund at termination. The fund ranks in the first quartile, which means that it belongs to the best performing funds of that category and vintage year. Gross IRR of 16.1 percent after 6 years of operations, and 11.3 percent net of fees represents a good performance.

The second fund exhibits, to date, very modest performance in terms of gross and net IRR, which indicates that the fund is still experiencing the J-curve effect. EVP II has returned 35 percent of capital drawn down to LPs and a residual value of 113 percent of capital drawn down, which indicates that despite the fund being in its early years, the GP has already managed a number of profitable exits and increased the value of the investment portfolio half way through the termination of the fund. Actual fund size significantly exceeds previous fund size and is an indication that the GP is gaining momentum in terms of fund raising, probably partly attributable to the strong performance of the first fund.

Solution to 2:

	Called-down (1)	Paid-in Capital (2)	Mgmt Fees (3)	Operating Results (4)	NAV before Distributions (5)	Carried Interest (6)	Distributions (7)	NAV after Distributions (8)
Cash Flows and Distributions (€ Million)								
Year								
2001	50	50	1.0	−5	44.0			44.0
2002	15	65	1.3	−15	42.7			42.7
2003	10	75	1.5	25	76.2			76.2
2004	25	100	2.0	45	144.2	3.8	25	115.4
2005	10	110	2.2	55	178.2	6.8	45	126.4
2006	5	115	2.3	105	234.1	11.2	75	147.9

Based on this table, the calculations of DPI, RVPI, and TVPI can be derived as follows:

▶ Paid-in capital = Cumulative capital called-down (shown in Column 2)

▶ Management fees = (2 Percent) × (Column 2)

▶ Carried interest: The first year that NAV is higher than committed capital (€125m), carried interest is 20 percent of the excess, or (20 Percent)([NAV in Column 5] − €125m). Thereafter, provided that NAV before distribution exceeds committed capital, carried interest is (20 Percent)(increase in NAV before distributions). For example, carried interest in 2006 is calculated as follows: (20 Percent)(234.1 − 178.2)

▶ NAV before distributions = NAV after distributions$_{t-1}$ + (Column 1) − (Column 3) + (Column 4)

▶ NAV after distributions = (Column 5) − (Column 6) − (Column 7)

▶ DPI = (25 + 45 + 75)/115 or 1.26x

▶ RVPI = 147.9/115 or 1.29x

▶ TVPI = 1.26 + 1.29 = 2.55x

The IRRs may be developed as follows:

▶ Gross IRRs are estimated by calculating the internal rate of return between the following cash flows: called down capital at the beginning of period (Column 1) and operating results (Column 4).

▶ Net IRRs are estimated by calculating the internal rate of return between the following cash flows: called down capital at the beginning of period (Column 1) and operating results (Column 4) net of management fees (Column 3) and carried interest (Column 6). The calculated IRRs are in the bottom row of the following table.

Year End	Cash Flows for Gross IRR	Cash Flows for Net IRR
2000	−50	−50.0
2001	−20	−21.0
2002	−25	−26.3
2003	0	−1.5
2004	35	29.2
2005	50	41.0
2006	105	91.5
IRR	16.1%	11.3%

PREFATORY COMMENTS ON THE CASE STUDY   5

The case study that follows is a complement to this private equity valuation reading and is included to show the reader how to apply in context valuation methodologies in a private equity setting.

A Note on Valuation of Venture Capital Deals
This technical note on the valuation of venture capital deals is meant to explain the foundations of the venture capital method for valuing venture capital investments, the specific issues and diligences that must be addressed, and illustrate the concept in action with a case study.

SUMMARY

This reading focuses on valuation issues confronting investors in a private equity fund and the methods that the funds use to make investment decisions.

▶ Private equity funds seek to add value by various means, including optimizing financial structures, incentivizing management, and creating operational improvements.

▶ Private equity can be thought of as an alternative system of governance for corporations: rather than ownership and control being separated as in most publicly quoted companies, private equity concentrates ownership and control. Many view this governance arbitrage as a fundamental source of the returns earned by the best private equity funds.

▶ A critical role for the GP is valuation of potential investments. But because these investments are usually privately owned, valuation encounters a myriad of challenges, some of which have been discussed in this reading.

▶ Valuation techniques differ according to the nature of the investment. Early stage ventures require very different techniques than leveraged buyouts. Private equity professionals tend to use multiple techniques when performing a valuation, and they explore many different scenarios for the future development of the business.

▶ In buyouts the availability of debt financing can have a big impact on the scale of private equity activity and also seems to impact the valuations observed in the market.

▶ Because private equity funds have incentives to acquire, add value, and then exit within the lifetime of the fund, they are considered buy-to-sell investors. Planning the exit route for the investment is a critical role for the GP, and a well-timed and executed investment can be a significant source of realized value.

▶ In addition to the problems encountered by the private equity funds in valuing potential portfolio investments, many challenges exist in valuing the investment portfolio on an ongoing basis. This is because the investments have no easily observed market value, and there is a high element of judgment involved in valuing each of the portfolio companies prior to their sale by the fund.

▶ The two main metrics for measuring the ongoing and ultimate performance of private equity funds are IRR and multiples. Comparisons of the observed returns from private equity across funds and with other assets are demanding because it is important to control for the timing of cash flows, differences in risk, portfolio composition, and vintage year effects.

APPENDIX 46

A NOTE ON VALUATION OF VENTURE CAPITAL DEALS

When times are mysterious serious numbers are eager to please.

—Musician, Paul Simon, in the lyrics to his song *When Numbers Get Serious*

In this note, I discuss some of the fundamental issues of valuation in venture capital deals. The topics discussed are not necessarily limited to venture capital-backed companies, but they frequently surface in entrepreneurial companies that are financed either by venture capitalists or other private equity investors.

In Section 1, I introduce the so-called venture capital method. This is really a simple net present value (NPV) method that takes the perspective of the investor instead of the firm. This method has the advantage of extreme simplicity, but it makes many strong assumptions that limit its usefulness. I focus on three main issues in the remaining sections. In Section 2, I examine the problem of determining the terminal value. In Section 3, I examine the treatment of risk. In Section 4, I examine how to determine the funding requirements and I examine a number of ways of dealing with multiple financing rounds. In Section 5, I briefly cover the use of these methods in actual negotiations.

THE BASIC VENTURE CAPITAL METHOD   1

1.1 An Example

There exists a simple approach to valuation that is sometimes referred to as the venture capital method. The method is sometimes explained in the language of internal rates of return (IRR) and sometimes in terms of NPV. Since most of you have been more exposed to the NPV framework, I will use that language. I will then show that it is in fact *identical* to the IRR framework.

To illustrate my method I will use a fictional start-up company called "Spiffy-Calc," which is seeking financing from a venture capital fund by the name of "Vulture Ventures." Studying their crystal ball, the founders of SpiffyCalc expect to be able to sell the company for $25 million in four years.[1] At this point they need to raise $3 million. Vulture Ventures considers this a risky business and wants to apply a discount rate of 50 percent to be adequately compensated for the risk they will bear.[2] The entrepreneurs also decided that whatever valuation they would get, they wanted to own 1 million shares, which they thought would be a cool number to brag about.

This note was prepared by Thomas Hellmann, Assistant Professor of Strategic Management, Stanford University, as the basis for class discussion rather than to illustrate either effective or ineffective handling of an administrative situation.

[1] In Section 2, I discuss how one might replace the crystal ball by a liquid crystal display screen, as a slight improvement in the art of future telling.

[2] In Section 3, I discuss discount rates in more detail.

It is useful to define variables for the key assumptions we have made.

V = terminal value (at time of exit) = $25 million (in four years)

t = time to exit event = 4 years

I = amount of investment = $3 million

r = discount return used by investors = 50 percent

x = number of existing shares (owned by the entrepreneurs) = 1 million

Step 1: Determine the Post-Money Valuation

The only positive cash flow in this model occurs at the time of exit (typically an IPO or an acquisition), where we measure the terminal value of the company, denoted by V = $25 million. This means that after receiving the required $3 million, the initial value of the company is simply the discounted terminal value in 4 years' time. If Vulture Ventures is using a discount rate of 50 percent, the NPV of the terminal value in four years is $V/(1 + r)^t$ = $25 million$/(1.5)^4$ = $4,938,272 = POST. This is called the post-money valuation, i.e., the value of the company once the initial investment has been made. Intuitively, this is the value that is being placed on the entire company. This value is obviously not realized at the time of financing, as it depends on the belief that there will be great financial returns in the future.

Step 2: Determine the Pre-Money Valuation

Subtracting the cost of the investment of $3 million from the post-money valuation yields PRE = $1,938,272. This is called the pre-money valuation.

Step 3: Determine the Ownership Fraction

Vulture Ventures is investing $3 million in a venture valued at $4,938,272. In order to get back its money it therefore needs to own a sufficient fraction of the company. If they own a fraction F = $3 million$/$4,938,272 = 60.75 percent, they get their required rate of return on their investment.

Step 4: Obtain the Number of Shares

The founders want to hold 1 million shares. When Vulture Ventures makes its investment it needs to calculate the number of shares required to achieve its desired ownership fraction. In order to obtain a 60.75 percent ownership share, Vulture Venture makes the following calculation: let x be the number of shares owned by the founders (x = 1 million) and y be the number of shares that Vulture Ventures requires, then $y/(1,000,000 + y)$ = F = 60.75 percent. After some algebraic transformation we get y = 1,000,000 [0.6075/(1–0.6075)] = 1,547,771. Vulture Ventures thus needs 1,547,771 shares to obtain their desired 60.75 percent of the company.

Step 5: Obtain the Price of Shares

The price of shares is thus given by $3 million/1,547,771 = $1.94.

1.2 The General Case

We can calculate all important variables of a deal in a simple five step procedure:

Step 1: $POST = V/(1 + r)^t$

POST is the post-money valuation.

Step 2: $PRE = POST - I$

PRE is the pre-money valuation.

Step 3: $F = I/POST$

F is the required ownership fraction for the investor.

Step 4: $y = x\,[F/(1 - F)]$

y is the number of shares the investors require to achieve their desired ownership fraction.

Step 5: $p_1 = I/y$

p_1 is the price per share.

1.3 Sensitivity Analysis with the Basic Venture Capital Method

It is interesting to do some sensitivity analysis. How will the value of the company change if we change our assumptions? We will examine the effect of changing the following assumptions:

Variation 1: reduce the terminal value by 10 percent

Variation 2: increase the discount rate by an absolute 10 percent

Variation 3: increase investment by 10 percent

Variation 4: increase time to exit by 10 percent

Variation 5: increase the number of exiting shares: this has no effect on any real values!

Single Period NPV Method		Base Model	Variation 1	Variation 2
Exit Value	V	$25,000,000	**$22,500,000**	$25,000,000
Time to exit	t	4	4	4
Discount rate	r	50.00%	50.00%	**60.00%**
Investment amount	I	$3,000,000	$3,000,000	$3,000,000
Number of existing shares	x	1,000,000	1,000,000	1,000,000
Post-Money	POST	$4,938,272	$4,444,444	$3,814,697
Pre-Money	PRE	$1,938,272	$1,444,444	$814,697
Ownership fraction of investors	F	60.75%	67.50%	78.64%
Ownership fraction of entrepreneurs	$1 - F$	39.25%	32.50%	21.36%

(Continued on next page . . .)

Single Period NPV Method		Base Model	Variation 1	Variation 2
Number of new shares	y	1,547,771	2,076,923	3,682,349
Price per share	p	$1.94	$1.44	$0.81
Final wealth of investors		$15,187,500	$15,187,500	$19,660,800
Final wealth of entrepreneurs		$9,812,500	$7,312,500	$5,339,200
NPV of investors' wealth		$3,000,000	$3,000,000	$3,000,000
NPV of entrepreneurs' wealth		$1,938,272	$1,444,444	$814,697

Single Period NPV Method		Variation 3	Variation 4	Variation 5
Exit Value	V	$25,000,000	$25,000,000	$25,000,000
Time to exit	t	4	**4.4**	4
Discount rate	r	50.00%	50.00%	50.00%
Investment amount	I	**$3,300,000**	$3,000,000	$3,000,000
Number of existing shares	x	1,000,000	1,000,000	**2,000,000**
Post-Money	POST	$4,938,272	$4,198,928	$4,938,272
Pre-Money	PRE	$1,638,272	$1,198,928	$1,938,272
Ownership fraction of investors	F	66.83%	71.45%	60.75%
Ownership fraction of entrepreneurs	$1-F$	33.18%	28.55%	39.25%
Number of new shares	y	2,014,318	2,502,235	3,095,541
Price per share	p	$1.64	$1.20	$0.97
Final wealth of investors		$16,706,250	$17,861,700	$15,187,500
Final wealth of entrepreneurs		$8,293,750	$7,138,300	$9,812,500
NPV of investors' wealth		$3,300,000	$3,000,000	$3,000,000
NPV of entrepreneurs' wealth		$1,638,272	$1,198,928	$1,938,272

1.4 The Treatment of Option Pools

One subtle point in this calculation is the treatment of an employee option pool. Most venture capital deals include a nontrivial amount of shares for the option pool. This option pool will be depleted over time as the company hires executives and other employees. How do we account for the option pool in these calculations? The norm is that the entrepreneurs' shares and the option pool are lumped into one. Consider an example where the entrepreneurs receive 2 million shares, the investors receive 2 million shares, and there is an option pool of 1 million shares. Investors are investing $2 million at $1 per share. We then say that the post-money valuation is $5 million and the pre-money valuation is $3 million. Note, however, that from the entrepreneurs' perspective they are getting only $2 million of the pre-money valuation. The other $1 million is reserved for the option pool.

1.5 An Alternative Phrasing of the Venture Capital Method in Terms of IRR

The so-called venture capital method is often explained in the language of IRRs. While the IRR is often a problematic method in finance, our venture capital method is sufficiently simple that the IRR and the NPV method give *exactly the same answer.* Below I use the above example to walk you through the logic of the IRR calculation in the way it is sometimes presented as the venture capital method.

Step 1: Determine the future wealth that Vulture Ventures needs to obtain in order to achieve their desired IRR.

When Vulture Ventures decides to invest in a company, it formulates a "desired rate of return." Suppose that Vulture Ventures is asking for 50 percent IRR. Also, SpiffyCalc needs an investment of $3 million. We can then determine how much money Vulture Ventures needs to accumulate in order to achieve its desired return. Vulture Ventures would want to make $3 million $\times$ $(1.5)^4$ = $15,187,500 in four years.

Step 2: Determine the fraction of shares that Vulture Ventures needs to hold in order to achieve the desired IRR.

To find out the required percentage of shares that Vulture Ventures needs to achieve a 50 percent IRR, we simply divide its required wealth by the estimated value of the company, i.e., $15,187,500/$25 million = 0.6075. Vulture Ventures would thus need 60.75 percent of the shares.

Step 3: Determine the number of shares.

When Vulture Ventures makes its investment it needs to calculate the number of shares required to achieve its desired ownership fraction. We assume that the founders of SpiffyCalc issued themselves 1,000,000 shares, and nobody else owns any other shares. We then calculate how many shares Vulture Ventures needs to obtain a 60.75 percent ownership share in the company. Using the same reasoning as before let x be the number of shares owned by the founders (x = 1,000,000) and y be the number of shares that Vulture Ventures requires, then $y/(1,000,000 + y)$ = 0.6075. After some algebraic transformation we have y = 1,000,000 $[0.6075/(1 - 0.6075)]$ = 1,547,771. Vulture Ventures thus needs 1,547,771 shares to obtain their desired 60.75 percent of the company.

Step 4: Determine the price of shares.

Given that Vulture Ventures is investing $3 million, the price of a share is $3 million/1,547,771 = $1.94.

Step 5: Determine post-money valuation.

The post-money valuation can actually be calculated in a number of ways. First, if an investment of $3 million buys 60.75 percent of the company, then it must be that 60.75 percent * post-money valuation = $3 million. It follows that the post-money valuation is given by $3 million/0.6075 = $4,938,272. Another way to obtain the post-money valuation is to note that there are 2,547,771 shares in the company that are valued at $1.94, so the post-money valuation is 2,547,771 * $1.94 $\approx$ $4.94 million (allowing for rounding error).

Step 6: Determine pre-money valuation.

To calculate the pre-money valuation we simply subtract the value of the VC's investment from the post-money valuation. This is $4,938,272 − $3 million = $1,938,272. Another way of calculating the pre-money valuation is to evaluate the existing shares at the new price, i.e., $1,000,000 \times \$1.94 \approx \$1.94$ million (again allowing for rounding error).

We note that all the values are exactly the same as for the NPV method. The only difference is that one additional step was needed in the IRR method, namely to calculate the required wealth of the investors at a future point in time.[3]

Again, we can write down the general case:

Step 1: $W = I \, (1 + r)^t$

W is the amount of wealth investors expect to accumulate.

Step 2: $F = W/V$

F is the fraction of share ownership required by investors.

Step 3: $y = x \, [F/(1 - F)]$

y is the number of shares the investors require to achieve their desired ownership fraction.

Step 4: $p_1 = I/y$

p_1 is the price per share.

Step 5: $POST = I/F$ or $POST = p_1 \times (x + y)$

POST is the post-money valuation.

Step 6: $PRE = POST - I$ or $PRE = p_1 \times x$

PRE is the pre-money valuation.

2   ESTIMATING THE TERMINAL VALUE

Conceptually the terminal value represents the value of the company at the time of an exit event, be it an IPO or an acquisition.[4] Probably the most frequently used method to determine the terminal value is to take a multiple of earnings at the time of exit. Typically an estimate is taken of what the earnings are before tax, and then an industry multiple is taken. The difficulty is obviously to come up with a good estimate of the earnings and to find an appropriate industry multiple. This is particularly difficult for highly innovative ventures that operate in new or emerging industries.

---

[3] In the spreadsheet that accompanies the case, future wealth is also discounted back into the present to obtain the NPV of the stakes for the entrepreneurs and investors.

[4] To be precise, the relevant value is the pre-money valuation at the exit event.

Instead of taking a multiple of earnings, one might also consider taking multiples of sales or assets, or indeed of whatever other accounting measure is meaningful in that specific industry. The common methodology of all these multiples calculations is to look at comparable firms in the industry. One problem is that it is often difficult to find truly comparable companies. Another problem is that one typically looks at recent comparable deals. If a company is financed at a time when the stock market peaks and it uses recent IPOs as a basis of comparison, it will obtain large multiples. But these multiples may not reflect the multiples that it will be able to obtain when it plans to go public several years later.[5]

In principle, better methods of estimating terminal value would be to use NPV, CAPM, APT, or whatever equilibrium valuation model we think fits the data best. The problem, however, is that it is exceedingly difficult to come up with reasonable cash flow projections. And indeed, again one would look at comparable firms in the industry to come up with these estimates. These calculations may therefore not be much more accurate than the rough estimates using the multiples method.

Note that the implicit assumption for these estimates of the terminal value is typically that they measure the value of the company in case of success. This leads us to examine the issue of risk more carefully.

ACCOUNTING FOR RISK 　　　　　3

In the venture capital method of valuation, the estimate of the terminal value is typically based on some kind of success scenario. Because there is considerable risk involved in a typical venture capital deal, venture capitalists usually apply a very high discount risk "to compensate for the risk." It is not hard to see why they use this method. Venture capitalists are negotiating with entrepreneurs who are often overconfident and have a strong tendency to overstate the prospects of their new ventures. Venture capitalists can argue with them for some time, but rather than having a long and aggravating debate about these estimates, the VCs can simply deflate them by applying a higher discount rate. I therefore suspect that the venture capital method is simply a victim of bargaining dynamics. The method, however, is rather confusing, as it combines two distinct reasons for discounting. One of the reasons is that VCs need to be compensated for holding significant (and typically nondiversifiable) risk. The second is that VCs do not believe that the venture will necessarily succeed. The problem here is that the earnings estimate does not represent the *expected* earnings, but the earnings in case of success.[6] There are two closely related ways of dealing with this.

The first method is to simply recognize the fact that the discount rate incorporates a "risk of failure" component, as well as a true risk–diversification component. Since venture capitalists are not diversified, they may use a high discount

---

[5] While one would think that venture capitalists take this effect into account (and indeed they typically use that argument to talk multiples down) it is still true that venture capital valuations appreciate in times of rising stock markets.

[6] Technically speaking, the first aspect is true risk as measured in terms of the variance (or covariance) of returns. The second aspect does not concern the variance, but the overestimation of the mean.

rate to account for the variability of returns around their expected value.[7] Suppose, for example, that the risk–aversion of the VC fund implies an approximate risk-adjusted discount rate of 20 percent. If it was certain that this company would succeed, then the post-money valuation would simply be given by $25 million/$(1.2)^4$ = $12,056,327. But suppose now that the investors actually believe that the company might simply falter (with no value left) and that the probability of that event happening is 20 percent each year. The probability of getting the terminal valuation is only $(80 \text{ percent})^4$ = 40.96 percent, so that that the expected post-money valuation is only $0.4096 * \$12,056,327 = \$4,938,272$. We chose those numbers such that we get the same post-money valuation as before. This can be seen from the following: Let π be the probability of failure in any one year, then

$$\text{POST} = \frac{(1 - \pi)^t X}{(1 + r)^t} = \left(\frac{1 - \pi}{1 + r}\right)^t X = \frac{X}{(1 + \tilde{r})^t} \text{ where } \tilde{r} = \frac{1 + r}{1 - \pi} - 1$$

$$= \frac{r + \pi}{1 - \pi}$$

In our case $\tilde{r} = \dfrac{1 + 0.2}{1 - 0.2} - 1 = 0.5$: a 20 percent failure rate, combined with a 20 percent discount rate, have the combined effect of a 50 percent discount rate. Note that these numbers do not simply add up, so we need to go through the above formulas.

The second method is to allow for a variety of scenarios to generate a less biased estimate of expected returns. Typically we would try to adjust the terminal value to better reflect our true expectations. For example, SpiffyCalc's estimate of $25 million may have been based on an estimated earnings of $2.5 million and a multiple of 10. Suppose now that $2.5 million earnings is in fact an optimistic estimate. Suppose that there is a possibility that SpiffyCalc's product won't work, in which case the company will have no earnings. Or it may work, but the opportunity is smaller than originally hoped for, so that earnings in year 3 are only $1 million and the multiple is only 5, reflecting a lower growth potential. Suppose now that each of these three scenarios are equally likely. The expected terminal value is not $25 million but only 1/3*$0 + 1/3*5*$1 million + 1/3*10*$2.5 million = $10 million.

When valuing the company, the VC may now use a lower discount rate that reflects only the true amount of risk in the venture. Using the corrected estimate of $10 million and applying a 20 percent discount rate as before leads to a post-money valuation of $4,822,531. The VC would need to own 62.21 percent of the company.

4   INVESTMENT AMOUNTS AND MULTIPLE ROUNDS OF FINANCE

How do we determine the amount of money that needs to be raised? Again, there are a variety of methods. A simple and powerful method is to go to the entrepreneurs' financial projections and look at their cash flow statement, which

---

[7] The limited partners of the VC funds, however, tend to be very diversified. This can lead to some conflicts of interest, which we will not dwell on here.

tracks the expected cash balances of the company over time. An important insight that comes out of this method is that it is often better to raise money in several rounds. We illustrate this with our hypothetical example of SpiffyCalc.

4.1 An Example

Starting with a cash balance of $0, the company projects the following cash balances:

End of Year 1	End of Year 2	End of Year 3	End of Year 4	End of Year 5
$(1,600,000)	$(2,700,000)	$(4,600,000)	$(2,600,000)	$1,200,000

Looking at these numbers, SpiffyCalc realized that raising $3 million would get the company through its first two years. But after two years the company would need some additional money to survive. Indeed, SpiffyCalc estimated that the lowest cash balance would occur at the end of year 3, and that it would generate positive cash flows thereafter. The company therefore recognized that it needed to raise a total of $4.6 million. It also thought that it was more prudent to leave itself with some safety cushion, so it decided to raise a total of $5 million dollars. When it put those numbers into its spreadsheet, however, the numbers demonstrated that investors needed to receive 101.25 percent of the company and that its pre-money valuation was $-\$61,728$. This obviously means that at $5 million, the project was a negative NPV project.

But SpiffyCalc also noticed that it didn't need to raise the entire $5 million right from the start. For example, it could initially raise $3 million, and then raise the remaining $2 million after two years. In this case, the valuation method needs to take into account that the equity that first-round investors put into the business will be diluted in future rounds. This is a difficult problem, as it requires that we make assumptions about the terms of financing of these future rounds. While these assumptions may be difficult to get by, ignoring them will almost certainly lead to an inaccurate valuation. Indeed, ignoring future dilution will lead the venture capitalist to pay too much. The NPV framework is the most flexible and powerful method to account for future dilution.[8]

Suppose now that SpiffyCalc has already identified "Slowtrain Investors" as a potential investor for that second round. Suppose also that all investors apply a 50 percent discount rate through the four years before SpiffyCalc expects to be acquired. At the end of the second year, when "Slowtrain Investors" makes the second round investment, it would be doing the same calculation as we did above. It would use $POST_2 = \$25$ million$/(1.5)^2 = \$11,111,111$ as the post-money valuation. It would ask for a $2,000,000/11,111,111 = 18.00$ percent ownership stake. This means that the existing owners of the firm (the founders) and

---

[8] It is sometimes argued that future dilution does not matter in efficient markets, but we have to be careful with this argument. In a typical venture capital situation the company can only meet its financial projections if it manages to raise additional capital. In that sense the future dilution applies not to new investment opportunities of the company, but to the realization of the current investment opportunity. As an early round investor we therefore want to take account of the future dilution. This is different from the scenario in which future dilution relates to raising money for future investment opportunities that are additively separable from the current investment.

the first round investors (Vulture Ventures) would jointly only retain 82 percent of the company, or $0.82 * \$11,111,111 = \$9,111,111$. This is also the pre-money valuation at the time of this second round of financing, and no coincidence, since the pre-money valuation measures precisely the value for the existing owners of the firm.

For the first round investment, Vulture Ventures can then expect the company to be worth \$9,111,111 at the time of the second round, i.e., in two years' time. It then uses the same method as above to calculate the post-money valuation at the time of the first round, i.e., $POST_1 = \$9,111,111/(1.5)^2 = \$4,049,383$. This implies that it will ask for $3,000,000/\$4,049,383 = 74.09$ percent of the shares of the company. Note, however, that Vulture Ventures will not own 74.09 percent after four years. Instead, it expects a future dilution that will bring its ownership down to $f_1 = 0.82 * 0.7409 = 60.75$ percent (the lower case notation indicates final ownership, after dilution). This is obviously a familiar number, as we have seen before that Vulture Ventures needs exactly 60.75 percent to get their required return on their investment of \$3 million.

So far we haven't said anything about the number of shares and the price of shares for either the first or second round. In fact, we cannot calculate the price and number of shares for the second round before we calculate the price and number of shares for the first round. For this first round, we use the usual method, i.e., $y_1 = x_1 F_1/(1 - F_1) = 1,000,000 * 0.7409/(1 - 0.7409) = 2,858,824$ and thus $p_1 = 3,000,000/2,858,824 = \$1.05$. For the second round we repeat the exercise. The important step, however, is to use the correct number of shares, namely the total number of existing shares (irrespective of whether they are owned by the entrepreneur or the investor). We have $x_2 = (x_1 + y_1) = 1,000,000 + 2,858,824 = 3,858,824$ as the number of existing shares at the time of the second round. The new number of shares required is thus $y_2 = x_2 F_2/(1 - F_2) = 3,858,824(0.18)/(1 - 0.18) = 847,059$. The price of the second round shares is then given by $\$2,000,000/847,059 = \$2.36$.

The following table summarizes these assumptions and results.

NPV Method with Two Rounds of Financing	Time of Exit	Second Round	First Round
Exit Value	$25,000,000		
Compound discount rate		2.25	2.25
Investment amount		2,000,000	3,000,000
Number of existing shares		3,858,824	1,000,000
Post-Money		$11,111,111	$4,049,383
Pre-Money		$9,111,111	$1,049,383
Ownership Fraction		18.00%	74.09%
Number of new shares		847,059	2,858,824
Price per share		$2.36	$1.05
Ownership shares of entrepreneurs	21.25%		
Wealth of entrepreneurs	$5,312,500	$2,361,111	$1,049,383
Ownership shares of first round investors	60.75%		
Wealth of first round investors	$15,187,500	$6,750,000	$3,000,000
Ownership shares of second round investors	18.00%		
Wealth of second round investors	$4,500,000	$2,000,000	

4.2 The General Case with Multiple Rounds of Financing

We are now in a position to examine the general case. We show the formulas for the case where there are two rounds of financing. All variables pertaining to round 1 (2) will have the subscript $_{1\ (2)}$. The case with an arbitrary number of rounds is a straightforward extension discussed at the end of the section.

Step 1: Define appropriate compound interest rates.
Suppose that the terminal value is expected to occur at some date T_3, the second round at some date T_2, and the first round is happening at date T_1. Define $(1 + R_2)$ as the compound discount rate between time T_2 and T_3. If, for example, there are three years between the second round and the exit time, and if the discount rate for these three years is 40 percent, 35 percent, and 30 percent, respectively, then $(1 + R_2) = 1.4*1.35*1.3$. The compound discount rate $(1 + R_1)$ is defined similarly for the time between dates T_1 and T_2 (not T_3!!!).

Step 2: $POST_2 = V/(1 + R_2)$
Where $POST_2$ is the post-money valuation at the time of the second round, V is the terminal value and R_2 is the compound discount rate between the time of the second round and the time of exit.

Step 3: $PRE_2 = POST_2 - I_2$
PRE_2 is the pre-money valuation at the time of the second round of financing and I_2 is the amount raised in the second round.

Step 4: $POST_1 = PRE_2/(1 + R_1)$
Where $POST_1$ is the post-money valuation at the time of the first round and R_1 is the compound discount rate between the time of the first and second rounds.

Step 5: $PRE_1 = POST_1 - I_1$
PRE_1 is the pre-money valuation at the time of the first round of financing, and I_1 is the amount raised in the first round.

Step 6: $F_2 = I_2/POST_2$
F_2 is the required ownership fraction for the investors in the second round.

Step 7: $F_1 = I_1/POST_1$
F_1 is the required ownership fraction for the investors in the first round (this is not their final ownership share, as they will get diluted by a factor of $(1 - F_2)$ in the second round).

Step 8: $y_1 = x_1 [F_1/(1 - F_1)]$
y_1 is the number of new shares that the investors in the first round require to achieve their desired ownership fraction, and x_1 is the number of existing shares.[9]

Step 9: $p_1 = I_1/y_1$
p_1 is the price per share in the first round.

---

[9] If there are no pre-existing shares, one may also fix a total number of shares and then simply allocate them according to the fractions F_1 and $(1 - F_1)$.

Step 10: $x_2 = x_1 + y_1$
x_2 is the number of existing shares at the time of the second round.

Step 11: $y_2 = x_2 [F_2/(1 - F_2)]$
y_2 is the number of new shares that the investors in the second round require to achieve their desired ownership fraction.

Step 12: $p_2 = I_2/y_2$
p_2 is the price per share in the second round.

The general case is a straightforward extension of the case with two rounds. First we need to define the compound discount rates between all the rounds. Then we find the post- and pre-money valuations working backwards from the terminal value to each round of financing, all the way back to the first round of financing. For each round we discount the pre-money valuation of the subsequent round to get the post-money valuation of the round. Once we have the post-money valuations for all rounds we can calculate all the required ownership shares. To get the number and prices of shares we begin with the usual formula for the first round and then count up for each round.

4.3 Some Further Examples

Consider a first variation of the model. Suppose that the discount rate is highest in the early years and becomes lower after a while. For example, assume that the discount rate is 60 percent in the first year, stays at 50 percent in years two and three, and falls to 40 percent in the fourth year. This changes our compound discount rates: we have $(1+R_2) = 1.5*1.4 = 2.1$ and $(1+R_1) = 1.6*1.5 = 2.4$

Variation 1	Time of Exit	Second Round	First Round
Exit Value	$25,000,000		
Compound discount rate		2.1	2.4
Investment amount		2,000,000	3,000,000
Number of existing shares		3,661,972	1,000,000
Post-Money		$11,904,762	$4,126,984
Pre-Money		$9,904,762	$1,126,984
Ownership Fraction		16.80%	72.69%
Number of new shares		739,437	2,661,972
Price per share		$2.70	$1.13
Ownership shares of entrepreneurs	22.72%		
Wealth of entrepreneurs	$5,680,000	$2,704,762	$1,126,984
Ownership shares of first round investors	60.48%		
Wealth of first round investors	$15,120,000	$7,200,000	$3,000,000
Ownership shares of second round investors	16.80%		
Wealth of second round investors	$4,200,000	$2,000,000	

There are many other variations that we can examine in this model. A second variation of particular interest is to examine the role of the timing of the second round. Suppose, for example, that SpiffyCalc might be able to delay the timing of the second round by one year. In this case the compound discount rates are given by $(1 + R_2) = 1.4$ and $(1 + R_1) = 1.6*1.5*1.5 = 3.6$. Delaying the second round of financing would improve the valuation of the company.

Variation 2	Time of Exit	Second Round	First Round
Exit Value	$25,000,000		
Compound discount rate		1.4	3.6
Investment amount		2,000,000	3,000,000
Number of existing shares		3,135,593	1,000,000
Post-Money		$17,857,143	$4,404,762
Pre-Money		$15,857,143	$1,404,762
Ownership Fraction		11.20%	68.11%
Number of new shares		395,480	2,135,593
Price per share		$5.06	$1.40
Ownership shares of entrepreneurs	28.32%		
Wealth of entrepreneurs	$7,080,000	$5,057,143	$1,404,762
Ownership shares of first round investors	60.48%		
Wealth of first round investors	$15,120,000	$10,800,000	$3,000,000
Ownership shares of second round investors	11.20%		
Wealth of second round investors	$2,800,000	$2,000,000	

THE DETERMINANTS OF VALUATION: LOOKING BEYOND THE NUMBERS   5

To put things in perspective, it should be said that any method of valuation depends critically on the assumptions we make. Indeed, any valuation number can be justified by an appropriate choice of the discount rates and the terminal value. There is a more fundamental point here. A valuation method is a sophisticated tool for determining how entrepreneurs and venture capitalists should split the returns of the new venture. But the actual split, i.e., the actual deal, is not really driven by the valuation method, but rather by the outcome of the bargaining between the entrepreneurs and the venture capitalists. The relative bargaining power is thus the true economic determinant of the valuation that entrepreneurs will obtain for their companies. The valuation method, however, is an important tool to master for all parties involved, as it often provides the quantitative basis for the negotiation.

PRACTICE PROBLEMS FOR READING 46

1. Jo Ann Ng is a senior analyst at SING INVEST, a large regional mid-market buyout manager in Singapore. She is considering the exit possibilities for an existing investment in a mature automotive parts manufacturer that was acquired 3 years ago at a multiple of 7.5 times EBITDA. SING INVEST originally anticipated exiting its investment in China Auto Parts, Inc. within 3 to 6 years. Ng noted that current market conditions have deteriorated and that companies operating in a similar business trade at an average multiple of 5.5 times EBITDA. She deemed, however, based on analyst reports and industry knowledge that the market is expected to recover strongly within the next two years because of the fast increasing demand for cars in emerging markets. Upon review of market opportunities, Ng also noted that China Gear Box, Inc., a smaller Chinese auto parts manufacturer presenting potential strong synergies with China Auto Parts, Inc., is available for sale at an EBITDA multiple of 4.5. Exits by means of an IPO or a trade sale to a financial or strategic (company) buyer are possible in China. How would you advise Ng to enhance value upon exit of China Auto Parts?

2. Wenda Lee, CFA, is a portfolio manager at a U.K.-based private equity institutional investor. She is considering an investment in a mid-market European buyout fund to achieve a better diversification of her firm's existing private equity portfolio. She short listed two funds that she deemed to have a similar risk return profile. Before deciding which one to invest in, she is carefully reviewing and comparing the terms of each fund.

	Mid-Market Fund A	Mid-Market Fund B
Management fees	2.5%	1.5%
Transaction fees	100% to the GP	50–50% split
Carried interest	15%	20%
Hurdle rate	6%	9%
Clawback provision	No	Yes
Distribution waterfall	Deal-by-deal	Total return

Based on the analysis of terms, which fund would you recommend to Lee?

3. Jean Pierre Dupont is the CIO of a French pension fund allocating a substantial portion of its assets to private equity. The existing private equity portfolio comprises mainly large buyout funds, mezzanine funds, and a limited allocation to a special situations fund. The pension fund decided to further increase its allocation to European venture capital. The investment committee of the pension fund requested Dupont present an analysis of five key investment characteristics specific to venture capital relative to buyout investing. Can you assist Dupont in this request?

4. Discuss the ways that private equity funds can create value.

5. What problems are encountered when using comparable publicly traded companies to value private acquisition targets?

6. What are the main ways in which the performance of private equity limited partnerships can be measured A) during the life of the fund, and B) once all investments have been exited?

The following information relates to Questions 7–12

Martha Brady is the chief investment officer (CIO) of the Upper Darby County (UDC) public employees' pension system. Brady is considering an allocation of a portion of the pension system's assets to private equity. She has asked two of her analysts, Jennifer Chau, CFA, and Matthew Hermansky, to provide more information about the workings of the private equity market.

Brady recognizes that the private equity asset class covers a broad spectrum of equity investments that are not traded in public markets. She asks Chau to describe the major differences between assets that constitute this asset class. Chau notes that the private equity class ranges from venture capital financing of early stage companies to complete buyouts of large publicly traded or even privately held companies. Chau describes some of the characteristics of venture capital and buyout investments.

Chau mentions that private equity firms take care to align the economic interests of the managers of the investments they control with the interests of the private equity firms. Various contractual clauses are inserted in the compensation contracts of the management team in order to reward or punish managers who do not meet agreed on target objectives.

One concern is the illiquidity of private equity investments over time. But some funds are returned to investors over the life of the fund because a number of investment opportunities are exited early. A number of provisions describe the distribution of returns to investors, some of which favor the limited partners. One such provision is the distribution waterfall mechanism that provides distributions to limited partners (LP) before the general partner (GP) receives the carried interest. This distribution mechanism is called the total return waterfall.

Chau prepares the following data to illustrate the distribution waterfall mechanism and the funds provided to limited partners when a private equity fund with a zero hurdle rate exits from its first three projects during a three-year period.

EXHIBIT 1	Investment Returns and Distribution Waterfalls
Private equity committed capital	$400 million
Carried interest	20%
First project investment capital	$20 million
Second project investment capital	$45 million
Third project investment capital	$50 million
Proceeds from first project	$25 million
Proceeds from second project	$35 million
Proceeds from third project	$65 million

Chau cautions that investors must understand the terminology used to describe the performance of private equity funds. Interpretation of performance numbers should be made with the awareness that much of the fund assets are illiquid during a substantial part of the fund's life. She provides the latest data in Exhibit 2 for Alpha, Beta, and Gamma Funds—diversified high-technology venture capital funds formed five years ago and each with five years remaining to termination.

Chau studies the data and comments: "Of the three funds, the Alpha Fund has the best chance to outperform over the remaining life. First, because the management has earned such a relatively high residual value on capital and will be able to earn a high return on the remaining funds called down. At termination, the RVPI will earn double the '0.65' value when the rest of the funds are called down. Second, its 'cash on cash' return as measured by DPI is already as high as that of the Beta Fund. PIC, or paid-in capital, provides information about the proportion of capital called by the GP. The PIC of Alpha is relatively low relative to Beta and Gamma."

EXHIBIT 2	Financial Performance of Alpha, Beta, and Gamma Funds		
Fund	**PIC**	**DPI**	**RVPI**
Alpha	0.30	0.10	0.65
Beta	0.85	0.10	1.25
Gamma	0.85	1.25	0.75

Hermansky notes that a private equity fund's ability to properly plan and execute its exit from an investment is vital for the fund's success. Venture funds such as Alpha, Beta, and Gamma take special care to plan for exiting from investments. Venture funds tend to focus on certain types of exits, especially when equity markets are strong.

Brady then asks the analysts what procedures private equity firms would use to value investments in their portfolios as well as any other investments that might be added to the portfolio. She is concerned about buying into a fund with existing assets that do not have public market prices to ascertain value. In such cases, the GP may overvalue the assets and new investors in the fund will pay a higher NAV for the fund assets than they are worth.

Hermansky makes three statements regarding the valuation methods used in private equity transactions during the early stages of selling a fund to investors.

Statement 1:   For venture capital investment in the early stages of analysis, emphasis is placed on the discounted cash flow approach to valuation.

Statement 2:   For buyout investments, income-based approaches are used frequently as a primary method of valuation.

Statement 3:   If a comparable group of companies exist, multiples of revenues or earnings are used frequently to derive a value for venture capital investments.

7. The characteristic that is *most likely* common to both the venture capital and buyout private equity investment is:

   A. measurable and assessable risk.

   B. the extensive use of financial leverage.

   C. the strength of the individual track record and ability of members of management.

8. The contractual term enabling management of the private equity controlled company to be rewarded with increased equity ownership as a result of meeting performance targets is called:

   A. a ratchet.

   B. the tag-along right.

   C. the clawback provision.

9. For the projects described in Exhibit 1, under a deal-by-deal method with a clawback provision and true-up every three years, the cumulative dollar amount the GP receives by the end of the three years is equal to:

   A. one million.

   B. two million.

   C. three million.

10. Are Chau's two reasons for interpreting Alpha Fund as the best performing fund over the remaining life correct?

   A. No.

   B. Yes.

   C. The first reason is correct, but the second reason is incorrect.

11. The exit route for a venture capital investment is *least likely* to be in the form of a(n):

   A. initial public offering (IPO).

   B. sale to other venture funds targeting the same sector.

   C. buyout by the management of the venture investment.

12. Which statement by Hermansky is the *least* valid?

   A. Statement 1.

   B. Statement 2.

   C. Statement 3.

SOLUTIONS FOR READING 46

1. The exit strategies available to SING INVEST to divest their holding in China Auto Parts, Inc. will largely depend on the following two factors:

   ▶ Time remaining until the fund's term expires. If the time remaining is sufficiently long, the fund's manager has more flexibility to work out an exit at more favorable market circumstances and terms.

   ▶ Amount of undrawn commitments from LPs in the fund. If sufficient LP commitments can be drawn, the fund manager may take advantage of current market investment opportunities at depressed market prices with the objective to enhance returns upon exit in an expected more favorable market environment.

   In the case of China Auto Parts Inc., depending on an analysis of the above, Ng could advise the acquisition of China Gear Box, Inc. subject to an indepth analysis of potential synergies with China Auto Parts, Inc. The objective here may thus be twofold: benefit from short-term market conditions and enhance the value of existing investments by reinforcing their market potential with a strategic merger.

2. Assuming that both funds have similar risk return characteristics, a closer analysis of economic and corporate governance terms should be instrumental in determining which fund to select.

   In economic terms, Mid-Market Fund B has a higher carried interest relative to Mid-Market Fund A, but Mid-Market Fund B has a fee structure that is better aligned with the interests of LPs. A larger proportion of Mid-Market Fund B's fees will be on achieving successful exits (through the carried interest), whereas Mid-Market Fund A will earn relatively larger fees on running the fund (management fees and transaction fees) without necessarily achieving high performance. In addition, the 9 percent hurdle rate of Mid-Market Fund B is indicative of a stronger confidence of the fund manager to achieve a minimum compounded 9 percent return to LPs under which no carried interest will be paid.

   In corporate governance terms, Mid-Market Fund B is far better aligned with the interests of LPs as a result of a clawback provision and a more favorable distribution waterfall to LPs that will allow payment of carried interest on a total return basis instead of deal-by-deal.

   The conclusion is that Mid-Market Fund B appears better aligned with the interests of LPs.

3.

Venture Capital	Buyout
Primarily equity funded. Use of leverage is rare and very limited.	Extensive use of leverage consisting of a large proportion of senior debt and a significant layer of junior and/or mezzanine debt.
Returns of investment portfolios are generally characterized by very high returns from a limited number of highly successful investments and a significant number of write-offs from low performing investments or failures.	Returns of investment portfolios are generally characterized by lower variance across returns from underlying investments. Bankruptcies are rare events.

Venture Capital	Buyout
Venture capital firm monitors achievement of milestones defined in business plan and growth management.	Buyout firm monitors cash flow management and strategic and business planning.
Expanding capital requirement if in the growth phase.	Low working capital requirement.
Assessment of risk is difficult because of new technologies, new markets, and lack of operating history.	Risk is measurable (e.g., mature businesses, long operating history, etc.).

4. The main ways that private equity funds can create value include the following:

   ▶ Operational improvements and clearly defined strategies. In the case of later stage companies and buyouts, private equity owners can often create value by focusing the business on its most profitable opportunities and providing new strategic direction for the business. In the case of venture capital deals, the private equity funds can provide valuable business experience, mentor management, and offer access to their network of contacts and other portfolio companies.

   ▶ Creating incentives for managers and aligning their goals with the investors. This is often achieved by providing significant monetary rewards to management if the private equity fund secures a profitable exit. In the case of buyouts, the free cash flow available to management is minimized by taking on significant amounts of debt financing.

   ▶ Optimizing the financial structure of the company. In the case of buyouts, the use of debt can reduce the tax payments made by the company and reduce the cost of capital. There may also be opportunities in certain market conditions to take advantage of any mispricing of risk by lenders, which can allow the private equity funds to take advantage of interest rates that do not fully reflect the risks being carried by the lenders. Many would point to the period from mid-2006 to mid-2007 as a period when such conditions prevailed.

5. There are many complexities in using comparable companies to value private targets, including the following:

   ▶ The lack of public comparison companies operating in the same business, facing the same risks, and at the same stage of development. It is often possible to identify "approximate" comparisons but very rare to find an exact match. It is essential, therefore, to use judgment when using comparison company information, rather than just taking the average multiples derived from a sample of disparate companies.

   ▶ Comparison companies may have different capital structures, so estimated beta coefficients and some financial ratios should be adjusted accordingly.

   ▶ Reported accounting numbers for earnings must be chosen carefully and adjusted for any exceptional items, atypical revenues, and costs in the reference year. Care must also be taken to decide which earnings figures to compare—the main choices are trailing earnings (the last 12 months), earnings from the last audited accounts, or prospective year-ahead earnings.

6. In the early years of a fund, all measures of returns are of little relevance because fees drag down the reported returns and investments are initially valued at cost. This produces the J-curve effect. After a few years (longer in the case of venture capital investments), performance measures become more meaningful and the two main measures used by investors are IRR and return multiples (of the initial sum invested). During the life of the fund it is necessary to value the non-exited investments and add them to the realized returns. The former inevitably involves an element of judgment on the part of the General Partner, especially when it is difficult to estimate the likely market value of the investment. Once all the investments have been exited, the multiples and IRR can be estimated easily, taking account of the exact timing of the cash flows into and out of the fund. The most relevant measures for investors are computed net of management fees and any carried interest earned by the General Partner.

7. C is correct. Members of both the firm being bought out and the venture capital investment usually have strong individual management track records. Extensive financial leverage is common in buyouts but not venture capital investments, whereas measurable risk is more common in buyouts than in venture capital situations.

8. A is correct.

9. B is correct. On a cumulative basis for three years, the fund earns $10 million, of which $2 million goes to the GP. The $2 million earned by the GP corresponds to 20 percent of the difference between total three-year proceeds and three-year invested capital, or $0.2[(25 + 35 + 65) - (20 + 45 + 50)]$.

10. A is correct. Chau misinterprets DPI, RVPI, and PIC. The returns earned to date are for each dollar of invested capital, that which has been drawn down, not total returns. Chau mistakenly believes (assuming the same management skill) the result for Alpha Fund at termination will be on the order of $3 \times 0.65 = 1.95$ instead of 0.65. In both cases, Alpha Fund has underperformed relative to the other two funds.

11. C is correct. Leverage needed to finance a management buyout is not readily available to firms with limited history.

12. A is correct. Statement 1 is the least likely to be valid.

INVESTING IN HEDGE FUNDS: A SURVEY

by Keith H. Black, CFA

LEARNING OUTCOMES

The candidate should be able to:	Mastery
a. distinguish between hedge funds and mutual funds in terms of leverage, use of derivatives, disclosure requirements and practices, lockup periods, and fee structures;	☐
b. describe hedge fund strategies;	☐
c. explain possible biases in reported hedge fund performance;	☐
d. describe factor models for hedge fund returns;	☐
e. describe sources of non-normality in hedge fund returns and implications for performance appraisal;	☐
f. describe motivations for hedge fund replication strategies;	☐
g. explain difficulties in applying traditional portfolio analysis to hedge funds;	☐
h. compare funds of funds to single manager hedge funds.	☐

Although the media and many investors perceive hedge funds to be uniformly risky, the facts are that little about the hedge fund universe is homogenous. Some hedge funds hedge, whereas others take directional market risks. As a result of the private and opaque nature of hedge fund investing, a multitude of data challenges exist because hedge funds are not required to report their returns to regulators or any single database. Much of the literature describes adjustments and caveats to working with as-reported hedge fund returns and risk data.

"Hedge fund" is a term used to describe a wide variety of investment strategies. As a general rule, these strategies are less regulated and more opaque than long-only funds offered by traditional investment managers. Rather than taking a long-only exposure to a single asset class, many hedge fund strategies involve the use of leverage, derivative products, multiple asset classes, and short selling. The net market exposure of hedge funds can vary over time, which makes it more difficult to analyze performance, manage risk, and decide on the proper allocation of hedge funds in investor portfolios.

Stulz (2007) draws several contrasts between mutual funds and hedge funds. Hedge fund assets have grown explosively to more than $1 trillion, which is now more than 10 percent of the size of the mutual fund industry.

In the United States, mutual funds are required to report to the U.S. Securities and Exchange Commission (SEC). This requirement includes filing a prospectus, full disclosure of portfolio holdings on a semiannual basis, and the daily dissemination of a net asset value (NAV). Mutual funds are also subject to limits on leverage. In exchange for this regulation, mutual fund providers are allowed to market their products to a wide variety of investors, ask for low minimum investments, and offer universal availability to investors.

Hedge funds may earn exemptions from many of these regulatory requirements. By choosing to not market their investments to the public and restricting fund investments to certain types of high-net-worth investors, hedge funds are exempt from disclosure requirements. The unregulated nature of hedge funds, then, simply refers to the ability to provide less disclosure to investors and little or no disclosure to noninvestors. The opaque nature of hedge funds makes it difficult to calculate exact statistics on the size and performance of hedge funds because even their existence may not be disclosed.

Although exempt from disclosure requirements, hedge funds are not entirely unregulated. Hedge fund managers must still follow other laws determined by securities regulators. Hedge funds may not misrepresent performance, steal client funds, or engage in insider trading, manipulative trading, or front running.

In contrast to the low minimum investment and daily liquidity of mutual fund shares, investments in hedge funds are much less liquid. Most hedge funds report a NAV at the end of each month or calendar quarter. Many hedge funds also have lockup periods that restrict withdrawals from the hedge fund for some period of time. Popular lockups at hedge funds are one and two years, and three-year lockups are becoming more common. A "hard lockup" states that no provisions exist for the redemption of hedge fund investments for the stated period of time. A "soft lockup" period suggests a minimum investment period, but investors have the ability to sell their shares before the expiration of the lockup period by paying a redemption fee, which is often in the range of 1–3 percent. As a result of regulatory requirements that limit the number of investors in each fund, hedge funds typically have high minimum investment requirements, generally ranging from $500,000 to $10 million per investor.

1   FEE STRUCTURES

Much has been written about hedge fund fee structures. Hedge fund performance is typically reported net of all fees. Stulz (2007) explains that hedge funds can earn both management fees and incentive fees. A typical management fee is 1–2 percent annually based on the assets under management. Incentive fees, also called performance fees, are calculated as a set percentage of the profits on the underlying pool of assets. A hedge fund manager might earn 15–25 percent of profits in addition to the management fee. Few mutual funds charge performance fees because U.S. regulations require the fees to be symmetrical, meaning the investment manager must share equally in both gains and losses.

Hedge fund incentive fees are paid on a quarterly or annual basis and are often subject to a high-water mark provision. These fees are earned by a manager only during time periods of positive investment performance. The high-water mark provision ensures that incentive fees are earned only once for a given dollar of investment return. For example, a hedge fund earns a 10 percent gain, net of fees, in a calendar year for which incentive fees are paid. If the fund posts a return of −9 percent the following year, no incentive fees are paid because performance was negative. In the next year, the hedge fund returns 15 percent. The incentive fees in that year are paid only on the gains in excess of the high-water mark, which is the 5 percent of gains in excess of the NAV of the fund at the end of the first year. Anson (2001) has described hedge fund incentive fees as a free call option because the manager earns high fees for large investment gains but does not share in any investor losses. This lack of sharing in losses could provide an incentive for the manager to take risks larger than the investor would choose. An offsetting factor to this asymmetrical fee structure is when the investment manager has invested a substantial portion of his or her net worth in the fund, which would cause the manager and the investor to simultaneously experience trading losses.

Although a large percentage of hedge funds use a high-water mark in their fee calculations, a small minority also use hurdle rates. Hedge funds with hurdle rates do not earn any incentive fee until a minimum return threshold has been reached. Typical hurdle rates may be a stated short-term interest rate or a fixed annual rate, such as 5 percent.

Some investors have chosen not to allocate assets to hedge funds because of the size of fees paid to hedge fund managers. Asness (2006) suggests several modifications to hedge fund fee structures. Higher hedge fund fees should be paid to managers that have demonstrated skill by earning alpha, which is a high return after adjusting for all applicable risks. Leveraged hedge funds may also justify higher fees because these strategies earn a greater benefit from the manager's insight for each dollar of invested capital. Hedge fund investors are starting to separate alpha from beta in their performance calculation, leading them to ask hedge funds to charge lower fees for beta exposures to traditional market factors. By replacing high beta hedge funds with index funds or hedge fund beta replications (see the section "Hedge Fund Replication"), investors can substantially reduce the fees they pay. As the hedge fund industry comes to rely more on institutional investors, such as pension plans, and less on high-net-worth individuals, hedge fund fees for larger investments are likely to decline.

A WIDE VARIETY OF HEDGE FUND STRATEGIES

2

Black (2004) provides a comprehensive overview of hedge fund strategies and follows the fund style classification methodology of the Credit Suisse/Tremont Hedge Fund Index (www.hedgeindex.com).

Arbitrage-based funds typically have a lower standard deviation of returns because they are the hedge funds that explicitly hedge. By design, the risk and size of the long positions are highly correlated with the risk and size of the short positions. In many cases, these funds have short volatility exposures that lead to gains in quiet markets and losses in turbulent markets. These strategies typically have annualized standard deviations of 5–7 percent, which result in the highest Sharpe ratios of all hedge fund strategies. Many of these strategies, however, make money slowly and lose money quickly, which leads to unattractive negative skewness and fat tail risk (i.e., large excess kurtosis).

Convertible bond arbitrage strategies purchase a portfolio of convertible bonds and take short positions in the related equity security. A convertible bond is typically a corporate debt issue that includes a call option on the stock price of the issuer. Investors accept a lower yield on convertible bonds compared with option-free debt of the same issuer because they are compensated for the lower yield through the call option. For example, a corporation that typically borrows at 7 percent in the bond market may issue a convertible bond with a 4 percent yield, which prices the call option at the present value of the foregone 3 percent interest. A convertible bond strategy is deemed to be market neutral when the price of the fund does not change with small changes in the underlying stock prices. Market neutrality is achieved when the size of the short-stock position matches the long-delta position of the embedded call options. Convertible bond arbitrage performs well in times of declining credit spreads and high stock price volatility. In times of rising credit spreads, convertible bond arbitrage funds can suffer steep losses because bond prices are falling quickly and liquidity of convertible bonds declines rapidly in a flight to quality market.

Equity market neutral funds seek to take, on average, a zero beta exposure to equity markets. Many funds aim for a zero exposure on average but may take temporary risks of up to a beta of ±0.20. Although beta risks are minimized in this strategy, fund managers may take substantial risks in other areas of the equity markets, such as market capitalization, value, growth, or industry. To reach beta neutrality, the size and beta of the long positions are closely matched through the size and beta of the short positions. Many market neutral funds are driven through a quantitative process. Quantitative funds with longer holding periods (months) may be based on factor models with such themes as value, growth, momentum, and earnings quality. Quantitative funds with shorter holding periods (minutes to days) may be called statistical arbitrage and are largely based on trading long–short pairs of stocks with a high long-term correlation with divergent short-term stock movements.

Event driven funds are focused on a single strategy, such as distressed investments or risk arbitrage. Multistrategy implementations of event driven investing can combine these two strategies with others, such as spinoffs, cross-ownership, or index reconstitution strategies. Distressed funds typically invest in debt securities of issuers currently in default or expected to default soon. Distressed funds have, perhaps, the most significant liquidity risk of any hedge fund strategy because many investors are not willing or able to buy the debt of firms currently in bankruptcy. Distressed investors can be passive, simply willing to earn the return on the bonds they purchase. Others, however, are very active investors who will become involved in the bankruptcy process. Capital structure arbitrage implementations of distressed investments include spreads between many parts of a given company's capital structure, perhaps by buying debt and selling short the stock or trading credit default swaps against stock options.

Risk arbitrage, or merger arbitrage, funds seek to predict the outcome of announced corporate merger transactions. The classic implementation is to purchase the stock of the target company and sell short the stock of the acquiring company in the ratio of the stock swap transaction. This strategy is the definition of event risk and higher moment risk because these funds make money slowly and lose money quickly. The target return of a successful investment may be only 5–10 percent, which is earned during the 3–18 months between the announcement and consummation of the deal. Risk arbitrage funds can experience substantial losses when a planned merger is cancelled because the stock of the target company can fall 30 percent or more in a single day. Risk arbitrage is considered a short volatility strategy because the hedge fund has sold insurance against a broken deal in consideration of the expected return of the completed deal.

Fixed-income arbitrage typically invests with a positive income orientation that benefits during times of declining credit spreads. Fixed-income arbitrage strategies purchase higher yielding bonds, which can be investment- or speculative-grade corporate bonds, mortgage-backed securities, or debt issued by emerging market governments. Higher quality debt is sold or leverage is acquired at lower rates. The strategy usually earns a positive income because the purchased bonds have a higher yield than the higher quality debt or the cost of the leverage. This strategy benefits when credit spreads are stable or tightening and markets are relatively liquid. Fixed-income arbitrage funds can suffer catastrophic losses during flight to quality markets because credit spreads widen quickly, leverage becomes more expensive, and markets for lower quality debt become much less liquid.

Medium volatility hedge fund strategies typically take both long and short positions, but these positions are not always designed as hedges. The long and short positions may differ dramatically in size and/or risk, often resulting in a net long position in an underlying stock, bond, commodity, or currency market. These strategies have an average volatility of 10–12 percent per year, which is slightly less than the volatility of the underlying markets.

Global macro funds typically focus on long and short investments in broad markets, such as equity indices, currencies, commodities, and interest rate markets. Rather than selecting specific securities, macro funds focus on the macroeconomic picture, selecting asset classes and countries that will benefit from the manager's market view. In many cases, these views will be driven by market changes related to governmental actions, such as the transition from fixed to floating rate currencies. Macro funds can take concentrated positions and be quite volatile. Because macro fund managers have the entire world of securities to choose from, they tend to be difficult to replicate and have a relatively low correlation with other managers trading the same strategy.

Long–short equity funds are the largest hedge fund strategy, earning nearly 40 percent of all investor dollars allocated to hedge funds. The implementation is very similar to that of equity market neutral hedge funds, except that long–short funds do not target a zero beta exposure to underlying equity markets. During long periods of time, these funds may average a net long beta of 0.3 to 0.6. When bear markets are expected, however, managers have the flexibility to take a neutral or short exposure to equity markets.

Managed futures funds, in which the managers are also called commodity trading advisers (CTAs), use a strategy dominated by systematic trend following that seeks to profit through the quantitative prediction of market trends. These funds will invest in currencies, commodities, equity indices, and interest rate futures. They seek to take long positions during times of rising prices and short positions during times of falling prices. Managed futures funds typically have no target for the mix of long and short positions but simply build a bottom-up portfolio of positions expected to benefit from the anticipated trends in market prices. Although the risk–return profile of the managed futures index does not seem to be attractive on a stand-alone basis, this strategy offers the best hedging and diversification characteristics of any hedge fund strategy. Valuation risk, liquidity risk, complexity risk, and counterparty risk are typically minimal in this sector.

Multistrategy funds are similar to funds of funds in that they diversify broadly among a variety of hedge fund strategies. A fund of funds invests with a number of underlying managers and charges a second layer of fees at the fund-of-funds level. Multistrategy funds charge only a single layer of fees but typically manage all of the assets with managers employed by a single hedge fund management company.

Directional hedge fund strategies are the most volatile of all because little to no hedging activity is used. As such, these strategies inherit the full volatility (15–17 percent or more) of the underlying markets in which the funds are invested.

Dedicated short bias funds typically invest exclusively in the short sale of equity securities. Although the funds often have a beta exposure close to −1.0, their returns can add significant value if the manager displays skill in predicting which stocks will underperform the market index.

Emerging market hedge funds are often long only because the ability to trade derivative securities or sell short is either not developed or is prohibitively expensive in these markets. Although some funds may focus on specific regions or trade exclusively fixed-income or equity market funds, others may invest globally and mix stocks and bonds in the same fund. When the debt of emerging market countries is rated below investment grade, these bonds may have risk and return characteristics similar to equity securities.

3   HEDGE FUND DATABASES AND PERFORMANCE BIASES

Hamza, Kooli, and Roberge (2006), Fung and Hsieh (2004), and Malkiel and Saha (2005) describe a number of features of hedge fund databases. A variety of databases exist, including Hedge Fund Research (HFR), Credit Suisse/Tremont, MSCI, Lipper TASS, EACM, Zurich, Eurekahedge, Tuna, and Center for International Securities and Derivatives Market (CISDM). Although each database contains hundreds, or thousands, of hedge funds and their associated returns, no database is complete. In fact, a surprisingly high number of hedge funds report only to a subset of available databases. Many academics and large hedge fund investors subscribe to multiple databases to get a more complete picture of the hedge fund universe.

Each hedge fund database provider has its own methodology for the inclusion of funds, style classification of funds, and the index weight. For example, HFR is equally weighted whereas Credit Suisse/Tremont is asset weighted. This difference in fund weighting methodology can lead to substantial differences in hedge fund index returns, risks, and correlations across databases. Although equally weighted databases are more representative of the "average" hedge fund, this methodology places a larger weight on funds with lower levels of assets under management (AUM). Equally weighted databases also require a rebalancing methodology, which may not be feasibly implemented in a world with large minimum investments and substantial lockup periods. An asset weighted database places a larger weight on hedge funds with larger AUM, which leads the index to be more representative of the hedge fund industry than of the average hedge fund.

As a result of the lack of disclosure requirements by hedge funds, reporting to databases is voluntary. Some analysts believe that managers with higher returns and lower risks are more likely to report returns to database providers, whereas managers of funds with less attractive track records are less likely to provide their track record to the database. This lack of reporting leads to selection bias or self-reporting bias, in which the risk–return trade-off of hedge funds represented by databases is more attractive than what is actually experienced by the full universe of hedge fund investors.

Selection bias is closely related to backfill bias, which is also termed instant history or incubation bias. When a manager decides to report to a database, he

analysis regression showed the hedge fund index's average exposure over time. Many hedge funds, however, do not have static beta exposures but vary their market exposures substantially over time. By splitting the sample into smaller time periods, such as January 1994 to September 1998 or April 2000 to December 2002, the R^2 of the regression climbed as high as 80 percent. Beckers et al. (2007) used a 36-month rolling window regression to explain the returns of funds of funds. Ideally, hedge funds will take greater exposure in rising markets and less exposure in declining markets. Unfortunately, these authors found evidence of negative market timing skill among fund-of-funds managers.

NON-NORMALITY OF HEDGE FUND RETURNS

5

Much of the traditional finance literature has made the implicit assumption that investment returns are normally distributed and linearly related to asset class returns. Sharpe ratios and Markowitz's efficient frontier analysis include return and standard deviation of return in their calculations of risk–return trade-offs. The calculation of beta, and the resulting Jensen's alpha, include the assumption that investment returns are earned from taking risk exposures to traditional market factors and that these exposures are relatively constant through time. Unfortunately, many of these assumptions are violated when investing in hedge funds. Because hedge fund returns are often not normally distributed or linearly related to traditional market exposures, Kat (2003) and Cremers, Kritzman, and Page (2005) show that applying many of the classical techniques and ratios to hedge fund returns without accounting for nonlinearities can cause investors to reach inappropriate conclusions about the attractiveness of hedge funds. As a result, some investors allocate too much of their portfolio to hedge funds and are disappointed when their assumptions are violated.

The Sharpe ratio and efficient frontier analysis assume that standard deviation is the only investment risk, but many hedge fund strategies have return profiles in which the skewness and kurtosis of returns do not closely match the assumptions of the normal distribution. Investors prefer a large mean and positive skewness of returns, while also preferring lower variance and smaller kurtosis. Hedge funds generally have higher moment risks, in which returns have negative skewness (i.e., the third moment of the return distribution) and large excess kurtosis (i.e., the fourth moment of the return distribution, also called fat tails). These return characteristics come from managers' spread trading strategies, which Kat (2004) deemed to be "pseudo" arbitrages and showed that these trades are far from risk free. Because these trades typically have a low volatility, leverage is frequently used.

Consider a merger arbitrage trade in which the fund manager purchases the target company and sells short the acquiring company with the intention of earning a 10 percent return during the next 12 months. When the deal is consummated at the time and terms as expected, it seems to be a low risk, low volatility strategy. In actuality, this trade is selling insurance. Investors sell the target company at a discount to its stated deal price to hedge the risk that the deal will fail. By offering the hedge fund the last 10 percent of return, the investor avoids the risk of a one-week decline of 30 percent or more in the target stock should the merger not proceed as planned. Notice that this trade is negatively skewed and highly kurtotic because the potential loss is larger than the potential gain and the losses come much more quickly than the gains.

Similar return profiles can be found in fixed-income arbitrage, option selling strategies, and currency carry trades. Evaluating the returns to these funds during quiet and converging market conditions can underestimate the potential losses that these funds could experience during turbulent markets in which credit spreads widen and stock prices decline quickly. Black (2006), Weisman (2002), and Kat (2003) demonstrate that these trading styles are short volatility, meaning these strategies incur substantial losses at times when equity market volatility is rising. Adding long volatility strategies, such as managed futures or purchased options, to a hedge fund portfolio can cause portfolio returns to be closer to normally distributed. When balancing long volatility and short volatility in a hedge fund portfolio, reported volatility will increase and the Sharpe ratio will decline, but the skewness and kurtosis exposures will be much more attractive to investors. Much of the nonlinearities in hedge fund returns can be traced back to extreme events, such as the demise of Long-Term Capital Management in 1998 (see Kazemi and Schneeweis 2004).

6   LIQUIDITY, COMPLEXITY, AND VALUATION RISKS

Hedge fund factor exposures vary in their ease of being added to a factor model compared with traditional market exposures, which are better understood and easy to add to a factor model. Hedge fund strategies and exotic betas are more difficult to derive, but once derived they are straightforward to add to the factor model. Some of the hedge fund returns attributed to alpha could simply be compensation for bearing liquidity and complexity risks. That is, some investments should offer higher returns simply because they are more difficult to understand or value.

Till (2004) discusses the costs of illiquidity in hedge funds. As mentioned earlier, investors should be compensated for longer lockup periods, and many hedge funds are now offering lower fees in exchange for investors agreeing to longer lockup periods. Investors should also be compensated for short volatility risk and event risk. Illiquid assets, such as emerging markets, over-the-counter derivatives, microcap stocks, and distressed fixed-income securities, are difficult to value and difficult to trade. Investors in these assets are taking the risk that the assets will be valued at a price far different from what would be realized when asking the market for liquidity. Should the hedge fund choose or be forced to sell during a liquidity crisis, prices will be even lower.

In these illiquid asset classes, many holdings are valued using a mark-to-model methodology. Because these assets do not have a liquid market, marking to market is not feasible. These assets also trade infrequently, so valuations change relatively slowly when compared with prices in more liquid markets. This tendency to change valuations slowly is termed stale pricing. When funds exhibit stale pricing, the risk of the fund's holdings will be understated because volatility and the correlation with freely traded assets are likely to be understated. Kat (2004) estimates that this artificial smoothing of net asset values can underestimate risk by as much as 40 percent. Although it seems logical to include illiquidity in a factor model, Kat (2004) states that no study has adequately modeled this common risk of hedge fund investing. The Sharpe ratio of funds with smoothed returns is dramatically overstated, as the standard deviation of reported returns is far below the true economic standard deviation.

Although it can be difficult to include illiquidity in a factor model, a number of authors have suggested adjustments to smoothed data to estimate the true, or unsmoothed, risk of these illiquid investments. Getmansky, Lo, and Makarov

(2004) explain the procedures for adjusting for stale prices, which can be detected through the use of serial correlation. When analysis shows that autocorrelation is present in hedge fund returns, it is said that the returns have been smoothed and that prior month returns can be used to predict the current month returns. The factor analysis equation given earlier can be modified as follows:

$$\text{Hedge fund return } (t) = \text{Alpha} + \text{Risk free rate} + \text{Hedge fund return } (t - 1)$$
$$+ \sum_i \text{Beta}_i \times \text{Factor}_i$$

By including the prior month's return, the analysis shows that this hedge fund trading strategy incurs illiquidity risks. When the prior month's return is statistically significant, a new explanatory factor is added to the analysis. The typical result is that the R^2 of the regression increases and the alpha of the hedge fund style declines. Some authors include lagged values of a hedge fund index or a traditional market beta source. When the current month and the prior month both have a statistically significant exposure to a given factor, Kazemi and Schneeweis (2004) show that the true risk to that factor is the sum of the current and prior month's factor betas. For example, rather than the fund beta being 0.3 from the S&P 500 Index return in the current month, the true beta would be 0.5 if the regression also showed a statistically significant beta of 0.2 from the prior month's return on the S&P 500 Index.

Getmansky, Lo, and Makarov (2004) show that stale pricing risks are most prominent in fixed-income and convertible bond strategies, as well as event driven and relative value strategies and emerging markets. These markets are known for their illiquidity and the need for mark-to-market valuation. Strategies that rely on trading in more liquid markets, such as large-cap stocks, currencies, and commodity futures, do not show evidence of stale pricing because fund managers can easily calculate NAV from each day's market settlement prices.

Beyond the effect of underestimated risks, stale pricing can have clear financial implications for investors. If the monthly NAV for a hedge fund is struck using stale prices, investors who sell hedge fund interests during a bull market may receive proceeds of less than the fair value for those assets. Conversely, investors who redeem hedge fund interests during a bear market will receive a higher than realistic price for their assets because future prices are likely to be lower when full markdowns of assets are taken.

ALPHA AND THE CAPACITY FOR HEDGE FUNDS TO INCREASE ASSETS

7

Géhin and Vaissié (2006) and Amenc and Martinelli (2002) discuss the proper calculation of the alpha earned by hedge funds. Alpha is the return to the hedge fund after accounting for the risks incurred by both traditional and alternative beta exposures. Amenc and Martinelli (2002) estimate the alpha of hedge funds to be 5.8 percent per year in excess of the exposure to traditional beta risks. After adding the exposure to alternative beta risks, the alpha declines to −1.0 percent. The implication of this analysis is that hedge funds, as a group, do not earn positive alpha but simply provide investors with the ability to access alternative beta exposures.

Of course, alpha varies over time and by strategy. Concerns exist that as the size of the hedge fund industry increases, the alpha earned by the average hedge fund will decline. More simply, Hsieh (2006) estimates that by exploiting market inefficiencies a static $30 billion in alpha is available to be earned by all hedge fund managers combined. This amount is based on 3 percent alpha from a hedge fund industry size of $1 trillion, but as hedge fund assets grow to $2 trillion, the percentage return to each fund in alpha terms would decline to 1.5 percent. This argument assumes that a finite capacity for AUM for hedge funds exists, both as an industry and in each strategy. As greater assets enter each strategy, the market inefficiencies disappear more quickly, making the future prognosis for hedge fund growth dim. Géhin and Vaissié (2006), however, find no clear evidence of a declining trend in alpha. The capacity for hedge fund managers to profitably invest is based on alpha and beta factors. If hedge funds derive most of their returns from beta factors, then the industry can continue to grow in terms of assets and managers. If hedge funds are dependent on alpha and disappearing market inefficiencies, then the capacity of AUM for the hedge fund industry is more limited.

Géhin and Vaissié (2006) believe that investors overstate the importance of alpha and understate the importance of beta when analyzing the returns to hedge funds. The three drivers of hedge fund returns are static beta exposures, dynamic beta exposures (market timing), and alpha (security selection skill). The authors estimate that approximately half of hedge fund variance comes from static betas, whereas the remaining variance is evenly split between dynamic betas and alpha. Nearly the entire return to hedge funds can be attributed to static betas, whereas dynamic betas incur losses over time and alpha adds value.

8   HEDGE FUND REPLICATION

Hedge fund replication is widely discussed in the literature, with Jaeger and Wagner (2005), Fung and Hsieh (2004), and Kat (2007) leading the discussion. The original discussion of hedge fund replication was based on the factor models mentioned earlier and the concept of alpha–beta separation. If traditional stock and bond market indices can explain the majority of hedge fund return variance, then investors may be able to replicate hedge fund returns by using index funds and swaps products. Replication strategies can be attractive when hedge fund managers are not earning a positive alpha, when investors are worried about the size of the fees paid to hedge fund managers, or because of the historical lack of liquidity and transparency of hedge fund investments. A common theme in the replication literature is that replication products are relatively simple to manage and can, therefore, be offered to investors at fees much lower than those charged by hedge fund managers.

The simplest form of replication uses static weights to invest in traditional market products. Jaeger and Wagner (2005) develop replicating factor strategies, which can replicate many hedge fund styles with just three or four traditional market exposures. Of 11 styles tested, 8 could be replicated with an R^2 above 49 percent. Long–short equity, emerging market, short selling, and distressed strategies can be most closely replicated, with an R^2 of between 68 percent and 88 percent. Less efficient replications can be developed for equity market neutral, risk arbitrage, fixed-income arbitrage, convertible bond arbitrage, global macro, and managed futures strategies. For example, a simple replication of a fixed-income arbitrage fund would take a long position in a credit fund, such as corporate bonds, high yield bonds, or mortgage-backed securities, and a short position in a Treasury securities fund of a similar duration. The weights for each fund would be determined through a linear regression of long-term hedge fund returns on the traditional bond market sector funds. A slightly more complex form of replication uses dynamic weights with the same traditional market factors. Rather than having static weights, the beta exposure to each market sector is determined through the use of rolling regressions, with common look-back periods of one to three years.

Fung and Hsieh (2004) add dynamic strategies to the factor mix, simulating the use of look-back straddles on bond, currency, and commodity indices. These dynamic factors can simulate the use of trend-following strategies, as well as short or long volatility exposures.

Berger, Crowell, and Kabiller (2008) seek to separate hedge fund beta from hedge fund replication. Hedge fund replication using factor models and liquid index products avoids many of the issues of liquidity and complex valuation faced by hedge funds that invest in specific securities. To capture the returns to event risk, illiquidity, and complex securities, the hedge fund beta strategy seeks to mechanically reproduce hedge fund strategies by investing in specific securities. A fund designed to provide merger arbitrage beta, for example, would purchase the target company and sell short the acquiring company in all announced merger transactions. Beta exposure to managed futures could be developed through a mechanical trend-following system that seeks to buy futures in any market with a trend of rising prices and sell short futures in any market in which prices are expected to decline. A distressed or convertible arbitrage beta could be devised through the purchase of those specific fixed-income securities, perhaps by selling short the related equity security.

HEDGE FUND PORTFOLIO ANALYSIS   9

Hedge fund investors are interested in how an allocation to hedge funds would modify the risk and return of their entire portfolio, including exposures to traditional stock and bond markets. Fund-of-funds managers are concerned with building the most efficient portfolio of hedge funds. In each case, the goal is to minimize the risk for each level of expected return. Ideally, adding hedge funds to a traditional investment portfolio would reduce portfolio risk without reducing portfolio return.

Traditional portfolio theory says that the calculation of efficient portfolios requires estimates of return, correlation, and volatility for each asset class. The factor analysis techniques discussed earlier can give clues to future correlation and volatility. For example, long–short equity funds are highly correlated with stock market indices in which volatility is scaled by the average beta through time. Géhin and Vaissié (2006) state that managed futures, fixed-income and convertible bond arbitrage, and market neutral equity funds provide the best diversification properties when added to an equity portfolio. Similarly, event driven, long–short equity, emerging market, and convertible bond arbitrage funds add diversification to a fixed-income portfolio.

Allison and Lin (2004) show that a number of caveats exist when attempting to model the addition of hedge funds to traditional portfolios. Specifically, it is difficult to develop expected return assumptions for hedge funds given the survivor, selection, stale pricing, and backfill biases inherent in hedge fund databases. Correlation and volatility of historical hedge fund returns, however, can be appropriately used to develop estimates of future risks. After determining the beta of each hedge fund strategy in relation to the underlying traditional market factors, an expected return assumption for the hedge fund style can be derived by adding estimated alpha to the beta-adjusted expected returns of the underlying asset classes.

Dopfel (2005) also uses the alpha and beta estimates of factor analysis to derive expected returns for hedge fund strategies. Investors need to be aware, however, that hedge fund performance can be quite dynamic, with correlation, volatility, and beta exposures that can change significantly over time. In addition, derivatives and short volatility trading strategies can add nonlinearities to the hedge fund return generation process. These properties can lead hedge funds to have asymmetrical beta exposures, in which the beta of the hedge fund differs according to the volatility and the direction of the underlying market. For example, managed futures and dedicated short bias funds have attractive asymmetrical exposures to equity index prices, with higher betas in rising markets and lower betas in falling markets. Multistrategy and market neutral equity funds have little exposure to asymmetrical beta. Unfortunately, all other hedge fund styles have negative asymmetrical beta exposures, and betas tend to rise in falling markets. Dopfel (2005) also discusses using factor analysis to target overall asset allocation. When the hedge fund portfolio has a persistent beta relative to equity markets, it is wise to reduce the portfolio's exposure to equity markets by a similar amount to ensure that equity market risk is consistent with the strategic asset allocation.

Kat (2004) warns about the use of mean–variance optimization and Sharpe ratios in building hedge fund portfolios because standard deviation is not a complete measure of risk for hedge funds. Some hedge fund styles are known to smooth returns, as well as experience negative skewness and excess kurtosis. In fact, the hedge fund styles with the lowest standard deviations and highest Sharpe ratios are often the ones with the most unattractive higher moment exposures. A high Sharpe ratio and high alpha are simply invitations to further research the hedge fund manager's trading strategy. Investors need to determine whether the trading strategy is a short volatility, convergence related, or event-risk-laden strategy in which future risks could potentially be larger than historical risk. The typical result of adding hedge funds to a portfolio of traditional investments is that standard deviation will decline and the Sharpe ratio will increase but at the cost of worsening higher moment exposures. This result is attributed to the variable correlation and asymmetrical beta exposures of hedge funds, in which losses to hedge fund portfolios tend to increase during times of extreme losses in stock and bond markets. Mean–variance optimization also assumes that assets have the same liquidity characteristics and return distributions. If mean–variance optimization is to be used to add hedge funds to traditional investment portfolios, constraints on the deterioration of skewness and kurtosis risks should be added to the optimization equation. Placing constraints on the nonlinearities of hedge funds will cause investors to choose lower allocations to hedge funds than when mean–variance optimization is used without considering higher moment risks.

Sharma (2004) states that higher moment risks are more prevalent in lower volatility strategies because 75 percent of nondirectional strategies have returns that are not normally distributed, whereas only 39 percent of directional strategies reject normality.

Kat (2004) discusses the differences in analyzing hedge fund index data and the returns to individual hedge funds. Individual hedge funds typically have a higher standard deviation than their style index because a less than perfect correlation exists between funds in the same style. When aggregating hedge funds into a style index, the standard deviation of the index is lower than the standard deviation of the average fund, but the index tends to have more negative skewness and a higher correlation with equity markets. Although each fund has its own specific risks and market timing, those exposures are averaged when funds are bundled into an index. Although it diversifies the specific risk of each fund, the indexing process reduces standard deviation but increases the exposures to common factor risks.

PERFORMANCE PERSISTENCE OF HEDGE FUNDS   10

Beckers et al. (2007) discuss the performance persistence of hedge funds and find that the persistence of alpha is higher than the persistence of total returns. The persistence of funds with high information ratios (i.e., alpha divided by the standard deviation of alpha) is greater than that of funds with high Sharpe ratios. Specifically, funds with top quartile rankings of information ratios during the trailing three years have a 51 percent chance of remaining in the top quartile of that same measure during the subsequent year. Persistence is also strong for lower quartile funds because a large percentage of funds repeat as below average performers. Funds of funds show much greater persistence than single strategy hedge funds. The common factor risks tend to dominate the performance of single strategy funds, which are often clustered around the average return for the strategy. Funds of funds diversify among hedge fund styles, which diversifies the risks of relying on returns from a specific market factor.

Naik and Agarwal (2000) analyzed the performance persistence of hedge funds by calculating the alpha of each fund relative to its style index using quarterly returns. Past performance was calculated by using a variety of methodologies, including regressions, contingency tables, and appraisal ratios, which explicitly consider volatility and leverage. The results indicated that persistence varies by hedge fund style because 6 to 8 of 13 strategies showed reasonable persistence using different methodologies. Losers tend to exhibit greater persistence than winners, which shows the importance of manager selection when building a portfolio of hedge funds.

FUNDS OF FUNDS   11

Funds of funds allow investors to one-stop shop for their hedge fund needs at a low minimum investment. Fothergill and Coke (2001) describe the advantages and disadvantages of investing in funds of funds. Funds of funds use investment managers that perform due diligence on single strategy hedge fund investments, with the goal of building a lower risk, well-diversified hedge fund portfolio. By investing in 15 to 20 single manager hedge funds across a variety of trading styles, funds of funds can reduce the standard deviation of a hedge fund portfolio. Smaller investors may be able to access a fund of funds portfolio with a minimum investment as low as $100,000, far lower than the $7 million to $20 million required to meet the minimum investment requirements of each of the underlying hedge fund managers. Funds of funds may offer preferential liquidity terms to investors, perhaps allowing monthly redemptions, which are preferable to the quarterly or annual redemptions of the underlying managers.

Smaller investors may appreciate the due diligence performed by funds-of-funds managers because this task can require significant investment skill, manager relationships, and research costs. Of course, the funds-of-funds manager gets paid for providing access, diversification, risk management, and due diligence benefits to investors. A common fee structure requires a 1 percent management fee and a 10 percent performance fee to be paid to the funds-of-funds manager, which is in addition to the 2 percent and 20 percent fees paid to the underlying hedge fund managers. Beckers et al. (2007) calculate that the average fund-of-funds fee is 1.3 percent plus 8.1 percent. This double layer of fees presents a high hurdle for funds of funds to earn an alpha in excess of the required return for taking risks in the traditional and exotic beta exposures. The fund-of-funds business is becoming increasingly concentrated—the largest 25 percent of funds of funds manage more than 75 percent of all assets in this sector.

Funds of funds, as a result of their diversification among strategies and managers, tend to have average performance. Although single hedge fund managers and strategies will dominate the top and bottom of the performance charts, funds of funds tend to approximate hedge fund index performance before adding their second layer of fees. Beckers et al. (2007) show that the lowest quartile of funds of funds outperforms the lowest quartile of single manager funds (i.e., 6.3 percent versus 5.5 percent annually), whereas the top quartile of funds of funds offers lower returns than the top hedge funds (i.e., 15.1 percent versus 23.2 percent). Funds of funds also tend to have lower mortality, survivor bias, and backfill bias than single manager hedge funds. On average, funds of funds tend to add more value through risk reduction rather than return enhancement.

Funds of funds tend to take less factor risk than is found through the analysis of a broad hedge fund index. The typical hedge fund examined by Beckers et al. (2007) has an R^2 to traditional market factors of only 40 percent, but those common factor risks are rising over time. The authors find that even the lowest quartile of funds of funds earned alpha in excess of traditional market factor exposures, but exotic and hedge fund betas were not included in the analysis. Unfortunately, funds of funds have consistently taken common factor bets at the wrong time because beta exposures reduced returns in 8 of the 12 years of the study.

Hsieh (2006) explains that many funds of funds take substantial risk in traditional market factors. Investors in these beta funds may be paying high fees for risk exposures that can be sourced more cheaply outside of the hedge fund universe. Hsieh (2006) predicts that the limited number of funds of funds that provide true alpha with low beta risks will rapidly grow as a share of the industry's AUM, whereas funds of funds that provide beta exposures with minimal value added will struggle to retain market share.

Fung, Hsieh, Naik, and Ramadorai (2008) calculated the alpha earned by funds of funds in three different time periods. Factor risks have statistically significant variations in exposure across three periods, with structural breaks at the time of the Long-Term Capital Management crisis and the end of the internet stocks era. They found that funds of funds did not earn statistically significant alpha between January 1995 and September 1998 or from April 2000 to December 2004. Funds of funds, however, did earn alpha from October 1998 to March 2000. Although the universe of hedge funds may not always earn alpha, some funds of funds always can. On average, 22 percent of funds of funds provided alpha, whereas the rest were simply providing factor exposures without value added. Of course, the portion of "have alpha" funds of funds varies over time, peaking at 42 percent in 2000.

Funds of funds with proven alpha tend to have longer lives and larger asset inflows. Unfortunately, the larger the inflows become, the more difficult it is to continue to earn high levels of alpha. Capital flows to alpha funds, presumably from sophisticated institutional investors, are relatively constant. Capital flows to beta funds are cyclical, with large flows from individual investors after times of high returns.

RISK MANAGEMENT 12

Some funds of funds will closely manage their risks, especially to traditional beta exposures. Beta risks can be limited in the portfolio construction process by closely understanding the beta exposures of individual hedge fund managers and increasing the allocation to funds with lower market risks. Alternatively, the funds of funds will allocate to managers with the highest alpha and then hedge away the common factor risks at the fund-of-funds level. Hedging can be accomplished through the use of futures that linearly reduce market risks. Equity index options are also used, which reduce downside risks of the portfolio without capping the upside return potential.

Beyond market risks, hedge fund investors need to understand and manage a number of other risks. These include event risk, operational risk, leverage, and counterparty risks. In fact, many of these risks tend to magnify market risks, so a global view of risk is very important for hedge fund investors and fund-of-funds managers.

Event risks are commonly focused in event driven funds, such as those following mergers and distressed or special situation investments. Although event driven funds may offer a lower correlation with market indices, their returns can change dramatically at the emergence of event risk, such as when a merger deal is not completed or when a company defaults on debt that the manager assumed was issued by a going concern. Event risk can also be present in a number of other hedge fund styles, either from hedge fund managers explicitly including event driven investments in their fund or from the effect that specific events may have on broader market risks.

Operational risks can lead to a total loss of investments in a specific hedge fund. Kundro and Feffer (2003, 2004) estimate that 54 percent of hedge fund failures can be attributed, at least in part, to operational risks. Of the funds that failed as a result of operational failures, they estimate that 6 percent of occurrences were because of inadequate resources, 14 percent were the result of unauthorized trading and style drift, 30 percent were from the theft of investor assets, and 41 percent were from the misrepresentation of investments and performance. Further, they estimate that 38 percent of hedge fund failures had only investment risk, meaning that the operational controls were in place and effective. Surprisingly, 54 percent of hedge fund failures were the result of operational risk, whereas the final 8 percent of hedge fund debacles could be attributed to business risk or a combination of different risks.

In a series of case studies, Black (2007) shows that a key way to minimize operational risks is to ensure a strict delineation of duties within a hedge fund. This structure means the portfolio manager is separate from the risk manager, the pricing process, and the auditing function. A proper system of checks and balances ensures that the hedge fund manager stays within the risk limits stated in the hedge fund documentation. Ideally, a hedge fund should be diversified among securities and have leverage and market exposure limits consistent with a low probability of catastrophic losses. The valuation of securities should be handled outside of the portfolio management group to ensure accurate statements of risk and return. The auditing of returns should be handled by a reputable third party because the misstatement of hedge fund returns can prolong fraudulent behavior and allow a manager to continue to attract assets from new investors. Clearly, assets should be appropriately segregated—client funds should be kept safe and separate from the hedge fund's corporate and the manager's personal accounts. Many hedge fund investors insist on separate accounts or managed accounts in which the assets are held in custody with the investor's broker. The investor allows the manager to trade his or her account, but the complete transparency disallows excessive concentration or leverage risks that can cause catastrophic losses. A separate account format also prevents the misstatement of investment performance or the theft of client assets. Many investors perform a background check on hedge fund managers to ensure that the biography is correct and that the manager has not previously been disciplined by regulatory authorities or sued by prior investors.

Brown, Goetzmann, Liang, and Schwarz (2009) derive a quantitative operational risk score, ω, that can be calculated from information in hedge fund databases. This quantitative factor score can be used as a supplement for qualitative due diligence, which includes manager interviews, on-site visits, and background checks. The score is used to define "problem funds" that subsequently have lower mean returns, lower Sharpe ratios, lower incentive fees, and less frequent high-water mark provisions than nonproblem funds. Similar to Altman's (1968) z-score, which is used to predict corporate bankruptcies, the ω-score can be used to predict operational risks and the demise of hedge funds because the half-life of funds with an ω-score exceeding one is just 4.2 years. Funds with lower returns, higher standard deviations, and lower incentive fees have characteristics that correlate with operational issues, such as conflicts of interests, concentrated ownership of the management company, relationships with investment advisers or broker/dealers, and the ability of fund staff to trade the same securities as the fund.

Counterparty risk arises whenever a hedge fund deals with investors, prime brokers, and other market participants. In the over-the-counter market, counterparty risk arises when a hedge fund is owed money on a swaps or options contract but the seller of the contract fails to deliver the required investment gains. Counterparty risk to prime brokers or investors is less obvious to discern but just as important.

A special concern is leverage that can magnify market risk and counterparty risk. Leverage allows a hedge fund manager to take economic exposure in excess of the assets invested by clients. Leverage can be explicit debt, borrowed either in the repurchase market or from a prime broker. For example, a fund with $100 million in client assets may be allowed to borrow $900 million and invest the entire $1 billion fund value in fixed-income securities. When the return to the investment exceeds the borrowing costs, returns are increased through leverage. Of course, losses are also magnified. So, a 10 percent loss on the $1 billion investment will cause a 100 percent loss of the clients' $100 million investment. Leverage can also be gained through the use of derivative products, such as swaps, options, and futures, which can increase market exposure with initial capital requirements ranging from 0 to 20 percent of the notional value of the investment.

Sharma (2004) describes the dangers of leverage and the interaction between leverage, counterparty risk, and market risk. Leverage increases the probability of large investment losses because the increase in assets beyond investor capital magnifies the beta of the investment portfolio. Leverage also increases the vulnerability to margin calls and forced liquidations. Counterparty risk and leverage are a dangerous mix because the prime broker sets the credit limit for each hedge fund. For example, consider the fund mentioned earlier that invested $1 billion based on only $100 million in investor capital. If the prime broker reduces the credit limit from $900 million to $400 million, the fund manager is required to sell half of the fund's assets in just a few days' time. Credit limits are typically reduced during turbulent markets when it is difficult to sell assets for their fair value. This forced liquidation can be sufficient to cause catastrophic losses for the hedge fund because rapidly selling assets in a falling market can incur market impact sufficient to wipe out the investors' equity in the fund. Investor redemptions can also cause forced liquidations because managers are forced to sell assets in less than 30 to 60 days to return investor capital on a timely basis.

It is important for hedge fund managers to align the lockup policies of the fund with the liquidity of the underlying assets and the terms of financing used in the investment strategy. A fund of funds offering monthly liquidity to investors but investing in hedge funds with an average lockup period of two years is a recipe for a liquidity crisis that can cause dramatic losses to a fund.

SUMMARY

When allocating assets to hedge funds, investors need to clearly understand the characteristics of these investments. It is important to delineate the differences between fund strategies and to understand the level and volatility of the resulting alpha and beta exposures. This analysis can show the value added by the fund manager, as well as the fit between the hedge fund investments and the investor's traditional investments in equity and fixed-income securities. Beyond market risks, investors also need to investigate fee structures, operational risks, and the capacity of the market to absorb increased levels of hedge fund assets.

REFERENCES

Editor's Note: References mentioned in the text are marked with an asterisk.

Ackermann, Carl, Richard McEnally, and David Ravenscraft. 1999. "The Performance of Hedge Funds: Risk, Return, and Incentives." *Journal of Finance,* vol. 54, no. 3 (June):833–874.

"Hedge funds display several interesting characteristics that may influence performance, including flexible investment strategies, strong managerial incentives, substantial managerial investment, sophisticated investors, and limited government oversight. Using a large sample of hedge fund data from 1988–1995, we find that hedge funds consistently outperform mutual funds, but not standard market indices. Hedge funds, however, are more volatile than both mutual funds and market indices. Incentive fees explain some of the higher performance, but not the increased total risk. The impact of six data-conditioning biases is explored. We find evidence that positive and negative survival-related biases offset each other." (p. 833)

Agarwal, Vikas, and Narayan Y. Naik. 2000. "Multi-Period Performance Persistence Analysis of Hedge Funds." *Journal of Financial and Quantitative Analysis,* vol. 35, no. 3 (September):327–342.

"Since hedge funds specify significant lockup periods, we investigate persistence in the performance of hedge funds using a multi-period framework in which the likelihood of observing persistence by chance is lower than that in the traditional two-period framework. Under the null hypothesis of no manager skill (no persistence), the theoretical distribution of observing wins or losses follows a binomial distribution. We test this hypothesis using the traditional two-period framework and compare the findings with the results obtained using our multi-period framework. We examine whether persistence is sensitive to the length of return measurement intervals by using quarterly, half-yearly and yearly returns. We find maximum persistence at the quarterly horizon indicating that persistence among hedge fund managers is short-term in nature. It decreases as one moves to yearly returns and this finding is not sensitive to whether returns are calculated on a pre- or post-fee basis suggesting that the intra-year persistence finding is not driven by the way

performance fees are imputed. The level of persistence in the multi-period framework is considerably smaller than that in the two-period framework with virtually no evidence of persistence using yearly returns under the multi-period framework. Finally persistence, whenever present, seems to be unrelated to whether the fund took directional bets or not." (p. 327)

————. 2004. "Risks and Portfolio Decisions Involving Hedge Funds." *Review of Financial Studies,* vol. 17, no. 1 (Spring):63–98.

"This article characterizes the systematic risk exposures of hedge funds using buy-and-hold and option-based strategies. Our results show that a large number of equity-oriented hedge fund strategies exhibit payoffs resembling a short position in a put option on the market index and, therefore, bear significant left-tail risk, risk that is ignored by the commonly used mean-variance framework. Using a mean-conditional value-at-risk framework, we demonstrate the extent to which the mean-variance framework underestimates the tail risk. Finally, working with the systematic risk exposures of hedge funds, we show that their recent performance appears significantly better than their long-run performance." (p. 63)

* Allison, Douglas T., and Felix T. Lin. 2004. "Including Hedge Funds in Private Client Portfolios." *AIMR Conference Proceedings: Integrating Hedge Funds into a Private Wealth Strategy* (February):6–20.

"Hedge funds can play a vital role in client portfolios, but clients need to be aware of all the issues involved—issues ranging from the impact of incorporating hedge funds into the portfolio mix to understanding the potential risks involved to the pros and cons of hedge fund investing. Once the decision has been made to include hedge funds in the portfolio mix, the allocation must be determined and should be based on future expectations for hedge fund performance. Finally, by using an optimizer, an ideal mix of hedge fund strategies can be established. The end result is a portfolio that meets client goals and objectives and has the potential to decrease risk and enhance return." (p. 6)

* Altman, Edward I. 1968. "Financial Ratios, Discriminant Analysis and the Prediction of Corporate Bankruptcy." *Journal of Finance*, vol. 23, no. 4 (September):589–609.

"Academicians seem to be moving toward the elimination of ratio analysis as an analytical technique in assessing the performance of the business enterprise. Theorists downgrade arbitrary rules of thumb, such as company ratio comparisons, widely used by practitioners. Since attacks on the relevance of ratio analysis emanate from many esteemed members of the scholarly world, does this mean that ratio analysis is limited to the world of 'nuts and bolts'? Or, has the significance of such an approach been unattractively garbed and therefore unfairly handicapped? Can we bridge the gap, rather than sever the link, between traditional ratio 'analysis' and the more rigorous statistical techniques which have become popular among academicians in recent years? The purpose of this paper is to attempt an assessment of this issue—the quality of ratio analysis as an analytical technique. The prediction of corporate bankruptcy is used as an illustrative case. Specifically, a set of financial and economic ratios will be investigated in a bankruptcy prediction context wherein a multiple discriminant statistical methodology is employed. The data used in the study are limited to manufacturing corporations." (p. 589)

* Amenc, N., and L. Martinelli. 2002. "Portfolio Optimization and Hedge Fund Style Allocation Decisions." *Journal of Alternative Investments*, vol. 5, no. 2 (Fall):7–20.

"This paper attempts to evaluate the out-of-sample performance of an improved estimator of the covariance structure of hedge fund index returns, focusing on its use for optimal portfolio selection. Using data from CSFB/Tremont hedge fund indices, we find that ex-post volatility of minimum variance portfolios generated using implicit factor based estimation techniques is between 1.5 and 6 times lower than that of a value-weighted benchmark, such differences being both economically and statistically significant. This strongly indicates that optimal inclusion of hedge funds in an investor portfolio can potentially generate a dramatic decrease in the portfolio volatility on an out-of-sample basis. Differences in mean returns, on the other hand, are not statistically significant, suggesting that the improvement in terms of risk control does not necessarily come at the cost of lower expected returns." (p. 7)

Amin, Gaurav S., and Harry M. Kat. 2003. "Hedge Fund Performance 1990–2000: Do the 'Money Machines' Really Add Value?" *Journal of Financial and Quantitative Analysis*, vol. 38, no. 2 (June):251–274.

"In this paper we investigate the claim that hedge funds offer investors a superior risk–return tradeoff. We do so using a continuous time version of Dybvig's (1988a, 1988b) payoff distribution pricing model. The evaluation model, which does not require any assumptions with regard to the return distribution of the funds in question, is applied to the monthly returns of 77 hedge funds and 13 hedge fund indices over the period May 1990–April 2000. The results show that as a stand-alone investment hedge funds do not offer a superior risk-return profile. We find 12 indices and 72 individual funds to be inefficient, with the average efficiency loss amounting to 2.76% per annum for indices and 6.42% for individual funds. Part of the inefficiency cost of individual funds can be diversified away. Funds of funds, however, are not the preferred vehicle for this as their performance appears to suffer badly from their double fee structure. Looking at hedge funds in a portfolio context results in a marked improvement in the evaluation outcomes. Seven of the 12 hedge fund indices and 58 of the 72 individual funds classified as inefficient on a stand-alone basis are capable of producing an efficient payoff profile when mixed with the S&P 500. The best results are obtained when 10–20% of the portfolio value is invested in hedge funds." (p. 251)

* Anson, Mark J.P. 2001. "Hedge Fund Incentive Fees and the 'Free Option.'" *Journal of Alternative Investments*, vol. 4, no. 2 (Fall):43–48.

"One of the ironies of hedge fund investing is that investors can provide conflicting incentives to the hedge fund manager. While hedge fund managers earn a management fee, which is a constant percentage applied to the amount of assets managed in the hedge fund, they receive an incentive fee, which is a form of profit sharing when a profitable return is earned for their investors. The standard Black-Scholes analysis is used to determine the value of the call option on hedge fund incentives. The article also discusses how this call option might provide an inconsistent incentive compared to the desires of investors in the hedge fund." (p. 43)

Asness, Clifford. 2004. "Sources of Change and Risk for Hedge Funds." *CFA Institute Conference Proceedings: Challenges and Innovation in Hedge Fund Management* (August):4–9.

"A lot of change is on the horizon for hedge funds, particularly given institutional investors' growing use of alternative investments. The changes will likely bring a greater focus on benchmarking, calls for increased transparency, a need for better articulation of investment strategies, rationalization of hedge fund fees, and the need for solid risk control mechanisms. The future also brings subtle shifts in hedge fund risk. And although the risk of blowups still exists, perhaps the larger future risk will relate to diminished returns." (p. 4)

* ———. 2006. "The Future Role of Hedge Funds." *CFA Institute Conference Proceedings Quarterly*, vol. 23, no. 2 (June):1–9.

"Hedge funds generate returns through managers' skill (measured by alpha) as well as managers' systematic risk taking (measured by hedge fund beta). Hedge funds combined with index funds are now poised to replace traditional active management. To position themselves for such a future role, hedge funds must correct some of the industry's negative characteristics, including high correlations with the market, the misuse of momentum strategies, and lags in marking to market. To appeal to institutional investors, hedge funds must also improve their professionalism by altering the way they make decisions, reducing their fees (or at least rationalizing them), and striving for increased transparency." (p. 1)

Asness, Clifford, Robert Krail, and John Liew. 2001. "Do Hedge Funds Hedge?" *Journal of Portfolio Management*, vol. 28, no. 1 (Fall):6–19.

"Many hedge funds claim to provide significant diversification for traditional portfolios, besides attractive returns. The authors provide empirical evidence regarding the return and diversification benefits of hedge fund investing using the CSFB/Tremont hedge fund indexes over 1994–2000. Like many others, they find that simple regressions of monthly hedge fund excess returns on monthly S&P 500 excess returns seem to support the claims about the benefits of hedge funds. The regressions show only modest market exposure and positive added value. This type of analysis can produce misleading results, however. Many hedge funds hold, to various degrees and combinations, illiquid exchange-traded securities or difficult-to-price over-the-counter securities. For the purposes of monthly reporting, hedge funds often price these securities using either the last available traded prices or estimates of current market prices. These practices can lead to reported monthly hedge fund returns that are not perfectly synchronous with monthly S&P 500 returns. Non-synchronous return data can lead to understated estimates of actual market exposure. When the authors apply standard techniques that account for this problem, they find that hedge funds in the aggregate have significantly more market exposure than simple estimates indicate. Furthermore, after accounting for this increased market exposure, they find that taken as a whole the broad universe of hedge funds does not add value over this period." (p. 6)

* Beckers, Stan, Ross Curds, and Simon Weinberger. 2007. "Funds of Hedge Funds Take the Wrong Risks." *Journal of Portfolio Management*, vol. 33, no. 3 (Spring):108–121.

"On average, the funds of hedge funds industry over the last 15 years has delivered alpha with a high information ratio. Unfortunately, these alphas come with significant common-factor exposures for which the typical fund was unrewarded. While funds of hedge funds can deliver a valuable product, sloppy manager selection and portfolio construction typically result in less-than-pure alpha generation. A naive selection of a fund of hedge funds may thus lead to assuming relatively expensive common-factor exposure without necessarily accessing significant skill-based returns. A multifactor modeling of fund of hedge fund returns can help to identify skillful value-added." (p. 108)

* Berger, A., B. Crowell, and D. Kabiller. 2008. "Is Alpha Just Beta Waiting To Be Discovered? What the Rise of Hedge Fund Beta Means for Investors." AQR Capital Management, Working paper (July): www.aqrcapital .com/research_15.htm.

"Alpha is shrinking, and it's good news for investors. This idea may seem paradoxical. But alpha is really just the portion of a portfolio's returns that cannot be explained by exposure to common risk factors (betas).

With the emergence of new betas, the unexplained portion (alpha) shrinks–alpha gets reclassified as beta. The rise of a group of risk factors we call hedge fund betas makes this transformation especially relevant today. Hedge fund betas are the common risk exposures shared by hedge fund managers pursuing similar strategies. We believe these risk factors can capture not just the fundamental insights of hedge funds, but also a meaningful portion of their returns. Hedge fund betas are available for investment and can also be used to enhance portfolio construction and risk management. Ultimately, we believe the rise of hedge fund betas will lead not only to the reclassification of alpha, but also to better-diversified portfolios with greater transparency, improved risk control, and—perhaps most importantly—higher net returns." (p. 1)

* Black, K. 2004. *Managing a Hedge Fund: A Complete Guide to Trading, Business Strategies, Risk Management and Regulations*. New York: McGraw-Hill.

This book covers an extensive array of topics concerning hedge funds, including a discussion of the impact of hedge funds on portfolios, measuring the performance of hedge funds, managing the risks of hedge funds, and appropriate hedge fund due diligence.

* ———. 2006. "Improving Hedge Fund Risk Exposures by Hedging Equity Market Volatility, or How the VIX Ate My Kurtosis." *Journal of Trading*, vol. 1, no. 2 (Spring):6–15.

"In 2004 investors began trading futures on the volatility index (VIX). Investors can directly trade the volatility implied in stock index options. Because the VIX has a negative correlation to the S&P 500 Index and most hedge fund styles, we find that adding a small VIX position to an investment portfolio significantly reduced portfolio volatility. This strategy may be more effective at improving the robustness of Sharpe ratios than other methods explored in the literature. Even more important, VIX rises quickly during the most risky market conditions, which dramatically improves the skewness and kurtosis characteristics of many hedge fund strategies." (p. 6)

* ———. 2007. "Preventing and Detecting Hedge Fund Failure Risk through Partial Transparency." *Derivatives Use, Trading Regulation*, vol. 12, no. 4 (February): 330–341.

"Some hedge fund investors may pay close attention to market risk while not spending enough time considering operational risks. The examples of Bayou, Wood River, and Lancer are used to illustrate the operational risks that are all too present in hedge funds. A proposal to gather and aggregate data directly from brokers and custodians could reveal a large portion of the data necessary to make well-informed risk management decisions. Investors do not really need to know the details of every position owned by a hedge fund. They only need to see the partial transparency of aggregated risk statistics. A risk management system that is less intrusive to managers and more useful to investors could be an invaluable tool to fight hedge fund fraud." (p. 330)

Brooks, Chris, and Harry M. Kat. 2002. "The Statistical Properties of Hedge Fund Index Returns and Their Implications for Investors." *Journal of Alternative Investments,* vol. 5, no. 2 (Fall):26–44.

"The monthly return distributions of many hedge fund indices exhibit highly unusual skewness and kurtosis properties as well as first-order serial correlation. This has important consequences for investors. Although many hedge fund indices are highly attractive in mean–variance terms, this is much less the case when skewness, kurtosis and autocorrelation are taken into account. Sharpe ratios will substantially overestimate the true risk–return performance of (portfolios containing) hedge funds. Similarly, mean-variance portfolio analysis will overestimate the benefits of including hedge funds in an investment portfolio and, therefore, overallocate to hedge funds. We also find substantial differences between indices that aim to cover the same type of strategy. Investors' perceptions of hedge fund performance and value added will, therefore, strongly depend on the indices used." (p. 26)

Brown, Stephen J., and William N. Goetzmann. 2003. "Hedge Funds with Style." *Journal of Portfolio Management,* vol. 29, no. 2 (Winter):101–112.

"The popular perception is that hedge funds follow a reasonably well-defined market-neutral investment style. Investigation of the monthly return history of hedge funds over 1989–2000, however, finds there are in fact distinct styles of management that account for about 20% of the cross-sectional variability in performance. This result is consistent across the years in the sample and robust as to the way investment style is determined. Appropriate style analysis and style management are crucial to success for investors looking to invest in hedge funds." (p. 101)

Brown, Stephen J., William N. Goetzmann, and Roger G. Ibbotson. 1999. "Offshore Hedge Funds: Survival and Performance, 1989-95." *Journal of Business,* vol. 72, no. 1 (January):91–117.

"We examine the performance of the off-shore hedge fund industry over the period 1989 through 1995 using a database that includes both defunct and currently operating funds. The industry is characterized by high attrition rates of funds, low covariance with the U.S. stock market, evidence consistent with positive risk-adjusted returns over the time, and little evidence of differential manager skill." (p. 91)

Brown, Stephen J., William N. Goetzmann, and James Park. 2001. "Careers and Survival: Competition and Risk in the Hedge Fund and CTA Industry." *Journal of Finance,* vol. 56, no. 5 (October):1869–1886.

"Investors in hedge funds and commodity trading advisors (CTAs) are concerned with risk as well as return. We investigate the volatility of hedge funds and CTAs in light of managerial career concerns. We find an association between past performance and risk levels consistent with previous findings for mutual fund managers. Variance shifts depend upon relative rather than absolute fund performance. The importance of relative rankings points to the importance of reputation costs in the investment industry. Our analysis of factors contributing to fund disappearance shows that survival depends on absolute and relative performance, excess volatility, and on fund age." (p. 1869)

* Brown, Stephen J., William N. Goetzmann, Bing Liang, and Christopher Schwarz. 2009. "Estimating Operational Risk for Hedge Funds: The ω-Score." *Financial Analysts Journal,* vol. 65, no. 1 (January/February):43–53.

"Using a complete set of U.S. SEC filing information on hedge funds (Form ADV) and data from the Lipper TASS Hedge Fund Database, the study reported here developed a quantitative model called the ω-score to measure hedge fund operational risk. The ω-score is related to conflict-of-interest issues, concentrated ownership, and reduced leverage in the Form ADV data. With a statistical methodology, the study further related the ω-score to such readily available information as fund performance, volatility, size, age, and fee structures. Finally, the study demonstrated that although operational risk is more significant than financial risk in explaining fund failure, a significant and positive interaction exists between operational risk and financial risk." (p. 43)

Brunnermeier, Markus K., and Stefan Nagel. 2004. "Hedge Funds and the Technology Bubble." *Journal of Finance,* vol. 59, no. 5 (October):2013–2040.

"This paper documents that hedge funds did not exert a correcting force on stock prices during the technology bubble. Instead, they were heavily invested in technology stocks. This does not seem to be the result of unawareness of the bubble: Hedge funds captured the upturn, but, by reducing their positions in stocks that were about to decline, avoided much of the downturn. Our findings question the efficient markets notion that rational speculators always stabilize prices. They are consistent with models in which rational investors may prefer to ride bubbles because of predictable investor sentiment and limits to arbitrage." (p. 2013)

* Cremers, Jan-Hein, Mark Kritzman, and Sebastien Page. 2005. "Optimal Hedge Fund Allocations." *Journal of Portfolio Management,* vol. 31, no. 3 (Spring):70–81.

"Hedge funds have return peculiarities not commonly associated with traditional investment vehicles. They are more inclined to produce return distributions with significantly non-normal skewness and kurtosis. Investor preferences may be better represented by bilinear utility functions or S-shaped value functions than by neoclassical utility functions, and mean–variance optimization is thus not appropriate for forming portfolios that include hedge funds. Portfolios of hedge funds formed using both mean–variance and full-scale optimization, given a wide range of assumptions about investor preferences, reveal that higher moments of hedge funds do not meaningfully compromise the efficacy of mean–variance optimization if investors have power utility; mean–variance optimization is not particularly effective for identifying optimal hedge fund allocations if preferences are bilinear or S-shaped; and, contrary to conventional wisdom, investors with S-shaped preferences are attracted to kurtosis as well as negative skewness." (p. 70)

* Dopfel, Frederick E. 2005. "How Hedge Funds Fit." *Journal of Portfolio Management*, vol. 31, no. 4 (Summer):9–20.

"Hedge funds fit in an institutional investor's portfolio only if one can evaluate how the inclusion of hedge fund strategies would improve the performance of the entire portfolio, after considering both beta and alpha characteristics. This is more challenging than it first appears because of the opaqueness and the complexity of most hedge fund strategies. The key is to identify institutional-quality hedge funds that permit a clear understanding of the normal portfolio and provide confidence in projecting a positive, pure alpha. If these conditions can be satisfied, there are two possible approaches to incorporating institutional-quality hedge funds: 1) hedge funds as an active overlay at the total portfolio level, or 2) hedge funds as portable alpha within a traditional asset class." (p. 9)

Edwards, Franklin R. 1999. "Hedge Funds and the Collapse of Long-Term Capital Management." *Journal of Economic Perspectives*, vol. 13, no. 2 (Spring):189–210.

"The Fed-engineered rescue of Long-Term Capital Management (LTCM) in September 1998 set off alarms throughout financial markets about the activities of hedge funds and the stability of financial markets in general. With only $4.8 billion in equity, LTCM managed to leverage itself to the hilt by borrowing more than $125 billion from banks and securities firms and entering into derivatives contracts totaling more than $1 trillion (notional). When LTCM's speculations went sour in the summer of 1998, the impending liquidation of LTCM's portfolio threatened to destabilize financial markets throughout the world. Public policy response to LTCM should focus on risks of systemic fragility and ways in which bank regulation can be improved." (p. 189)

Edwards, Franklin R., and Mustafa Onur Caglayan. 2001. "Hedge Fund Performance and Manager Skill." *Journal of Futures Markets*, vol. 21, no. 11 (November):1003–1028.

"Using data on the monthly returns of hedge funds during the period January 1990 to August 1998, we estimate six-factor Jensen alphas for individual hedge funds, employing eight different investment styles. We find that about 25 percent of the hedge funds earn positive excess returns and that the frequency and magnitude of funds' excess returns differ markedly with investment style. Using six-factor alphas as a measure of performance, we also analyze performance persistence over 1-year and 2-year horizons and find evidence of significant persistence among both winners and losers. These findings, together with our finding that hedge funds that pay managers higher incentive fees also have higher excess returns, are consistent with the view that fund manager skill may be a partial explanation for the positive excess returns earned by hedge funds." (p. 1003)

Eichengreen, Barry, and Donald Mathieson, eds. 1998. *Hedge Funds and Financial Market Dynamics*. Washington, DC: International Monetary Fund.

This book discusses many aspects of hedge funds, including their operations, the hedge fund industry, hedge fund market dynamics, regulation, and recent crises and hedge funds.

* Fothergill, Martin, and Carolyn Coke. 2001. "Funds of Hedge Funds: An Introduction to Multi-Manager Funds." *Journal of Alternative Investments*, vol. 4, no. 2 (Fall):7–16.

"In addition to the enhanced risk–return profile of funds of hedge funds, there are numerous additional structural benefits to investment in multi-manager hedge funds. This article both reviews the characteristics of various hedge fund strategies and emphasizes the unique structural characteristics of multi-manager hedge funds." (p. 7)

Fung, William, and David A. Hsieh. 1997. "Empirical Characteristics of Dynamic Trading Strategies: The Case of Hedge Funds." *Review of Financial Studies*, vol. 10, no. 2 (Summer):275–302.

"This article presents some new results on an unexplored dataset on hedge fund performance. The results indicate that hedge funds follow strategies that are dramatically different from mutual funds, and support the claim that these strategies are highly dynamic. The article finds five dominant investment styles in hedge funds, which when added to Sharpe's (1992) asset class factor model can provide an integrated framework for style analysis of both buy-and-hold and dynamic trading strategies." (p. 275)

———. 1999. "A Primer on Hedge Funds." *Journal of Empirical Finance*, vol. 6, no. 3 (September):309–331.

"In this paper, we provide a rationale for how hedge funds are organized and some insight on how hedge fund performance differs from traditional mutual funds. Statistical differences among hedge fund styles are used to supplement qualitative differences in the way hedge fund strategies are described. Risk factors associated with different trading styles are discussed. We give examples where standard linear statistical techniques are unlikely to capture the risk of hedge fund investments where the returns are primarily driven by non-linear dynamic strategies." (p. 309)

———. 2000. "Performance Characteristics of Hedge Funds and Commodity Funds: Natural vs. Spurious Biases." *Journal of Financial and Quantitative Analysis*, vol. 35, no. 3 (September):291–307.

"It is well known that the pro forma performance of a sample of investment funds contains biases. These biases are documented in Brown, Goetzmann, Ibbotson, and Ross (1992) using mutual funds as subjects. The organization structure of hedge funds, as private and often offshore vehicles, makes data collection a much more onerous task, amplifying the impact of performance measurement biases. This paper reviews these biases in hedge funds. We also propose using funds of hedge funds to measure aggregate hedge fund performance, based on the idea that the investment experience of hedge fund investors can be used to estimate the performance of hedge funds." (p. 291)

———. 2001. "The Risk in Hedge Fund Strategies: Theory and Evidence from Trend Followers." *Review of Financial Studies*, vol. 14, no. 2 (Summer):313–341.

"Hedge fund strategies typically generate option-like returns. Linear-factor models using benchmark asset indices have difficulty explaining them. Following the suggestions in Glosten and Jagannathan (1994), this article shows how to model hedge fund returns by focusing on the popular 'trend-following' strategy. We use lookback straddles to model trend-following strategies, and show that they can explain trend-following funds' returns better than standard asset indices. Though standard straddles lead to similar empirical results, lookback straddles are theoretically closer to the concept of trend-following. Our model should be useful in the design of performance benchmarks for trend-following funds." (p. 313)

* ———. 2004. "Hedge Fund Benchmarks: A Risk-Based Approach." *Financial Analysts Journal,* vol. 60, no. 5 (September/October):65–80.

"Following a review of the data and methodological difficulties in applying conventional models used for traditional asset class indices to hedge funds, this article argues against the conventional approach. Instead, in an extension of previous work on asset-based style (ABS) factors, the article proposes a model of hedge fund returns that is similar to models based on arbitrage pricing theory, with dynamic risk-factor coefficients. For diversified hedge fund portfolios (as proxied by indices of hedge funds and funds of hedge funds), the seven ABS factors can explain up to 80 percent of monthly return variations. Because ABS factors are directly observable from market prices, this model provides a standardized framework for identifying differences among major hedge fund indexes that is free of the biases inherent in hedge fund databases." (p. 65)

* Fung, William, David A. Hsieh, Narayan Y. Naik, and Tarun Ramadorai. 2008. "Hedge Funds: Performance, Risk, and Capital Formation." *Journal of Finance,* vol. 63, no. 4 (August):1777–1803.

"We use a comprehensive data set of funds of funds to investigate performance, risk, and capital formation in the hedge fund industry from 1995 to 2004. While the average fund of funds delivers alpha only in the period between October 1998 and March 2000, a subset of funds of funds consistently delivers alpha. The alpha-producing funds are not as likely to liquidate as those that do not deliver alpha and experience far greater and steadier capital inflows than their less fortunate counterparts. These capital inflows attenuate the ability of the alpha producers to continue to deliver alpha in the future." (p. 1777)

* Géhin, Walter, and Mathieu Vaissié. 2006. "The Right Place for Alternative Betas in Hedge Fund Performance: An Answer to the Capacity Effect Fantasy." *Journal of Alternative Investments,* vol. 9, no. 1 (Summer):9–18.

"In recent months, concerns have been raised about the profitability prospects for hedge funds. This article argues that market participants' pessimistic view of the hedge fund industry's capacity to generate long-term returns is a direct result of their continued focus on alpha. It illustrates the importance of considering not only the exposure to the market (the traditional beta), but also other exposures (the alternative betas) to characterize alternative sources of hedge fund returns. It also revisits the capacity issue by distinguishing

between market capacity and manager capacity. The results show that alternative betas are an important source of hedge fund returns that reduce the importance of alpha. The authors conclude that capacity issues do not significantly impact alpha by illustrating that alpha is generated by successful bets on numerous exposures rather than by exploiting market opportunities." (p. 9)

* Getmansky, Mila, Andrew W. Lo, and Igor Makarov. 2004. "An Econometric Model of Serial Correlation and Illiquidity in Hedge Fund Returns." *Journal of Financial Economics,* vol. 74, no. 3 (December):529–609.

"The returns to hedge funds and other alternative investments are often highly serially correlated. In this paper, we explore several sources of such serial correlation and show that the most likely explanation is illiquidity exposure and smoothed returns. We propose an econometric model of return smoothing and develop estimators for the smoothing profile as well as a smoothing-adjusted Sharpe ratio. For a sample of 908 hedge funds drawn from the TASS database, we show that our estimated smoothing coefficients vary considerably across hedge-fund style categories and may be a useful proxy for quantifying illiquidity exposure." (p. 529)

* Gregoriou, Greg N., Georges Hübner, Nicolas Papageorgiou, and Fabrice Rouah. 2005. "Survival of Commodity Trading Advisors: 1990-2003." *Journal of Futures Markets,* vol. 25, no. 8 (August):795–815.

"This article investigates the mortality of Commodity Trading Advisors (CTAs) over the 1990–2003 period, a longer horizon than any encompassed in the literature. A detailed survival analysis over the full range of CTA classifications is provided, and it is found that the median lifetime of CTAs in this sample is different than previously documented. Through the implementation of nonparametric, parametric, and semiparametric statistical techniques, it is emphasized that CTA survivorship is heavily contingent on the strategy followed by the fund. Furthermore, a significant positive size effect on survival is shown, whereas poor returns, and to a lesser extent, high-risk exposure, appear to hasten mortality." (p. 795)

* Hamza, Olfa, Maher Kooli, and Mathieu Roberge. 2006. "Further Evidence on Hedge Fund Return Predictability." *Journal of Wealth Management,* vol. 9, no. 3 (Winter):68–79.

"In this article, the authors provide new evidence of the out-of-sample predictability of hedge fund returns. They first adopt a rigorous model-construction process to find the best predictive variables for each hedge fund style. They then examine whether the perceived predictability could translate into profitable 'tactical style' allocation strategies. Nine out of ten hedge funds strategies outperform the passive benchmark. For robustness, they test the performance of optimized strategies and confirm the profitability of tactical style allocation based on the prediction of our multifactor models." (p. 68)

Henriksson, Roy D. 1984. "Market Timing and Mutual Fund Performance: An Empirical Investigation." *Journal of Business,* vol. 57, no. 1 (January):73–96.

"The evaluation of the performance of investment managers is a topic of considerable interest to practitioners and academics alike. Using both the parametric and non-parametric tests for the evaluation of forecasting ability presented by Henriksson and Merton, the market-timing ability of 116 open-end mutual funds is evaluated for the period 1968–80. The empirical results do not support the hypothesis that mutual fund managers are able to follow an investment strategy that successfully times the return on the market portfolio." (p. 73)

* Hsieh, David A. 2006. "The Search for Alpha—Sources of Future Hedge Fund Returns." *CFA Institute Conference Proceedings Quarterly,* vol. 23, no. 3 (September):79–89.

"Two types of hedge fund investors exist: alpha seekers and beta chasers. If alpha seekers dominate the market, the decline in alpha per dollar invested in the hedge fund industry is likely to continue as long as the supply of alpha is finite. If, however, beta chasers dominate, growth in the industry should be sustainable because beta return is easily replicated and, therefore, the supply of beta virtually unlimited." (p. 79)

* Jaeger, L., and C. Wagner. 2005. "Factor Modeling and Benchmarking of Hedge Funds: Can Passive Investments in Hedge Fund Strategies Deliver?" *Journal of Alternative Investments,* vol. 8, no. 3 (Winter):9–36.

"The hedge fund industry is starting to recognize that the main component of its returns corresponds to risk premia rather than market inefficiencies, i.e., from 'beta' instead of 'alpha.' This has some implication for the industry and investors, among which is the endeavor to construct investable benchmarks for hedge funds on the basis of an analysis of the underlying systematic risk factors. This issue is closely linked to the rationale for constructing investable versions of hedge fund indices. An important question is whether investable benchmarks based on risk factor analysis offer a valid, more theoretically sound, and cheaper alternative to the hedge fund index products currently available? This article reflects on this most recent discussion within the global hedge fund industry about the 'beta versus alpha' controversy, investable hedge fund indices, and finally, capacity issues. It illustrates how the current research might turn the hedge fund industry upside down in coming years." (p. 9)

* Kat, Harry M. 2003. "Taking the Sting Out of Hedge Funds." *Journal of Wealth Management,* vol. 6, no. 3 (Winter):67–76.

"Although the inclusion of hedge funds in an investment portfolio can significantly improve that portfolio's mean–variance characteristics, it can also be expected to lead to significantly lower skewness and higher kurtosis. In this article, the author shows how this highly undesirable side effect can be neutralized by allocating a fraction of wealth to out-of-the-money put options on the relevant stock index. Roughly speaking, the costs of the proposed skewness reduction strategy will be higher 1) the higher the hedge fund allocation, 2) the lower the expected equity risk premium, and 3) the higher the bond allocation relative to the equity allocation. In the current low interest rate environment, for portfolios with a more or less equal allocation to stocks and bonds, the costs of skewness reduction are unlikely to be much higher than 1 percent per annum. For portfolios with relatively high bond allocations, however, the costs could amount to 3 percent or even more. This confirms that the benefits of hedge funds heavily depend on the portfolio they are added to and that the attractive mean-variance properties of (portfolios including) hedge funds may come at a significant price." (p. 67)

* ———. 2004. "Hedge Funds versus Common Sense: An Illustration of the Dangers of Mechanical Investment Decision Making." In *Intelligent Hedge Fund Investing.* Edited by Barry Schachter. London: Risk Books.

"It has become clear that hedge funds are a lot more complicated than common stocks and investment grade bonds and may not be as phenomenally attractive as many hedge fund managers and marketers want investors to believe. Hedge fund investing requires a more elaborate approach to investment decision making than most investors are used to. Mechanically applying the same decision-making processes that are typically used for stock and bond investment may lead to some very nasty surprises." (p. 9)

———. 2005. "Integrating Hedge Funds into the Traditional Portfolio." *Journal of Wealth Management,* vol. 7, no. 4 (Spring):51–57.

"In this summary article, the author shows how investors can neutralize the unwanted skewness and kurtosis effects from investing in hedge funds by 1) purchasing out-of-the-money equity puts, 2) investing in managed futures, and/or by 3) overweighting equity market neutral and global macro and avoiding distressed securities and emerging market funds. The analysis suggests that all three alternatives are up to the job but also come with their own specific price tag." (p. 51)

* ———. 2007. "Alternative Routes to Hedge Fund Return Replication." *Journal of Wealth Management,* vol. 10, no. 3 (Winter):25–39.

"The author starts with the observation that although institutions are still pouring more and more money into hedge funds, hedge fund performance is clearly deteriorating. In part, this reflects lower interest rates and a global decline in risk premiums. Part of hedge funds' disappointing performance, however, is also due to the huge inflow of institutional money itself. The author then notes that, driven by a desire to reduce costs and improve investor returns, the market has recently seen several attempts to 'replicate' hedge fund index returns. Stating that the driving force behind hedge fund replication is the realization that the majority of hedge fund managers do not have enough skill to make up for the fees they charge, the author argues that it may be worthwhile to replace the managers in question with a synthetic hedge fund. Synthetic hedge funds produce no pre-fee alpha, but they don't cost a fortune to run and may therefore very well produce significant after-fee alpha. In addition, synthetic hedge funds come with great improvements in liquidity, transparency, capacity, etc. The article proceeds to discuss three different approaches to replications." (p. 25)

* Kazemi, Hossein B., and Thomas Schneeweis. 2004. "Hedge Funds: Stale Prices Revisited." Working paper, CISDM (April).

"The growth in hedge fund has in part been due to their historical return to risk performance. Concern, however, has been expressed that one reason for the superior return to risk tradeoff for hedge funds, is that, unlike traditional mutual funds, hedge funds often trade in illiquid securities and may have the ability to smooth prices such that reported volatility and systematic risk are less than actual volatility and systematic risk. In this paper we show that previous research which has used the lagged values of S&P 500 returns to test the potential impact of stale prices may simply reflect a unique historical anomaly in the relationship between hedge fund returns and lagged returns on the S&P 500. While price smoothing may still exist in various hedge fund strategies, we show that the empirical results presented in previous papers have an alternative explanation that is unrelated to stale prices or data smoothing." (p. 1)

* Kundro, Christopher, and Stuart Feffer. 2003. "Understanding and Mitigating Operational Risk in Hedge Fund Investments." Capco white paper series (March): www.capco.com/content/knowledge-ideas?q=content/research.

"As the hedge fund industry has grown explosively, so too has the list of fund failures and burned investors. To better understand the reason why hedge funds fail in ways that often result in substantial investor losses and how such failures could be prevented or at least avoided, Capco initiated a study. Our initial analysis shows that operational issues account for an alarmingly high proportion of hedge fund failures (50%) and that expanding due diligence and monitoring practices to understand 'back office' capabilities can make a big difference in preventing or avoiding these failures." (p. 3)

* ———. 2004. "Valuation Issues and Operational Risk in Hedge Funds." Working paper, Capco (March).

"In our recent study on the root causes of hedge fund failures, we identified a number of operational risk factors that together seem to account for approximately half of catastrophic cases. Issues related to valuation—the determination of fair-market value for all of the positions that make up a fund—underlie many of these operational risk factors. Recently, valuation problems have also been much in the news. These headlines suggest that the industry is not yet taking the steps needed to address problems in the valuation process. In fact, we believe that issues related to valuation of portfolios will likely become the next major 'black eye' for the hedge fund industry. Unless certain practices discussed in this paper become more widespread, we believe that hedge funds face a potential crisis of confidence with institutional and high net worth investors. Therefore, we are using this paper to consider the issues related to the valuation of hedge fund portfolios more closely, in particular as they pertain to the issue of managing operational risks associated with hedge fund investments." (p. 1)

Liang, Bing. 1999. "On the Performance of Hedge Funds." *Financial Analysts Journal*, vol. 55, no. 4 (July/August):72–85.

"Empirical evidence indicates that hedge funds differ substantially from traditional investment vehicles, such as mutual funds. Unlike mutual funds, hedge funds follow dynamic trading strategies and have low systematic risk. Hedge funds' special fee structures apparently align managers' incentives with fund performance. Funds with 'high watermarks' (under which managers are required to make up previous losses before receiving any incentive fees) significantly outperform those without. Hedge funds provide higher Sharpe ratios than mutual funds, and their performance in the period of January 1992 through December 1996 reflects better manager skills, although hedge fund returns are more volatile. Average hedge fund returns are related positively to incentive fees, fund assets, and the lockup period." (p. 72)

———. 2000. "Hedge Funds: The Living and the Dead." *Journal of Financial and Quantitative Analysis*, vol. 35, no. 3 (September):309–326.

"In this paper, we examine survivorship bias in hedge fund returns by comparing two large databases. We find that the survivorship bias exceeds 2 percent per year. We reconcile the conflicting results about survivorship bias in previous studies by showing that the two major hedge fund databases contain different amounts of dissolved funds. Empirical results show that poor performance is the main reason for a fund's disappearance. Furthermore, we find that there are significant differences in fund returns, inception date, net assets value, incentive fee, management fee, and investment styles for the 465 common funds covered by both databases. One database has more return and NAV observations, longer fund return history, and more funds with fee information than the other database. There are at least 5 percent return numbers and 5 percent NAV numbers which differ dramatically across the two databases. Mismatching between reported returns and the percentage changes in NAVs can partially explain the difference. The two databases also have different style classifications. Results of survivorship bias by styles indicate that the biases are different across styles and significant for ten out of fifteen styles in one database but none is significant for the other one." (p. 309)

Lo, Andrew W. 2001. "Risk Management for Hedge Funds: Introduction and Overview." *Financial Analysts Journal*, vol. 57, no. 6 (November/December):16–33.

"Although risk management has been a well-plowed field in financial modeling for more than two decades, traditional risk management tools such as mean–variance analysis, beta, and value-at-risk do not capture many of the risk exposures of hedge-fund investments. In this article, I review several unique aspects of risk management for hedge funds—survivorship bias, dynamic risk analytics, liquidity, and nonlinearities—and provide examples that illustrate their potential importance to hedgefund managers and investors. I propose a research agenda for developing a new set of risk analytics specifically designed for hedge-fund investments, with the ultimate goal of creating risk transparency without compromising the proprietary nature of hedge-fund investment strategies." (p. 16)

————. 2002. "The Statistics of Sharpe Ratios." *Financial Analysts Journal,* vol. 58, no. 4 (July/August):36–52.

"The building blocks of the Sharpe ratio—expected returns and volatilities—are unknown quantities that must be estimated statistically and are, therefore, subject to estimation error. This raises the natural question: How accurately are Sharpe ratios measured? To address this question, I derive explicit expressions for the statistical distribution of the Sharpe ratio using standard asymptotic theory under several sets of assumptions for the return-generating process—independently and identically distributed returns, stationary returns, and with time aggregation. I show that monthly Sharpe ratios cannot be annualized by multiplying by $\sqrt{12}$ except under very special circumstances, and I derive the correct method of conversion in the general case of stationary returns. In an illustrative empirical example of mutual funds and hedge funds, I find that the annual Sharpe ratio for a hedge fund can be overstated by as much as 65 percent because of the presence of serial correlation in monthly returns, and once this serial correlation is properly taken into account, the rankings of hedge funds based on Sharpe ratios can change dramatically." (p. 36)

Lowenstein, Roger. 2000. *When Genius Failed: The Rise and Fall of Long-Term Capital Management.* New York: Random House.

This book tells the compelling story of Long-Term Capital Management. In 1993, the best and brightest bond arbitrageurs allied themselves with two future Nobel Prize winners to form a firm that was so sure of its models, it believed it could use leverage without limit to generate fabulous profits. But by 1997, when the Russia default touched off a scenario not anticipated by the models, the staggering amounts of leverage used by LTCM threatened to bring down the world's financial system.

*Malkiel, Burton G., and Atanu Saha. 2005. "Hedge Funds: Risk and Return." *Financial Analysts Journal,* vol. 61, no. 6 (November/December):80–88.

"From a database that is relatively free of bias, this article provides measures of the returns of hedge funds and of the distinctly non-normal characteristics of the data. The results include risk-adjusted measures of performance and tests of the degree to which hedge funds live up to their claim of market neutrality. The substantial attrition of hedge funds is examined, the determinants of hedge fund demise are analyzed, and results of tests of return persistence are presented. The conclusion is that hedge funds are riskier and provide lower returns than is commonly supposed." (p. 80)

* Naik, Narayan Y., and Vikas Agarwal. 2000. "On Taking the 'Alternative' Route: The Risks, Rewards, and Performance Persistence of Hedge Funds." *Journal of Alternative Investments,* vol. 2, no. 4 (Spring):6–23.

"The risk–return characteristics, risk exposures, and performance persistence of various hedge fund strategies remains an area of interest to alternative asset investors. Using a database on hedge fund indices and individual hedge fund managers in a mean-variance framework, results show that a combination of alternative investments and passive indexing provides a significantly better risk–return trade-off than passively investing in the different asset classes. Moreover, using parametric and nonparametric methods, a reasonable degree of persistence is found for hedge fund managers. This seems to be attributable more to the losers continuing to be losers instead of winners continuing to be winners and highlights the importance of manager selection in case of hedge funds." (p. 6)

* Sharma, Milind. 2004. "A.I.R.A.P.—Alternative Views on Alternative Investments." Working paper (January).

"This paper investigates issues of risk-adjusted performance, value added and leverage for hedge funds. It applies AIRAP (Alternative Investments Risk Adjusted Performance), which is the power utility implied certain return that a risk-averse investor would trade off for holding risky assets, to hedge fund indices and individual hedge fund data. Inferences are made about the value added by hedge funds and the difference between directional and non-directional strategies. Evidence of nonnormality, higher moment risks, and the trade-off between mean–variance profile vis-à-vis skewness and kurtosis is noted across style categories. Further, survivorship bias is estimated across style categories in the first four moments." (p. 1)

* Stulz, René. 2007. "Hedge Funds: Past, Present, and Future." *Journal of Economic Perspectives,* vol. 21, no. 2 (Spring):175–194.

"Assets managed by hedge funds have grown faster over the last 10 years than assets managed by mutual funds. Hedge funds and mutual funds perform the same economic function, but hedge funds are largely unregulated while mutual funds are tightly regulated. This paper compares the organization, performance, and risks of hedge funds and mutual funds. It then examines whether one can expect increasing convergence between these two investment vehicles and concludes that the performance gap between hedge funds and mutual funds will narrow, that regulatory developments will limit the flexibility of hedge funds, and that hedge funds will become more institutionalized." (p. 175)

* Till, Hilary. 2004. "Benefits and Costs of Illiquidity." In *Intelligent Hedge Fund Investing.* Edited by Barry Schachter. London: Risk Books.

"Illiquidity affects the valuation of hedge fund investments in several ways. Despite the quantitative definition of illiquidity, some of those effects are behavioral. Further, and somewhat surprising, not all the effects might be considered as negative. We discuss what we know about the various impacts of illiquidity on the decision to invest in hedge funds, and, where appropriate, how an investor may take aspects of illiquidity into account to compare investments with dissimilar liquidity." (p. 75)

*Weisman, Andrew. 2002. "Informationless Investing and Hedge Fund Performance Measurement Bias." *Journal of Portfolio Management,* vol. 28, no. 4 (Summer):80–91.

"Asset managers have the ability to engage in essentially 'informationless' investment strategies that can produce the appearance of return enhancement without necessarily providing any value to an investor. Statistical estimates of risk, return, and association therefore frequently mischaracterize investment returns. These mischaracterizations, the author argues, have significant negative implications for both the asset allocation process and the validity of related academic research. He presents three specific informationless investment strategies, which he believes are endemic to the hedge fund industry, and assesses their consequences with respect to performance measurement and asset allocation." (p. 80)

PRACTICE PROBLEMS FOR READING 47

The following information relates to Questions 1–6[1]

Ian Wang is an alternative investments analyst for the U.S. investment management firm Garnier Brothers. The firm has $500 million of assets under management and a 25-year track record. Garnier's current asset allocation consists of 55% domestic equities (equity mutual funds that invest in S&P 500 companies), 40% fixed-income (U.S. government and U.S. corporate bonds), and 5% direct equity investments in U.S. commercial real estate. Garnier's CIO, Michelle Perez, has informed Wang that over the next 1 to 2 months she wants to reduce the amount invested in traditional asset classes and to invest the proceeds in hedge funds. Wang's current assignment is to analyze the hedge fund industry including different investment strategies as potential investment opportunities for Garnier Brothers. As a basis for his analysis Wang will use the CISDM Hedge Fund Composite Index (HFCI) as a benchmark for the hedge fund universe. To complete his analysis he gathers the selected returns data in Exhibits 1 and 2.

EXHIBIT 1	HFCI and Garnier's S&P 500 Equity Holdings Selected Returns Data			
	1990–2007		2000–2007	
Measure	HFCI	S&P 500	HFCI	S&P 500
Average Monthly Return (Annualized)	13.5%	10.9%	6.8%	−2.3%
Monthly Standard Deviation (Annualized)	5.7%	14.7%	4.8%	16.4%
Sharpe ratio	1.61	0.45	0.86	−0.31

EXHIBIT 2	Hedge Fund Investment Strategies Selected Returns Data 1990–2007		
Strategy or Index	Average Monthly Return (Annualized)	Monthly Standard Deviation (Annualized)	Sharpe Ratio
HFCI	13.5%	5.7%	1.61
Event driven	13.5	5.6	1.64
Equity market neutral	9.2	2.5	1.96
Fixed-income arbitrage	7.6	3.6	0.92
Convertible arbitrage	10.2	4.0	1.48
Fund of Funds	7.0	2.0	1.35

---

[1]Developed by Mark Bhasin, CFA (New York, New York, USA).

After reviewing his research materials as well as Exhibits 1 and 2, Wang formulates the following conclusions:

Conclusion 1: The primary reasons that the hedge fund universe (as proxied by the HFCI) outperformed Garnier's S&P 500 equity holdings during the 2000–2007 period are the hedge funds' ability to short sell securities; to utilize financial leverage; and to employ derivatives.

Conclusion 2: The greater return exhibited by event driven funds relative to equity market neutral funds is due to event driven funds capturing a significant liquidity premium and equity market neutral funds minimizing risk exposures to market capitalization, value, growth, and industry.

Conclusion 3: Hedge fund managers implementing event driven strategies have historically outperformed the S&P 500 because of alpha creation.

Conclusion 4: The Sharpe ratio is not the optimal risk-adjusted return measure for hedge funds because of the negative skewness and negative excess kurtosis exhibited by hedge fund returns.

Wang notes that the relatively high fees charged by hedge funds make them an unattractive investment. His research indicates that replication strategies can be an attractive alternative to hedge funds when investors wish to avoid the large fees charged by hedge fund managers. Wang describes two such replication strategies in his report:

Replication Strategy 1: A long position in high yield corporate bonds and a short position in U.S. Treasury securities with a similar duration.

Replication Strategy 2: A long position in convertible bonds and a short position in the equity of the firm issuing the convertible bond.

After reading Wang's report on hedge funds, Perez concludes that the performance data are more reliable for fund-of-funds rather than the single manager hedge fund; therefore, implementing Garnier's hedge fund exposure should be accomplished through a fund-of-funds vehicle rather than a single manager hedge fund.

1. Wang's Conclusion 1 is:
   A. correct.
   B. incorrect because short selling is not permitted.
   C. incorrect because the use of financial leverage is not permitted.

2. Wang's Conclusion 2 is:
   A. correct.
   B. incorrect because liquidity premiums are insignificant for event driven hedge funds.
   C. incorrect because equity market neutral funds do not minimize risk exposures to market capitalization, value, growth, and industry.

3. Wang's Conclusion 3 is:

   A. correct.

   B. incorrect because event driven hedge funds assume greater risk-adjusted returns through higher traditional betas.

   C. incorrect because event driven hedge funds earn excess returns from taking significant risks in untraditional market factors.

4. Wang's Conclusion 4 is:

   A. correct.

   B. incorrect because the Sharpe ratio is unaffected by higher moment exposures.

   C. incorrect because hedge fund returns exhibit negative skewness and positive excess kurtosis.

5. Which of the following hedge fund strategies can be replicated by Replication Strategy 1 and Replication Strategy 2?

   A. Fixed-income arbitrage for both strategies.

   B. Fixed-income arbitrage for Replication Strategy 1 and convertible arbitrage for Replication Strategy 2.

   C. Convertible arbitrage for Replication Strategy 1 and fixed-income arbitrage for Replication Strategy 2.

6. Which of the following statements most likely supports Perez's conclusion relating to implementing Garnier's hedge fund exposure?

   A. Fund-of-fund returns are less risky than single manager returns.

   B. Fund-of-fund returns are prone to smaller backfill and selection bias.

   C. Fund-of-funds tend to exhibit more average performance than single manager hedge funds.

SOLUTIONS FOR READING 47

1. A is correct.

2. C is correct. Equity market neutral funds may take substantial risks in other areas of the equity markets, such as market capitalization, value, growth, or industry.

3. C is correct. Event driven hedge funds exhibit strong risk-adjusted returns by taking significant risks in untraditional market factors.

4. C is correct. Many hedge fund styles have higher moment risks in which returns have negative skewness and fat tails (i.e., large excess kurtosis).

5. B is correct. Fixed-income arbitrage replication would take a long position in a credit fund, such as high yield bonds or mortgage-backed securities, and a short position in a Treasury securities fund of a similar duration. Convertible arbitrage replication would be achieved by purchasing convertible bonds and shorting the equity of the firm issuing the convertible bond.

6. B is correct. Fund of funds, as a result of their diversification among strategies and managers, tend to exhibit lower mortality, survivor bias, and backfill bias than single manager hedge funds.

FIXED INCOME

TOPIC LEVEL LEARNING OUTCOME

The candidate should be able to estimate the risks and expected returns for fixed income instruments, analyze the term structure of interest rates and yield spreads, and evaluate fixed income instruments with embedded options and unique features.

4⅝ 4¹¹⁄₁₆ – ⅜
5½ 5½ –
5½ 21³⁄₁₆ – ¹⁄₁₆
20⅝ 21³⁄₁₆
17⅜ 18⅛ + ⅞
6½ 6½ – ½
7¼ 6½ 3¹⁄₃₂ – ⅛
15⁄₁₆ ⁹⁄₁₆
9⁄₁₆
7¹⁵⁄₁₆ 7¹³⁄₁₆ 7¹⁵⁄₁₆
2⅝ 2¹¹⁄₃₂ 2½ +
2¾ 2¼ 2¼
6½ 12¹⁄₁₆ 11⅜ 11¾ +
87 33¾ 33 33¹⁄₁₆ –
5½ 25⅝ 24⁹⁄₁₆ 25⅜ +
833 12 11⅝ 11⅛ +
16 10½ 10½ 10½ –
78 15⅞ 15¹³⁄₁₆ 15⅛ –
5 45⅜ 9⁵⁄₁₆ 8¼ 8⅛ +
430 11¼ 10⅛

STUDY SESSION 14
FIXED INCOME:
Valuation Concepts

This study session demonstrates the primary skills needed for the valuation of fixed income investments. It begins with a discussion of the key valuation tools used in credit analysis and how credit standards affect liquidity. Interest rate volatility and term structure are presented next and are then followed by an introduction to embedded options in fixed income securities.

READING ASSIGNMENTS

Reading 48   General Principles of Credit Analysis
             Fixed Income Analysis for the Chartered Financial Analyst®
             Program, Second Edition, by Frank J. Fabozzi, CFA

Reading 49   Term Structure and Volatility of Interest Rates
             Fixed Income Analysis for the Chartered Financial Analyst®
             Program, Second Edition, by Frank J. Fabozzi, CFA

Reading 50   Valuing Bonds with Embedded Options
             Fixed Income Analysis for the Chartered Financial Analyst®
             Program, Second Edition, by Frank J. Fabozzi, CFA

4⅝ 4¹¹/₁₆
5½ 5½ − ⅜
5½ 21³/₁₆ − ⅛
20⅝ 21³/₁₆ − ⅛
17⅜ 18⅛ + ⅞
6½ 6½ − ½
7¼ 6½ 3¹/₃₂ −
15/₁₆ ⅝
9/₁₆ ⅝
1¹/₃₂ 7¹³/₁₆ 7¹⁵/₁₆
7¹⁵/₁₆
2⅝ 2¹¹/₃₂ 2½ +
2¼ 2¼
2¾ 2¼
6⅛ 12¹/₁₆ 11⅜ 11¼ +
87 33¾ 33 33¼ −
6⅛ 25⅝ 24⁹/₁₆ 25⅝ +
11⅝ 11⅛ +
833 12 11⅝
16 10½ 10½ 10½ −
78 15⅞ 15¹³/₁₆ 15⅞ −
9¹/₁₆ 8¼ 8¼ +
430 11¼ 10⅝

GENERAL PRINCIPLES
OF CREDIT ANALYSIS
by Frank J. Fabozzi, CFA

LEARNING OUTCOMES

The candidate should be able to:	Mastery
a. distinguish among default risk, credit spread risk, and downgrade risk;	☐
b. explain and analyze capacity, collateral, covenants, and character as components of credit analysis;	☐
c. calculate and interpret key financial ratios used by credit analysts;	☐
d. evaluate the credit quality of an issuer of a corporate bond, given such data as key financial ratios for the issuer and the industry;	☐
e. analyze why and how cash flow from operations is used to assess the ability of an issuer to service its debt obligations and to assess the financial flexibility of a company;	☐
f. explain and interpret typical elements of the corporate structure and debt structure of a high-yield issuer and the effect of these elements on the risk position of the lender;	☐
g. describe factors considered by rating agencies in rating asset-backed securities;	☐
h. explain how the credit worthiness of municipal bonds is assessed, and contrast the analysis of tax-backed debt with the analysis of revenue obligations;	☐
i. describe considerations used by Standard & Poor's in assigning sovereign ratings, and explain why two ratings are assigned to each national government;	☐
j. contrast the credit analysis required for corporate bonds to that required for 1) asset-backed securities, 2) municipal securities, and 3) sovereign debt.	☐

1   INTRODUCTION

The credit risk of a bond includes:

1) the risk that the issuer will default on its obligation and

2) the risk that the bond's value will decline and/or the bond's price performance will be worse than that of other bonds against which the investor is compared because either a) the market requires a higher spread due to a perceived increase in the risk that the issuer will default or b) companies that assign ratings to bonds will lower a bond's rating.

The first risk is referred to as default risk. The second risk is labeled based on the reason for the adverse or inferior performance. The risk attributable to an increase in the spread, or more specifically the credit spread, is referred to as credit spread risk; the risk attributable to a lowering of the credit rating (i.e., a downgrading) is referred to as downgrade risk.[1]

Credit analysis of any entity—a corporation, a municipality, or a sovereign government—involves the analysis of a multitude of quantitative and qualitative factors over the past, present, and future. There are four general approaches to gauging credit risk:

▶ credit ratings;

▶ traditional credit analysis;

▶ credit scoring models;

▶ credit risk models.

In this reading, we discuss each approach. Our primary focus is on the credit analysis of corporate bonds.

2   CREDIT RATINGS

A credit rating is a formal opinion given by a specialized company of the default risk faced by investing in a particular issue of debt securities. The specialized companies that provide credit ratings are referred to as "rating agencies." The three nationally recognized rating agencies in the United States are Moody's Investors Service, Standard & Poor's Corporation, and Fitch Ratings. The symbols used by these rating agencies and a summary description of each rating can be found elsewhere.

---

[1] These types of credit risk were discussed in detail at Level I.

A. Rating Process, Surveillance, and Review

The rating process begins when a rating agency receives a formal request from an entity planning to issue a bond in which it seeks a rating for the bond issue (i.e., an "issue specific credit rating"). The cost associated with obtaining a credit rating is paid by the entity making the request for a rating. The request for a rating is made because without one, it would be difficult for the entity to issue a bond. The rating assigned applies to the specific bond to be issued, *not* to the entity requesting the rating. A rating agency may also be requested to provide a rating for a company that has no public debt outstanding (i.e., an "issuer credit rating"). This is done for companies that are parties in derivative transactions, such as swaps, so that market participants can assess counterparty risk.[2]

Once a credit rating is assigned to a corporate debt obligation, a rating agency monitors the credit quality of the issuer and can reassign a different credit rating to its bonds. An "upgrade" occurs when there is an improvement in the credit quality of an issue; a "downgrade" occurs when there is a deterioration in the credit quality of an issue. As noted earlier, downgrade risk is the risk that an issue will be downgraded.

Typically, before an issue's rating is changed, the rating agency will announce in advance that it is reviewing the issue with the potential for upgrade or downgrade. The issue in such cases is said to be on "rating watch" or "credit watch." In the announcement, the rating agency will state the direction of the potential change in rating—upgrade or downgrade. Typically, a decision will be made within three months.

In addition, rating agencies will issue rating outlooks. A rating outlook is a projection of whether an issue in the long term (from six months to two years) is likely to be upgraded, downgraded, or maintain its current rating. Rating agencies designate a rating outlook as either positive (i.e., likely to be upgraded), negative (i.e., likely to be downgraded), or stable (i.e., likely to be no change in the rating).

B. Gauging Default Risk and Downgrade Risk

The information available to investors from rating agencies about credit risk are: 1) ratings, 2) rating watches or credit watches, and 3) rating outlooks. Moreover, periodic studies by the rating agencies provide information to investors about credit risk. Below we describe how the information provided by rating agencies can be used to gauge two forms of credit risk: default risk and downgrade risk.

For long-term debt obligations, a credit rating is a forward-looking assessment of 1) the probability of default and 2) the relative magnitude of the loss should a default occur. For short-term debt obligations (i.e., obligations with initial maturities of one year or less), a credit rating is a forward-looking assessment of the probability of default. Consequently, credit ratings are the rating agencies' assessment of the default risk associated with a bond issue.

Periodic studies by rating agencies provide information about two aspects of default risk—default rates and default loss rates. First, rating agencies study and make available to investors the percentage of bonds of a given rating at the beginning of a period that have defaulted at the end of the period. This percentage is referred to as the default rate.[3] For example, a rating agency might

---

[2] Counterparty risk is the risk that a party to a financial transaction will default on its obligation.

[3] There are several ways that default rates can be measured.

report that the one-year default rate for triple B rated bonds is 1.8%. These studies have shown that the lower the credit rating, the higher the default rate. Rating agency studies also show default loss rates by rating and other characteristics of the issue (e.g., level of seniority and industry). A default loss rate is a measure of the magnitude of the potential of the loss should a default occur.[4]

A study by Moody's found that for a corporate bond, its ratings combined with its rating watches and rating outlook status provide a better gauge for default risk than using the ratings alone.[5] The authors of the study looked at one-year and three-year default rates from 1996 through 2003 for senior unsecured rated bonds and within each rating by rating watch (watch upgrade and watch downgrade) and rating outlook status (positive, stable, and negative). The one-year default rate results for three selected ratings are shown below:

Rating	Watch Up	Positive	Stable	Negative	Watch Down
Baa3	NA	0.20%	0.60%	1.25%	2.26%
B1	NA	0.98%	2.53%	5.07%	12.03%
Caa1	3.7%	3.82%	8.43%	14.93%	42.21%

Notice that as one moves from left to right for a given credit rating in the above table that the default rate increases. Look at the Caa1 rating. For issues that were on rating watch for a potential upgrade at the beginning of the period, 3.7% defaulted in one year. However, for those on rating watch for a potential downgrade at the beginning of the period, 42.21% defaulted in one year. This suggests that rating watches contain useful information in gauging default risk. Look at the rating outlook status for Caa1. Issues that had a negative rating outlook at the beginning of the year had a one-year default rate that was almost four times greater than issues that had a positive rating outlook.

Moody's makes the following suggestion as to how an analyst can combine the information contained in rating watches and outlook rating status to adjust the senior unsecured rating of a corporate bond:

For issues on:	*Suggestion:*
downgrade watch	reduce current rating by two rating notches[6]
upgrade watch	increase current rating by two rating notches
negative outlook	reduce current rating by one rating notch
stable outlook	keep current rating
positive outlook	increase current rating by one rating notch

Of course, portfolio managers may elect to develop their own system for adjusting the current rating of a bond based on their assessment of the findings of the study by Moody's. What is essential, however, is that in assessing the default risk when using credit ratings, portfolio managers should take into consideration rating watches and rating outlook status.

---

[4] The default loss rate is described at Level I.

[5] David T. Hamilton and Richard Cantor, *Rating Transitions and Defaults Conditional on Watchlist, Outlook and Rating History,* Moody's Investors Service, February 2004.

[6] A rating "notch" is a rating based on the modified rating (i.e., in the case of Moody's with the "1", "2", and "3" modifiers). For example, if an issue is rated Baa2, then a reduction of one rating notch would be a rating of Baa3. A reduction of two rating notches would be a rating of Ba1.

While the discussion above has focused on default risk, other studies by rating agencies also provide information. The rating transition matrix published periodically by the rating agencies has previously been explained. A rating transition table shows the percentage of issues of each rating at the beginning of a period that was downgraded or upgraded by the end of the time period. Consequently, by looking at the percentage of downgrades for a given rating, an estimate can be obtained of the probability of a downgrade and this can serve as a measure of downgrade risk.[7]

TRADITIONAL CREDIT ANALYSIS
3

In traditional credit analysis, the analyst considers the four C's of credit:

- ► capacity;
- ► collateral;
- ► covenants;
- ► character.

Capacity is the ability of an issuer to repay its obligations. Collateral is looked at not only in the traditional sense of assets pledged to secure the debt, but also to the quality and value of those unpledged assets controlled by the issuer. In both senses the collateral is capable of supplying additional aid, comfort, and support to the debt and the debtholder. Assets form the basis for the generation of cash flow which services the debt in good times as well as bad. Covenants are the terms and conditions of the lending agreement. They lay down restrictions on how management operates the company and conducts its financial affairs. Covenants can restrict management's discretion. A default or violation of any covenant may provide a meaningful early warning alarm enabling investors to take positive and corrective action before the situation deteriorates further. Covenants have value as they play an important part in minimizing risk to creditors. They help prevent the transfer of wealth from debt holders to equity holders. Character of management is the foundation of sound credit. This includes the ethical reputation as well as the business qualifications and operating record of the board of directors, management, and executives responsible for the use of the borrowed funds and repayment of those funds.

A. Analysis of the Capacity to Pay

A corporation will generate the funds to service its debt from its cash flow. The cash flow is generated from revenues and reduced by the costs of operations. Therefore, in assessing the ability of an issuer to pay, an analysis of the financial statements as discussed later in this reading is undertaken. In addition to management quality, the factors examined by analysts at Moody's are:[8]

1. industry trends

2. the regulatory environment

---

[7] An illustration of a rating transition matrix and the calculation of the probability of downgrade were provided at Level I.

[8] "Industrial Company Rating Methodology," Moody's Investors Services: Global Credit Research (July 1998), p. 3.

3. basic operating and competitive position

4. financial position and sources of liquidity

5. company structure (including structural subordination and priority of claim)

6. parent company support agreements

7. special event risk

In considering industry trends, analysts look at the vulnerability of the company to economic cycles, the barriers to entry, and the exposure of the company to technological changes. For firms in regulated industries, proposed changes in regulations must be analyzed to assess their impact on future cash flows. At the company level, diversification of the product line and the cost structure are examined in assessing the basic operating position of the firm.

In addition to the measures described later in this reading for assessing a company's financial position over the past three to five years, an analyst must look at the capacity of a firm to obtain additional financing and back-up credit facilities. There are various forms of back-up credit facilities. The strongest forms of back-up credit facilities are those that are contractually binding and do not include provisions that permit the lender to refuse to provide funds. An example of such a provision is one that allows the bank to refuse funding if the bank feels that the borrower's financial condition or operating position has deteriorated significantly. (Such a provision is called a material adverse change clause.) Non-contractual facilities such as lines of credit that make it easy for a bank to refuse funding should be of concern to the analyst. The analyst must also examine the quality of the bank providing the back-up facility.

Analysts should also assess whether the company can use securitization as a funding source for generating liquidity. Asset securitization involves using a pool of loans or receivables as collateral for a security. The decision of whether to securitize assets to borrow or use traditional borrowing sources is done on the basis of cost. However, if traditional sources dry up when a company faces a liquidity crisis, securitization may provide the needed liquidity. An analyst should investigate the extent to which management has considered securitization as a funding source.

Other sources of liquidity for a company may be third-party guarantees, the most common being a contractual agreement with its parent company. When such a financial guarantee exists, the analyst must undertake a credit analysis of the parent company.

In the analysis of an issuer's ability to pay, the analyst will analyze the issuer's financial statements (income statement, balance sheet, and statement of cash flows), project future financial statements based on certain assumptions, and compute various measures. These measures include traditional ratio measures and cash flow measures. Below we review these measures and explain how an additional analysis of cash flows provides a better early warning alarm of potential financial difficulties than traditional ratios.

1. Traditional Ratios

Traditional ratios to evaluate the ability of an issuer to meet its obligations include:

▶ profitability ratios,

▶ debt and coverage ratios.

a. Profitability Ratios

Equity analysts focus on the earnings of a firm, particularly the earnings per share. While a holder of the debt obligation of a firm does not have the opportunity to share in the economic growth of the firm, this does not mean that a credit analyst should ignore a firm's profitability. It is from revenues that a firm will continue to grow in order to generate cash flow to meet obligations.

Profitability ratios are utilized to explore the underlying causes of a change in the company's earnings. They show the combined effects of liquidity and asset and debt management on the profitability of the firm. These ratios break earnings per share into its basic determinants for purposes of assessing the factors underlying the profitability of the firm. They help to assess the adequacy of historical profits, and to project future profitability through better understanding of its underlying causes.

Standards for a given ratio will vary according to operating characteristics of the company being analyzed and general business conditions; such standards cannot be stated as fixed and immutable. It is assumed that the analyst has made all adjustments deemed necessary to reflect comparable and true earning power of the corporation before calculating the ratios discussed below. It is important to stress that ratios are utilized to raise significant questions requiring further analysis, not to provide answers.

Equity analysts use the DuPont formula (explained in textbooks on equity analysis) to assess the determinants of a company's earnings per share. The profitability ratios analyzed to assess earnings per share are:

- ▶ return on stockholders' equity;
- ▶ return on total assets;
- ▶ profit margin;
- ▶ asset turnover.

Each of these measures and their limitations are explained in textbooks on financial statement analysis and equity analysis so they will not be repeated here.

b. Debt and Coverage Analysis

There are three sets of ratios that are used by credit analysts as indicators to assess the ability of a firm to satisfy its debt obligations:

- ▶ short-term solvency ratios;
- ▶ capitalization (or financial leverage) ratios;
- ▶ coverage ratios.

i. Short-Term Solvency Ratios Short-term solvency ratios are used to judge the adequacy of liquid assets for meeting short-term obligations as they come due. A complete analysis of the adequacy of working capital for meeting current liabilities as they come due and assessing management's efficiency in using working capital would require a thorough analysis of cash flows and forecasts of fund flows in future periods that will be discussed in the next section. However, ratios provide a crude but useful assessment of working capital. The following two ratios are calculated to assess the adequacy of working capital for a firm:

- ▶ the current ratio,
- ▶ the acid-test ratio.

The current ratio is calculated by dividing current assets by current liabilities:

$$\text{Current ratio} = \frac{\text{Current assets}}{\text{Current liabilities}}$$

The current ratio indicates the company's coverage of current liabilities by current assets. For example, if the ratio were 2:1, the firm could realize only half of the values stated in the balance sheet in liquidating current assets and still have adequate funds to pay all current liabilities.

A general standard for this ratio (such as 2:1) is *not* useful. Such a standard fails to recognize that an appropriate current ratio is a function of the nature of a company's business and would vary with differing operating cycles of different businesses. The **operating cycle** of a company is the duration from the time cash is invested in goods and services to the time that investment produces cash.[9]

A **current asset** is one that is expected to be converted into cash in the ordinary operating cycle of a business. Inventory, therefore, is a current asset. In a tobacco or liquor manufacturing company, inventory may be as much as 80% to 90% of current assets. However, for a liquor company that inventory may have to age four years or more before it can be converted into a salable asset. Such a company typically would require a much higher current ratio than average to have adequate liquidity to meet current liabilities maturing in one year. For a public utility company where there is no inventory or receivables collection problem, a current ratio of 1.1 or 1.2 to 1 has proved satisfactory. Industry averages are published by organizations such as Dun & Bradstreet and Robert Morris Associates. While industry averages have their faults, they are preferable to general standards that do not recognize operating differences among classes of companies.

The current ratio has a major weakness as an analytical tool. It ignores the composition of current assets, which may be as important as their relationship with current liabilities. Therefore, current ratio analysis must be supplemented by other working capital ratios.

Since the problem in meeting current liabilities may rest on slowness or even inability to convert inventories into cash to meet current obligations, the **acid-test ratio** (also called the **quick ratio**) is recommended. This is the ratio of current assets minus inventories to current liabilities; that is:

$$\text{Acid-test ratio} = \frac{\text{Current assets} - \text{Inventories}}{\text{Current liabilities}}$$

This ratio does assume that receivables are of good quality and will be converted into cash over the next year.

ii. Capitalization Ratios   Credit analysts also calculate capitalization ratios to determine the extent to which the corporation is using financial leverage. These ratios, also called **financial leverage ratios**, can be interpreted only in the context of the stability of industry and company earnings and cash flow. The assumption is that the greater the stability of industry and company earnings and cash flow,

---

[9] For example, a firm that produces and sells goods has an operating cycle comprising four phases: 1) purchase raw material and produce goods, investing in inventory; 2) sell goods, generating sales, which may or may not be for cash; 3) extend credit, creating accounts receivable; and, 4) collect accounts receivable, generating cash. The four phases make up the cycle of cash use and generation. The operating cycle would be somewhat different for companies that produce services rather than goods, but the idea is the same—the operating cycle is the length of time it takes to generate cash through the investment of cash.

the more the company is able to accept the risk associated with financial leverage, and the higher the allowable ratio of debt to total capitalization (the total dollar amount of all long-term sources of funds in the balance sheet).

There are many variations to be found within the industry to calculate capitalization ratios. Two such ratios are shown below:

$$\text{Long-term debt to capitalization} = \frac{\text{Long-term debt}}{\text{Long-term debt} + \text{Shareholders' equity including minority interest}}$$

$$\text{Total debt to capitalization}$$
$$= \frac{\text{Current liabilities} + \text{Long-term debt}}{\text{Long-term debt} + \text{Current liabilities} + \text{Shareholders' equity including minority interest}}$$

where shareholders' equity includes preferred stock.

For both ratios, the higher the ratio, the greater the financial leverage. The value used to measure debt in both ratios is book value. It is useful to calculate stockholders' equity at market as well as at book value for the purpose of determining these ratios. A market calculation for common equity may indicate considerably more or less financial leverage than a book calculation.

Commercial rating companies and most Wall Street analysts rely heavily upon the long-term debt to capitalization ratio, and this is often provided in research reports sent out to clients. While this ratio can be useful, it should be noted that in recent years, given the uncertain interest rate environment, many corporations have taken to financing a good deal of their business with short-term debt. Indeed, an imaginative treasurer with a keen insight into money market activities can earn as much for a company as a plant manager, simply by switching debt from long term to short term and vice versa, at the right time.

Other considerations in using the long-term debt to capitalization ratio involves leased assets. Many corporations rent buildings and equipment under long-term lease contracts. Required rental payments are contractual obligations similar to bond coupon and repayment obligations. However, assets acquired through leasing (i.e., those leases classified as operating leases) may not be capitalized and shown in the balance sheet. Two companies, therefore, might work with the same amount of fixed assets and produce the same profits before interest or rental payments, but the one leasing a high proportion of its productive equipment could show significantly lower financial leverage.

iii. Coverage Tests   Coverage ratios are used to test the adequacy of cash flows generated through earnings for purposes of meeting debt and lease obligations. The four most commonly used coverage ratios are:

▶ EBIT interest coverage ratio;
▶ EBITDA interest coverage ratio;
▶ funds from operations/total debt ratio;
▶ free operating cash flow/total debt ratio.

EBIT stands for "earnings before interest and taxes." The EBIT interest coverage ratio is simply EBIT divided by the annual interest expense. (Interest expense includes "capitalized interest." This is effectively interest expense imputed for capitalized assets, the most important of which is leased assets.) Interest expense is tax-deductible and, therefore, all earnings before taxes are available for paying such charges. Also, the interest should be added back to determine the amount available to meet annual interest expenses.

EBITDA stands for "earnings before interest, taxes, depreciation, and amortization." The EBITDA interest coverage ratio is simply the ratio of EBITDA divided by the annual interest expense.

The last two ratios listed above indicate the amount of funds from operations relative to the amount of total debt. The funds from operations includes net income plus the following: depreciation, amortization, deferred income taxes, and other noncash items. The definition of free operating cash flows varies by rating agency. In the next section we describe one variant of free operating cash flow.

Suggested standards for coverage ratios are based on experience and empirical studies relating the incidence of defaults over a number of years to such ratios. Different standards are needed for a highly cyclical company than for a stable company. In the case study presented in the appendix to this reading, benchmark ratios (as measured in terms of median ratios) by credit rating are presented for the coverage ratios described above, as well as for the capitalization ratios.

2. Cash Flow Analysis

Will the ratios just described be sufficient to help an analyst identify companies that may encounter financial difficulties? Consider the study by Largay and Stickney, who analyzed the financial statements of W.T. Grant during the 1966–1974 period preceding its bankruptcy in 1975 and ultimate liquidation.[10] They noted that financial indicators such as profitability ratios, turnover ratios, and liquidity ratios showed some down trends, but provided no definite clues to the company's impending bankruptcy. A study of cash flows from operations, however, revealed that company operations were causing an increasing drain on cash, rather than providing cash.[11] This necessitated an increased use of external financing, the required interest payments on which exacerbated the cash flow drain. Cash flow analysis clearly was a valuable tool in this case since W.T. Grant had been running a negative cash flow from operations for years. Yet none of the traditional ratios discussed above take into account the cash flow from operations.

The need to look at cash flow is emphasized by Standard & Poor's:

> Cash flow analysis is the single most critical aspect of all credit rating decisions. It takes on added importance for speculative-grade issuers. While companies with investment-grade ratings generally have ready access to external cash to cover temporary shortfalls, junk-bond issuers lack this degree of flexibility and have fewer alternatives to internally generated cash for servicing debt.[12]

S&P also notes that: "Discussions about cash flow often suffer from lack of uniform definition of terms."[13] Below we describe how S&P's terminology with respect to four cash flow concepts: operating cash flow, free operating cash flow, discretionary cash flow, and prefinancing cash flow. In addition, we discuss the various ratios employing these cash flow measures.

---

[10] J.A. Largay III and C.P. Stickney, "Cash Flows, Ratio Analysis and the W.T. Grant Company Bankruptcy," *Financial Analysts Journal* (July–August 1980), pp. 51–54.

[11] For the period investigated, a statement of changes of financial position (on a working capital basis) was required prior to 1988.

[12] Standard & Poor's, *Corporate Ratings Criteria*, undated, p. 26.

[13] *Corporate Ratings Criteria*, p. 27.

a. Cash Flow Measures

Prior to the adoption of the statement of cash flows in 1987, the information regarding a firm's cash flows was quite limited. The **statement of cash flows** is a summary over a period of time of a firm's cash flows from operating, investing, and financing activities. The firm's statement of cash flows lists separately its:

- ▶ cash flows from operating activities;
- ▶ cash flows from investing;
- ▶ cash flow financing activities.

Typically the corresponding cash flows are referred to as:[14]

- ▶ cash provided by operating activities;
- ▶ cash provided by/(used for) investing activities;
- ▶ cash used for financing activities.

"Cash provided by operating activities" is also referred to as "cash flow from operations."

By analyzing these individual statement of cash flows, creditors can examine such aspects of the business as:

- ▶ the source of financing for business operations, whether through internally generated funds or external sources of funds.
- ▶ the ability of the company to meet debt obligations (interest and principal payments).
- ▶ the ability of the company to finance expansion through cash flow from its operating activities.
- ▶ the ability of the company to pay dividends to shareholders.
- ▶ the flexibility the business has in financing its operations.

A firm that generates cash flows only by selling off its assets (obtaining cash flows from investing) or by issuing more securities (obtaining cash flows from financing) cannot keep that up for very long. For future prosperity and the ability to meet its obligations, the firm must be able to generate cash flows from its operations.

Analysts have reformatted the information from the firm's income statement and statement of cash flows to obtain what they view as a better description of the company's activities. S&P begins with what it refers to as funds from operations. The funds from operations is defined as net income adjusted for depreciation

---

[14] Some firms use different labels. For example, Microsoft refers to these cash flows as: Net cash from operations, Net cash used for financing, and Net cash used for investing.

and other noncash debits and credits. Then from the funds from operation, the following cash flow measures are computed:[15]

> **Funds from operations**
>> Decrease (increase) in noncash current assets
>> Increase (decrease) in nondebt current liabilities
>
> **Operating cash flow**
>> Decrease by capital expenditures
>
> **Free operating cash flow**
>> Decrease by cash dividends
>
> **Discretionary cash flow**
>> Decrease by acquisitions
>> Increase by asset disposals
>> Net other sources (uses) of cash
>
> **Prefinancing cash flow**

Operating cash flow is therefore funds from operations reduced by changes in the investment in working capital (current assets less current liabilities). Subtracting capital expenditures gives what S&P defines as free operating cash flow. It is this cash flow measure that can be used to pay dividends and make acquisitions.[16] Reducing free operating cash flow by cash dividends gives discretionary cash flow. Adjusting discretionary cash flow for managerial discretionary decisions for acquisition of other companies, the disposal of assets (e.g., lines of business or subsidiaries), and other sources or uses of cash gives prefinancing cash flow. As stated by S&P, prefinancing cash flow "represents the extent to which company cash flow from all internal sources have been sufficient to cover all internal needs."[17]

b. Cash Flow Ratios

S&P uses the following cash flow ratios (based on its cash flow definitions described above) in analyzing a company in addition to the measures described earlier for coverage ratios:

$$\frac{\text{Funds from operations}}{\text{Total debt (adjusted for off-balance sheet liabilities)}}$$

$$\frac{\text{Free operating cash flow} + \text{Interest}}{\text{Interest}}$$

$$\frac{\text{Free operating cash flow} + \text{Interest}}{\text{Interest} + \text{Annual principal repayment obligation}}$$

(the above ratio is referred to as the "debt service coverage ratio")

---

[15] *Corporate Ratings Criteria*, p. 27.

[16] One of the most popular measures of cash flow in equity analysis is the "free cash flow." This cash flow measure is defined as "the cash flow available to the company's suppliers of capital after all operating expenses (including taxes) have been paid and necessary investments in working capital (e.g., inventory) and fixed capital (e.g., equipment) have been made." (See, John D. Stowe, Thomas R. Robinson, Jerald E. Pinto, and Dennis W. McLeavey, *Analysis of Equity Investments: Valuation* [Charlottesville, VA: Association for Investment Management and Research, 2002], p. 115.) Analysts will make different adjustments to the statement of cash flows to obtain the free cash flow depending on the accounting information that is available. The procedure for calculating free cash flow starting with net income or statement of cash flows is explained in Stowe, Robinson, Pinto, and McLeavey, *Analysis of Equity Investments: Valuation*, pp. 119–124.

[17] *Corporate Ratings Criteria*, p. 27.

$$\frac{\text{Total debt}}{\text{Discretionary cash flow}}$$

(the above ratio is called the "debt payback period")

$$\frac{\text{Funds from operations}}{\text{Capital spending requirements}}$$

The particular cash flow ratios that S&P focuses on depend on the type of company being analyzed. According to S&P:

> Where long-term viability is more assured (i.e., higher in the rating spectrum) there can be greater emphasis on the level of funds from operations and its relation to total debt burden. These measures clearly differentiate between levels of protection over time. Focusing on debt service coverage and free cash flow becomes more critical in the analysis of a weaker company. Speculative-grade issuers typically face near-term vulnerabilities, which are better measured by free cash flow ratios.[18]

B. Analysis of Collateral

A corporate debt obligation can be secured or unsecured. In the case of a liquidation, proceeds from a bankruptcy are distributed to creditors based on the absolute priority rule. However, in the case of a reorganization, the absolute priority rule rarely holds. That is, an unsecured creditor may receive distributions for the entire amount of his or her claim and common stockholders may receive something, while a secured creditor may receive only a portion of its claim. The reason is that a reorganization requires approval of all the parties. Consequently, secured creditors are willing to negotiate with both unsecured creditors and stockholders in order to obtain approval of the plan of reorganization.

The question is then, what does a secured position mean in the case of a reorganization if the absolute priority rule is not followed in a reorganization? The claim position of a secured creditor is important in terms of the negotiation process. However, because absolute priority is not followed and the final distribution in a reorganization depends on the bargaining ability of the parties, some analysts place less emphasis on collateral compared to the other factors discussed earlier and covenants discussed next.

We have previously discussed the various types of collateral used for a corporate debt issue and features that analysts should be cognizant of in looking at an investor's secured position. Other important features are covered in our discussion of covenants below.

C. Analysis of Covenants

Covenants deal with limitations and restrictions on the borrower's activities. Some covenants are common to all indentures, such as:

▶ to pay interest, principal, and premium, if any, on a timely basis;

▶ to pay all taxes and other claims when due unless contested in good faith;

---

[18] *Corporate Ratings Criteria*, p. 27.

► to maintain all properties used and useful in the borrower's business in good condition and working order;

► to submit periodic certificates to the trustee stating whether the debtor is in compliance with the loan agreement.

These covenants are called affirmative covenants since they call upon the debtor to make promises to do certain things.

Negative covenants are those which require the borrower not to take certain actions. There are an infinite variety of restrictions that can be placed on borrowers, depending on the type of debt issue, the economics of the industry and the nature of the business, and the lenders' desires. Some of the more common restrictive covenants include various limitations on the company's ability to incur debt, since unrestricted borrowing can lead a company and its debtholders to ruin. Thus, debt restrictions may include limits on the absolute dollar amount of debt that may be outstanding or may require a ratio test—for example, debt may be limited to no more than 60% of total capitalization or that it cannot exceed a certain percentage of net tangible assets.

There may be an interest or fixed charge coverage test. The two common tests are:

► **maintenance test**: This test requires the borrower's ratio of earnings available for interest or fixed charges to be at least a certain minimum figure on each required reporting date (such as quarterly or annually) for a certain preceding period.

► **debt incurrence test**: only comes into play when the company wishes to do additional borrowing. In order to take on additional debt, the required interest or fixed charge coverage figure adjusted for the new debt must be at a certain minimum level for the required period prior to the financing. Debt incurrence tests are generally considered less stringent than maintenance provisions.

There could also be cash flow tests (or cash flow requirements) and working capital maintenance provisions.

Some indentures may prohibit subsidiaries from borrowing from all other companies except the parent. Indentures often classify subsidiaries as restricted or unrestricted. Restricted subsidiaries are those considered to be consolidated for financial test purposes; unrestricted subsidiaries (often foreign and certain special-purpose companies) are those excluded from the covenants governing the parent. Often, subsidiaries are classified as unrestricted in order to allow them to finance themselves through outside sources of funds.

Limitations on dividend payments and stock repurchases may be included in indentures. Often, cash dividend payments will be limited to a certain percentage of net income earned after a specific date (often the issuance date of the debt, called the "peg date") plus a fixed amount. Sometimes the dividend formula might allow the inclusion of the net proceeds from the sale of common stock sold after the peg date. In other cases, the dividend restriction might be so worded as to prohibit the declaration and payment of cash dividends if tangible net worth (or other measures, such as consolidated quick assets) declines below a certain amount.

D. Character of a Corporation

Character analysis involves the analysis of the quality of management. In discussing the factors it considers in assigning a credit rating, Moody's Investors Service notes the following regarding the quality of management:[19]

> Although difficult to quantify, management quality is one of the most important factors supporting an issuer's credit strength. When the unexpected occurs, it is a management's ability to react appropriately that will sustain the company's performance.

In assessing management quality, the analysts at Moody's, for example, try to understand the business strategies and policies formulated by management. Following are factors that are considered: 1) strategic direction, 2) financial philosophy, 3) conservatism, 4) track record, 5) succession planning, and 6) control systems.

In recent years, focus has been on the corporate governance of the firm and the role of the board of directors.

1. Corporate Governance

The bylaws are the rules of governance for the corporation. The bylaws define the rights and obligations of officers, members of the board of directors, and shareholders. In most large corporations, it is not possible for each owner to participate in monitoring of the management of the business. Therefore, the owners of a corporation elect a board of directors to represent them in the major business decisions and to monitor the activities of the corporation's management. The board of directors, in turn, appoints and oversees the officers of the corporation. Directors who are also employees of the corporation are called inside directors; those who have no other position within the corporation are outside directors or independent directors.

It is the board of directors that decides whether to hire, retain, or dismiss the chief executive officer, to establish the compensation system for senior management, and to ensure that the proper internal corporate control systems are in place to monitor management. Generally it is believed that the greater the proportion of outside directors, the greater the board independence from the management of the company. The proportion of outside directors on corporate boards varies significantly.

Recently, there have been a number of scandals and allegations regarding the financial information that is being reported to shareholders and the market. Financial results reported in the income statements and balance sheets of some companies indicated much better performance than the true performance or much better financial condition than actual.[20] Along with these financial reporting issues, the independence of the auditors and the role of financial analysts have been brought to the forefront.

The eagerness of managers to present favorable results to shareholders and the market appears to be a major factor in several of the scandals. Personal enrichment at the expense of shareholders seems to explain some of the scandals. Whatever the motivation, chief executive officers (CEOs), chief financial

---

[19] "Industrial Company Rating Methodology," p. 6.

[20] Examples include Xerox, which was forced to restate earnings for several years because it had inflated pre-tax profits by $1.4 billion, Enron, which is accused of inflating earnings and hiding substantial debt, and Worldcom, which failed to properly account for $3.8 billion of expenses.

officers (CFOs), and board members are being held directly accountable for financial disclosures. For example, in 2002, the U.S. Securities and Exchange Commission ordered sworn statements attesting to the accuracy of financial statements. The first deadline for such statements resulted in several companies restating financial results.

The accounting scandals are creating an awareness of the importance of corporate governance, the importance of the independence of the public-accounting auditing function, the role of financial analysts, and the responsibilities of CEOs and CFOs.

2. Agency Problem

Corporate financial theory helps us understand how the abuses that diminish shareholder value arise and the potential for mitigating the abuse. In a publicly traded company, typically the managers of a corporation are not the major owners. The managers make decisions for owners. Thus, the managers act as agents. An agent is a person who acts for—and exerts powers on behalf of—another person or group of persons. The person (or group of persons) the agent represents is referred to as the **principal**. The relationship between the agent and his or her principal is an **agency relationship**. There is an agency relationship between the managers and the shareholders of corporations.[21]

In an agency relationship, the agent is charged with the responsibility of acting for the principal. As a result, it is possible that the agent may not act in the best interest of the principal, but instead act in his or her own self-interest. This is because the agent has his or her own objective of maximizing personal wealth. In a large corporation, for example, the managers may enjoy many fringe benefits, such as golf club memberships, access to private jets, and company cars. These benefits (also called perquisites, or "perks") may be useful in conducting business and may help attract or retain management personnel, but there is room for abuse. The abuse of perquisites imposes costs on the firm—and ultimately on the owners of the firm. There is also a possibility that managers who feel secure in their positions may not bother to expend their best efforts toward the business. Finally, there is the possibility that managers will act in their own self-interest, rather than in the interest of the shareholders when those interests clash. For example, management may fight the acquisition of their firm by some other firm even if the acquisition would benefit shareholders. This is because in most takeovers, the management of the acquired firm generally lose their jobs. Consequently, a manager's self-interest may be placed ahead of those of shareholders who may be offered an attractive price for their stock in the acquisition.

There are costs involved with any effort to minimize the potential for conflict between the principal's interest and the agent's interest. Such costs are called **agency costs**, and they are of three types: monitoring costs, bonding costs, and residual loss.

Monitoring costs are costs incurred by the principal to monitor or limit the actions of the agent. In a corporation, shareholders may require managers to periodically report on their activities via audited accounting statements, which are sent to shareholders. The accountants' fees and the management time lost in preparing such statements are monitoring costs. Another example is the implicit cost incurred when shareholders limit the decision-making power of managers.

---

[21] The seminal paper on the agency-principal relationship in corporate finance is Michael Jensen and William Meckling, "Theory and the Firm: Managerial Behavior, Agency Costs and Ownership Structure," *Journal of Financial Economics* (October 1976), pp. 305–360.

By doing so, the owners may miss profitable investment opportunities; the forgone profit is a monitoring cost.

The board of directors of a corporation has a fiduciary duty to shareholders; that is, the legal responsibility to make decisions (or to see that decisions are made) that are in the best interests of shareholders. Part of that responsibility is to ensure that managerial decisions are also in the best interests of the shareholders. Therefore, at least part of the cost of having directors is a monitoring cost.

Bonding costs are incurred by agents to assure principals that they will act in the principal's best interest. The name comes from the agent's promise or bond to take certain actions. A manager may enter into a contract that requires him or her to stay on with the firm even though another company acquires it; an implicit cost is then incurred by the manager, who forgoes other employment opportunities. Even when monitoring and bonding devices are used, there may be some divergence between the interests of principals and those of agents. The resulting cost, called the **residual loss**, is the implicit cost that results because the principal's and the agent's interests cannot be perfectly aligned even when monitoring and bonding costs are incurred.

3. Stakeholders and Corporate Governance

When managers of a corporation assess a potential investment in a new product, they examine the risks and the potential benefits and costs. Similarly, managers assess current investments for the same purpose; if benefits do not continue to outweigh costs, they will not continue to invest in the product but will shift their investment elsewhere. This is consistent with the goal of shareholder wealth maximization and with the allocative efficiency of the market economy.

Discontinuing investment in an unprofitable business may mean closing down plants, laying off workers, and, perhaps destroying an entire town that depends on the business for income. So decisions to invest or disinvest may affect great numbers of people. All but the smallest business firms are linked in some way to groups of persons who are dependent to a degree on the business. These groups may include suppliers, customers, the community itself, and nearby businesses, as well as employees and shareholders. The various groups of persons that depend on a firm are referred to as its stakeholders; they all have some *stake* in the outcomes of the firm. For example, if the Boeing Company lays off workers or increases production, the effects are felt by Seattle and the surrounding communities.

Can a firm maximize the wealth of shareholders and stakeholders at the same time? Probably. If a firm invests in the production of goods and services that meet the demand of consumers in such a way that benefits exceed costs, then the firm will be allocating the resources of the community efficiently, employing assets in their most productive use. If later the firm must disinvest—perhaps close a plant—it has a responsibility to assist employees and other stakeholders who are affected. Failure to do so could tarnish its reputation, erode its ability to attract new stakeholder groups to new investments, and ultimately act to the detriment of shareholders.

The effects of a firm's actions on others are referred to as **externalities**. Pollution is an important example. Suppose the manufacturer of a product creates air pollution. If the polluting firm acts to reduce this pollution, it incurs a cost that either increases the price of its product or decreases profit and the market value of its stock. If competitors do not likewise incur costs to reduce their pollution, the firm is at a disadvantage and may be driven out of business through competitive pressure.

The firm may try to use its efforts at pollution control to enhance its reputation in the hope that this will lead to a sales increase large enough to make up for the cost of reducing pollution. This is a market solution: the market places a value on the pollution control and rewards the firm (or an industry) for it. If society really believes that pollution is bad and that pollution control is good, the interests of owners and society can be aligned.

It is more likely, however, that pollution control costs will be viewed as reducing owners' wealth. Then firms must be forced to reduce pollution through laws or government regulations. But such laws and regulations also come with a cost—the cost of enforcement. Again, if the benefits of mandatory pollution control outweigh the cost of government action, society is better off. In such a case, if the government requires all firms to reduce pollution, then pollution control costs simply become one of the conditions under which owner wealth-maximizing decisions are to be made.

4. Mitigating the Agency Problem: Standard and Codes of Best Practices for Corporate Governance

Let's focus on just shareholders and the agency problem as it relates to shareholders. There are three ways that shareholders can reduce the likelihood that management will act in its self-interest. First, the compensation of the manager can be tied to the price performance of the firm. Second, managers can be granted a significant equity interest in the company. While an interesting solution, in practice most CEOs and boards have an extremely small equity interest in their firms. For example, a study of 1,000 of the largest U.S. corporations found that the median holdings of CEOs was less than 0.2% of the outstanding equity.[22]

Finally, the firm's internal corporate control systems can provide a means for effectively monitoring the performance and decision-making behavior of management. The timely removal of the CEO by the board of directors who believe that a CEO's performance is not in the best interest of the shareholders is one example of how an internal corporate control system can work. In general, there are several key elements of an internal corporate control system that are necessary for the effective monitoring of management. It is the breakdown of the internal corporate control systems that lead to corporate difficulties and the destruction of shareholder wealth.

Because of the important role placed by the board of directors, the structure and composition of the board is critical for effective corporate governance. The key is to remove the influence of the CEO on board members. This can be done in several ways. First, while there is no optimal board size, the more members the less likely the influence of the CEO. With more board members, a larger number of committees can be formed to deal with important matters of the firm. At a minimum, there should be an auditing committee, a nominating committee (for board members), and a compensation committee. Second, the composition of the board should have a majority of independent directors and the committees should include only independent directors. Third, the nominating committee should develop sound criteria for the selection of potential directors and the retention of current board members. The nominating committee should use the services of recruiting agencies to identify potential independent board members rather than rely on the CEO or management to put forth a slate of candidates. Fourth, the sole chairman of the board of directors should not be the CEO. This

---

[22] Michael Jensen, "The Modern Industrial Revolution, Exist, and the Failure of Internal Control Systems," in Donald H. Chew, Jr. (ed.), *The New Corporate Finance: Second Edition* (New York, NY: McGraw-Hill, 1999).

practice allows the CEO to exert too much influence over board members and set agenda items at board meetings. A compromise position is having the chair of the board being jointly held by the CEO and an independent board member.

The standards and codes of best practice for effective corporate governance are evolving. Unlike securities laws or regulatory requirements (such as exchange listing requirements) which set forth rules that affect corporate governance, standards and codes of best practice go beyond the applicable securities law of the country and are adopted voluntarily by a corporation. The expectation is that the adoption of best practice for corporate governance is a signal to investors about the character of management. The standards of best practice that have become widely accepted as a benchmark are those set forth by the Organisation of Economic Cooperation and Development (OECD) in 1999. The OECD Principles of Corporate Governance cover:

▶ the basic rights of shareholders;

▶ equitable treatment of shareholders;

▶ the role of stakeholders;

▶ disclosure and transparency;

▶ the role of the board of directors.

Other entities that have established standards and codes for corporate governance are the Commonwealth Association for Corporate Governance, the International Corporate Governance Network, and the Business Roundtable. Countries have established their own code and standards using the OECD principles.[23]

A survey of more than 200 institutional investors throughout the world conducted between April and May 2002 by McKinsey & Company found that investors "put corporate governance on a par with financial indicators when evaluating investment decisions."[24] The investors surveyed indicated that they were prepared to pay a premium for the stock of companies that they felt exhibited high governance standards.

5. *Corporate Governance and Bond Ratings*

Empirically, there have been several studies that have investigated the impact of corporate governance on stockholder returns.[25] Our interest in this reading is the relationship between corporate governance and bond ratings (and hence bond yields). A study by Bhojraj and Sengupta investigates this relationship using a large sample of 1,001 industrial bonds for the period 1991–1996.[26]

They note that a firm's likelihood of default can be decomposed into two risks, information risk and agency risk. Information risk is the risk that the available information for evaluating default risk is not credible. There are two studies that support the position that corporate governance mechanisms reduce information risk. Beasley found that the greater the proportion of a board composed of

---

[23] The World Bank updates country progress on corporate governance on its website: www.worldbank.org/html/fpd/privatesector/cg/codes.htm.

[24] *McKinsey & Company's Global Investor Opinion Survey,* May 2002.

[25] For a review of the impact of various corporate governance mechanism on shareholder returns, as well as the experiences and perspective of the California Public Employee Pension Fund (CalPERS), see Chapter 22 in Mark J.P. Anson, *Handbook of Alternative Assets* (Hoboken, NJ: John Wiley & Sons, 2002).

[26] Sanjeev Bhojraj and Partha Sengupta, "Effect of Corporate Governance on Bond Ratings and Yields: The Role of Institutional Investors and Outside Directors," *Journal of Business,* Vol. 76, No. 3 (2003), pp. 455–476.

outsiders, the lower the probability of financial statement fraud.[27] Sengupta found that the higher the quality of corporate disclosure, the higher the bond rating.[28] Agency risk is the risk that management will make decisions in its own self-interest, thereby reducing firm value. There is mixed evidence on how the different types of corporate governance mechanism affect equity returns.

Bhojraj and Sengupta argue that if corporate governance mechanisms reduce agency risk and information risk, the result is that strong corporate governance should be associated with superior bond ratings and therefore lower yields. They find that companies that have greater institutional ownership and stronger outside control of the board benefited from lower bond yields and higher ratings on their new bond issues. Bhojraj and Sengupta conclude that their findings "are consistent with the view that institutional owners and outside directors play an active role in reducing management opportunism and promoting firm value."

They also investigate the effect of governance mechanisms on lower rated corporate bonds. Bhojraj and Sengupta argue that the monitoring role of governance mechanisms would be more important when dealing with such bonds because traditional measures for assessing default risk described earlier in this reading (profitability ratios, debt and coverage ratios, and cash flow measures) may not be informative about future prospects for satisfying debt obligations. Their results are consistent with a greater role for corporate governance mechanisms in reducing default risk for corporations that issue lower rated bonds.

6. Corporate Governance Ratings

Several firms have developed services that assess corporate governance. One type of service provides confidential assessment of the relative strength of a firm's corporate governance practices. The customer for this service is a corporation seeking external evaluations of its current practice. The second is a service that rates (or scores) the corporate governance mechanisms of companies. Generally, these ratings are made public at the option of the company requesting an evaluation. The motivation for developing a corporate governance rating is described by one of the firms that provides this service, Governance Metrics International (GMI), as follows:

> Why are we undertaking this challenge? Our premise is simple: companies that focus on corporate governance and transparency will, over time, generate superior returns and economic performance and lower their cost of capital. The opposite is also true: companies weak in corporate governance and transparency represent increased investment risks and result in a higher cost of capital. Our hope is that GMI research and ratings will help diligent investors and corporations focus on governance on an ongoing basis, identify companies and particular items that need improvement and, just as important, recognize companies that are clearly trying to set the best example with a positive rating.[29]

Firms that provide corporate governance ratings for companies fall into two categories. The first are those that provide ratings for companies within a country. Examples of countries where firms have produced or plan to produce corporate

---

[27] M. Beasley, "An Empirical Analysis of the Relation Between the Board of Director Composition and Financial Statement Fraud," *Accounting Review* (October 1996), pp. 443–465.

[28] Partha Sengupta, "Corporate Disclosure Quality and the Cost of Debt," *Accounting Review* (October 1998), pp. 459–474.

[29] Howard Sherman, "Corporate Governance Ratings," *Corporate Governance* (January 2004), p. 6.

governance ratings are Australia, Brazil, Greece, India, Malaysia, Philippines, Russia, South Korea, and Thailand.[30] The second category includes firms that rate across country borders. Examples of firms that fall into this category are Standard & Poor's, Governance Metrics International, The Corporate Library, and Deminor. We discuss each below.

Standard & Poor's produces a Corporate Governance Score which, at the option of the company, may be disclosed to the public. The score or rating is based on a review of both publicly available information, interviews with senior management and directors, and confidential information that S&P may have available from its credit rating of the corporation's debt.

S&P believes that its Corporate Governance Score helps companies in the following ways:

▶ Benchmark their current governance practices against global best practices;

▶ Communicate both the substance and form of their governance practices to investors, insurers, creditors, customers, regulators, employees, and other stakeholders;

▶ Enhance the investor relations process when used as part of a program designed to highlight governance effectiveness to both potential and current investors, thus differentiating the company from its competitors.[31]

The score is based on four key elements evaluated by S&P:[32]

1. *Ownership structure and external influences*
    ▶ Transparency of ownership structure
    ▶ Concentration and influence of ownership and external stakeholders

2. *Shareholder rights and stakeholder relations*
    ▶ Shareholder meeting and voting procedures
    ▶ Ownership rights and takeover defenses
    ▶ Stakeholder relations

3. *Transparency, disclosure, and audit*
    ▶ Content of public disclosure
    ▶ Timing of and access to public disclosure
    ▶ Audit process

4. *Board structure and effectiveness*
    ▶ Board structure and independence
    ▶ Role and effectiveness of the board
    ▶ Director and senior executive compensation

Based on the S&P's analysis of the four key elements listed above, its assessment of the company's corporate governance practices and policies and how its policies serve shareholders and other stakeholders is reflected in the Corporate Governance Score. The score ranges from 10 (the highest score) to 1 (the lowest score).

---

[30] Sherman, "Corporate Governance Ratings," p. 5.

[31] Standard & Poor's, *Corporate Governance Evaluations & Scores*, undated, p. 2.

[32] *Corporate Governance Evaluations & Scores*, p. 2.

Governance Metrics International (GMI) provides two types of ratings. The first is what GMI refers to as a "basic" rating; the information for this rating is based on publicly available information (regulatory filings, company websites, and news services); no fee is charged to a company receiving a basic rating. The second is a fee-based "comprehensive" rating obtained from interviews with outside directors and senior management. The seven categories analyzed by GMI are shareholder rights, compensation policies, accountability of the board, financial disclosure, market for control, shareholder base, and corporate reputation. There are more than 600 metrics that are used in generating the rating. GMI's scoring model calculates a value between 1 (lowest score) and 10 (highest score). The scores are relative to the other companies that are included in the universe researched by GMI. The ratings provided include a global rating (which allows a comparison to all the companies in the universe), a home market rating (which allows a comparison to all of the companies in the home country or region), and corresponding ratings for each of the seven categories analyzed by GMI.

The Corporate Library (TCL) has a rating service it calls "Board Effectiveness Rating." Rather than using best practice standards or codes in developing its corporate governance indicators, ratings are based on what this firm believes are "proven dynamics indicators of interest to shareholders and investors."[33] The indicators include compensation, outside director shareholdings, board structure and make-up, accounting and audit oversight, and board decision-making. The focus is on "which boards are most likely to enhance and preserve shareholder value, and which boards might actually increase investor risk."[34] The ratings are expressed on a scale ranging from A (highest effectiveness) to F (lowest effectiveness). TCL does not intend for its ratings to be used on a stand-alone basis. Rather, the ratings are intended to improve current investment research methods employed by investors.

Finally, Deminor focuses on corporate governance ratings for Western European firms. The rating is based on 300 corporate governance indicators obtained from public and non-public information provided by the company being rated, as well as on interviews with members of the board of directors and executive committee. The ratings are based on standards that are internationally recognized such as the OECD Principles of Corporate Governance. The four categories analyzed are 1) rights and duties of shareholders, 2) commitment to shareholder value, 3) disclosure on corporate governance, and 4) board structure and functioning. The ratings range from 1 (lowest) to 10 (highest). There is an overall rating and a rating for each of the four categories.

E. Special Considerations for High-Yield Corporate Bonds

The discussion thus far has focused on credit analysis for any issuer regardless of credit rating. There are some unique factors that should be considered in the analysis of high-yield bonds. We will discuss the following:

▶ analysis of debt structure;

▶ analysis of corporate structure;

▶ analysis of covenants.

---

[33] www.thecorporatelibrary.net/products/ratings2003.html.

[34] Indicators that best practice might suggest such as a split chairman of the board/CEO role or a lead independent director are not considered by TCL because the firm does not believe they are significant in improving board effectiveness.

In addition, we will discuss the reasons why an equity analysis approach to high-yield bond issuers is being used.

1. Analysis of Debt Structure

In January 1990, the Association for Investment Management and Research held a conference on high-yield bonds. One of the presenters at the conference was William Cornish, then President of Duff & Phelps Credit Rating Company.[35] In his presentation he identified a unique factor in the credit analysis of high-yield issuers—the characteristics of the types of debt obligations comprising a high-yield issuer's debt structure.[36]

Cornish explained why it was necessary for an analyst to examine a high-yield issuer's debt structure. At the time of his presentation, new types of bonds were being introduced into the high-yield market such as deferred coupon bonds. He noted that the typical debt structure of a high-yield issuer includes:

- ▶ bank debt;
- ▶ brokers loans or "bridge loans;"
- ▶ reset notes;
- ▶ senior debt;
- ▶ senior subordinated debt;
- ▶ subordinated debt (payment in kind bonds).

Cornish then went on to explain the importance of understanding the characteristics of the diverse debt obligations that are included in a typical high-yield debt structure.

Consider first bank loans. While investment-grade issuers also have bank debt in their capital structure, high-yield issuers rely to a greater extent on this form of debt because of a lack of alternative financing sources. Banks loans have three key characteristics. First, holders of bank debt have a priority over other debt holders on the firm's assets. Second, bank debt is typically short-term (usually it is not greater than two years). Finally, the rate on bank debt floats with the level of interest rates.

There are three implications of these characteristics of bank debt for the analysis of the credit-worthiness of high-yield issuers. First, because the cost of this source of debt financing is affected by changes in short-term interest rates, the analyst must incorporate changing interest rate scenarios into cash flow projections. A rise in short-term interest rates can impose severe cash flow problems for an issuer heavily financed by bank debt.

Second, because the debt is short term, bank debt must be repaid in the near future. The challenge that the analyst faces is determining where the funds will be obtained to pay off maturing bank debt. There are three sources available:

1. repayment from operating cash flow
2. refinancing
3. sale of assets

---

[35] Duff & Phelps was acquired by Fitch.

[36] William A. Cornish, "Unique Factors in the Credit Analysis of High-Yield Bonds," in Frank K. Reilly (ed.), *High-Yield Bonds: Analysis and Risk Assessment* (Charlottesville, VA: Association for Investment Management and Research, 1990).

Typically, it is a combination of these three sources that a high-yield issuer will use. The implication is that the analyst must carefully examine the timing and amount of maturing bank debt and consider the sources for repayment.

If the repayment is to come from operations, the projections of cash flow from operations become even more critical than for a high-grade issuer which can rely on a wider range of funding sources such as commercial paper. When refinancing is the source of funds for loan repayment, there is the issue discussed earlier that future conditions in the financial market must be incorporated into the analyst's projections in order to assess future funding costs.

If the source of the loan repayment is the sale of assets, the analyst must consider which assets will be sold and how the sale of such assets will impact future cash flow from operations. If key assets must be sold to pay off maturing bank debt, management is adversely impacting the ability to repay other debt in the future from cash flow from operations. In leveraged buyouts, the new management will have a specific plan for the disposal of certain assets in order to pay off bank debt and other debt or related payments. One credit analyst, Jane Tripp Howe, suggests that the analyst ask the following questions regarding asset sales:[37]

> Can the company meet its cash obligations if the sale of assets is delayed?
> How liquid are the assets that are scheduled for sale?
> Are the appraised values for these assets accurate?

Banks will not provide short-term funds where there are insufficient assets to cover a loan in the case of liquidation. If short-term to intermediate-term funds are needed, a high-yield issuer will turn to broker loans (or bridge loans) and/or reset notes. A reset note is a security where the coupon rate is reset periodically such that the security price will trade at some specified premium above par value. The presence of reset notes in the debt structure is of particular concern to the analyst for two reasons. First, there is the need to analyze the impact of future interest rates and spreads to assess the impact of higher borrowing costs. Second, to avoid a higher reset rate when interest rates rise due to rising interest rates in general and/or because of a higher spread demanded by the market for the particular issuer, the issuer may seek to dispose of assets. Again the assets sold may have an adverse impact on future cash flow from operations.

While there are typically longer term bonds referred to as "senior bonds" in a high-yield issuer's debt structure, the term "senior bonds" is misleading in the presence of bank loans. Moreover, there are deferred coupon bonds. One such bond structure is a zero-coupon bond. Deferred coupon bonds permit the issuer to postpone interest payment to some future year. As a result, the interest burden is placed on future cash flow to meet the interest obligations. Because of this burden, the presence of deferred coupon bonds may impair the ability of the issuer to improve its credit quality in future periods. Moreover, if senior bonds have deferred coupon payments, the subordinated bonds will be adversely affected over time as the amount of senior bonds increases over time relative to the amount of subordinated bonds. For example, one type of deferred coupon bond that was commonly issued at one time was the payment-in-kind (PIK) bond. With this bond structure, a high-yield issuer has the option to either pay interest in cash or pay the equivalent of interest with another bond with the same coupon rate. If the issuer does not have the ability to pay the interest in cash,

---

[37] Jane Tripp Howe, "Credit Considerations in Evaluating High-Yield Bonds," Chapter 21 in Frank J. Fabozzi (ed.), *Handbook of Fixed Income Securities* (Burr Ridge, IL: Irwin Professional Publishing, 1997), p. 408.

payment with another bond will increase future interest expense and thereby adversely impact the issuer's future cash flow. If the PIK bonds are senior bonds, subordinated bonds are adversely affected over time as more senior bonds are added to the capital structure and future interest expense is increased further.

2. Analysis of Corporate Structure

High-yield issuers usually have a holding company structure. The assets to pay creditors of the holding company will come from the operating subsidiaries. Cornish explains why it is critical to analyze the corporate structure for a high-yield issuer. Specifically, the analyst must understand the corporate structure in order to assess how cash will be passed between subsidiaries and the parent company and among the subsidiaries. The corporate structure may be so complex that the payment structure can be confusing.

Cornish provides an illustration of this. At the time of his presentation (January 1990), Farley Inc. had the following debt structure: senior subordinated debt, subordinated notes, and junior subordinated debt. The question raised by Cornish was where Farley Inc. was going to obtain cash flow to make payments to its creditors. One possibility was to obtain funds from its operating subsidiaries. At the time, Farley Inc. had three operating subsidiaries: Fruit of the Loom, Acme Boot, and West Point Pepperell. An examination of the debt structure of Fruit of the Loom (20% owned by Farley Inc.) indicated that there was bank debt and no intercompany loans were permitted. While there were restrictions on dividend payments, none were being paid at the time. An examination of the Acme Boot (100% owned by Farley Inc.) showed that there was bank debt, and while there were restrictions but no prohibitions on intercompany loans, Farley Inc. had in fact put cash into this operating subsidiary. Finally, West Point Pepperell (95% owned by Farley Inc.) had bridge loans that restricted asset sales and dividend payments. Moreover, any payments that could be made to Farley Inc. from West Point Pepperell had to be such that they would not violate West Point Pepperell's financial ratio requirements imposed by its bridge loan. The key point of the illustration is that an analyst evaluating the ability of Farley Inc. to meet its obligations to creditors would have to look very closely at the three operating subsidiaries. Just looking at financial ratios for the entire holding company structure would not be adequate. At the time, it was not likely that the three operating subsidiaries would be able to make any contribution to assist the parent company in paying off its creditors.

3. Analysis of Covenants

While an analyst should of course consider covenants when evaluating any bond issue (investment grade or high yield), it is particularly important for the analysis of high-yield issuers. The importance of understanding covenants was summarized by one high-yield portfolio manager, Robert Levine, as follows:[38]

> Covenants provide insight into a company's strategy. As part of the credit process, one must read covenants within the context of the corporate strategy. It is not sufficient to hire a lawyer to review the covenants because a lawyer might miss the critical factors necessary to make the appropriate decision. Also, loopholes in covenants often provide clues about the intentions of management teams.

---

[38] Robert Levine, "Unique Factors in Managing High-Yield Bond Portfolios," in *High-Yield Bonds*, p. 35.

4. Equity Analysis Approach

Historically, the return on high-yield bonds has been greater than that of high-grade corporate bonds but less than that of common stocks. The risk (as measured in terms of the standard deviation of returns) has been greater than the risk of high-grade bonds but less than that of common stock. Moreover, high-yield bond returns have been found to be more highly correlated to equity returns than to investment grade bond returns. This is why, for example, managers hedging high-yield bond portfolios have found that a combination of stock index futures contracts and Treasury futures contracts has offered a better hedging alternative than just hedging with Treasury bond futures.[39]

Consequently, some portfolio managers strongly believe that high-yield bond analysis should be viewed from an equity analyst's perspective. As Stephen Esser notes:[40]

> Using an equity approach, or at least considering the hybrid nature of high-yield debt, can either validate or contradict the results of traditional credit analysis, causing the analyst to dig further.

He further states:[41]

> For those who work with investing in high-yield bonds, whether issued by public or private companies, dynamic, equity-oriented analysis is invaluable. If analysts think about whether they would want to buy a particular high-yield company's stock and what will happen to the future equity value of that company, they have a useful approach because, as equity values go up, so does the equity cushion beneath the company's debt. All else being equal, the bonds then become better credits and should go up in value relative to competing bond investments.

We will not review the equity analysis framework here. But, there has been strong sentiment growing in the investment community that an equity analysis approach will provide a better framework for high-yield bond analysis than a traditional credit approach.

F. Credit Analysis of Non-Corporate Bonds

In this section we will look at the key factors analyzed in assessing the credit of the following non-corporate bonds:

▶ asset-backed securities and non-agency mortgage-backed securities;

▶ municipal bonds;

▶ sovereign bonds.

---

[39] Kenneth S. Choie, "How to Hedge a High-Yield Bond Portfolio," Chapter 13 in Frank J. Fabozzi (ed.), *The New High-Yield Debt Market* (New York, NY: HarperBusiness, 1990).

[40] Stephen F. Esser, "High-Yield Bond Analysis: The Equity Perspective," in Ashwinpaul C. Sondhi (ed.), *Credit Analysis of Nontraditional Debt Securities* (Charlottesville, VA: Association for Investment Management and Research, 1995), p. 47.

[41] Esser, "High-Yield Bond Analysis: The Equity Perspective," p. 54.

1. Asset-Backed Securities and Non-Agency Mortgage-Backed Securities

Asset-backed securities and non-agency mortgage-backed securities expose investors to credit risk. The three nationally recognized statistical rating organizations rate asset-backed securities. We begin with the factors considered by rating agencies in assigning ratings to asset-backed securities. Then we will discuss how the agencies differ with respect to rating asset-backed securities versus corporate bonds.

a. Factors Considered by Rating Agencies

In analyzing credit risk, the rating companies focus on: 1) credit quality of the collateral, 2) quality of the seller/servicer, 3) cash flow stress and payment structure, and 4) legal structure.[42] We discuss each below.

i. Credit Quality of the Collateral   Analysis of the credit quality of the collateral depends on the asset type. The rating companies will look at the underlying borrower's ability to pay and the borrower's equity in the asset. The latter will be a key determinant as to whether the underlying borrower will default or sell the asset and pay off a loan. The rating companies will look at the experience of the originators of the underlying loans and will assess whether the loans underlying a specific transaction have the same characteristics as the experience reported by the issuer.

The concentration of loans is examined. The underlying principle of asset securitization is that the large number of borrowers in a pool will reduce the credit risk via diversification. If there are a few borrowers in the pool that are significant in size relative to the entire pool balance, this diversification benefit can be lost, resulting in a higher level of default risk. This risk is called concentration risk. In such instances, rating companies will set concentration limits on the amount or percentage of receivables from any one borrower. If the concentration limit at issuance is exceeded, the issue will receive a lower credit rating than if the concentration limit was not exceeded. If after issuance the concentration limit is exceeded, the issue may be downgraded.

Based on its analysis of the collateral and other factors described below, a rating company will determine the amount of credit enhancement necessary for an issue to receive a particular rating. Credit enhancement levels are determined relative to a specific rating desired for a security and can be either internal or external. External credit enhancement can be either insurance, corporate guarantees, letters of credit, or cash collateral reserves. Internal credit enhancements include reserve funds, overcollateralization, and senior/subordinated structures.

ii. Quality of the Seller/Servicer   All loans must be serviced. Servicing involves collecting payments from borrowers, notifying borrowers who may be delinquent, and, when necessary, recovering and disposing of the collateral if the borrower does not make loan repayments by a specified time. These responsibilities are fulfilled by a third-party to an asset-backed securities transaction called a servicer. The servicer may be the originator of the loans used as the collateral.

In addition to the administration of the loan portfolio as just described, the servicer is responsible for distributing the proceeds collected from the borrowers to the different bondholders according to the payment priorities. Where there are floating-rate securities in the transaction, the servicer will determine the

---

[42] Suzanne Michaud, "A Rating Agency Perspective on Asset-Backed Securities," Chapter 16 in Anand K. Bhattacharya and Frank J. Fabozzi (eds.), *Asset-Backed Securities* (New Hope, PA: Frank J. Fabozzi Associates, 1997).

interest rate for the period. The servicer may also be responsible for advancing payments when there are delinquencies in payments (that are likely to be collected in the future), resulting in a temporary shortfall in the payments that must be made to the bondholders.

The role of the servicer is critical in a securitization transaction. Therefore, rating agencies look at the ability of a servicer to perform its duties before assigning a rating to the bonds in a transaction. For example, the following factors are reviewed when evaluating servicers: servicing history, experience, underwriting standard for loan originations, servicing capabilities, human resources, financial condition, and growth/competition/business environment.

As explained in the reading on the asset-backed sector of the bond market, the issuer is the special purpose vehicle or trust. There are no employees. The trust simply has loans and receivables. The servicer therefore plays an important role in assuring that the payments are made to the bondholders. Shortly we will see how the characteristics of the servicer affect the way in which an issue is evaluated in terms of credit quality in comparison to the rating of a corporate bond issue.

iii. Cash Flow Stress and Payment Structure   As explained in the reading on the asset-backed sector of the bond market, the waterfall describes how the cash flow (i.e., interest and principal payments) from the collateral will be distributed to pay trustee fees, servicing fees, other administrative fees, and interest and principal to the bondholders in the structure. In determining a rating for bond class, the process begins with an analysis of the cash flow from the collateral under different assumptions about losses and delinquencies and economic scenarios established by the rating agency. (That is, the rating agencies perform a scenario analysis.) Then in each scenario, the cash flow is distributed to all bond classes in accordance with the structure's waterfall. Once a determination of what loss to the different bonds in the structure can occur, a rating can be assigned.

iv. Legal Structure   A corporation using structured financing seeks a rating on the securities it issues that is higher than its own corporate bond rating. If that is not possible, the corporation seeking funds would be better off simply issuing a corporate bond.

The corporation seeking funds will sell collateral to a special purpose vehicle (SPV). The corporation selling the collateral to the SPV is called the "seller." It is the SPV that issues the securities and is therefore referred to as the "issuer." The SPV is used so that the collateral is no longer an asset of the corporation that sold it and therefore available to the seller's creditors. The key in a securitization is to protect the buyers of the asset-backed securities issued by the SPV from having a bankruptcy judge redirect the collateral to the creditors of the selling corporation. Consequently, the rating agencies examine the legal structure and the underlying legal documents to assure that this will not happen in a bankruptcy.

b. Corporate Bond versus Asset-Backed Securities Credit Analysis

Let's look at how the rating of an asset-backed security differs from that of a corporate bond issue. To understand the difference, it is important to appreciate how the cash flow that must be generated differs for a corporate bond issue and a securitization transaction from which the asset-backed securities are created.

In a corporate bond issue, management through its operations must undertake the necessary activities that will produce revenues and collect revenues. Management will incur costs in creating products and services. These costs include management compensation, employee salaries, the costs of raw materials, and financial costs. Consequently, in evaluating the credit risk of a corporate bond issue, an analyst will examine the factors discussed earlier in this reading regarding the corporation's capacity to pay and the corporation's character.

In contrast, in a securitization transaction, there are assets (loans or receivables) that are to be collected and distributed to bondholders (i.e., investors in the asset-backed securities). There are no operating or business risks such as the competitive environment or existence of control systems that are needed to assess the cash flow. What is important is the quality of the collateral in generating the cash flow needed to make interest and principal payments. The assurance of cash flow is based on different scenarios regarding defaults and delinquencies that the rating agencies will review. The rating agencies will review the likelihood of the cash flow based on different scenarios regarding defaults and delinquencies. It is the greater predictability of the cash flow in an asset-backed security transaction due to the absence of operational risks that distinguishes it from a corporate bond issue.

In a "true" securitization transaction, the role of the servicer is to simply collect the cash flow. There is no active management with respect to the collateral as is the case of the management necessary to operate a corporation to generate cash flow to pay bondholders. Standard & Poor's defines a "true securitization" as follows:

> In a true securitization, repayment is not dependent on the ability of the servicer to replenish the pool with new collateral or to perform more than routine administrative functions.[43]

There are securitization transactions where the role of the servicer is more than administrative. Where the role of the servicer is more than administrative, Standard & Poor's, for example, refers to such transactions as hybrid transactions. This is because such transactions have elements of an asset-backed security transaction and a corporation performing a service. According to Standard & Poor's:

> In a hybrid transaction, the role of the servicer is akin to that of a business manager. The hybrid servicer performs not only administrative duties, as in a true securitization, but also . . . [other] services that are needed to generate cash flow for debt service.[44]

Moreover, Standard & Poor's notes that:

> Unlike a true securitization, where the servicer is a fungible entity replaceable with few, if any, consequences to the transaction, bondholders depend on the expertise of the hybrid servicer for repayment. . . . Not coincidentally, these are the same attributes that form the basis of a corporate rating of the hybrid servicer. They also explain the rating linkage between the securitization and its hybrid servicer.[45]

Standard & Poor's provides an illustration of the distinction between a true asset-backed securitization transaction and one requiring a more active role for the servicer.[46] Consider a railcar company that has several hundred leases and

---

[43] Standard & Poor's, "Rating Hybrid Securitizations," *Structured Finance* (October 1999), p. 2.

[44] "Rating Hybrid Securitizations," p. 3.

[45] "Rating Hybrid Securitizations," p. 3.

[46] "Rating Hybrid Securitizations," p. 3.

the leases are with a pool of diversified highly rated companies. Suppose that each lease is for 10 years and it is the responsibility of the customers—not the railcar company—to perform the necessary maintenance on the leased railcars. If there is an asset-backed security transaction backed by these leases and the term of the transaction is 10 years, then the role of the servicer is minimal. Since the leases are for 10 years and the securities issued are for 10 years, the servicer is just collecting the lease payments and distributing them to the holders of the securities. In such a transaction, it *is* possible for this issue to obtain a high investment-grade rating as a true asset-backed security transaction.

Suppose we change the assumptions as follows. The securities issued are for 25 years, not 10 years. Also assume that the railcar company, not the customers, is responsible for the servicing. Now the role of the servicer changes. The servicer will be responsible for finding new companies to release the railcars to when the original leases terminate in 10 years. This is necessary because the securities issued have a maturity of 25 years but the original leases only cover payments to securityholders for the first 10 years. It is the releasing of the railcars that is required for the last 15 years. The servicer under this new set of assumptions is also responsible for the maintenance of the railcars leased. Thus, the servicer must be capable of maintaining the railcars or have ongoing arrangements with one or more companies that have the ability to perform such maintenance.

How do rating agencies evaluate hybrid transactions? These transactions will be rated both in terms of a standard methodology for rating an asset-backed security transaction and using a "quasi-corporate approach" (in the words of Standard & Poor's) which involves an analysis of the servicer. The relative weight of the evaluations in assigning a rating to an asset-backed security transaction will depend on the involvement of the servicer. The more important the role of the servicer, the more weight will be assigned to the quasi-corporate approach analysis.

2. Municipal Bonds

We have previously discussed municipal bonds available in the United States—tax-backed debt and revenue bonds. However, municipal governments in other countries are making greater use of bonds with similar structures to raise funds. Below we discuss the factors that should be considered in assessing the credit risk of an issue.

a. Tax-Backed Debt

In assessing the credit risk of tax-backed debt, there are four basic categories that should be considered. The first category includes information on the issuer's debt structure to determine the overall debt burden.[47] The second category relates to the issuer's ability and political discipline to maintain sound budgetary policy. The focus of attention here usually is on the issuer's general operating funds and whether it has maintained at least balanced budgets over three to five years. The third category involves determining the specific local taxes and intergovernmental revenues available to the issuer, as well as obtaining historical information both on tax collection rates, which are important when looking at property tax levies, and on the dependence of local budgets on specific revenue sources. The final category of information necessary to the credit analysis is an assessment of the issuer's overall socioeconomic environment. The determinations that have to be made here include trends of local employment distribution

---

[47] For municipalities, the debt burden usually is composed of the debt per capita as well as the debt as percentages of real estate valuations and personal incomes.

and composition, population growth, real estate property valuation, and personal income, among other economic factors.

b. Revenue Bonds

Revenue bonds are issued for either project or enterprise financings where the bond issuers pledge to the bondholders the revenues generated by the operating projects financed, or for general public-purpose financings in which the issuers pledge to the bondholders the tax and revenue resources that were previously part of the general fund.

While there are numerous security structures for revenue bonds, the underlying principle in assessing an issuer's credit-worthiness is whether the project being financed will generate sufficient cash flows to satisfy the obligations due bondholders. Consequently, the analysis of revenue bonds is similar to the analysis of corporate bonds.

In assessing the credit risk of revenue bonds, the trust indenture and legal opinion should provide legal comfort in the following bond-security areas: 1) the limits of the basic security, 2) the flow-of-funds structure, 3) the rate, or user-charge, covenant, 4) the priority-of-revenue claims, 5) the additional-bonds tests, and 6) other relevant covenants.

i. Limits of the Basic Security   The trust indenture and legal opinion should explain the nature of the revenues for the bonds and how they realistically may be limited by federal, state, and local laws and procedures. The importance of this is that while most revenue bonds are structured and appear to be supported by identifiable revenue streams, those revenues sometimes can be negatively affected directly by other levels of government.

ii. Flow-of-Funds Structure for Revenue Bonds   For a revenue bond, the revenue of the enterprise is pledged to service the debt of the issue. The details of how revenue received by the enterprise will be disbursed are set forth in the trust indenture. Typically, the flow of funds for a revenue bond is as follows. First, all revenues from the enterprise are put into a revenue fund. It is from the revenue fund that disbursements for expenses are made to the following funds: operation and maintenance fund, sinking fund, debt service reserve fund, renewal and replacement fund, reserve maintenance fund, and surplus fund.

There are structures in which it is legally permissible for others to tap the revenues of the enterprise prior to the disbursement set forth in the flow-of-funds structure just described. For example, it is possible that the revenue bond could be structured such that the revenue is first applied to the general obligation of the municipality that has issued the bond.

Operations of the enterprise have priority over the servicing of the issue's debt, and cash needed to operate and maintain the enterprise is deposited from the revenue fund into the operation and maintenance fund. The pledge of revenue to the bondholders is a net revenue pledge, "net" meaning after operation expenses, so cash required to service the debt is deposited next into the sinking fund. Disbursements are then made to bondholders as specified in the trust indenture. Any remaining cash is then distributed to the reserve funds.

The purpose of the debt service reserve fund is to accumulate cash to cover any shortfall of future revenue to service the issue's debt. The specific amount that must be deposited is stated in the trust indenture. The function of the renewal and replacement fund is to accumulate cash for regularly scheduled major repairs and equipment replacement. The function of the reserve maintenance fund is to accumulate cash for extraordinary maintenance or replacement costs that might arise. Finally, if any cash remains after disbursement for operations, debt servicing, and reserves, it is deposited in the surplus fund. The entity issuing the bond can use the cash in this fund in any way it deems appropriate.

iii. Rate, or User-Charge, Covenants   There are various restrictive covenants included in the trust indenture for a revenue bond to protect the bondholders. A rate covenant (or user-charge covenant) dictates how charges will be sct on the product or service sold by the enterprise. The covenant could specify that the minimum charges be set so as to satisfy both expenses and debt servicing, or to yield a higher rate to provide for a certain amount of reserves.

iv. Priority-of-Revenue Claims   The legal opinion as summarized in the official statement should clearly indicate whether or not others can legally tap the revenue of the issuer even before they start passing through the issuer's flow-of-funds structure.

v. Additional-Bonds Test   An additional-bonds test covenant indicates whether additional bonds with the same lien (i.e., claim against property) may be issued. If additional bonds with the same lien may be issued, the conditions that must first be satisfied are specified. Other covenants specify that the facility may not be sold, the amount of insurance to be maintained, requirements for recordkeeping and for the auditing of the enterprise's financial statements by an independent accounting firm, and requirements for maintaining the facilities in good order.

vi. Other Relevant Covenants   There are other relevant covenants for the bond-holder's protection that the trust indenture and legal opinion should cover. These usually include pledges by the issuer of the bonds to have insurance on the project, to have accounting records of the issuer annually audited by an outside certified public accountant, to have outside engineers annually review the condition of the facility, and to keep the facility operating for the life of the bonds.

c. Corporate versus Municipal Bond Credit Analysis

The credit analysis of municipal bonds involves the same factors and quantitative measures as in corporate credit analysis. For tax-backed debt, the analysis of the character of the public officials is the same as that of the analysis of the character of management for a corporate bond. The analysis of the ability to pay in the case of tax-backed debt involves looking at the ability of the issuing entity to generate taxes and fees. As a corporate analyst would look at the composition of the revenues and profits by product line for a corporation, the municipal analyst will look at employment, industry, and real estate valuation trends needed to generate taxes and fees.

The credit analysis of municipal revenue bonds is identical to that of a corporate bond analysis. Effectively, the enterprise issuing a municipal revenue bond must generate cash flow from operations to satisfy the bond payments. For example, here are the types of questions that a municipal analyst evaluating a toll road, bridge, or tunnel revenue bond would ask. As you read these questions you will see that they are the same types of questions that a corporate analyst would ask in evaluating a corporate issuer if it could issue a bond for a toll road, bridge, or tunnel.[48]

1. What is the traffic history and how sensitive is the demand to the toll charged? Equivalently, does the toll road, bridge, or tunnel provide a vital

---

[48] Sylvan G. Feldstein and Frank J. Fabozzi, *The Dow Jones-Irwin Guide to Municipal Bonds* (Homewood, IL: Dow Jones-Irwin, 1987), p. 72.

transportation link or does it face competition from interstate highways, toll-free bridges, or mass transportation?

2. How well is the facility maintained? Has the issuer established a maintenance reserve fund at a reasonable level to use for such repair work as road resurfacing and bridge painting?

3. What is the history of labor-management relations, and can public employee strikes substantially reduce toll collections?

The covenants that are unique to a municipal revenue bond and impact the credit analysis are the rate covenants and the priority-of-revenue covenants. The former dictates how the user charges will be set to meet the bond obligations. Also, just as in the case of a bond issue of a regulated corporate entity, restrictions on pricing must be recognized. In a municipal revenue bond the analyst must determine whether changes in the user charge require approval of other governmental entities such as the governor or state legislature. Priority-of-revenue covenants specify if other parties can legally tap the revenue of the enterprise before the revenue can be passed through to bondholders.

3. Sovereign Bonds

The debt of national governments is rated by nationally recognized statistical rating organizations. These ratings are referred to as sovereign ratings. Standard & Poor's and Moody's rate sovereign debt. We will first look at the factors considered by rating agencies in assigning sovereign ratings and then look at a structured approach that an analyst familiar with corporate credit analysis can use in assessing sovereign credits.

The categories used by S&P in deriving their ratings are listed in Exhibit 1. The two general categories are economic risk and political risk. The former category represents S&P's assessment of the ability of a government to satisfy its obligations. Both quantitative and qualitative analyses are used in assessing economic risk. Political risk is an assessment of the willingness of a government to satisfy its obligations. A government may have the ability to pay, but may be unwilling to pay. Political risk is assessed based on qualitative analysis of the economic and political factors that influence a government's economic policies.

There are two ratings assigned to each national government. One is a local currency debt rating and the other is a foreign currency debt rating. The reason for distinguishing between the two types of debt is that historically, the default frequency differs by the currency denomination of the debt. Specifically, defaults have been greater on foreign currency denominated debt.[49]

The reason for the difference in default rates for local currency debt and foreign currency debt is that if a government is willing to raise taxes and control its domestic financial system, it can generate sufficient local currency to meet its local currency debt obligation. This is not the case with foreign currency denominated debt. A national government must purchase foreign currency to meet a debt obligation in that foreign currency and therefore has less control with respect to its exchange rate. Thus, a significant depreciation of the local currency relative to a foreign currency in which a debt obligation is denominated will impair a national government's ability to satisfy a foreign currency obligation.

The implication of this is that the factors S&P analyzes in assessing the creditworthiness of a national government's local currency debt and foreign currency

---

[49] David T. Beers and Marie Cavanaugh, "Sovereign Ratings: A Primer," Chapter 6 in Frank J. Fabozzi and Alberto Franco (eds.), *Handbook of Emerging Fixed Income & Currency Markets* (New Hope, PA: Frank J. Fabozzi Associates, 1997).

EXHIBIT 1	S&P Sovereign Ratings Methodology Profile

Political Risk

▶ Form of government and adaptability of political institutions
▶ Extent of popular participation
▶ Orderliness of leadership succession
▶ Degree of consensus on economic policy objectives
▶ Integration in global trade and financial system
▶ Internal and external security risks

Income and Economic Structure

▶ Living standards, income, and wealth distribution
▶ Market, non-market economy
▶ Resource endowments, degree of diversification

Economic Growth Prospects

▶ Size, composition of savings, and investment
▶ Rate, pattern of economic growth

Fiscal Flexibility

▶ General government operating and total budget balances
▶ Tax competitiveness and tax-raising flexibility
▶ Spending pressures

Public Debt Burden

▶ General government financial assets
▶ Public debt and interest burden
▶ Currency composition, structure of public debt
▶ Pension liabilities
▶ Contingent liabilities

Price Stability

▶ Trends in price inflation
▶ Rates of money and credit growth
▶ Exchange rate policy
▶ Degree of central bank autonomy

Balance of Payments Flexibility

▶ Impact on external accounts of fiscal and monetary policies
▶ Structure of the current account
▶ Composition of capital flows

External Debt and Liquidity

▶ Size and currency composition of public external debt
▶ Importance of banks and other public and private entities as contingent liabilities of the sovereign
▶ Maturity structure and debt service burden
▶ Debt service track record
▶ Level, composition of reserves and other public external assets

Source: David T. Beers and Marie Cavanaugh, "Sovereign Ratings: A Primer," Chapter 6 in Frank J. Fabozzi and Alberto Franco (eds.), *Handbook of Emerging Fixed Income & Currency Markets* (New Hope, PA: Frank J. Fabozzi Associates, 1997), p. 67.

debt will differ to some extent. In assessing the credit quality of local currency debt, for example, S&P emphasizes domestic government policies that foster or impede timely debt service. The key factors looked at by S&P are:

▶ the stability of political institutions and degree of popular participation in the political process;

▶ income and economic structure;

▶ fiscal policy and budgetary flexibility;

▶ monetary policy and inflation pressures; and

▶ public debt burden and debt service track record.[50]

For foreign currency debt, credit analysis by S&P focuses on the interaction of domestic and foreign government policies. S&P analyzes a country's balance of payments and the structure of its external balance sheet. The area of analysis with respect to its external balance sheet are the net public debt, total net external debt, and net external liabilities.

---

[50] Beers and Cavanaugh, "Sovereign Credit Ratings: A Primer," p. 68.

CREDIT SCORING MODELS 4

The previous section described the traditional ratios and other measures that credit analysts use in assessing default risk. Several researchers have used these measures as input to assess the default risk of issuers using the statistical technique of multiple discriminant analysis (MDA). This statistical technique is primarily a classification technique that is helpful in distinguishing between or among groups of objects and in identifying the characteristics of objects responsible for their inclusion in one or another group. One of the chief advantages of MDA is that it permits a simultaneous consideration of a large number of characteristics and does not restrict the investigator to a sequential evaluation of each individual attribute. For example, MDA permits a credit analyst studying ratings of corporate bonds to examine, at one time, the total and joint impact on ratings of multiple financial ratios, financial measures, and qualitative factors. Thus, the analyst is freed from the cumbersome and possibly misleading task of looking at each characteristic in isolation from the others. MDA seeks to form groups that are internally as similar as possible but that are as different from one another as possible.

From the above description of MDA it can be seen why it has been applied to problems of why bonds get the ratings they do and what variables seem best able to account for a bond's rating. Moreover, MDA has been used as a predictor of bankruptcy. While the steps involved in MDA for predicting bond ratings and corporate bankruptcies are a specialist topic, we will discuss the results of the work by Edward Altman, the primary innovator of MDA for predicting corporate bankruptcy.[51] The models of Altman and others involved in this area are updated periodically. Our purpose here is only to show what an MDA model looks like.

In one of Altman's earlier models, referred to as the "Z-score model," he found that the following MDA could be used to predict corporate bankruptcy:[52]

$$Z = 1.2 \, X_1 + 1.4 \, X_2 + 3.3 \, X_3 + 0.6 \, X_4 + 1.0 \, X_5$$

where

X_1 = Working capital/Total assets (in decimal)
X_2 = Retained earnings/Total assets (in decimal)
X_3 = Earnings before interest and taxes/Total assets (in decimal)
X_4 = Market value of equity/Total liabilities (in decimal)
X_5 = Sales/Total assets (number of times)
Z = Z-score

Given the value of the five variables for a given firm, a Z-score is computed. It is the Z-score that is used to classify firms with respect to whether or not there is potentially a serious credit problem that would lead to bankruptcy. Specifically, Altman found that Z-scores less than 1.81 indicated a firm with serious credit problems while a Z-score in excess of 3.0 indicated a healthy firm.

---

[51] See Chapters 8 and 9 in Edward I. Altman, *Corporate Financial Distress and Bankruptcy: A Complete Guide to Predicting and Avoiding Distress and Profiting from Bankruptcy* (Hoboken, NJ: John Wiley & Sons, 1993). For discussion of MDA applied to predicting municipal bond ratings, see Michael G. Ferri and Frank J. Fabozzi, "Statistical Techniques for Predicting the Credit Worthiness of Municipal Bonds," Chapter 44 in Frank J. Fabozzi, Sylvan G. Feldstein, Irving M. Pollack, and Frank G. Zarb (eds.), *The Municipal Bond Handbook: Volume I* (Homewood, IL: Dow-Jones Irwin 1983).

[52] Edward I. Altman, "Financial Bankruptcies, Discriminant Analysis and the Prediction of Corporate Bankruptcy," *Journal of Finance* (September 1968), pp. 589–699.

Subsequently, Altman and his colleagues revised the Z-score model based on more recent data. The resulting model, referred to as the "Zeta model," found that the following seven variables were important in predicting corporate bankruptcies and were highly correlated with bond ratings:[53]

▶ Earnings before interest and taxes (EBIT)/Total assets;

▶ Standard error of estimate of EBIT/Total assets (normalized) for 10 years;

▶ EBIT/Interest charges;

▶ Retained earnings/Total assets;

▶ Current assets/Current liabilities;

▶ Five-year average market value of equity/Total capitalization;

▶ Total tangible assets, normalized.

While credit scoring models have been found to be helpful to analysts and bond portfolio managers, they do have limitations as a replacement for human judgment in credit analysis. Marty Fridson, for example, provides the following sage advice about using MDA models:

> . . . quantitative models tend to classify as troubled credits not only most of the companies that eventually default, but also many that do not default. Often, firms that fall into financial peril bring in new management and are revitalized without ever failing in their debt service. If faced with a huge capital loss on the bonds of a financially distressed company, an institutional investor might wish to assess the probability of a turnaround—an inherently difficult-to-quantify prospect—instead of selling purely on the basis of a default model.[54]

Fridson then goes on to explain that credit analysts must bear in mind that "companies can default for reasons that a model based on reported financial data cannot pick up" and provides several actual examples of companies that filed for bankruptcy for such reasons.

5   CREDIT RISK MODELS

Historically, credit risk modeling has focused on credit ratings, default rates, and traditional credit analysis. In recent years, models for assessing credit risk to value corporate bonds have been introduced. The models can be divided into two groups: structural models and reduced form models. In this section we briefly describe these models.

A. Structural Models

Structural models are credit risk models developed on the basis of option pricing theory presented by Fischer Black and Myron Scholes[55] and Robert

---

[53] Edward J. Altman, Robert G. Haldeman, and Paul Narayann, "Zeta Analysis: A New Model to Identify Bankruptcy Risk of Corporations," *Journal of Banking and Finance* (June 1977), pp. 29–54.

[54] Martin S. Fridson, *Financial Statement Analysis: A Practitioner's Guide, Second Edition* (Hoboken, NJ: John Wiley & Sons, 1995), p. 195.

[55] Fischer Black and Myron Scholes, "The Pricing of Options and Corporate Liabilities," *Journal of Political Economy* (May–June 1973), pp. 637–654.

Merton.[56] The basic idea, common to all structural-type models, is that a company defaults on its debt if the value of the assets of the company falls below a certain default point. For this reason, these models are also known as "firm-value models."[57] In these models it has been demonstrated that default can be modeled as an option to the stockholders granted by the bondholders and, as a result, an analyst can apply the same principles used for option pricing to the valuation of risky corporate securities.[58]

The use of the option pricing theory set forth by Black-Scholes-Merton (BSM) provides a significant improvement over traditional methods for valuing default risky bonds. Subsequent to the work of BSM, there have been many extensions on both a theoretical and practical level. The BSM framework has been used by a number of credit software/consulting companies, including Moody's KMV Corporation and JP Morgan's Credit Metrics (co-developed with Reuters). Both systems use the BSM approach to model defaults and obtain the probability of default. (Moody's KMV refers to this probability as the "expected default frequency.") To make the BSM model operational, model developers define default occurring when the equity price falls below a certain barrier. This simplification is due to the fact that equity prices are much more available than asset values of the company.

B. Reduced Form Models

In structural models, the default process of a corporation is driven by the value of its assets. Since the value of any option depends on the volatility of the underlying (the volatility of the asset value in structural models), the probability of default is explicitly linked to the expected volatility of a corporation's asset value. Thus, in structural models both the default process and recovery rates should a bankruptcy occur depend on the corporation's structural characteristics.

In contrast, reduced form models do not look "inside the firm," but instead model directly the probability of default or downgrade.[59] That is, the default process and the recovery process are 1) modeled independently of the corporation's structural features and 2) are independent of each other.

The two most popular reduced form models are the Jarrow and Turnbull model[60] and the Duffie and Singleton model.[61] The statistical tools for modeling the default process and the recovery process are a specialized topic.[62]

---

[56] Robert Merton, "Theory of Rational Option Pricing," *Bell Journal of Economics and Management* (Spring 1973), pp. 141–183, and "On the Pricing of Corporate Debt: The Risk Structure of Interest Rates," *Journal of Finance,* Vol. 29, No. 2 (1974), pp. 449–470.

[57] For a more detailed discussion of these models, see Chapter 8 in Mark J.P. Anson, Frank J. Fabozzi, Moorad Choudhry, and Ren Raw Chen, *Credit Derivatives: Instruments, Applications, and Pricing* (Hoboken, NJ: John Wiley & Sons, 2004).

[58] For the underlying theory and an illustration, see Don M. Chance, *Analysis of Derivatives for the CFA Program* (Charlottesville, VA: Association for Investment Management and Research, 2003), pp. 588–591.

[59] The name "reduced form" was first given by Darrell Duffie to differentiate these models from the structural form models of the Black-Scholes-Merton type.

[60] Robert Jarrow and Stuart Turnbull, "Pricing Derivatives on Financial Securities Subject to Default Risk," *Journal of Finance,* Vol. 50, No. 1 (1995), pp. 53–86.

[61] Darrell Duffie and Kenneth Singleton, "Modeling Term Structures of Defaultable Bonds," *Review of Financial Studies,* Vol. 12 (1999), pp. 687–720.

[62] For a further discussion of reduced form models, see Chapter 9 in Anson, Fabozzi, Choudhry, and Chen, *Credit Derivatives: Instruments, Applications, and Pricing;* Darrell Duffie and Kenneth J. Singleton, *Credit Risk: Pricing Measurement, and Management* (Princeton, NJ: Princeton University Press, 2003), or Srichander Ramaswamy, *Managing Credit Risk in Corporate Bond Portfolios* (Hoboken, NJ: John Wiley & Sons, 2003).

SUMMARY

- There are three types of credit risk: default risk, credit spread risk, and downgrade risk.

- Default risk is the risk that the issuer will fail to meet its obligation to make timely payment of interest and principal.

- Credit spread risk is the risk that the spread that the market demands for an issue will increase or widen, resulting in inferior performance of an issue relative to other issues.

- Downgrade risk is the risk that the issue will be downgraded, resulting in an increase in the credit spread demanded by the market.

- For long-term debt obligations, a credit rating is a forward-looking assessment of 1) the probability of default and 2) the relative magnitude of the loss should a default occur. For short-term debt obligations (i.e., obligations with initial maturities of one year or less), a credit rating is a forward-looking assessment of the probability of default.

- A rating agency monitors the credit quality of the issuer and can reassign a different credit rating to its bonds (an upgrade or a downgrade).

- Before an issue's rating is changed, typically a rating agency will place on rating watch or credit watch that it is reviewing the issue with the potential for upgrade or downgrade.

- Rating agencies issue rating outlooks, a projection as to whether an issue in the long term is likely to be upgraded, downgraded, or maintain its current rating.

- A credit analyst must consider the four C's of credit—character, capacity, collateral, and covenants.

- Character relates to the ethical reputation as well as the business qualifications and operating record of the board of directors, management, and executives responsible for the use of the borrowed funds and its repayment.

- Capacity deals with the ability of an issuer to repay its obligations.

- Collateral involves not only the traditional pledging of assets to secure the debt, but also the quality and value of those unpledged assets controlled by the issuer.

- Covenants are important because they impose restrictions on how management operates the company and conducts its financial affairs.

- The statement of cash flows is used in the analysis of an entity's ability to repay its financial obligations and to gain insight into an entity's financing methods, capital investment strategies, and dividend policy.

- To assess the ability of a company to meet its financial obligations, an analyst looks at profitability ratios that help explain the underlying causes of a change in the company's earnings.

- One of the best ways an analyst can predict future downward earnings is through a careful analysis of accounts receivable and inventories; two signs that can indicate problems are a larger than average accounts receivable balance situation and/or a bloated inventory.

- There are three sets of ratios that are used by credit analysts as indicators to assess the ability of a firm to satisfy its debt obligations: 1) short-term solvency ratios which assess the ability of the firm to meet debts maturing over the coming year, 2) capitalization (or financial leverage) ratios which assess the extent to which the firm relies on debt financing, and 3) coverage ratios which assess the ability of the firm to meet the fixed obligations brought about by debt financing.

▶ Analysts have reformatted the information from the firm's income statement and statement of cash flows to obtain what they view as a better description of the company's activities; these measures include funds from operations, operating cash flow, free operating cash flow, discretionary cash flow, and prefinancing cash flow.

▶ Negative covenants are covenants which require the borrower not to take certain actions; some of the more common restrictive covenants include various limitations on the company's ability to incur debt.

▶ There are two types of interest or fixed charge coverage tests: 1) a maintenance test which requires the borrower's ratio of earnings available for interests or fixed charges to be at least a certain minimum figure and 2) a debt incurrence test when the company wishes to do additional borrowing; in addition, there could be cash flow tests or requirements and working capital maintenance provisions.

▶ In assessing management quality, analysts consider the corporation's 1) strategic direction, 2) financial philosophy, 3) conservatism, 4) track record, 5) succession planning, and 6) control systems.

▶ Corporate financial theory helps us understand how the abuses that diminish shareholder value arise (agency problem) and the potential for mitigating the abuse.

▶ The corporate bylaws are the rules of governance; independent organizations have developed corporate governance ratings.

▶ In analyzing the credit-worthiness of high-yield corporate bond issuers, the analyst will want to pay close attention to the characteristics of the debt obligations in the capital structure.

▶ The corporate structure is particularly important to investigate when assessing the credit-worthiness of high-yield corporate bond issuers where there is a holding company structure because of potential limitations or restrictions on cash flow from operating subsidiaries to the parent company and among operating subsidiaries.

▶ Covenants in high-yield corporate bond issues should be reviewed in conjunction with the issuer's overall strategy.

▶ Some analysts believe that in assessing the credit quality of a high-yield corporate bond issuer an equity analysis approach is more informative than simply a traditional credit analysis approach.

▶ In analyzing the credit risk of an asset-backed security, rating companies basically look at four factors: 1) the credit quality of the collateral; 2) the quality of the seller/servicer, 3) cash flow stress test and payment (financial) structures, and 4) legal structure.

▶ A key factor in assessing the quality of the collateral is the amount of equity the borrower has in the asset.

▶ To reduce concentration risk in an asset-backed security, rating companies impose concentration limits.

▶ Based on their analysis of the four factors in assigning ratings, rating companies will determine the amount of credit enhancement needed for an issue to receive a particular rating.

► Fundamentally, because of the absence of operational risk, an asset-backed security transaction generally has greater certainty about the cash flow than a corporate bond issue.

► A true asset-backed security transaction involves minimal involvement by the servicer beyond administrative functions.

► In a hybrid asset-backed security transaction, the servicer has more than an administrative function; the greater the importance of the servicer, the more the transaction should be evaluated as a quasi-corporate entity.

► In assessing the credit risk of tax-backed debt, four basic informational categories should be considered: 1) information on the issuer's debt structure to determine the overall debt burden; 2) information on the issuer's ability and political discipline to maintain sound budgetary policy; 3) information on the specific local taxes and intergovernmental revenues available to the issuer; and 4) information on the issuer's overall socioeconomic environment.

► While there are numerous security structures for revenue bonds, the underlying principle in rating is whether the project being financed will generate sufficient cash flows to satisfy the obligations due bondholders.

► The principles involved in analyzing the credit risk of a revenue bond are the same as for a corporate bond.

► In assessing the credit risk for revenue bonds, the trust indenture and legal opinion should provide legal comfort in the following bond-security areas: 1) the limits of the basic security, 2) the flow-of-funds structure, 3) the rate, or user-charge, covenant, 4) the priority-of-revenue claims, 5) the additional-bonds tests, and 6) other relevant covenants.

► Sovereign credits are rated by Standard & Poor's and Moody's.

► In deriving ratings, the two general categories analyzed are economic risk (the ability to pay) and political risk (the willingness to pay).

► There are two ratings assigned to each central government: a local currency debt rating and a foreign currency debt rating.

► Historically, defaults have been greater on foreign currency denominated debt.

► In assessing the credit quality of local currency debt, rating agencies emphasize domestic government policies that foster or impede timely debt service.

► For foreign currency debt, rating agencies analyze a country's balance of payments and the structure of its external balance sheet.

► Analysts familiar with corporate credit analysis can build a structure for the analysis of quantitative and qualitative information of a sovereign issuer.

► Analysts must assess qualitative factors in assessing the credit risk of both a sovereign and corporate entity.

► A structure developed for corporate credit analysis can be developed for assessing the credit risk of a sovereign.

► Multiple discriminant analysis, a statistical classification technique, has been used by some analysts to predict corporate bankruptcies.

► Credit risk models for assessing credit risk to value corporate bonds include structural models and reduced form models.

APPENDIX 48

CASE STUDY: BERGEN BRUNSWIG CORPORATION

The purpose of this case is to illustrate how the analysis of financial statements based on traditional ratios discussed in this reading can be used to identify a corporate issuer that might be downgraded. The corporation used in the illustration is Bergen Brunswig Corporation.

Background Information

Bergen Brunswig Corporation is a supply channel management company that provides pharmaceuticals, medical-surgical supplies, and specialty products. The company also provides information management solutions and outsourcing services, as well as develops disease-specific treatment protocols and pharmacoeconomic initiatives to assist in the reduction of healthcare costs.

The original corporate bond rating was BBB+. On December 17, 1999, S&P lowered the company's rating to BBB− citing "disappointing results at the company's two recently acquired businesses, PharMerica and Statlander." PharMerica, an institutional pharmacy, suffered from changes in Medicare reimbursement policies which reduced hospital patient occupancy and the use of high-margin drugs.

On February 2, 2000, S&P decided to downgrade the company's corporate rating again to BB. S&P's rationale was "deteriorating conditions in the company's core drug distribution business as well as continued losses at Statlander, a specialty drug distributor acquired in 1999."

Analysis

Exhibit 1 shows the financial data for the 1996–1999 fiscal years and various financial ratios. (The financial ratios are shaded in the exhibit.) The company's fiscal year ends on September 30th. Since each rating agency uses slightly different inputs for the ratios it computes, we have included the ratio definitions used by S&P in Exhibit 2.

Exhibit 3 provides a summary of all the ratios that show a deteriorating trend of Bergen Brunswig's financial condition. The eight ratios shown in the exhibit strongly suggest that Bergen Brunswig was losing its financial strength and could possibly be a candidate for downgrade. To show the degree of deterioration, Exhibit 3 also displays for the eight ratios the median ratios for BBB and BB ratings.

Exhibit 4 highlights the trending of two key ratios—EBIT interest coverage and funds from operations/total debt—relative to the BBB benchmark. For 1999, the EBIT fell below 4 times, the median for BBB rated firms. For 1999, the ratio of funds from operations to total debt fell below the median for BB rated firms.

EXHIBIT 1	Financial Data and Selected Ratios for Bergen Brunswig: Fiscal Years 1996–1999 Based on 10K Data			
		1999	**1998**	**1997**	**1996**

			1999	1998	1997	1996
1	Revenue	1	$17,244,905	$13,720,017	$11,659,127	
	COGS	1	$(16,145,378)	$(12,969,752)	$(11,004,696)	
	SG & A		$(837,700)	$(534,119)	$(479,399)	
	EBIT		$261,827	$216,146	$175,032	
	Interest Expense	2	$74,143	$39,996	$30,793	
	EBIT interest coverage		**3.53**	**5.40**	**5.68**	
2	EBIT		$261,827	$216,146	$175,032	
	Depreciation & Amortization		$66,031	$37,465	$40,756	
	EBITDA		$327,858	$253,611	$215,788	
	Interest Expense		$74,143	$39,996	$30,793	
	EBITDA interest coverage		**4.42**	**6.34**	**7.01**	
3	Net Income		$70,573	$3,102	$81,679	
	Depreciation & Amortization		$66,031	$37,465	$40,756	
	Current Deferred Income Taxes		$10,840	$41,955	$10,577	
	Other Noncash Items					
	Deferred Compensation		$2,552	$2,809	$2,266	
	Doubtful Receivables		$85,881	$11,934	$11,899	
	Writedown of goodwill			$87,271		
	Abandonment of capitalized			$5,307		
	Funds from operations		$235,877	$189,843	$147,177	
	Long-Term Debt		$1,041,983	$464,778	$437,956	$419,275
	Lease Debt Equivalent		$82	$53	$59	$43
	Long-Term Debt*		$1,042,065	$464,831	$438,015	$419,318
	Current Maturity of LTD		$545,923	$6,029	$1,021	$1,125
	Total Debt		$1,587,988	$470,860	$439,036	$420,443
	Funds from operations/Total debt		**14.85%**	**40.32%**	**33.52%**	
4	Funds from operations		$235,877	$189,843	$147,177	
	Capital Expenditure		($305,535)	($52,361)	($23,806)	
	Working Capital		$1,199,527	$518,443	$474,910	$643,607
	Change in WC		$(681,084)	$(43,533)	$168,697	
	Free operating cash flow	3	$(750,742)	$93,949	$292,068	
	Total Debt		$1,587,988	$470,860	$439,036	
	Free operating cash flow/Total debt		**−47.28%**	**19.95%**	**66.52%**	
5	EBIT		$261,827	$216,146	$175,032	
	Total debt		$1,587,988	$470,860	$439,036	$420,443
	Equity		$1,495,490	$629,064	$644,861	$666,877
	Non-current deferred taxes				$1,791	
	Total Capital		$3,083,478	$1,099,924	$1,085,688	$1,087,320
	Average Capital		2,091,701.10	1,092,806.15	1,086,503.89	
	Pretax return on capital		**12.52%**	**19.78%**	**16.11%**	

(Exhibit continued on next page . . .)

EXHIBIT 1	(continued)			
	1999	**1998**	**1997**	**1996**
6 Operating Income	$261,827	$216,146	$175,032	
Sales	$17,244,905	$13,720,017	$11,659,127	
Operating Income/Sales	1.52%	1.58%	1.50%	
7 Long-Term Debt*	$1,042,065	$464,831	$438,015	
Long-term debt	$1,041,983	$464,778	$437,956	
Shareholders' equity	$1,495,490	$629,064	$644,861	
Capitalization	$2,537,473	$1,093,842	$1,082,817	
Long-term debt/Capitalization	41.07%	42.50%	40.45%	
8 Total Debt	$1,587,988	$470,860	$439,036	
Shareholders' equity	$1,495,490	$629,064	$644,861	
Capitalization	$3,083,478	$1,099,924	$1,083,897	
Total debt/Capitalization	51.50%	42.81%	40.51%	

*Bergen Brunswig fiscal year ends September 30th.

1. Revenues and Cost of Goods Sold excludes bulk shipment to customers' warehouse sites. The Company only serves as an intermediary and there is no material impact on the Company's operating earnings.

2. a) Does not include pre-tax distributions on the Company's Preferred Securities.

   b) Although the S&P formulas call for "Gross Interest Expense" net interest is used because Gross Interest Expense was unavailable in the filings and could not be inferred.

3. Free operating cash flow = Funds from operations + Capital expenditure + Change in WC.

Note for the above formula for free operating cash flow:
a) Capital expenditure is shown as a negative in the exhibit. That is why it is added to obtain free operating cash flow. (This is consistent with S&P's formula for free operating cash flow as given in Formula 4 in Exhibit 2.)
b) Increase in working capital for 1998 and 1999 is shown as a negative, so is added to free operating cash flow as per the S&P Formula 4 in Exhibit 2.

EXHIBIT 2	S&P's Formulas for Key Ratios

1. EBIT interest coverage = $\dfrac{\text{Earnings from continuing operations** before interest and taxes}}{\substack{\text{Gross interest incurred before subtracting 1) capitalized interest and}\\ \text{2) interest income}}}$

2. EBITDA interest coverage = $\dfrac{\substack{\text{Earnings from continuing operations** before interest and taxes,}\\ \text{depreciation, and amortization}}}{\substack{\text{Gross interest incurred before subtracting 1) capitalized interest and}\\ \text{2) interest income}}}$

3. Funds from operations/Total debt = $\dfrac{\substack{\text{Net income from continuing operations plus depreciation,}\\ \text{amortization, deferred taxes, and other noncash items}}}{\substack{\text{Long-term debt* plus current maturities, commercial paper, and}\\ \text{other short-term borrowings}}}$

4. Free operating cash flow/Total debt = $\dfrac{\substack{\text{Funds from operations minus capital expenditures, minus (plus) the}\\ \text{increase (decrease) in working capital (excluding changes in cash)}}}{\substack{\text{Long-term debt* plus current maturities, commercial paper, and}\\ \text{other short-term borrowings}}}$

5. Pretax return on capital = $\dfrac{\text{EBIT}}{\substack{\text{Average of beginning of year and end of year capital, including short-term debt,}\\ \text{current maturities, long-term debt*, non-current deferred taxes, and equity}}}$

6. Operating income/Sales = $\dfrac{\substack{\text{Sales minus cost of goods manufactured (before depreciation and}\\ \text{amortization), selling, general and administrative, and}\\ \text{research and development costs}}}{\text{Sales}}$

7. Long-term debt/Capitalization = $\dfrac{\text{Long-term debt*}}{\substack{\text{Long-term debt + Shareholders' equity (including preferred stock)}\\ \text{plus minority interest}}}$

8. Total debt/Capitalization = $\dfrac{\substack{\text{Long-term debt* plus current maturities, commercial paper, and other}\\ \text{short-term borrowings}}}{\substack{\text{Long-term debt* plus current maturities, commercial paper, and other}\\ \text{short-term borrowings + Shareholder's equity (including preferred}\\ \text{stock) plus minority interest}}}$

*Including amount for operating lease debt equivalent.

**Including interest income and equity earnings; excluding nonrecurring items.

EXHIBIT 3	Summary of Ratios Showing Deteriorating Trend and Median Ratio for S&P BBB and BB Ratings				
	1999	**1998**	**1997**	**BBB Median**	**BB Median**
EBIT interest coverage	3.53	5.40	5.68	4.10	2.5
EBITDA interest coverage	4.42	6.34	7.01	6.30	3.9
Funds from operations/Total debt	14.85%	40.32%	33.52%	32.30%	20.10%
Free operating cash flow/Total debt	−47.28%	19.95%	66.52%	6.30%	1.00%
Pretax return on capital	12.52%	19.78%	16.11%	15.40%	12.60%
Operating income/Sales	1.52%	1.58%	1.50%	15.80%	14.40%
Long-term debt/Capitalization	41.07%	42.50%	40.45%	40.80%	55.30%
Total debt/Capitalization	51.50%	42.81%	40.51%	46.40%	58.50%

EXHIBIT 4	Trending of EBIT Interest Leverage and Funds from Operating/Total Debt Ratios Relative to BBB and BB Benchmark

EBIT Interest Coverage

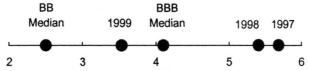

Funds from Operations/Total Debt

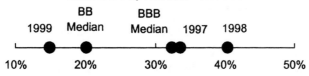

Conclusion

An analysis of the key ratios would have clearly signaled by December 1999 that Bergen Brunswig was a candidate for downgrading. As noted earlier, S&P lowered the company's corporate credit rating from BBB+ to BBB− on December 17, 1999 and then lowered it again on February 2, 2000 to BB. Among the reasons for the downgrade, S&P indicated that it expected EBITDA/interest to drop below 4 times in fiscal year 2000.

While wc have demonstrated that traditional analysis could have identified a potential downgrade, what we did not address was the timing of information for preparing the analysis and reaching our conclusion. Specifically, S&P downgraded Bergen Brunswig the first time on December 17, 1999, but the company did not file its 10K (annual filing with the SEC) until December 29, 1999. Although we use the 10K numbers (since they are more accurate) for this project, an analyst would most probably estimate the ratios by looking at the 10Qs (the quarterly filings with the SEC).

Exhibit 5 shows how this would be done for the first two ratios (EBIT interest coverage and EBITDA interest coverage). An analyst would add the results from the first 9 months of 1999 (fiscal year) to the last quarter of 1998 in order to estimate the annual ratio and show the trend.

As we can see from Exhibit 5, the annualized EBITDA interest coverage ratio (5.65) is much lower than the 1998 ratio. If we take a closer look, the ratio for the first nine months of 1999 is even lower. This strongly suggests a deteriorating trend. Bergen Brunswig filed its 1999 third quarter 10Q on August 17, 1999, so the information was available to the analyst before December 1999.

We believe S&P further lowered Bergen Brunswig's rating because of the first quarter result. Again, S&P's action date (February 2) is slightly earlier than the date that the company filed with the SEC (February 17). However, the weakening of Bergen Brunswig's financial position is apparent by the fact that the full-year 1999 ratios are even weaker than those for the first nine months of 1999.

EXHIBIT 5	Using Quarterly Financial Data from Bergen Brunswig to Compute EBIT and EBITDA Interest Coverage Ratios		
	1999 9 months	1998 4Q	Annualized Estimate
Revenue	$12,716,939	$3,666,166	$16,383,105
COGS	$(11,938,185)	$(3,466,355)	$(15,404,540)
SG & A	$(559,142)	$(144,725)	$(703,867)
EBIT	$219,612	$55,086	$274,698
Interest Expense	$47,906	$9,657	$57,563
EBIT interest coverage	4.58	5.70	4.77
EBIT	$219,612	$55,086	$274,698
Depreciation & Amortization	$40,497	$9,847	$50,344
EBITDA	$260,109	$64,933	$325,042
Interest Expense	$47,906	$9,657	$57,563
EBITDA interest coverage	5.43	6.72	5.65

PRACTICE PROBLEMS FOR READING 48

1. Explain whether you agree or disagree with the following statement: "The credit risk of a bond is the risk that the issuer will fail to meet its obligation to make timely payment of interest and principal."

2. A. In addition to credit ratings, what other information is provided by rating agencies that investors can use to gauge the credit risk of an issuer?

    B. How do long-term credit ratings differ from short-term credit ratings?

3. What are some of the major factors considered by rating agencies in assessing the quality of management?

4. A. There are various forms of back-up credit facilities available to a corporation. What factors should an analyst consider in assessing the back-up credit facilities available to an issuer?

    B. What is a "material adverse change clause provision" in a back-up credit facility and what is its significance in terms of the strength of a back-up credit facility?

5. In 1998 there were several developments in Europe leading to the liberalization of the European telecommunication industry. In October 1998, Moody's Investors Service published a report ("Rating Methodology: European Telecoms") addressing the issues in the rating of European telecommunication companies. Below are quotes from the report followed by questions that should be answered.

    A. "We look carefully at a company's general funding strategy—the debt and equity markets the company accesses, and the sources of bank financing it arranges. . . . This becomes more important the lower down the rating scale, particularly in the case of high yield issuers . . ." Why is the funding strategy of high-yield issuers of particular concern to Moody's analysts?

    B. "As a very general rule of thumb, the larger the company's cushion of cash and assets above fixed payments due, the more able it will be to meet maturing debt obligations in potentially adverse conditions, and the higher the rating. In many cases, the size of this cushion may be less important than its predictability or sustainability. Moody's views the telecom industry as having generally very predictable revenue streams, which accounts for the relatively high level of ratings of the telecom industry compared to other industries." Explain why "predictability and sustainability" may be more important than size of a coverage ratio.

    C. In discussing the financial measures it uses, the report explains the importance of "cash flow to debt figures." The report stated, "We also look at adjusted retained cash flow which includes any items which we view as non-discretionary to gauge the financial flexibility of a company, . . ." What is meant by "financial flexibility of a company"?

    D. The quote in the previous part ends with "as well as adjusted debt figures which include unfunded pension liabilities and guarantees." Why would Moody's adjust debt figures for these items?

    E. In the report, Moody's looks at various measures considered in ratings such as coverage ratios and capitalization ratios, and shows these ratios for a sample of European telecom companies. In each case when discussing ratios, Moody's notes the "loose correlation" between ratings

Practice Problems and Solutions: 1–24 taken from *Fixed Income Analysis for the Chartered Financial Analyst® Program*, Second Edition, by Frank J. Fabozzi, CFA. Copyright © 2005 by CFA Institute. Reprinted with permission. All other problems and solutions copyright © CFA Institute.

and ratios; that is, it is not necessarily the case that companies with the best ratios will always receive a better rating. Moody's noted that "inconsistencies underscore the limitations of ratio analysis." Explain why one might expect a loose correlation between ratios and ratings.

6. What type of information can a credit analyst obtain from an analysis of the statement of cash flows?

7. **A.** Using S&P's definitions, what is the relationship between free cash flow, discretionary cash, and prefinancing cash flow?

  B. What is the meaning of free cash flow, discretionary cash flow, and prefinancing cash flow?

8. **A.** Why is the analysis of covenants important in credit analysis?

  B. What is a negative covenant?

  C. Why is covenant analysis particularly important for assessing the credit-worthiness of high-yield corporate issuers?

9. What is meant by agency risk?

10. **A.** What is the motivation for corporate governance ratings?

  B. What are some of the characteristics of a firm considered in assigning a corporate governance rating?

11. Explain the following two statements made by Robert Levine in "Unique Factors in Managing High-Yield Bond Portfolios," in Frank K. Reilly (ed.), *High-Yield Bonds: Analysis and Risk Assessment* (Charlottesville, VA: Association for Investment Management and Research, 1990), p. 36.

  A. "One must understand the structure because not all debt that is listed as senior is actually senior debt."

  B. "Intellectually zero-coupon bonds are troublesome when they are not at the bottom of the capital structure . . . From a credit standpoint, it is not desirable to have more senior debt growing faster than the subordinated cash-pay securities, thus offering less protection to the subordinated holders in bankruptcy. We prefer to see less debt that is less senior growing faster than the debt that is more senior—e.g., less above us in the event of bankruptcy."

12. Explain why an understanding of the corporate structure of a high-yield issuer that has a holding company structure is important.

13. The following statement was made by Stephen Esser in "High-Yield Bond Analysis: The Equity Perspective," in Ashwinpaul C. Sondhi (ed.), *Credit Analysis of Nontraditional Debt Securities* (Charlottesville, VA: Association for Investment Management and Research, 1995), p. 54: "An equity perspective on high-yield bond analysis can be an important edge for an active manager." Explain why.

14. In the analysis of an asset-backed security, the analysis of the collateral allows the analyst to project the cash flow from the underlying collateral under different scenarios. However, this is not sufficient to assess the credit-worthiness of an asset-backed security transaction. Explain why?

15. Why is it necessary for an analyst to assess the financial condition of a servicer in an asset-backed security transaction?

16. **A.** Some asset-backed security transactions may be characterized as "true securitizations," while others may be more properly classified as "hybrid transactions." What is the distinguishing feature of a "true securitization" and a "hybrid transaction"?

  B. How is the credit quality of a "hybrid transaction" evaluated?

17. What are the four basic categories that are considered in assessing the credit quality of tax-backed municipal debt?

18. A. What is the underlying principle in assessing the credit-worthiness of municipal revenue bonds?

B. In a municipal revenue bond, what is a "rate covenant" and why is such a covenant included?

19. You are reviewing a publication of Moody's Investors Service entitled "Moody's Approach to Rating Regional and Local Governments in Latin America," published in August 1997. On page 3 of the publication, the following was written:

"A Moody's credit rating is an independent opinion of the relative ability and willingness of an issuer of fixed-income securities to make full and timely payments of amounts due on the security over its life."

Why in the case of a sovereign entity is the "willingness" of an issuer to pay important?

20. A. Why do rating agencies assign both a local currency debt rating and a foreign currency debt rating to the bonds of a sovereign government?

B. How do the factors considered in deriving a local currency debt rating differ from those for a foreign currency debt rating?

21. Comment on the following statement: "The difficulty with analyzing bonds issued by foreign governments is the intangible and non-quantitative elements involved in the credit analysis. I would not encounter such complexities when analyzing the credit worthiness of domestic corporate bonds or domestic municipal bonds."

22. Krane Products Inc. is a manufacturer of ski equipment. The company has been in operation since 1997. Ms. Andrews is a credit analyst for an investment management company. She has been asked to analyze Krane Products as a possible purchase for the bond portfolio of one of her firm's accounts. At the time of the analysis, Krane Products Inc. was rated BB by S&P. The bonds of the company trade in the market with the same spread as other comparable BB bonds.

Ms. Andrews collected financial data for Krane Products Inc. for the years 2000 and 1999 and computed several financial ratios. Information for selected ratios is given below:

Ratios	2000	1999
EBIT interest coverage	3.8	2.7
EBITDA interest coverage	5.9	4.1
Funds from operations/Total debt	28.3%	24.5%
Free operating cash flow/Total debt	19.2%	1.2%
Pretax return on capital	24.4%	17.1%
Operating income/Sales	25.5%	19.5%
Long-term debt/Capitalization	55.0%	57.4%
Total debt/Capitalization	57.1%	59.5%

Based on the first three quarters of fiscal year 2001, Ms. Andrews projected the following ratios for 2001:

Ratios	2001
EBIT interest coverage	4.5
EBITDA interest coverage	6.9
Funds from operations/Total debt	41.5%
Free operating cash flow/Total debt	22.5%
Pretax return on capital	24.2%
Operating income/Sales	25.12%
Long-term debt/Capitalization	40.5%
Total debt/Capitalization	45.2%

Ms. Andrews obtained from S&P information about median ratios by credit rating. These ratios are reproduced below:

	AAA	AA	A	BBB	BB	B
EBIT interest coverage	12.9	9.2	7.2	4.1	2.5	1.2
EBITDA interest coverage	18.7	14.0	10.0	6.3	3.9	2.3
Funds from operations/Total debt	89.7	67.0	49.5	32.3	20.1	10.5
Free operating cash flow/Total debt	40.5	21.6	17.4	6.3	1.0	(4.0)
Pretax return on capital	30.6	25.1	19.6	15.4	12.6	9.2
Operating income/Sales	30.9	25.2	17.9	15.8	14.4	11.2
Long-term debt/Capitalization	21.4	29.3	33.3	40.8	55.3	68.8
Total debt/Capitalization	31.8	37.0	39.2	46.4	58.5	71.4

What do you think Ms. Andrews' recommendation will be with respect to the purchase of the bonds of Krane Products Inc.? Explain why.

23. Credit scoring models have been found to be helpful to analysts and bond portfolio managers. What are their limitations as a replacement for human judgment in credit analysis?

24. What are the two types of credit risk models used to value corporate bonds?

The following information relates to Questions 25–30

Felipe Santos is a fixed-income analyst for an investment research firm. Santos is performing a credit analysis on Hansen Print Solutions (HPS), a small company specializing in the manufacture and distribution of equipment for the printing and publishing industries. The outstanding bonds of HPS are secured by the factory and its contents. Selected financial data for HPS are shown in Exhibit 1.

EXHIBIT 1	Selected Financial Data for Hansen Print Solutions

Balance Sheet (000's)			Income Statement (000's)		
31 December	**2006**	**2005**	**Year Ending 31 December**	**2006**	**2005**
Assets			**Total Revenue**	**274,140**	**129,851**
Current Assets			Cost of Revenue	192,144	87,387
Cash and Cash Equivalents	5,615	8,739	**Gross Profit**	**81,996**	**42,464**
Net Receivables	44,088	38,946	Operating Expenses		
Inventory	50,083	44,229	Research & Development	7,335	6,460
Other Current Assets	1,175	1,499	Selling General and Administrative	61,583	31,461
Total Current Assets	**100,961**	**93,413**	Non Recurring	874	−392
Property Plant and Equipment	45,250	47,372	Other Operating Expenses	2,724	0
Goodwill	23,089	18,888			
Intangible Assets	11,974	10,460	**Total Operating Expenses**	**72,516**	**37,529**
Other Assets	213	1,185	**Operating Income**	9,480	4,935
Total Assets	**181,487**	**171,318**	Total Other Income (Expenses)	239	53
Liabilities			**Earnings Before Interest and Taxes**	**9,719**	**4,988**
Current Liabilities					
Accounts Payable	37,917	24,026	Interest Expense	2,459	923
Short/Current Long-Term Debt	13,073	12,322	Income Tax Expense	1,174	200
Other Current Liabilities	8,579	16,068	**Net Income**	**6,086**	**3,865**
Total Current Liabilities	**59,569**	**52,416**			
Long-Term Debt	23,285	29,500			
Total Liabilities	**82,854**	**81,916**			
Stockholders' Equity					
Common Stock	354	349			
Retained Earnings	−7,930	−14,016			
Capital Surplus	106,268	102,962			
Other Stockholders' Equity	−59	107			
Total Stockholders' Equity	**98,633**	**89,402**			
Total Debt & Equity	**181,487**	**171,318**			

(Exhibit continued on next page . . .)

EXHIBIT 1   (continued)

Statement of Cash Flows
(000's)

Year Ending 31 December	2006	2005
Net Income	**6,086**	**3,865**
Operating Activities, Cash Flows Provided By or Used In		
Depreciation	10,949	9,106
Adjustments to Net Income	4,130	3,011
Changes in Accounts Receivables	−7,344	−6,513
Changes in Liabilities	4,792	3,346
Changes in Inventories	−7,054	−6,471
Changes in Other Operating Activities	171	−370
Total Cash Flow from Operating Activities	**11,730**	**5,974**
Investing Activities, Cash Flows Provided By or Used In		
Capital Expenditures	−6,129	−2,194
Investments	0	0
Other Cash Flows from Investing Activities	−5,519	−55,463
Total Cash Flows from Investing Activities	**−11,648**	**−57,657**
Financing Activities, Cash Flows Provided By or Used In		
Dividends Paid	0	0
Sale Purchase of Stock	3,113	5,200
Net Borrowings	−6,289	27,026
Total Cash Flows from Financing Activities	**−3,176**	**32,226**
Effect of Exchange Rate Changes	−30	—
Change in Cash and Cash Equivalents	**(3,124)**	**(19,457)**

The HPS bond indenture contains the following covenants that require the company to:

Covenant 1:   Maintain a total debt-to-capitalization ratio of no more than 50%.

Covenant 2:   Maintain properties and other assets in good repair.

Covenant 3:   Pay interest and principal on a timely basis.

Santos's analysis of the company includes the following statements:

Statement 1:   "HPS has a strong track record of solid strategic planning and their management is well-qualified to run the company."

Statement 2:   "HPS has a back-up credit facility with a highly-rated commercial bank."

HPS is also considering financing its account receivables by issuing asset-backed securities. Management believes this will allow the company to increase credit sales and improve overall profitability and liquidity. In response, Santos included the following statement in his analysis:

> Statement 3: "HPS's asset-backed securities are expected to receive a AAA-rating from the credit agencies."

25. Based on the current ratio and the acid-test ratio, has the short-term solvency position for HPS *most likely* improved or deteriorated from December 2005 to December 2006?

    A. Improved. Both the current ratio and acid-test ratio have shown improvements from 2005–2006.

    B. Deteriorated. Both the current ratio and the acid-test ratio have shown deterioration from 2005–2006.

    C. Inconclusive. The current ratio and acid-test ratios moved in opposite directions from 2005–2006.

26. The EBIT interest coverage ratio and the long-term debt to capitalization ratio for HPS for 2006 are *closest* to:

	EBIT interest coverage	Long-term debt to capitalization
A.	2.47	12.8%
B.	3.95	12.8%
C.	3.95	19.1%

27. HPS's debt payback period for 2006 is *closest* to:

    A. 11.83.

    B. 12.16.

    C. 14.79.

28. Which of the HPS covenants is *most likely* a negative covenant?

    A. Covenant 1.

    B. Covenant 2.

    C. Covenant 3.

29. Which of the "4 C's of Credit" do each of Santos's first two statements *most likely* support?

	Statement 1	Statement 2
A.	Capacity	Collateral
B.	Character	Capacity
C.	Collateral	Character

30. Santos's third statement about the credit agencies' ratings of HPS's asset-backed securities is *most likely* related to which of the following?

    A. Profit margin.

    B. Credit quality of HPS.

    C. Credit quality of the collateral.

The following information relates to Questions 31–36

Trumbull Partners specializes in fixed income portfolio management. It focuses on buying corporate bonds it perceives to be undervalued. Claire Simone is a junior analyst at the firm and is analyzing whether Trumbull should buy Fiber Optics Inc.'s bonds.

The bonds have an 8.875% semi-annual pay coupon, are non-callable, and mature in 2017. They are currently quoted at 119.193 and have carried a rating of BBB+ from Standard and Poor's (S&P) since 2005 with no review announcements. These are the only bonds issued by the company.

Selected summary financial statement data for Fiber Optics for the first quarter of 2009 are presented in Exhibit 1. Simone believes that there is no seasonality and the first quarter numbers are good estimates for the full year ratios (after adjustments, where necessary). She also assumes that average capitalization measures at the end of the year will be the same as the end of first quarter figures. The company did not have any interest income or capitalized interest in the first quarter of 2009.

EXHIBIT 1	Fiber Optics Inc. Selected Financial Information, 2009Q1
	Euros (Million)
Net income	456
Earnings before interest and taxes (EBIT)	533
Free operating cash flow	156
Pre-financing cash flow	140
Depreciation	150
Amortization	3
Other non-cash items	54
Increase (decrease) in net working capital	(245)
Short-term debt	2,231
Long-term debt	3,286
Stockholders' equity	7,644

In her report, Simone discusses the short-term credit risk factors associated with Fiber Optics bonds. She also discusses the change in key financial ratios of the firm over the years.

Key ratios for Fiber Optics are presented in Exhibit 2:

EXHIBIT 2	Fiber Optics Inc., Key Financial Ratios		
Ratios	**2008**	**2007**	**2006**
EBIT interest coverage (x)*	22.68	11.83	6.61
EBITDA interest coverage (x)*	32.22	17.54	10.12
Funds from operations (FFO)/Total debt (%)	44.03	31.14	19.37
Free operating cash flow (FOCF)/Total debt (%)	20.62	5.45	5.92

* EBIT is earnings before interest and taxes and EBITDA is earnings before interest, taxes, depreciation, and amortization.

During the analysis of indentures, Simone found that existing covenants included in the bonds of Fiber Optics:

I. Required Fiber Optics to certify every year that all plant and equipment was in good working order and property taxes had been paid.

II. Stipulated that EBIT Interest coverage ratio be higher than 5 for every quarter.

III. Stipulated that total debt of Fiber Optics cannot exceed 70% of capitalization.

31. Which of the following is the *most* significant short-term risk being faced by holders of Fiber Optics bonds?
   A. Default risk.
   B. Downgrade risk.
   C. Credit spread risk.

32. Based on the information provided in Exhibit 1, the funds from operations (FFO)/total debt ratio for 2009Q1 is *closest* to:
   A. 11.04%.
   B. 12.02%.
   C. 16.46%.

33. Based on Exhibit 1, the pre-tax return on capital for 2009Q1 is *closest* to:
   A. 4.05%.
   B. 4.88%.
   C. 6.97%.

34. Given EBITDA coverage ratio of 33 and based on Exhibit 1, the interest expense for 2009Q1 is *closest* to:
   A. €16.15 million.
   B. €20.79 million.
   C. €22.42 million.

35. Based only on FFO/Total debt and FOCF/Total debt ratios for 2006 through 2008 in Exhibit 2, which of the following is the *most likely* conclusion that can be drawn regarding Fiber Optics?

   A. The financial flexibility of the company has improved.

   B. Reliance on outside funding for financing has declined.

   C. Internally generated sources of funding have grown at a faster rate than external sources.

36. Of the covenants listed by Simone, which one is an example of a negative covenant?

   A. I.

   B. II.

   C. III.

SOLUTIONS FOR READING 48

1. Credit risk is more general than the statement in the quote. Credit risk encompasses three types of risk: default risk, credit spread risk, and downgrade risk. The quote in the question refers to default risk only. (Credit spread risk is the risk that the credit spread will increase. Downgrade risk is the risk that the issue will be downgraded.) Thus, one should disagree with the statement in the question.

2. **A.** Information in addition to the credit rating that is provided by a rating agency includes rating watches (or credit watches), rating outlooks, and transition tables. The first two are useful in assessing default risk, while the last is useful for assessing downgrade risk.

    When an issue is put on rating watch (credit watch), this means that the rating agency is reviewing the issue with the potential for an upgrade or a downgrade. A rating outlook is a projection of whether an issue in the long term (from six months to two years) is likely to be upgraded (positive outlook), downgraded (negative outlook), or maintain its current rating (stable outlook).

    A rating transition table is published periodically by a rating agency. It shows the percentage of issues of each rating at the beginning of a period that was downgraded or upgraded by the end of the time period.

    B. A credit rating is a forward-looking assessment of credit risk. For long-term debt obligations, it is an assessment of 1) the probability of default and 2) the relative magnitude of the loss should a default occur. For short-term debt obligations, a credit rating is an assessment of only the probability of default.

3. The factors considered include strategic direction of management, financial philosophy, management's track record, succession planning, and control systems.

4. **A.** While there are various forms of back-up credit facilities, some forms are stronger than others. A back-up credit facility where the lender is contractually bound and contains no provisions that permit the lender to refuse to provide funds is the strongest form. There are non-contractual facilities such as lines of credit. For such facilities, the analyst should be concerned because the lender has the right to refuse to lend funds.

    B. A "material adverse change clause" in a back-up credit facility allows a bank to refuse funding if the bank feels that the borrower's financial condition or operating position has deteriorated significantly. Consequently, as explained in Part A, this is a weaker form of back-up credit facility.

5. **A.** With high-yield issuers there tends to be more bank loans in the debt structure and the loans tend to be short term. Also, the loans tend to be floating rate rather than fixed. As a result, the analyst must look at the ability of the issuer to access short-term funding sources for liquidity to meet not only possible higher interest payments (when interest rates rise), but to pay off a maturing loan. High-yield issuers, however, have fewer alternatives for short-term funding sources than high-grade issuers.

B. At any given point in time, the cushion (as measured by coverage ratios) may be high. However, the concern is with future cash flows to satisfy obligations. If the coverage ratio is adequate and is predicted to change little in the future and the degree of confidence in the prediction is high, that situation would give greater comfort to a bondholder than one where the coverage ratio is extremely high but can fluctuate substantially in the future. Because of this variability it is difficult to assign a high degree of confidence to coverage ratios that are projected, and there must be recognition that the coverage ratio may fall well below acceptable levels.

C. Financial flexibility means the ability to sustain operations should there be a down turn in business and to sustain current dividends without reliance on external funding.

D. Unfunded pension liabilities may not be listed as debt, but they are effectively a form of borrowing by the firm. Hence, Moody's is considering them as part of the debt obligation. Guarantees represent potential liabilities if the corporate entity whose debt is guaranteed does not meet its obligations. If Moody's views the obligation as one that the company may have to satisfy, the obligation of the corporate entity whose debt is guaranteed is a form of borrowing and should be included in total debt.

E. Ratios represent a snapshot of a particular aspect of a firm's financial position at a given point in time. Ratings reflect an assessment of the future financial position and the assessment of future cash flows. This involves looking at a myriad of factors that impact future cash flows such as competition, potential earnings growth, and future capital requirements. This is a major limitation of ratio analysis as a sole indicator of an entity's financial strength—it is not forward looking in that it does not look at how factors in the future can alter cash flows.

6. By analyzing the statement of cash flows, creditors can examine such aspects of the business as 1) the source of financing for business operations, 2) the company's ability to meet its debt obligations, 3) the company's ability to finance expansion through operating cash flow, 4) the company's ability to pay dividends, and 5) the flexibility given to management in financing its operations.

7. A. Free operating cash flow, according to S&P, is obtained by reducing operating cash flow by capital expenditures.

Discretionary cash flow is found by reducing free operating cash flow by cash dividends.

Prefinancing financing cash flow is found by adjusting discretionary cash flow by 1) decreasing it by acquisitions and 2) increasing it by asset disposals, and then further adjusting by the net of other sources (uses) of cash.

B. Free operating cash flow according to S&P is the cash flow that can be used to pay dividends and make acquisitions. Reducing free operating cash flow by cash dividends gives discretionary cash flow that management can use to make acquisitions. Adjusting discretionary cash flow for managerial discretionary decisions for acquisition of other companies, the disposal of assets (e.g., lines of business or subsidiaries), and other sources or uses of cash gives prefinancing cash flow, which represents the extent to which company cash flow from all internal sources has been sufficient to cover all internal needs.

8. A. Since covenants deal with limitations and restrictions on the borrower's activities, certain covenants provide protection for a bondholder and this protection must be factored into the credit analysis.

   B. A negative covenant is one that requires the borrower not to take certain actions. An example of a negative covenant is a restriction on the company's ability to incur additional debt.

   C. A review of the covenants in a high-yield corporate issue may help the analyst understand management strategy regarding future funding and operational strategies to determine if they are consistent with what management is stating to investors. Loopholes in covenants may provide further clues as to management's future plans.

9. Agency risk is the risk that management will make decisions in its own self-interest, thereby reducing firm value.

10. A. The motivation for developing a corporate governance rating is the belief that in the long run firms that focus on corporate governance and transparency will generate superior returns and economic performance and lower their cost of capital.

   B. Every firm that has developed a corporate governance rating uses its own criteria. Typically what is considered (using the S&P criteria) is ownership structure and external influences, shareholder rights and stakeholder relations, transparency, disclosure and audit process, and board structure and effectiveness.

11. A. The typical structure for a high-yield corporate issuer includes bank debt. This debt is senior to all other debt claims. As a result, bonds that are labeled "senior bonds" are subordinated to bank debt despite their title.

   B. The interest for a zero-coupon bond increases over time due to the accrual of the unpaid interest. As a result, assuming no other changes in the firm's debt structure, the percentage of a zero-coupon bond in the firm's debt structure increases over time. If these bonds are senior bonds (senior relative to the subordinated bonds, not to bank debt as discussed in part a), then the zero-coupon bond's percentage increases relative to the subordinated bonds. This may increase the credit risk of the subordinated bonds over time and adversely impact subordinated bondholders in the event of bankruptcy. Hence, in the quote Mr. Levine is stating that it is preferred to have zero-coupon bonds (or any deferred coupon bonds) as subordinated bonds rather than senior bonds.

12. In a holding company structure, the parent company issues debt as well as the operating subsidiaries. Consequently, the analyst in projecting the cash flows available to pay the creditors of the holding company must understand any restrictions on payments that can be made to the parent company (dividends or loans) by the operating subsidiaries.

13. In the risk-return spectrum, high-yield bonds are between high-grade corporate bonds and common stocks. High-yield corporate bonds have an equity component as evidenced by the higher correlation between stock returns and high-yield bond returns compared to high-grade bond returns and high-yield bond returns. Consequently, some portfolio managers such as Mr. Esser firmly believe that high-yield bond analysis should be viewed from an equity analyst's perspective. It is believed that the equity approach can provide more insight than traditional credit analysis. A manager using an equity approach, it is believed by Mr. Esser, will give that manager an edge in identifying attractive issues for purchase or avoiding or disposing of unattractive issues relative to other managers who rely solely on traditional credit analysis.

14. Given the projected cash flow for the collateral under various scenarios, the next step is to determine how the cash flow would be distributed among the different tranches in the structure. So, by itself projection of the cash flow is insufficient because it will not indicate if any, or all, of the tranches (i.e., bonds) will realize a loss. The allocation of the cash flow in a given scenario will permit the determination of which tranches may realize losses and the extent of those losses.

15. A servicer may be required to make advances to cover interest payments to bondholders when there are delinquencies. Consequently, the servicer must have the financial capacity to fulfill this obligation. This requires an assessment of the financial condition of the servicer.

16. A. In a "true securitization" the role of the servicer is basically routine. There are basic daily administrative tasks performed and the cash flow does not depend to any significant extent on the servicer to perform. Where the role of the servicer is more than administrative in order to generate the cash flow, the transaction is referred to as a "hybrid transaction."

  B. The analysis of a "hybrid transaction" uses both the standard methodology for evaluating an asset-backed security transaction and the analysis of a corporate entity—basically as a service business. The latter approach is referred to by S&P as a "quasi-corporate" approach. The final assessment of a rating agency is a subjective weighting of the credit quality using the two approaches. The more the transaction's cash flow is dependent on the performance of the servicer, the greater the weight given to the quasi-corporate approach.

17. The four basic categories are 1) the issuer's debt structure; 2) the issuer's ability and political discipline to maintain sound budgetary policy; 3) the specific local taxes and intergovernmental revenues available to the issuer, as well as obtaining historical information on tax collection rates; and 4) the issuer's overall socioeconomic environment.

18. A. The payment of the obligations of a revenue bond must come from the cash flow generated from the enterprise for which the bonds were issued. Thus, just as in the case of a corporate bond, the underlying principle in assessing an issuer's credit-worthiness is whether or not sufficient cash flow will be generated to satisfy the obligations due bondholders.

  B. A rate covenant specifies how charges will be set on the product or service sold by the enterprise. A rate covenant is included so the enterprise will set charges so as to satisfy both expenses and debt servicing, or to create a certain amount of reserves.

19. Because the issuer is a sovereign entity, if the issuer refuses to pay, there is little legal remedy for the debt holder. Thus, it becomes necessary to understand the factors other than legal recourse that will increase the likelihood that the issuer will repay.

20. A. The reason for assigning two ratings is that the currency denomination of the payments may be either the local currency or a foreign currency. (Historically, the default frequency had differed by the currency denomination of the debt. It has been observed by rating agencies that defaults have been greater on foreign currency denominated debt.)

B. To generate sufficient local currency to satisfy its debt obligations denominated in its local currency, a government must be willing to raise taxes and control its domestic financial system. In contrast, a national government must purchase foreign currency to meet a debt obligation in that foreign currency. Consequently, a government has less control with respect to its exchange rate and faces exchange rate risk (i.e., depreciation of its currency) when it issues a foreign currency denominated bond.

The implication of this is that the factors a rating agency will emphasize in assessing the credit-worthiness of a national government's local currency debt and foreign currency debt will differ to some extent. S&P, for example, focuses on domestic government policies that affect the likelihood of the government's ability to repay local currency denominated debt. For foreign currency debt, the same rating agency focuses on the interaction of domestic and foreign government policies. Specifically, the areas of analysis that S&P assesses is a country's balance of payments and the structure of its external balance sheet (i.e., the net public debt, total net external debt, and net external liabilities).

21. When analyzing domestic corporate bonds, an analyst does factor in intangible and non-quantitative elements, the most important of which is the quality of management. Moreover, a factor that is considered in assessing the credit quality of a tax-backed municipal bond issue is the willingness of the issuing entity to generate funds to repay the obligation by raising taxes. So, the statement that intangible and non-quantitative elements are not considered in analyzing domestic corporate and domestic municipal bonds but only with sovereign bonds is incorrect.

22. All the financial ratios—actual and projected for 2001—clearly indicate that the credit-worthiness of Krane Products is improving. Using as benchmarks the S&P median ratios, the coverage ratios were already by fiscal year 2000 approaching that of the median BBB rated issuer. The capitalization ratios, while improving, were still well below that of the median BBB rated issuer. Consequently, by fiscal year 2000 an analyst would have been well advised to monitor this issuer's credit for a possible upgrade and to examine how it was trading in the market. That is, was it trading like a BB or BBB credit?

If Ms. Andrews' projections are correct for fiscal year 2001, the ratios shown in the table are at least as good as the median BBB rated company. Consequently, based on her projections she would recommend the purchase of Krane Products Inc. bonds if that issuer's bonds continue to trade like a BB credit since, based on her analysis, the bonds are likely to be upgraded to BBB.

23. Credit scoring models tend to classify firms as likely to default, not only most of the firms that do eventually default, but also many firms that do not default. Some of the firms that appear to be classified as troubled credits by credit scoring models hire new management and are then revitalized without defaulting. Thus, a credit analyst must recognize the possibility of a turnaround for a firm that the model has classified as likely to default. Furthermore, there are reasons why a firm may default that have nothing to do with the financial variables used in a credit scoring model.

24. Structural models and reduced form models are the two types of credit risk models for valuing corporate bonds.

The foundation of structural models, also known as "firm-value models," is the Black-Scholes-Merton option pricing model. The basic idea of these models is that a company defaults on its debt if the value of the assets of the company falls below a certain default point. The default process of a corporation is driven by the value of its assets. Since the value of any option depends on the volatility of the asset value in structural models, the probability of default is explicitly linked to the expected volatility of a corporation's asset value. Thus, in structural models, both the default process and recovery rates should a bankruptcy occur depend on the corporation's structural characteristics.

Reduced form models do not look "inside the firm," but instead model directly the probability of default or downgrade. That is, the default process and the recovery process are 1) modeled independently of the corporation's structural features and 2) are independent of each other.

25. B is correct. Both the current ratio and acid-test ratio declined from 2005 to 2006. A lower number indicates lower solvency.

> Current ratio = (Current assets/Current liabilities)
> 2005 Current ratio = (93,413/52,416) = 1.78
> 2006 Current ratio = (100,961/59,569) = 1.69
>
> Acid-test ratio = ((Current assets − Inventories)/Current liabilities)
> 2005 Acid-test ratio = ((93,413 − 44,229)/52,416) = 0.94
> 2006 Acid-test ratio = ((100,961 − 50,083)/59,569) = 0.85

26. C is correct.

EBIT interest coverage = Earnings before interest & taxes/Annual interest expense = (9,719/2,459) = 3.95

Long-term debt to capitalization = Long-term debt/(Long-term debt + Shareholders' equity) = 23,285/(23,285 + 98,633) = 19.1%

27. C is correct. The Debt payback period = Total debt/Discretionary cash flow

= Total debt/(Operating cash flow − Capital expenditures − Cash dividends)

= 82,854/(11,730 − 6,129 − 0)

= 14.79

28. A is correct. Covenant 1 is an example of a negative covenant, which prohibits the borrower from taking certain actions. Affirmative covenants, in contrast, require the borrower to take specific actions.

29. B is correct. Statement 1 describes strategic direction and management qualifications, both of which are examples of a corporation's character, whereas Statement 2 describes liquidity sources which demonstrate the capacity to repay the debt obligation.

30. C is correct. When analyzing credit risk of an asset-backed security, the rating agencies consider the following: credit quality of the collateral, quality of the seller/servicer, cash flow stress and payment structure, and legal structure.

31. C is correct. Credit spread risk has an external factor component, so it is most significant. Credit spreads can change irrespective of firm performance.

32. B is correct.

FFO = Net Income + Depreciation + Amortization + Non cash items
   = 456 + 150 + 3 + 54 = 663

Total debt = Short-term debt + Long-term debt
      = 2,231 + 3,286 = 5,517

FFO/Total debt ratio = 663/5517 = 12.02%

33. A is correct.

Pre-tax return on capital = EBIT/(Short-term debt + Long-term debt
              + Stockholders' equity)
       = 533/(2,231 + 3,286 + 7,644) = 4.05%

34. B is correct.

EBITDA coverage = EBITDA/(Gross interest before interest income
          and capitalized interest)
OR   EBITDA/Interest expense
OR   Interest expense = EBITDA/EBITDA coverage
OR   Interest expense = (EBIT + Depreciation + Amortization)/
          EBITDA coverage
Interest expense = (533 + 150 + 3)/33 = €20.79 million

35. A is correct. Both FFO/TD and FOCF/TD have been increasing, indicating improved financial flexibility for the company.

36. C is correct. III is an example of a negative covenant. It requires the borrower not to take certain actions, i.e., total debt of Fiber Optics cannot exceed 70% of capitalization.

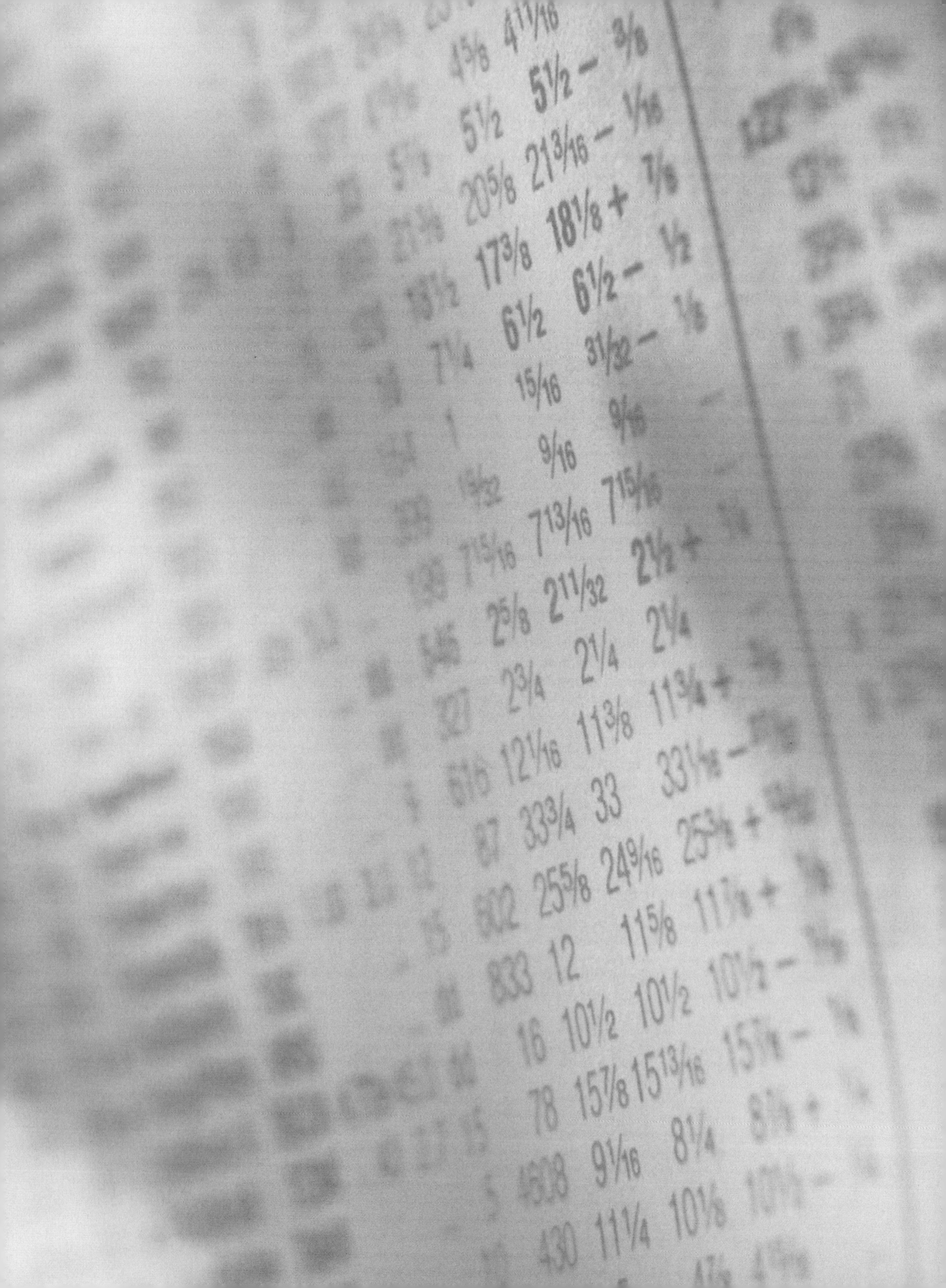

TERM STRUCTURE AND VOLATILITY OF INTEREST RATES

by Frank J. Fabozzi, CFA

LEARNING OUTCOMES

The candidate should be able to:	Mastery
a. explain parallel and nonparallel shifts in the yield curve, a yield curve twist, and a change in the curvature of the yield curve (i.e., a butterfly shift);	☐
b. describe factors that drive U.S. Treasury security returns, and evaluate the importance of each factor;	☐
c. explain various universes of Treasury securities that are used to construct the theoretical spot rate curve, and evaluate their advantages and disadvantages;	☐
d. explain the swap rate curve (LIBOR curve) and why market participants have used the swap rate curve rather than a government bond yield curve as a benchmark;	☐
e. explain the pure expectations, liquidity, and preferred habitat theories of the term structure of interest rates and the implications of each for the shape of the yield curve;	☐
f. calculate and interpret the yield curve risk of a security or a portfolio by using key rate duration;	☐
g. calculate and interpret yield volatility, distinguish between historical yield volatility and implied yield volatility, and explain how yield volatility is forecasted.	☐

INTRODUCTION 1

Market participants pay close attention to yields on Treasury securities. An analysis of these yields is critical because they are used to derive interest rates which are used to value securities. Also, they are benchmarks used to establish the minimum yields that investors want when investing in a non-Treasury security. We distinguish between the on-the-run (i.e., the most recently auctioned

Fixed Income Analysis for the Chartered Financial Analyst® Program, Second Edition, by Frank J. Fabozzi, CFA.
Copyright © 2005 by CFA Institute. Reprinted with permission.

Treasury securities) Treasury yield curve and the term structure of interest rates. The on-the-run Treasury yield curve shows the relationship between the yield for on-the-run Treasury issues and maturity. The term structure of interest rates is the relationship between the theoretical yield on zero-coupon Treasury securities and maturity. The yield on a zero-coupon Treasury security is called the Treasury spot rate. The term structure of interest rates is thus the relationship between Treasury spot rates and maturity. The importance of this distinction between the Treasury yield curve and the Treasury spot rate curve is that it is the latter that is used to value fixed-income securities.

We demonstrated how to derive the Treasury spot rate curve from the on-the-run Treasury issues using the method of bootstrapping and then how to obtain an arbitrage-free value for an option-free bond. In this reading we will describe other methods to derive the Treasury spot rates. In addition, we explained that another benchmark that is being used by practitioners to value securities is the swap curve. We discuss the swap curve in this reading.

Previously, the theories of the term structure of interest rates were explained. Each of these theories seeks to explain the shape of the yield curve. The concept of forward rates also was explained. In this reading, we explain the role that forward rates play in the theories of the term structure of interest rates. In addition, we critically evaluate one of these theories, the pure expectations theory, because of the economic interpretation of forward rates based on this theory.

We also mentioned the role of interest rate volatility or yield volatility in valuing securities and in measuring interest rate exposure of a bond. We will continue to see the importance of this measure. Specifically, we will see the role of interest rate volatility in valuing bonds with embedded options, valuing mortgage-backed and certain asset-backed securities, and valuing derivatives. Consequently, in this reading, we will explain how interest rate volatility is estimated and the issues associated with computing this measure.

In the opening sections of this reading we provide some historical information about the Treasury yield curve. In addition, we set the stage for understanding bond returns by looking at empirical evidence on some of the factors that drive returns.

2   HISTORICAL LOOK AT THE TREASURY YIELD CURVE

The yields offered on Treasury securities represent the base interest rate or minimum interest rate that investors demand if they purchase a non-Treasury security. For this reason market participants continuously monitor the yields on Treasury securities, particularly the yields of the on-the-run issues. In this reading we will discuss the historical relationship that has been observed between the yields offered on on-the-run Treasury securities and maturity (i.e., the yield curve).

A. Shape of the Yield Curve

Exhibit 1 shows some yield curves that have been observed in the U.S. Treasury market and in the government bond market of other countries. Four shapes have been observed. The most common relationship is a yield curve in which the longer the maturity, the higher the yield as shown in panel a. That is, investors are rewarded for holding longer maturity Treasuries in the form of a higher potential yield. This shape is referred to as a normal or positively sloped yield curve. A flat yield curve is one in which the yield for all maturities is approximately equal, as shown in panel b. There have been times when the relationship between maturities and yields was such that the longer the maturity the lower the yield. Such a downward-sloping yield curve is referred to as an inverted or a negatively sloped yield curve and is shown in panel c. In panel d, the yield curve shows yields increasing with maturity for a range of maturities and then the yield curve becoming inverted. This is called a humped yield curve.

Market participants talk about the difference between long-term Treasury yields and short-term Treasury yields. The spread between these yields for two maturities is referred to as the steepness or slope of the yield curve. There is no industry-wide accepted definition of the maturity used for the long-end and the

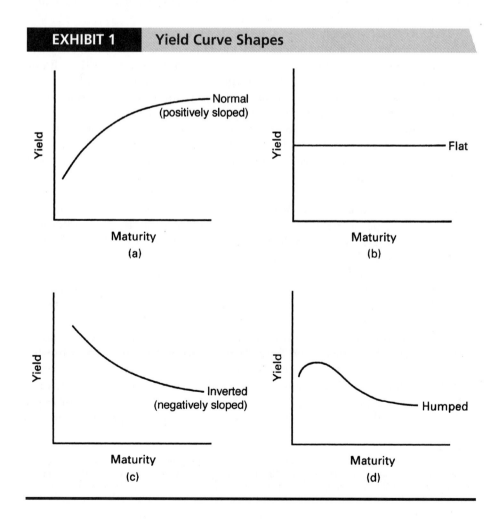

EXHIBIT 1   Yield Curve Shapes

maturity used for the short-end of the yield curve. Some market participants define the slope of the yield curve as the difference between the 30-year yield and the 3-month yield. Other market participants define the slope of the yield curve as the difference between the 30-year yield and the 2-year yield. The more common practice is to use the spread between the 30-year and 2-year yield. While as of June 2003 the U.S. Treasury has suspended the issuance of the 30-year Treasury issue, most market participants view the benchmark for the 30-year issue as the last issued 30-year bond which as of June 2003 had a maturity of approximately 27 years. (Most market participants use this issue as a barometer of long-term interest rates; however, it should be noted that in daily conversations and discussions of bond market developments, the 10-year Treasury rate is frequently used as a barometer of long-term interest rates.)

The slope of the yield curve varies over time. For example, in the U.S., over the period 1989 to 1999, the slope of the yield curve as measured by the difference between the 30-year Treasury yield and the 2-year Treasury yield was steepest at 348 basis points in September and October 1992. It was negative—that is, the 2-year Treasury yield was greater than the 30-year Treasury yield—for most of 2000. In May 2000, the 2-year Treasury yield exceeded the 30-year Treasury yield by 65 basis points (i.e., the slope of the yield curve was −65 basis points).

It should be noted that not all sectors of the bond market view the slope of the yield curve in the same way. The mortgage sector of the bond—which we cover in the reading on the mortgage-backed sector of the bond market—views the yield curve in terms of the spread between the 10-year and 2-year Treasury yields. This is because it is the 10-year rates that affect the pricing and refinancing opportunities in the mortgage market.

Moreover, it is not only within the U.S. bond market that there may be different interpretations of what is meant by the slope of the yield curve, but there are differences across countries. In Europe, the only country with a liquid 30-year government market is the United Kingdom. In European markets, it has become increasingly common to measure the slope in terms of the swap curve (in particular, the euro swap curve) that we will cover later in this reading.

Some market participants break up the yield curve into a "short end" and "long end" and look at the slope of the short end and long end of the yield curve. Once again, there is no universal consensus that defines the maturity break points. In the United States, it is common for market participants to refer to the short end of the yield curve as up to the 10-year maturity and the long end as from the 10-year maturity to the 30-year maturity. Using the 2-year as the shortest maturity, the slope of the short end of the yield curve is then the difference between the 10-year Treasury yield and the 2-year Treasury yield. The slope of the long end of the yield curve is the difference between the 30-year Treasury yield and the 10-year Treasury yield. Historically, the long end of the yield curve has been flatter than the short-end of the yield curve. For example, in October 1992 when the slope of the yield curve was the greatest at 348 basis points, the slope of the long end of the yield curve was only 95 basis points.

Market participants often decompose the yield curve into three maturity sectors: short, intermediate, and long. Again, there is no consensus as to what the maturity break points are and those break points can differ by sector and by country. In the United States, a common breakdown has the 1–5 year sector as the short end (ignoring maturities less than 1 year), the 5–10 year sector as the intermediate end, and greater than 10-year maturities as the long end.[1] In

---

[1] Index constructors such as Lehman Brothers when constructing maturity sector indexes define "short-term sector" as up to three years, the "intermediate sector" as maturities greater than three years but less than 10 years (note the overlap with the short-term sector), and the "long-term sector" as greater than 10 years.

Continental Europe where there is little issuance of bonds with a maturity greater than 10 years, the long end of the yield sector is the 10-year sector.

B. Yield Curve Shifts

A shift in the yield curve refers to the relative change in the yield for each Treasury maturity. A parallel shift in the yield curve refers to a shift in which the change in the yield for all maturities is the same. A nonparallel shift in the yield curve means that the yield for different maturities does not change by the same number of basis points. Both of these shifts are graphically portrayed in Exhibit 2.

Historically, two types of nonparallel yield curve shifts have been observed: 1) a twist in the slope of the yield curve and 2) a change in the humpedness or curvature of the yield curve. A twist in the slope of the yield curve refers to a flattening or steepening of the yield curve. A flattening of the yield curve means that the slope of the yield curve (i.e., the spread between the yield on a long-term and short-term Treasury) has decreased; a steepening of the yield curve means that the slope of the yield curve has increased. This is depicted in panel b of Exhibit 2.

The other type of nonparallel shift is a change in the curvature or humpedness of the yield curve. This type of shift involves the movement of yields at the short maturity and long maturity sectors of the yield curve relative to the movement of yields in the intermediate maturity sector of the yield curve. Such nonparallel shifts in the yield curve that change its curvature are referred to as butterfly shifts. The name comes from viewing the three maturity sectors (short, intermediate, and long) as three parts of a butterfly. Specifically, the intermediate maturity sector is viewed as the body of the butterfly and the short maturity and long maturity sectors are viewed as the wings of the butterfly.

A positive butterfly means that the yield curve becomes less humped (i.e., has less curvature). This means that if yields increase, for example, the yields in the short maturity and long maturity sectors increase more than the yields in the intermediate maturity sector. If yields decrease, the yields in the short and long maturity sectors decrease less than the intermediate maturity sector. A negative butterfly means the yield curve becomes more humped (i.e., has more curvature). So, if yields increase, for example, yields in the intermediate maturity sector will increase more than yields in the short maturity and long maturity sectors. If, instead, yields decrease, a negative butterfly occurs when yields in the intermediate maturity sector decrease less than the short maturity and long maturity sectors. Butterfly shifts are depicted in panel c of Exhibit 2.

Historically, these three types of shifts in the yield curve have not been found to be independent. The two most common types of shifts have been 1) a downward shift in the yield curve combined with a steepening of the yield curve and 2) an upward shift in the yield curve combined with a flattening of the yield curve. Positive butterfly shifts tend to be associated with an upward shift in yields and negative butterfly shifts with a downward shift in yields. Another way to state this is that yields in the short-term sector tend to be more volatile than yields in the long-term sector.

TREASURY RETURNS RESULTING FROM YIELD CURVE MOVEMENTS

3

A yield measure is a promised return if certain assumptions are satisfied; but total return (return from coupons and price change) is a more appropriate measure of the potential return from investing in a Treasury security. The total return for a short investment horizon depends critically on how interest rates change, reflected by how the yield curve changes.

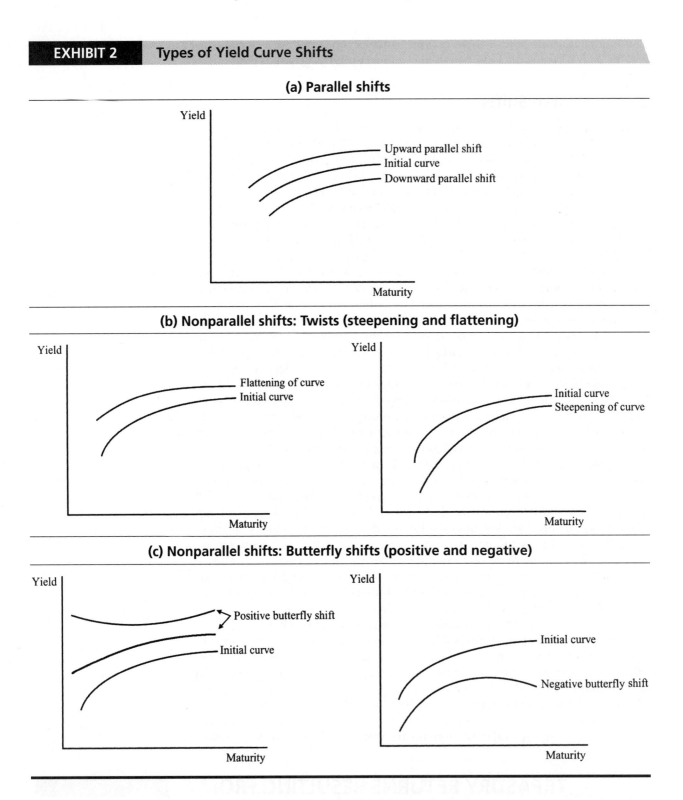

EXHIBIT 2   Types of Yield Curve Shifts

There have been several published and unpublished studies of how changes in the shape of the yield curve affect the total return on Treasury securities. The first such study by two researchers at Goldman Sachs (Robert Litterman and José Scheinkman) was published in 1991.[2] The results reported in more recent studies

[2] Robert Litterman and José Scheinkman, "Common Factors Affecting Bond Returns," *Journal of Fixed Income* (June 1991), pp. 54–61.

support the findings of the Litterman-Scheinkman study, so we will just discuss their findings. Litterman and Scheinkman found that three factors explained historical returns for zero-coupon Treasury securities for all maturities. The first factor was changes in the level of rates, the second factor was changes in the slope of the yield curve, and the third factor was changes in the curvature of the yield curve.

Litterman and Scheinkman employed regression analysis to determine the relative contribution of these three factors in explaining the returns on zero-coupon Treasury securities of different maturities. They determined the importance of each factor by its coefficient of determination, popularly referred to as the "R^2." In general, the R^2 measures the percentage of the variance in the dependent variable (i.e., the total return on the zero-coupon Treasury security in their study) explained by the independent variables (i.e., the three factors).[3] For example, an R^2 of 0.8 means that 80% of the variation of the return on a zero-coupon Treasury security is explained by the three factors. Therefore, 20% of the variation of the return is not explained by these three factors. The R^2 will have a value between 0% and 100%. In the Litterman-Scheinkman study, the R^2 was very high for all maturities, meaning that the three factors had a very strong explanatory power.

The first factor, representing changes in the level of rates, holding all other factors constant (in particular, yield curve slope), had the greatest explanatory power for all the maturities, averaging about 90%. The implication is that the most important factor that a manager of a Treasury portfolio should control for is exposure to changes in the level of interest rates. For this reason it is important to have a way to measure or quantify this risk. Duration is in fact the measure used to quantify exposure to a parallel shift in the yield curve.

The second factor, changes in the yield curve slope, was the second largest contributing factor. The average relative contribution for all maturities was 8.5%. Thus, changes in the yield curve slope were, on average, about one-tenth as significant as changes in the level of rates. While the relative contribution was only 8.5%, this can still have a significant impact on the return for a Treasury portfolio, and a portfolio manager must control for this risk. We briefly explained how a manager can do this using key rate duration and will discuss this further in this reading.

The third factor, changes in the curvature of the yield curve, contributed relatively little to explaining historical returns for Treasury zero-coupon securities.

CONSTRUCTING THE THEORETICAL SPOT RATE CURVE FOR TREASURIES

4

Our focus thus far has been on the shape of the Treasury yield curve. In fact, often the financial press in its discussion of interest rates focuses on the Treasury yield curve. However, it is the default-free spot rate curve as represented by the Treasury spot rate curve that is used in valuing fixed-income securities. But how does one obtain the default-free spot rate curve? This curve can be constructed from the yields on Treasury securities. The Treasury issues that are candidates for inclusion are:

1. Treasury coupon strips

2. on-the-run Treasury issues

---

[3] For a further explanation of the coefficient of determination, see Richard A. DeFusco, Dennis W. McLeavey, Jerald E. Pinto, and David E. Runkle, *Quantitative Methods for Investment Analysis* (Charlottesville, VA: Association for Investment Management and Research, 2002), pp. 388–390.

3. on-the-run Treasury issues and selected off-the-run Treasury issues

4. all Treasury coupon securities and bills

Once the securities that are to be included in the construction of the theoretical spot rate curve are selected, the methodology for constructing the curve must be determined. The methodology depends on the securities included. If Treasury coupon strips are used, the procedure is simple since the observed yields are the spot rates. If the on-the-run Treasury issues with or without selected off-the-run Treasury issues are used, then the methodology of bootstrapping is used.

Using an estimated Treasury par yield curve, bootstrapping is a repetitive technique whereby the yields prior to some maturity, same m, are used to obtain the spot rate for year m. For example, suppose that the yields on the par yield curve are denoted by $y_1, \ldots, y_T$ where the subscripts denote the time periods. Then the yield for the first period, y_1, is the spot rate for the first period. Let the first period spot rate be denoted as s_1. Then y_2 and s_1 can be used to derive s_2 using arbitrage arguments. Next, y_3, s_1, and s_2 are used to derive s_3 using arbitrage arguments. The process continues until all the spot rates are derived, $s_1, \ldots, s_m$.

In selecting the universe of securities used to construct a default-free spot rate curve, one wants to make sure that the yields are not biased by any of the following: 1) default, 2) embedded options, 3) liquidity, and 4) pricing errors. To deal with default, U.S. Treasury securities are used. Issues with embedded options are avoided because the market yield reflects the value of the embedded options. In the U.S. Treasury market, there are only a few callable bonds so this is not an issue. In other countries, however, there are callable and putable government bonds. Liquidity varies by issue. There are U.S. Treasury issues that have less liquidity than bonds with a similar maturity. In fact, there are some issues that have extremely high liquidity because they are used by dealers in repurchase agreements. Finally, in some countries the trading of certain government bond issues is limited, resulting in estimated prices that may not reflect the true price.

Given the theoretical spot rate for each maturity, there are various statistical techniques that are used to create a continuous spot rate curve. A discussion of these statistical techniques is a specialist topic.

A. Treasury Coupon Strips

It would seem simplest to use the observed yield on Treasury coupon strips to construct an actual spot rate curve, but there are three problems with using the observed rates on Treasury strips. First, the liquidity of the strips market is not as great as that of the Treasury coupon market. Thus, the observed rates on strips reflect a premium for liquidity.

Second, the tax treatment of strips is different from that of Treasury coupon securities. Specifically, the accrued interest on strips is taxed even though no cash is received by the investor. Thus they are negative cash flow securities to taxable entities, and, as a result, their yield reflects this tax disadvantage.

Finally, there are maturity sectors where non-U.S. investors find it advantageous to trade off yield for tax advantages associated with a strip. Specifically, certain foreign tax authorities allow their citizens to treat the difference between the maturity value and the purchase price as a capital gain and tax this gain at a favorable tax rate. Some will grant this favorable treatment only when the strip is created from the principal rather than the coupon. For this reason, those who use Treasury strips to represent theoretical spot rates restrict the issues included to coupon strips.

B. On-the-Run Treasury Issues

The on-the-run Treasury issues are the most recently auctioned issues of a given maturity. In the U.S., these issues include the 1-month, 3-month, and 6-month Treasury bills, and the 2-year, 5-year, and 10-year Treasury notes. Treasury bills are zero-coupon instruments; the notes are coupon securities.[4]

There is an observed yield for each of the on-the-run issues. For the coupon issues, these yields are not the yields used in the analysis when the issue is not trading at par. Instead, for each on-the-run coupon issue, the estimated yield necessary to make the issue trade at par is used. The resulting on-the-run yield curve is called the par coupon curve. The reason for using securities with a price of par is to eliminate the effect of the tax treatment for securities selling at a **discount** or premium. The differential tax treatment distorts the yield.

C. On-the-Run Treasury Issues and Selected Off-the-Run Treasury Issues

One of the problems with using just the on-the-run issues is the large gap between maturities, particularly after five years. To mitigate this problem, some dealers and vendors use selected off-the-run Treasury issues. Typically, the issues used are the 20-year issue and 25-year issue.[5] Given the par coupon curve including any off-the-run selected issues, a linear interpolation method is used to fill in the gaps for the other maturities. The bootstrapping method is then used to construct the theoretical spot rate curve.

D. All Treasury Coupon Securities and Bills

Using only on-the-run issues and a few off-the-run issues fails to recognize the information embodied in Treasury prices that are not included in the analysis. Thus, some market participants argue that it is more appropriate to use all outstanding Treasury coupon securities and bills to construct the theoretical spot rate curve. Moreover, a common practice is to filter the Treasury securities universe to eliminate securities that are on special (trading at a lower yield than their true yield) in the repo market.[6]

When all coupon securities and bills are used, methodologies more complex than bootstrapping must be employed to construct the theoretical spot rate curve since there may be more than one yield for each maturity. There are various methodologies for fitting a curve to the points when all the Treasury securities are used. The methodologies make an adjustment for the effect of taxes.[7] A discussion of the various methodologies is a specialist topic.

---

[4] At one time, the Department of the Treasury issued 3-year notes, 7-year notes, 15-year bonds, 20-year bonds, and 30-year bonds.

[5] See, for example, Philip H. Galdi and Shenglin Lu, *Analyzing Risk and Relative Value of Corporate and Government Securities,* Merrill Lynch & Co., Global Securities Research & Economics Group, Fixed Income Analytics, 1997, p. 11.

[6] There must also be an adjustment for what is known as the "specials effect." This has to do with a security trading at a lower yield than its true yield because of its value in the repurchase agreement market. In a repurchase agreement, a security is used as collateral for a loan. If the security is one that is in demand by dealers, referred to as "hot collateral" or "collateral on special," then the borrowing rate is lower if that security is used as collateral. As a result of this favorable feature, a security will offer a lower yield in the market if it is on special so that the investor can finance that security cheaply. As a result, the use of the yield of a security on special will result in a biased yield estimate. The 10-year on-the-run U.S. Treasury issue is typically on special.

[7] See Oldrich A. Vasicek and H. Gifford Fong, "Term Structure Modeling Using Exponential Splines," *Journal of Finance* (May 1982), pp. 339–358.

5   THE SWAP CURVE (LIBOR CURVE)

In the United States it is common to use the Treasury spot rate curve for purposes of valuation. In other countries, either a government spot rate curve is used (if a liquid market for the securities exists) or the swap curve is used (or as explained shortly, the *LIBOR curve*). LIBOR is the London interbank offered rate and is the interest rate which major international banks offer each other on Eurodollar certificates of deposit (CD) with given maturities. The maturities range from overnight to five years. So, references to "3-month LIBOR" indicate the interest rate that major international banks are offering to pay to other such banks on a CD that matures in three months. A swap curve can be constructed that is unique to a country where there is a swap market for converting fixed cash flows to floating cash flows in that country's currency.

A.   Elements of a Swap and a Swap Curve

To discuss a swap curve, we need the basics of a generic (also called a "plain vanilla" interest rate) swap. In a generic interest rate swap two parties are exchanging cash flows based on a notional amount where 1) one party is paying fixed cash flows and receiving floating cash flows and 2) the other party is paying floating cash flows and receiving fixed cash flows. It is called a "swap" because the two parties are "swapping" payments: 1) one party is paying a floating rate and receiving a fixed rate, and 2) the other party is paying a fixed rate and receiving a floating rate. While the swap is described in terms of a "rate," the amount the parties exchange is expressed in terms of a currency and determined by using the notional amount as explained below.

For example, suppose the swap specifies that 1) one party is to pay a fixed rate of 6%, 2) the notional amount is $100 million, 3) the payments are to be quarterly, and 4) the term of the swap is 7 years. The fixed rate of 6% is called the swap rate, or equivalently, the swap fixed rate. The swap rate of 6% multiplied by the notional amount of $100 million gives the amount of the annual payment, $6 million. If the payment is to be made quarterly, the amount paid each quarter is $1.5 million ($6 million/4) and this amount is paid every quarter for the next 7 years.[8]

The floating rate in an interest rate swap can be any short-term interest rate. For example, it could be the rate on a 3-month Treasury bill or the rate on 3-month LIBOR. The most common reference rate used in swaps is 3-month LIBOR. When LIBOR is the reference rate, the swap is referred to as a "LIBOR-based swap."

Consider the swap we just used in our illustration. We will assume that the reference rate is 3-month LIBOR. In that swap, one party is paying a fixed rate of 6% (i.e., the swap rate) and receiving 3-month LIBOR for the next 7 years. Hence, the 7-year swap rate is 6%. But entering into this swap with a swap rate of 6% is equivalent to locking in 3-month LIBOR for 7 years (rolled over on a quarterly basis). So, casting this in terms of 3-month LIBOR, the 7-year maturity rate for 3-month LIBOR is 6%.

---

[8] Actually the payments are slightly different each quarter because the amount of the quarterly payment depends on the actual number of days in the quarter.

So, suppose that the swap rates for the maturities quoted in the swap market are as shown below:

Maturity (years)	Swap Rate (%)
2	4.2
3	4.6
4	5.0
5	5.3
6	5.7
7	6.0
8	6.2
9	6.4
10	6.5
15	6.7
30	6.8

This would be the swap curve. But this swap curve is also telling us how much we can lock in 3-month LIBOR for a specified future period. By locking in 3-month LIBOR it is meant that a party that pays the floating rate (i.e., agrees to pay 3-month LIBOR) is locking in a borrowing rate; the party receiving the floating rate is locking in an amount to be received. Because 3-month LIBOR is being exchanged, the swap curve is also called the LIBOR curve.

Note that we have not indicated the currency in which the payments are to be made for our hypothetical swap curve. Suppose that the swap curve above refers to swapping U.S. dollars (i.e., the notional amount is in U.S. dollars) from a fixed to a floating (and vice versa). Then the swap curve above would be the U.S. swap curve. If the notional amount was for euros, and the swaps involved swapping a fixed euro amount for a floating euro amount, then it would be the euro swap curve.

Finally, let's look at how the terms of a swap are quoted. Rather than quote a swap rate for a given maturity, the convention in the swap market is to quote a **swap spread**. The spread can be over any benchmark desired, typically a government bond yield. The swap spread is defined as follows for a given maturity:

Swap spread = Swap rate − Government yield on a bond with the same maturity as the swap

For euro-denominated swaps (i.e., swaps in which the currency in which the payments are made is the euro), the government yield used as the benchmark is the German government bond with the same maturity as the swap.

For example, consider our hypothetical 7-year swap. Suppose that the currency of the swap payments is in U.S. dollars and the estimated 7-year U.S. Treasury yield is 5.4%. Then since the swap rate is 6%, the swap spread is:

Swap spread = 6% − 5.4% = 0.6% = 60 basis points

Suppose, instead, the swap was denominated in euros and the swap rate is 6%. Also suppose that the estimated 7-year German government bond yield is 5%. Then the swap spread would be quoted as 100 basis points (6% − 5%).

Effectively the swap spread reflects the risk of the counterparty to the swap failing to satisfy its obligation. Consequently, it primarily reflects credit risk. Since the counterparties in swaps are typically bank-related entities, the swap spread is a rough indicator of the credit risk of the banking sector. Therefore, the swap rate curve is not a default-free curve. Instead, it is an inter-bank or AA rated curve.

Notice that the swap rate is compared to a government bond yield to determine the swap spread. Why would one want to use a swap curve if a government bond yield curve is available? We answer that question next.

B. Reasons for Increased Use of Swap Curve

Investors and issuers use the swap market for hedging and arbitrage purposes, and the swap curve as a benchmark for evaluating performance of fixed income securities and the pricing of fixed income securities. Since the swap curve is effectively the LIBOR curve and investors borrow based on LIBOR, the swap curve is more useful to funded investors than a government yield curve.

The increased application of the swap curve for these activities is due to its advantages over using the government bond yield curve as a benchmark. Before identifying these advantages, it is important to understand that the drawback of the swap curve relative to the government bond yield curve could be poorer liquidity. In such instances, the swap rates would reflect a liquidity premium. Fortunately, liquidity is not an issue in many countries as the swap market has become highly liquid, with narrow bid–ask spreads for a wide range of swap maturities. In some countries swaps may offer better liquidity than that country's government bond market.

The advantages of the swap curve over a government bond yield curve are:[9]

1. There is almost no government regulation of the swap market. The lack of government regulation makes swap rates across different markets more comparable. In some countries, there are some sovereign issues that offer various tax benefits to investors and, as a result, for global investors it makes comparative analysis of government rates across countries difficult because some market yields do not reflect their true yield.

2. The supply of swaps depends only on the number of counterparties that are seeking or are willing to enter into a swap transaction at any given time. Since there is no underlying government bond, there can be no effect of market technical factors[10] that may result in the yield for a government bond issue being less than its true yield.

3. Comparisons across countries of government yield curves is difficult because of the differences in sovereign credit risk. In contrast, the credit risk as reflected in the swaps curve are similar and make comparisons across countries more meaningful than government yield curves. Sovereign risk is not present in the swap curve because, as noted earlier, the swap curve is viewed as an inter-bank yield curve or AA yield curve.

4. There are more maturity points available to construct a swap curve than a government bond yield curve. More specifically, what is quoted in the swap market are swap rates for 2, 3, 4, 5, 6, 7, 8, 9, 10, 15, and 30 year maturities.

---

[9] See Uri Ron, "A Practical Guide to Swap Curve Construction," Chapter 6 in Frank J. Fabozzi (ed.), *Interest Rate, Term Structure, and Valuation Modeling* (NY: John Wiley & Sons, 2002).

[10] For example, a government bond issue being on "special" in the repurchase agreement market.

Thus, in the swap market there are 10 market interest rates with a maturity of 2 years and greater. In contrast, in the U.S. Treasury market, for example, there are only three market interest rates for on-the-run Treasuries with a maturity of 2 years or greater (2, 5, and 10 years) and one of the rates, the 10-year rate, may not be a good benchmark because it is often on special in the repo market. Moreover, because the U.S. Treasury has ceased the issuance of 30-year bonds, there is no 30-year yield available.

C. Constructing the LIBOR Spot Rate Curve

In the valuation of fixed income securities, it is not the Treasury yield curve that is used as the basis for determining the appropriate discount rate for computing the present value of cash flows but the Treasury spot rates. The Treasury spot rates are derived from the Treasury yield curve using the bootstrapping process.

Similarly, it is not the swap curve that is used for discounting cash flows when the swap curve is the benchmark but the spot rates. The spot rates are derived from the swap curve in exactly the same way—using the bootstrapping methodology. The resulting spot rate curve is called the LIBOR spot rate curve. Moreover, a forward rate curve can be derived from the spot rate curve. The same thing is done in the swap market. The forward rate curve that is derived is called the LIBOR forward rate curve. Consequently, if we understand the mechanics of moving from the yield curve to the spot rate curve to the forward rate curve in the Treasury market, there is no reason to repeat an explanation of that process here for the swap market; that is, it is the same methodology, just different yields are used.[11]

EXPECTATIONS THEORIES OF THE TERM STRUCTURE OF INTEREST RATES

6

So far we have described the different types of curves that analysts and portfolio managers focus on. The key curve is the spot rate curve because it is the spot rates that are used to value the cash flows of a fixed-income security. The spot rate curve is also called the term structure of interest rates, or simply term structure. Now we turn to another potential use of the term structure. Analysts and portfolio managers are interested in knowing if there is information contained in the term structure that can be used in making investment decisions. For this purpose, market participants rely on different theories about the term structure.

We explained four theories of the term structure of interest rates—pure expectations theory, liquidity preference theory, preferred habitat theory, and market segmentation theory. Unlike the market segmentation theory, the first

---

[11] The question is what yields are used to construct the swap rate curve. Practitioners use yields from two related markets: the Eurodollar CD futures contract and the swap market. We will not review the Eurodollar CD futures contract here. For now, the only important fact to note about this contract is that it provides a means for locking in 3-month LIBOR in the future. In fact, it provides a means for doing so for an extended time into the future.

Practitioners use the Eurodollar CD futures rate up to four years to get 3-month LIBOR for every quarter. While there are Eurodollar CD futures contracts that settle further out than four years, for technical reasons (having to do with the convexity of the contract), analysts use only the first four years. (In fact, this actually varies from practitioner to practitioner. Some will use the Eurodollar CD futures from two years up to four years.) For maturities after four years, the swap rates are used to get 3-month LIBOR. As noted above, there is a swap rate for maturities for each year 10, and then swap rates for 15 years and 30 years.

three theories share a hypothesis about the behavior of short-term forward rates and also assume that the forward rates in current long-term bonds are closely related to the market's expectations about future short-term rates. For this reason, the pure expectations theory, liquidity preference theory, and preferred habitat theory are referred to as expectations theories of the term structure of interest rates.

What distinguishes these three expectations theories is whether there are systematic factors other than expectations of future interest rates that affect forward rates. The pure expectations theory postulates that no systematic factors other than expected future short-term rates affect forward rates; the liquidity preference theory and the preferred habitat theory assert that there are other factors. Accordingly, the last two forms of the expectations theory are sometimes referred to as biased expectations theories. The relationship among the various theories is described below and summarized in Exhibit 3.

A. The Pure Expectations Theory

According to the pure expectations theory, forward rates exclusively represent expected future spot rates. Thus, the entire term structure at a given time reflects the market's current expectations of the family of future short-term rates. Under this view, a rising term structure must indicate that the market expects short-term rates to rise throughout the relevant future. Similarly, a flat term structure reflects an expectation that future short-term rates will be mostly constant, while a falling term structure must reflect an expectation that future short-term rates will decline.

1. Drawbacks of the Theory

The pure expectations theory suffers from one shortcoming, which, qualitatively, is quite serious. It neglects the risks inherent in investing in bonds. If forward rates were perfect predictors of future interest rates, then the future prices of bonds would be known with certainty. The return over any investment period would be certain and independent of the maturity of the instrument acquired. However, with the uncertainty about future interest rates and, therefore, about

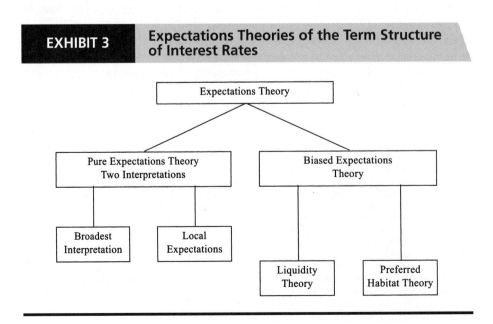

EXHIBIT 3   Expectations Theories of the Term Structure of Interest Rates

future prices of bonds, these instruments become risky investments in the sense that the return over some investment horizon is unknown.

There are two risks that cause uncertainty about the return over some investment horizon. The first is the uncertainty about the price of the bond at the end of the investment horizon. For example, an investor who plans to invest for five years might consider the following three investment alternatives:

Alternative 1:   Invest in a 5-year zero-coupon bond and hold it for five years.
Alternative 2:   Invest in a 12-year zero-coupon bond and sell it at the end of five years.
Alternative 3:   Invest in a 30-year zero-coupon bond and sell it at the end of five years.

The return that will be realized in Alternatives 2 and 3 is not known because the price of each of these bonds at the end of five years is unknown. In the case of the 12-year bond, the price will depend on the yield on 7-year bonds five years from now; and the price of the 30-year bond will depend on the yield on 25-year bonds five years from now. Since forward rates implied in the current term structure for a 7-year bond five years from now and a 25-year bond five years from now are not perfect predictors of the actual future rates, there is uncertainty about the price for both bonds five years from now. Thus, there is interest rate risk; that is, the price of the bond may be lower than currently expected at the end of the investment horizon due to an increase in interest rates. An important feature of interest rate risk is that it increases with the length of the bond's maturity.

The second risk involves the uncertainty about the rate at which the proceeds from a bond that matures prior to the end of the investment horizon can be reinvested until the maturity date, that is, reinvestment risk. For example, an investor who plans to invest for five years might consider the following three alternative investments:

Alternative 1:   Invest in a 5-year zero-coupon bond and hold it for five years.
Alternative 2:   Invest in a 6-month zero-coupon instrument and, when it matures, reinvest the proceeds in 6-month zero-coupon instruments over the entire 5-year investment horizon.
Alternative 3:   Invest in a 2-year zero-coupon bond and, when it matures, reinvest the proceeds in a 3-year zero-coupon bond.

The risk for Alternatives 2 and 3 is that the return over the 5-year investment horizon is unknown because rates at which the proceeds can be reinvested until the end of the investment horizon are unknown.

2. Interpretations of the Theory

There are several interpretations of the pure expectations theory that have been put forth by economists. These interpretations are not exact equivalents nor are they consistent with each other, in large part because they offer different treatments of the two risks associated with realizing a return that we have just explained.[12]

---

[12] These formulations are summarized by John Cox, Jonathan Ingersoll, Jr., and Stephen Ross, "A Re-examination of Traditional Hypotheses About the Term Structure of Interest Rates," *Journal of Finance* (September 1981), pp. 769–799.

a. Broadest Interpretation

The broadest interpretation of the pure expectations theory suggests that investors expect the return for any investment horizon to be the same, regardless of the maturity strategy selected.[13] For example, consider an investor who has a 5-year investment horizon. According to this theory, it makes no difference if a 5-year, 12-year, or 30-year bond is purchased and held for five years since the investor expects the return from all three bonds to be the same over the 5-year investment horizon. A major criticism of this very broad interpretation of the theory is that, because of price risk associated with investing in bonds with a maturity greater than the investment horizon, the expected returns from these three very different investments should differ in significant ways.[14]

b. Local Expectations Form of the Pure Expectations Theory

A second interpretation, referred to as the local expectations form of the pure expectations theory, suggests that the return will be the same over a short-term investment horizon starting today. For example, if an investor has a 6-month investment horizon, buying a 1-year, 5-year or 10-year bond will produce the same 6-month return.

To illustrate this, we will use the hypothetical yield curve shown in Exhibit 4. We have previously used the yield curve in Exhibit 4 to show how to compute spot rates and forward rates. Exhibit 5 shows all the 6-month forward rates. We will focus on the 1-year, 5-year, and 10-year issues.

Our objective is to look at what happens to the total return over a 6-month investment horizon for the 1-year, 5-year, and 10-year issues if all the 6-month forward rates are realized. Look first at panel a in Exhibit 6. This shows the total return for the 1-year issue. At the end of 6 months, this issue is a 6-month issue. The 6-month forward rate is 3.6%. This means that if the forward rate is realized, the 6-month yield 6 months from now will be 3.6%. Given a 6-month issue that must offer a yield of 3.6% (the 6-month forward rate), the price of this issue will decline from 100 (today) to 99.85265 six months from now. The price must decline because if the 6-month forward rate is realized 6 months from now, the yield increases from 3.3% to 3.6%. The total dollars realized over the 6 months are coupon interest adjusted for the decline in the price. The total return for the 6 months is 3%.

What the local expectations theory asserts is that over the 6-month investment horizon even the 5-year and the 10-year issues will generate a total return of 3% if forward rates are realized. Panels b and c show this to be the case. We need only explain the computation for one of the two issues. Let's use the 5-year issue. The 6-month forward rates are shown in the third column of panel b. Now we apply a few principles discussed previously. We demonstrate that to value a security each cash flow should be discounted at the spot rate with the same maturity. We also demonstrate that 6-month forward rates can be used to value the cash flows of a security and that the results will be identical using the forward rates to value a security. For example, consider the cash flow in period 3 for the 5-year issue. The cash flow is $2.60. The 6-month forward rates are 3.6%, 3.92%,

---

[13] F. Lutz, "The Structure of Interest Rates," *Quarterly Journal of Economics* (1940–41), pp. 36–63.

[14] Cox, Ingersoll, and Ross, pp. 774–775.

EXHIBIT 4	Hypothetical Treasury Par Yield Curve			
Period	**Years**	**Annual Yield to Maturity (BEY)(%)[a]**	**Price**	**Spot Rate (BEY)(%)**
1	0.5	3.00	—	3.0000
2	1.0	3.30	—	3.3000
3	1.5	3.50	100.00	3.5053
4	2.0	3.90	100.00	3.9164
5	2.5	4.40	100.00	4.4376
6	3.0	4.70	100.00	4.7520
7	3.5	4.90	100.00	4.9622
8	4.0	5.00	100.00	5.0650
9	4.5	5.10	100.00	5.1701
10	5.0	5.20	100.00	5.2772
11	5.5	5.30	100.00	5.3864
12	6.0	5.40	100.00	5.4976
13	6.5	5.50	100.00	5.6108
14	7.0	5.55	100.00	5.6643
15	7.5	5.60	100.00	5.7193
16	8.0	5.65	100.00	5.7755
17	8.5	5.70	100.00	5.8331
18	9.0	5.80	100.00	5.9584
19	9.5	5.90	100.00	6.0863
20	10.0	6.00	100.00	6.2169

[a] The yield to maturity and the spot rate are annual rates. They are reported as **bond-equivalent yields**. To obtain the semiannual yield or rate, one half the annual yield or annual rate is used.

EXHIBIT 5	Six-Month Forward Rates: The Short-Term Forward Rate Curve (Annualized Rates on a Bond-Equivalent Basis)		
Notation	**Forward Rate**	**Notation**	**Forward Rate**
$_1f_0$	3.00	$_1f_{10}$	6.48
$_1f_1$	3.60	$_1f_{11}$	6.72
$_1f_2$	3.92	$_1f_{12}$	6.97
$_1f_3$	5.15	$_1f_{13}$	6.36
$_1f_4$	6.54	$_1f_{14}$	6.49
$_1f_5$	6.33	$_1f_{15}$	6.62
$_1f_6$	6.23	$_1f_{16}$	6.76
$_1f_7$	5.79	$_1f_{17}$	8.10
$_1f_8$	6.01	$_1f_{18}$	8.40
$_1f_9$	6.24	$_1f_{19}$	8.72

and 5.15%. These are annual rates. So, half these rates are 1.8%, 1.96%, and 2.575%. The present value of $2.60 using the 6-month forward is:

$$\frac{\$2.60}{(1.018)\,(1.0196)\,(1.02575)} = \$2.44205$$

This is the present value shown in the third column of panel b. In a similar manner, all of the other present values in the third column are computed. The arbitrage-free value for this 5-year issue 6 months from now (when it is a 4.5-year issue) is 98.89954. The total return (taking into account the coupon interest and the loss due to the decline in price from 100) is 3%. Thus, if the 6-month forward rates are realized, all three issues provide a short-term (6-month) return of 3%.[15]

EXHIBIT 6	Total Return over 6-Month Investment Horizon if 6-Month Forward Rates Are Realized

a: Total return on 1-year issue if forward rates are realized

Period	Cash Flow ($)	Six-Month Forward Rate (%)	Price at Horizon ($)
1	101.650	3.60	99.85265

Price at horizon: 99.85265   Total proceeds: 101.5027
Coupon: 1.65   Total return: 3.00%

b: Total return on 5-year issue if forward rates are realized

Period	Cash Flow ($)	Six-Month Forward Rate (%)	Present Value ($)
1	2.60	3.60	2.55403
2	2.60	3.92	2.50493
3	2.60	5.15	2.44205
4	2.60	6.54	2.36472
5	2.60	6.33	2.29217
6	2.60	6.23	2.22293
7	2.60	5.79	2.16039
8	2.60	6.01	2.09736
9	102.60	6.24	80.26096
		Total	98.89954

Price at horizon: 98.89954   Total proceeds: 101.4995
Coupon: 2.60   Total return: 3.00%

(Exhibit continued on next page . . .)

---

[15] It has been demonstrated that the local expectations formulation, which is narrow in scope, is the only interpretation of the pure expectations theory that can be sustained in equilibrium. See Cox, Ingersoll, and Ross, "A Re-examination of Traditional Hypotheses About the Term Structure of Interest Rates."

EXHIBIT 6   (continued)

c: Total return on 10-year issue if forward rates are realized

Period	Cash Flow ($)	Six-Month Forward Rate (%)	Present Value ($)
1	3.00	3.60	2.94695
2	3.00	3.92	2.89030
3	3.00	5.15	2.81775
4	3.00	6.54	2.72853
5	3.00	6.33	2.64482
6	3.00	6.23	2.56492
7	3.00	5.79	2.49275
8	3.00	6.01	2.42003
9	3.00	6.24	2.34681
10	3.00	6.48	2.27316
11	3.00	6.72	2.19927
12	3.00	6.97	2.12520
13	3.00	6.36	2.05970
14	3.00	6.49	1.99497
15	3.00	6.62	1.93105
16	3.00	6.76	1.86791
17	3.00	8.10	1.79521
18	3.00	8.40	1.72285
19	103.00	8.72	56.67989
		Total	98.50208

Price at horizon: 98.50208   Total proceeds: 101.5021

Coupon: 3.00   Total return: 3.00%

c. Forward Rates and Market Consensus

We have already seen how various types of forward rates can be computed. That is, how to compute the forward rate for any length of time beginning at any future period of time. So, it is possible to compute the 2-year forward rate beginning 5 years from now or the 3-year forward rate beginning 8 years from now. We showed how, using arbitrage arguments, forward rates can be derived from spot rates.

Previously, no interpretation was given to the forward rates. The focus was just on how to compute them from spot rates based on arbitrage arguments. Let's provide two interpretations now with a simple illustration. Suppose that an investor has a 1-year investment horizon and has a choice of investing in either a 1-year Treasury bill or a 6-month Treasury bill and rolling over the proceeds from the maturing 6-month issue in another 6-month Treasury bill. Since the Treasury bills are zero-coupon securities, the rates on them are spot rates and can be used to compute the 6-month forward rate six months from now. For example, if the 6-month Treasury bill rate is 5% and the 1-year Treasury bill rate is 5.6%, then the 6-month forward rate six months from now is 6.2%. To verify this, suppose an investor invests $100 in a 1-year investment. The $100 investment in a zero-coupon instrument will grow at a rate of 2.8% (one-half 5.6%) for two 6-month periods to:

$$\$100\,(1.028)^2 = \$105.68$$

If $100 is invested in a six month zero-coupon instrument at 2.5% (one-half 5%) and the proceeds reinvested at the 6-month forward rate of 3.1% (one-half 6.2%), the $100 will grow to:

$$\$100\,(1.025)(1.031) = \$105.68$$

Thus, the 6-month forward rate generates the same future dollars for the $100 investment at the end of 1 year.

One interpretation of the forward rate is that it is a "break-even rate." That is, a forward rate is the rate that will make an investor indifferent between investing for the full investment horizon and part of the investment horizon and rolling over the proceeds for the balance of the investment horizon. So, in our illustration, the forward rate of 6.2% can be interpreted as the break-even rate that will make an investment in a 6-month zero-coupon instrument with a yield of 5% rolled-over into another 6-month zero-coupon instrument equal to the yield on a 1-year zero-coupon instrument with a yield of 5.6%.

Similarly, a 2-year forward rate beginning four years from now can be interpreted as the break-even rate that will make an investor indifferent between investing in 1) a 4-year zero-coupon instrument at the 4-year spot rate and rolling over the investment for two more years in a zero-coupon instrument and 2) investing in a 6-year zero-coupon instrument at the 6-year spot rate.

A second interpretation of the forward rate is that it is a rate that allows the investor to lock in a rate for some future period. For example, consider once again our 1-year investment. If an investor purchases this instrument rather than the 6-month instrument, the investor has locked in a 6.2% rate six months from now regardless of how interest rates change six months from now. Similarly, in the case of a 6-year investment, by investing in a 6-year zero-coupon instrument rather than a 4-year zero-coupon instrument, the investor has locked in the 2-year zero-coupon rate four years from now. That locked in rate is the 2-year forward rate four years from now. The 1-year forward rate five years from now is the rate that is locked in by buying a 6-year zero-coupon instrument rather than investing in a 5-year zero-coupon instrument and reinvesting the proceeds at the end of five years in a 1-year zero-coupon instrument.

There is another interpretation of forward rates. Proponents of the pure expectations theory argue that forward rates reflect the "market's consensus" of future interest rates. They argue that forward rates can be used to predict future interest rates. A natural question about forward rates is then how well they do at predicting future interest rates. Studies have demonstrated that forward rates do not do a good job at predicting future interest rates.[16] Then, why is it so important to understand forward rates? The reason is that forward rates indicate how an investor's expectations must differ from the "break-even rate" or the "lock-in rate" when making an investment decision.

Thus, even if a forward rate may not be realized, forward rates can be highly relevant in deciding between two alternative investments. Specifically, if an

---

[16] Eugene F. Fama, "Forward Rates as Predictors of Future Spot Rates," *Journal of Financial Economics*, Vol. 3, No. 4, 1976, pp. 361–377.

investor's expectation about a rate in the future is less than the corresponding forward rate, then he would be better off investing now to lock in the forward rate.

B. Liquidity Preference Theory

We have explained that the drawback of the pure expectations theory is that it does not consider the risks associated with investing in bonds. We know that the interest rate risk associated with holding a bond for one period is greater the longer the maturity of a bond. (Recall that duration increases with maturity.)

Given this uncertainty, and considering that investors typically do not like uncertainty, some economists and financial analysts have suggested a different theory—the liquidity preference theory. This theory states that investors will hold longer-term maturities if they are offered a long-term rate higher than the average of expected future rates by a risk premium that is positively related to the term to maturity.[17] Put differently, the forward rates should reflect both interest rate expectations and a "liquidity" premium (really a risk premium), and the premium should be higher for longer maturities.

According to the liquidity preference theory, forward rates will not be an unbiased estimate of the market's expectations of future interest rates because they contain a liquidity premium. Thus, an upward-sloping yield curve may reflect expectations that future interest rates either 1) will rise, or 2) will be unchanged or even fall, but with a liquidity premium increasing fast enough with maturity so as to produce an upward-sloping yield curve. That is, any shape for either the yield curve or the term structure of interest rates can be explained by the biased expectations theory.

C. The Preferred Habitat Theory

Another theory, known as the preferred habitat theory, also adopts the view that the term structure reflects the expectation of the future path of interest rates as well as a risk premium. However, the preferred habitat theory rejects the assertion that the risk premium must rise uniformly with maturity.[18] Proponents of the preferred habitat theory say that the latter conclusion could be accepted if all investors intend to liquidate their investment at the shortest possible date while all borrowers are anxious to borrow long. This assumption can be rejected since institutions have holding periods dictated by the nature of their liabilities.

The preferred habitat theory asserts that if there is an imbalance between the supply and demand for funds within a given maturity range, investors and borrowers will not be reluctant to shift their investing and financing activities out of their preferred maturity sector to take advantage of any imbalance. However, to do so, investors must be induced by a yield premium in order to accept the risks associated with shifting funds out of their preferred sector. Similarly, borrowers can only be induced to raise funds in a maturity sector other than their preferred sector by a sufficient cost savings to compensate for the corresponding funding risk.

Thus, this theory proposes that the shape of the yield curve is determined by both expectations of future interest rates and a risk premium, positive or negative,

---

[17] John R. Hicks, *Value and Capital* (London: Oxford University Press, 1946), Second Ed., pp. 141–145.

[18] Franco Modigliani and Richard Sutch, "Innovations in Interest Rate Policy," *American Economic Review* (May 1966), pp. 178–197.

to induce market participants to shift out of their preferred habitat. Clearly, according to this theory, yield curves that slope up, down, or flat are all possible.

7   MEASURING YIELD CURVE RISK

We now know how to construct the term structure of interest rates and the potential information content contained in the term structure that can be used for making investment decisions under different theories of the term structure. Next we look at how to measure exposure of a portfolio or position to a change in the term structure. This risk is referred to as yield curve risk.

Yield curve risk can be measured by changing the spot rate for a particular key maturity and determining the sensitivity of a security or portfolio to this change holding the spot rate for the other key maturities constant. The sensitivity of the change in value to a particular change in spot rate is called rate duration. There is a rate duration for every point on the spot rate curve. Consequently, there is not one rate duration, but a vector of durations representing each maturity on the spot rate curve. The total change in value if all rates change by the same number of basis points is simply the effective duration of a security or portfolio to a parallel shift in rates. Recall that effective duration measures the exposure of a security or portfolio to a parallel shift in the term structure, taking into account any embedded options.

This rate duration approach was first suggested by Donald Chambers and Willard Carleton in 1988,[19] who called it "duration vectors." Robert Reitano suggested a similar approach in a series of papers and referred to these durations as "partial durations."[20] The most popular version of this approach is that developed by Thomas Ho in 1992.[21]

Ho's approach focuses on 11 key maturities of the spot rate curve. These rate durations are called key rate durations. The specific maturities on the spot rate curve for which a key rate duration is measured are 3 months, 1 year, 2 years, 3 years, 5 years, 7 years, 10 years, 15 years, 20 years, 25 years, and 30 years. Changes in rates between any two key rates are calculated using a linear approximation.

The impact of any type of yield curve shift can be quantified using key rate durations. A level shift can be quantified by changing all key rates by the same number of basis points and determining, based on the corresponding key rate durations, the effect on the value of a portfolio. The impact of a steepening of the yield curve can be found by 1) decreasing the key rates at the short end of the yield curve and determining the positive change in the portfolio's value using the corresponding key rate durations, and 2) increasing the key rates at the long end of the yield curve and determining the negative change in the portfolio's value using the corresponding key rate durations.

To simplify the key rate duration methodology, suppose that instead of a set of 11 key rates, there are only three key rates—2 years, 16 years, and 30 years.[22] The duration of a zero-coupon security is approximately the number of years

---

[19] Donald Chambers and Willard Carleton, "A Generalized Approach to Duration," *Research in Finance* 7 (1988).

[20] See, for example, Robert R. Reitano, "Non-Parallel Yield Curve Shifts and Durational Leverage," *Journal of Portfolio Management* (Summer 1990), pp. 62–67, and "A Multivariate Approach to Duration Analysis," *ARCH* 2 (1989).

[21] Thomas S.Y. Ho, "Key Rate Durations: Measures of Interest Risk," *The Journal of Fixed Income* (September 1992), pp. 29–44.

[22] This is the numerical example used by Ho, "Key Rate Durations," p. 33.

to maturity. Thus, the three key rate durations are 2, 16, and 30. Consider the following two $100 portfolios composed of 2-year, 16-year, and 30-year issues:

Portfolio	2-Year Issue ($)	16-Year Issue ($)	30-Year Issue ($)
I	50	0	50
II	0	100	0

The key rate durations for these three points will be denoted by $D(1)$, $D(2)$, and $D(3)$ and defined as follows:

$D(1)$ = key rate duration for the 2-year part of the curve
$D(2)$ = key rate duration for the 16-year part of the curve
$D(3)$ = key rate duration for the 30-year part of the curve

The key rate durations for the three issues and the duration are as follows:

Issue	$D(1)$	$D(2)$	$D(3)$	Crash Duration
2-year	2	0	0	2
16-year	0	16	0	16
30-year	0	0	30	30

A portfolio's key rate duration is the weighted average of the key rate durations of the securities in the portfolio. The key rate duration and the effective duration for each portfolio are calculated below:

Portfolio I
$D(1) = (50/100) \times 2 + (0/100) \times 0 + (50/100) \times 0 = 1$
$D(2) = (50/100) \times 0 + (0/100) \times 16 + (50/100) \times 0 = 0$
$D(3) = (50/100) \times 0 + (0/100) \times 0 + (50/100) \times 30 = 15$

Effective duration $= (50/100) \times 2 + (0/100) \times 16 + (50/100) \times 30 = 16$

Portfolio II
$D(1) = (0/100) \times 2 + (100/100) \times 0 + (0/100) \times 0 = 0$
$D(2) = (0/100) \times 0 + (100/100) \times 16 + (0/100) \times 0 = 16$
$D(3) = (0/100) \times 0 + (100/100) \times 0 + (0/100) \times 30 = 0$

Effective duration $= (0/100) \times 2 + (100/100) \times 16 + (0/100) \times 30 = 16$

Thus, the key rate durations differ for the two portfolios. However, the effective duration for each portfolio is the same. Despite the same effective duration, the performance of the two portfolios will not be the same for a nonparallel shift in the spot rates. Consider the following three scenarios:

Scenario 1: All spot rates shift down 10 basis points.
Scenario 2: The 2-year key rate shifts up 10 basis points and the 30-year rate shifts down 10 basis points.

Scenario 3: The 2-year key rate shifts down 10 basis points and the 30-year rate shifts up 10 basis points.

Let's illustrate how to compute the estimated total return based on the key rate durations for Portfolio I for scenario 2. The 2-year key rate duration [D(1)] for Portfolio I is 1. For a 100 basis point increase in the 2-year key rate, the portfolio's value will decrease by approximately 1%. For a 10 basis point increase (as assumed in scenario 2), the portfolio's value will decrease by approximately 0.1%. Now let's look at the change in the 30-year key rate in scenario 2. The 30-year key rate duration [D(3)] is 15. For a 100 basis point decrease in the 30-year key rate, the portfolio's value will increase by approximately 15%. For a 10 basis point decrease (as assumed in scenario 2), the increase in the portfolio's value will be approximately 1.5%. Consequently, for Portfolio I in scenario 2 we have:

change in portfolio's value due to 2-year key rate change	−0.1%
change in portfolio's value due to 30-year key rate change	+1.5%
change in portfolio value	+1.4%

In the same way, the total return for both portfolios can be estimated for the three scenarios. The estimated total returns are shown below:

Portfolio	Scenario 1 (%)	Scenario 2 (%)	Scenario 3 (%)
I	1.6	1.4	−1.4
II	1.6	0	0

Thus, only for the parallel yield curve shift (scenario 1) do the two portfolios have identical performance based on their durations.

Key rate durations are different for ladder, barbell, and bullet portfolios. A ladder portfolio is one with approximately equal dollar amounts (market values) in each maturity sector. A barbell portfolio has considerably greater weights given to the shorter and longer maturity bonds than to the intermediate maturity bonds. A bullet portfolio has greater weights concentrated in the intermediate maturity relative to the shorter and longer maturities.

The key rate duration profiles for a ladder, a barbell, and a bullet portfolio are graphed in Exhibit 7.[23] All these portfolios have the same effective duration. As can be seen, the ladder portfolio has roughly the same key rate duration for all the key maturities from year 2 on. For the barbell portfolio, the key rate durations are much greater for the 5-year and 20-year key maturities and much smaller for the other key maturities. For the bullet portfolio, the key rate duration is substantially greater for the 10-year maturity than the duration for other key maturities.

---

[23] The portfolios whose key rate durations are shown in Exhibit 7 were hypothetical Treasury portfolios constructed on April 23, 1997.

EXHIBIT 7	Key Rate Duration Profile for Three Treasury Portfolios (April 23, 1997): Ladder, Barbell, and Bullet

(a) Ladder Portfolio

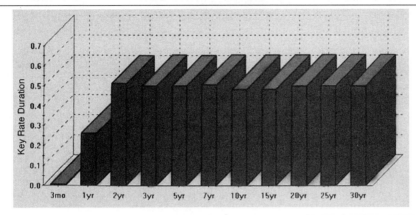

(b) Barbell Portfolio

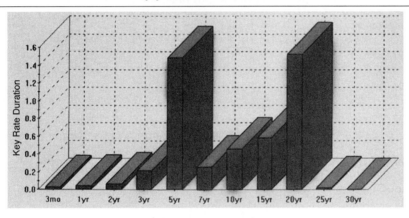

(c) Bullet Portfolio

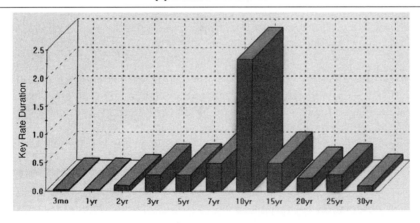

Source: Barra.

8

YIELD VOLATILITY AND MEASUREMENT

In assessing the interest rate exposure of a security or portfolio one should combine effective duration with yield volatility because effective duration alone is not sufficient to measure interest rate risk. The reason is that effective duration says that if interest rates change, a security's or portfolio's market value will change by approximately the percentage projected by its effective duration. However, the risk exposure of a portfolio to rate changes depends on how likely and how much interest rates may change, a parameter measured by yield volatility. For example, consider a U.S. Treasury security with an effective duration of 6 and a government bond of an emerging market country with an effective duration of 4. Based on effective duration alone, it would seem that the U.S. Treasury security has greater interest rate risk than the emerging market government bond. Suppose that yield volatility is substantial in the emerging market country relative to in the United States. Then the effective durations alone are not sufficient to identify the interest rate risk.

There is another reason why it is important to be able to measure yield or interest rate volatility: it is a critical input into a valuation model. An assumption of yield volatility is needed to value bonds with embedded options and structured products. The same measure is also needed in valuing some interest rate derivatives (i.e., options, caps, and floors).

In this section, we look at how to measure yield volatility and discuss some techniques used to estimate it. Volatility is measured in terms of the standard deviation or variance. We will see how yield volatility as measured by the daily percentage change in yields is calculated from historical yields. We will see that there are several issues confronting an investor in measuring historical yield volatility. Then we turn to modeling and forecasting yield volatility.

A. Measuring Historical Yield Volatility

Market participants seek a measure of yield volatility. The measure used is the standard deviation or variance. Here we will see how to compute yield volatility using historical data.

The sample variance of a random variable using historical data is calculated using the following formula:

$$\text{Variance} = \frac{\sum_{t=1}^{T} (X_t - \overline{X})^2}{T - 1} \qquad (1)$$

and then

$$\text{Standard deviation} = \sqrt{\text{Variance}}$$

where

X_t = observation t of variable X
$\overline{X}$ = the sample mean for variable X
T = the number of observations in the sample

Our focus is on yield volatility. More specifically, we are interested in the change in the daily yield relative to the previous day's yield. So, for example, suppose the yield on a zero-coupon Treasury bond was 6.555% on Day 1 and 6.593% on Day 2. The relative change in yield would be:

$$\frac{6.593\% - 6.555\%}{6.555\%} = 0.005797$$

This means if the yield is 6.555% on Day 1 and grows by 0.005797 in one day, the yield on Day 2 will be:

$$6.555\% \, (1.005797) = 6.593\%$$

If instead of assuming simple compounding it is assumed that there is continuous compounding, the relative change in yield can be computed as the natural logarithm of the ratio of the yield for two days. That is, the relative yield change can be computed as follows:

$$\text{Ln} \, (6.593\%/6.555\%) = 0.0057804$$

where "Ln" stands for the natural logarithm. There is not much difference between the relative change of daily yields computed assuming simple compounding and continuous compounding.[24] In practice, continuous compounding is used. Multiplying the natural logarithm of the ratio of the two yields by 100 scales the value to a percentage change in daily yields.

Therefore, letting y_t be the yield on day t and y_{t-1} be the yield on day $t-1$, the percentage change in yield, X_t, is found as follows:

$$X_t = 100[\text{Ln}(y_t/y_{t-1})]$$

In our example, y_t is 6.593% and y_{t-1} is 6.555%. Therefore,

$$X_t = 100[\text{Ln}(6.593/6.555)] = 0.57804\%$$

To illustrate how to calculate a daily standard deviation from historical data, consider the data in Exhibit 8 which show the yield on a Treasury zero for 26 consecutive days. From the 26 observations, 25 days of percentage yield changes are calculated in Column 3. Column 4 shows the square of the deviations of the observations from the mean. The bottom of Exhibit 8 shows the calculation of the daily mean for 25 yield changes, the variance, and the standard deviation. The daily standard deviation is 0.6360%.

The daily standard deviation will vary depending on the 25 days selected. It is important to understand that the daily standard deviation is dependent on the period selected, a point we return to later in this reading.

1. Determining the Number of Observations

In our illustration, we used 25 observations for the daily percentage change in yield. The appropriate number of observations depends on the situation at hand. For example, traders concerned with overnight positions might use the 10 most recent trading days (i.e., two weeks). A bond portfolio manager who is concerned with longer term volatility might use 25 trading days (about one month). The selection of the number of observations can have a significant effect on the calculated daily standard deviation.

[24] See DeFusco, McLeavey, Pinto, and Runkle, *Quantitative Methods for Investment Analysis.*

EXHIBIT 8		Calculation of Daily Standard Deviation Based on 26 Daily Observations for a Treasury Zero	
(1) t	**(2)** y_t	**(3)** $X_t = 100 [Ln(y_t/y_{t-1})]$	**(4)** $(X_t - \bar{X})^2$
0	6.6945		
1	6.699	0.06720	0.02599
2	6.710	0.16407	0.06660
3	6.675	−0.52297	0.18401
4	6.555	−1.81411	2.95875
5	6.583	0.42625	0.27066
6	6.569	−0.21290	0.01413
7	6.583	0.21290	0.09419
8	6.555	−0.42625	0.11038
9	6.593	0.57804	0.45164
10	6.620	0.40869	0.25270
11	6.568	−0.78860	0.48246
12	6.575	0.10652	0.04021
13	6.646	1.07406	1.36438
14	6.607	−0.58855	0.24457
15	6.612	0.07565	0.02878
16	6.575	−0.56116	0.21823
17	6.552	−0.35042	0.06575
18	6.515	−0.56631	0.22307
19	6.533	0.27590	0.13684
20	6.543	0.15295	0.06099
21	6.559	0.24424	0.11441
22	6.500	−0.90360	0.65543
23	6.546	0.70520	0.63873
24	6.589	0.65474	0.56063
25	6.539	−0.76173	0.44586
	Total	−2.35020	9.7094094

$$\text{Sample mean} = \bar{X} = \frac{-2.35020\%}{25} = -0.09401\%$$

$$\text{Variance} = \frac{9.7094094\%}{25 - 1} = 0.4045587\%$$

$$\text{Std dev} = \sqrt{0.4045587\%} = 0.6360493\%$$

2. Annualizing the Standard Deviation

The daily standard deviation can be annualized by multiplying it by the square root of the number of days in a year.[25] That is,

$$\text{Daily standard deviation} \times \sqrt{\text{Number of days in a year}}$$

Market practice varies with respect to the number of days in the year that should be used in the annualizing formula above. Some investors and traders use the number of days in the year, 365 days, to annualize the daily standard deviation. Some investors and traders use only either 250 days or 260 days to annualize. The latter is simply the number of trading days in a year based on five trading days per week for 52 weeks. The former reduces the number of trading days of 260 for 10 non-trading holidays.

Thus, in calculating an annual standard deviation, the investor must decide on:

1. the number of daily observations to use.

2. the number of days in the year to use to annualize the daily standard deviation.

The annual standard deviation for the daily standard deviation based on the 25-daily yield changes shown in Exhibit 8 (0.6360493%) using 250 days, 260 days, and 365 days to annualize are as follows:

250 Days	260 Days	365 Days
10.06%	10.26%	12.15%

Now keep in mind that all of these decisions regarding the number of days to use in the daily standard deviation calculation, which set of days to use, and the number of days to use to annualize are not merely an academic exercise. Eventually, the standard deviation will be used in either the valuation of a security or in the measurement of risk exposure and can have a significant impact on the resulting value.

3. Using the Standard Deviation with Yield Estimation

What does it mean if the annual standard deviation for the *change in* the Treasury zero yield is 12%? It means that if the prevailing yield is 8%, then the annual standard deviation of the yield change is 96 basis points. This is found by multiplying the annual standard deviation of the yield change of 12% by the prevailing yield of 8%.

Assuming that yield volatility is approximately normally distributed, we can use the normal distribution to construct a confidence interval for the future yield.[26] For example, we know that there is a 68.3% probability that an interval

---

[25] For any probability distribution, it is important to assess whether the value of a random variable in one period is affected by the value that the random variable took on in a prior period. Casting this in terms of yield changes, it is important to know whether the yield today is affected by the yield in a prior period. The term *serial correlation* is used to describe the correlation between the yield in different periods. Annualizing the daily yield by multiplying the daily standard deviation by the square root of the number of days in a year assumes that serial correlation is not significant.

[26] See Chapter 4 in DeFusco, McLeavey, Pinto, and Runkle, *Quantitative Methods for Investment Analysis*.

PRACTICE QUESTION 1

A. The daily yields for 26 days are given below. Compute the daily percentage change in yield for each day assuming continuous compounding.

t	y_t
0	7.17400
1	7.19400
2	7.21800
3	7.15100
4	7.02500
5	7.02400
6	7.03000
7	7.02000
8	6.96400
9	6.90400
10	6.89671
11	6.85300
12	6.87100
13	6.88300
14	6.87500
15	6.87800
16	6.80400
17	6.84300
18	6.79500
19	6.79500
20	6.85400
21	6.81000
22	6.77300
23	6.86700
24	6.88700
25	6.88100

B. Compute the daily standard deviation.

PRACTICE QUESTION 2

Based on the daily standard deviation computed in Practice Question 1, compute the annualized standard deviation based on the following number of days: a) 250, b) 260, and c) 365.

between *one* standard deviation below and above the sample expected value will bracket the future yield. The sample expected value is the prevailing yield. If the annual standard deviation is 96 basis points and the prevailing yield is 8%, then there is a 68.3% probability that the range between 7.04% (8% minus 96 basis points) and 8.96% (8% plus 96 basis points) will include the future yield. For *three* standard deviations below and above the prevailing yield, there is a 99.7% probability. Using the numbers above, three standard deviations are 288 basis points (3 times 96 basis points). The interval is then 5.12% (8% minus 288 basis points) and 10.88% (8% plus 288 basis points).

The interval or range constructed is called a "confidence interval."[27] Our first interval of 7.04% to 8.96% is a 68.3% confidence interval. Our second interval of 5.12% to 10.88% is a 99.7% confidence interval. A confidence interval with any probability can be constructed.

B. Historical versus Implied Volatility

Market participants estimate yield volatility in one of two ways. The first way is by estimating historical yield volatility. This is the method that we have thus far described in this reading. The resulting volatility is called historical volatility. The second way is to estimate yield volatility based on the observed prices of interest rate options and caps. Yield volatility calculated using this approach is called **implied volatility**.

The implied volatility is based on some option pricing model. One of the inputs to any option pricing model in which the underlying is a Treasury security or Treasury futures contract is expected yield volatility. If the observed price of an option is assumed to be the fair price and the option pricing model is assumed to be the model that would generate that fair price, then the implied yield volatility is the yield volatility that, when used as an input into the option pricing model, would produce the observed option price.

There are several problems with using implied volatility. First, it is assumed the option pricing model is correct. Second, option pricing models typically assume that volatility is constant over the life of the option. Therefore, interpreting an implied volatility becomes difficult.[28]

C. Forecasting Yield Volatility

As has been seen, the yield volatility as measured by the standard deviation can vary based on the time period selected and the number of observations. Now we turn to the issue of forecasting yield volatility. There are several methods. Before describing these methods, let's address the question of what mean value should be used in the calculation of the forecasted standard deviation.

Suppose at the end of Day 12 a trader was interested in a forecast for volatility using the 10 most recent days of trading and updating that forecast at the end of each trading day. What mean value should be used?

The trader can calculate a 10-day moving average of the daily percentage yield change. Exhibit 8 shows the daily percentage change in yield for the

---

[27] See Chapter 6 in DeFusco, MacLeavey, Pinto, and Runkle, *Quantitative Methods for Investment Analysis*.

[28] For a further discussion, see Frank J. Fabozzi and Wai Lee, "Measuring and Forecasting Yield Volatility," Chapter 16 in Frank J. Fabozzi (ed.), *Perspectives on Interest Rate Risk Management for Money Managers and Traders* (New Hope, PA: Frank J. Fabozzi Associates, 1998).

EXHIBIT 9	10-Day Moving Average of Daily Yield Change for Treasury Zero

10-Trading Days Ending	Daily Average (%)
Day 12	−0.20324
Day 13	−0.04354
Day 14	0.07902
Day 15	0.04396
Day 16	0.00913
Day 17	−0.04720
Day 18	−0.06121
Day 19	−0.09142
Day 20	−0.11700
Day 21	−0.01371
Day 22	−0.11472
Day 23	−0.15161
Day 24	−0.02728
Day 25	−0.11102

Treasury zero from Day 1 to Day 25. To calculate a moving average of the daily percentage yield change at the end of Day 12, the trader would use the 10 trading days from Day 3 to Day 12. At the end of Day 13, the trader will calculate the 10-day average by using the percentage yield change on Day 13 and would exclude the percentage yield change on Day 3. The trader will use the 10 trading days from Day 4 to Day 13.

Exhibit 9 shows the 10-day moving average calculated from Day 12 to Day 25. Notice the considerable variation over this period. The 10-day moving average ranged from −0.20324% to 0.07902%.

Thus far, it is assumed that the moving average is the appropriate value to use for the expected value of the change in yield. However, there are theoretical arguments that suggest it is more appropriate to assume that the expected value of the change in yield will be zero.[29] In the equation for the variance given by Equation 1, the value of zero is used for $\overline{X}$ rather than the moving average. If zero is substituted into Equation 1, the equation for the variance becomes:

$$\text{Variance} = \frac{\sum_{t=1}^{T} X_t^2}{T - 1} \tag{2}$$

There are various methods for forecasting daily volatility. The daily standard deviation given by Equation 2 assigns an equal weight to all observations. So, if a trader is calculating volatility based on the most recent 10 days of trading, each day is given a weight of 0.10.

---

[29]Jacques Longerstacey and Peter Zangari, *Five Questions about RiskMetrics™*, JP Morgan Research Publication 1995.

EXHIBIT 10	Moving Averages of Daily Standard Deviations Based on 10 Days of Observations

10-Trading Days Ending	Moving Average Daily Standard Deviation (%)
Day 12	0.75667
Day 13	0.81874
Day 14	0.58579
Day 15	0.56886
Day 16	0.59461
Day 17	0.60180
Day 18	0.61450
Day 19	0.59072
Day 20	0.57705
Day 21	0.52011
Day 22	0.59998
Day 23	0.53577
Day 24	0.54424
Day 25	0.60003

For example, suppose that a trader is interested in the daily volatility of our hypothetical Treasury zero yield and decides to use the 10 most recent trading days. Exhibit 10 reports the 10-day volatility for various days using the data in Exhibit 8 and the standard deviation derived from the formula for the variance given by Equation 2.

There is reason to suspect that market participants give greater weight to recent movements in yield or price when determining volatility. To give greater importance to more recent information, observations farther in the past should be given less weight. This can be done by revising the variance as given by Equation 2 as follows:

$$\text{Variance} = \frac{\sum_{t=1}^{T} W_t X_t^2}{T-1} \tag{3}$$

where W_t is the weight assigned to observation t such that the sum of the weights is equal to T (i.e., $\Sigma\ W_t = T$) and the farther the observation is from today, the lower the weight. The weights should be assigned so that the forecasted volatility reacts faster to a recent major market movement and declines gradually as we move away from any major market movement.

Finally, a time series characteristic of financial assets suggests that a period of high volatility is followed by a period of high volatility. Furthermore, a period of relative stability in returns appears to be followed by a period that can be characterized in the same way. This suggests that volatility today may depend upon recent prior volatility. This can be modeled and used to forecast volatility. The statistical model used to estimate this time series property of volatility is called an autoregressive conditional heteroskedasticity (ARCH) model.[30] The term "conditional" means that the value of the variance depends on or is conditional on the value of the random variable. The term heteroskedasticity means that the variance is not equal for all values of the random variable. The foundation for ARCH models is a specialist topic.[31]

[30] See Robert F. Engle, "Autoregressive Conditional Heteroskedasticity with Estimates of Variance of U.K. Inflation," *Econometrica* 50 (1982), pp. 987–1008.

[31] See Chapter 9 in DeFusco, McLeavey, Pinto, and Runkle, *Quantitative Methods for Investment Analysis*.

SUMMARY

- Historically, four shapes have been observed for the yield curve: 1) normal or positively sloped (i.e., the longer the maturity, the higher the yield), 2) flat (i.e., the yield for all maturities is approximately equal), 3) inverted or negatively sloped (i.e., the longer the maturity, the lower the yield), and 4) a humped yield curve.

- The spread between long-term Treasury yields and short-term Treasury yields is referred to as the steepness or slope of the yield curve.

- Some investors define the slope of the yield curve as the spread between the 30-year yield and the 3-month yield and others as the spread between the 30-year yield and the 2-year yield.

- A shift in the yield curve refers to the relative change in the yield for each Treasury maturity.

- A parallel shift in the yield curve refers to a shift in which the change in the yield for all maturities is the same; a nonparallel shift in the yield curve means that the yield for all maturities does not change by the same number of basis points.

- Historically, the two types of nonparallel yield curve shifts that have been observed are a twist in the slope of the yield curve and a change in the curvature of the yield curve.

- A flattening of the yield curve means that the slope of the yield curve has decreased; a steepening of the yield curve means that the slope has increased.

- A butterfly shift is the other type of nonparallel shift—a change in the curvature or humpedness of the yield curve.

- Historically, the factors that have been observed to drive Treasury returns are 1) a shift in the level of interest rates, 2) a change in the slope of the yield curve, and 3) a change in the curvature of the yield curve.

- The most important factor driving Treasury returns is a shift in the level of interest rates. Two other factors, in decreasing importance, include changes in the yield curve slope and changes in the curvature of the yield curve.

- The universe of Treasury issues that can be used to construct the theoretical spot rate curve is 1) on-the-run Treasury issues, 2) on-the-run Treasury issues and selected off-the-run Treasury issues, 3) all Treasury coupon securities and bills, and 4) Treasury strips.

- There are three methodologies that have been used to derive the theoretical spot rate curve: 1) bootstrapping when the universe is on-the-run Treasury issues (with and without selected off-the-run issues), 2) econometric modeling for all Treasury coupon securities and bills, and 3) simply the observed yields on Treasury coupon strips.

- The problem with using Treasury coupon strips is that the observed yields may be biased due to a liquidity premium or an unfavorable tax treatment.

- The swap rate is the rate at which fixed cash flows can be exchanged for floating cash flows.

- In a LIBOR-based swap, the swap curve provides a yield curve for LIBOR.

- A swap curve can be constructed that is unique to a country where there is a swap market.

- The swap spread is primarily a gauge of the credit risk associated with a country's banking sector.

▶ The advantages of using a swap curve as the benchmark interest rate rather than a government bond yield curve are 1) there is almost no government regulation of the swap market making swap rates across different markets more comparable, 2) the supply of swaps depends only on the number of counterparties that are seeking or are willing to enter into a swap transaction at any given time, 3) comparisons across countries of government yield curves is difficult because of the differences in sovereign credit risk, and 4) there are more maturity points available to construct a swap curve than a government bond yield curve.

▶ From the swap yield curve a LIBOR spot rate curve can be derived using the bootstrapping methodology and the LIBOR forward rate curve can be derived.

▶ The three forms of the expectations theory (the pure expectations theory, the liquidity preference theory, and the preferred habitat theory) assume that the forward rates in current long-term bonds are closely related to the market's expectations about future short-term rates.

▶ The three forms of the expectations theory differ on whether or not other factors also affect forward rates, and how.

▶ The pure expectations theory postulates that no systematic factors other than expected future short-term rates affect forward rates.

▶ Because forward rates are not perfect predictors of future interest rates, the pure expectations theory neglects the risks (interest rate risk and reinvestment risk) associated with investing in Treasury securities.

▶ The broadest interpretation of the pure expectations theory suggests that investors expect the return for any investment horizon to be the same, regardless of the maturity strategy selected.

▶ The local expectations form of the pure expectations theory suggests that the return will be the same over a short-term investment horizon starting today, and it is this narrow interpretation that economists have demonstrated is the only interpretation that can be sustained in equilibrium.

▶ Two interpretations of forward rates based on arbitrage arguments are that they are 1) "break-even rates" and 2) rates that can be locked in.

▶ Advocates of the pure expectations theory argue that forward rates are the market's consensus of future interest rates.

▶ Forward rates have not been found to be good predictors of future interest rates; however, an understanding of forward rates is still extremely important because of their role as break-even rates and rates that can be locked in.

▶ The liquidity preference theory and the preferred habitat theory assert that there are other factors that affect forward rates and these two theories are therefore referred to as biased expectations theories.

▶ The liquidity preference theory states that investors will hold longer-term maturities only if they are offered a risk premium and therefore forward rates should reflect both interest rate expectations and a liquidity risk premium.

▶ The preferred habitat theory, in addition to adopting the view that forward rates reflect the expectation of the future path of interest rates as well as a risk premium, argues that the yield premium need not reflect a liquidity risk but instead reflects the demand and supply of funds in a given maturity range.

▶ A common approach to measure yield curve risk is to change the yield for a particular maturity of the yield curve and determine the sensitivity of a security or portfolio to this change holding all other key rates constant.

▶ Key rate duration is the sensitivity of a portfolio's value to the change in a particular key rate.

▶ The most popular version of key rate duration uses 11 key maturities of the spot rate curve (3 months, 1, 2, 3, 5, 7, 10, 15, 20, 25, and 30 years).

▶ Variance is a measure of the dispersion of a random variable around its expected value.

▶ The standard deviation is the square root of the variance and is a commonly used measure of volatility.

▶ Yield volatility can be estimated from daily yield observations.

▶ The observation used in the calculation of the daily standard deviation is the natural logarithm of the ratio of one day's and the previous day's yield.

▶ The selection of the time period (the number of observations) can have a significant effect on the calculated daily standard deviation.

▶ A daily standard deviation is annualized by multiplying it by the square root of the number of days in a year.

▶ Typically, either 250 days, 260 days, or 365 days are used to annualize the daily standard deviation.

▶ Implied volatility can also be used to estimate yield volatility based on some option pricing model.

▶ In forecasting volatility, it is more appropriate to use an expectation of zero for the mean value.

▶ The simplest method for forecasting volatility is weighting all observations equally.

▶ A forecasted volatility can be obtained by assigning greater weight to more recent observations.

▶ Autoregressive conditional heteroskedasticity (ARCH) models can be used to capture the time series characteristic of yield volatility in which a period of high volatility is followed by a period of high volatility and a period of relative stability appears to be followed by a period that can be characterized in the same way.

PRACTICE PROBLEMS FOR READING 49

1. What are the four types of shapes observed for the yield curve?

2. How is the slope of the yield curve defined and measured?

3. Historically, how has the slope of the long end of the yield curve differed from that of the short end of the yield curve at a given point in time?

4. **A.** What are the three factors that have empirically been observed to affect Treasury returns?

   B. What has been observed to be the most important factor in affecting Treasury returns?

   C. Given the most important factor identified in Part B, justify the use of duration as a measure of interest rate risk.

   D. What has been observed to be the second most important factor in affecting Treasury returns?

   E. Given the second most important factor identified in Part D, justify the use of a measure of interest rate risk in addition to duration.

5. **A.** What are the limitations of using just the on-the-run Treasury issues to construct the theoretical spot rate curve?

   B. Why if all Treasury bills and Treasury coupon securities are used to construct the theoretical spot rate curve is it not possible to use the bootstrapping method?

6. **A.** What are the problems with using the yield on Treasury strips to construct the theoretical spot rate curve?

   B. Why, even if a practitioner decides to use the yield on Treasury strips to construct the theoretical spot rate curve despite the problems identified in Part A, will the practitioner restrict the analysis to Treasury coupon strips?

7. What are the advantages of using the swap curve as a benchmark of interest rates relative to a government bond yield curve?

8. How can a spot rate curve be constructed for a country that has a liquid swap market?

9. **A.** What is a swap spread?

   B. What is the swap spread indicative of?

10. **A.** What is the pure expectations theory?

    B. What are the shortcomings of the pure expectations theory?

11. Based on the broadest interpretation of the pure expectations theory, what would be the difference in the 4-year total return if an investor purchased a 7-year zero-coupon bond or a 15-year zero-coupon bond?

12. Based on the local expectations form of the pure expectations theory, what would be the difference in the 6-month total return if an investor purchased a 5-year zero-coupon bond or a 2-year zero-coupon bond?

13. Comment on the following statement made by a portfolio manager to a client:

> Proponents of the unbiased expectations theory argue that the forward rates built into the term structure of interest rates are the market's consensus of future interest rates. We disagree with the theory because studies suggest that forward rates are poor predictors of future interest rates. Therefore, the position that our investment management firm takes is that forward rates are irrelevant and provide no information to our managers in managing a bond portfolio.

14. Based on arbitrage arguments, give two interpretations for each of the following three forward rates:

   A. The 1-year forward rate seven years from now is 6.4%.

   B. The 2-year forward rate one year from now is 6.2%.

   C. The 8-year forward rate three years from now is 7.1%.

15. There are two forms of the "biased" expectations theory. Why are these two forms referred to as "biased" expectations?

16. You are the financial consultant to a pension fund. After your presentation to the trustees of the fund, you asked the trustees if they have any questions. You receive the two questions below. Answer each one.

   A. "The yield curve is upward-sloping today. Doesn't this suggest that the market consensus is that interest rates are expected to increase in the future and therefore you should reduce the interest rate risk exposure for the portfolio that you are managing for us?"

   B. "I am looking over one of the pages in your presentation that shows spot rates and I am having difficulty in understanding it. The spot rates at the short end (up to three years) are increasing with maturity. For maturities greater than three years but less than eight years, the spot rates are declining with maturity. Finally, for maturities greater than eight years the spot rates are virtually the same for each maturity. There is simply no expectations theory that would explain that type of shape for the term structure of interest rates. Is this market simply unstable?"

17. Below are the key rate durations for three portfolios of U.S. Treasury securities, all with the same duration for a parallel shift in the yield curve.

A. For each portfolio describe the type of portfolio (barbell, ladder, or bullet).

Key Rate Maturity	Portfolio A	Portfolio B	Portfolio C
3-month	0.04	0.04	0.03
1-year	0.06	0.29	0.07
2-year	0.08	0.67	0.31
3-year	0.28	0.65	0.41
5-year	0.38	0.65	1.90
7-year	0.65	0.64	0.35
10-year	3.38	0.66	0.41
15-year	0.79	0.67	0.70
20-year	0.36	0.64	1.95
25-year	0.12	0.62	0.06
30-year	0.06	0.67	0.01

B. Which portfolio will benefit the most if the spot rate for the 10-year decreases by 50 basis points while the spot rate for all other key maturities changes very little?

C. What is the duration for a parallel shift in the yield curve for the three portfolios?

18. Compute the 10-day daily standard deviation of the percentage change in yield assuming continuous compounding and assuming the following daily yields.

t	y_t
0	5.854
1	5.843
2	5.774
3	5.719
4	5.726
5	5.761
6	5.797
7	5.720
8	5.755
9	5.787
10	5.759

19. For the daily yield volatility computed in the previous question, what is the annual yield volatility assuming the following number of days in the year?

   A. 250 days.

   B. 260 days.

   C. 365 days.

20. Comment on the following statement: "Two portfolio managers with the same set of daily yields will compute the same historical annual volatility."

21. Suppose that the annualized standard deviation for the change in the 2-year Treasury yield based on daily yields is 7% and the current level of the 2-year Treasury yield is 5%. Assuming that the probability distribution for the percentage change in 2-year Treasury yields is approximately normally distributed, how would you interpret the 7% annualized standard deviation?

22. A. What is implied volatility?

   B. What are the problems associated with using implied volatility as a measure of yield volatility?

23. A. In forecasting yield volatility, why would a manager not want to weight each daily yield change equally?

   B. In forecasting yield volatility, what is recommended for the sample mean in the formula for the variance or standard deviation?

The following information relates to Questions 24–29 and is based on "General Principles of Credit Analysis" and this reading

Sheila Lane, a U.S.-based fixed income portfolio manager, is considering adding asset-backed or sovereign debt securities to her managed portfolios. For asset-backed securities (ABS), Lane is considering only true securitization structures where the seller is AA-rated. For sovereign securities, she is considering only securities issued by national governments. She asks two analysts to assist her in evaluating the credit ratings of these securities.

    Frank Bauer, an ABS analyst, states:

  1. "When assigning credit ratings, the rating agencies consider four different factors: the credit quality of the collateral, the quality of the servicer, the seller's operating cash flow, and the ABS cash flow payment structure."

  2. "Because only true securitizations are being considered, the role of the servicer is to collect and distribute collateral cash flow."

    Benjamin Hinault, a sovereign debt analyst, remarks:

  1. "Sovereign debt from the same issuer can receive different credit ratings depending on whether the debt is denominated in local currency or foreign currency."

  2. "Different portfolio strategies within a specific government bond market and over the same time horizon will have the same return assuming forward interest rates are realized."

After reviewing the asset-backed and sovereign debt securities markets, Lane decides to invest in UK Gilt Strips. She considers the following investments:

#1:   £50 million market value of a 5-year strip bond;

#2:   £35 million market value of a 2-year strip bond and £15 million market value in a 12-year strip bond;

#3:   £37.5 million market value of a 5-year strip bond and £12.5 million market value of a 30-year strip bond.

Lane wishes to determine the estimated change in value for these investments using key rate duration analysis. In her analysis, she assumes the 2-year interest rate increases by 50 basis points instantaneously and that all other interest rates remain constant.

24. Is Bauer's first statement *most likely* correct?

   A. Yes.

   B. No, the quality of the servicer is not considered by the rating agencies.

   C. No, the seller's operating cash flow is not considered by the rating agencies.

25. Is Bauer's second statement *most likely* correct?

   A. Yes.

   B. No, the servicer is responsible for collateral maintenance so that it generates sufficient net cash flow.

   C. No, the servicer is required to maintain collateral quality so that the asset-backed securities remain investment grade.

26. Is Hinault's first remark *most likely* correct?

   A. Yes.

   B. No, because sovereign debt will carry the same rating no matter the currency of denomination.

   C. No, because differential credit ratings on sovereign debt depend on the country's fiscal and monetary policy when the debt is issued.

27. Under which theory of the term structure of interest rates would Hinault's second remark *most likely* be correct?

   A. Preferred habitat theory.

   B. Pure expectations theory.

   C. Liquidity preference theory.

28. Given Lane's expected change in interest rates, which of the following best describes the relation between Investments #1 and #2?

   A. Investment #1 would have approximately a 0.7% greater value than Investment #2.

   B. Investment #2 would have approximately a 0.7% greater value than Investment #1.

   C. Investment #1 would have approximately a 1.0% greater value than Investment #2.

29. The duration of Investment #3 is *closest* to:

   A. 7.5.

   B. 11.3.

   C. 17.5.

The following information relates to Questions 30–35 and is based on "General Principles of Credit Analysis" and this reading

Kate Campbell is the manager of a U.S. Treasury bond portfolio. She is considering increasing the portfolio's exposure to zero-coupon U.S. Treasury securities and asks her assistant, Naomi Moss, to investigate what determines the return on these bonds. Moss replies that three factors determine the return on zero-coupon U.S. Treasury bonds:

▶ the level of the yield curve;
▶ the slope of the yield curve;
▶ the curvature of the yield curve.

Intrigued by the role of the slope of yield curve, Campbell asks Moss for more information on the determinants of the term structure of interest rates. Moss replies:

> "The pure expectations theory and preferred habitat theory both assume that the forward rates in current long-term bonds are closely related to the market's expectations about future short-term rates."

Campbell learns that the investment mandate of her portfolio has been expanded to allow investments in asset-backed bonds, U.S. municipal revenue bonds, and non-dollar sovereign bonds. Campbell asks Moss to investigate the potential risks and credit rating issues involved with these bonds. Moss writes a report that makes the following statements:

1. "The role of the servicer in a securitization transaction is critical for asset-backed bonds. Therefore the rating agencies analyze servicing history and costs to the special purpose vehicle before assigning a credit rating."

2. "For U.S. municipal revenue bonds, the three areas that the legal opinion should address are: the flow-of-funds structure; limits of the basic security; and the stability of the excess spread."

3. "For non-dollar sovereign bonds, the key factors considered by S&P in assigning the local currency credit rating are a) the balance of payments, b) fiscal policy and budgetary flexibility, and c) monetary policy and inflation pressures."

After reading Moss's report, Campbell has decided to invest in the German government bond market. Campbell asks Moss to help structure this portion of the portfolio. Moss proposes the following alternative portfolios, each consisting solely of zero-coupon German government bonds:

EXHIBIT 1	Alternative Portfolio Weights		
	Portfolio I (%)	Portfolio II (%)	Portfolio III (%)
2-year maturity	50	—	25
16-year maturity	—	100	50
30-year maturity	50	—	25
TOTAL	**100**	**100**	**100**

30. Which factor in Moss's list has the least impact on zero-coupon
U.S. Treasury bond returns?

   A. The level of the yield curve.

   B. The slope of the yield curve.

   C. The curvature of the yield curve.

31. Is Moss's response regarding theories about the term structure of interest
rates correct?

   A. Yes.

   B. No, preferred habitat theory does not make an assumption of market's
   expectations.

   C. No, pure expectations theory does not make an assumption of market's
   expectations.

32. Is the first statement from Moss's report correct?

   A. Yes.

   B. No, servicing history is not a factor.

   C. No, costs to the special purpose vehicle are not a factor.

33. Is the second statement from Moss's report correct?

   A. Yes.

   B. No, flow-of-funds structure is not addressed in the legal opinion.

   C. No, stability of the excess spread is not addressed in the legal opinion.

34. The third statement from Moss's report is *most likely* incorrect with respect
to the:

   A. balance of payments.

   B. fiscal policy and budgetary flexibility.

   C. monetary policy and inflation pressures.

35. If the 2-year key rate shifts up by 10 bps and the 30-year key rate shifts down
by 20 bps, the difference in total return between portfolio III and portfolio
I would be *closest* to:

   A. 1.45%.

   B. 2.90%.

   C. 4.35%.

SOLUTIONS FOR READING 49

1. Historically, four shapes have been observed for the yield curve. A positively sloping or normal yield curve is where the longer the maturity, the higher the yield. A flat yield curve is where the yield for all maturities is approximately the same. A negatively sloped or inverted yield curve is where yield decreases as maturity increases. A humped yield curve is where yield increases for a range of maturities and then decreases.

2. The slope of the yield curve is measured by the difference between long-term Treasury yields and short-term Treasury yields. While there is no industrywide accepted definition of the maturity used for the long-end and the maturity for the short-end of the yield curve, some market participants define the slope of the yield curve as the difference between the 30-year yield and the 3-month yield while other market participants define the slope of the yield curve as the difference between the 30-year yield and the 2-year yield. The more accepted measure is the latter. However, for some sectors of the bond market such as the mortgage sector, the slope of the yield curve is measured by the spread between the 10-year yield and 2-year yield.

3. Historically, the slope of the long end of the yield curve has been flatter than the slope of the short end of the yield curve.

4. **A.** Studies have shown that there have been three factors that affect Treasury returns: 1) changes in the level of yields, 2) changes in the slope of the yield curve, and 3) changes in the curvature of the yield curve.

   B. The most important factor is the change in the level of interest rates.

   C. The implication is that the manager of a Treasury portfolio should control for its exposure to changes in the level of interest rates. For this reason it is important to have a measure such as duration to quantify exposure to a parallel shift in the yield curve.

   D. The second most important factor is changes in the yield curve slope.

   E. The implication is that a measure such as duration must be supplemented with information about a portfolio's exposure to changes in the slope of the yield curve—a measure such as key rate duration.

5. **A.** One limitation is that there is a large gap between maturities for the on-the-run issues, and a linear extrapolation is used to get the yield for maturities between the on-the-runs. A second limitation is that information is lost about the yield on other Treasury securities. Finally, one or more of the on-the-run issues may be on special in the repo market and thereby distort the true yield for these issues.

   B. Since there may be more than one Treasury issue for a given maturity and since there are callable securities and securities trading at a price different from par (leading to tax issues), a methodology for handling these problems must be used. The bootstrapping methodology does not deal with such problems.

6. **A.** There are three problems with using the observed rates on Treasury strips: 1) there is a liquidity premium for the observed yields in the strips market because strips are not as liquid as Treasury coupon securities; 2) the tax treatment of strips is different from that of

Treasury coupon securities—the accrued interest on strips is taxed even though no cash is received by the investor—resulting in the yield on strips reflecting this tax disadvantage; and 3) there are maturity sectors where non-U.S. investors find it advantageous to trade off yield for tax advantages in their country that are associated with a strip.

B. A practitioner may restrict the use of Treasury strips to construct the theoretical spot rate curve to coupon strips because of the tax aspect mentioned in Part A. Specifically, certain foreign tax authorities allow their citizens to treat the difference between the maturity value and the purchase price as a capital gain and tax this gain at a favorable tax rate. Some will grant this favorable treatment only when the strip is created from the principal rather than the coupon. Any such bias can be avoided by just using coupon strips.

7. The advantages are that 1) there are typically more points available to construct a swap curve than a government bond yield curve; 2) there are no distortions in yields caused by bonds being on special in the repo market; and 3) comparisons across countries are easier because there is almost no government regulation and no distortions caused by tax benefits.

8. If the country has a liquid swap market with a wide spectrum of maturities, a swap curve can be developed. By the bootstrapping methodology, the spot rate curve for that country can be derived.

9. A. The convention in the swap market is to quote the fixed rate (i.e., the swap rate) as a spread over an estimated government yield for a bond with the same maturity as the swap. That spread is called the swap spread.

B. Since the credit risk in a swap is that the counterparty will fail to make the contractual payments and typically the counterparty is a high credit quality bank, the swap spread is a gauge of the credit risk associated with the banking sector.

10. A. The pure expectations theory postulates that no systematic factors other than expected future short-term rates affect forward rates. According to the pure expectations theory, forward rates exclusively represent expected future rates. Thus, the entire term structure at a given time reflects the market's current expectations of the family of future short-term rates.

B. The pure expectations theory neglects the risks inherent in investing in bonds. If forward rates were perfect predictors of future interest rates, then the future prices of bonds would be known with certainty. The return over any investment period would be certain and independent of the maturity of the instrument acquired. However, with the uncertainty about future interest rates and, therefore, about future prices of bonds, these instruments become risky investments in the sense that the return over some investment horizon is unknown.

11. The broadest interpretation of the pure expectations theory asserts that there is no difference in the 4-year total return if an investor purchased a 7-year zero-coupon bond or a 15-year zero-coupon bond.

12. The local expectations form of the pure expectations theory asserts that the total return over a 6-month horizon for a 5-year zero-coupon bond would be the same as for a 2-year zero-coupon bond.

13. The first sentence of the statement is correct. Moreover, it is correct that studies have shown that forward rates are poor predictors of future interest rates. However, the last sentence of the statement is incorrect. Forward rates should not be ignored because they indicate break-even rates and rates that can be locked in. So, they play an important role in investment decisions.

14. The two interpretations of forward rates are that they are break-even rates and they are rates that can be locked in.

   A. For the 1-year forward rate seven years from now of 6.4% the two interpretations are as follows:

     i. 6.4% is the rate that will make an investor indifferent between buying an 8-year zero-coupon bond or investing in a 7-year zero-coupon bond and when it matures reinvesting in a zero-coupon bond that matures in one year, and

     ii. 6.4% is the rate that can be locked in today by buying an 8-year zero-coupon bond rather than investing in a 7-year zero-coupon bond and when it matures reinvesting in a zero-coupon bond that matures in one year.

   B. For the 2-year forward rate one year from now of 6.2% the two interpretations are as follows:

     i. 6.2% is the rate that will make an investor indifferent between buying a 3-year zero-coupon bond or investing in a 1-year zero-coupon bond and when it matures reinvesting in a zero-coupon bond that matures in two years, and

     ii. 6.2% is the rate that can be locked in today by buying a 3-year zero-coupon bond rather than investing in a 1-year zero-coupon bond and when it matures reinvesting in a zero-coupon bond that matures in two years.

   C. For the 8-year forward rate three years from now of 7.1% the two interpretations are as follows:

     i. 7.1% is the rate that will make an investor indifferent between buying an 11-year zero-coupon bond or investing in a 3-year zero-coupon bond and when it matures reinvesting in a zero-coupon bond that matures in eight years, and

     ii. 7.1% is the rate that can be locked in today by buying an 11-year zero-coupon bond rather than investing in a 3-year zero-coupon bond and when it matures reinvesting in a zero-coupon bond that matures in eight years.

15. All expectations theories—the pure expectations theory, the liquidity preference theory, and the preferred habitat theory—share a hypothesis about the behavior of short-term forward rates and also assume that the forward rates in current long-term bonds are closely related to the market's expectations about future short-term rates. While the pure expectations theory postulates that no systematic factors other than expected future short-term rates affect forward rates, the liquidity preference theory and the preferred habitat theory postulate that there are other factors and therefore are referred to as biased expectations theories. The liquidity preference theory asserts that investors demand a liquidity premium for extending maturity so that the forward rates are biased by this premium. The preferred habitat theory asserts that investors must be induced by a yield premium in order to accept the risks associated with shifting funds out of their preferred sector and forward rates embody the premium for this inducement.

16. A. Proponents of the pure expectations theory would assert that an upward-sloping yield curve is a market's forecast of a rise in interest rates. If that is correct, an expected rise in interest rates would mean that the manager should shorten or reduce the duration (i.e., interest rate risk) of the portfolio. However, the pure expectations theory has serious pitfalls and the forward rates are not good predictors of future interest rates.

B. The preferred habitat form of the biased expectations theory is consistent with the shape of the spot rate curve observed. The preferred habitat theory asserts that if there is an imbalance between the supply and demand for funds within a given maturity sector, market participants (i.e., borrowers and investors) will agree to shift their financing and investing activities out of their preferred maturity sector to take advantage of any such imbalance. However, participants will demand compensation for shifting out of their preferred maturity sector in the form of a yield premium. Consequently, any shape for the spot rate curve (and yield curve) can result, such as the one observed in the question. Therefore, the trustee's statement is incorrect.

(*Note*: The question only asked about *expectations* theories of the term structure of interest rates. Another theory, the market segmentation theory, asserts that when there are supply and demand imbalances within a maturity sector, market participants will not shift out of their preferred maturity sector. Consequently, different maturity sectors reflect supply and demand imbalances within each sector, and the type of yield curve observed in the question is possible.)

17. A. Portfolio A is the bullet portfolio because its 10-year key rate duration dominates by far the key rate duration for the other maturities. Portfolio B is the laddered portfolio because the key rate durations after year 2 are roughly equal. Portfolio C is the barbell portfolio with the short end of the barbell at 5 years and the long end of the barbell at 20 years.

B. The bullet portfolio has the highest 10-year key rate duration and will therefore increase the most if the 10-year spot rate decreases while the key rates for the other maturities do not change much.

C. Adding up the key rate durations for each portfolio gives 6.2. This is the duration of all three portfolios if the spot rate for all key maturities changes by the same number of basis points—that is, a parallel shift in the spot rate for the key maturities.

18. The information for computing the daily standard deviation for yield volatility is shown below:

t	y_t	$X_t = 100 [Ln (y_t/y_{t-1})]$	$(X_t - \bar{X})^2$
0	5.854		
1	5.843	−0.18808	0.00060
2	5.774	−1.18793	1.04922
3	5.719	−0.95711	0.62964
4	5.726	0.12232	0.08176
5	5.761	0.60939	0.59753
6	5.797	0.62295	0.61868
7	5.720	−1.33717	1.37724
8	5.755	0.61002	0.59851
9	5.787	0.55450	0.51568
10	5.759	−0.48502	0.10330
	Total	−1.63613	5.57216825

$$\text{Sample mean} = \bar{X} = \frac{-1.63613}{10} = -0.163613\%$$

$$\text{Variance} = \frac{5.57216825}{10-1} = 0.6191298$$

$$\text{Std dev} = \sqrt{0.6191298} = 0.786848\%$$

19. A. Using 250 days: $\sqrt{250}\ (0.786848\%) = 12.44\%$

   B. Using 260 days: $\sqrt{260}\ (0.786848\%) = 12.69\%$

   C. Using 365 days: $\sqrt{365}\ (0.786848\%) = 15.03\%$

20. This is not necessarily the case because with the same data there are still choices that the managers must make that may result in quite different estimates of historical volatility. These choices include the number of days to use and the annualization of the daily standard deviation.

21. Since the current level of the 2-year Treasury yield is 5%, then the annual standard deviation of 7% translates into a 35 basis point (5% times 7%) standard deviation. Assuming that yield volatility is approximately normally distributed, we can use the normal distribution to construct an interval or range for what the future yield will be. There is a 68.3% probability that the yield will be between one standard deviation below and above the expected value. The expected value is the prevailing yield. If the annual standard deviation is 35 basis points and the prevailing yield is 5%, then there is a 68.3% probability that the yield next year will be between 4.65% (5% minus 35 basis points) and 5.35% (5% plus 35 basis points). There is a 99.7% probability that the yield next year will be within three standard deviations. In our case, three standard deviations is 105 basis points. Therefore there is a 99.7% probability that the yield will be between 3.95% (5% minus 105 basis points) and 6.05% (5% plus 105 basis points).

22. A. Yield volatility can be estimated from the observed prices of interest rate options and caps. A yield volatility estimated in this way is called implied volatility and is based on some option pricing model. An input to any option pricing model in which the underlying is a Treasury security or Treasury futures contract is expected yield volatility. If the observed price of an option is assumed to be the fair price and the option pricing model is assumed to be the model that would generate that fair price, then the implied yield volatility is the yield volatility that when used as an input into the option pricing model would produce the observed option price.

   B. The problems with using implied volatility are that 1) it is assumed the option pricing model is correct, and 2) since option pricing models typically assume that volatility is constant over the life of the option, interpreting an implied volatility becomes difficult.

23. A. There are reasons to believe that market participants give greater weight to recent movements in yield when determining volatility. To incorporate this belief into the estimation of historical volatility, different weights can be assigned to the observed changes in daily yields. More specifically, observations further in the past should be given less weight.

   B. Some market practitioners argue that in forecasting volatility the expected value or mean that should be used in the formula for the variance is zero.

24. C is correct. The factors considered by rating agencies are the credit quality of the collateral, quality of the servicer, cash flow stress and payment structure, and legal structure. The seller's operating cash flow is irrelevant to the ABS credit quality because the ABS is not determined by the seller's corporate credit—in fact the ABS is issued apart from the seller and can often carry a higher credit rating than that of the seller.

25. A is correct. In a true securitization, the servicer's role is simply to collect and distribute cash flow.

26. A is correct. Historically, the default frequency is greater for foreign currency debt than local currency debt. A sovereign issuer must obtain foreign currency in the open market or through trade to service foreign currency denominated debt. A sovereign issuer can raise local currency through taxes or other controls on its domestic financial system. Therefore, it is easier to repay debt denominated in local currency.

27. B is correct. If the pure expectations theory holds and if the forward rates implied by the expectations are actually realized, then the return for any given horizon (say six months) is the same whether a 1-year note is purchased and then sold after six months, or a 5-year note is purchased and then sold after six months, or if a 10-year bond is purchased and sold after six months.

28. A is correct. Investment #1 consists of just one 5-year duration strip bond, and thus its price does not change with a change in the 2-year key rate. Investment #2 will see a decline in value of approximately 0.70%. This is because 70 percent of Investment #2 is in the 2-year strip bond. Thus, the key rate duration for Investment #2 is $0.70 \times 2 = 1.40$. Given a 50 basis point increase in 2-year rates, the price of Investment #2 will fall by approximately $1.40 \times 0.50 = 0.70\%$.

29. B is correct. The duration of a portfolio is simply the weighted average of the component securities' durations. In this case, Investment #3 places £37.5 million into a 5-year strip bond and £12.5 million into a 30-year strip bond. The total investment is £50 million. The weighted average duration is therefore $(37.5/50) \times 5 + (12.5/50) \times 30 = 11.25$.

30. C is correct. The curvature of the yield has the least impact in explaining the return of zero-coupon bonds.

31. A is correct. Both theories assume that the forward rates in current long-term bonds are closely related to the market's expectations about future short-term rates.

32. C is correct. The credit rating agency will not be looking at the costs to the special purpose vehicle of the servicer, but rather how well they service the assets.

33. C is correct. This is a term used in asset-backed securities and does not apply to revenue bonds. In addition, the legal opinion would not address this as it is an investment decision.

34. A is correct. Balance of payments affects the foreign currency debt rating, not the local currency debt rating.

35. A is correct. The return calculation for each bond is:

Bond duration $\times$ $-$Basis point change $\times$ % Weight in portfolio for each bond

We then add together the bond returns for each bond in the portfolio. The key rate durations are the same as the maturities because all bonds are zero-coupon bonds. This gives a return of:

Portfolio I: $(2 \times -0.10 \times 50\%) + (16 \times 0.00 \times 0\%) +$
$(30 \times 0.20 \times 50\%) = +2.90\%$

Portfolio III: $(2 \times -0.10 \times 25\%) + (16 \times 0.00 \times 50\%) +$
$(30 \times 0.20 \times 25\%) = +1.45\%$

Therefore the difference in return would be: $1.45\% - 2.90\% = -1.45\%$

SOLUTIONS FOR READING 49

Solutions are for Practice Questions found in Reading

1. A. The daily percentage change in yield for each trading day is shown below in the next to the last column:

t	y_t	$X_t = 100 [\text{Ln} (y_t/y_{t-1})]$	$(X_t - \bar{X})^2$
0	7.17400		
1	7.19400	0.27840	0.19820
2	7.21800	0.33306	0.24985
3	7.15100	−0.93257	0.58641
4	7.02500	−1.77770	2.59500
5	7.02400	−0.01424	0.02328
6	7.03000	0.08538	0.06360
7	7.02000	−0.14235	0.00060
8	6.96400	−0.80092	0.40211
9	6.90400	−0.86531	0.48792
10	6.89671	−0.10565	0.00374
11	6.85300	−0.63580	0.21996
12	6.87100	0.26231	0.18414
13	6.88300	0.17449	0.11648
14	6.87500	−0.11630	0.00255
15	6.87800	0.04363	0.04428
16	6.80400	−1.08172	0.83709
17	6.84300	0.57156	0.54517
18	6.79500	−0.70392	0.28850
19	6.79500	0.00000	0.02782
20	6.85400	0.86454	1.06365
21	6.81000	−0.64403	0.22775
22	6.77300	−0.54480	0.14289
23	6.86700	1.37832	2.38739
24	6.88700	0.29082	0.20942
25	6.88100	−0.08716	0.00634
Total		−4.16994	10.91412

B. The daily standard deviation is computed as follows:

$$\text{Sample mean} = \overline{X} = \frac{-4.16994\%}{25} = -0.166798\%$$

$$\text{Variance} = \frac{10.91412\%}{25 - 1} = 0.4547550\%$$

$$\text{Std dev} = \sqrt{0.4547550\%} = 0.67436\%$$

2. The daily standard deviation is 0.67436% and the annualized standard deviation based on an assumed number of trading days in a year is:

250 days	260 days	365 days
10.66%	10.87%	12.88%

VALUING BONDS WITH EMBEDDED OPTIONS

by Frank J. Fabozzi, CFA

LEARNING OUTCOMES

The candidate should be able to:	Mastery
a. evaluate, using relative value analysis, whether a security is undervalued or overvalued;	☐
b. evaluate the importance of benchmark interest rates in interpreting spread measures;	☐
c. describe the backward induction valuation methodology within the binomial interest rate tree framework;	☐
d. calculate the value of a callable bond from an interest rate tree;	☐
e. explain the relations among the values of a callable (putable) bond, the corresponding option-free bond, and the embedded option;	☐
f. explain the effect of volatility on the arbitrage-free value of an option;	☐
g. interpret an option-adjusted spread with respect to a nominal spread and to benchmark interest rates;	☐
h. explain how effective duration and effective convexity are calculated using the binomial model;	☐
i. calculate the value of a putable bond, using an interest rate tree;	☐
j. describe and evaluate a convertible bond and its various component values;	☐
k. compare the risk-return characteristics of a convertible bond with the risk-return characteristics of ownership of the underlying common stock.	☐

1   INTRODUCTION

The presence of an embedded option in a bond structure makes the valuation of such bonds complicated. In this reading, we present a model to value bonds that have one or more embedded options and where the value of the embedded options depends on future interest rates. Examples of such embedded options are call and put provisions and caps (i.e., maximum interest rate) in floating-rate securities. While there are several models that have been proposed to value bonds with embedded options, our focus will be on models that provide an "arbitrage-free value" for a security. At the end of this reading, we will discuss the valuation of convertible bonds. The complexity here is that these bonds are typically callable and may be putable. Thus, the valuation of convertible bonds must take into account not only embedded options that depend on future interest rates (i.e., the call and the put options) but also the future price movement of the common stock (i.e., the call option on the common stock).

In order to understand how to value a bond with an embedded option, there are several fundamental concepts that must be reviewed. We will do this in Sections 2, 3, 4, and 5. In Section 2, the key elements involved in developing a bond valuation model are explained. In Section 3, an overview of the bond valuation process is provided. Since the valuation of bonds requires benchmark interest rates, the various benchmarks are described in Section 4. In this section we also explain how to interpret spread measures relative to a particular benchmark. In Section 5, the valuation of an option-free bond is reviewed using a numerical illustration. The bond used in the illustration in this section to show how to value an option-free bond is then used in the remainder of the reading to show how to value that bond if there is one or more embedded options.

2   ELEMENTS OF A BOND VALUATION MODEL

The valuation process begins with determining benchmark interest rates. As will be explained later in this section, there are three potential markets where benchmark interest rates can be obtained:

▶ the Treasury market;
▶ a sector of the bond market;
▶ the market for the issuer's securities.

An arbitrage-free value for an option-free bond is obtained by first generating the spot rates (or forward rates). When used to discount cash flows, the spot rates are the rates that would produce a model value equal to the observed market price for each on-the-run security in the benchmark. For example, if the Treasury market is the benchmark, an arbitrage-free model would produce a value for each on-the-run Treasury issue that is equal to its observed market price. In the Treasury market, the on-the-run issues are the most recently auctioned issues. (Note that all such securities issued by the U.S. Department of the Treasury are option free.) If the market used to establish the benchmark is a sector of the bond market or the market for the issuer's securities, the on-the-run issues are estimates of what the market price would be if newly issued *option-free* securities with different maturities are sold.

In deriving the interest rates that should be used to value a bond with an embedded option, the same principle must be maintained. No matter how complex the valuation model, when each on-the-run issue for a benchmark security is valued using the model, the value produced should be equal to the on-the-run issue's market price. The on-the-run issues for a given benchmark are assumed to be fairly priced.[1]

The first complication in building a model to value bonds with embedded options is that the future cash flows will depend on what happens to interest rates in the future. This means that future interest rates must be considered. This is incorporated into a valuation model by considering how interest rates can change based on some assumed interest rate volatility. In the reading on term structure and volatility of interest rates, we explained what interest rate volatility is and how it is estimated. Given the assumed interest rate volatility, an interest rate "tree" representing possible future interest rates consistent with the volatility assumption can be constructed. It is from the interest rate tree that two important elements in the valuation process are obtained. First, the interest rates on the tree are used to generate the cash flows taking into account the embedded option. Second, the interest rates on the tree are used to compute the present value of the cash flows.

For a given interest rate volatility, there are several interest rate models that have been used in practice to construct an interest rate tree. An interest rate model is a probabilistic description of how interest rates can change over the life of the bond. An interest rate model does this by making an assumption about the relationship between the level of short-term interest rates and the interest rate volatility as measured by the standard deviation. A discussion of the various interest rate models that have been suggested in the finance literature and that are used by practitioners in developing valuation models is beyond the scope of this reading.[2] What is important to understand is that the interest rate models commonly used are based on how short-term interest rates can evolve (i.e., change) over time. Consequently, these interest rate models are referred to as one-factor models, where "factor" means only one interest rate is being modeled over time. More complex models would consider how more than one interest rate changes over time. For example, an interest rate model can specify how the short-term interest rate and the long-term interest rate can change over time. Such a model is called a two-factor model.

Given an interest rate model and an interest rate volatility assumption, it can be assumed that interest rates can realize one of two possible rates in the next period. A valuation model that makes this assumption in creating an interest rate tree is called a **binomial model**. There are valuation models that assume that interest rates can take on three possible rates in the next period and these models are called trinomial models. There are even more complex models that assume in creating an interest rate tree that more than three possible rates in the next period can be realized. These models that assume discrete change in interest

---

[1] Market participants also refer to this characteristic of a model as one that "calibrates to the market."

[2] An excellent source for further explanation of many of these models is Gerald W. Buetow Jr. and James Sochacki, *Term Structure Models Using Binomial Trees: Demystifying the Process* (Charlottesville, VA: Association of Investment Management and Research, 2000).

rates are referred to as "discrete-time option pricing models." It makes sense that option valuation technology is employed to value a bond with an embedded option because the valuation requires an estimate of what the value of the embedded option is worth. However, a discussion of the underlying theory of discrete-time pricing models in general and the binomial model in particular are beyond the scope of this reading.[3]

As we will see later in this reading, when a discrete-time option pricing model is portrayed in graph form, it shows the different paths that interest rates can take. The graphical presentation looks like a lattice.[4] Hence, discrete-time option pricing models are sometimes referred to as "lattice models." Since the pattern of the interest rate paths also look like the branches of a tree, the graphical presentation is referred to as an interest rate tree.

Regardless of the assumption about how many possible rates can be realized in the next period, the interest rate tree generated must produce a value for the securities in the benchmark that is equal to their observed market price—that is, it must produce an arbitrage-free value. Consequently, if the Treasury market is used for the benchmark interest rates, the interest rate tree generated must produce a value for each on-the-run Treasury issue that is equal to its observed market price. Moreover, the intuition and the methodology for using the interest rate tree (i.e., the backward induction methodology described later) are the same. Once an interest rate tree is generated that 1) is consistent with both the interest rate volatility assumption and the interest rate model and 2) generates the observed market price for the securities in the benchmark, the next step is to use the interest rate tree to value a bond with an embedded option. The complexity here is that a set of rules must be introduced to determine, for any period, when the embedded option will be exercised. For a callable bond, these rules are called the "call rules." The rules vary from model builder to model builder.

While the building of a model to value bonds with embedded options is more complex than building a model to value option-free bonds, the basic principles are the same. In the case of valuing an option-free bond, the model that is built is simply a set of spot rates that are used to value cash flows. The spot rates will produce an arbitrage-free value. For a model to value a bond with embedded options, the interest rate tree is used to value future cash flows, and the interest rate tree is combined with the call rules to generate the future cash flows. Again, the interest rate tree will produce an arbitrage-free value.

Let's move from theory to practice. Only a few practitioners will develop their own model to value bonds with embedded options. Instead, it is typical for a portfolio manager or analyst to use a model developed by either a dealer firm or a vendor of analytical systems. A fair question is then: Why bother covering a valuation model that is readily available from a third party? The answer is that a valuation model should not be a black box to portfolio managers and analysts. *The models in practice share all of the principles described in this reading, but differ with respect to certain assumptions that can produce quite different values.* The reasons for these differences in valuation must be understood. Moreover, third-party models give the user a choice of changing the assumptions. A user who has not "walked through" a valuation model has no appreciation of the significance of these assumptions and therefore how to assess the impact of these assumptions on the value produced by the model. "Modeling risk" is the risk that the underlying assumptions of a model may be incorrect. Understanding a valuation model permits the user to effectively determine the significance of an assumption.

---

[3] For a discussion of the binomial model and the underlying theory, see Chapter 4 in Don M. Chance, *Analysis of Derivatives for the CFA Program* (Charlottesville, VA: Association for Investment Management and Research, 2003).

[4] A lattice is an arrangement of points in a regular periodic pattern.

As an example of the importance of understanding the assumptions of a model, consider interest rate volatility. Suppose that the market price of a bond is $89. Suppose further that a valuation model produces a value for a bond with an embedded option of $90 based on a 12% interest rate volatility assumption. Then, according to the valuation model, this bond is cheap by one point. However, suppose that the same model produces a value of $87 if a 15% volatility is assumed. This tells the portfolio manager or analyst that the bond is two points rich. Which is correct? The answer clearly depends on what the investor believes interest rate volatility will be in the future.

In this reading, we will use the binomial model to demonstrate all of the issues and assumptions associated with valuing a bond with embedded options. This model is available on Bloomberg, as well as from other commercial vendors and several dealer firms.[5] We show how to create an interest rate tree (more specifically, a binomial interest rate tree) given a volatility assumption and how the interest rate tree can be used to value an option-free bond. Given the interest rate tree, we then show how to value several types of bonds with an embedded option—a callable bond, a putable bond, a step-up note, and a floating-rate note with a cap.

Once again, it must be emphasized that while the binomial model is used in this reading to demonstrate how to value bonds with embedded options, other models that allow for more than one interest rate in the next period all follow the same principles—they begin with on-the-run yields, they produce an interest rate tree that generates an arbitrage-free value, and they depend on assumptions regarding the volatility of interest rates and rules for when an embedded option will be exercised.

OVERVIEW OF THE BOND VALUATION PROCESS

3

In this section we review the bond valuation process and the key concepts that were previously introduced. This will help us tie together the concepts that have already been covered and how they relate to the valuation of bonds with embedded options.

Regardless if a bond has an embedded option, the following can be done:

1. Given a required yield to maturity, we can compute the value of a bond. For example, if the required yield to maturity of a 9-year, 8% coupon bond that pays interest semiannually is 7%, its price is 106.59.

2. Given the observed market price of a bond we can calculate its yield to maturity. For example, if the price of a 5-year, 6% coupon bond that pays interest semiannually is 93.84, its yield to maturity is 7.5%.

3. Given the yield to maturity, a yield spread can be computed. For example, if the yield to maturity for a 5-year, 6% coupon bond that pays interest semiannually is 7.5% and its yield is compared to a benchmark yield of 6.5%, then the yield spread is 100 basis points (7.5% minus 6.5%). We refer to the yield spread as the *nominal spread.*

---

[5] The model described in this reading was first presented in Andrew J. Kalotay, George O. Williams, and Frank J. Fabozzi, "A Model for the Valuation of Bonds and Embedded Options," *Financial Analysts Journal* (May–June 1993), pp. 35–46.

The problem with using a single interest rate when computing the value of a bond (as in 1) on the preceding page) or in computing a yield to maturity (as in 2) on the preceding page) is that it fails to recognize that each cash flow is unique and warrants its own discount rate. Failure to discount each cash flow at an appropriate interest unique to when that cash flow is expected to be received results in an arbitrage opportunity.

It is at this point in the valuation process that the notion of theoretical spot rates are introduced to overcome the problem associated with using a single interest rate. The spot rates are the appropriate rates to use to discount cash flows. There is a theoretical spot rate that can be obtained for each maturity. The procedure for computing the spot rate curve (i.e., the spot rate for each maturity) was previously explained and discussed in the previous reading.

Using the spot rate curve, one obtains the bond price. However, how is the spot rate curve used to compute the yield to maturity? Actually, there is no equivalent concept to a yield to maturity in this case. Rather, there is a yield spread measure that is used to overcome the problem of a single interest rate. This measure is the zero-volatility spread. The zero-volatility spread, also called the Z-spread and the static spread, is the spread that when added to all of the spot rates will make the present value of the bond's cash flow equal to the bond's market price.

At this point, we have not introduced any notion of how to handle bonds with embedded options. We have simply dealt with the problem of using a single interest rate for discounting cash flows. But there is still a critical issue that must be resolved. When a bond has an embedded option, a portion of the yield, and therefore a portion of the spread, is attributable to the embedded option. When valuing a bond with an embedded option, it is necessary to adjust the spread for the value of the embedded option. The measure that does this is called the option-adjusted spread (OAS). In this reading, we show how this spread measure is computed for bonds with embedded options.

A. The Benchmark Interest Rates and Relative Value Analysis

Yield spread measures are used in assessing the relative value of securities. Relative value analysis involves identifying securities that can potentially enhance return relative to a benchmark. Relative value analysis can be used to identify securities as being overpriced ("rich"), underpriced ("cheap"), or fairly priced. A portfolio manager can use relative value analysis in ranking issues within a sector or sub-sector of the bond market or different issues of a specific issuer.

Two questions that need to be asked in order to understand spread measures were identified:

1. What is the benchmark for computing the spread? That is, what is the spread measured relative to?
2. What is the spread measuring?

The different spread measures begin with benchmark interest rates. The benchmark interest rates can be one of the following:

▶ the Treasury market;
▶ a specific bond sector with a given credit rating;
▶ a specific issuer.

A specific bond sector with a given credit rating, for example, would include single-A rated corporate bonds or double-A rated banks. The LIBOR curve discussed in the previous reading is an example, since it is viewed by the market as an inter-bank or AA rated benchmark.

Moreover, the benchmark interest rates can be based on either:

▶ an estimated yield curve,
▶ an estimated spot rate curve.

A yield curve shows the relationship between yield and maturity for coupon bonds; a spot rate curve shows the relationship between spot rates and maturity.

Consequently, there are six potential benchmark interest rates as summarized below:

	Treasury Market	Specific Bond Sector with a Given Credit Rating	Specific Issuer
Yield curve	Treasury yield curve	Sector yield curve	Issuer yield curve
Spot rate curve	Treasury spot rate curve	Sector spot rate curve	Issuer spot rate curve

We illustrated how the Treasury spot rate curve can be constructed from the Treasury yield curve. Rather than start with yields in the Treasury market as the benchmark interest rates, an estimated on-the-run yield curve for a bond sector with a given credit rating or a specific issuer can be obtained. To obtain a sector with a given credit rating or a specific issuer's on-the-run yield curve, an appropriate credit spread is added to each on-the-run Treasury issue. The credit spread need not be constant for all maturities. For example, the credit spread may increase with maturity. Given the on-the-run yield curve, the theoretical spot rates for the bond sector with a given credit rating or issuer can be constructed using the same methodology to construct the Treasury spot rates given the Treasury yield curve.

B. Interpretation of Spread Measures

Given the alternative benchmark interest rates, in this section we will see how to interpret the three spread measures that were previously described: nominal spread, zero-volatility spread, and option-adjusted spread.

1. Treasury Market Benchmark

In the United States, yields in the U.S. Treasury market are typically used as the benchmark interest rates. The benchmark can be either the Treasury yield curve or the Treasury spot rate curve. The nominal spread is a spread measured relative to the Treasury yield curve and the zero-volatility spread is a spread relative to the Treasury spot rate curve. As we will see in this reading, the OAS is a spread relative to the Treasury spot rate curve.

If the Treasury market rates are used, then the benchmark for the three spread measures and the risks for which the spread is compensating are summarized below:

Spread Measure	Benchmark	Reflects Compensation for...
Nominal	Treasury yield curve	Credit risk, option risk, liquidity risk
Zero-volatility	Treasury spot rate curve	Credit risk, option risk, liquidity risk
Option-adjusted	Treasury spot rate curve	Credit risk, liquidity risk

where "credit risk" is relative to the default-free rate since the Treasury market is viewed as a default-free market.

In the case of an OAS, if the computed OAS is greater than what the market requires for credit risk and liquidity risk, then the security is undervalued. If the computed OAS is less than what the market requires for credit risk and liquidity risk, then the security is overvalued. Only using the nominal spread or zero-volatility spread masks the compensation for the embedded option.

For example, assume the following for a non-Treasury security, Bond W, a triple B rated corporate bond with an embedded call option:

Benchmark: Treasury market
Nominal spread based on Treasury yield curve: 170 basis points
Zero-volatility spread based on Treasury spot rate curve: 160 basis points
OAS based on Treasury spot rate curve: 125 basis points

Suppose that in the market *option-free* bonds with the same credit rating, maturity, and liquidity as Bond W trade at a nominal spread of 145 basis points. It would seem, based solely on the nominal spread, Bond W is undervalued (i.e., cheap) since its nominal spread is greater than the nominal spread for comparable bonds (170 versus 145 basis points). Even comparing Bond W's zero-volatility spread of 160 basis points to the market's 145 basis point nominal spread for option-free bonds (not a precise comparison since the Treasury benchmarks are different), the analysis would suggest that Bond W is cheap. However, after removing the value of the embedded option—which as we will see is precisely what the OAS measure does—the OAS tells us that the bond is trading at a spread that is less than the nominal spread of otherwise comparable option-free bonds. Again, while the benchmarks are different, the OAS tells us that Bond W is overvalued.

C. Specific Bond Sector with a Given Credit Rating Benchmark

Rather than use the Treasury market as the benchmark, the benchmark can be a specific bond sector *with a given credit rating*. The interpretation for the spread measures would then be:

Spread Measure	Benchmark	Reflects Compensation for ...
Nominal	Sector yield curve	Credit risk, option risk, liquidity risk
Zero-volatility	Sector spot rate curve	Credit risk, option risk, liquidity risk
Option-adjusted	Sector spot rate curve	Credit risk, liquidity risk

where "Sector" means the sector with a specific credit rating. "Credit risk" in this case means the *credit risk of a security under consideration relative to the credit risk of the sector used as the benchmark*, and "liquidity risk" is the *liquidity risk of a security under consideration relative to the liquidity risk of the sector used as the benchmark.*

Let's again use Bond W, a triple B rated corporate bond with an embedded call option to illustrate. Assume the following spread measures were computed:

Benchmark: double A rated corporate bond sector
Nominal spread based on benchmark: 110 basis points
Zero-volatility spread based benchmark spot rate curve: 100 basis points
OAS based on benchmark spot rate curve: 80 basis points

Suppose that in the market *option-free* bonds with the same credit rating, maturity, and liquidity as Bond W trade at a nominal spread *relative to the double A corporate bond sector* of 90 basis points. Based solely on the nominal spread as a relative yield measure using the same benchmark, Bond W is undervalued (i.e., cheap) since its nominal spread is greater than the nominal spread for comparable bonds (110 versus 90 basis points). Even naively comparing Bond W's zero-volatility spread of 100 basis points (relative to the double A corporate spot rate curve) to the market's 90 basis point nominal spread for option-free bonds relative to the double A corporate bond yield curve, the analysis would suggest that Bond W is cheap. However, the proper assessment of Bond W's relative value will depend on what its OAS is in comparison to the OAS (relative to the same double A corporate benchmark) of other triple B rated bonds. For example, if the OAS of other triple B rated corporate bonds is less than 80 basis points, then Bond W is cheap.

D. Issuer-Specific Benchmark

Instead of using as a benchmark the Treasury market or a bond market sector to measure relative value for a specific issue, one can use an estimate of the issuer's yield curve or an estimate of the issuer's spot rate curve as the benchmark. Then we would have the following interpretation for the three spread measures:

Spread Measure	Benchmark	Reflects Compensation for ...
Nominal	Issuer yield curve	Option risk, liquidity risk
Zero-volatility	Issuer spot rate curve	Option risk, liquidity risk
Option-adjusted	Issuer spot rate curve	Liquidity risk

Note that there is no credit risk since it is assumed that the specific issue analyzed has the same credit risk as the embedded option in the issuer benchmark. Using the nominal spread, a value that is positive indicates that, ignoring any embedded option, the issue is cheap relative to how the market is pricing other bonds of the issuer. A negative value would indicate that the security is expensive. The same interpretation holds for the zero-volatility spread, ignoring any embedded option. For the OAS, a positive spread means that even after adjusting for the embedded option, the value of the security is cheap. If the OAS is zero, the security is fairly priced and if it is negative, the security is expensive.

Once again, let's use our hypothetical Bond W, a triple B rated corporate bond with an embedded call option. Assume this bond is issued by RJK Corporation. Then suppose for Bond W:

Benchmark: RJK Corporation's bond issues
Nominal spread based on RJK Corporation's yield curve: 30 basis points
Zero-volatility spread based on RJK Corporation's spot rate curve:
    20 basis points
OAS based on RJK Corporation's spot rate curve: −25 basis points

Both the nominal spread and the zero-volatility spread would suggest that Bond W is cheap (i.e., both spread measures have a positive value). However, once the embedded option is taken into account, the appropriate spread measure, the OAS, indicates that there is a negative spread. This means that Bond W is expensive and should be avoided.

E. OAS, the Benchmark, and Relative Value

Our focus in this reading is the valuation of bonds with an embedded option. While we have yet to describe how an OAS is calculated, here we summarize how to interpret OAS as a relative value measure based on the benchmark.

Consider first when the benchmark is the Treasury spot rate curve. A zero OAS means that the security offers no spread over Treasuries. Hence, a security with a zero OAS in this case should be avoided. A negative OAS means that the security is offering a spread that is less than Treasuries. Therefore, it should be avoided. A positive value alone does not mean a security is fairly priced or cheap. It depends on what spread relative to the Treasury market the market is demanding for comparable issues. Whether the security is rich, fairly priced, or cheap depends on the OAS for the security compared to the OAS for comparable securities. We will refer to the OAS offered on comparable securities as the "required OAS" and the OAS computed for the security under consideration as the "security OAS." Then,

if security OAS is greater than required OAS, the security is cheap
if security OAS is less than required OAS, the security is rich
if security OAS is equal to the required OAS, the security is fairly priced

When a sector of the bond market with the same credit rating is the benchmark, the credit rating of the sector relative to the credit rating of the security being analyzed is important. In the discussion, *it is assumed that the credit rating of the bond sector that is used as a benchmark is higher than the credit rating of the security being analyzed.* A zero OAS means that the security offers no spread over the bond sector benchmark and should therefore be avoided. A negative OAS means that the security is offering a spread that is less than the bond sector benchmark and hence should be avoided. As with the Treasury benchmark, when there is a positive OAS, relative value depends on the security OAS compared to the required OAS. Here the required OAS is the OAS of comparable securities relative to the bond sector benchmark. Given the security OAS and the required OAS, then

if security OAS is greater than required OAS, the security is cheap
if security OAS is less than required OAS, the security is rich
if security OAS is equal to the required OAS, the security is fairly priced

EXHIBIT 1	Relationship between the Benchmark, OAS, and Relative Value		
Benchmark	**Negative OAS**	**Zero OAS**	**Positive OAS**
Treasury market	Overpriced (rich) security	Overpriced (rich) security	Comparison must be made between security OAS and OAS of comparable securities (required OAS): if security OAS > required OAS, security is cheap if security OAS < required OAS, security is rich if security OAS = required OAS, security is fairly priced
Bond sector with a given credit rating (*assumes credit rating higher than security being analyzed*)	Overpriced (rich) security (*assumes credit rating higher than security being analyzed*)	Overpriced (rich) security (*assumes credit rating higher than security being analyzed*)	Comparison must be made between security OAS and OAS of comparable securities (required OAS): if security OAS > required OAS, security is cheap if security OAS < required OAS, security is rich if security OAS = required OAS, security is fairly priced
Issuer's own securities	Overpriced (rich) security	Fairly valued	Underpriced (cheap) security

The terms "rich," "cheap," and "fairly priced" are only relative to the benchmark. If an investor is a funded investor who is assessing a security relative to his or her borrowing costs, then a different set of rules exists. For example, suppose that the bond sector used as the benchmark is the LIBOR spot rate curve. Also assume that the funding cost for the investor is a spread of 40 basis points over LIBOR. Then the decision to invest in the security depends on whether the OAS exceeds the 40 basis point spread by a sufficient amount to compensate for the credit risk.

Finally, let's look at relative valuation when the issuer's spot rate curve is the benchmark. If a particular security by the issuer is fairly priced, its OAS should be equal to zero. Thus, unlike when the Treasury benchmark or bond sector benchmark is used, a zero OAS is a fairly valued security. A positive OAS means that the security is trading cheap relative to other securities of the issuer and a negative OAS means that the security is trading rich relative to other securities of the same issuer.

The relationship between the benchmark, OAS, and relative value is summarized in Exhibit 1.

REVIEW OF HOW TO VALUE AN OPTION-FREE BOND   4

Before we illustrate how to value a bond with an embedded option, we will review how to value an option-free bond. We will then take the same bond and explain how it would be valued if it has an embedded option.

We have previously explained how to compute an arbitrage-free value for an option-free bond using spot rates. We also showed the relationship between spot rates and forward rates, and then how forward rates can be used to derive the same arbitrage-free value as using spot rates. What we will review in this section is how to value an option-free bond using both spot rates and forward rates. We will use as our benchmark in the rest of this reading, the securities of the issuer whose bond we want to value. Hence, *we will start with the issuer's on-the-run yield curve.*

To obtain a particular issuer's on-the-run yield curve, an appropriate credit spread is added to each on-the-run Treasury issue. The credit spread need not be constant for all maturities. In our illustration, we use the following hypothetical *on-the-run issue for the issuer whose bond we want to value*:

Maturity (Years)	Yield to Maturity (%)	Market Price
1	3.5	100
2	4.2	100
3	4.7	100
4	5.2	100

Each bond is trading at par value (100) so the coupon rate is equal to the yield to maturity. We will simplify the illustration by assuming annual-pay bonds.

Using the bootstrapping methodology, the spot rates are given below:

Year	Spot Rate (%)
1	3.5000
2	4.2148
3	4.7352
4	5.2706

We will use the above spot rates shortly to value a bond.

We explained how to derive forward rates from spot rates. Recall that forward rates can have different interpretations based on the theory of the term structure to which one subscribes. However, in the valuation process, *we are not relying on any theory*. The forward rates below are mathematically derived from the spot rates and, as we will see, when used to value a bond will produce the same value as the spot rates. The 1-year forward rates are:

Current 1-year forward rate	3.500%
1-year forward rate one year from now	4.935%
1-year forward rate two years from now	5.784%
1-year forward rate three years from now	6.893%

Now consider an option-free bond with four years remaining to maturity and a coupon rate of 6.5%. The value of this bond can be calculated in one of two ways, both producing the same value. First, the cash flows can be discounted at the spot rates as shown below:

$$\frac{\$6.5}{(1.035)^1} + \frac{\$6.5}{(1.042148)^2} + \frac{\$6.5}{(1.047352)^3} + \frac{\$100 + \$6.5}{(1.052706)^4} = \$104.643$$

The second way is to discount by the 1-year forward rates as shown below:

$$\frac{\$6.5}{(1.035)} + \frac{\$6.5}{(1.035)(1.04935)} + \frac{\$6.5}{(1.035)(1.04935)(1.05784)}$$
$$+ \frac{\$100 + \$6.5}{(1.035)(1.04935)(1.05784)(1.06893)} = \$104.643$$

As can be seen, discounting by spot rates or forward rates will produce the same value for a bond.

Remember this value for the option-free bond, $104.643. When we value the same bond using the binomial model later in this reading, that model should produce a value of $104.643 or else our model is flawed.

VALUING A BOND WITH AN EMBEDDED OPTION USING THE BINOMIAL MODEL

5

As explained in Section 2, there are various models that have been developed to value a bond with embedded options. The one that we will use to illustrate the issues and assumptions associated with valuing bonds with embedded options is the binomial model. The interest rates that are used in the valuation process are obtained from a binomial interest rate tree. We'll explain the general characteristics of this tree first. Then we see how to value a bond using the binomial interest rate tree. We will then see how to construct this tree from an on-the-run yield curve. Basically, the derivation of a binomial interest rate tree is the same in principle as deriving the spot rates using the bootstrapping method—that is, there is no arbitrage.

A. Binomial Interest Rate Tree

Once we allow for embedded options, consideration must be given to interest rate volatility. The reason is, the decision of the issuer or the investor (depending upon who has the option) will be affected by what interest rates are in the future. This means that the valuation model must explicitly take into account how interest rates may change in the future. In turn, this recognition is achieved by incorporating interest rate volatility into the valuation model. In the reading on term structure and volatility of interest rates, we explained what interest rate volatility is and how it can be measured.

Let's see how interest rate volatility is introduced into the valuation model. More specifically, let's see how this can be done in the binomial model using Exhibit 2. Look at panel a of the exhibit which shows the beginning or *root* of the interest rate tree. The time period shown is "Today." At the dot, denoted N, in the exhibit is an interest rate denoted by r_0, which represents the interest rate today.

Notice that there are two arrows as we move to the right of N. Here is where we are introducing interest rate volatility. The dot in the exhibit is referred to as a *node*. What takes place at a node is either a *random event* or a *decision*. We will see

| EXHIBIT 2 | Binomial Interest Rate Tree |

Panel a: One-Year Binomial Interest Rate Tree   *Panel b: Two-Year Binomial Interest Rate Tree*

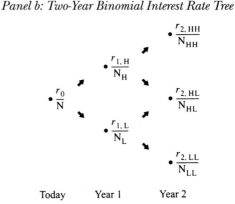

that in building a binomial interest rate tree, at each node there is a random event. The change in interest rates represents a random event. Later when we show how to use the binomial interest rate tree to determine the value of a bond with an embedded option, at each node there will be a decision. Specifically, the decision will be whether or not the issuer or bondholders (depending on the type of embedded option) will exercise the option.

In the binomial model, it is assumed that the random event (i.e., the change in interest rates) will take on only two possible values. Moreover, it is assumed that the probability of realizing either value is equal. The two possible values are the interest rates shown by $r_{1,H}$ and $r_{1,L}$ in panel a.[6] If you look at the time frame at the bottom of panel a, you will notice that it is in years.[7] What this means is that the interest rate at r_0 is the current (i.e., today's) 1-year rate and at year 1, the two possible 1-year interest rates are $r_{1,H}$ and $r_{1,L}$. Notice the notation that is used for the two subscripts. The first subscript, 1, means that it is the interest rate starting in year 1. The second subscript indicates whether it is the higher (H) or lower (L) of the two interest rates in year 1.

Now we will grow the binomial interest rate tree. Look at panel b of Exhibit 2 which shows today, year 1, and year 2. There are two nodes at year 1 depending on whether the higher or the lower interest rate is realized. At both of the nodes a random event occurs. N_H is the node if the higher interest rate ($r_{1,H}$) is realized. In the binomial model, the interest rate that can occur in the next year (i.e., year 2) can be one of two values: $r_{2,HH}$ or $r_{2,HL}$. The subscript 2 indicates year 2. This would get us to either the node N_{HH} or N_{HL}. The subscript "HH" means that the path to get to node N_{HH} is the higher interest rate in year 1 and in year 2. The subscript "HL" means that the path to get to node N_{HL} is the higher interest rate in year 1 and the lower interest rate in year 2.

Similarly, N_L is the node if the lower interest rate ($r_{1,L}$) is realized in year 1. The interest rate that can occur in year 2 is either $r_{2,LH}$ or $r_{2,LL}$. This would get us to either the node N_{LH} or N_{LL}. The subscript "LH" means that the path to get to node N_{LH} is the lower interest rate in year 1 and the higher interest rate in year 2. The subscript "LL" means that the path to get to node N_{LL} is the lower interest rate in year 1 and in year 2.

---

[6] If we were using a trinomial model, there would be three possible interest rates shown in the next year.

[7] In practice, much shorter time periods are used to construct an interest rate tree.

Notice that in panel b, at year 2 only N_{HL} is shown but no N_{LH}. The reason is that if the higher interest rate is realized in year 1 and the lower interest rate is realized in year 2, we would get to the same node as if the lower interest rate is realized in year 1 and the higher interest rate is realized in year 2. Rather than clutter up the interest rate tree with notation, only one of the two paths is shown.

In our illustration of valuing a bond with an embedded option, we will use a 4-year bond. Consequently, we will need a 4-year binomial interest rate tree to value this bond. Exhibit 3 shows the tree and the notation used.

EXHIBIT 3	**Four-Year Binomial Interest Rate Tree**

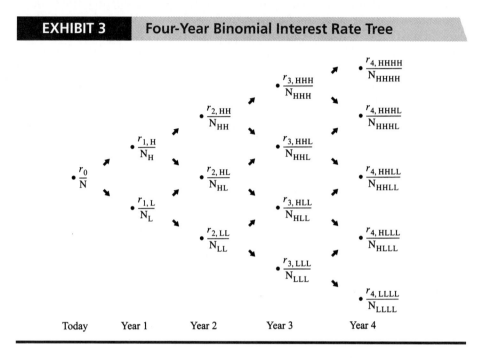

The interest rates shown in the binomial interest rate tree are actually forward rates. Basically, they are the one-period rates starting in period t. (A period in our illustration is one year.) Thus, in valuing an option-free bond we know that it is valued using forward rates, and we have illustrated this by using 1-period forward rates. For each period, there is a unique forward rate. When we value bonds with embedded options, we will see that we continue to use forward rates, but there is not just one forward rate for a given period but a set of forward rates.

There will be a relationship between the rates in the binomial interest rate tree. The relationship depends on the interest rate model assumed. Based on some interest rate volatility assumption, the interest rate model selected would show the relationship between:

$r_{1,L}$ and $r_{1,H}$ for year 1
$r_{2,LL}$, $r_{2,HL}$, and $r_{2,HH}$ for year 2
etc.

For our purpose of understanding the valuation model, it is not necessary that we show the mathematical relationships here.

B. Determining the Value at a Node

Now we want to see how to use the binomial interest rate tree to value a bond. To do this, we first have to determine the value of the bond at each node. To find the value of the bond at a node, we begin by calculating the bond's value at the high and low nodes to the right of the node for which we are interested in obtaining a value. For example, in Exhibit 3, suppose we want to determine the bond's value at node N_H. The bond's value at node N_{HH} and N_{HL} must be determined. Hold aside for now how we get these two values because, as we will see, the process involves starting from the last (right-most) year in the tree and working backwards to get the final solution we want. Because the procedure for solving for the final solution in any interest rate tree involves moving backwards, the methodology is known as backward induction.

Effectively what we are saying is that if we are at some node, then the value at that node will depend on the future cash flows. In turn, the future cash flows depend on 1) the coupon payment one year from now and 2) the bond's value one year from now. The former is known. The bond's value depends on whether the rate is the higher or lower rate reported at the two nodes to the right of the node that is the focus of our attention. So, the cash flow at a node will be either 1) the bond's value if the 1-year rate is the higher rate plus the coupon payment, or 2) the bond's value if the 1-year rate is the lower rate plus the coupon payment. Let's return to the bond's value at node N_H. The cash flow will be either the bond's value at N_{HH} plus the coupon payment, or the bond's value at N_{HL} plus the coupon payment.

In general, to get the bond's value at a node we follow the fundamental rule for valuation: the value is the present value of the expected cash flows. The appropriate discount rate to use is the 1-year rate at the node where we are computing the value. Now there are two present values in this case: the present value if the 1-year rate is the higher rate and one if it is the lower rate. Since it is assumed that the probability of both outcomes is equal (i.e., there is a 50% probability for each), an average of the two present values is computed. This is illustrated in Exhibit 4 for any node assuming that the 1-year rate is $r*$ at the node where the valuation is sought and letting:

V_H = the bond's value for the higher 1-year rate
V_L = the bond's value for the lower 1-year rate
C = coupon payment

Using our notation, the cash flow at a node is either:

$V_H + C$ for the higher 1-year rate
$V_L + C$ for the lower 1-year rate

EXHIBIT 4   Calculating a Value at a Node

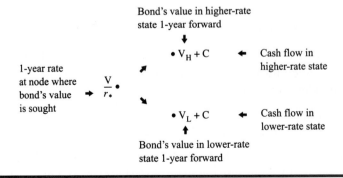

The present value of these two cash flows using the 1-year rate at the node, r^*, is:

$$\frac{V_H + C}{(1 + r^*)} = \text{present value for the higher 1-year rate}$$

$$\frac{V_L + C}{(1 + r^*)} = \text{present value for the lower 1-year rate}$$

Then, the value of the bond at the node is found as follows:

$$\text{Value at a node} = \frac{1}{2}\left[\frac{V_H + C}{(1 + r^*)} + \frac{V_L + C}{(1 + r^*)}\right]$$

C. Constructing the Binomial Interest Rate Tree

The construction of any interest rate tree is complicated, although the principle is simple to understand. This applies to the binomial interest rate tree or a tree based on more than two future rates in the next period. *The fundamental principle is that when a tree is used to value an on-the-run issue for the benchmark, the resulting value should be arbitrage free.* That is, the tree should generate a value for an on-the-run issue equal to its observed market value. Moreover, the interest rate tree should be consistent with the interest rate volatility assumed.

Here is a brief overview of the process for constructing the interest rate tree. It is not essential to know how to derive the interest rate tree; rather, it should be understood how to value a bond given the rates on the tree. The interest rate at the first node (i.e., the root of the tree) is the 1-year interest rate for the on-the-run issue. (This is because in our simplified illustration we are assuming that the length of the time between nodes is one year.) The tree is grown just the same way that the spot rates were obtained using the bootstrapping method based on arbitrage arguments.

The interest rates for year 1 (there are two of them and remember they are forward rates) are obtained from the following information:

1. the coupon rate for the 2-year on-the-run issue
2. the interest rate volatility assumed
3. the interest rate at the root of the tree (i.e., the current 1-year on-the-run rate)

Given the above, a *guess* is then made of the lower rate at node N_L, which is $r_{1,L}$. The upper rate, $r_{1,H}$, is not guessed at. Instead, it is determined by the assumed volatility of the 1-year rate ($r_{1,L}$). The formula for determining $r_{1,H}$ given $r_{1,L}$ is specified by the interest rate model used. Using the $r_{1,L}$ that was guessed and the corresponding $r_{1,H}$, the 2-year on-the-run issue can be valued. If the resulting value computed using the backward induction method is not equal to the market value of the 2-year on-the-run issue, then the $r_{1,L}$ that was tried is not the rate that should be used in the tree. If the value is too high, then a higher rate guess should be tried; if the value is too low, then a lower rate guess should be tried. The process continues in an iterative (i.e., trial and error) process until a value for $r_{1,L}$ and the corresponding $r_{1,H}$ produce a value for the 2-year on-the-run issue equal to its market value.

| EXHIBIT 5 | Binomial Interest Rate Tree for Valuing an Issuer's Bond with a Maturity up to 4 Years (10% Volatility Assumed) |

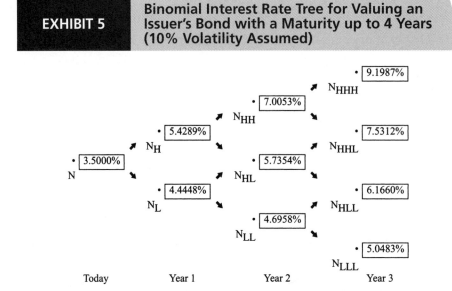

After this stage, we have the rate at the root of the tree and the two rates for year 1—$r_{1,L}$ and $r_{1,H}$. Now we need the three rates for year 2—$r_{2,LL}$, $r_{2,HL}$, and $r_{2,HH}$. These rates are determined from the following information:

1. the coupon rate for the 3-year on-the-run issue
2. the interest rate model assumed
3. the interest rate volatility assumed
4. the interest rate at the root of the tree (i.e., the current 1-year on-the-run rate)
5. the two 1-year rates (i.e., $r_{1,L}$ and $r_{1,H}$)

A guess is made for $r_{2,LL}$. The interest rate model assumed specifies how to obtain $r_{2,HL}$, and $r_{2,HH}$ given $r_{2,LL}$ and the assumed volatility for the 1-year rate. This gives the rates in the interest rate tree that are needed to value the 3-year on-the-run issue. The 3-year on-the-run issue is then valued. If the value generated is not

| EXHIBIT 6 | Demonstration That the Binomial Interest Rate Tree in Exhibit 5 Correctly Values the 3-Year 4.7% On-the-Run Issue |

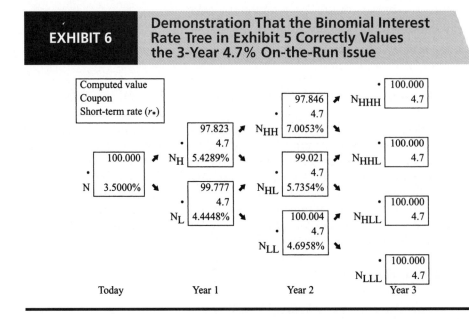

PRACTICE QUESTION 1

For the hypothetical issuer whose on-the-run yield was given in Section 4, the binomial interest rate tree below is based on 20% volatility. Using the 4-year on-the-run issue, show that the binomial interest tree below does produce a value equal to the price of the 4-year issue (i.e., par value).

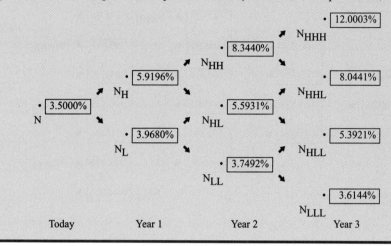

equal to the market value of the 3-year on-the-run issue, then the $r_{2,LL}$ value tried is not the rate that should be used in the tree. An iterative process is again followed until a value for $r_{2,LL}$ produces rates for year 2 that will make the value of the 3-year on-the-run issue equal to its market value.

The tree is grown using the same procedure as described above to get $r_{1,L}$ and $r_{1,H}$ for year 1 and $r_{2,LL}$, $r_{2,HL}$, and $r_{2,HH}$ for year 2. Exhibit 5 shows the binomial interest rate tree for this issuer for valuing issues up to four years of maturity assuming volatility for the 1-year rate of 10%. The interest rate model used is not important. How can we be sure that the interest rates shown in Exhibit 5 are the correct rates? Verification involves using the interest rate tree to value an on-the-run issue and showing that the value obtained from the binomial model is equal to the observed market value. For example, let's just show that the interest rates in the tree for years 0, 1, and 2 in Exhibit 5 are correct. To do this, we use the 3-year on-the-run issue. The market value for the issue is 100. Exhibit 6 shows the valuation of this issue using the backward induction method. Notice that the value at the root (i.e., the value derived by the model) is 100. Thus, the value derived from the interest rate tree using the rates for the first two years produces the observed market value of 100 for the 3-year on-the-run issue. This verification is the same as saying that the model has produced an arbitrage-free value.

D. Valuing an Option-Free Bond with the Tree

To illustrate how to use the binomial interest rate tree shown in Exhibit 5, consider a 6.5% option-free bond with four years remaining to maturity. Also assume that the *issuer's on-the-run yield curve* is the one given earlier and hence the

PRACTICE QUESTION 2

Show that the value of an option-free bond with four years to maturity and a coupon rate of 6.5% is $104.643 if volatility is assumed to be 20%.

EXHIBIT 7
Valuing an Option-Free Bond with Four Years to Maturity and a Coupon Rate of 6.5% (10% Volatility Assumed)

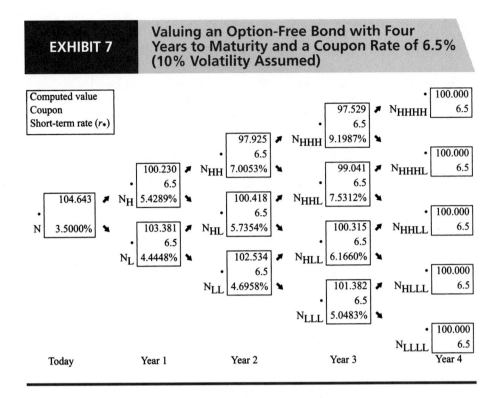

appropriate binomial interest rate tree is the one in Exhibit 5. Exhibit 7 shows the various values in the discounting process, and produces a bond value of $104.643.

It is important to note that this value is identical to the bond value found earlier when we discounted at either the spot rates or the 1-year forward rates. We should expect to find this result since our bond is option free. This clearly demonstrates that the valuation model is consistent with the arbitrage-free valuation model for an option-free bond.

6   VALUING AND ANALYZING A CALLABLE BOND

Now we will demonstrate how the binomial interest rate tree can be applied to value a callable bond. The valuation process proceeds in the same fashion as in the case of an option-free bond, but with one exception: when the call option may be exercised by the issuer, the bond value at a node must be changed to reflect the lesser of its values if it is not called (i.e., the value obtained by applying the backward induction method described above) and the call price. As explained earlier, at a node either a random event or a decision must be made. In constructing the binomial interest rate tree, there is a random event at a node. When valuing a bond with an embedded option, at a node there will be a decision made as to whether or not an option will be exercised. In the case of a callable bond, the issuer must decide whether or not to exercise the call option.

For example, consider a 6.5% bond with four years remaining to maturity that is callable in one year at $100. Exhibit 8 shows two values at each node of the binomial interest rate tree. The discounting process explained above is used to calculate the first of the two values at each node. The second value is the value based on whether the issue will be called. For simplicity, let's assume that this issuer calls the issue if it exceeds the call price.

In Exhibit 9 two portions of Exhibit 8 are highlighted. Panel a of the exhibit shows nodes where the issue is not called (based on the simple call rule used in the illustration) in year 2 and year 3. The values reported in this case are the same as in the valuation of an option-free bond. Panel b of the exhibit shows some nodes where the issue is called in year 2 and year 3. Notice how the methodology changes the cash flows. In year 3, for example, at node N_{HLL} the backward induction method produces a value (i.e., cash flow) of 100.315. However, given the simplified call rule, this issue would be called. Therefore, 100 is shown as the second value at the node and it is this value that is then used in the backward induction methodology. From this we can see how the binomial method changes the cash flow based on future interest rates and the embedded option.

The root of the tree, shown in Exhibit 8, indicates that the value for this callable bond is $102.899.

EXHIBIT 8   **Valuing a Callable Bond with Four Years to Maturity, a Coupon Rate of 6.5%, and Callable in One Year at 100 (10% Volatility Assumed)**

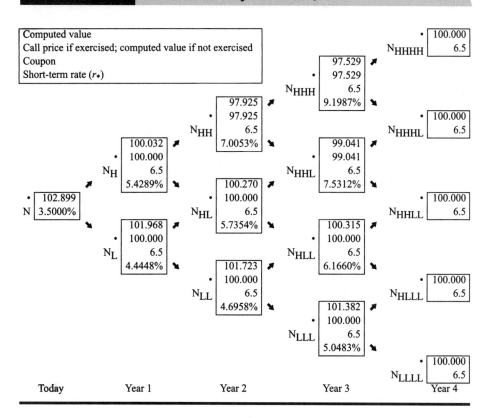

EXHIBIT 9	Highlighting Nodes in Years 2 and 3 for a Callable Bond

(a) Nodes where call option is not exercised

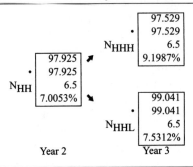

Year 2   Year 3

(b) Selected nodes where the call option is exercised

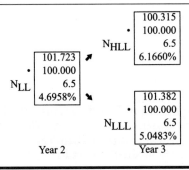

Year 2   Year 3

The question that we have not addressed in our illustration, which is nonetheless important, is the circumstances under which the issuer will actually call the bond. A detailed explanation of the call rule is beyond the scope of this reading. Basically, it involves determining when it would be economical for the issuer on an after-tax basis to call the issue.

Suppose instead that the call price schedule is 102 in year 1, 101 in year 2, and 100 in year 3. Also assume that the bond will not be called unless it exceeds the call price for that year. Exhibit 10 shows the value at each node and the value of the callable bond. The call price schedule results in a greater value for the callable bond, $103.942 compared to $102.899 when the call price is 100 in each year.

A. Determining the Call Option Value

The value of a callable bond is equal to the value of an option-free bond minus the value of the call option. This means that:

Value of a call option = Value of an option-free bond − Value of a callable bond

We have just seen how the value of an option-free bond and the value of a callable bond can be determined. The difference between the two values is therefore the value of the call option.

In our illustration, the value of the option-free bond is $104.643. If the call price is $100 in each year and the value of the callable bond is $102.899 assuming

EXHIBIT 10	Valuing a Callable Bond with Four Years to Maturity, a Coupon Rate of 6.5%, and with a Call Price Schedule (10% Volatility Assumed)

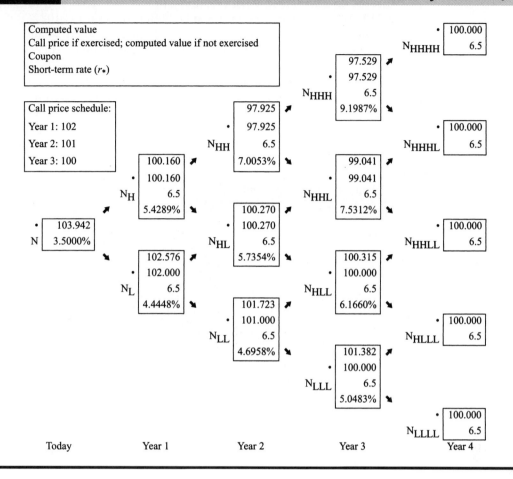

10% volatility for the 1-year rate, the value of the call option is $1.744 (= $104.643 − $102.899).

B. Volatility and the Arbitrage-Free Value

In our illustration, interest rate volatility was assumed to be 10%. The volatility assumption has an important impact on the arbitrage-free value. More specifically, the higher the expected volatility, the higher the value of an option. The same is true for an option embedded in a bond. Correspondingly, this affects the value of a bond with an embedded option.

For example, for a callable bond, a higher interest rate volatility assumption means that the value of the call option increases and, since the value of the option-free bond is not affected, the value of the callable bond must be lower.

We can see this using the on-the-run yield curve in our previous illustrations. In the previous illustrations, we assumed interest rate volatility of 10%. To show the effect of higher volatility, we will assume volatility of 20%. The solution to Practice Question 1 gives the corresponding binomial interest rate tree using the same interest rate model. The solution to Practice Question 2 verifies that the binomial interest rate tree provides the same value for the option-free bond, $104.643.

The solution to Practice Question 3 shows the calculation for the callable bond assuming interest rate volatility of 20%. For the callable bond it is assumed that the issue is callable at par beginning in year 1. The value of the callable bond is $102.108 if volatility is assumed to be 20% compared to $102.899 if volatility is assumed to be 10%. Notice that at the higher assumed volatility (20%), the callable bond has a lower value than at the lower assumed volatility (10%). The reason for this is that the value of an option increases with the higher assumed volatility. So, at 20% volatility the value of the embedded call option is higher than at 10% volatility. But the embedded call option is subtracted from the option-free value to obtain the value of the callable bond. Since a higher value for the embedded call option is subtracted from the option-free value at 20% volatility rather than at 10% volatility, the value of the callable bond is lower at 20% volatility.

PRACTICE QUESTION 3

Suppose that the volatility assumption is 20% rather than 10% and therefore the binomial interest rate tree is the one shown in Practice Question 1.

A. Compute the arbitrage-free value for the 4-year 6.5% coupon bond callable at par beginning Year 1 based on 20% volatility.

B. Compare the arbitrage-free value for this bond based on 20% volatility and 10% volatility as computed in Exhibit 8.

C. Option-Adjusted Spread

Suppose the market price of the 4-year 6.5% callable bond is $102.218 and the theoretical value assuming 10% volatility is $102.899. This means that this bond is cheap by $0.681 according to the valuation model. Bond market participants prefer to think not in terms of a bond's price being cheap or expensive in dollar terms but rather in terms of a yield spread—a cheap bond trades at a higher yield spread and an expensive bond at a lower yield spread.

The option-adjusted spread is the constant spread that when added to all the 1-year rates on the binomial interest rate tree will make the arbitrage-free value (i.e., the value produced by the binomial model) equal to the market price. In our illustration, if the market price is $102.218, the OAS would be the constant spread added to every rate in Exhibit 5 that will make the arbitrage-free value equal to $102.218. The solution in this case would be 35 basis points. This can be verified in Exhibit 11, which shows the value of this issue by adding 35 basis points to each rate.

As with the value of a bond with an embedded option, the OAS will depend on the volatility assumption. For a given bond price, the higher the interest rate volatility assumed, the lower the OAS for a callable bond. For example, if volatility is 20% rather than 10%, the OAS would be −6 basis points. This illustration clearly demonstrates the importance of the volatility assumption. Assuming volatility of 10%, the OAS is 35 basis points. At 20% volatility, the OAS declines and, in this case is negative and therefore the bond is overvalued relative to the model.

What the OAS seeks to do is remove from the nominal spread the amount that is due to the option risk. The measure is called an OAS because 1) it is a spread and 2) it adjusts the cash flows for the option when computing the spread

EXHIBIT 11	Demonstration That the Option-Adjusted Spread Is 35 Basis Points for a 6.5% Callable Bond Selling at 102.218 (Assuming 10% Volatility)

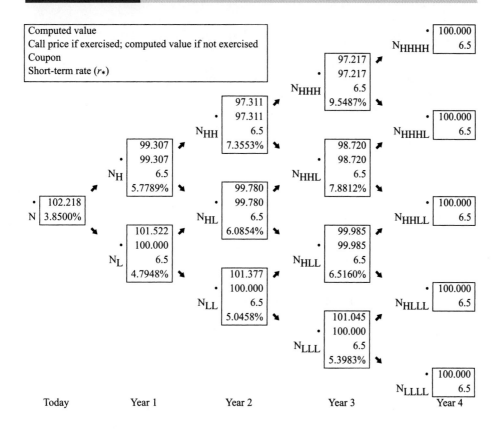

Note: Each 1-year rate is 35 basis points greater than in Exhibit 5.

to the benchmark interest rates. The second point can be seen from Exhibits 8 and 9. Notice that at each node the value obtained from the backward induction method is adjusted based on the call option and the call rule. Thus, the resulting spread is "option adjusted."

What does the OAS tell us about the relative value for our callable bond? As explained in Section 3, the answer depends on the benchmark used. Exhibit 1 provides a summary of how to interpret the OAS. In valuing the callable bond in our illustration, the benchmark is the issuer's own securities. As can be seen in Exhibit 1, a positive OAS means that the callable bond is cheap (i.e., under-priced). At a 10% volatility, the OAS is 35 basis points. Consequently, assuming a 10% volatility, on a relative value basis the callable bond is attractive. However, and this is critical to remember, the OAS depends on the assumed interest rate volatility. When a 20% interest rate volatility is assumed, the OAS is −6 basis points. Hence, if an investor assumes that this is the appropriate interest rate volatility that should be used in valuing the callable bond, the issue is expensive (overvalued) on a relative value basis.

PRACTICE QUESTION 4

Show that if 20% volatility is assumed, the OAS is −6 basis points.

D. Effective Duration and Effective Convexity

We previously explained the meaning of duration and convexity measures and explained how these two measures can be computed. Specifically, duration is the approximate percentage change in the value of a security for a 100 basis point change in interest rates (assuming a parallel shift in the yield curve). The convexity measure allows for an adjustment to the estimated price change obtained by using duration. The formulas for duration and convexity are repeated below:

$$\text{Duration} = \frac{V_- - V_+}{2V_0(\Delta y)}$$

$$\text{Convexity} = \frac{V_+ + V_- - 2V_0}{2V_0(\Delta y)^2}$$

where

Δy = change in rate used to calculate new values
V_+ = estimated value if yield is increased by Δy
V_- = estimated value if yield is decreased by Δy
V_0 = initial price (per $100 of par value)

We also made a distinction between "modified" duration and convexity and "effective" duration and convexity. **Modified duration** and convexity do not allow for the fact that the cash flows for a bond with an embedded option may change due to the exercise of the option. In contrast, effective duration and convexity do take into consideration how changes in interest rates in the future may alter the cash flows due to the exercise of the option. But, we did not demonstrate how to compute effective duration and convexity because they require a model for valuing bonds with embedded options and we did not introduce such models until this reading.

So, let's see how effective duration and convexity are computed using the binomial model. With effective duration and convexity, the values V_- and V_+ are obtained from the binomial model. Recall that in using the binomial model, the cash flows at a node are adjusted for the embedded call option as was demonstrated in Exhibit 8 and highlighted in the lower panel of Exhibit 9.

The procedure for calculating the value of V_+ is as follows:

Step 1:   Given the market price of the issue calculate its OAS using the procedure described earlier.

Step 2:   Shift the on-the-run yield curve up by a small number of basis points (Δy).

Step 3:   Construct a binomial interest rate tree based on the new yield curve in Step 2.

Step 4:   To each of the 1-year rates in the binomial interest rate tree, add the OAS to obtain an "adjusted tree." That is, the calculation of the effective duration and convexity assumes that the OAS will not change when interest rates change.

Step 5:   Use the adjusted tree found in Step 4 to determine the value of the bond, which is V_+.

To determine the value of V_-, the same five steps are followed except that in Step 2, the on-the-run yield curve is shifted down by a small number of basis points (Δy).

To illustrate how V_+ and V_- are determined in order to calculate effective duration and effective convexity, we will use the same on-the-run yield curve that we have used in our previous illustrations assuming a volatility of 10%. The 4-year callable bond with a coupon rate of 6.5% and callable at par selling at 102.218 will be used in this illustration. The OAS for this issue is 35 basis points.

Exhibit 12 shows the adjusted tree by shifting the yield curve up by an arbitrarily small number of basis points, 25 basis points, and then adding 35 basis points (the OAS) to each 1-year rate. The adjusted tree is then used to value the bond. The resulting value, V_+, is 101.621. Exhibit 13 shows the adjusted tree by shifting the yield curve down by 25 basis points and then adding 35 basis points to each 1-year rate. The resulting value, V_-, is 102.765.

The results are summarized below:

$$\Delta y = 0.0025$$
$$V_+ = 101.621$$
$$V_- = 102.765$$
$$V_0 = 102.218$$

EXHIBIT 12	Determination of V_+ for Calculating Effective Duration and Convexity[a]

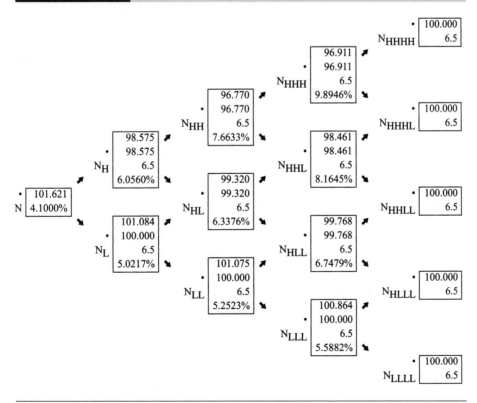

[a]+25 basis point shift in on-the-run yield curve.

EXHIBIT 13   Determination of V_ for Calculating Effective Duration and Convexity[a]

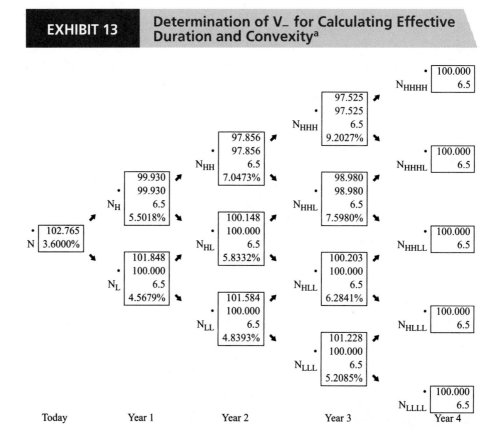

[a]−25 basis point shift in on-the-run yield curve.

Therefore,

$$\text{Effective duration} = \frac{102.765 - 101.621}{2(102.218)(0.0025)} = 2.24$$

$$\text{Effective convexity} = \frac{101.621 + 102.765 - 2(102.218)}{2(102.218)(0.0025)^2} = -39.1321$$

Notice that this callable bond exhibits negative convexity.

7   VALUING A PUTABLE BOND

A putable bond is one in which the bondholder has the right to force the issuer to pay off the bond prior to the maturity date. To illustrate how the binomial model can be used to value a putable bond, suppose that a 6.5% bond with four years remaining to maturity is putable in one year at par ($100). Also assume that the appropriate binomial interest rate tree for this issuer is the one in Exhibit 5, and the bondholder exercises the put if the bond's price is less than par.

Exhibit 14 shows the binomial interest rate tree with the values based on whether or not the investor exercises the option at a node. Exhibit 15 highlights selected nodes for year 2 and year 3 just as we did in Exhibit 9. The right

EXHIBIT 14	Valuing a Putable Bond with Four Years to Maturity, a Coupon Rate of 6.5%, and Putable in One Year at 100 (10% Volatility Assumed)

Computed value
Put price if exercised; computed value if not exercised
Coupon
Short-term rate (r_*)

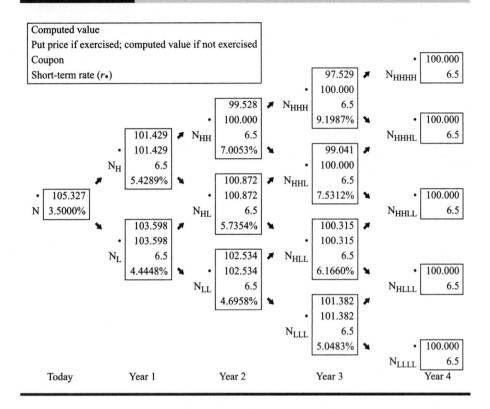

Today   Year 1   Year 2   Year 3   Year 4

EXHIBIT 15	Highlighting Nodes in Years 2 and 3 for a Putable Bond

(a) Selected nodes where put option is exercised

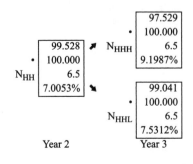

Year 2   Year 3

(b) Nodes where put option is not exercised

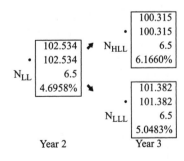

Year 2   Year 3

side of the exhibit shows the nodes where the put option is not exercised, and therefore the value at each node is the same as when the bond is option free. In contrast, the left side of the exhibit shows where the value obtained from the backward induction method is overridden, and 100 is used because the put option is exercised.

The value of the putable bond is $105.327, a value that is greater than the value of the corresponding option-free bond. The reason for this can be seen from the following relationship:

Value of a putable bond = Value of an option-free bond
+ Value of the put option

The reason for adding the value of the put option is that the investor has purchased the put option.

We can rewrite the above relationship to determine the value of the put option:

Value of the put option = Value of a putable bond
− Value of an option-free bond

In our example, since the value of the putable bond is $105.327 and the value of the corresponding option-free bond is $104.643, the value of the put option is −$0.684. The negative sign indicates the issuer has sold the option, or equivalently, the investor has purchased the option.

We have stressed that the value of a bond with an embedded option is affected by the volatility assumption. Unlike a callable bond, the value of a putable bond increases if the assumed volatility increases. It can be demonstrated

EXHIBIT 16   **Valuing a Putable/Callable Issue (10% Volatility Assumed)**

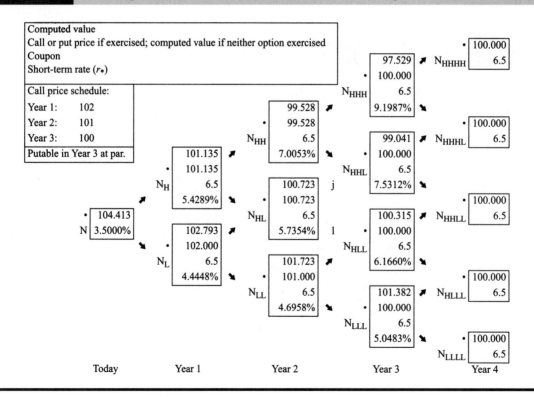

that if a 20% volatility is assumed, the value of this putable bond increases from 105.327 at 10% volatility to 106.010.

Suppose that a bond is both putable and callable. The procedure for valuing such a structure is to adjust the value at each node to reflect whether the issue would be put or called. To illustrate this, consider the 4-year callable bond analyzed earlier that had a call schedule. The valuation of this issue is shown in Exhibit 10. Suppose the issue is putable in year 3 at par value. Exhibit 16 shows how to value this callable/putable issue. At each node there are two decisions about the exercising of an option that must be made. First, given the valuation from the backward induction method at a node, the call rule is invoked to determine whether the issue will be called. If it is called, the value at the node is replaced by the call price. The valuation procedure then continues using the call price at that node. Second, if the call option is not exercised at a node, it must be determined whether or not the put option is exercised. If it is exercised, then the value from the backward induction method is overridden and the put price is substituted at that node and is used in subsequent calculations.

PRACTICE QUESTION 5

Using the binomial interest rate tree based on 20%, show that the value of this putable bond is 106.010. (Assume that the bond is noncallable.)

VALUING A STEP-UP CALLABLE NOTE 8

Step-up callable notes are callable instruments whose coupon rate is increased (i.e., "stepped up") at designated times. When the coupon rate is increased only once over the security's life, it is said to be a single step-up callable note. A multiple step-up callable note is a step-up callable note whose coupon is increased more than one time over the life of the security. Valuation using the binomial model is similar to that for valuing a callable bond except that the cash flows are altered at each node to reflect the coupon changing characteristics of a step-up note.

To illustrate how the binomial model can be used to value step-up callable notes, let's begin with a single step-up callable note. Suppose that a 4-year step-up callable note pays 4.25% for two years and then 7.5% for two more years. Assume that this note is callable at par at the end of Year 2 and Year 3. We will use the binomial interest rate tree given in Exhibit 5 to value this note.

Exhibit 17 shows the value of a corresponding single step-up *noncallable* note. The valuation procedure is identical to that performed in Exhibit 8 except that the coupon in the box at each node reflects the step-up terms. The value is $102.082. Exhibit 18 shows that the value of the single step-up callable note is $100.031. The value of the embedded call option is equal to the difference in the step-up noncallable note value and the step-up callable note value, $2.051.

The procedure is the same for a multiple step-up callable note. Suppose that a multiple step-up callable note has the following coupon rates: 4.2% in Year 1, 5% in Year 2, 6% in Year 3, and 7% in Year 4. Also assume that the note is callable at the end of Year 1 at par. Exhibit 19 shows that the value of this note if it *is* noncallable is $101.012. The value of the multiple step-up callable note is $99.996 as shown in Exhibit 20. Therefore, the value of the embedded call option is $1.016 (= 101.012 − 99.996).

EXHIBIT 17	Valuing a Single Step-Up Noncallable Note with Four Years to Maturity (10% Volatility Assumed)

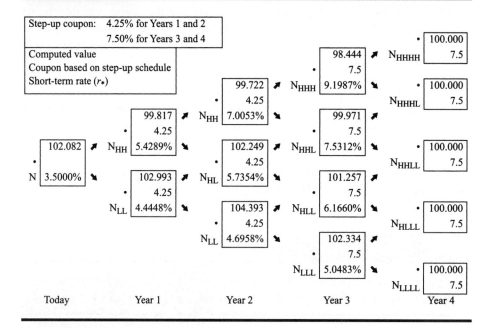

Step-up coupon: 4.25% for Years 1 and 2
7.50% for Years 3 and 4

Computed value
Coupon based on step-up schedule
Short-term rate (r_*)

EXHIBIT 18	Valuing a Single Step-Up Callable Note with Four Years to Maturity, Callable in Two Years at 100 (10% Volatility Assumed)

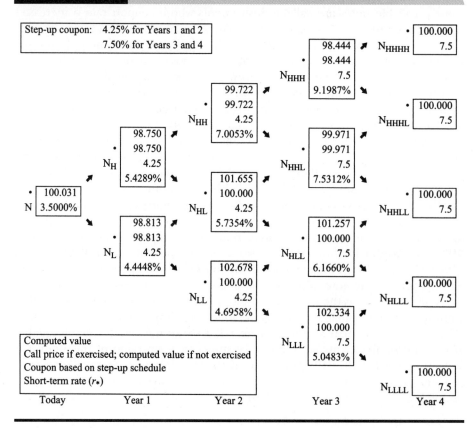

Step-up coupon: 4.25% for Years 1 and 2
7.50% for Years 3 and 4

Computed value
Call price if exercised; computed value if not exercised
Coupon based on step-up schedule
Short-term rate (r_*)

EXHIBIT 19

Valuing a Multiple Step-Up Noncallable Note with Four Years to Maturity (10% Volatility Assumed)

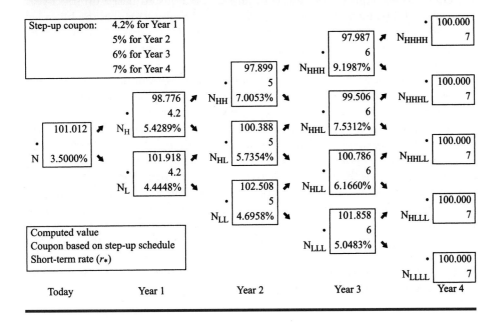

Step-up coupon: 4.2% for Year 1
5% for Year 2
6% for Year 3
7% for Year 4

Computed value
Coupon based on step-up schedule
Short-term rate (r_*)

Today   Year 1   Year 2   Year 3   Year 4

EXHIBIT 20

Valuing a Multiple Step-Up Callable Note with Four Years to Maturity, and Callable in One Year at 100 (10% Volatility Assumed)

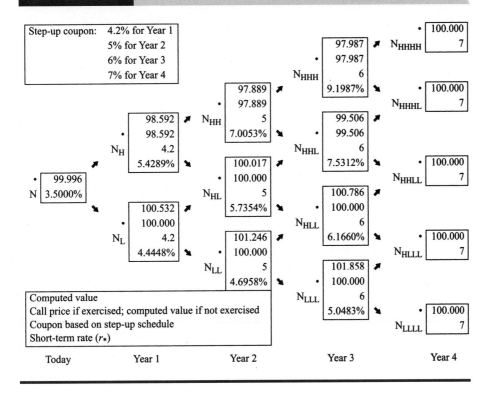

Step-up coupon: 4.2% for Year 1
5% for Year 2
6% for Year 3
7% for Year 4

Computed value
Call price if exercised; computed value if not exercised
Coupon based on step-up schedule
Short-term rate (r_*)

Today   Year 1   Year 2   Year 3   Year 4

9   VALUING A CAPPED FLOATER

The valuation of a floating-rate note with a cap (i.e., a capped floater) using the binomial model requires that the coupon rate be adjusted based on the 1-year rate (which is assumed to be the reference rate). Exhibit 21 shows the binomial tree and the relevant values at each node for a floater whose coupon rate is the 1-year rate flat (i.e., no margin over the reference rate) and in which there are no restrictions on the coupon rate.

What is important to recall about floaters is that the coupon rate is set at the beginning of the period but paid at the end of the period (i.e., beginning of the next period). That is, the coupon interest is paid in arrears.

The valuation procedure is identical to that for the other structures described above except that an adjustment is made for the characteristic of a floater that the coupon rate is set at the beginning of the year and paid in arrears. Here is how the payment in arrears characteristic affects the backward induction method. Look at the top node for year 2 in Exhibit 21. The coupon rate shown at that node is 7.0053% as determined by the 1-year rate at that node. Since the coupon payment will not be made until year 3 (i.e., paid in arrears), the value of 100 shown at the node is determined using the backward induction method but discounting the coupon rate shown at the node. For example, let's see how we get the value of 100 in the top box in year 2. The procedure is to calculate the average of the two present values of the bond

---

EXHIBIT 21   **Valuing a Floater with No Cap (10% Volatility Assumed)**

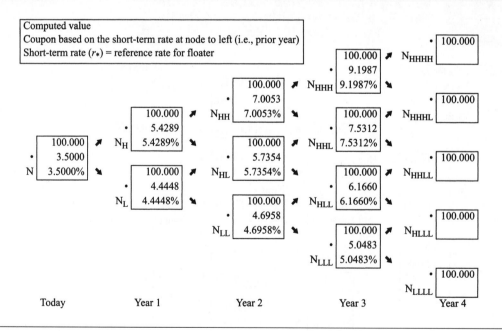

Note: The coupon rate shown at a node is the coupon rate to be received in the next year.

value and coupon. Since the bond values and coupons are the same, the present value is simply:

$$\frac{100 + 7.0053}{1.070053} = 100$$

Suppose that the floater has a cap of 7.25%. Exhibit 22 shows how this floater would be valued. At each node where the 1-year rate exceeds 7.25%, a coupon of $7.25 is substituted. The value of this capped floater is 99.724. Thus, the cost of the cap is the difference between par and 99.724. If the cap for this floater was 7.75% rather than 7.25%, it can be shown that the value of this floater would be 99.858. That is, the higher the cap, the closer the capped floater will trade to par.

Thus, it is important to emphasize that the valuation mechanics are being modified slightly only to reflect the characteristics of the floater's cash flow. All of the other principles regarding valuation of bonds with embedded options are the same. For a capped floater there is a rule for determining whether or not to override the cash flow at a node based on the cap. Since a cap embedded in a floater is effectively an option granted by the investor to the issuer, it should be no surprise that the valuation model described in this reading can be used to value a capped floater.

EXHIBIT 22	Valuing a Floating Rate Note with a 7.25% Cap (10% Volatility Assumed)

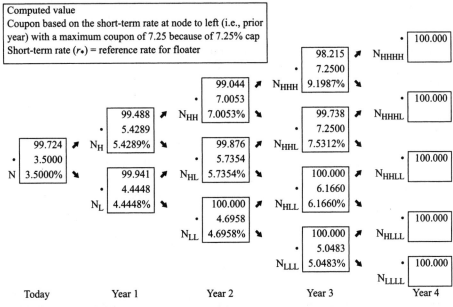

Computed value
Coupon based on the short-term rate at node to left (i.e., prior year) with a maximum coupon of 7.25 because of 7.25% cap
Short-term rate (r_*) = reference rate for floater

Note: The coupon rate shown at a node is the coupon rate to be received in the next year.

10   ANALYSIS OF CONVERTIBLE BONDS

A convertible bond is a security that can be converted into common stock at the option of the investor. Hence, it is a bond with an embedded option where the option is granted to the investor. Moreover, since a convertible bond may be callable and putable, it is a complex bond because the value of the bond will depend on both how interest rates change (which affects the value of the call and any put option) *and* how changes in the market price of the stock affects the value of the option to convert to common stock.

A. Basic Features of Convertible Securities

The conversion provision of a convertible security grants the securityholder the right to convert the security into a predetermined number of shares of common stock of the issuer. A convertible security is therefore a security with an embedded call option to buy the common stock of the issuer. An exchangeable security grants the securityholder the right to exchange the security for the common stock of a firm *other* than the issuer of the security. Throughout this reading we use the term convertible security to refer to both convertible and exchangeable securities.

In illustrating the calculation of the various concepts described below, we will use a hypothetical convertible bond issue. The issuer is the All Digital Component Corporation (ADC) 5¾% convertible issue due in 9+ years. Information about this hypothetical bond issue and the stock of this issuer is provided in Exhibit 23.

The number of shares of common stock that the securityholder will receive from exercising the call option of a convertible security is called the conversion ratio. The conversion privilege may extend for all or only some portion of the security's life, and the stated conversion ratio may change over time. It is always adjusted proportionately for stock splits and stock dividends. For the ADC convertible issue, the conversion ratio is 25.32 shares. This means that for each $1,000 of par value of this issue the securityholder exchanges for ADC common stock, he will receive 25.32 shares.

At the time of issuance of a convertible bond, the effective price at which the buyer of the convertible bond will pay for the stock can be determined as follows. The prospectus will specify the number of shares that the investor will receive by exchanging the bond for the common stock. The number of shares is called the conversion ratio. So, for example, assume the conversion ratio is 20. If the investor converts the bond for stock, the investor will receive 20 shares of common stock. Now, suppose that the par value for the convertible bond is $1,000 and is sold to investors at issuance at that price. Then effectively by buying the convertible bond for $1,000 at issuance, investors are purchasing the common stock for $50 per share ($1,000/20 shares). This price is referred to in the prospectus as the conversion price, and some investors refer to it as the stated conversion price. For a bond not issued at par (for example, a zero-coupon bond), the market or effective conversion price is determined by dividing the issue price per $1,000 of par value by the conversion ratio.

The ADC convertible was issued for $1,000 per $1,000 of par value and the conversion ratio is 25.32. Therefore, the conversion price at issuance for the ADC convertible issue is $39.49 ($1,000/25.32 shares).

Almost all convertible issues are callable. The ADC convertible issue has a non-call period of three years. The call price schedule for the ADC convertible issue is shown in Exhibit 23. There are some issues that have a provisional call feature that allows the issuer to call the issue during the non-call period if the price of the stock reaches a certain price.

Some convertible bonds are putable. Put options can be classified as "hard" puts and "soft" puts. A hard put is one in which the convertible security must be redeemed by the issuer for cash. In the case of a soft put, while the investor has the option to exercise the put, the *issuer* may select how the payment will be made. The issuer may redeem the convertible security for cash, common stock, subordinated notes, or a combination of the three.

EXHIBIT 23	Information about All Digital Component Corporation (ADC) 5¾% Convertible Bond Due in 9+ Years and Common Stock

Convertible bond

Current market price: $106.50   Maturity date: 9+ years

Non-call for 3 years

Call Price Schedule

In Year 4	103.59
In Year 5	102.88
In Year 6	102.16
In Year 7	101.44
In Year 8	100.72
In Year 9	100.00
In Year 10	100.00

Coupon rate: 5¾%

Conversion ratio: 25.320 shares of ADC shares per $1,000 par value

Rating: A3/A−

ADC common stock

     Expected volatility: 17%   Current dividend yield: 2.727%

     Dividend per share: $0.90 per year   Stock price: $33

B. Traditional Analysis of Convertible Securities

Traditional analysis of convertible bonds relies on measures that do not attempt to directly value the embedded call, put, or common stock options. We present and illustrate these measures below and later discuss an option-based approach to valuation of convertible bonds.

1. Minimum Value of a Convertible Security

The conversion value or parity value of a convertible security is the value of the security if it is converted immediately.[8] That is,

Conversion value = Market price of common stock × Conversion ratio

The minimum price of a convertible security is the greater of[9]

1. Its conversion value, or

2. Its value as a security without the conversion option—that is, based on the convertible security's cash flows if not converted (i.e., a plain vanilla security). This value is called its straight value or investment value. The straight value is found by using the valuation model described earlier in this reading because almost all issues are callable.

If the convertible security does not sell for the greater of these two values, arbitrage profits could be realized. For example, suppose the conversion value is greater than the straight value, and the security trades at its straight value. An investor can buy the convertible security at the straight value and immediately convert it. By doing so, the investor realizes a gain equal to the difference between the conversion value and the straight value. Suppose, instead, the straight value is greater than the conversion value, and the security trades at its conversion value. By buying the convertible at the conversion value, the investor will realize a higher yield than a comparable straight security.

Consider the ADC convertible issue. Suppose that the straight value of the bond is $98.19 per $100 of par value. Since the market price per share of common stock is $33, the conversion value per $1,000 of par value is:

Conversion value = $33 × 25.32 = $835.56

Consequently, the conversion value is 83.556% of par value. Per $100 of par value the conversion value is $83.556. Since the straight value is $98.19 and the conversion value is $83.556, the minimum value for the ADC convertible has to be $98.19.

2. Market Conversion Price

The price that an investor effectively pays for the common stock if the convertible bond is purchased and then converted into the common stock is called the market conversion price or conversion parity price. It is found as follows:

$$\text{Market conversion price} = \frac{\text{Market price of convertible security}}{\text{Conversion ratio}}$$

---

[8] Technically, the standard textbook definition of conversion value given here is theoretically incorrect because as bondholders convert, the price of the stock will decline. The theoretically correct definition for the conversion value is that it is the product of the conversion ratio and the stock price *after* conversion.

[9] If the conversion value is the greater of the two values, it is possible for the convertible bond to trade below the conversion value. This can occur for the following reasons: 1) there are restrictions that prevent the investor from converting, 2) the underlying stock is illiquid, and 3) an anticipated forced conversion will result in loss of accrued interest of a high coupon issue. See Mihir Bhattacharya, "Convertible Securities and Their Valuation," Chapter 51 in Frank J. Fabozzi (ed.), *The Handbook of Fixed Income Securities: Sixth Edition* (New York: McGraw Hill, 2001), p. 1128.

The market conversion price is a useful benchmark because once the actual market price of the stock rises above the market conversion price, any further stock price increase is certain to increase the value of the convertible bond by at least the same percentage. Therefore, the market conversion price can be viewed as a break-even price.

An investor who purchases a convertible bond rather than the underlying stock, effectively pays a premium over the current market price of the stock. This premium per share is equal to the difference between the market conversion price and the current market price of the common stock. That is,

$$\text{Market conversion premium per share} = \text{Market conversion price} \\ - \text{Current market price}$$

The market conversion premium per share is usually expressed as a percentage of the current market price as follows:

$$\text{Market conversion premium ratio} = \frac{\text{Market conversion premium per share}}{\text{Market price of common stock}}$$

Why would someone be willing to pay a premium to buy the stock? Recall that the minimum price of a convertible security is the greater of its conversion value or its straight value. Thus, as the common stock price declines, the price of the convertible bond will not fall below its straight value. The straight value therefore acts as a floor for the convertible security's price. However, it is a moving floor as the straight value will change with changes in interest rates.

Viewed in this context, the market conversion premium per share can be seen as the price of a call option. The buyer of a call option limits the downside risk to the option price. In the case of a convertible bond, for a premium, the securityholder limits the downside risk to the straight value of the bond. The difference between the buyer of a call option and the buyer of a convertible bond is that the former knows precisely the dollar amount of the downside risk, while the latter knows only that the most that can be lost is the difference between the convertible bond's price and the straight value. The straight value at some future date, however, is unknown; the value will change as market interest rates change or if the issuer's credit quality changes.

The calculation of the market conversion price, market conversion premium per share, and market conversion premium ratio for the ADC convertible issue is shown below:

$$\text{Market conversion price} = \frac{\$1,065}{25.32} = \$42.06$$

Thus, if the investor purchased the convertible and then converted it to common stock, the effective price that the investor paid per share is $42.06.

$$\text{Market conversion premium per share} = \$42.06 - \$33 = \$9.06$$

The investor is effectively paying a premium per share of $9.06 by buying the convertible rather than buying the stock for $33.

$$\text{Market conversion premium ratio} = \frac{\$9.06}{\$33} = 0.275 = 27.5\%$$

The premium per share of $9.06 means that the investor is paying 27.5% above the market price of $33 by buying the convertible.

3. Current Income of Convertible Bond versus Common Stock

As an offset to the market conversion premium per share, investing in the convertible bond rather than buying the stock directly, generally means that the investor realizes higher current income from the coupon interest from a convertible bond than would be received from common stock dividends based on the number of shares equal to the conversion ratio. Analysts evaluating a convertible bond typically compute the time it takes to recover the premium per share by computing the premium payback period (which is also known as the break-even time). This is computed as follows:

$$\text{Premium payback period} = \frac{\text{Market conversion premium per share}}{\text{Favorable income differential per share}}$$

where the favorable income differential per share is equal to the following:

$$\frac{\text{Coupon interest} - (\text{Conversion ratio} \times \text{Common stock dividend per share})}{\text{Conversion ratio}}$$

The numerator of the formula is the difference between the coupon interest for the issue and the dividends that would be received if the investor converted the issue into common stock. Since the investor would receive the number of shares specified by the conversion ratio, then multiplying the conversion ratio by the dividend per share of common stock gives the total dividends that would be received if the investor converted. Dividing the difference between the coupon interest and the total dividends that would be received if the issue is converted by the conversion ratio gives the favorable income differential on a per share basis by owning the convertible rather than the common stock or changes in the dividend over the period.

Notice that the premium payback period does *not* take into account the time value of money or changes in the dividend over the period.

For the ADC convertible issue, the market conversion premium per share is $9.06. The favorable income differential per share is found as follows:

Coupon interest from bond = 0.0575 × $1,000 = $57.50
Conversion ratio × Dividend per share = 25.32 × $0.90 = $22.79

Therefore,

$$\text{Favorable income differential per share} = \frac{\$57.50 - \$22.79}{25.32} = \$1.37$$

and

$$\text{Premium payback period} = \frac{\$9.06}{\$1.37} = 6.6 \text{ years}$$

Without considering the time value of money, the investor would recover the market conversion premium per share assuming unchanged dividends in about 6.6 years.

4. Downside Risk with a Convertible Bond

Unfortunately, investors usually use the straight value as a measure of the downside risk of a convertible security, because it is assumed that the price of the convertible cannot fall below this value. Thus, some investors view the straight value as the floor for the price of the convertible bond. The downside risk is measured as a percentage of the straight value and computed as follows:

$$\text{Premium over straight value} = \frac{\text{Market price of convertible bond}}{\text{Straight value}} - 1$$

The higher the premium over straight value, all other factors constant, the less attractive the convertible bond.

Despite its use in practice, this measure of downside risk is flawed because the straight value (the floor) changes as interest rates change. If interest rates rise (fall), the straight value falls (rises) making the floor fall (rise). Therefore, the downside risk changes as interest rates change.

For the ADC convertible issue, since the market price of the convertible issue is 106.5 and the straight value is 98.19, the premium over straight value is

$$\text{Premium over straight value} = \frac{\$106.50}{\$98.19} - 1 = 0.085 = 8.5\%$$

5. The Upside Potential of a Convertible Security

The evaluation of the upside potential of a convertible security depends on the prospects for the underlying common stock. Thus, the techniques for analyzing common stocks discussed in books on equity analysis should be employed.

C. Investment Characteristics of a Convertible Security

The investment characteristics of a convertible bond depend on the common stock price. If the price is low, so that the straight value is considerably higher than the conversion value, the security will trade much like a straight security. The convertible security in such instances is referred to as a fixed income equivalent or a busted convertible.

When the price of the stock is such that the conversion value is considerably higher than the straight value, then the convertible security will trade as if it were an equity instrument; in this case it is said to be a common stock equivalent. In such cases, the market conversion premium per share will be small.

Between these two cases, fixed income equivalent and common stock equivalent, the convertible security trades as a hybrid security, having the characteristics of both a fixed income security and a common stock instrument.

D. An Option-Based Valuation Approach

In our discussion of convertible bonds, we did not address the following questions:

1. What is a fair value for the conversion premium per share?

2. How do we handle convertible bonds with call and/or put options?

3. How does a change in interest rates affect the stock price?

Consider first a noncallable/nonputable convertible bond. The investor who purchases this security would be effectively entering into two separate transactions: 1) buying a noncallable/nonputable straight security and 2) buying a call option (or warrant) on the stock, where the number of shares that can be purchased with the call option is equal to the conversion ratio.

The question is: What is the fair value for the call option? The fair value depends on the factors that affect the price of a call option. One key factor is the expected price volatility of the stock: the higher the expected price volatility, the greater the value of the call option. The theoretical value of a call option can be valued using the Black-Scholes option pricing model. This model will be discussed in the reading on option markets and contracts and is explained in more detail in investment textbooks. As a first approximation to the value of a convertible bond, the formula would be:

Convertible security value = Straight value + Value of the call option on the stock

The value of the call option is added to the straight value because the investor has purchased a call option on the stock.

Now let's add in a common feature of a convertible bond: the issuer's right to call the issue. Therefore, the value of a convertible bond that is callable is equal to:

Convertible bond value = Straight value + Value of the call option on the stock
              − Value of the call option on the bond

Consequently, the analysis of convertible bonds must take into account the value of the issuer's right to call. This depends, in turn, on 1) future interest rate volatility and 2) economic factors that determine whether or not it is optimal for the issuer to call the security. The Black-Scholes option pricing model cannot handle this situation.

Let's add one more wrinkle. Suppose that the callable convertible bond is also putable. Then the value of such a convertible would be equal to:

Convertible bond value = Straight value + Value of the call option on the stock
              − Value of the call option on the bond
              + Value of the put option on the bond

To link interest rates and stock prices together (the third question we raise on the previous page), statistical analysis of historical movements of these two variables must be estimated and incorporated into the model.

Valuation models based on an option pricing approach have been suggested by several researchers.[10] These models can generally be classified as one-factor or multi-factor models. By "factor" we mean the stochastic (i.e., random) variables that are assumed to drive the value of a convertible or bond. The obvious candidates for factors are the price movement of the underlying common stock and the movement of interest rates. According to Mihir Bhattacharya and Yu Zhu, the most widely used convertible valuation model has been the one-factor model, and the factor is the price movement of the underlying common stock.[11]

---

[10] See, for example: Michael Brennan and Eduardo Schwartz, "Convertible Bonds: Valuation and Optimal Strategies for Call and Conversion," *Journal of Finance* (December 1977), pp. 1699–1715; Jonathan Ingersoll, "A Contingent-Claims Valuation of Convertible Securities," *Journal of Financial Economics* (May 1977), pp. 289–322; Michael Brennan and Eduardo Schwartz, "Analyzing Convertible Bonds," *Journal of Financial and Quantitative Analysis* (November 1980), pp. 907–929; and, George Constantinides, "Warrant Exercise and Bond Conversion in Competitive Markets," *Journal of Financial Economics* (September 1984), pp. 371–398.

[11] Mihir Bhattacharya and Yu Zhu, "Valuation and Analysis of Convertible Securities," Chapter 42 in Frank J. Fabozzi (ed.), *The Handbook of Fixed Income Securities: Fifth Edition* (Chicago: Irwin Professional Publishing, 1997).

E. The Risk/Return Profile of a Convertible Security

Let's use the ADC convertible issue and the valuation model to look at the risk/return profile by investing in a convertible issue or the underlying common stock.

Suppose an investor is considering the purchase of either the common stock of ADC or the convertible issue. The stock can be purchased in the market for $33. By buying the convertible bond, the investor is effectively purchasing the stock for $42.06 (the market conversion price per share). Exhibit 24 shows the total return for both alternatives one year later assuming 1) the stock price does not change, 2) it changes by ±10%, and 3) it changes by ±25%. The convertible's theoretical value is based on some valuation model not discussed here.

If the ADC's stock price is unchanged, the stock position will underperform the convertible position despite the fact that a premium was paid to purchase the stock by acquiring the convertible issue. The reason is that even though the convertible's theoretical value decreased, the income from coupon more than compensates for the capital loss. In the two scenarios where the price of ADC stock declines, the convertible position outperforms the stock position because the straight value provides a floor for the convertible.

One of the critical assumptions in this analysis is that the straight value does not change except for the passage of time. If interest rates rise, the straight value will decline. Even if interest rates do not rise, the perceived credit-worthiness of the issuer may deteriorate, causing investors to demand a higher yield. The illustration clearly demonstrates that there are benefits and drawbacks of investing in convertible securities. The disadvantage is the upside potential give-up because a premium per share must be paid. An advantage is the reduction in downside risk (as determined by the straight value).

Keep in mind that the major reason for the acquisition of the convertible bond is the potential price appreciation due to the increase in the price of the stock. An analysis of the growth prospects of the issuer's earnings and stock price is beyond the scope of this book but is described in all books on equity analysis.

EXHIBIT 24	Comparison of 1-Year Return for ADC Stock and Convertible Issue for Assumed Changes in Stock Price

Beginning of horizon: October 7, 1993

End of horizon: October 7, 1994

Price of ADC stock on October 7, 1993: $33.00

Assumed volatility of ADC stock return: 17%

Stock Price Change (%)	ADC Stock Return (%)	Convertible's Theoretical Value	Convertible's Return (%)
−25	−22.27	100.47	−0.26
−10	−7.27	102.96	2.08
0	2.73	105.27	4.24
10	12.73	108.12	6.92
25	27.73	113.74	12.20

SUMMARY

▶ The potential benchmark interest rates that can be used in bond valuation are those in the Treasury market, a specific bond sector with a given credit rating, or a specific issuer.

▶ Benchmark interest rates can be based on either an estimated yield curve or an estimated spot rate curve.

▶ Yield spread measures are used in assessing the relative value of securities.

▶ Relative value analysis is used to identify securities as being overpriced ("rich"), underpriced ("cheap"), or fairly priced relative to benchmark interest rates.

▶ The interpretation of a spread measure depends on the benchmark used.

▶ The option-adjusted spread is a spread after adjusting for the option risk.

▶ Depending on the benchmark interest rates used to generate the interest rate tree, the option-adjusted spread may or may not capture credit risk.

▶ The option-adjusted spread is not a spread off of one maturity of the benchmark interest rates; rather, it is a spread over the forward rates in the interest rate tree that were constructed from the benchmark interest rates.

▶ A valuation model must produce arbitrage-free values; that is, a valuation model must produce a value for each on-the-run issue that is equal to its observed market price.

▶ There are several arbitrage-free models that can be used to value bonds with embedded options, but they all follow the same principle—they generate a tree of interest rates based on some interest rate volatility assumption, they require rules for determining when any of the embedded options will be exercised, and they employ the backward induction methodology.

▶ A valuation model involves generating an interest rate tree based on 1) benchmark interest rates, 2) an assumed interest rate model, and 3) an assumed interest rate volatility.

▶ The assumed volatility of interest rates incorporates the uncertainty about future interest rates into the analysis.

▶ The interest rate tree is constructed using a process that is similar to bootstrapping but requires an iterative procedure to determine the interest rates that will produce a value for the on-the-run issues equal to their market value.

▶ At each node of the tree there are interest rates and these rates are effectively forward rates; thus, there is a set of forward rates for each year.

▶ Using the interest rate tree the arbitrage-free value of any bond can be determined.

▶ In valuing a callable bond using the interest rate tree, the cash flows at a node are modified to take into account the call option.

▶ The value of the embedded call option is the difference between the value of an option-free bond and the value of the callable bond.

▶ The volatility assumption has an important impact on the arbitrage-free value.

▶ The option-adjusted spread is the constant spread that when added to the short rates in the binomial interest rate tree will produce a valuation for the bond (i.e., arbitrage-free value) equal to the market price of the bond.

▶ The interpretation of the OAS, or equivalently, what the OAS is compensating an investor for, depends on what benchmark interest rates are used.

▶ The required values for calculating effective duration and effective convexity are found by shifting the on-the-run yield curve, calculating a new binomial interest rate tree, and then determining the required values after adjusting the tree by adding the OAS to each short rate.

▶ For a bond with any embedded option or options, application of the binomial model requires that the value at each node of the tree be adjusted based on whether or not the option will be exercised; the binomial model can be used to value bonds with multiple or interrelated embedded options by determining at each node of the tree whether or not one of the options will be exercised.

▶ With a putable bond, the option will be exercised if the value at a node is less than the price at which the bondholder can put the bond to the issuer.

▶ The value of a putable bond is greater than the value of an otherwise option-free bond.

▶ The binomial model can be used to value a single step-up callable note or a multiple step-up callable note.

▶ To value a floating-rate note that has a cap, the coupon at each node of the tree is adjusted by determining whether or not the cap is reached at a node; if the rate at a node does exceed the cap, the rate at the node is the capped rate rather than the rate determined by the floater's coupon formula.

▶ For a floating-rate note, the binomial method must be adjusted to account for the fact that a floater pays in arrears; that is, the coupon payment is determined in a period but not paid until the next period.

▶ Convertible and exchangeable securities can be converted into shares of common stock.

▶ The conversion ratio is the number of common stock shares for which a convertible security may be converted.

▶ Almost all convertible securities are callable and some are putable.

▶ The conversion value is the value of the convertible bond if it is immediately converted into the common stock.

▶ The market conversion price is the price that an investor effectively pays for the common stock if the convertible security is purchased and then converted into the common stock.

▶ The premium paid for the common stock is measured by the market conversion premium per share and market conversion premium ratio.

▶ The straight value or investment value of a convertible security is its value if there was no conversion feature.

▶ The minimum value of a convertible security is the greater of the conversion value and the straight value.

▶ A fixed income equivalent (or a busted convertible) refers to the situation where the straight value is considerably higher than the conversion value so that the security will trade much like a straight security.

▶ A common stock equivalent refers to the situation where the conversion value is considerably higher than the straight value so that the convertible security trades as if it were an equity instrument.

▶ A hybrid equivalent refers to the situation where the convertible security trades with characteristics of both a fixed income security and a common stock instrument.

▶ While the downside risk of a convertible security usually is estimated by calculating the premium over straight value, the limitation of this measure is that the straight value (the floor) changes as interest rates change.

▶ An advantage of buying the convertible rather than the common stock is the reduction in downside risk.

▶ The disadvantage of a convertible relative to the straight purchase of the common stock is the upside potential give-up because a premium per share must be paid.

▶ An option-based valuation model is a more appropriate approach to value convertible securities than the traditional approach because it can handle multiple embedded options.

▶ There are various option-based valuation models: one-factor and multiple-factor models.

▶ The most common convertible bond valuation model is the one-factor model in which the one factor is the stock price movement.

PRACTICE PROBLEMS FOR READING 50

1. Comment on the following statement:

"There are several arbitrage-free models for valuing callable bonds. These models differ significantly in terms of how interest rates may change in the next period. There are models that allow the rate in the next period to take on only one of two values. Such a model is called a binomial model. There are models that allow the rate in the next period to take on more than two possible values. For example, there is a model that allows the rate in the next period to take on three possible values. Such a model is called a trinomial model. All these models represent a significantly different approach to valuation and involve different procedures for obtaining the arbitrage-free value."

2. Why is the procedure for valuing a bond with an embedded option called "backward induction"?

3. Why is the value produced by a binomial model and any similar models referred to as an "arbitrage-free value"?

4. A. When valuing an option-free bond, short-term forward rates can be used. When valuing a bond with an embedded option, there is not one forward rate for a period but a set of forward rates for a given period. Explain why.

B. Explain why the set of forward rates for a given period depend on the assumed interest rate volatility.

5. The on-the-run issue for the Inc.Net Company is shown below:

Maturity (Years)	Yield to Maturity (%)	Market Price
1	7.5	100
2	7.6	100
3	7.7	100

Using the bootstrapping methodology, the spot rates are:

Maturity (Years)	Spot Rate (%)
1	7.500
2	7.604
3	7.710

Assuming an interest rate volatility of 10% for the 1-year rate, the binomial interest rate tree for valuing a bond with a maturity of up to three years is shown below:

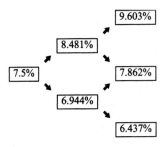

A. Demonstrate using the 2-year on-the-run issue that the binomial interest rate tree above is in fact an arbitrage-free tree.

B. Demonstrate using the 3-year on-the-run issue that the binomial interest rate tree above is in fact an arbitrage-free tree.

C. Using the spot rates given above, what is the arbitrage-free value of a 3-year 8.5% coupon issue of Inc.Net Company?

D. Using the binomial tree, determine the value of an 8.5% 3-year option-free bond.

E. Suppose that the 3-year 8.5% coupon issue is callable starting in year 1 at par (100) (that is, the call price is 100). Also assume that the following call rule is used: if the price exceeds 100, the issue will be called. What is the value of this 3-year 8.5% coupon callable issue?

F. What is the value of the embedded call option for the 3-year 8.5% coupon callable issue?

6. In discussing the approach taken by its investment management firm in valuing bonds, a representative of the firm made the following statement:

> "Our managers avoid the use of valuation methodologies such as the binomial model or other fancier models because of the many assumptions required to determine the value. Instead, our managers are firm believers in the concept of option-adjusted spread."

Comment on this statement.

7. A portfolio manager must mark a bond position to market. One issue, a callable issue, has not traded in the market recently. So to obtain a price that can be used to mark a position to market, the manager requested a bid from a dealer and a value from a pricing service. The dealer bid's price was 92. The pricing service indicated a bid price of 93 would be a fair value. The manager could not understand the reason for the 1 point difference in the bid prices.

Upon questioning the trader at the dealer firm that gave a bid of 92, the manager found that the trader based the price on the dealer's valuation model. The model used is the binomial model and the benchmark interest rates the model uses are the on-the-run Treasury issues. The manager then contacted a representative from the pricing service and asked what type of valuation model it used. Again, the response was that the binomial model is used and that the on-the-run Treasury issues are used as the benchmark interest rates.

The manager is puzzled why there is a 1 point difference even though the dealer and the pricing service used the same model and the same benchmark interest rates. The manager has asked you to explain why. Provide an explanation to the manager.

8. The manager of an emerging market bond portfolio is approached by a broker about purchasing a new corporate bond issue in Brazil. The issue is callable, and the broker's firm estimates that the option-adjusted spread is 220 basis points. What questions would you ask the broker with respect to the 220 basis points OAS?

9. In explaining the option-adjusted spread to a client, a manager stated the following: "The option-adjusted spread measures the yield spread using the Treasury on-the-run yield curve as benchmark interest rates." Comment on this statement.

10. A. Explain why the greater the assumed interest rate volatility the lower the value of a callable bond?

  B. Explain why the greater the assumed interest rate volatility the higher the value of a putable bond?

11. An assistant portfolio manager described the process for valuing a bond that is both callable and putable using the binomial model as follows:

> "The process begins by first valuing one of the embedded options, say the call option. Then the model is used to value the put option. The value of the corresponding option-free bond is then computed. Given the value of the call option, the value of the put option, and the value of the option-free bond, the value of the bond that is callable and putable is found by adding to the value of the option-free bond the value of the put option and then subtracting the value of the call option."

Explain why you agree or disagree with this assistant portfolio manager's description of the process for valuing a bond that is both callable and putable.

12. Explain why, when the binomial model is used to obtain the values to be used in the formula for computing duration and convexity, the measures computed are an effective duration and effective convexity.

13. An assistant portfolio manager is trying to find the duration of a callable bond of FeedCo Corp. One vendor of analytical systems reported the duration for the issue is 5.4. A dealer firm reported that the duration is 4.5. The assistant portfolio manager was confused by the difference in the reported durations for the FeedCo Corp. issue. He discussed the situation with the senior portfolio manager. In the discussion, the assistant portfolio manager commented: "I don't understand how such a difference could occur. After all, there is a standard formula for computing any duration." How should the senior portfolio manager respond?

14. In computing the effective duration and convexity of a bond with an embedded option, what assumption is made about the option-adjusted spread when rates change?

15. Four portfolio managers are discussing the meaning of option-adjusted spread. Here is what each asserted:

Manager 1: "The option-adjusted spread is a measure of the value of the option embedded in the bond. That is, it is the compensation for accepting option risk."

Manager 2: "The option-adjusted spread is a measure of the spread relative to the Treasury on-the-run yield curve and reflects compensation for credit risk."

Manager 3: "The option-adjusted spread is a measure of the spread relative to the Treasury on-the-run yield curve and reflects compensation for credit risk and liquidity risk."

Manager 4: "The option-adjusted spread is a measure of the spread relative to the issuer's on-the-run yield curve and reflects compensation for credit risk and liquidity risk."

Comment on each manager's interpretation of OAS.

16. Suppose that a callable bond is valued using as the benchmark interest rates the on-the-run yield curve of the issuer and that the yield for the 10-year issue is 6%. Suppose further that the option-adjusted spread computed for a 10-year callable bond of this issuer is 20 basis points. Is it proper to interpret the OAS as meaning that the 10-year callable bond is offering a spread of 20 basis points over the 6% yield on the 10-year on-the-run issue? If not, what is the proper interpretation of the 20 basis point OAS?

17. Suppose that a callable bond has an option-adjusted spread of zero. Does that mean the corporate bond is being overvalued in the market (i.e., trading rich)?

18. In valuing a floating rate note, it is necessary to make a modification to the backward induction method.
   A. Why is the adjustment necessary?
   B. What adjustment is made?
   C. If the floating rate note has a cap, how is that handled by the backward induction method?

19. A. In what sense does a convertible bond typically have multiple embedded options?
   B. Why is it complicated to value a convertible bond?

20. In the October 26, 1992, prospectus summary of the Staples 5% convertible subordinated debentures due 1999, the offering stated: "Convertible into Common Stock at a conversion price of $45 per share. . ." Since the par value is $1,000, what is the conversion ratio?

21. Consider the convertible bond by Miser Electronics:

par value = $1,000
coupon rate = 8.5%
market price of convertible bond = $900
conversion ratio = 30
estimated straight value of bond = $700

Assume that the price of Miser Electronics common stock is $25 and that the dividend per share is $1 per annum.

Calculate each of the following:

A. conversion value.

B. market conversion price.

C. conversion premium per share.

D. conversion premium ratio.

E. premium over straight value.

F. favorable income differential per share.

G. premium payback period.

22. Suppose that the price of the common stock of Miser Electronics whose convertible bond was described in the previous question increases from $25 to $54.

A. What will be the approximate return realized from investing in the convertible bond if an investor had purchased the convertible for $900?

B. What would be the return realized if $25 had been invested in the common stock?

C. Why would the return be higher by investing in the common stock directly rather than by investing in the convertible bond?

23. Suppose that the price of the common stock declines from $25 to $10.

A. What will be the approximate return realized from investing in the convertible bond if an investor had purchased the convertible for $900 *and* the straight value does not change?

B. What would be the return realized if $25 had been invested in the common stock?

C. Why would the return be higher by investing in the convertible bond rather than by investing in the common stock directly?

24. The following excerpt is taken from an article entitled "Caywood Looks for Convertibles," that appeared in the January 13, 1992 issue of *BondWeek*, p. 7:

Caywood Christian Capital Management will invest new money in its $400 million high-yield portfolio in "busted convertibles," double- and triple-B rated convertible bonds of companies whose stock . . . , said James Caywood, CEO. Caywood likes these convertibles as they trade at discounts and are unlikely to be called, he said.

A. What is a "busted convertible"?

B. What is the premium over straight value that these bonds would trade?

C. Why does Mr. Caywood seek convertibles with higher investment grade ratings?

D. Why is Mr. Caywood interested in call protection?

25. Explain the limitation of using premium over straight value as a measure of the downside risk of a convertible bond?

26. A. The valuation of a convertible bond using an options approach requires a two-factor model. What is meant by a two-factor model and what are the factors?

   B. In practice, is a two-factor model used to value a convertible bond?

The following information relates to Questions 27–32

Mary Merton is a fixed income analyst. She is considering three bonds: a callable bond issued by Wentz Electronics, a non-callable bond issued by AGP Foods Inc., and a convertible bond issued by Ashling Enterprises.

Merton has developed the binomial interest rate tree in Exhibit 1 to use in valuing the Wentz Electronics callable bond. In each non-empty cell of Exhibit 1, there is the one-year interest rate for that node and the expected value at that node of a *non-callable* bond with originally four years to maturity and annual coupons of 8%. The expected values show the ex-coupon price of the bond, the 8% coupon payment, and the cum-coupon price of the bond, each expressed as a percent of par. Some of the data is indicated as missing.

The Wentz Electronics callable bond has four years to maturity, pays an annual coupon of 8%, and is callable any time after today at par plus one-half of the annual coupon (i.e., callable at 104).

In applying the binomial tree to this problem, Merton assumes that the probability of an up move equals the probability of a down move. In other words, at every node of the tree, there is a 50% chance of moving to the higher interest rate node in the next period and a 50% chance of moving to the lower interest rate node in the next period. Merton uses annual compounding in all of her calculations.

The AGP Foods bond has ten years to maturity and pays an annual coupon of 8%. The yield-to-maturity of this bond is 8%.

Merton is also considering a convertible bond issued by Ashling Enterprises. The convertible bond has three years to maturity and a coupon rate of 5.75% with coupons paid annually. Par value of the bond is $1,000. The bond can be converted into 40 shares of Ashling stock. Ashling Enterprises stock closed today at $28.80 per share. Ashling has never paid cash dividends on its stock and does not plan to pay dividends in the near future. Non-convertible bonds of equivalent risk and maturity to the Ashling bond currently have a yield-to-maturity of 6%.

EXHIBIT 1	Binomial Interest Rate Tree with Certain Prices of a Four-Year Non-Callable Bond with an 8% Coupon			
Today	Year 1	Year 2	Year 3	Year 4
				10% 100.00 + 8.00 108.00
			9.00% 99.0826 + 8.00 107.0826	
		8.00% 100.0079 + 8.00 108.0079		8.00% 100.00 + 8.00 108.00
	7.00% 102.6557 + 8.00 110.6557		7.00% 100.9346 + 8.00 108.9346	
6.00% missing		6.00% 103.6753 + 8.00 111.6753		6.00% 100.00 + 8.00 108.00
	5.00% missing + 8.00 missing		5.00% 102.8571 + 8.00 110.8571	
		4.00% missing + 8.00 missing		4.00% 100.00 + 8.00 108.00
			3.00% 104.8544 + 8.00 112.8544	
				2.00% 100.00 + 8.00 108.00

27. Today's ex-coupon price of a *non-callable* bond with four years to maturity and an 8% coupon rate like the Wentz bond is *closest* to:

   A. 99.4623.

   B. 107.0094.

   C. 107.0437.

28. Today's ex-coupon price of the *callable* Wentz bond is *closest* to:

   A. 96.0000.

   B. 104.5688.

   C. 105.0263.

29. Holding all other factors constant, if Merton revises her analysis and uses a higher estimate of the volatility of interest rates, the price of the callable Wentz bond:

   A. is likely to fall.

   B. will not change.

   C. is likely to increase.

30. Merton has calculated the price of the AGP Foods bond if its YTM increases to 9%. The price is $935.82. On the other hand, if the YTM of the bond falls to 7%, the price of the bond would be $1,070.24. Using these two prices, the price of the bond at an 8% YTM, and the 100bps change in interest rates, the effective duration of the AGP Foods bond is *closest* to:

   A. 6.72.

   B. 7.00.

   C. 7.25.

31. Today's minimum market price of the Ashling Enterprises convertible bond is *most likely*:

   A. $993.32.

   B. $1,006.72.

   C. $1,152.00.

32. Which of the following provides the best rationale for purchasing the Ashling Enterprises convertible bond rather than the common stock of Ashling?

   A. The convertible bond is more liquid than the common stock.

   B. The convertible bond provides current income; the common stock does not.

   C. The convertible bond is, in effect, a leveraged position in Ashling stock and therefore offers the opportunity for dramatically higher returns.

The following information relates to Questions 33–38 and is based on "General Principles of Credit Analysis" and this reading

Eero Jokinen is a portfolio manager at Northern Lights Pension Fund in Finland. Given the overall low level of interest rates currently in Europe, Jokinen is looking for ways to enhance the yield of Northern Lights' portfolio. The investment guidelines have recently been amended to allow investments in corporate bonds and bonds with embedded options. Jokinen is analyzing three different bonds as possible investments for Northern Lights: Thor Products bonds, France Telecom bonds, and a particular dual currency bond.

Thor Products Bonds

Selected financial data for Thor Products are provided in Exhibit 1.

EXHIBIT 1	Selected Financial Data for Thor Products (€ Thousands)

Balance Sheet

Current assets	230	Current liabilities	120
Property, plant, and equipment	1,039	Long-term debt	850
		Shareholders' equity	299
Total assets	1,269	Total debt and equity	1,269

Income Statement

Sales	2,000
Cost of sales and operating expenses	1,400
Depreciation expense	200
Income from operations	400
Interest expense	75
Income tax expense	98
Net income	227

The covenants on Thor's outstanding bonds require the company to maintain:

1. a dividend payout ratio below 30 percent.
2. timely interest and principal payments.
3. a total debt-to-capitalization ratio of no more than 60 percent.

Jokinen expects that the current environment of low interest rates and low interest rate volatility may not continue. So, he analyzes the effects of an increase in interest rates and volatility on the value of any callable bonds in the portfolio. Jokinen states:

▶ "If interest rates rise and interest rate volatility remains unchanged, the value of callable bonds should decrease."

▶ "If interest rate volatility increases and interest rates remain unchanged, the value of the callable bonds should increase."

Jokinen will use a binomial model to value a Thor Products bond with a 5.75 percent coupon and a maturity of 3 years. The bond is callable at par every year starting one year from now. Jokinen assumes that Thor would call the bonds if their price rose above par. A binomial interest rate tree for a *non-callable* Thor Products bond is shown in Exhibit 2. The probability of each interest rate move in the tree is 0.50.

EXHIBIT 2	Option-Free Binomial Interest Rate Tree (10% Volatility Assumed) for Valuing a 3-Year Option-Free Bond with a 5.75% Coupon

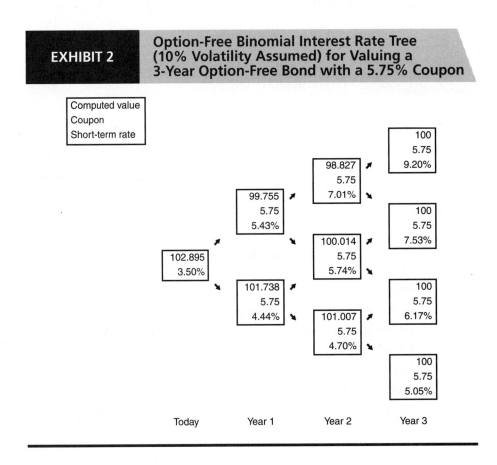

France Telecom Bonds

Jokinen is considering investing in a France Telecom (FRTEL) convertible bond because of the favorable outlook for the industry. His 12-month price forecast is €27.50 per FRTEL share. The convertible bond has the following characteristics:

▶ FRTEL 1.6% 01 January 2012;

▶ conversion ratio is 100 shares per bond;

▶ par value is €2,581;

▶ current price of the bond is €2,825;

▶ FRTEL common stock has a current price of €25.75 per share and pays no dividend;

▶ bond is callable at €2,581 on 31 December 2009.

Dual Currency Bond

Finally, Jokinen is considering a dual currency bond with coupon payments in euros and principal repayment in Turkish lira. He states that the bond would not have any currency exposure to the Turkish lira until it matured and the Turkish lira were actually paid.

33. The total debt-to-capitalization and the EBITDA interest coverage ratios for Thor Products are *closest* to:

	Total Debt-to-Capitalization	EBITDA Interest Coverage
A.	68.4%	5.3
B.	76.4%	8.0
C.	84.4%	2.7

34. Which of the three covenants on Thor's bonds is an affirmative covenant?
   A. #1.
   B. #2.
   C. #3.

35. Are Jokinen's statements regarding the effects on callable bonds of an increase in interest rates and an increase in interest rate volatility, respectively, correct?

	Interest Rates	Interest Rate Volatility
A.	No	No
B.	No	Yes
C.	Yes	No

36. From Exhibit 2, the current price of the Thor callable bond is *closest* to:
   A. 102.05.
   B. 102.17.
   C. 103.01.

37. The premium payback period (in years) for the France Telecom convertible bond is *closest* to:
   A. 1.60.
   B. 1.81.
   C. 6.05.

38. Is Jokinen's statement about the currency exposure to investing in the dual currency bond (euro and Turkish lira) correct?
   A. No, the bond has exposure to the Turkish lira from the date of purchase.
   B. Yes, the bond has appreciation exposure to the Turkish lira only at maturity.
   C. Yes, the bond has depreciation exposure to the Turkish lira only at maturity.

SOLUTIONS FOR READING 50

1. This statement is incorrect. While there are different models such as the binomial and trinomial models, the basic features of all these models are the same. They all involve assessing the cash flow at each node in the interest rate tree and determining whether or not to adjust the cash flow based on the embedded options. All these models require a rule for calling the issue and all require an assumption about the volatility of interest rates. The backward induction method is used for all these models.

2. The procedure for determining the value of a bond with an embedded option starts at the maturity date on the interest rate tree (i.e., the end of the tree) and values the bond moving backward to the root of the tree—which is today's value. Hence the procedure is called backward induction.

3. The reason is that in constructing the interest rate tree the on-the-run issues are used and interest rates on the tree must be such that if the on-the-run issue is valued using the tree, the model will produce the market value of the on-the-run issue. When a model produces the market value of the on-the-run issues, it is said to be "calibrated to the market" or "arbitrage free."

4. **A.** In the interest rate tree, the forward rates for a given period are shown at each node. (In the illustrations in the reading, each period is one year.) Since there is more than one node for each period (after the root of the tree), there is not one forward rate for a given period but several forward rates.

    B. The binomial interest rate tree is constructed based on an assumption about interest rate volatility. If a different volatility assumption is made, a new interest rate tree is constructed, and therefore there are different interest rates at the nodes for a given period and therefore a different set of forward rates.

5. **A.**

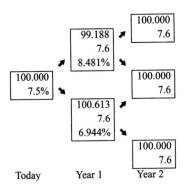

B.

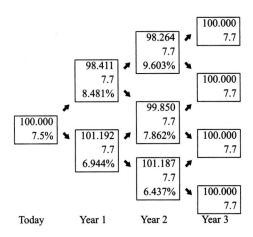

C. The value of an 8.5% coupon 3-year bond using the spot rates is as follows:

$$\frac{8.5}{(1.07500)} + \frac{8.5}{(1.07604)^2} + \frac{108.5}{(1.07710)^3} = \$102.076$$

D.

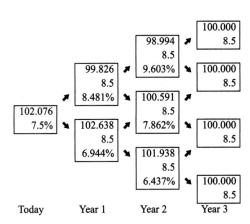

E. The value of this callable bond is 100.722.

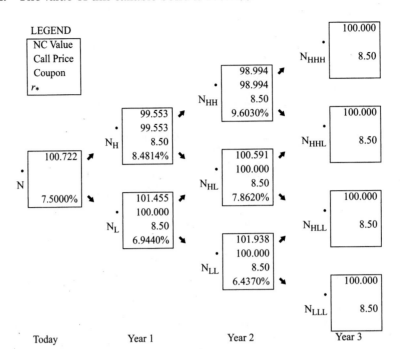

LEGEND

NC Value
Call Price
Coupon
r_*

Today   Year 1   Year 2   Year 3

F. The value of the embedded call option is $1.354, which is equal to the value of the option-free bond ($102.076) minus the value of the callable bond ($100.722).

6. The statement is wrong. The option-adjusted spread is a byproduct (i.e., is obtained from) of a valuation model. Any assumptions that must be made in a valuation model to obtain the arbitrage-value of a bond also apply to the option-adjusted spread. For example, if a valuation model assumes that interest rate volatility is $x\%$, then the OAS is based on a volatility of $x\%$.

7. Despite the fact that both the dealer and the pricing service used the same model and same benchmark, there are other inputs to the model that could cause a 1 point difference. The major reason is probably that the two may have used a different volatility assumption. A second reason is that the call rule used by the two may be quite different.

8. One of the first questions should be what is the benchmark that the spread is relative to. The other key question is what is the assumed interest rate volatility.

9. This statement is not necessarily correct. An OAS can be computed based on any benchmark interest rates. For example, the on-the-run rates for the issuer or the on-the-run rates for issuers in the same bond sector and having the same credit rating can be used.

10. A. The value of a callable bond is equal to the value of an otherwise option-free bond minus the value of the embedded call option. The value of the embedded call option is higher the greater the assumed interest rate volatility. Therefore, a higher value for the embedded call option is subtracted from the value of the option-free bond, resulting in a lower value for the callable bond.

B. The value of a putable bond is equal to the value of an otherwise option-free bond plus the value of the embedded put option. The value of the embedded put option is higher the greater the assumed interest rate volatility. Therefore, a higher value for the embedded put option is added to the value of the option-free bond, resulting in a higher value of the putable bond.

11. While it is true that the value of a bond that is callable and putable is conceptually equal to the value of the option-free bond adjusted for the value of the put option and the value of the call option, this is not the procedure used in a model such as the binomial model that uses the backward induction method. The reason is that these embedded options exist simultaneously so that the exercise of one option would extinguish the value of the other option. What is done in the backward induction method is to value the callable/putable bond by simultaneously considering the two embedded options. The way this works is at each node it will be determined whether or not the call option will be exercised based on the call rule and then whether or not the put option will be exercised. If either option is exercised, the corresponding exercise value for the bond is used in subsequent calculations in the backward induction process.

12. There are two types of duration and convexity—modified and effective. Modified forms of duration and convexity assume that when interest rates change the cash flows do not change. In contrast, the effective forms assume that when interest rates change the cash flows may change. When the binomial model is used to determine the values when rates are increased and decreased, the new values reflect how the cash flows may change. That is, the cash flow at each node of the binomial interest tree when rates are shifted up and down are allowed to change depending on the rules for when an option will be exercised. Thus, the resulting duration and convexity are effective duration and convexity.

13. It is true that there is a standard formula for computing duration by shocking (i.e., changing) interest rates and substituting the values computed in the duration formula. However, for a bond with an embedded option, such as a callable bond, it is necessary to have a valuation model (such as the binomial model) to determine the value of the bond when interest rates are changed. Valuation models can give different values for the same bond depending on the assumptions used. For example, suppose that the vendor and the dealer use the same valuation model but employ 1) a different volatility assumption, 2) different benchmark interest rates, and 3) a different call rule. The values produced by the two models that are substituted into the (effective) duration formula can result in the difference of 5.4 versus 4.5.

14. It is assumed that the option-adjusted spread is constant when interest rates change.

15. The starting point is defining what the benchmark interest rates are that the spread is being measured relative to. It is based on the benchmark that one interprets what the option-adjusted spread is compensation for.

Manager 1 is wrong. The option-adjusted spread is adjusting any spread for the option risk. That is, it is netting out from the spread the option risk.

Manager 2 is partially correct. If the benchmark interest rates are the on-the-run Treasury issues, then the option-adjusted spread is indicating compensation for credit risk. But it also captures liquidity risk. Moreover, it is not necessarily true that the benchmark interest rates are the on-the-run Treasury rates.

Manager 3 is correct if the benchmark interest rates are the on-the-run Treasury issues. However, other benchmark interest rates have been used, and in such cases Manager 3's interpretation would be incorrect.

Manager 4 is incorrect. Even if the benchmark interest rates are the rates for the issuer's on-the-run issues, the spread would not reflect compensation for credit risk.

16. It is incorrect to state that the 20 basis point OAS is a spread over the issuer's 10-year on-the-run issue. That is, it is not a spread over one point on the yield curve. Rather, from the issuer's on-the-run yield curve, the rates at each node on the interest rate tree are determined. These rates are the one-period forward rates. The OAS is the spread that when added to all these forward rates will produce a value for the callable bond equal to the market price of the bond. So, it is a spread over the forward rates in the interest rate tree which are in turn generated from the benchmark interest rates.

17. Without knowing the benchmark interest rate used to compute the OAS, no statement can be made. If the benchmark is the Treasury sector or a corporate sector with a higher credit quality than the issue being analyzed, then the statement is correct. However, if the benchmark is the issuer's yield curve, then an OAS of zero means that the issue is fairly priced.

18. **A.** The coupon rate on a floater is paid in arrears. This means that for a floater the rate determined in the current period is not paid until the end of the period (or beginning of the next period). This requires that an adjustment be made to the backward induction method.

    B. The adjustment is made to the backward induction method by discounting the coupon payment to be made in the next period for a floater based on the beginning of the period reference rate.

    C. A cap on a floater is handled by determining at each node if the cap is reached. At a node where the coupon rate exceeds the cap, the coupon rate is replaced by the capped rate.

19. **A.** A convertible bond grants the investor the option to call the common stock of the issuer. Thus, a convertible bond has an embedded call option on the common stock. However, most convertible bonds are callable. That is, there is a second embedded call option granting the issuer the right to retire the bond.

    B. The complication that arises is that one of the options, the call on the common stock granted to the investor, depends on the future price of the common stock. However, the call on the bond granted to the issuer depends on future interest rates. Thus, valuing a callable convertible bond requires including in one valuation model both future stock price movements and future interest rate movements.

20. The conversion ratio is found by dividing the par value of $1,000 by the conversion price stated in the prospectus of $45 per share. The conversion ratio is then 22.22 ($1,000/$45).

21. **A.** Conversion value = Market price of common stock × Conversion ratio

    $$= \$25 \times 30 = \$750$$

    B. Market conversion price

    $$= \frac{\text{Market price of convertible bond}}{\text{Conversion ratio}} = \frac{\$900}{30} = \$30$$

    C. Conversion premium per share

    = Market conversion price − Market price of common stock

    = $30 − $25 = $5

D. Conversion premium ratio

$$= \frac{\text{Conversion premium per share}}{\text{Market price of common stock}} = \frac{\$5}{\$25} = 20\%$$

E. Premium over straight value $= \dfrac{\text{Market price of convertible bond}}{\text{Straight value}} - 1$

$$= \frac{\$900}{\$700} - 1 = 28.6\%$$

F. Favorable income differential per share

$$= \frac{\text{Coupon interest from bond} - \text{Conversion ratio} \times \text{Dividend per share}}{\text{Conversion ratio}}$$

$$= \frac{\$85 - (30 \times \$1)}{30} = \$1.833$$

G. Premium payback period $= \dfrac{\text{Market conversion premium per share}}{\text{Favorable income differential per share}}$

$$= \frac{\$5}{\$1.833} = 2.73 \text{ years}$$

22. A. If the price increases to $54, the conversion value will be

Conversion value $= \$54 \times 30 = \$1,620$

Assuming that the convertible bond's price does not exceed the conversion value (that is why the question asked for an approximate return), then the return on the $900 investment in the convertible bond is:

$$\frac{\$1,620}{\$900} - 1 = 0.8 = 80\%$$

B. The return realized if $25 had been invested in the common stock is equal to:

$$\frac{\$54 - \$25}{\$25} = 1.16 = 116\%$$

C. The reason for the lower return by buying the convertible bond rather than the stock directly is that the investor has effectively paid $5 more for the stock.

23. A. If the price decreases to $10, the conversion value will be

Conversion value $= \$10 \times 30 = \$300$

However, it is assumed in the question that the straight value is unchanged at $700. The convertible bond will trade at the greater of the straight value or the conversion value. In this case, it is $700. The return is then:

$$\frac{\$700}{\$900} - 1 = -0.22 = -22\%$$

B. The return realized if $25 had been invested in the common stock is equal to:

$$\frac{\$10 - \$25}{\$25} = -0.6 = -60\%$$

C. The return is greater for the convertible bond because of the assumption made that the straight value did not change. If the straight value did decline, the loss would be greater than -22% but it would still be probably less than the loss on the direct purchase of the stock. The key here is that the floor (straight value) is what cushions the decline—but it is a moving floor.

24. A. If the stock price is low so that the straight value is considerably higher than the conversion value, the bond will trade much like a straight bond. The convertible in such instances is referred to as a "busted convertible."

B. Since the market value of a busted convertible is very close to that of a straight bond, the premium over straight value would be very small.

C. By restricting the convertible bonds in which Mr. Caywood would invest to higher investment grade ratings, he is reducing credit risk.

D. By seeking bonds not likely to be called, Mr. Caywood is reducing call risk that would result in a forced conversion to the common stock.

25. The measure assumes that the straight value does not decline.

26. A. A "factor" is the stochastic (or random) variable that is assumed to affect the value of a security. The two factors in valuing a convertible bond are the price movement of the underlying common stock (which affects the value of the embedded call option on the common stock) and the movement of interest rates (which affects the value of the embedded call option on the bond).

B. In practice, models used to value convertible bonds have been one-factor models with the factor included being the price movement of the underlying common stock.

27. B is correct. To answer this question, you need to find the missing values. The ex-coupon missing value at Year 2 is $((110.8571 + 112.8544)/2)/1.04 = 107.5536$. This is the expected value of the cash flows at the end of year 2 (beginning of year 3) discounted by the year 2 one-year interest rate of 4%. The cum-coupon value is 115.5536. Once the missing value for Year 2 is found, the missing value for Year 1 can be calculated. The missing ex-coupon value at Year 1 is $((111.6753 + (107.5536 + 8))/2)/1.05 = 108.2042$. Add the coupon to get the cum-coupon value of 116.2042. The ex-coupon value of the non-callable bond today is then calculated as $[(110.6557 + 116.2042)/2]/1.06 = 107.0094$.

28. C is correct. At each node in Exhibit 1 where the ex-coupon value exceeds 104 the bond will be called. Therefore, at each node in Exhibit 1 where the ex-coupon value exceeds 104, replace that value with 104. Year 4 needs no adjustment. The first required adjustment occurs in the Year 3 column. Replace the ex-coupon value of 104.8544 with 104. The cum-coupon becomes 112. Since a Year 3 value changed, at least one Year 2 value must change. The ex-coupon missing value in Year 2 for a *callable* bond now becomes $((110.8571 + 112.0000)/2)/1.04 = 107.1428$. As this value exceeds 104, replace it with 104 and add 8 to get a cum-coupon value of

112. No other year 2 value has to be adjusted (no other year 2 node has a cum-coupon value in excess of 104). The year 1 ex-coupon missing value is [(111.6753 + 112.0000)/2]/1.05 = 106.5120. As this value exceeds 104, replace it with 104 and add 8 to get a cum-coupon value of 112. The other year 1 node requires no adjustment. Finally, solve for the ex-coupon value of the bond today by [(110.6557 + 112.0000)/2]/1.06 = 105.0263.

29. A is correct. An increase in volatility, holding other factors constant, will increase the value of the call. Because the value of a callable bond equals the value of an otherwise identical non-callable bond minus the value of the call, an increase in the value of the call decreases the value of the callable bond.

30. A is correct. Effective duration is a measure of the bond's price sensitivity to a change in interest rates. $ED = (BV_{-\Delta y} - BV_{+\Delta y})/(2 \times BV_0 \times \Delta y) = (1{,}070.24 - 935.82)/(2 \times 1{,}000 \times 0.01) = 6.72$.

31. C is correct. The minimum market price of a convertible bond is the higher of its straight-debt value and its conversion value. The straight-debt value of the convertible bond is \$993.32 (found using a financial calculator: N = 3, I/Y = 6, PMT = 57.50, FV = 1,000 and solve for PV). The conversion value of the bond is 40 × \$28.80 = \$1,152. \$1,152 is the minimum value of the bond.

32. B is correct. Ashling common does not pay a dividend. Buying the convertible provides the investor with current income (the coupon) while allowing the investor to benefit from an increase in the price of Ashling common.

33. B is correct. Total debt to capitalization = (120 + 850)/(850 + 120 + 299) = 76.4%. EBITDA interest coverage = (2000 − 1400)/75 = 8.0.

34. B is correct. Covenant #2, to pay interest and principal, is an affirmative covenant requiring action. The other two covenants are negative covenants restricting actions.

35. C is correct. The value of a callable bond equals the value of an otherwise identical non-callable bond minus the value of the call. A rise in interest rates will reduce the value of the non-callable bond portion and thus reduce the value of the callable bond. Jokinen's first statement is correct. If volatility increases, the value of the call portion of the bond increases and the value of the callable bond decreases. Jokinen's second statement is incorrect.

36. A is correct. The bond will be called when the price exceeds par so replace all the bond values above par with 100 and recalculate the tree. The current price is [.5(99.748 + 5.75) + .5(100 + 5.75)]/1.035 = 102.05.

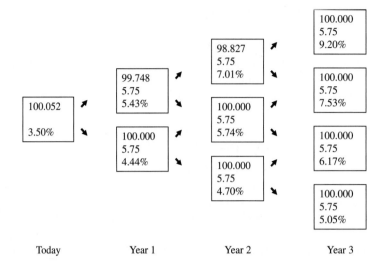

37. C is correct. The coupon interest = €2581 × 1.60% = €41.30

Favorable income difference per share = [€41.30 − (100 × 0)]/100 = €0.413

Market conversion price = (€2825)/100 = €28.25

Market conversion premium per share = €28.25 − €25.75 = €2.50

Then the premium payback period = €2.50/€0.413 = 6.05 years

38. A is correct. The bond has currency exposure to the Turkish lira from the date of purchase.

SOLUTIONS FOR READING 50

Solutions are for Practice Questions found in Reading

1.

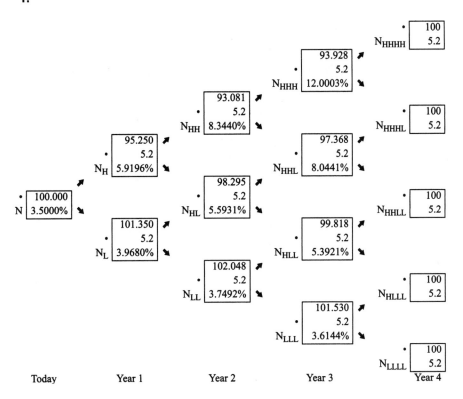

2. The binomial interest rate tree is the one in Practice Question 1. Below is the tree with the values completed at each node. As can be seen, the root of the tree is 104.643, the arbitrage-free value found in the reading for this option-free bond.

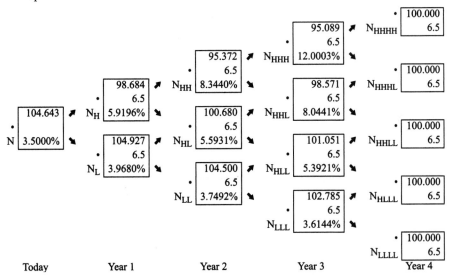

Fixed Income Analysis for the Chartered Financial Analyst® Program, Second Edition, by Frank J. Fabozzi, CFA.

3. A. The root of the binomial interest rate tree below shows that the arbitrage-free value of this bond is 102.108.

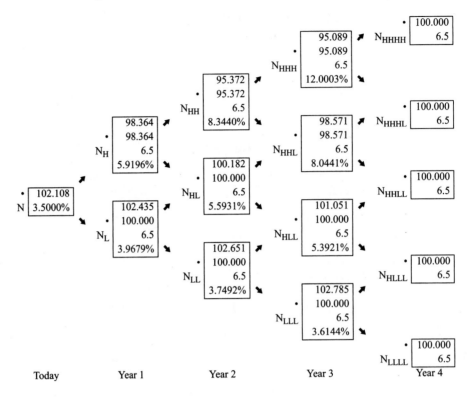

B. The arbitrage-free value at 20% is less than the arbitrage-free value at 10% (102.108 versus 102.899). This is because the value of the embedded call option is greater the higher the volatility.

4. The tree below shows that the OAS is −6 basis points for the 6.5% callable bond assuming 20% volatility. (Each 1-year rate is 6 basis points less than in Practice Question 1.)

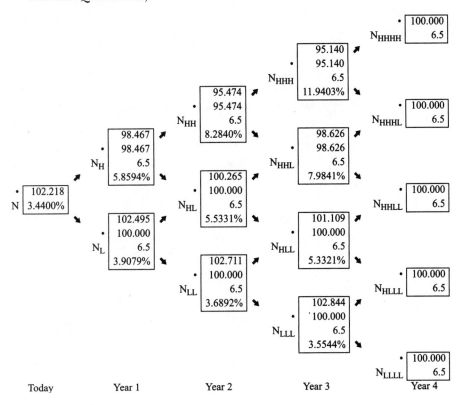

Today   Year 1   Year 2   Year 3   Year 4

5. The tree below shows the arbitrage-free value for a putable bond with four years to maturity, a coupon rate of 6.5%, and putable in one year at 100 assuming a 20% volatility is 106.010.

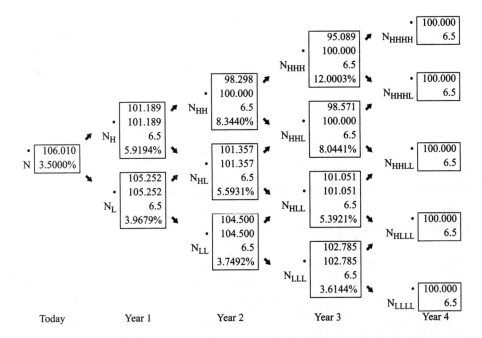

Today   Year 1   Year 2   Year 3   Year 4

$4\frac{5}{8}$ $4\frac{11}{16}$ — $\frac{3}{8}$

$5\frac{1}{2}$ $5\frac{1}{2}$ —

$20\frac{5}{8}$ $21\frac{3}{16}$ — $\frac{1}{16}$

$17\frac{3}{8}$ $18\frac{1}{8}$ + $\frac{7}{8}$

$15\frac{1}{2}$ $6\frac{1}{2}$ $6\frac{1}{2}$ — $\frac{1}{2}$

$7\frac{1}{4}$ $31\frac{32}{}$ — $\frac{1}{8}$

$15/16$ $\frac{9}{8}$

$9/16$

$1\frac{9}{32}$ $7\frac{13}{16}$ $7\frac{15}{8}$

$7\frac{15}{16}$

$2\frac{5}{8}$ $2\frac{11}{32}$ $2\frac{1}{2}$ +

$2\frac{3}{4}$ $2\frac{1}{4}$ $2\frac{1}{4}$

$12\frac{1}{16}$ $11\frac{3}{8}$ $11\frac{3}{4}$ +

87 $33\frac{3}{4}$ 33 $33\frac{1}{8}$ —

662 $25\frac{5}{8}$ $24\frac{9}{16}$ $25\frac{3}{8}$ +

633 12 $11\frac{5}{8}$ $11\frac{5}{8}$ +

16 $10\frac{1}{2}$ $10\frac{1}{2}$ $10\frac{1}{2}$ —

78 $15\frac{7}{8}$ $15\frac{13}{16}$ $15\frac{7}{8}$ —

808 $9\frac{1}{16}$ $8\frac{1}{4}$ $8\frac{1}{2}$ +

430 $11\frac{1}{4}$ $10\frac{1}{8}$

STUDY SESSION 15
FIXED INCOME:
Structured Securities

This study session provides information on the knowledge and skills needed for valuing a unique segment of the fixed income market–structured securities. It begins with an in-depth study of the structure and characteristics of mortgage-backed and asset-backed markets and securities and concludes with a study of valuation techniques for these fixed income instruments.

READING ASSIGNMENTS

Reading 51 Mortgage-Backed Sector of the Bond Market
Fixed Income Analysis for the Chartered Financial Analyst®
Program, Second Edition, by Frank J. Fabozzi, CFA

Reading 52 Asset-Backed Sector of the Bond Market
Fixed Income Analysis for the Chartered Financial Analyst®
Program, Second Edition, by Frank J. Fabozzi, CFA

Reading 53 Valuing Mortgage-Backed and Asset-Backed Securities
Fixed Income Analysis for the Chartered Financial Analyst®
Program, Second Edition, by Frank J. Fabozzi, CFA

$4^{5}/_{8}$ $4^{11}/_{16}$ $-$ $^{3}/_{8}$

$5^{1}/_{2}$ $5^{1}/_{2}$ $-$ $^{1}/_{8}$

$20^{5}/_{8}$ $21^{3}/_{16}$ $-$ $^{7}/_{8}$

$17^{3}/_{8}$ $18^{1}/_{8}$ $+$ $^{1}/_{2}$

$8^{1}/_{2}$ $6^{1}/_{2}$ $6^{1}/_{2}$ $-$ $^{1}/_{8}$

$7^{1}/_{4}$ $15^{}/_{16}$ $31^{}/_{32}$ $-$

$9^{}/_{16}$ $^{9}/_{}$

$1^{}/_{32}$ $7^{13}/_{16}$ $7^{15}/_{16}$

$7^{15}/_{16}$ $2^{5}/_{8}$ $2^{11}/_{32}$ $2^{1}/_{2}$ $+$

$2^{3}/_{4}$ $2^{1}/_{4}$ $2^{1}/_{4}$

$5^{1}/_{8}$ $12^{1}/_{16}$ $11^{3}/_{8}$ $11^{3}/_{8}$ $+$

87 $33^{3}/_{4}$ 33 $33^{1}/_{8}$ $-$

602 $25^{5}/_{8}$ $24^{9}/_{16}$ $25^{5}/_{8}$ $+$

833 12 $11^{5}/_{8}$ $11^{5}/_{8}$ $+$

16 $10^{1}/_{2}$ $10^{1}/_{2}$ $10^{1}/_{2}$ $-$

78 $15^{5}/_{8}$ $15^{13}/_{16}$ $15^{5}/_{8}$ $-$

4508 $9^{1}/_{16}$ $8^{1}/_{4}$ $8^{1}/_{}$

430 $11^{1}/_{4}$ $10^{1}/_{8}$

MORTGAGE-BACKED SECTOR OF THE BOND MARKET
by Frank J. Fabozzi, CFA

LEARNING OUTCOMES

The candidate should be able to:	Mastery
a. describe a mortgage loan, and explain the cash flow characteristics of a fixed-rate, level payment, and fully amortized mortgage loan;	☐
b. explain investment characteristics, payment characteristics, and risks of mortgage passthrough securities;	☐
c. calculate the prepayment amount for a month, given the single monthly mortality rate;	☐
d. compare the conditional prepayment rate (CPR) with the Public Securities Association (PSA) prepayment benchmark;	☐
e. explain why the average life of a mortgage-backed security is more relevant than the security's maturity;	☐
f. explain factors that affect prepayments and the types of prepayment risks;	☐
g. explain how a collateralized mortgage obligation (CMO) is created and how it provides a better matching of assets and liabilities for institutional investors;	☐
h. distinguish among the sequential pay tranche, the accrual tranche, the planned amortization class tranche, and the support tranche in a CMO;	☐
i. evaluate the risk characteristics and relative performance of each type of CMO tranche, given changes in the interest rate environment;	☐
j. explain investment characteristics of stripped mortgage-backed securities;	☐
k. compare agency and nonagency mortgage-backed securities;	☐
l. compare credit risk analysis of commercial and residential nonagency mortgage-backed securities;	☐
m. describe the basic structure of a commercial mortgage-backed security (CMBS), and explain the ways in which a CMBS investor may realize call protection at the loan level and by means of the CMBS structure.	☐

Fixed Income Analysis for the Chartered Financial Analyst® Program, Second Edition, by Frank J. Fabozzi, CFA.
Copyright © 2005 by CFA Institute. Reprinted with permission.

1

INTRODUCTION

In this reading we will discuss securities backed by a pool of loans or receivables—mortgage-backed securities and asset-backed securities. The mortgage-backed securities sector, simply referred to as the **mortgage sector** of the bond market, includes securities backed by a pool of mortgage loans. There are securities backed by residential mortgage loans, referred to as **residential mortgage-backed securities**, and securities backed by commercial loans, referred to as **commercial mortgage-backed securities**.

In the United States, the securities backed by residential mortgage loans are divided into two sectors: 1) those issued by federal agencies (one federally related institution and two government sponsored enterprises) and 2) those issued by private entities. The former securities are called **agency mortgage-backed securities** and the latter **nonagency mortgage-backed securities**.

Securities backed by loans other than traditional residential mortgage loans or commercial mortgage loans and backed by receivables are referred to as **asset-backed securities**. There is a long and growing list of loans and receivables that have been used as collateral for these securities. Together, mortgage-backed securities and asset-backed securities are referred to as **structured financial products**.

It is important to understand the classification of these sectors in terms of bond market indexes. A popular bond market index, the Lehman Aggregate Bond Index, has a sector that it refers to as the "mortgage passthrough sector." Within the "mortgage passthrough sector," Lehman Brothers includes only agency mortgage-backed securities that are mortgage passthrough securities. To understand why it is essential to understand this sector, consider that the "mortgage passthrough sector" represents more than one-third of the Lehman Aggregate Bond Index. It is the largest sector in the bond market index. The commercial mortgage-backed securities sector represents about 2% of the bond market index. The mortgage sector of the Lehman Aggregate Bond Index includes the mortgage passthrough sector and the commercial mortgage-backed securities.

In this reading, our focus will be on the mortgage sector. Although many countries have developed a mortgage-backed securities sector, our focus in this reading is the U.S. mortgage sector because of its size and its important role in U.S. bond market indexes. Credit risk does not exist for agency mortgage-backed securities issued by a federally related institution and is viewed as minimal for securities issued by government sponsored enterprises. The significant risk is prepayment risk, and there are ways to redistribute prepayment risk among the different bond classes created. Historically, it is important to note that the agency mortgage-backed securities market developed first. The technology developed for creating agency mortgage-backed security was then transferred to the securitization of other types of loans and receivables. In transferring the technology to create securities that expose investors to credit risk, mechanisms had to be developed to create securities that could receive investment grade credit ratings sought by the issuer. We will discuss these mechanisms in the reading on the asset-backed sector of the market.

Outside the United States, market participants treat asset-backed securities more generically. Specifically, asset-backed securities include mortgage-backed securities as a subsector. While that is actually the proper way to classify these securities, it was not the convention adopted in the United States. The development of the asset-backed securities (including mortgage-backed securities) outside the United States will also be covered in the reading on the asset-backed sector of the market.

Residential mortgage-backed securities include 1) mortgage passthrough securities, 2) collateralized mortgage obligations, and 3) stripped mortgage-backed securities. The latter two mortgage-backed securities are referred to as derivative mortgage-backed securities because they are created from mortgage passthrough securities.

RESIDENTIAL MORTGAGE LOANS   `2`

A mortgage is a loan secured by the collateral of some specified real estate property which obliges the borrower to make a predetermined series of payments. The mortgage gives the lender the right to "foreclose" on the loan if the borrower defaults and to seize the property in order to ensure that the debt is paid off. The interest rate on the mortgage loan is called the mortgage rate or contract rate. Our focus in this section is on residential mortgage loans.

When the lender makes the loan based on the credit of the borrower and on the collateral for the mortgage, the mortgage is said to be a conventional mortgage. The lender may require that the borrower obtain mortgage insurance to guarantee the fulfillment of the borrower's obligations. Some borrowers can qualify for mortgage insurance which is guaranteed by one of three U.S. government agencies: the Federal Housing Administration (FHA), the Veteran's Administration (VA), and the Rural Housing Service (RHS). There are also private mortgage insurers. The cost of mortgage insurance is paid by the borrower in the form of a higher mortgage rate.

There are many types of mortgage designs used throughout the world. A mortgage design is a specification of the interest rate, term of the mortgage, and the manner in which the borrowed funds are repaid. In the United States, the alternative mortgage designs include 1) fixed-rate, level-payment fully amortized mortgages, 2) adjustable-rate mortgages, 3) balloon mortgages, 4) growing equity mortgages, 5) reverse mortgages, and 6) tiered payment mortgages. Other countries have developed mortgage designs unique to their housing finance market. Some of these mortgage designs relate the mortgage payment to the country's rate of inflation. Below we will look at the most common mortgage design in the United States—the fixed-rate, level-payment, fully amortized mortgage. All of the principles we need to know regarding the risks associated with investing in mortgage-backed securities and the difficulties associated with their valuation can be understood by just looking at this mortgage design.

A. Fixed-Rate, Level-Payment, Fully Amortized Mortgage

A fixed-rate, level-payment, fully amortized mortgage has the following features:

▶ the mortgage rate is fixed for the life of the mortgage loan;

▶ the dollar amount of each monthly payment is the same for the life of the mortgage loan (i.e., there is a "level payment");

▶ when the last scheduled monthly mortgage payment is made, the remaining mortgage balance is zero (i.e., the loan is fully amortized).

The monthly mortgage payments include principal repayment and interest. The frequency of payment is typically monthly. Each monthly mortgage payment for this mortgage design is due on the first of each month and consists of:

1. interest of $\frac{1}{12}$ of the fixed annual interest rate times the amount of the outstanding mortgage balance at the beginning of the previous month, and

2. a repayment of a portion of the outstanding mortgage balance (principal).

The difference between the monthly mortgage payment and the portion of the payment that represents interest equals the amount that is applied to reduce the outstanding mortgage balance. The monthly mortgage payment is designed so that after the last scheduled monthly mortgage payment is made, the amount of the outstanding mortgage balance is zero (i.e., the mortgage is fully repaid).

To illustrate this mortgage design, consider a 30-year (360-month), $100,000 mortgage with an 8.125% mortgage rate. The monthly mortgage payment would be $742.50. Exhibit 1 shows for selected months how each monthly mortgage payment is divided between interest and scheduled principal repayment. At the beginning of month 1, the mortgage balance is $100,000, the amount of the original loan. The mortgage payment for month 1 includes interest on the $100,000 borrowed for the month. Since the interest rate is 8.125%, the monthly interest rate is 0.0067708 (0.08125 divided by 12). Interest for month 1 is therefore $677.08 ($100,000 times 0.0067708). The $65.41 difference between the monthly mortgage payment of $742.50 and the interest of $677.08 is the portion of the monthly mortgage payment that represents the scheduled principal repayment. It is also referred to as the scheduled amortization, and we shall use the terms scheduled principal repayment and scheduled amortization interchangeably throughout this reading. This $65.41 in month 1 reduces the mortgage balance.

The mortgage balance at the end of month 1 (beginning of month 2) is then $99,934.59 ($100,000 minus $65.41). The interest for the second monthly mortgage payment is $676.64, the monthly interest rate (0.0067708) times the mortgage balance at the beginning of month 2 ($99,934.59). The difference between the $742.50 monthly mortgage payment and the $676.64 interest is $65.86, representing the amount of the mortgage balance paid off with that monthly mortgage payment. Notice that the mortgage payment in month 360—the final payment—is sufficient to pay off the remaining mortgage balance.

As Exhibit 1 clearly shows, *the portion of the monthly mortgage payment applied to interest declines each month and the portion applied to principal repayment increases.* The reason for this is that as the mortgage balance is reduced with each monthly mortgage payment, the interest on the mortgage balance declines. Since the monthly mortgage payment is a fixed dollar amount, an increasingly larger portion of the monthly payment is applied to reduce the mortgage balance outstanding in each subsequent month.

EXHIBIT 1	Amortization Schedule for a Level-Payment, Fixed-Rate, Fully Amortized Mortgage

Mortgage loan: $100,000   Monthly payment: $742.50

Mortgage rate: 8.125%   Term of loan: 30 years (360 months)

Month	Beginning of Month Mortgage Balance ($)	Mortgage Payment ($)	Interest ($)	Scheduled Repayment ($)	End of Month Mortgage Balance ($)
1	100,000.00	742.50	677.08	65.41	99,934.59
2	99,934.59	742.50	676.64	65.86	99,868.73
3	99,868.73	742.50	676.19	66.30	99,802.43
4	99,802.43	742.50	675.75	66.75	99,735.68
...	...	...	...	...	...
25	98,301.53	742.50	665.58	76.91	98,224.62
26	98,224.62	742.50	665.06	77.43	98,147.19
27	98,147.19	742.50	664.54	77.96	98,069.23
...	...	...	...	...	...
74	93,849.98	742.50	635.44	107.05	93,742.93
75	93,742.93	742.50	634.72	107.78	93,635.15
76	93,635.15	742.50	633.99	108.51	93,526.64
...	...	...	...	...	...
141	84,811.77	742.50	574.25	168.25	84,643.52
142	84,643.52	742.50	573.11	169.39	84,474.13
143	84,474.13	742.50	571.96	170.54	84,303.59
...	...	...	...	...	...
184	76,446.29	742.50	517.61	224.89	76,221.40
185	76,221.40	742.50	516.08	226.41	75,994.99
186	75,994.99	742.50	514.55	227.95	75,767.04
...	...	...	...	...	...
233	63,430.19	742.50	429.48	313.02	63,117.17
234	63,117.17	742.50	427.36	315.14	62,802.03
235	62,802.03	742.50	425.22	317.28	62,484.75
...	...	...	...	...	...
289	42,200.92	742.50	285.74	456.76	41,744.15
290	41,744.15	742.50	282.64	459.85	41,284.30
291	41,284.30	742.50	279.53	462.97	40,821.33
...	...	...	...	...	...
321	25,941.42	742.50	175.65	566.85	25,374.57
322	25,374.57	742.50	171.81	570.69	24,803.88
323	24,803.88	742.50	167.94	574.55	24,229.32
...	...	...	...	...	...
358	2,197.66	742.50	14.88	727.62	1,470.05
359	1,470.05	742.50	9.95	732.54	737.50
360	737.50	742.50	4.99	737.50	0.00

1. Servicing Fee

Every mortgage loan must be serviced. Servicing of a mortgage loan involves collecting monthly payments and forwarding proceeds to owners of the loan; sending payment notices to mortgagors; reminding mortgagors when payments are overdue; maintaining records of principal balances; initiating foreclosure proceedings if necessary; and, furnishing tax information to borrowers (i.e., mortgagors) when applicable.

The servicing fee is a portion of the mortgage rate. If the mortgage rate is 8.125% and the servicing fee is 50 basis points, then the investor receives interest of 7.625%. The interest rate that the investor receives is said to be the net interest or net coupon. The servicing fee is commonly called the servicing spread.

The dollar amount of the servicing fee declines over time as the mortgage amortizes. This is true for not only the mortgage design that we have just described, but for all mortgage designs.

2. Prepayments and Cash Flow Uncertainty

Our illustration of the cash flow from a level-payment, fixed-rate, fully amortized mortgage assumes that the homeowner does not pay off any portion of the mortgage balance prior to the scheduled due date. But homeowners can pay off all or part of their mortgage balance prior to the maturity date. A payment made in excess of the monthly mortgage payment is called a prepayment. The prepayment could be to pay off the entire outstanding balance or a partial paydown of the mortgage balance. When a prepayment is not for the entire outstanding balance it is called a curtailment.

The effect of prepayments is that the amount and timing of the cash flow from a mortgage loan are not known with certainty. This risk is referred to as prepayment risk. For example, all that the lender in a $100,000, 8.125% 30-year mortgage knows is that as long as the loan is outstanding and the borrower does not default, interest will be received and the principal will be repaid at the scheduled date each month; then at the end of the 30 years, the investor would have received $100,000 in principal payments. What the investor does not know—the uncertainty—is for how long the loan will be outstanding, and therefore what the timing of the principal payments will be. This is true for all mortgage loans, not just the level-payment, fixed-rate, fully amortized mortgage. Factors affecting prepayments will be discussed later in this reading.

Most mortgages have no prepayment penalty. The outstanding loan balance can be repaid at par. However, there are mortgages with prepayment penalties. The purpose of the penalty is to deter prepayment when interest rates decline. A prepayment penalty mortgage has the following structure. There is a period of time over which if the loan is prepaid in full or in excess of a certain amount of the outstanding balance, there is a prepayment penalty. This period is referred to as the lockout period or penalty period. During the penalty period, the borrower may prepay up to a specified amount of the outstanding balance without a penalty. Over that specified amount, the penalty is set in terms of the number of months of interest that must be paid.

3   MORTGAGE PASSTHROUGH SECURITIES

A mortgage passthrough security is a security created when one or more holders of mortgages form a collection (pool) of mortgages and sell shares or participation certificates in the pool. A pool may consist of several thousand or only a few mortgages. When a mortgage is included in a pool of mortgages that is used as collateral for a mortgage passthrough security, the mortgage is said to be securitized.

A. Cash Flow Characteristics

The cash flow of a mortgage passthrough security depends on the cash flow of the underlying pool of mortgages. As we explained in the previous section, the cash flow consists of monthly mortgage payments representing interest, the scheduled repayment of principal, and any prepayments.

Payments are made to security holders each month. However, neither the amount nor the timing of the cash flow from the pool of mortgages is identical to that of the cash flow passed through to investors. The monthly cash flow for a passthrough is less than the monthly cash flow of the underlying pool of mortgages by an amount equal to servicing and other fees. The other fees are those charged by the issuer or guarantor of the passthrough for guaranteeing the issue (discussed later). The coupon rate on a passthrough is called the passthrough rate. The passthrough rate is less than the mortgage rate on the underlying pool of mortgages by an amount equal to the servicing and guaranteeing fees.

The timing of the cash flow is also different. The monthly mortgage payment is due from each mortgagor on the first day of each month, but there is a delay in passing through the corresponding monthly cash flow to the security holders. The length of the delay varies by the type of passthrough security.

Not all of the mortgages that are included in a pool of mortgages that are securitized have the same mortgage rate and the same maturity. Consequently, when describing a passthrough security, a weighted average coupon rate and a weighted average maturity are determined. A weighted average coupon rate, or WAC, is found by weighting the mortgage rate of each mortgage loan in the pool by the percentage of the mortgage outstanding relative to the outstanding amount of all the mortgages in the pool. A weighted average maturity, or WAM, is found by weighting the remaining number of months to maturity for each mortgage loan in the pool by the amount of the outstanding mortgage balance.

For example, suppose a mortgage pool has just five loans and the outstanding mortgage balance, mortgage rate, and months remaining to maturity of each loan are as follows:

Loan	Outstanding Mortgage Balance ($)	Weight in Pool (%)	Mortgage Rate (%)	Months Remaining
1	125,000	22.12	7.50	275
2	85,000	15.04	7.20	260
3	175,000	30.97	7.00	290
4	110,000	19.47	7.80	285
5	70,000	12.39	6.90	270
Total	565,000	100.00	7.28	279

The WAC for this mortgage pool is:

$$0.2212\ (7.5\%) + 0.1504\ (7.2\%) + 0.3097\ (7.0\%) + 0.1947\ (7.8\%)$$
$$+ 0.1239\ (6.90\%) = 7.28\%$$

The WAM for this mortgage pool is

$$0.2212\ (275) + 0.1504\ (260) + 0.3097\ (290) + 0.1947\ (285)$$
$$+ 0.1239\ (270) = 279 \text{ months (rounded)}$$

B. Types of Mortgage Passthrough Securities

In the United States, the three major types of passthrough securities are guaranteed by agencies created by Congress to increase the supply of capital to the residential mortgage market. Those agencies are the Government National Mortgage Association (Ginnie Mae), the Federal Home Loan Mortgage Corporation (Freddie Mac), and the Federal National Mortgage Association (Fannie Mae).

While Freddie Mac and Fannie Mae are commonly referred to as "agencies" of the U.S. government, both are corporate instrumentalities of the U.S. government. That is, they are government sponsored enterprises; therefore, their guarantee does not carry the full faith and credit of the U.S. government. In contrast, Ginnie Mae is a federally related institution; it is part of the Department of Housing and Urban Development. As such, its guarantee carries the full faith and credit of the U.S. government. The passthrough securities issued by Fannie Mae and Freddie Mac are called conventional passthrough securities. However, in this reading we shall refer to those passthrough securities issued by all three entities (Ginnie Mae, Fannie Mae, and Freddie Mac) as agency passthrough securities. It should be noted, however, that market participants do reserve the term "agency passthrough securities" for those issued only by Ginnie Mae.[1]

In order for a loan to be included in a pool of loans backing an agency security, it must meet specified underwriting standards. These standards set forth the maximum size of the loan, the loan documentation required, the maximum loan-to-value ratio, and whether or not insurance is required. If a loan satisfies the underwriting standards for inclusion as collateral for an agency mortgage-backed security, it is called a conforming mortgage. If a loan fails to satisfy the underwriting standards, it is called a nonconforming mortgage.

Nonconforming mortgages used as collateral for mortgage passthrough securities are privately issued. These securities are called nonagency mortgage passthrough securities and are issued by thrifts, commercial banks, and private conduits. Private conduits may purchase nonconforming mortgages, pool them, and then sell passthrough securities whose collateral is the underlying pool of nonconforming mortgages. Nonagency passthrough securities are rated by the nationally recognized statistical rating organizations. These securities are supported by credit enhancements so that they can obtain an investment grade rating. We shall describe these securities in the next reading.

C. Trading and Settlement Procedures

Agency passthrough securities are identified by a pool prefix and pool number provided by the agency. The prefix indicates the type of passthrough. There are specific rules established by the Bond Market Association for the trading and

---

[1] The name of the passthrough issued by Ginnie Mae and Fannie Mae is a *Mortgage-Backed Security* or *MBS*. So, when a market participant refers to a Ginnie Mae MBS or Fannie Mae MBS, what is meant is a passthrough issued by these two entities. The name of the passthrough issued by Freddie Mac is a *Participation Certificate* or *PC*. So, when a market participant refers to a Freddie Mac PC, what is meant is a passthrough issued by Freddie Mac. Every agency has different "programs" under which passthroughs are issued with different types of mortgage pools (e.g., 30-year fixed-rate mortgages, 15-year fixed-rate mortgages, adjustable-rate mortgages). We will not review the different programs here.

settlement of mortgage-backed securities. Many trades occur while a pool is still unspecified, and therefore no pool information is known at the time of the trade. This kind of trade is known as a TBA trade (to-be-announced trade). In a TBA trade the two parties agree on the agency type, the agency program, the coupon rate, the face value, the price, and the settlement date. The actual pools of mortgage loans underlying the agency passthrough are not specified in a TBA trade. However, this information is provided by the seller to the buyer before delivery. There are trades where more specific requirements are established for the securities to be delivered. An example is a Freddie Mac with a coupon rate of 8.5% and a WAC between 9.0% and 9.2%. There are also specified pool trades wherein the actual pool numbers to be delivered are specified.

Passthrough prices are quoted in the same manner as U.S. Treasury coupon securities. A quote of 94-05 means 94 and 5 32nds of par value, or 94.15625% of par value. The price that the buyer pays the seller is the agreed upon sale price plus accrued interest. Given the par value, the dollar price (excluding accrued interest) is affected by the amount of the pool mortgage balance outstanding. The pool factor indicates the percentage of the initial mortgage balance still outstanding. So, a pool factor of 90 means that 90% of the original mortgage pool balance is outstanding. The pool factor is reported by the agency each month.

The dollar price paid for just the principal is found as follows given the agreed upon price, par value, and the month's pool factor provided by the agency:

$$\text{Price} \times \text{Par value} \times \text{Pool factor}$$

For example, if the parties agree to a price of 92 for $1 million par value for a passthrough with a pool factor of 0.85, then the dollar price paid by the buyer in addition to accrued interest is:

$$0.92 \times \$1{,}000{,}000 \times 0.85 = \$782{,}000$$

The buyer does not know what he will get unless he specifies a pool number. There are many seasoned issues of the same agency with the same coupon rate outstanding at a given point in time. For example, in early 2000 there were more than 30,000 pools of 30-year Ginnie Mae MBSs outstanding with a coupon rate of 9%. One passthrough may be backed by a pool of mortgage loans in which all the properties are located in California, while another may be backed by a pool of mortgage loans in which all the properties are in Minnesota. Yet another may be backed by a pool of mortgage loans in which the properties are from several regions of the country. So which pool are dealers referring to when they talk about Ginnie Mae 9s? They are not referring to any specific pool but instead to a generic security, despite the fact that the prepayment characteristics of passthroughs with underlying pools from different parts of the country are different. Thus, the projected prepayment rates for passthroughs reported by dealer firms (discussed later) are for generic passthroughs. A particular pool purchased may have a materially different prepayment rate from the generic. Moreover, when an investor purchases a passthrough without specifying a pool number, the seller has the option to deliver the worst-paying pools as long as the pools delivered satisfy good delivery requirements.

D. Measuring the Prepayment Rate

A prepayment is any payment toward the repayment of principal that is in excess of the scheduled principal payment. In describing prepayments, market participants refer to the prepayment rate or prepayment speed. In this section we will see how the historical prepayment rate is computed for a month. We then look at how to annualize a monthly prepayment rate and then explain the convention in the residential mortgage market for describing a pattern of prepayment rates over the life of a mortgage pool.

There are three points to keep in mind in the discussion in this section. First, we will look at how the actual or historical prepayment rate of a mortgage pool is calculated. Second, we will see later how in projecting the cash flow of a mortgage pool, an investor uses the same prepayment measures to project prepayments given a prepayment rate. The third point is that we are just describing the mechanics of calculating prepayment measures. The difficult task of projecting the prepayment rate is not discussed here. In fact, this task is beyond the scope of this reading. However, the factors that investors use in prepayment models (i.e., statistical models used to project prepayments) will be described in Section F.

1. Single Monthly Mortality Rate

Given the amount of the prepayment for a month and the amount that was available to prepay that month, a monthly prepayment rate can be computed. The amount available to prepay in a month is *not* the outstanding mortgage balance of the pool in the previous month. The reason is that there will be scheduled principal payments for the month and therefore by definition this amount cannot be prepaid. Thus, the amount available to prepay in a given month, say month t, is the beginning mortgage balance in month t reduced by the scheduled principal payment in month t.

The ratio of the prepayment in a month and the amount available to prepay that month is called the single monthly mortality rate[2] or simply SMM. That is, the SMM for month t is computed as follows

$$\text{SMM}_t = \frac{\text{Prepayment in month } t}{\text{Beginning mortgage balance for month } t - \text{Scheduled principal payment in month } t}$$

Let's illustrate the calculation of the SMM. Assume the following:

beginning mortgage balance in month 33 = $358,326,766
scheduled principal payment in month 33 = $297,825
prepayment in month 33   = $1,841,347

The SMM for month 33 is therefore:

$$\text{SMM}_{33} = \frac{\$1,841,347}{\$358,326,766 - \$297,825} = 0.005143 = 0.5143\%$$

The SMM_{33} of 0.5143% is interpreted as follows: In month 33, 0.5143% of the outstanding mortgage balance available to prepay in month 33 prepaid.

Let's make sure we understand the two ways in which the SMM can be used. First, given the prepayment for a month for a mortgage pool, an investor can calculate the SMM as we just did in our illustration to determine the SMM for month 33. Second given an *assumed* SMM, an investor will use it to project the prepayment for a month. The prepayment for a month will then be used to

---

[2] It may seem strange that the term "mortality" is used to describe this prepayment measure. This term reflects the influence of actuaries who in the early years of the development of the mortgage market migrated to dealer firms to assist in valuing mortgage-backed securities. Actuaries viewed the prepayment of a mortgage loan as the "death" of a mortgage.

determine the cash flow of a mortgage pool for the month. We'll see this later in this section when we illustrate how to calculate the cash flow for a passthrough security. For now, it is important to understand that given an assumed SMM for month t, the prepayment for month t is found as follows:

Prepayment for month t = SMM × (Beginning mortgage balance for month t − Scheduled principal payment for month t) **(1)**

For example, suppose that an investor owns a passthrough security in which the remaining mortgage balance at the beginning of some month is $290 million and the scheduled principal payment for that month is $3 million. The investor believes that the SMM next month will be 0.5143%. Then the projected prepayment for the month is:

$$0.005143 \times (\$290,000,000 - \$3,000,000) = \$1,476,041$$

2. Conditional Prepayment Rate

Market participants prefer to talk about prepayment rates on an annual basis rather than a monthly basis. This is handled by annualizing the SMM. The annualized SMM is called the conditional prepayment rate or CPR.[3] Given the SMM for a given month, the CPR can be demonstrated to be:[4]

$$CPR = 1 - (1 - SMM)^{12}$$ **(2)**

For example, suppose that the SMM is 0.005143. Then the CPR is

$$CPR = 1 - (1 - 0.005143)^{12}$$
$$= 1 - (0.994857)^{12} = 0.06 = 6\%$$

A CPR of 6% means that, ignoring scheduled principal payments, approximately 6% of the outstanding mortgage balance at the beginning of the year will be prepaid by the end of the year.

Given a CPR, the corresponding SMM can be computed by solving Equation 2 for the SMM:

$$SMM = 1 - (1 - CPR)^{1/12}$$ **(3)**

To illustrate Equation 3, suppose that the CPR is 6%; then the SMM is

$$SMM = 1 - (1 - 0.06)^{1/12} = 0.005143 = 0.5143\%$$

3. PSA Prepayment Benchmark

An SMM is the prepayment rate for a month. A CPR is a prepayment rate for a year. Market participants describe prepayment rates (historical/actual prepayment rates and those used for projecting future prepayments) in terms of a prepayment pattern or benchmark over the life of a mortgage pool. In the early

---

[3] It is referred to as a "conditional" prepayment rate because the prepayments in one year depend upon (i.e., are conditional upon) the amount available to prepay in the previous year. Sometimes market participants refer to the CPR as the "constant" prepayment rate.

[4] The derivation of the CPR for a given SMM is beyond the scope of this chapter. The proof is provided in Lakhbir S. Hayre and Cyrus Mohebbi, "Mortgage Mathematics," in Frank J. Fabozzi (ed.), *Handbook of Mortgage-Backed Securities: Fifth Edition* (New York, NY: McGraw-Hill, 2001), pp. 844–845.

1980s, the Public Securities Association (PSA), later renamed the Bond Market Association, undertook a study to look at the pattern of prepayments over the life of a typical mortgage pool. Based on the study, the PSA established a prepayment benchmark which is referred to as the PSA prepayment benchmark. Although sometimes referred to as a "prepayment model," it is a convention and not a model to predict prepayments.

The PSA prepayment benchmark is expressed as a monthly series of CPRs. The PSA benchmark assumes that prepayment rates are low for newly originated mortgages and then will speed up as the mortgages become seasoned. The PSA benchmark assumes the following prepayment rates for 30-year mortgages: 1) a CPR of 0.2% for the first month, increased by 0.2% per year per month for the next 30 months until it reaches 6% per year, and 2) a 6% CPR for the remaining months.

This benchmark, referred to as "100% PSA" or simply "100 PSA," is graphically depicted in Exhibit 2. Mathematically, 100 PSA can be expressed as follows:

if $t < 30$ then CPR = 6% $(t/30)$
if $t \geq 30$ then CPR = 6%

where t is the number of months since the mortgages were originated.

It is important to emphasize that the CPRs and corresponding SMMs apply to a mortgage pool *based on the number of months since origination*. For example, if a mortgage pool has loans that were originally 30-year (360-month) mortgage loans and the WAM is currently 357 months, this means that the mortgage pool is seasoned three months. So, in determining prepayments for the next month, the CPR and SMM that are applicable are those for month 4.

Slower or faster speeds are then referred to as some percentage of PSA. For example, "50 PSA" means one-half the CPR of the PSA prepayment benchmark; "150 PSA" means 1.5 times the CPR of the PSA prepayment benchmark; "300 PSA" means three times the CPR of the prepayment benchmark. A prepayment rate of 0 PSA means that no *prepayments* are assumed. While there are no prepayments at 0 PSA, there are scheduled principal repayments.

In constructing a schedule for monthly prepayments, the CPR (an annual rate) must be converted into a monthly prepayment rate (an SMM) using

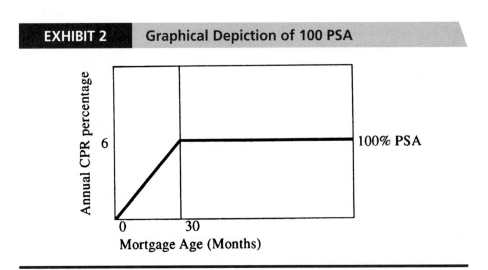

EXHIBIT 2   Graphical Depiction of 100 PSA

Equation 3. For example, the SMMs for month 5, month 20, and months 31 through 360 assuming 100 PSA are calculated as follows:

for month 5:

CPR = 6% (5/30) = 1% = 0.01

SMM = $1 - (1 - 0.01)^{1/12} = 1 - (0.99)^{0.083333} = 0.000837$

for month 20:

CPR = 6% (20/30) = 4% = 0.04

SMM = $1 - (1 - 0.04)^{1/12} = 1 - (0.96)^{0.083333} = 0.003396$

for months 31–360:

CPR = 6%

SMM = $1 - (1 - 0.06)^{1/12} = 1 - (0.94)^{0.083333} = 0.005143$

What if the PSA were 165 instead? The SMMs for month 5, month 20, and months 31 through 360 assuming 165 PSA are computed as follows:

for month 5:

CPR = 6% (5/30) = 1% = 0.01

165 PSA = 1.65 (0.01) = 0.0165

SMM = $1 - (1 - 0.0165)^{1/12} = 1 - (0.9835)^{0.08333} = 0.001386$

for month 20:

CPR = 6% (20/30) = 4% = 0.04

165 PSA = 1.65 (0.04) = 0.066

SMM = $1 - (1 - 0.066)^{1/12} = 1 - (0.934)^{0.08333} = 0.005674$

for months 31–360:

CPR = 6%

165 PSA = 1.65 (0.06) = 0.099

SMM = $1 - (1 - 0.099)^{1/12} = 1 - (0.901)^{0.08333} = 0.008650$

Notice that the SMM assuming 165 PSA is not just 1.65 times the SMM assuming 100 PSA. It is the CPR that is a multiple of the CPR assuming 100 PSA.

4. Illustration of Monthly Cash Flow Construction

As our first step in valuing a hypothetical passthrough given a PSA assumption, we must construct a monthly cash flow. For the purpose of this illustration, the underlying mortgages for this hypothetical passthrough are assumed to be fixed-rate, level-payment, fully amortized mortgages with a weighted average coupon (WAC) rate of 8.125%. It will be assumed that the passthrough rate is 7.5% with a weighted average maturity (WAM) of 357 months.

Exhibit 3 shows the cash flow for selected months assuming 100 PSA. The cash flow is broken down into three components: 1) interest (based on the

EXHIBIT 3   Monthly Cash Flow for a $400 Million Passthrough with a 7.5% Passthrough Rate, a WAC of 8.125%, and a WAM of 357 Months Assuming 100 PSA

Months from Now (1)	Months Seasoned[a] (2)	Outstanding Balance ($) (3)	SMM (4)	Mortgage Payment ($) (5)	Net Interest ($) (6)	Scheduled Principal ($) (7)	Prepayment ($) (8)	Total Principal ($) (9)	Cash Flow ($) (10)
1	4	400,000,000	0.00067	2,975,868	2,500,000	267,535	267,470	535,005	3,035,005
2	5	399,464,995	0.00084	2,973,877	2,496,656	269,166	334,198	603,364	3,100,020
3	6	398,861,631	0.00101	2,971,387	2,492,885	270,762	400,800	671,562	3,164,447
4	7	398,190,069	0.00117	2,968,399	2,488,688	272,321	467,243	739,564	3,228,252
5	8	397,450,505	0.00134	2,964,914	2,484,066	273,843	533,493	807,335	3,291,401
6	9	396,643,170	0.00151	2,960,931	2,479,020	275,327	599,514	874,841	3,353,860
7	10	395,768,329	0.00168	2,956,453	2,473,552	276,772	665,273	942,045	3,415,597
8	11	394,826,284	0.00185	2,951,480	2,467,664	278,177	730,736	1,008,913	3,476,577
9	12	393,817,371	0.00202	2,946,013	2,461,359	279,542	795,869	1,075,410	3,536,769
10	13	392,741,961	0.00219	2,940,056	2,454,637	280,865	860,637	1,141,502	3,596,140
11	14	391,600,459	0.00236	2,933,608	2,447,503	282,147	925,008	1,207,155	3,654,658
27	30	364,808,016	0.00514	2,766,461	2,280,050	296,406	1,874,688	2,171,094	4,451,144
28	31	362,636,921	0.00514	2,752,233	2,266,481	296,879	1,863,519	2,160,398	4,426,879
29	32	360,476,523	0.00514	2,738,078	2,252,978	297,351	1,852,406	2,149,758	4,402,736
30	33	358,326,766	0.00514	2,723,996	2,239,542	297,825	1,841,347	2,139,173	4,378,715
100	103	231,249,776	0.00514	1,898,682	1,445,311	332,928	1,187,608	1,520,537	2,965,848
101	104	229,729,239	0.00514	1,888,917	1,435,808	333,459	1,179,785	1,513,244	2,949,052
102	105	228,215,995	0.00514	1,879,202	1,426,350	333,990	1,172,000	1,505,990	2,932,340
103	106	226,710,004	0.00514	1,869,538	1,416,938	334,522	1,164,252	1,498,774	2,915,712
104	107	225,211,230	0.00514	1,859,923	1,407,570	335,055	1,156,541	1,491,596	2,899,166
105	108	223,719,634	0.00514	1,850,357	1,398,248	335,589	1,148,867	1,484,456	2,882,703

(Exhibit continued on next page . . .)

EXHIBIT 3 (continued)

Months from Now (1)	Months Seasoned[a] (2)	Outstanding Balance ($) (3)	SMM (4)	Mortgage Payment ($) (5)	Net Interest ($) (6)	Scheduled Principal ($) (7)	Prepayment ($) (8)	Total Principal ($) (9)	Cash Flow ($) (10)
200	203	109,791,339	0.00514	1,133,751	686,196	390,372	562,651	953,023	1,639,219
201	204	108,838,316	0.00514	1,127,920	680,239	390,994	557,746	948,740	1,628,980
202	205	107,889,576	0.00514	1,122,119	674,310	391,617	552,863	944,480	1,618,790
203	206	106,945,096	0.00514	1,116,348	668,407	392,241	548,003	940,243	1,608,650
300	303	32,383,611	0.00514	676,991	202,398	457,727	164,195	621,923	824,320
301	304	31,761,689	0.00514	673,510	198,511	458,457	160,993	619,449	817,960
302	305	31,142,239	0.00514	670,046	194,639	459,187	157,803	616,990	811,629
303	306	30,525,249	0.00514	666,600	190,783	459,918	154,626	614,545	805,328
352	355	3,034,311	0.00514	517,770	18,964	497,226	13,048	510,274	529,238
353	356	2,524,037	0.00514	515,107	15,775	498,018	10,420	508,437	524,213
354	357	2,015,600	0.00514	512,458	12,597	498,811	7,801	506,612	519,209
355	358	1,508,988	0.00514	509,823	9,431	499,606	5,191	504,797	514,228
356	359	1,004,191	0.00514	507,201	6,276	500,401	2,591	502,992	509,269
357	360	501,199	0.00514	504,592	3,132	501,199	0	501,199	504,331

[a] Since the WAM is 357 months, the underlying mortgage pool is seasoned an average of three months, and therefore based on 100 PSA, the CPR is 0.8% in month 1 and the pool seasons at 6% in month 27.

passthrough rate), 2) the scheduled principal repayment (i.e., scheduled amortization), and 3) prepayments based on 100 PSA.

Let's walk through Exhibit 3 column by column.

Column 1:   This is the number of months from now when the cash flow will be received.

Column 2:   This is the number of months of seasoning. Since the WAM for this mortgage pool is 357 months, this means that the loans are seasoned an average of 3 months (360 months–357 months) now.

Column 3:   This column gives the outstanding mortgage balance at the beginning of the month. It is equal to the outstanding balance at the beginning of the previous month reduced by the total principal payment in the previous month.

Column 4:   This column shows the SMM based on the number of months the loans are seasoned—the number of months shown in Column 2. For example, for the first month shown in the exhibit, the loans are seasoned three months going into that month. Therefore, the CPR used is the CPR that corresponds to four months. From the PSA benchmark, the CPR is 0.8% (4 times 0.2%). The corresponding SMM is 0.00067. The mortgage pool becomes fully seasoned in Column 1 corresponding to month 27 because by that time the loans are seasoned 30 months. When the loans are fully seasoned the CPR at 100 PSA is 6% and the corresponding SMM is 0.00514.

Column 5:   The total monthly mortgage payment is shown in this column. Notice that the total monthly mortgage payment declines over time as prepayments reduce the mortgage balance outstanding. There is a formula to determine what the monthly mortgage balance will be for each month given prepayments.[5]

Column 6:   The *net* monthly interest (i.e., amount available to pay bondholders after the servicing fee) is found in this column. This value is determined by multiplying the outstanding mortgage balance at the beginning of the month by the passthrough rate of 7.5% and then dividing by 12.

Column 7:   This column gives the scheduled principal repayment (i.e., scheduled amortization). This is the difference between the total monthly mortgage payment (the amount shown in Column 5) and the gross coupon interest for the month. The gross coupon interest is found by multiplying 8.125% by the outstanding mortgage balance at the beginning of the month and then dividing by 12.

Column 8:   The prepayment for the month is reported in this column. The prepayment is found by using Equation 1. For example, in month 100, the beginning mortgage balance is $231,249,776, the scheduled principal payment is $332,928, and the SMM at 100 PSA is 0.00514301 (only 0.00514 is shown in the exhibit to save space), so the prepayment is:

$$0.00514301 \times (\$231,249,776 - \$332,928) = \$1,187,608$$

Column 9:   The total principal payment, which is the sum of columns 7 and 8, is shown in this column.

Column 10:   The projected monthly cash flow for this passthrough is shown in this last column. The monthly cash flow is the sum of the interest paid (Column 6) and the total principal payments for the month (Column 9).

---

[5] The formula is presented in Chapter 19 of Frank J. Fabozzi, *Fixed Income Mathematics* (Chicago: Irwin Professional Publishing, 1997).

Let's look at what happens to the cash flows for this passthrough if a different PSA assumption is made. Suppose that instead of 100 PSA, 165 PSA is assumed. Prepayments are assumed to be faster. Exhibit 4 shows the cash flow for this passthrough based on 165 PSA. Notice that the cash flows are greater in the early years compared to Exhibit 3 because prepayments are higher. The cash flows in later years are less for 165 PSA compared to 100 PSA because of the higher prepayments in the earlier years.

E. Average Life

It is standard practice in the bond market to refer to the maturity of a bond. If a bond matures in five years, it is referred to as a "5-year bond." However, the typical bond repays principal only once: at the maturity date. Bonds with this characteristic are referred to as "bullet bonds." We know that the maturity of a bond affects its interest rate risk. More specifically, for a given coupon rate, the greater the maturity the greater the interest rate risk.

For a mortgage-backed security, we know that the principal repayments (scheduled payments and prepayments) are made over the life of the security. While a mortgage-backed has a "legal maturity," which is the date when the last scheduled principal payment is due, the legal maturity does not tell us much about the characteristic of the security as its pertains to interest rate risk. For example, it is incorrect to think of a 30-year corporate bond and a mortgage-backed security with a 30-year legal maturity with the same coupon rate as being equivalent in terms of interest rate risk. Of course, duration can be computed for both the corporate bond and the mortgage-backed security. (We will see how this is done for a mortgage-backed security in the reading on valuing mortgage-backed and asset-backed securities.) Instead of duration, another measure widely used by market participants is the weighted average life or simply average life. This is the convention-based average time to receipt of principal payments (scheduled principal payments and projected prepayments).

Mathematically, the average life is expressed as follows:

$$\text{Average life} = \sum_{t=1}^{T} \frac{t \times \text{Projected principal received at time } t}{12 \times \text{Total principal}}$$

where T is the number of months.

The average life of a passthrough depends on the prepayment assumption. To see this, the average life is shown below for different prepayment speeds for the pass-through we used to illustrate the cash flow for 100 PSA and 165 PSA in Exhibits 3 and 4:

PSA Speed	50	100	165	200	300	400	500	600	700
Average Life (years)	15.11	11.66	8.76	7.68	5.63	4.44	3.68	3.16	2.78

F. Factors Affecting Prepayment Behavior

The factors that affect prepayment behavior are:

1. prevailing mortgage rate
2. housing turnover
3. characteristics of the underlying residential mortgage loans

The current mortgage rate affects prepayments. The spread between the prevailing mortgage rate in the market and the rate paid by the homeowner

EXHIBIT 4   Monthly Cash Flow for a $400 Million Passthrough with a 7.5% Passthrough Rate, a WAC of 8.125%, and a WAM of 357 Months Assuming 165 PSA

Months (1)	Months Seasoned[a] (2)	Outstanding Balance ($) (3)	SMM (4)	Mortgage Payment ($) (5)	Net Interest ($) (6)	Scheduled Principal ($) (7)	Prepayment ($) (8)	Total Principal ($) (9)	Cash Flow ($) (10)
1	4	400,000,000	0.00111	2,975,868	2,500,000	267,535	442,389	709,923	3,209,923
2	5	399,290,077	0.00139	2,972,575	2,495,563	269,048	552,847	821,896	3,317,459
3	6	398,468,181	0.00167	2,968,456	2,490,426	270,495	663,065	933,560	3,423,986
4	7	397,534,621	0.00195	2,963,513	2,484,591	271,873	772,949	1,044,822	3,529,413
5	8	396,489,799	0.00223	2,957,747	2,478,061	273,181	882,405	1,155,586	3,633,647
6	9	395,334,213	0.00251	2,951,160	2,470,839	274,418	991,341	1,265,759	3,736,598
7	10	394,068,454	0.00279	2,943,755	2,462,928	275,583	1,099,664	1,375,246	3,838,174
8	11	392,693,208	0.00308	2,935,534	2,454,333	276,674	1,207,280	1,483,954	3,938,287
9	12	391,209,254	0.00336	2,926,503	2,445,058	277,690	1,314,099	1,591,789	4,036,847
10	13	389,617,464	0.00365	2,916,666	2,435,109	278,631	1,420,029	1,698,659	4,133,769
11	14	387,918,805	0.00393	2,906,028	2,424,493	279,494	1,524,979	1,804,473	4,228,965
27	30	347,334,116	0.00865	2,633,950	2,170,838	282,209	3,001,955	3,284,164	5,455,002
28	31	344,049,952	0.00865	2,611,167	2,150,312	281,662	2,973,553	3,255,215	5,405,527
29	32	340,794,737	0.00865	2,588,581	2,129,967	281,116	2,945,400	3,226,516	5,356,483
30	33	337,568,221	0.00865	2,566,190	2,109,801	280,572	2,917,496	3,198,067	5,307,869
100	103	170,142,350	0.00865	1,396,958	1,063,390	244,953	1,469,591	1,714,544	2,777,933
101	104	168,427,806	0.00865	1,384,875	1,052,674	244,478	1,454,765	1,699,243	2,751,916
102	105	166,728,563	0.00865	1,372,896	1,042,054	244,004	1,440,071	1,684,075	2,726,128
103	106	165,044,489	0.00865	1,361,020	1,031,528	243,531	1,425,508	1,669,039	2,700,567
104	107	163,375,450	0.00865	1,349,248	1,021,097	243,060	1,411,075	1,654,134	2,675,231
105	108	161,721,315	0.00865	1,337,577	1,010,758	242,589	1,396,771	1,639,359	2,650,118

(Exhibit continued on next page . . . .)

EXHIBIT 4 (continued)

Months (1)	Months Seasoned[a] (2)	Outstanding Balance ($) (3)	SMM (4)	Mortgage Payment ($) (5)	Net Interest ($) (6)	Scheduled Principal ($) (7)	Prepayment ($) (8)	Total Principal ($) (9)	Cash Flow ($) (10)
200	203	56,746,664	0.00865	585,990	354,667	201,767	489,106	690,874	1,045,540
201	204	56,055,790	0.00865	580,921	350,349	201,377	483,134	684,510	1,034,859
202	205	55,371,280	0.00865	575,896	346,070	200,986	477,216	678,202	1,024,273
203	206	54,693,077	0.00865	570,915	341,832	200,597	471,353	671,950	1,013,782
300	303	11,758,141	0.00865	245,808	73,488	166,196	100,269	266,465	339,953
301	304	11,491,677	0.00865	243,682	71,823	165,874	97,967	263,841	335,664
302	305	11,227,836	0.00865	241,574	70,174	165,552	95,687	261,240	331,414
303	306	10,966,596	0.00865	239,485	68,541	165,232	93,430	258,662	327,203
352	355	916,910	0.00865	156,460	5,731	150,252	6,631	156,883	162,614
353	356	760,027	0.00865	155,107	4,750	149,961	5,277	155,238	159,988
354	357	604,789	0.00865	153,765	3,780	149,670	3,937	153,607	157,387
355	358	451,182	0.00865	152,435	2,820	149,380	2,611	151,991	154,811
356	359	299,191	0.00865	151,117	1,870	149,091	1,298	150,389	152,259
357	360	148,802	0.00865	149,809	930	148,802	0	148,802	149,732

[a] Since the WAM is 357 months, the underlying mortgage pool is seasoned an average of three months, and therefore based on 165 PSA, the CPR is 0.8% × 1.65 in month 1 and the pool seasons at 6% × 1.65 in month 27.

affects the incentive to refinance. Moreover, the path of mortgage rates since the loan was originated affects prepayments through a phenomenon referred to as refinancing burnout. Both the spread and path of mortgage rates affect prepayments that are the product of refinancing.

By far, the single most important factor affecting prepayments because of refinancing is the current level of mortgage rates relative to the borrower's contract rate. The greater the difference between the two, the greater the incentive to refinance the mortgage loan. For refinancing to make economic sense, the interest savings must be greater than the costs associated with refinancing the mortgage. These costs include legal expenses, origination fees, title insurance, and the value of the time associated with obtaining another mortgage loan. Some of these costs will vary proportionately with the amount to be financed. Other costs such as the application fee and legal expenses are typically fixed.

Historically it had been observed that mortgage rates had to decline by between 250 and 350 basis points below the contract rate in order to make it worthwhile for borrowers to refinance. However, the creativity of mortgage originators in designing mortgage loans such that the refinancing costs are folded into the amount borrowed has changed the view that mortgage rates must drop dramatically below the contract rate to make refinancing economic. Moreover, mortgage originators now do an effective job of advertising to make homeowners cognizant of the economic benefits of refinancing.

The historical pattern of prepayments and economic theory suggests that it is not only the level of mortgage rates that affects prepayment behavior but also the path that mortgage rates take to get to the current level. To illustrate why, suppose the underlying contract rate for a pool of mortgage loans is 11% and that three years after origination, the prevailing mortgage rate declines to 8%. Let's consider two possible paths of the mortgage rate in getting to the 8% level. In the first path, the mortgage rate declines to 8% at the end of the first year, then rises to 13% at the end of the second year, and then falls to 8% at the end of the third year. In the second path, the mortgage rate rises to 12% at the end of the first year, continues its rise to 13% at the end of the second year, and then falls to 8% at the end of the third year.

If the mortgage rate follows the first path, those who can benefit from refinancing will more than likely take advantage of this opportunity when the mortgage rate drops to 8% in the first year. When the mortgage rate drops again to 8% at the end of the third year, the likelihood is that prepayments because of refinancing will not surge; those who want to benefit by taking advantage of the refinancing opportunity will have done so already when the mortgage rate declined for the first time. This is the prepayment behavior referred to as the refinancing burnout (or simply, burnout) phenomenon. In contrast, the expected prepayment behavior when the mortgage rate follows the second path is quite different. Prepayment rates are expected to be low in the first two years. When the mortgage rate declines to 8% in the third year, refinancing activity and therefore prepayments are expected to surge. Consequently, the burnout phenomenon is related to the path of mortgage rates.

There is another way in which the prevailing mortgage rate affects prepayments: through its effect on the affordability of housing and housing turnover. The level of mortgage rates affects housing turnover to the extent that a lower rate increases the affordability of homes. However, even without lower interest rates, there is a normal amount of housing turnover. This is attributed to economic growth. The link is as follows: a growing economy results in a rise in personal income and in opportunities for worker migration; this increases family mobility and as a result increases housing turnover. The opposite holds for a weak economy.

Two characteristics of the underlying residential mortgage loans that affect prepayments are the amount of seasoning and the geographical location of the underlying properties. Seasoning refers to the aging of the mortgage loans. Empirical evidence suggests that prepayment rates are low after the loan is originated and increase after the loan is somewhat seasoned. Then prepayment rates tend to level off, in which case the loans are referred to as fully seasoned. This is the underlying theory for the PSA prepayment benchmark discussed earlier in this chapter. In some regions of the country the prepayment behavior tends to be faster than the average national prepayment rate, while other regions exhibit slower prepayment rates. This is caused by differences in local economies that affect housing turnover.

G. Contraction Risk and Extension Risk

An investor who owns passthrough securities does not know what the cash flow will be because that depends on actual prepayments. As we noted earlier, this risk is called prepayment risk.

To understand the significance of prepayment risk, suppose an investor buys a 9% coupon passthrough security at a time when mortgage rates are 10%. Let's consider what will happen to prepayments if mortgage rates decline to, say, 6%. There will be two adverse consequences. First, a basic property of fixed income securities is that the price of an option-free bond will rise. But in the case of a passthrough security, the rise in price will not be as large as that of an option-free bond because a fall in interest rates will give the borrower an incentive to prepay the loan and refinance the debt at a lower rate. This results in the same adverse consequence faced by holders of callable bonds. As in the case of those instruments, the upside price potential of a passthrough security is compressed because of prepayments. (This is the negative convexity characteristic.) The second adverse consequence is that the cash flow must be reinvested at a lower rate. Basically, the faster prepayments resulting from a decline in interest rates causes the passthrough to shorten in terms of the timing of its cash flows. Another way of saying this is that "shortening" results in a decline in the average life. Consequently, the two adverse consequences from a decline in interest rates for a passthrough security are referred to as contraction risk.

Now let's look at what happens if mortgage rates rise to 15%. The price of the passthrough, like the price of any bond, will decline. But again it will decline more because the higher rates will tend to slow down the rate of prepayment, in effect increasing the amount invested at the coupon rate, which is lower than the market rate. Prepayments will slow down, because homeowners will not refinance or partially prepay their mortgages when mortgage rates are higher than the contract rate of 10%. Of course this is just the time when investors want prepayments to speed up so that they can reinvest the prepayments at the higher market interest rate. Basically, the slower prepayments associated with a rise in interest rates that causes these adverse consequences are due to the passthrough lengthening in terms of the timing of its cash flows. Another way of saying this is that "lengthening" results in an increase in the average life. Consequently, the adverse consequence from a rise in interest rates for a passthrough security is referred to as extension risk.

Therefore, prepayment risk encompasses contraction risk and extension risk. Prepayment risk makes passthrough securities unattractive for certain financial institutions to hold from an asset/liability management perspective. Some institutional investors are concerned with extension risk and others with contraction risk when they purchase a passthrough security. This applies even for assets supporting specific types of insurance contracts. Is it possible to alter the cash flow of a passthrough so as to reduce the contraction risk or extension risk for institutional investors? This can be done, as we shall see, when we describe collateralized mortgage obligations.

COLLATERALIZED MORTGAGE OBLIGATIONS

As we noted, there is prepayment risk associated with investing in a mortgage passthrough security. Some institutional investors are concerned with extension risk and others with contraction risk. This problem can be mitigated by redirecting the cash flows of mortgage-related products (passthrough securities or a pool of loans) to different bond classes, called tranches,[6] so as to create securities that have different exposure to prepayment risk and therefore different risk/return patterns than the mortgage-related product from which they are created.

When the cash flows of mortgage-related products are redistributed to different bond classes, the resulting securities are called collateralized mortgage obligations (CMO). The mortgage-related products from which the cash flows are obtained are referred to as the collateral. Since the typical mortgage-related product used in a CMO is a pool of passthrough securities, sometimes market participants will use the terms "collateral" and "passthrough securities" interchangeably. The creation of a CMO cannot eliminate prepayment risk; it can only distribute the various forms of this risk among different classes of bondholders. The CMO's major financial innovation is that the securities created more closely satisfy the asset/liability needs of institutional investors, thereby broadening the appeal of mortgage-backed products.

There is a wide range of CMO structures.[7] We review the major ones below.

A. Sequential-Pay Tranches

The first CMO was structured so that each class of bond would be retired sequentially. Such structures are referred to as sequential-pay CMOs. The rule for the monthly distribution of the principal payments (scheduled principal plus prepayments) to the tranches would be as follows:

▶ Distribute all principal payments to Tranche 1 until the principal balance for Tranche 1 is zero. After Tranche 1 is paid off,

▶ distribute all principal payments to Tranche 2 until the principal balance for Tranche 2 is zero. After Tranche 2 is paid off,

▶ distribute all principal payments to Tranche 3 until the principal balance for Tranche 3 is zero. After Tranche 3 is paid off, . . .

and so on.

---

[6] "Tranche" is from an old French word meaning "slice." In the case of a collateralized mortgage obligation it refers to a "slice of the cash flows."

[7] The issuer of a CMO wants to be sure that the trust created to pass through the interest and principal payments is not treated as a taxable entity. A provision of the Tax Reform Act of 1986, called the Real Estate Mortgage Investment Conduit (REMIC), specifies the requirements that an issuer must fulfill so that the legal entity created to issue a CMO is not taxable. Most CMOs today are created as REMICs. While it is common to hear market participants refer to a CMO as a REMIC, not all CMOs are REMICs.

To illustrate a sequential-pay CMO, we discuss FJF-01, a hypothetical deal made up to illustrate the basic features of the structure. The collateral for this hypothetical CMO is a hypothetical passthrough with a total par value of $400 million and the following characteristics: 1) the passthrough coupon rate is 7.5%, 2) the weighted average coupon (WAC) is 8.125%, and 3) the weighted average maturity (WAM) is 357 months. This is the same passthrough that we used in Section 3 to describe the cash flow of a passthrough based on some PSA assumption.

From this $400 million of collateral, four bond classes or tranches are created. Their characteristics are summarized in Exhibit 5. The total par value of the four tranches is equal to the par value of the collateral (i.e., the passthrough security).[8] In this simple structure, the coupon rate is the same for each tranche and also the same as the coupon rate on the collateral. There is no reason why this must be so, and, in fact, typically the coupon rate varies by tranche.

Now remember that a CMO is created by redistributing the cash flow—interest and principal—to the different tranches based on a set of payment rules. The payment rules at the bottom of Exhibit 5 describe how the cash flow from the passthrough (i.e., collateral) is to be distributed to the four tranches. There are separate rules for the distribution of the coupon interest and the payment of principal (the principal being the total of the scheduled principal payment and any prepayments).

While the payment rules for the disbursement of the principal payments are known, the precise amount of the principal in each month is not. This will depend on the cash flow, and therefore principal payments, of the collateral, which depends on the actual prepayment rate of the collateral. An assumed PSA speed allows the cash flow to be projected. Exhibit 6 shows the cash flow (interest, scheduled principal repayment, and prepayments) assuming 165 PSA. Assuming that the collateral does prepay at 165 PSA, the cash flow available to all four tranches of FJF-01 will be precisely the cash flow shown in Exhibit 6.

EXHIBIT 5   FJF-01—A Hypothetical 4-Tranche Sequential-Pay Structure

Tranche	Par Amount ($)	Coupon Rate (%)
A	194,500,000	7.5
B	36,000,000	7.5
C	96,500,000	7.5
D	73,000,000	7.5
Total	400,000,000	

Payment rules:

1. *For payment of monthly coupon interest:* Disburse monthly coupon interest to each tranche on the basis of the amount of principal outstanding for each tranche at the beginning of the month.

2. *For disbursement of principal payments:* Disburse principal payments to tranche A until it is completely paid off. After tranche A is completely paid off, disburse principal payments to tranche B until it is completely paid off. After tranche B is completely paid off, disburse principal payments to tranche C until it is completely paid off. After tranche C is completely paid off, disburse principal payments to tranche D until it is completely paid off.

[8] Actually, a CMO is backed by a pool of passthrough securities.

EXHIBIT 6	Monthly Cash Flow for Selected Months for FJF-01 Assuming 165 PSA					
	Tranche A			Tranche B		
Month	Balance ($)	Principal ($)	Interest ($)	Balance ($)	Principal ($)	Interest ($)
1	194,500,000	709,923	1,215,625	36,000,000	0	225,000
2	193,790,077	821,896	1,211,188	36,000,000	0	225,000
3	192,968,181	933,560	1,206,051	36,000,000	0	225,000
4	192,034,621	1,044,822	1,200,216	36,000,000	0	225,000
5	190,989,799	1,155,586	1,193,686	36,000,000	0	225,000
6	189,834,213	1,265,759	1,186,464	36,000,000	0	225,000
7	188,568,454	1,375,246	1,178,553	36,000,000	0	225,000
8	187,193,208	1,483,954	1,169,958	36,000,000	0	225,000
9	185,709,254	1,591,789	1,160,683	36,000,000	0	225,000
10	184,117,464	1,698,659	1,150,734	36,000,000	0	225,000
11	182,418,805	1,804,473	1,140,118	36,000,000	0	225,000
12	180,614,332	1,909,139	1,128,840	36,000,000	0	225,000
75	12,893,479	2,143,974	80,584	36,000,000	0	225,000
76	10,749,504	2,124,935	67,184	36,000,000	0	225,000
77	8,624,569	2,106,062	53,904	36,000,000	0	225,000
78	6,518,507	2,087,353	40,741	36,000,000	0	225,000
79	4,431,154	2,068,807	27,695	36,000,000	0	225,000
80	2,362,347	2,050,422	14,765	36,000,000	0	225,000
81	311,926	311,926	1,950	36,000,000	1,720,271	225,000
82	0	0	0	34,279,729	2,014,130	214,248
83	0	0	0	32,265,599	1,996,221	201,660
84	0	0	0	30,269,378	1,978,468	189,184
85	0	0	0	28,290,911	1,960,869	176,818
95	0	0	0	9,449,331	1,793,089	59,058
96	0	0	0	7,656,242	1,777,104	47,852
97	0	0	0	5,879,138	1,761,258	36,745
98	0	0	0	4,117,879	1,745,550	25,737
99	0	0	0	2,372,329	1,729,979	14,827
100	0	0	0	642,350	642,350	4,015
101	0	0	0	0	0	0

(Exhibit continued on next page . . .)

| EXHIBIT 6 | (continued) |

	Tranche C			Tranche D		
Month	Balance ($)	Principal ($)	Interest ($)	Balance ($)	Principal ($)	Interest ($)
1	96,500,000	0	603,125	73,000,000	0	456,250
2	96,500,000	0	603,125	73,000,000	0	456,250
3	96,500,000	0	603,125	73,000,000	0	456,250
4	96,500,000	0	603,125	73,000,000	0	456,250
5	96,500,000	0	603,125	73,000,000	0	456,250
6	96,500,000	0	603,125	73,000,000	0	456,250
7	96,500,000	0	603,125	73,000,000	0	456,250
8	96,500,000	0	603,125	73,000,000	0	456,250
9	96,500,000	0	603,125	73,000,000	0	456,250
10	96,500,000	0	603,125	73,000,000	0	456,250
11	96,500,000	0	603,125	73,000,000	0	456,250
12	96,500,000	0	603,125	73,000,000	0	456,250
95	96,500,000	0	603,125	73,000,000	0	456,250
96	96,500,000	0	603,125	73,000,000	0	456,250
97	96,500,000	0	603,125	73,000,000	0	456,250
98	96,500,000	0	603,125	73,000,000	0	456,250
99	96,500,000	0	603,125	73,000,000	0	456,250
100	96,500,000	1,072,194	603,125	73,000,000	0	456,250
101	95,427,806	1,699,243	596,424	73,000,000	0	456,250
102	93,728,563	1,684,075	585,804	73,000,000	0	456,250
103	92,044,489	1,669,039	575,278	73,000,000	0	456,250
104	90,375,450	1,654,134	564,847	73,000,000	0	456,250
105	88,721,315	1,639,359	554,508	73,000,000	0	456,250
175	3,260,287	869,602	20,377	73,000,000	0	456,250
176	2,390,685	861,673	14,942	73,000,000	0	456,250
177	1,529,013	853,813	9,556	73,000,000	0	456,250
178	675,199	675,199	4,220	73,000,000	170,824	456,250
179	0	0	0	72,829,176	838,300	455,182
180	0	0	0	71,990,876	830,646	449,943
181	0	0	0	71,160,230	823,058	444,751
182	0	0	0	70,337,173	815,536	439,607
183	0	0	0	69,521,637	808,081	434,510
184	0	0	0	68,713,556	800,690	429,460
185	0	0	0	67,912,866	793,365	424,455
350	0	0	0	1,235,674	160,220	7,723
351	0	0	0	1,075,454	158,544	6,722
352	0	0	0	916,910	156,883	5,731
353	0	0	0	760,027	155,238	4,750
354	0	0	0	604,789	153,607	3,780
355	0	0	0	451,182	151,991	2,820
356	0	0	0	299,191	150,389	1,870
357	0	0	0	148,802	148,802	930

Note: The cash flow for a tranche in each month is the sum of the principal and interest.

To demonstrate how the payment rules for FJF-01 work, Exhibit 6 shows the cash flow for selected months assuming the collateral prepays at 165 PSA. For each tranche, the exhibit shows 1) the balance at the end of the month, 2) the principal paid down (scheduled principal repayment plus prepayments), and 3) interest. In month 1, the cash flow for the collateral consists of a principal payment of $709,923 and an interest payment of $2.5 million (0.075 times $400 million divided by 12). The interest payment is distributed to the four tranches based on the amount of the par value outstanding. So, for example, tranche A receives $1,215,625 (0.075 times $194,500,000 divided by 12) of the $2.5 million. The principal, however, is all distributed to tranche A. Therefore, the cash flow for tranche A in month 1 is $1,925,548. The principal balance at the end of month 1 for tranche A is $193,790,076 (the original principal balance of $194,500,000 less the principal payment of $709,923). No principal payment is distributed to the three other tranches because there is still a principal balance outstanding for tranche A. This will be true for months 2 through 80. The cash flow for tranche A for each month is found by adding the amounts shown in the "Principal" and "Interest" columns. So, for tranche A, the cash flow in month 8 is $1,483,954 plus $1,169,958 or $2,653,912. The cash flow from months 82 on is zero based on 165 PSA.

After month 81, the principal balance will be zero for tranche A. For the collateral, the cash flow in month 81 is $3,318,521, consisting of a principal payment of $2,032,197 and interest of $1,286,325. At the beginning of month 81 (end of month 80), the principal balance for tranche A is $311,926. Therefore, $311,926 of the $2,032,196 of the principal payment from the collateral will be disbursed to tranche A. After this payment is made, no additional principal payments are made to this tranche as the principal balance is zero. The remaining principal payment from the collateral, $1,720,271, is distributed to tranche B. Based on an assumed prepayment speed of 165 PSA, tranche B then begins receiving principal payments in month 81. The cash flow for tranche B for each month is found by adding the amounts shown in the "Principal" and "Interest" columns. For months 1 though 80, the cash flow is just the interest. There is no cash flow after month 100 for Tranche B.

Exhibit 6 shows that tranche B is fully paid off by month 100, when tranche C begins to receive principal payments. Tranche C is not fully paid off until month 178, at which time tranche D begins receiving the remaining principal payments. The maturity (i.e., the time until the principal is fully paid off) for these four tranches assuming 165 PSA would be 81 months for tranche A, 100 months for tranche B, 178 months for tranche C, and 357 months for tranche D. The cash flow for each month for tranches C and D is found by adding the principal and the interest for the month.

The principal paydown window or principal window for a tranche is the time period between the beginning and the ending of the principal payments to that tranche. So, for example, for tranche A, the principal paydown window would be month 1 to month 81 assuming 165 PSA. For tranche B it is from month 81 to month 100.[9] In confirmation of trades involving CMOs, the principal paydown window is specified in terms of the initial month that principal is expected to be received to the final month that principal is expected to be received.

Let's look at what has been accomplished by creating the CMO. Earlier we saw that the average life of the passthrough is 8.76 years assuming a prepayment speed of 165 PSA. Exhibit 7 reports the average life of the collateral and the four

---

[9] The window is also specified in terms of the length of the time from the beginning of the principal paydown window to the end of the principal paydown window. For tranche A, the window would be stated as 81 months; for tranche B, 20 months.

EXHIBIT 7	Average Life for the Collateral and the Four Tranches of FJF-01				
Prepayment Speed (PSA)	**Average Life (in Years) for**				
	Collateral	**Tranche A**	**Tranche B**	**Tranche C**	**Tranche D**
50	15.11	7.48	15.98	21.02	27.24
100	11.66	4.90	10.86	15.78	24.58
165	8.76	3.48	7.49	11.19	20.27
200	7.68	3.05	6.42	9.60	18.11
300	5.63	2.32	4.64	6.81	13.36
400	4.44	1.94	3.70	5.31	10.34
500	3.68	1.69	3.12	4.38	8.35
600	3.16	1.51	2.74	3.75	6.96
700	2.78	1.38	2.47	3.30	5.95

tranches assuming different prepayment speeds. Notice that the four tranches have average lives that are both shorter and longer than the collateral, thereby attracting investors who have a preference for an average life different from that of the collateral.

There is still a major problem: there is considerable variability of the average life for the tranches. We'll see how this can be handled later on. However, there is some protection provided for each tranche against prepayment risk. This is because prioritizing the distribution of principal (i.e., establishing the payment rules for principal) effectively protects the shorter-term tranche A in this structure against extension risk. This protection must come from somewhere, so it comes from the three other tranches. Similarly, tranches C and D provide protection against extension risk for tranches A and B. At the same time, tranches C and D benefit because they are provided protection against contraction risk, the protection coming from tranches A and B.

B. Accrual Tranches

In our previous example, the payment rules for interest provided for all tranches to be paid interest each month. In many sequential-pay CMO structures, at least one tranche does not receive current interest. Instead, the interest for that tranche would accrue and be added to the principal balance. Such a tranche is commonly referred to as an accrual tranche or a Z bond. The interest that would have been paid to the accrual tranche is used to pay off the principal balance of earlier tranches.

To see this, consider FJF-02, a hypothetical CMO structure with the same collateral as our previous example and with four tranches, each with a coupon rate of 7.5%. The last tranche, Z, is an accrual tranche. The structure for FJF-02 is shown in Exhibit 8.

Exhibit 9 shows cash flows for selected months for tranches A and B. Let's look at month 1 and compare it to month 1 in Exhibit 6. Both cash flows are based on 165 PSA. The principal payment from the collateral is $709,923. In FJF-01, this is the principal paydown for tranche A. In FJF-02, the interest for

EXHIBIT 8	FJF-02—A Hypothetical 4-Tranche Sequential-Pay Structure with an Accrual Tranche	

Tranche	Par Amount ($)	Coupon Rate (%)
A	194,500,000	7.5
B	36,000,000	7.5
C	96,500,000	7.5
Z (Accrual)	73,000,000	7.5
Total	400,000,000	

Payment rules:

1. *For payment of monthly coupon interest:* Disburse monthly coupon interest to tranches A, B, and C on the basis of the amount of principal outstanding for each tranche at the beginning of the month. For tranche Z, accrue the interest based on the principal plus accrued interest in the previous month. The interest for tranche Z is to be paid to the earlier tranches as a principal paydown.

2. *For disbursement of principal payments:* Disburse principal payments to tranche A until it is completely paid off. After tranche A is completely paid off, disburse principal payments to tranche B until it is completely paid off. After tranche B is completely paid off, disburse principal payments to tranche C until it is completely paid off. After tranche C is completely paid off, disburse principal payments to tranche Z until the original principal balance plus accrued interest is completely paid off.

tranche Z, $456,250, is not paid to that tranche but instead is used to pay down the principal of tranche A. So, the principal payment to tranche A in Exhibit 9 is $1,166,173, the collateral's principal payment of $709,923 plus the interest of $456,250 that was diverted from tranche Z.

The expected final maturity for tranches A, B, and C has shortened as a result of the inclusion of tranche Z. The final payout for tranche A is 64 months rather than 81 months; for tranche B it is 77 months rather than 100 months; and, for tranche C it is 113 months rather than 178 months.

The average lives for tranches A, B, and C are shorter in FJF-02 compared to our previous non-accrual, sequential-pay tranche example, FJF-01, because of the inclusion of the accrual tranche. For example, at 165 PSA, the average lives are as follows:

Structure	Tranche A	Tranche B	Tranche C
FJF-02	2.90	5.86	7.87
FJF-01	3.48	7.49	11.19

The reason for the shortening of the non-accrual tranches is that the interest that would be paid to the accrual tranche is being allocated to the other tranches. Tranche Z in FJF-02 will have a longer average life than tranche D in FJF-01 because in tranche Z the interest payments are being diverted to tranches A, B, and C.

Thus, shorter-term tranches and a longer-term tranche are created by including an accrual tranche in FJF-02 compared to FJF-01. The accrual tranche has appeal to investors who are concerned with reinvestment risk. Since there are no coupon payments to reinvest, reinvestment risk is eliminated until all the other tranches are paid off.

EXHIBIT 9	Monthly Cash Flow for Selected Months for Tranches A and B for FJF-02 Assuming 165 PSA					
	Tranche A			**Tranche B**		
Month	Balance ($)	Principal ($)	Interest ($)	Balance ($)	Principal ($)	Interest ($)
1	194,500,000	1,166,173	1,215,625	36,000,000	0	225,000
2	193,333,827	1,280,997	1,208,336	36,000,000	0	225,000
3	192,052,829	1,395,531	1,200,330	36,000,000	0	225,000
4	190,657,298	1,509,680	1,191,608	36,000,000	0	225,000
5	189,147,619	1,623,350	1,182,173	36,000,000	0	225,000
6	187,524,269	1,736,446	1,172,027	36,000,000	0	225,000
7	185,787,823	1,848,875	1,161,174	36,000,000	0	225,000
8	183,938,947	1,960,543	1,149,618	36,000,000	0	225,000
9	181,978,404	2,071,357	1,137,365	36,000,000	0	225,000
10	179,907,047	2,181,225	1,124,419	36,000,000	0	225,000
11	177,725,822	2,290,054	1,110,786	36,000,000	0	225,000
12	175,435,768	2,397,755	1,096,474	36,000,000	0	225,000
60	15,023,406	3,109,398	93,896	36,000,000	0	225,000
61	11,914,007	3,091,812	74,463	36,000,000	0	225,000
62	8,822,195	3,074,441	55,139	36,000,000	0	225,000
63	5,747,754	3,057,282	35,923	36,000,000	0	225,000
64	2,690,472	2,690,472	16,815	36,000,000	349,863	225,000
65	0	0	0	35,650,137	3,023,598	222,813
66	0	0	0	32,626,540	3,007,069	203,916
67	0	0	0	29,619,470	2,990,748	185,122
68	0	0	0	26,628,722	2,974,633	166,430
69	0	0	0	23,654,089	2,958,722	147,838
70	0	0	0	20,695,367	2,943,014	129,346
71	0	0	0	17,752,353	2,927,508	110,952
72	0	0	0	14,824,845	2,912,203	92,655
73	0	0	0	11,912,642	2,897,096	74,454
74	0	0	0	9,015,546	2,882,187	56,347
75	0	0	0	6,133,358	2,867,475	38,333
76	0	0	0	3,265,883	2,852,958	20,412
77	0	0	0	412,925	412,925	2,581
78	0	0	0	0	0	0
79	0	0	0	0	0	0
80	0	0	0	0	0	0

C. Floating-Rate Tranches

The tranches described thus far have a fixed rate. There is a demand for tranches that have a floating rate. The problem is that the collateral pays a fixed rate and therefore it would be difficult to create a tranche with a floating rate. However, a floating-rate tranche can be created. This is done by creating from any fixed-rate tranche a floater and an inverse floater combination. We will illustrate the creation of a floating-rate tranche and an inverse floating-rate tranche using the hypothetical CMO structure—the 4-tranche sequential-pay structure with an accrual tranche (FJF-02).[10] We can select any of the tranches from which to create a floating-rate and inverse floating-rate tranche. In fact, we can create these two securities for more than one of the four tranches or for only a portion of one tranche.

In this case, we create a floater and an inverse floater from tranche C. A floater could have been created from any of the other tranches. The par value for this tranche is $96.5 million, and we create two tranches that have a combined par value of $96.5 million. We refer to this CMO structure with a floater and an inverse floater as FJF-03. It has five tranches, designated A, B, FL, IFL, and Z, where FL is the floating-rate tranche and IFL is the inverse floating-rate tranche. Exhibit 10 describes FJF-03. Any reference rate can be used to create a floater and the corresponding inverse floater. The reference rate for setting the coupon rate for FL and IFL in FJF-03 is 1-month LIBOR.

EXHIBIT 10	FJF-03—A Hypothetical 5-Tranche Sequential-Pay Structure with Floater, Inverse Floater, and Accrual Bond Tranches	
Tranche	**Par Amount ($)**	**Coupon Rate (%)**
A	194,500,000	7.50
B	36,000,000	7.50
FL	72,375,000	1-month LIBOR + 0.50
IFL	24,125,000	$28.50 - 3 \times$ (1-month LIBOR)
Z (Accrual)	73,000,000	7.50
Total	400,000,000	

Payment rules:

1. *For payment of monthly coupon interest:* Disburse monthly coupon interest to tranches A, B, FL, and IFL on the basis of the amount of principal outstanding at the beginning of the month. For tranche Z, accrue the interest based on the principal plus accrued interest in the previous month. The interest for tranche Z is to be paid to the earlier tranches as a principal paydown. The maximum coupon rate for FL is 10%; the minimum coupon rate for IFL is 0%.

2. *For disbursement of principal payments:* Disburse principal payments to tranche A until it is completely paid off. After tranche A is completely paid off, disburse principal payments to tranche B until it is completely paid off. After tranche B is completely paid off, disburse principal payments to tranches FL and IFL until they are completely paid off. The principal payments between tranches FL and IFL should be made in the following way: 75% to tranche FL and 25% to tranche IFL. After tranches FL and IFL are completely paid off, disburse principal payments to tranche Z until the original principal balance plus accrued interest are completely paid off.

---

[10] The same principle for creating a floating-rate tranche and inverse floating-rate tranche could have been accomplished using the 4-tranche sequential-pay structure without an accrual tranche (FJF-01).

The amount of the par value of the floating-rate tranche will be some portion of the $96.5 million. There are an infinite number of ways to slice up the $96.5 million between the floater and inverse floater, and final partitioning will be driven by the demands of investors. In the FJF-03 structure, we made the floater from $72,375,000 or 75% of the $96.5 million. The coupon formula for the floater is 1-month LIBOR plus 50 basis points. So, for example, if LIBOR is 3.75% at the reset date, the coupon rate on the floater is 3.75% + 0.5%, or 4.25%. There is a cap on the coupon rate for the floater (discussed later).

Unlike a floating-rate note in the corporate bond market whose principal is unchanged over the life of the instrument, the floater's principal balance declines over time as principal payments are made. The principal payments to the floater are determined by the principal payments from the tranche from which the floater is created. In our CMO structure, this is tranche C.

Since the floater's par value is $72,375,000 of the $96.5 million, the balance is par value for the inverse floater. Assuming that 1-month LIBOR is the reference rate, the coupon formula for the inverse floater takes the following form:

$$K - L \times (\text{1-month LIBOR})$$

where K and L are constants whose interpretation will be explained shortly.

In FJF-03, K is set at 28.50% and L at 3. Thus, if 1-month LIBOR is 3.75%, the coupon rate for the month is:

$$28.50\% - 3 \times (3.75\%) = 17.25\%$$

K is the cap or maximum coupon rate for the inverse floater. In FJF-03, the cap for the inverse floater is 28.50%. The determination of the inverse floater's cap rate is based on 1) the amount of interest that would have been paid to the tranche from which the floater and the inverse floater were created, tranche C in our hypothetical deal, and 2) the coupon rate for the floater if 1-month LIBOR is zero.

We will explain the determination of K by example. Let's see how the 28.5% for the inverse floater is determined. The total interest to be paid to tranche C if it was not split into the floater and the inverse floater is the principal of $96,500,000 times 7.5%, or $7,237,500. The maximum interest for the inverse floater occurs if 1-month LIBOR is zero. In that case, the coupon rate for the floater is

$$\text{1-month LIBOR} + 0.5\% = 0.5\%$$

Since the floater receives 0.5% on its principal of $72,375,000, the floater's interest is $361,875. The remainder of the interest of $7,237,500 from tranche C goes to the inverse floater. That is, the inverse floater's interest is $6,875,625 (= $7,237,500 − $361,875). Since the inverse floater's principal is $24,125,000, the cap rate for the inverse floater is

$$\frac{\$6,875,625}{\$24,125,000} = 28.5\%$$

In general, the formula for the cap rate on the inverse floater, K, is

$$K = \frac{\text{Inverse floater interest when reference rate for floater is zero}}{\text{Principal for inverse floater}}$$

The *L* or multiple in the coupon formula to determine the coupon rate for the inverse floater is called the *leverage*. The higher the leverage, the more the inverse floater's coupon rate changes for a given change in 1-month LIBOR. For example, a coupon leverage of 3 means that a 1-basis point change in 1-month LIBOR will change the coupon rate on the inverse floater by 3 basis points.

As in the case of the floater, the principal paydown of an inverse floater will be a proportionate amount of the principal paydown of tranche C.

Because 1-month LIBOR is always positive, the coupon rate paid to the floater cannot be negative. If there are no restrictions placed on the coupon rate for the inverse floater, however, it is possible for its coupon rate to be negative. To prevent this, a floor, or minimum, is placed on the coupon rate. In most structures, the floor is set at zero. Once a floor is set for the inverse floater, a cap or ceiling is imposed on the floater.

In FJF-03, a floor of zero is set for the inverse floater. The floor results in a cap or maximum coupon rate for the floater of 10%. This is determined as follows. If the floor for the inverse floater is zero, this means that the inverse floater receives no interest. All of the interest that would have been paid to tranche C, $7,237,500, would then be paid to the floater. Since the floater's principal is $72,375,000, the cap rate on the floater is $7,237,500/$72,375,000, or 10%.

In general, the cap rate for the floater *assuming a floor of zero for inverse floater* is determined as follows:

$$\text{Cap rate for floater} = \frac{\text{Collateral tranche interest}}{\text{Principal for floater}}$$

The cap for the floater and the inverse floater, the floor for the inverse floater, the leverage, and the floater's spread are not determined independently. Any cap or floor imposed on the coupon rate for the floater and the inverse floater must be selected so that the weighted average coupon rate does not exceed the collateral tranche's coupon rate.

D. Structured Interest-Only Tranches

CMO structures can be created so that a tranche receives only interest. Interest only (IO) tranches in a CMO structure are commonly referred to as structured IOs to distinguish them from IO mortgage strips that we will describe later in this reading. The basic principle in creating a structured IO is to set the coupon rate below the collateral's coupon rate so that excess interest can be generated. It is the excess interest that is used to create one or more structured IOs.

Let's look at how a structured IO is created using an illustration. Thus far, we used a simple CMO structure in which all the tranches have the same coupon rate (7.5%), and that coupon rate is the same as the collateral. A structured IO is created from a CMO structure where the coupon rate for at least one tranche is different from the collateral's coupon rate. This is seen in FJF-04 shown in Exhibit 11. In this structure, notice that the coupon interest rate for each tranche is less than the coupon interest rate for the collateral. That means that there is excess interest from the collateral that is not being paid to all the tranches. At one time, all of that excess interest not paid to the tranches was paid to a bond class called a "residual." Eventually (due to changes in the tax law that do not concern us here), structures of CMO began allocating the excess interest to the tranche that receives only interest. This is tranche IO in FJF-04.

Notice that for this structure the par amount for the IO tranche is shown as $52,566,667 and the coupon rate is 7.5%. Since this is an IO tranche there is no par amount. The amount shown is the amount upon which the interest payments

EXHIBIT 11	FJF-04: A Hypothetical Five-Tranche Sequential Pay with an Accrual Tranche, an Interest-Only Tranche, and a Residual Class

Tranche	Par Amount ($)	Coupon Rate (%)
A	194,500,000	6.00
B	36,000,000	6.50
C	96,500,000	7.00
Z	73,000,000	7.25
IO	52,566,667 (Notional)	7.50
Total	400,000,000	

Payment rules:

1. *For payment of monthly coupon interest:* Disburse monthly coupon interest to tranches A, B, and C on the basis of the amount of principal outstanding for each class at the beginning of the month. For tranche Z, accrue the interest based on the principal plus accrued interest in the previous month. The interest for tranche Z is to be paid to the earlier tranches as a principal paydown. Disburse periodic interest to the IO tranche based on the notional amount for all tranches at the beginning of the month.

2. *For disbursement of principal payments:* Disburse monthly principal payments to tranche A until it is completely paid off. After tranche A is completely paid off, disburse principal payments to tranche B until it is completely paid off. After tranche B is completely paid off, disburse principal payments to tranche C until it is completely paid off. After tranche C is completely paid off, disburse principal payments to tranche Z until the original principal balance plus accrued interest is completely paid off.

3. *No principal is to be paid to the IO tranche:* The notional amount of the IO tranche declines based on the principal payments to all other tranches.

will be determined, not the amount that will be paid to the holder of this tranche. Therefore, it is called a notional amount. The resulting IO is called a notional IO.

Let's look at how the notional amount is determined. Consider tranche A. The par value is $194.5 million and the coupon rate is 6%. Since the collateral's coupon rate is 7.5%, the excess interest is 150 basis points (1.5%). Therefore, an IO with a 1.5% coupon rate and a notional amount of $194.5 million can be created from tranche A. But this is equivalent to an IO with a notional amount of $38.9 million and a coupon rate of 7.5%. Mathematically, this notional amount is found as follows:

$$\text{Notional amount for 7.5\% IO} = \frac{\text{Original tranche's par value} \times \text{Excess interest}}{0.075}$$

where

Excess interest = Collateral tranche's coupon rate − Tranche coupon rate

For example, for tranche A:

Excess interest = 0.075 − 0.060 = 0.015

Tranche's par value = $194,500,000

$$\text{Notional amount for 7.5\% IO} = \frac{\$194,500,000 \times 0.015}{0.075} = \$38,900,000$$

Similarly, from tranche B with a par value of $36 million, the excess interest is 100 basis points (1%) and therefore an IO with a coupon rate of 1% and a notional amount of $36 million can be created. But this is equivalent to creating an IO with a notional amount of $4.8 million and a coupon rate of 7.5%. This procedure is shown in Exhibit 12 for all four tranches.

EXHIBIT 12	Creating a Notional IO Tranche		
Tranche	Par Amount ($)	Excess Interest (%)	Notional Amount for a 7.5% Coupon Rate IO ($)
A	194,500,000	1.50	38,900,000
B	36,000,000	1.00	4,800,000
C	96,500,000	0.50	6,433,333
Z	73,000,000	0.25	2,433,333

Notional amount for 7.5% IO = $52,566,667

E. Planned Amortization Class Tranches

The CMO structures discussed above attracted many institutional investors who had previously either avoided investing in mortgage-backed securities or allocated only a nominal portion of their portfolio to this sector of the bond market. While some traditional corporate bond buyers shifted their allocation to CMOs, a majority of institutional investors remained on the sidelines, concerned about investing in an instrument they continued to perceive as posing significant prepayment risk. This concern was based on the substantial average life variability, despite the innovations designed to mitigate prepayment risk.

In 1987, several structures came to market that shared the following characteristic: if the prepayment speed is within a specified band over the collateral's life, the cash flow pattern is known. The greater predictability of the cash flow for these classes of bonds, now referred to as planned amortization class (PAC) bonds, occurs because there is a principal repayment schedule that must be satisfied. PAC bondholders have priority over all other classes in the CMO structure in receiving principal payments from the collateral. The greater certainty of the cash flow for the PAC bonds comes at the expense of the non-PAC tranches, called the support tranches or companion tranches. It is these tranches that absorb the prepayment risk. Because PAC tranches have protection against both extension risk and contraction risk, they are said to provide two-sided prepayment protection.

To illustrate how to create a PAC bond, we will use as collateral the $400 million passthrough with a coupon rate of 7.5%, an 8.125% WAC, and a WAM of 357 months. The creation requires the specification of two PSA prepayment rates—a *lower PSA prepayment assumption* and an *upper PSA prepayment assumption*. In our illustration the lower PSA prepayment assumption will be 90 PSA and the upper PSA prepayment assumption will be 300 PSA. A natural question is: How does one select the lower and upper PSA prepayment assumptions? These are dictated by market conditions. For our purpose here, how they are determined is not important. The lower and upper PSA prepayment assumptions are referred to as the initial PAC collar or the initial PAC band. In our illustration the initial PAC collar is 90-300 PSA.

The second column of Exhibit 13 shows the principal payment (scheduled principal repayment plus prepayments) for selected months assuming a prepayment speed of 90 PSA, and the next column shows the principal payments for selected months assuming that the passthrough prepays at 300 PSA.

The last column of Exhibit 13 gives the minimum principal payment if the collateral prepays at 90 PSA or 300 PSA for months 1 to 349. (After month 349, the outstanding principal balance will be paid off if the prepayment speed is between 90 PSA and 300 PSA.) For example, in the first month, the principal payment would be $508,169 if the collateral prepays at 90 PSA and $1,075,931 if the collateral prepays at 300 PSA. Thus, the minimum principal payment is $508,169, as reported in the last column of Exhibit 13. In month 103, the minimum principal payment is also the amount if the prepayment speed is 90 PSA, $1,446,761, compared to $1,458,618 for 300 PSA. In month 104, however, a prepayment speed of 300 PSA would produce a principal payment of $1,433,539, which is less than the principal payment of $1,440,825 assuming 90 PSA. So, $1,433,539 is reported in the last column of Exhibit 13. From month 104 on, the minimum principal payment is the one that would result assuming a prepayment speed of 300 PSA.

In fact, if the collateral prepays at any one speed between 90 PSA and 300 PSA over its life, the minimum principal payment would be the amount reported in the last column of Exhibit 13. For example, if we had included principal payment figures assuming a prepayment speed of 200 PSA, the minimum principal payment would not change: from month 1 through month 103, the minimum principal payment is that generated from 90 PSA, but from month 104 on, the minimum principal payment is that generated from 300 PSA.

This characteristic of the collateral allows for the creation of a PAC tranche, assuming that the collateral prepays over its life at a speed between 90 PSA to 300 PSA. A schedule of principal repayments that the PAC bondholders are entitled to receive before any other tranche in the CMO structure is specified. The monthly schedule of principal repayments is as specified in the last column of Exhibit 13, which shows the minimum principal payment. That is, this minimum principal payment in each month is the principal repayment schedule (i.e., planned amortization schedule) for investors in the PAC tranche. While there is no assurance that the collateral will prepay at a constant speed between these two speeds over its life, a PAC tranche can be structured to assume that it will.

Exhibit 14 shows a CMO structure, FJF-05, created from the $400 million, 7.5% coupon passthrough with a WAC of 8.125% and a WAM of 357 months. There are just two tranches in this structure: a 7.5% coupon PAC tranche created assuming 90 to 300 PSA with a par value of $243.8 million, and a support tranche with a par value of $156.2 million.

Exhibit 15 reports the average life for the PAC tranche and the support tranche in FJF-05 assuming various *actual* prepayment speeds. Notice that between 90 PSA and 300 PSA, the average life for the PAC bond is stable at 7.26 years. However, at slower or faster PSA speeds, the schedule is broken, and the average life changes, extending when the prepayment speed is less than 90 PSA and contracting when it is greater than 300 PSA. Even so, there is much greater variability for the average life of the support tranche.

1. Creating a Series of PAC Tranches

Most CMO PAC structures have more than one class of PAC tranches. A sequence of six PAC tranches (i.e., PAC tranches paid off in sequence as specified by a principal schedule) is shown in Exhibit 16 and is called FJF-06. The total

EXHIBIT 13	Monthly Principal Payment for $400 Million, 7.5% Coupon Passthrough with an 8.125% WAC and a 357 WAM Assuming Prepayment Rates of 90 PSA and 300 PSA

Month	At 90 PSA ($)	At 300 PSA ($)	Minimum Principal Payment Available to PAC Investors—the PAC Schedule ($)
1	508,169	1,075,931	508,169
2	569,843	1,279,412	569,843
3	631,377	1,482,194	631,377
4	692,741	1,683,966	692,741
5	753,909	1,884,414	753,909
6	814,850	2,083,227	814,850
7	875,536	2,280,092	875,536
8	935,940	2,474,700	935,940
9	996,032	2,666,744	996,032
10	1,055,784	2,855,920	1,055,784
11	1,115,170	3,041,927	1,115,170
12	1,174,160	3,224,472	1,174,160
13	1,232,727	3,403,265	1,232,727
14	1,290,844	3,578,023	1,290,844
15	1,348,484	3,748,472	1,348,484
16	1,405,620	3,914,344	1,405,620
17	1,462,225	4,075,381	1,462,225
18	1,518,274	4,231,334	1,518,274
101	1,458,719	1,510,072	1,458,719
102	1,452,725	1,484,126	1,452,725
103	1,446,761	1,458,618	1,446,761
104	1,440,825	1,433,539	1,433,539
105	1,434,919	1,408,883	1,408,883
211	949,482	213,309	213,309
212	946,033	209,409	209,409
213	942,601	205,577	205,577
346	618,684	13,269	13,269
347	617,071	12,944	12,944
348	615,468	12,626	12,626
349	613,875	12,314	3,432
350	612,292	12,008	0
351	610,719	11,708	0
352	609,156	11,414	0
353	607,603	11,126	0
354	606,060	10,843	0
355	604,527	10,567	0
356	603,003	10,295	0
357	601,489	10,029	0

EXHIBIT 14	FJF-05 CMO Structure with One PAC Tranche and One Support Tranche	
Tranche	**Par Amount ($)**	**Coupon Rate (%)**
P (PAC)	243,800,000	7.5
S (Support)	156,200,000	7.5
Total	400,000,000	

Payment rules:

1. *For payment of monthly coupon interest:* Disburse monthly coupon interest to each tranche on the basis of the amount of principal outstanding for each tranche at the beginning of the month.

2. *For disbursement of principal payments:* Disburse principal payments to tranche P based on its schedule of principal repayments. Tranche P has priority with respect to current and future principal payments to satisfy the schedule. Any excess principal payments in a month over the amount necessary to satisfy the schedule for tranche P are paid to tranche S. When tranche S is completely paid off, all principal payments are to be made to tranche P regardless of the schedule.

par value of the six PAC tranches is equal to $243.8 million, which is the amount of the single PAC tranche in FJF-05. The schedule of principal repayments for selected months for each PAC bond is shown in Exhibit 17.

Exhibit 18 shows the average life for the six PAC tranches and the support tranche in FJF-06 at various prepayment speeds. From a PAC bond in FJF-05 with an average life of 7.26, six tranches have been created with an average life as short as 2.58 years (P-A) and as long as 16.92 years (P-F) if prepayments stay within 90 PSA and 300 PSA.

EXHIBIT 15	Average Life for PAC Tranche and Support Tranche in FJF-05 Assuming Various Prepayment Speeds (Years)	
Prepayment Rate (PSA)	**PAC Bond (P)**	**Support Bond (S)**
0	15.97	27.26
50	9.44	24.00
90	7.26	20.06
100	7.26	18.56
150	7.26	12.57
165	7.26	11.16
200	7.26	8.38
250	7.26	5.37
300	7.26	3.13
350	6.56	2.51
400	5.92	2.17
450	5.38	1.94
500	4.93	1.77
700	3.70	1.37

EXHIBIT 16	FJF-06: CMO Structure with Six PAC Tranches and a Support Tranche	
Tranche	**Par Amount ($)**	**Coupon Rate (%)**
P-A	85,000,000	7.5
P-B	8,000,000	7.5
P-C	35,000,000	7.5
P-D	45,000,000	7.5
P-E	40,000,000	7.5
P-F	30,800,000	7.5
S	156,200,000	7.5
Total	400,000,000	

Payment rules:

1. *For payment of monthly coupon interest:* Disburse monthly coupon interest to each tranche on the basis of the amount of principal outstanding of each tranche at the beginning of the month.

2. *For disbursement of principal payments:* Disburse monthly principal payments to tranches P-A to P-F based on their respective schedules of principal repayments. Tranche P-A has priority with respect to current and future principal payments to satisfy the schedule. Any excess principal payments in a month over the amount necessary to satisfy the schedule for tranche P-A are paid to tranche S. Once tranche P-A is completely paid off, tranche P-B has priority, then tranche P-C, etc. When tranche S is completely paid off, all principal payments are to be made to the remaining PAC tranches in order of priority regardless of the schedule.

As expected, the average lives are stable if the prepayment speed is between 90 PSA and 300 PSA. Notice that even outside this range the average life is stable for several of the PAC tranches. For example, the PAC P-A tranche is stable even if prepayment speeds are as high as 400 PSA. For the PAC P-B, the average life does not vary when prepayments are in the initial collar until prepayments are greater than 350 PSA. Why is it that the shorter the PAC, the more protection it has against faster prepayments?

To understand this phenomenon, remember there are $156.2 million in support tranches that are protecting the $85 million of PAC P-A. Thus, even if prepayments are faster than the initial upper collar, there may be sufficient support tranches to assure the satisfaction of the schedule. In fact, as can be seen from Exhibit 18, even if prepayments are 400 PSA over the life of the collateral, the average life is unchanged.

Now consider PAC P-B. The support tranches provide protection for both the $85 million of PAC P-A and $93 million of PAC P-B. As can be seen from Exhibit 18, prepayments could be 350 PSA and the average life is still unchanged. From Exhibit 18 it can be seen that the degree of protection against contraction risk increases the shorter the PAC. Thus, while the initial collar may be 90 to 300 PSA, the effective collar is wider for the shorter PAC tranches.

2. PAC Window

The length of time over which expected principal repayments are made is referred to as the window. For a PAC tranche it is referred to as the PAC window. A PAC window can be wide or narrow. The narrower a PAC window, the more it resembles a corporate bond with a bullet payment. For example, if the PAC schedule calls for just one principal payment (the narrowest window) in month

EXHIBIT 17	Mortgage Balance ($) for Selected Months for FJF-06 Assuming 165 PSA						
	Tranche						
Month	A	B	C	D	E	F	Support
1	85,000,000	8,000,000	35,000,000	45,000,000	40,000,000	30,800,000	156,200,000
2	84,491,830	8,000,000	35,000,000	45,000,000	40,000,000	30,800,000	155,998,246
3	83,921,987	8,000,000	35,000,000	45,000,000	40,000,000	30,800,000	155,746,193
4	83,290,609	8,000,000	35,000,000	45,000,000	40,000,000	30,800,000	155,444,011
5	82,597,868	8,000,000	35,000,000	45,000,000	40,000,000	30,800,000	155,091,931
6	81,843,958	8,000,000	35,000,000	45,000,000	40,000,000	30,800,000	154,690,254
7	81,029,108	8,000,000	35,000,000	45,000,000	40,000,000	30,800,000	154,239,345
8	80,153,572	8,000,000	35,000,000	45,000,000	40,000,000	30,800,000	153,739,635
9	79,217,631	8,000,000	35,000,000	45,000,000	40,000,000	30,800,000	153,191,621
10	78,221,599	8,000,000	35,000,000	45,000,000	40,000,000	30,800,000	152,595,864
11	77,165,814	8,000,000	35,000,000	45,000,000	40,000,000	30,800,000	151,952,989
12	76,050,644	8,000,000	35,000,000	45,000,000	40,000,000	30,800,000	151,263,687
13	74,876,484	8,000,000	35,000,000	45,000,000	40,000,000	30,800,000	150,528,708
52	5,170,458	8,000,000	35,000,000	45,000,000	40,000,000	30,800,000	109,392,664
53	3,379,318	8,000,000	35,000,000	45,000,000	40,000,000	30,800,000	108,552,721
54	1,595,779	8,000,000	35,000,000	45,000,000	40,000,000	30,800,000	107,728,453
55	0	7,819,804	35,000,000	45,000,000	40,000,000	30,800,000	106,919,692
56	0	6,051,358	35,000,000	45,000,000	40,000,000	30,800,000	106,126,275
57	0	4,290,403	35,000,000	45,000,000	40,000,000	30,800,000	105,348,040
58	0	2,536,904	35,000,000	45,000,000	40,000,000	30,800,000	104,584,824
59	0	790,826	35,000,000	45,000,000	40,000,000	30,800,000	103,836,469
60	0	0	34,052,132	45,000,000	40,000,000	30,800,000	103,102,817
61	0	0	32,320,787	45,000,000	40,000,000	30,800,000	102,383,711
62	0	0	30,596,756	45,000,000	40,000,000	30,800,000	101,678,995
78	0	0	3,978,669	45,000,000	40,000,000	30,800,000	92,239,836
79	0	0	2,373,713	45,000,000	40,000,000	30,800,000	91,757,440
80	0	0	775,460	45,000,000	40,000,000	30,800,000	91,286,887
81	0	0	0	44,183,878	40,000,000	30,800,000	90,828,046
82	0	0	0	42,598,936	40,000,000	30,800,000	90,380,792
83	0	0	0	41,020,601	40,000,000	30,800,000	89,944,997
108	0	0	0	3,758,505	40,000,000	30,800,000	82,288,542
109	0	0	0	2,421,125	40,000,000	30,800,000	82,030,119
110	0	0	0	1,106,780	40,000,000	30,800,000	81,762,929
111	0	0	0	0	39,815,082	30,800,000	81,487,234
112	0	0	0	0	38,545,648	30,800,000	81,203,294
113	0	0	0	0	37,298,104	30,800,000	80,911,362

(Exhibit continued on next page . . .)

EXHIBIT 17	(continued)

| | | | | Tranche | | | |
Month	A	B	C	D	E	F	Support
153	0	0	0	0	1,715,140	30,800,000	65,030,732
154	0	0	0	0	1,107,570	30,800,000	64,575,431
155	0	0	0	0	510,672	30,800,000	64,119,075
156	0	0	0	0	0	30,724,266	63,661,761
157	0	0	0	0	0	30,148,172	63,203,587
158	0	0	0	0	0	29,582,215	62,744,644
347	0	0	0	0	0	29,003	1,697,536
348	0	0	0	0	0	16,058	1,545,142
349	0	0	0	0	0	3,432	1,394,152
350	0	0	0	0	0	0	1,235,674
351	0	0	0	0	0	0	1,075,454
352	0	0	0	0	0	0	916,910
353	0	0	0	0	0	0	760,026
354	0	0	0	0	0	0	604,789
355	0	0	0	0	0	0	451,182
356	0	0	0	0	0	0	299,191
357	0	0	0	0	0	0	148,801

120 and only interest payments up to month 120, this PAC tranche would resemble a 10-year (120-month) corporate bond.

PAC buyers appear to prefer tight windows, although institutional investors facing a liability schedule are generally better off with a window that more closely matches their liabilities. Investor demand dictates the PAC windows that dealers will create. Investor demand in turn is governed by the nature of investor liabilities.

3. Effective Collars and Actual Prepayments

The creation of a mortgage-backed security cannot make prepayment risk disappear. This is true for both a passthrough and a CMO. Thus, the reduction in prepayment risk (both extension risk and contraction risk) that a PAC offers investors must come from somewhere.

Where does the prepayment protection come from? It comes from the support tranches. It is the support tranches that defer principal payments to the PAC tranches if the collateral prepayments are slow; support tranches do not receive any principal until the PAC tranches receive the scheduled principal repayment. This reduces the risk that the PAC tranches will extend. Similarly, it is the support tranches that absorb any principal payments in excess of the scheduled principal payments that are made. This reduces the contraction risk of the PAC tranches. Thus, the key to the prepayment protection offered by a PAC tranche is the amount of support tranches outstanding. If the support tranches are paid off quickly because of faster-than-expected prepayments, then

EXHIBIT 18	Average Life for the Six PAC Tranches in FJF-06 Assuming Various Prepayment Speeds					

Prepayment Rate (PSA)	PAC Bonds					
	P-A	**P-B**	**P-C**	**P-D**	**P-E**	**P-F**
0	8.46	14.61	16.49	19.41	21.91	23.76
50	3.58	6.82	8.36	11.30	14.50	18.20
90	2.58	4.72	5.78	7.89	10.83	16.92
100	2.58	4.72	5.78	7.89	10.83	16.92
150	2.58	4.72	5.78	7.89	10.83	16.92
165	2.58	4.72	5.78	7.89	10.83	16.92
200	2.58	4.72	5.78	7.89	10.83	16.92
250	2.58	4.72	5.78	7.89	10.83	16.92
300	2.58	4.72	5.78	7.89	10.83	16.92
350	2.58	4.72	5.44	6.95	9.24	14.91
400	2.57	4.37	4.91	6.17	8.33	13.21
450	2.50	3.97	4.44	5.56	7.45	11.81
500	2.40	3.65	4.07	5.06	6.74	10.65
700	2.06	2.82	3.10	3.75	4.88	7.51

there is no longer any protection for the PAC tranches. *In fact, in FJF-06, if the support tranche is paid off, the structure effectively becomes a sequential-pay CMO.*

The support tranches can be thought of as bodyguards for the PAC bondholders. When the bullets fly—i.e., prepayments occur—it is the bodyguards that get killed off first. The bodyguards are there to absorb the bullets. Once all the bodyguards are killed off (i.e., the support tranches paid off with faster-than-expected prepayments), the PAC tranches must fend for themselves: they are exposed to all the bullets. A PAC tranche in which all the support tranches have been paid off is called a busted PAC or broken PAC.

With the bodyguard metaphor for the support tranches in mind, let's consider two questions asked by investors in PAC tranches:

1. Will the schedule of principal repayments be satisfied if prepayments are faster than the initial upper collar?

2. Will the schedule of principal repayments be satisfied as long as prepayments stay within the initial collar?

a. Actual Prepayments Greater than the Initial Upper Collar

Let's address the first question. The initial upper collar for FJF-06 is 300 PSA. Suppose that actual prepayments are 500 PSA for seven consecutive months. Will this disrupt the schedule of principal repayments? The answer is: It depends!

There are two pieces of information we will need to answer this question. First, when does the 500 PSA occur? Second, what has been the actual prepayment experience up to the time that prepayments are 500 PSA? For example, suppose six years from now is when the prepayments reach 500 PSA, and also suppose that for the past six years the actual prepayment speed has been 90 PSA every month. What this means is that there are more bodyguards (i.e., support tranches) around than were expected when the PAC was structured at the initial collar. In establishing the schedule of principal repayments, it is assumed that the bodyguards would be killed off at 300 PSA. (Recall that 300 PSA is the upper collar prepayment assumption used in creating FJF-06.) But the actual prepayment experience results in them being killed off at only 90 PSA. Thus, six years from now when the 500 PSA is assumed to occur, there are more bodyguards than expected. In turn, a 500 PSA for seven consecutive months may have no effect on the ability of the schedule of principal repayments to be met.

In contrast, suppose that the actual prepayment experience for the first six years is 300 PSA (the upper collar of the initial PAC collar). In this case, there are no extra bodyguards around. As a result, any prepayment speeds faster than 300 PSA, such as 500 PSA in our example, jeopardize satisfaction of the principal repayment schedule and increase contraction risk. This does not mean that the schedule will be "busted"—the term used in the CMO market when the support tranches are fully paid off. What it does mean is that the prepayment protection is reduced.

It should be clear from these observations that the initial collars are not particularly useful in assessing the prepayment protection for a seasoned PAC tranche. This is most important to understand, as it is common for CMO buyers to compare prepayment protection of PACs in different CMO structures and conclude that the greater protection is offered by the one with the wider initial collar. This approach is inadequate because it is actual prepayment experience that determines the degree of prepayment protection, as well as the expected future prepayment behavior of the collateral.

The way to determine this protection is to calculate the effective collar for a seasoned PAC bond. An effective collar for a seasoned PAC is the lower and the upper PSA that can occur in the future and still allow maintenance of the schedule of principal repayments. For example, consider two seasoned PAC tranches in two CMO structures where the two PAC tranches have the same average life and the prepayment characteristics of the remaining collateral (i.e., the remaining mortgages in the mortgage pools) are similar. The information about these PAC tranches is as follows:

	PAC Tranche X	PAC Tranche Y
Initial PAC collar	180 PSA–350 PSA	170 PSA–410 PSA
Effective PAC collar	160 PSA–450 PSA	240 PSA–300 PSA

Notice that at issuance PAC tranche Y offered greater prepayment protection than PAC tranche X as indicated by the *wider* initial PAC collar. However, that protection is irrelevant for an investor who is considering the purchase of one of these two tranches today. Despite PAC tranche Y's greater prepayment protection at issuance than PAC tranche X, tranche Y has a much narrower effective PAC collar than PAC tranche X and therefore less prepayment protection.

The effective collar changes every month. An extended period over which actual prepayments are below the upper range of the initial PAC collar will result in an increase in the upper range of the effective collar. This is because there will be more bodyguards around than anticipated. An extended period of prepayments slower than the lower range of the initial PAC collar will raise the lower range of the effective collar. This is because it will take faster prepayments to make up the shortfall of the scheduled principal payments not made plus the scheduled future principal payments.

b. Actual Prepayments within the Initial Collar

The PAC schedule may not be satisfied even if the actual prepayments never fall outside of the *initial* collar. This may seem surprising since our previous analysis indicated that the average life would not change if prepayments are at either extreme of the initial collar. However, recall that all of our previous analysis has been based on a single PSA speed for the life of the structure.

The table below shows for FJF-05 what happens to the effective collar if prepayments are 300 PSA for the first 24 months but another prepayment speed for the balance of the life of the structure.

PSA from Year 2 On	Average Life
95	6.43
105	6.11
115	6.01
120	6.00
125	6.00
300	6.00
305	5.62

Notice that the average life is stable at six years if the prepayments for the subsequent months are between 115 PSA and 300 PSA. That is, the effective PAC collar is no longer the initial collar. Instead, the lower collar has shifted upward. This means that the protection from year 2 on is for 115 to 300 PSA, a narrower band than initially (90 to 300 PSA), even though the earlier prepayments did not exceed the initial upper collar.

F. Support Tranches

The support tranches are the bonds that provide prepayment protection for the PAC tranches. Consequently, support tranches expose investors to the greatest level of prepayment risk. Because of this, investors must be particularly careful in assessing the cash flow characteristics of support tranches to reduce the likelihood of adverse portfolio consequences due to prepayments.

The support tranche typically is divided into different tranches. All the tranches we have discussed earlier are available, including sequential-pay support tranches, floater and inverse floater support tranches, and accrual support tranches.

The support tranche can even be partitioned to create support tranches with a schedule of principal payments. That is, support tranches that are PAC tranches can be created. In a structure with a PAC tranche and a support tranche with a PAC schedule of principal payments, the former is called a PAC I tranche or Level I PAC tranche and the latter a PAC II tranche or Level II PAC tranche or scheduled tranche (denoted SCH in a prospectus). While PAC II tranches have greater prepayment protection than the support tranches without a schedule of principal repayments, the prepayment protection is less than that provided PAC I tranches.

The support tranche without a principal repayment schedule can be used to create any type of tranche. In fact, a portion of the non-PAC II support tranche can be given a schedule of principal repayments. This tranche would be called a PAC III tranche or a Level III PAC tranche. While it provides protection against prepayments for the PAC I and PAC II tranches and is therefore subject to considerable prepayment risk, such a tranche has greater protection than the support tranche without a schedule of principal repayments.

G. An Actual CMO Structure

Thus far we have presented some hypothetical CMO structures in order to demonstrate the characteristics of the different types of tranches. Now let's look at an actual CMO structure, one that we will look at further when we discuss how to analyze a CMO deal in the reading on valuing mortgage-backed and asset-backed securities.

The CMO structure we will discuss is the Freddie Mac (FHLMC) Series 1706 issued in early 1994. The collateral for this structure is Freddie Mac 7% coupon passthroughs. A summary of the deal is provided in Exhibit 19.

There are 17 tranches in this structure: 10 PAC tranches, three scheduled tranches, a floating-rate support tranche, and an inverse floating-rate support tranche.[11] There are also two "TAC" support tranches. We will explain a TAC tranche below. Let's look at all tranches.

First, we know what a PAC tranche is. There are 10 of them: tranches A, B, C, D, E, G, H, J, K, and IA. The initial collar used to create the PAC tranches was 95 PSA to 300 PSA. The PAC tranches except for tranche IA are simply PACs that pay off in sequence. Tranche IA is structured such that the underlying collateral's interest not allocated to the other PAC tranches is paid to the IO tranche. This is a notional IO tranche and we described earlier in this section how it is created. In this deal the tranches from which the interest is stripped are the PAC tranches. So, tranche IA is referred to as a PAC IO. (As of the time of this writing, tranches A and B had already paid off all of their principal.)

The prepayment protection for the PAC bonds is provided by the support tranches. The support tranches in this deal are tranches LA, LB, M, O, OA, PF, and PS. Notice that the support tranches have been carved up in different ways. First, there are scheduled (SCH) tranches. These are what we have called the PAC II tranches earlier in this section. The scheduled tranches are LA, LB, and M. The initial PAC collar used to create the scheduled tranches was 190 PSA to 250 PSA.

There are two support tranches that are designed such that they are created with a schedule that provides protection against contraction risk but not against extension. We did not discuss these tranches in this reading. They are called target amortization class (TAC) tranches. The support tranches O and OA are TAC tranches. The schedule of principal payments is created by using just a single PSA. In this structure the single PSA is 225 PSA.

Finally, the support tranche without a schedule (that must provide support for the scheduled bonds and the PACs) was carved into two tranches—a floater (tranche PF) and an inverse floater (tranche PS). In this structure the creation of the floater and inverse floater was from a support tranche.

Now that we know what all these tranches are, the next step is to analyze them in terms of their relative value and their price volatility characteristics when rates change. We will do this in the reading on valuing mortgage-backed and asset-backed securities.

---

[11] Actually there were two other tranches, R and RS, called "residuals." These tranches were not described in the reading. They receive any excess cash flows remaining after the payment of all the tranches. The residual is actually the equity part of the deal.

EXHIBIT 19	Summary of Federal Home Loan Mortgage Corporation—Multiclass Mortgage Participation Certificates (Guaranteed), Series 1706

Total Issue: $300,000,000   Original Settlement Date: 3/30/94

Issue Date: 2/18/94

Tranche	Original Balance ($)	Coupon (%)	Average Life (Yrs)
A (PAC Bond)	24,600,000	4.50	1.3
B (PAC Bond)	11,100,000	5.00	2.5
C (PAC Bond)	25,500,000	5.25	3.5
D (PAC Bond)	9,150,000	5.65	4.5
E (PAC Bond)	31,650,000	6.00	5.8
G (PAC Bond)	30,750,000	6.25	7.9
H (PAC Bond)	27,450,000	6.50	10.9
J (PAC Bond)	5,220,000	6.50	14.4
K (PAC Bond)	7,612,000	7.00	18.8
LA (SCH Bond)	26,673,000	7.00	3.5
LB (SCH Bond)	36,087,000	7.00	3.5
M (SCH Bond)	18,738,000	7.00	11.2
O (TAC Bond)	13,348,000	7.00	2.5
OA (TAC Bond)	3,600,000	7.00	7.2
IA (IO, PAC Bond)	30,246,000	7.00	7.1
PF (FLTR, Support Bond)	21,016,000	6.75[a]	17.5
PS (INV FLTR, Support Bond)	7,506,000	7.70[a]	17.5

[a] Coupon at issuance.

Structural Features:

Cash Flow Allocation: Commencing on the first principal payment date of the Class A Bonds, principal equal to the amount specified in the Prospectus will be applied to the Class A, B, C, D, E, G, H, J, K, LA, LB, M, O, OA, PF, and PS Bonds. After all other Classes have been retired, any remaining principal will be used to retire the Class O, OA, LA, LB, M, A, B, C, D, E, G, H, J, and K Bonds. The Notional Class IA Bond will have its notional principal amount retired along with the PAC Bonds.

Other: The PAC Range is 95% to 300% PSA for the A–K Bonds, 190% to 250% PSA for the LA, LB, and M Bonds, and 225% PSA for the O and OA Bonds.

STRIPPED MORTGAGE-BACKED SECURITIES   5

In a CMO, there are multiple bond classes (tranches) and separate rules for the distribution of the interest and the principal to the bond classes. There are mortgage-backed securities where there are only two bond classes and the rule for the distribution for interest and principal is simple: one bond class receives all of the principal and one bond class receives all of the interest. This mortgage-backed security is called a stripped mortgage-backed security. The bond class that receives all of the principal is called the principal-only class or PO class. The bond class that receives all of the interest is called the interest-only class or IO class. These securities are also called mortgage strips. The POs are called principal-only mortgage strips and the IOs are called interest-only mortgage strips.

We have already seen interest-only type mortgage-backed securities: the structured IO. This is a product that is created within a CMO structure. A structured IO is created from the excess interest (i.e., the difference between the interest paid on the collateral and the interest paid to the bond classes). There is no corresponding PO class within the CMO structure. In contrast, in a stripped mortgage-backed security, the IO class is created by simply specifying that all interest payments be made to that class.

A. Principal-Only Strips

A principal-only mortgage strip is purchased at a substantial discount from par value. The return an investor realizes depends on the speed at which prepayments are made. The faster the prepayments, the higher the investor's return. For example, suppose that a pool of 30-year mortgages has a par value of $400 million and the market value of the pool of mortgages is also $400 million. Suppose further that the market value of just the principal payments is $175 million. The dollar return from this investment is the difference between the par value of $400 million that will be repaid to the investor in the principal mortgage strip and the $175 million paid. That is, the dollar return is $225 million.

Since there is no interest that will be paid to the investor in a principal-only mortgage strip, the investor's return is determined solely by the speed at which he or she receives the $225 million. In the extreme case, if all homeowners in the underlying mortgage pool decide to prepay their mortgage loans immediately, PO investors will realize the $225 million immediately. At the other extreme, if all homeowners decide to remain in their homes for 30 years and make no prepayments, the $225 million will be spread out over 30 years, which would result in a lower return for PO investors.

Let's look at how the price of the PO would be expected to change as mortgage rates in the market change. When mortgage rates decline below the contract rate, prepayments are expected to speed up, accelerating payments to the PO investor. Thus, the cash flow of a PO improves (in the sense that principal repayments are received earlier). The cash flow will be discounted at a lower interest rate because the mortgage rate in the market has declined. The result is that the PO price will increase when mortgage rates decline. When mortgage rates rise above the contract rate, prepayments are expected to slow down. The cash flow deteriorates (in the sense that it takes longer to recover principal repayments). Couple this with a higher discount rate, and the price of a PO will fall when mortgage rates rise.

Exhibit 20 shows the general relationship between the price of a principal-only mortgage strip when interest rates change and compares it to the relationship for the underlying passthrough from which it is created.

B. Interest-Only Strips

An interest-only mortgage strip has no par value. In contrast to the PO investor, the IO investor wants prepayments to be slow. The reason is that the IO investor receives interest only on the amount of the principal outstanding. When prepayments are made, less dollar interest will be received as the outstanding principal declines. In fact, *if prepayments are too fast, the IO investor may not recover the amount paid for the IO even if the security is held to maturity.*

Let's look at the expected price response of an IO to changes in mortgage rates. If mortgage rates decline below the contract rate, prepayments are expected to accelerate. This would result in a deterioration of the expected cash flow for an IO. While the cash flow will be discounted at a lower rate, the net

EXHIBIT 20	Relationship between Price and Mortgage Rates for a Passthrough, PO, and IO

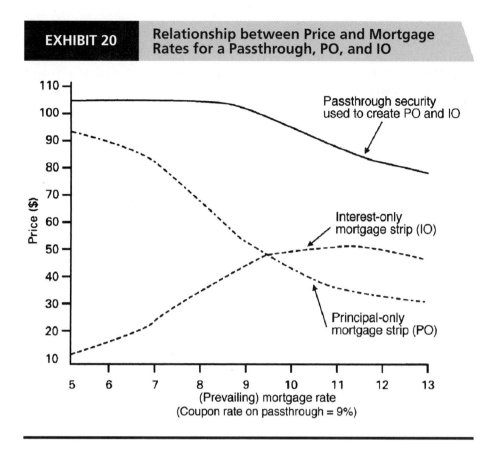

effect typically is a decline in the price of an IO. If mortgage rates rise above the contract rate, the expected cash flow improves, but the cash flow is discounted at a higher interest rate. The net effect may be either a rise or fall for the IO.

Thus, we see an interesting characteristic of an IO: its price tends to move in the same direction as the change in mortgage rates 1) when mortgage rates fall below the contract rate and 2) for some range of mortgage rates above the contract rate. Both POs and IOs exhibit substantial price volatility when mortgage rates change. The greater price volatility of the IO and PO compared to the passthrough from which they were created is due to the fact that the combined price volatility of the IO and PO must be equal to the price volatility of the passthrough.

Exhibit 20 shows the general relationship between the price of an interest-only mortgage strip when interest rates change and compares it to the relationship for the corresponding principal-only mortgage strip and underlying passthrough from which it is created.

An average life for a PO can be calculated based on some prepayment assumption. However, an IO receives no principal payments, so technically an average life cannot be computed. Instead, for an IO a cash flow average life is computed, using the projected interest payments in the average life formula instead of principal.

C. Trading and Settlement Procedures

The trading and settlement procedures for stripped mortgage-backed securities are similar to those set by the Public Securities Association for agency passthroughs described in Section 3.C. IOs and POs are extreme premium and discount securities and consequently are very sensitive to prepayments, which are driven by the specific characteristics (weighted average coupon, weighted average maturity, geographic concentration, average loan size) of the underlying loans. Therefore, almost all secondary trades in IOs and POs are on a specified pool basis rather than on a TBA basis.

All IOs and POs are given a trust number. For instance, Fannie Mae Trust 1 is a IO/PO trust backed by specific pools of Fannie Mae 9% mortgages. Fannie Mae Trust 2 is backed by Fannie Mae 10% mortgages. Fannie Mae Trust 23 is another IO/PO trust backed by Fannie Mae 10% mortgages. Therefore, a portfolio manager must specify which trust he or she is buying.

The total proceeds of a PO trade are calculated the same way as with a passthrough trade except that there is no accrued interest. The market trades IOs based on notional principal. The proceeds include the price on the notional amount and the accrued interest.

6   NONAGENCY RESIDENTIAL MORTGAGE-BACKED SECURITIES

In the previous sections we looked at agency mortgage-backed securities in which the underlying mortgages are 1- to 4-single-family residential mortgages. The mortgage-backed securities market includes other types of securities. These securities are called nonagency mortgage-backed securities (referred to as nonagency securities hereafter).

The underlying mortgage loans for nonagency securities can be for any type of real estate property. There are securities backed by 1- to 4-single family residential mortgages with a first lien (i.e., the lender has a first priority or first claim) on the mortgaged property. There are nonagency securities backed by other types of single family residential loans. These include home equity loan-backed securities and manufactured housing-loan backed securities. Our focus in this section is on nonagency securities in which the underlying loans are first-lien mortgages for 1- to 4-single-family residential properties.

As with an agency mortgage-backed security, the servicer is responsible for the collection of interest and principal. The servicer also handles delinquencies and foreclosures. Typically, there will be a master servicer and subservicers. The servicer plays a key role. In fact, in assessing the credit risk of a nonagency security, rating companies look carefully at the quality of the servicers.

A. Underlying Mortgage Loans

The underlying loans for agency securities are those that conform to the underwriting standards of the agency issuing or guaranteeing the issue. That is, only conforming loans are included in pools that are collateral for an agency mortgage-backed security. The three main underwriting standards deal with

1. the maximum loan-to-value ratio
2. the maximum payment-to-income ratio
3. the maximum loan amount

The loan-to-value ratio (LTV) is the ratio of the amount of the loan to the market value or appraised value of the property. The *lower* the LTV, the *greater* the protection afforded the lender. For example, an LTV of 0.90 means that if the lender has to repossess the property and sell it, the lender must realize at least 90% of the market value in order to recover the amount lent. An LTV of 0.80 means that the lender only has to sell the property for 80% of its market value in order to recover the amount lent.[12] Empirical studies of residential mortgage loans have found that the LTV is a key determinant of whether a borrower will default: the higher the LTV, the greater the likelihood of default.

As mentioned earlier in this reading, a nonconforming mortgage loan is one that does not conform to the underwriting standards established by any of the agencies. Typically, the loans for a nonagency security are nonconforming mortgage loans that fail to qualify for inclusion because the amount of the loan exceeds the limit established by the agencies. Such loans are referred to as jumbo loans. Jumbo loans do not necessarily have greater credit risk than conforming mortgages.

Loans that fail to qualify because of the first two underwriting standards expose the lender to greater credit risk than conforming loans. There are specialized lenders who provide mortgage loans to individuals who fail to qualify for a conforming loan because of their credit history. These specialized lenders classify borrowers by credit quality. Borrowers are classified as A borrowers, B borrowers, C borrowers, and D borrowers. A borrowers are those that are viewed as having the best credit record. Such borrowers are referred to as prime borrowers. Borrowers rated below A are viewed as subprime borrowers. However, there is no industry-wide classification system for prime and subprime borrowers.

B. Differences between Agency and Nonagency Securities

Nonagency securities can be either passthroughs or CMOs. In the agency market, CMOs are created from pools of passthrough securities. In the nonagency market, CMOs are created from unsecuritized mortgage loans. Since a mortgage loan not securitized as a passthrough is called a whole loan, nonagency CMOs are commonly referred to as whole-loan CMOs.

The major difference between agency and nonagency securities has to do with guarantees. With a nonagency security there is no explicit or implicit government guarantee of payment of interest and principal as there is with an agency security. The absence of any such guarantee means that the investor in a nonagency security is exposed to credit risk. The nationally recognized statistical rating organizations rate nonagency securities.

Because of the credit risk, all nonagency securities are credit enhanced. By credit enhancement it means that additional support against defaults must be obtained. The amount of credit enhancement needed is determined relative to a specific rating desired for a security rating agency. There are two general types of credit enhancement mechanisms: external and internal. We describe each of these types of credit enhancement in the reading on the asset-backed sector of the bond market where we cover asset-backed securities.

---

[12] This ignores the costs of repossession and selling the property.

7

COMMERCIAL MORTGAGE-BACKED SECURITIES

Commercial mortgage-backed securities (CMBSs) are backed by a pool of commercial mortgage loans on income-producing property—multifamily properties (i.e., apartment buildings), office buildings, industrial properties (including warehouses), shopping centers, hotels, and health care facilities (i.e., senior housing care facilities). The basic building block of the CMBS transaction is a commercial loan that was originated either to finance a commercial purchase or to refinance a prior mortgage obligation.

There are two types of CMBS deal structures that have been of primary interest to bond investors: 1) multiproperty single borrower and 2) multiproperty conduit. Conduits are commercial-lending entities that are established for the sole purpose of generating collateral to securitize.

CMBS have been issued outside the United States. The dominant issues have been U.K. based (more than 80% in 2000), with the primary property types being retail and office properties. Starting in 2001, there was a dramatic increase in the number of CMBS deals issued by German banks. An increasing number of deals include multi-country properties. The first pan-European securitization was Pan European Industrial Properties in 2001.[13]

A. Credit Risk

Unlike residential mortgage loans where the lender relies on the ability of the borrower to repay and may have recourse to the borrower if the payment terms are not satisfied, commercial mortgage loans are nonrecourse loans. This means that the lender can only look to the income-producing property backing the loan for interest and principal repayment. If there is a default, the lender looks to the proceeds from the sale of the property for repayment and has no recourse to the borrower for any unpaid balance. The lender must view each property as a stand-alone business and evaluate each property using measures that have been found useful in assessing credit risk.

While fundamental principles of assessing credit risk apply to all property types, traditional approaches to assessing the credit risk of the collateral differs between CMBS and nonagency mortgage-backed securities and real estate-backed securities that fall into the asset-backed securities sector (those backed by home equity loans and manufactured housing loans). For mortgage-backed securities and asset-backed securities in which the collateral is residential property, typically the loans are lumped into buckets based on certain loan characteristics, and then assumptions regarding default rates are made regarding each bucket. In contrast, for commercial mortgage loans, the unique economic characteristics of each income-producing property in a pool backing a CMBS require that credit analysis be performed on a loan-by-loan basis not only at the time of issuance, but monitored on an ongoing basis.

Regardless of the type of commercial property, the two measures that have been found to be key indicators of the potential credit performance is the debt-to-service coverage ratio and the loan-to-value ratio.

The debt-to-service coverage ratio (DSC) is the ratio of the property's net operating income (NOI) divided by the debt service. The NOI is defined as

---

[13] Christopher Flanagan and Edward Reardon, *European Structures Products: 2001 Review and 2002 Outlook*, Global Structured Finance Research, J.P. Morgan Securities Inc. (January 11, 2002), pp. 12–13.

the rental income reduced by cash operating expenses (adjusted for a replacement reserve). A ratio greater than 1 means that the cash flow from the property is sufficient to cover debt servicing. The higher the ratio, the more likely that the borrower will be able to meet debt servicing from the property's cash flow.

For all properties backing a CMBS deal, a weighted average DSC ratio is computed. An analysis of the credit quality of an issue will also look at the dispersion of the DSC ratios for the underlying loans. For example, one might look at the percentage of a deal with a DSC ratio below a certain value.

As explained in Section 6.A, in computing the LTV, the figure used for "value" in the ratio is either market value or appraised value. In valuing commercial property, it is typically the appraised value. There can be considerable variation in the estimates of the property's appraised value. Thus, analysts tend to be skeptical about estimates of appraised value and the resulting LTVs reported for properties.

B. Basic CMBS Structure

As with any structured finance transaction, a rating agency will determine the necessary level of credit enhancement to achieve a desired rating level. For example, if certain DSC and LTV ratios are needed, and these ratios cannot be met at the loan level, then "subordination" is used to achieve these levels. By subordination it is meant that there will be bond classes in the structure whose claims on the cash flow of the collateral are subordinated to that of other bond classes in the structure.

The rating agencies will require that the CMBS transaction be retired sequentially, with the highest-rated bonds paying off first. Therefore, any return of principal caused by amortization, prepayment, or default will be used to repay the highest-rated tranche.

Interest on principal outstanding will be paid to all tranches. In the event of a delinquency resulting in insufficient cash to make all scheduled payments, the transaction's servicer will advance both principal and interest. Advancing will continue from the servicer for as long as these amounts are deemed recoverable.

Losses arising from loan defaults will be charged against the principal balance of the lowest-rated CMBS tranche outstanding. The total loss charged will include the amount previously advanced as well as the actual loss incurred in the sale of the loan's underlying property.

1. Call Protection

A critical investment feature that distinguishes residential MBS and commercial MBS is the call protection afforded an investor. An investor in a residential MBS is exposed to considerable prepayment risk because the borrower has the right to prepay a loan, in whole or in part, before the scheduled principal repayment date. Typically, the borrower does not pay any penalty for prepayment. When we discussed CMOs, we saw how certain types of tranches (e.g., sequential-pay and PAC tranches) can be purchased by an investor to reduce prepayment risk.

With CMBS, there is considerable call protection afforded investors. In fact, it is this protection that results in CMBS trading in the market more like corporate bonds than residential MBS. This call protection comes in two forms: 1) call protection at the loan level and 2) call protection at the structure level. We discuss both below.

a. Protection at the Loan Level

At the commercial loan level, call protection can take the following forms:

1. prepayment lockout
2. defeasance
3. prepayment penalty points
4. yield maintenance charges

A prepayment lockout is a contractual agreement that prohibits any prepayments during a specified period of time, called the lockout period. The lockout period at issuance can be from 2 to 5 years. After the lockout period, call protection comes in the form of either prepayment penalty points or yield maintenance charges. Prepayment lockout and defeasance are the strongest forms of prepayment protection.

With defeasance, rather than loan prepayment, the borrower provides sufficient funds for the servicer to invest in a portfolio of Treasury securities that replicates the cash flows that would exist in the absence of prepayments. Unlike the other call protection provisions discussed next, there is no distribution made to the bondholders when the defeasance takes place. So, since there are no penalties, there is no issue as to how any penalties paid by the borrower are to be distributed amongst the bondholders in a CMBS structure. Moreover, the substitution of the cash flow of a Treasury portfolio for that of the borrower improves the credit quality of the CMBS deal.

Prepayment penalty points are predetermined penalties that must be paid by the borrower if the borrower wishes to refinance. (A point is equal to 1% of the outstanding loan balance.) For example, 5-4-3-2-1 is a common prepayment penalty point structure. That is, if the borrower wishes to prepay during the first year, the borrower must pay a 5% penalty for a total of $105 rather than $100 (which is the norm in the residential market). Likewise, during the second year, a 4% penalty would apply, and so on.

When there are prepayment penalty points, there are rules for distributing the penalty among the tranches. Prepayment penalty points are not common in new CMBS structures. Instead, the next form of call protection discussed, yield maintenance charges, is more commonly used.

Yield maintenance charge, in its simplest terms, is designed to make the lender indifferent as to the timing of prepayments. The yield maintenance charge, also called the make-whole charge, makes it uneconomical to refinance solely to get a lower mortgage rate. While there are several methods used in practice for calculating the yield maintenance charge, the key principle is to make the lender whole. However, when a commercial loan is included as part of a CMBS deal, there must be an allocation of the yield maintenance charge amongst the tranches. Several methods are used in practice for distributing the yield maintenance charge and, depending on the method specified in a deal, not all tranches may be made whole.

b. Structural Protection

The other type of call protection available in CMBS transactions is structural. Because the CMBS bond structures are sequential-pay (by rating), the AA-rated tranche cannot pay down until the AAA is completely retired, and the AA-rated bonds must be paid off before the A-rated bonds, and so on. However, principal losses due to defaults are impacted from the bottom of the structure upward.

2. *Balloon Maturity Provisions*

Many commercial loans backing CMBS transactions are balloon loans that require substantial principal payment at the end of the term of the loan. If the borrower fails to make the balloon payment, the borrower is in default. The lender may extend the loan, and in so doing may modify the original loan terms. During the workout period for the loan, a higher interest rate will be charged, called the default interest rate.

The risk that a borrower will not be able to make the balloon payment because either the borrower cannot arrange for refinancing at the balloon payment date or cannot sell the property to generate sufficient funds to pay off the balloon balance is called balloon risk. Since the term of the loan will be extended by the lender during the workout period, balloon risk is a type of "extension risk." This is the same risk that we referred to earlier in describing residential mortgage-backed securities.

Although many investors like the "bullet bond-like" paydown of the balloon maturities, it does present difficulties from a structural standpoint. That is, if the deal is structured to completely pay down on a specified date, an event of default will occur if any delays occur. However, how such delays impact CMBS investors is dependent on the bond type (premium, par, or discount) and whether the servicer will advance to a particular tranche after the balloon default.

Another concern for CMBS investors in multitranche transactions is the fact that all loans must be refinanced to pay off the most senior bondholders. Therefore, the balloon risk of the most senior tranche (i.e., AAA) may be equivalent to that of the most junior tranche (i.e., B).

SUMMARY

▶ The basic mortgage-backed security is the mortgage passthrough security created from a pool of mortgage loans.

▶ Agency passthrough securities are those issued/guaranteed by Ginnie Mae, Fannie Mae, and Freddie Mac.

▶ The cash flow of a passthrough includes net interest, scheduled principal repayments (i.e., scheduled amortization), and prepayments.

▶ Any amount paid in excess of the required monthly mortgage payment is a prepayment; the cash flow of a mortgage-backed security is unknown because of prepayments.

▶ A projection of prepayments is necessary to project the cash flow of a passthrough security.

▶ The single monthly mortality (SMM) rate is the ratio of the amount of prepayments divided by the amount available to prepay (i.e., outstanding mortgage balance at the beginning of the month minus the scheduled principal payment for the month).

▶ The PSA prepayment benchmark is a series of conditional prepayment rates and is simply a market convention that describes in general the pattern of prepayments.

▶ A measure commonly used to estimate the life of a passthrough is its average life.

▶ The prepayment risk associated with investing in mortgage passthrough securities can be decomposed into contraction risk and extension risk.

▶ Prepayment risk makes passthrough securities unattractive for certain financial institutions to hold from an asset/liability perspective.

▶ The three factors that affect prepayments are 1) the prevailing mortgage rate, 2) normal housing turnover, and 3) characteristics of the underlying mortgage pool.

▶ Collateralized mortgage obligations are bond classes created by redirecting the interest and principal from a pool of passthroughs or whole loans.

▶ The creation of a CMO cannot eliminate prepayment risk; it can only transfer the various forms of this risk among different classes of bonds called tranches.

▶ From a fixed-rate CMO tranche, a floating-rate tranche and an inverse floating-rate tranche can be created.

▶ A notional interest-only tranche (also called a structured IO) can be created from the excess interest available from other tranches in the structure; excess interest is the difference between the collateral's coupon rate and a tranche's coupon rate.

▶ The amortization schedule for a planned amortization class is structured based on a lower PSA prepayment assumption and an upper PSA prepayment assumption—called the initial PAC collar.

▶ A planned amortization class (PAC) tranche has reduced average life variability, the better prepayment protection provided by the support tranches.

▶ If the collateral from which a PAC bond is created pays at a constant PSA rate that is anywhere within the initial PAC collar, the amortization schedule will be satisfied.

▶ Over time, the prepayment collar that will be able to support the PAC tranches (i.e., provide the prepayment protection) changes as the amount of the support tranches change.

▶ The effective collar is the lower and upper PSA prepayment rates that can occur in the future and still be able to satisfy the amortization schedule for the PAC tranche.

▶ The key to the prepayment protection for the PAC tranches is the support tranches.

▶ The support tranches are exposed to the greatest prepayment risk of all the tranches in a CMO structure and greater prepayment risk than the collateral (i.e., passthrough securities) from which a deal is created.

▶ Support tranches with a PAC schedule can be created from the support tranches; these tranches are still support tranches but they have better prepayment protection than other support tranches in the structure that do not have a schedule.

▶ A stripped mortgage-backed security is a derivative mortgage-backed security that is created by redistributing the interest and principal payments to two different classes.

▶ A principal-only mortgage strip (PO) benefits from declining interest rates and fast prepayments.

▶ An interest-only mortgage strip (IO) benefits from rising interest rates and a slowing of prepayments; if rates fall instead, the investor in an interest-only security may not realize the amount invested even if the security is held to maturity.

▶ Nonagency securities are not backed by any federal government agency guarantee.

▶ The underlying loans for nonagency securities are nonconforming mortgage loans—loans that do not qualify for inclusion in mortgage pools that underlie agency mortgage-backed securities.

▶ Credit enhancement is needed to support nonagency mortgage-backed securities.

▶ Credit enhancement levels are determined relative to a specific rating desired for a security and there are two general types of credit enhancement structures—external and internal.

▶ Commercial mortgage-backed securities are backed by a pool of commercial mortgage loans—loans on income-producing property.

▶ Unlike residential mortgage loans where the lender relies on the ability of the borrower to repay and has recourse to the borrower if the payment terms are not satisfied, commercial mortgage loans are nonrecourse loans, and as a result the lender can only look to the income-producing property backing the loan for interest and principal repayment.

▶ Two measures that have been found to be key indicators of the potential credit performance of a commercial mortgage loan are the debt-to-service coverage ratio (i.e., the property's net operating income divided by the debt service) and the loan-to-value ratio.

▶ The degree of call protection available to a CMBS investor is a function of 1) call protection available at the loan level and 2) call protection afforded from the actual CMBS structure.

▶ At the commercial loan level, call protection can be in the form of a prepayment lockout, defeasance, prepayment penalty points, or yield maintenance charges.

▶ Many commercial loans backing CMBS transactions are balloon loans that require substantial principal payment at the end of the balloon term and therefore the investor faces balloon risk—the risk that the loan will extend beyond the scheduled maturity date.

PRACTICE PROBLEMS FOR READING 51

1. A. Complete the following schedule for a 30-year fully amortizing mortgage loan with a mortgage rate of 7.25% where the amount borrowed is $150,000. The monthly mortgage payment is $1,023.26.

Month	Beginning Mortgage ($)	Mortgage Payment ($)	Interest ($)	Sch. Prin. Repayment ($)	End-of-Month Balance ($)
1	150,000.00	1,023.26			
2		1,023.26			
3		1,023.26			
4		1,023.26			
5		1,023.26			
6		1,023.26			
7		1,023.26			
8		1,023.26			
9		1,023.26			
10		1,023.26			
11		1,023.26			
12		1,023.26			
13		1,023.26			
14		1,023.26			

B. Complete the following schedule for the mortgage loan in part A given the following information:

Month	Beginning Mortgage ($)	Mortgage Payment ($)	Interest ($)	Sch. Prin. Repayment ($)	End-of-Month Balance ($)
357	4,031.97	1,023.26			
358		1,023.26			
359		1,023.26			
360		1,023.26			

2. A. Suppose that the servicing fee for a mortgage loan is 0.5%. Complete the following schedule for the mortgage loan in the previous question. The column labeled "Servicing Fee" is the dollar amount of the servicing fee for the month. The column labeled "Net Interest" is the monthly interest after the servicing fee for the month.

Month	Beginning Mortgage ($)	Mortgage Payment ($)	Servicing Fee ($)	Net Interest ($)	Sch. Prin. Repayment ($)	End-of-Month Balance ($)
1						
2						
3						
4						
5						
6						

B. Determine for the first six months the cash flow for an investor who purchases this mortgage loan after the servicing fee is paid.

3. Explain why you agree or disagree with the following statement: "Since mortgage passthrough securities issued by Ginnie Mae are guaranteed by the full faith and credit of the U.S. government, there is no uncertainty about the cash flow for the security."

4. Consider the following mortgage pool.

Loan	Outstanding Mortgage Balance ($)	Mortgage Rate (%)	Months Remaining
1	215,000	6.75	200
2	185,000	7.75	185
3	125,000	7.25	192
4	100,000	7.00	210
5	200,000	6.50	180
Total	825,000		

A. What is the weighted average coupon rate for this mortgage pool?

B. What is the weighted average maturity for this mortgage pool?

5. Mr. Jamison is looking at the historical prepayment for a passthrough security. He finds the following:

mortgage balance in month 42	=	$260,000,000
scheduled principal payment in month 42	=	$1,000,000
prepayment in month 42	=	$2,450,000

  A. What is the SMM for month 42?
  B. How should Mr. Jamison interpret the SMM computed?
  C. What is the CPR for month 42?
  D. How should Mr. Jamison interpret the CPR computed?

6. Using the Public Securities Association Prepayment benchmark, complete the following table:

Month	PSA	CPR	SMM
5	100		
15	80		
20	175		
27	50		
88	200		
136	75		
220	225		

7. Explain why 30 months after the origination of a mortgage pool, discussing prepayments in terms of one CPR and a PSA are identical.

8. Suppose that in month 140 the mortgage balance for a mortgage pool underlying a passthrough security is $537 million and that the scheduled principal repayment for month 140 is $440,000. Assuming 175 PSA, what is the amount of the prepayment for month 140?

9. Comment on the following statement: "The PSA model is a prepayment model."

10. Robert Reed is an assistant portfolio manager who has been recently given the responsibility of assisting Joan Soprano, the portfolio manager for the mortgage-backed securities portfolio. Ms. Soprano gave Mr. Reed a copy of the Prudential Securities publication for November 1999 entitled *Mortgage and Asset-Backed Prepayment and Issuance*. An excerpt from the publication is given below:

GNMA 30 Year	Projected PSA				
	Dec	Jan	Feb	One Year	Long Term
6.0　1998	73	68	60	60	65
6.5　1998	113	102	92	91	90
7.0　1998	154	137	124	126	116
7.5　1993	181	166	150	155	138
8.0　1996	220	211	181	185	159
8.5　1994	283	272	223	205	173
9.0　1986	269	263	232	209	195

The mortgage rate at the time of the report was 8.13%.

Mr. Reed asks the following questions about the information in the above excerpt. Respond to each question.

A. What does "GNMA 30 YEAR" mean?

B. What does "8.5 1994" mean?

C. What do the numbers under "PROJECTED" mean?

D. Do the prepayment rates for "7.5 1993" apply to all GNMA issues in the market?

E. Why are the projected prepayments for "one year" and "long term" such that they increase with the coupon rate?

11. Suppose that you are analyzing prepayments of a passthrough security that was issued more than 15 years ago. The weighted average coupon (WAC) for the underlying mortgage pool was 13%. Suppose that the mortgage rate over the year of the analysis declined from 8% to 7% but prepayments for this mortgage pool you are analyzing did not increase. Explain why there is no increase in prepayments despite the lower mortgage rate relative to 13% being paid by borrowers and the decline in the mortgage rates over the year.

12. What type of prepayment risk is an investor interested in a short-term security concerned with when purchasing a mortgage-backed security?

13. Suppose that a portfolio manager is considering a collateralized mortgage obligation structure KMF-01. This structure has three tranches. The deal is a simple sequential pay and was issued several years ago. The tranches are A, B, and C with a coupon rate paid to each tranche each month and principal payments are made first to tranche A, then to tranche B, and finally to tranche C. Here is the status of the deal as of the time of the analysis:

Tranche	Coupon Rate (%)	Par Amount Outstanding ($)
A	6	3 million
B	7	8 million
C	8	30 million

Based on some prepayment rate, the projected principal payments (prepayments plus scheduled principal repayment) for the next four years for the collateral underlying this deal are as follows:

Month	Sch. Principal Repayment + Prepayments ($)	Month	Sch. Principal Repayment + Prepayments ($)
1	520,000	25	287,000
2	510,000	26	285,000
3	490,000	27	283,000
4	450,000	28	280,000
5	448,000	29	278,000
6	442,000	30	275,000
7	410,000	31	271,000
8	405,000	32	270,000
9	400,000	33	265,000
10	396,000	34	260,000
11	395,000	35	255,000
12	390,000	36	252,000
13	388,000	37	250,000
14	385,000	38	245,000
15	380,000	39	240,000
16	377,000	40	210,000
17	375,000	41	200,000
18	370,000	42	195,000
19	369,000	43	190,000
20	366,000	44	185,000
21	300,000	45	175,000
22	298,000	46	170,000
23	292,000	47	166,000
24	290,000	48	164,000

- **A.** Compute the principal, interest, and cash flow for tranche A for the 48 months.
- **B.** Compute the principal, interest, and cash flow for tranche B for the 48 months.
- **C.** Compute the principal, interest, and cash flow for tranche C for the 48 months.
- **D.** Compute the average life for tranche A.

14. Suppose that in the previous CMO structure, KMF-01, that tranche C is an accrual tranche that accrues coupon interest monthly. We will refer to this new CMO structure as KMF-02.
    - **A.** What is the principal repayment, interest, and cash flow for tranche A in KMF-02?
    - **B.** What is the principal balance for tranche C for the first five months?
    - **C.** What is the average life for tranche A in KMF-02 and contrast this with the average life for tranche A in KMF-01?

15. Explain why it is necessary to have a cap for the floater when a fixed-rate tranche is split into a floater and an inverse floater.

16. Suppose that a tranche from which a floater and an inverse floater are created has an average life of six years. What will be the average life of the floater and the inverse floater?

17. How does a CMO alter the cash flow from mortgages so as to redistribute the prepayment risk across various tranches in a deal?

18. "By creating a CMO, an issuer eliminates the prepayment risk associated with the underlying mortgages loans." Explain why you agree or disagree with this statement.

19. Ellen Morgan received a phone call from the trustee of a pension fund. Ms. Morgan is the portfolio manager for the pension fund's bond portfolio. The trustee expressed concerns about the inclusion of CMOs in the portfolio. The trustee's concern arose after reading several articles in the popular press where the CMO market was characterized as the sector of the mortgage-backed securities market with the greatest prepayment risk and the passthrough sector as the safest sector in terms of prepayment risk. What should Ms. Morgan say to this trustee regarding such statements made in the popular press?

20. What is the role of a support tranche in a CMO structure?

21. Suppose that the manager of a savings & loan association portfolio has decided to invest in mortgage-backed securities and is considering the following two securities: i) a Fannie Mae passthrough security with a WAM of 310 months or ii) a PAC tranche of a Fannie Mae CMO issue with an average life of 2 years. Which mortgage-backed security would probably be better from an asset/liability perspective?

22. Suppose that a PAC bond is created using prepayment speeds of 90 PSA and 240 PSA and the average life is 5 years. Will the average life for this PAC tranche be shorter than, longer than, or equal to 5 years if the collateral pays at 140 PSA over its life? Explain your answer.

23. Suppose that $1 billion of passthroughs are used to create a CMO structure, KMF-05. This structure includes a PAC tranche with a par value of $650 million and a support tranche with a par value of $350 million.

   A. Which of the following will have the least average life variability: i) the collateral, ii) the PAC tranche, or iii) the support tranche? Why?

   B. Which of the following will have the greatest average life variability: i) the collateral, ii) the PAC tranche, or iii) the support tranche? Why?

24. Suppose that the $1 billion of collateral in the CMO structure KMF-05 in the previous question was divided into a PAC tranche with a par value of $800 million and a support tranche with a par value of $200 million (instead of $650 million and $350 million). The new structure is KMF-06. Will the PAC tranche in KMF-06 have more or less protection than the PAC tranche in KMF-05?

25. Suppose that $500 million of passthroughs are used to create a CMO structure with a PAC tranche with a par value of $350 million (PAC I), a support tranche with a schedule (PAC II) with a par value of $100 million, and a support tranche without a schedule with a par value of $200 million.

   A. Will the PAC I or PAC II have less average life variability? Why?

   B. Will the support tranche without a schedule or the PAC II have the greater average life variability? Why?

26. In a CMO structure with several PAC tranches that pay off sequentially, explain what the structure effectively becomes once all the support tranches are paid off.

27. Suppose that for the first four years of a CMO, prepayments are well below the initial upper PAC collar and within the initial lower PAC collar. What will happen to the effective upper collar?

28. Consider the following CMO structure backed by 8% collateral:

Tranche	Par Amount ($)	Coupon Rate (%)
A	400,000,000	6.25
B	200,000,000	6.75
C	225,000,000	7.50
D	175,000,000	7.75

Suppose that the structurer of this CMO wants to create a notional IO tranche with a coupon rate of 8%. Calculate the notional amount for this notional IO tranche.

29. An issuer is considering the following two CMO structures:

Structure I:

Tranche	Par Amount ($)	Coupon Rate (%)
A	150 million	6.50
B	100 million	6.75
C	200 million	7.25
D	150 million	7.75
E	100 million	8.00
F	500 million	8.50

Tranches A–E are a sequence of PAC Is, and F is the support tranche.

Structure II:

Tranche	Par Amount ($)	Coupon Rate (%)
A	150 million	6.50
B	100 million	6.75
C	200 million	7.25
D	150 million	7.75
E	100 million	8.00
F	200 million	8.25
G	300 million	?????

Tranches A–E are a sequence of PAC Is, F is a PAC II, and G is a support tranche without a schedule.

A. In Structure II tranche G is created from tranche F in Structure I. What is the coupon rate for tranche G assuming that the combined coupon rate for tranches F and G in Structure II should be 8.5%?

B. What is the effect on the value and average life of tranches A–E by including the PAC II in Structure II?

C. What is the difference in the average life variability of tranche G in Structure II and tranche F in Structure I?

30. What is a broken or busted PAC?

31. Assume that in FJF-01 (see Exhibit 5 in the reading), tranche C had been split to create a floater with a principal of $80,416,667 and an inverse floater with a principal of $16,083,333.

A. What would be the cap rate for the inverse floater if the coupon rate for the floater is 1-month LIBOR plus 1%?

B. Assuming that 1) the coupon formula for the floater is 1-month LIBOR plus 1% and 2) a floor is imposed on the inverse floater of zero, what would be the cap rate on the floater?

32. A. In assessing the prepayment protection offered by a seasoned PAC tranche, explain why the initial collars may provide limited insight?

B. What measure provides better information about the prepayment protection offered by a seasoned PAC tranche?

33. A. For a mortgage loan, is a higher or lower loan-to-value ratio an indication of greater credit risk? Explain why.

B. What is the empirical relationship between defaults and loan-to-value ratio observed by studies of residential mortgage loans?

34. A. What is a principal-only mortgage strip and an interest-only mortgage strip?

B. How does an interest-only mortgage strip differ with respect to the certainty about the cash flow from a Treasury strip created from the coupon interest?

C. How is the price of an interest-only mortgage strip expected to change when interest rates change?

35. A. An investor purchased $10 million par value of a 7% Ginnie Mae passthrough security agreeing to pay 102. The pool factor is 0.72. How much does the investor pay to the seller?

B. Why would an investor who wants to purchase a principal-only mortgage strip not want to do so on a TBA basis?

36. Why can't all residential mortgage loans be securitized by either Ginnie Mae, Fannie Mae, or Freddie Mac?

37. Why is credit enhancement needed for a nonagency mortgage-backed security?

38. With respect to a default by the borrower, how does a residential mortgage loan differ from a commercial mortgage loan?

39. Why is the debt-to-service coverage ratio used to assess the credit risk of a commercial mortgage loan?

40. A. What types of provisions are usually included in a commercial loan to protect the lender against prepayment risk?

B. In a commercial mortgage-backed securities deal, explain why the investor in a security may be afforded prepayment protection at the deal level.

41. What is balloon risk and how is it related to extension risk?

The following information relates to Questions 42–47

Ellen Hurst, a fixed income portfolio manager at a private foundation, is considering the purchase of a mortgage-backed security for the foundation's portfolio. The mortgage market has shown recent signs of turmoil due to a spike in mortgage rates and a decline in new and existing home sales, and Hurst believes that yields on MBS are at attractive levels.

Hurst is considering the two securities described in Exhibits 1 and 2. Both are specified-pool, seasoned issues. Security A is a non-conforming private-issue mortgage passthrough and Security B is a conventional Fannie Mae passthrough. Both are rated AAA.

EXHIBIT 1	MBS Descriptions					
	Par Value ($)	Passthrough Rate (%)	Pool Factor	Average Life (years)	WAC	WAM
Security A	1,175,000	5.60	0.72	10.44		
Security B	1,225,000	5.50	0.85	11.50	6.10%	136 months

EXHIBIT 2	Collateral Description Mortgage Pool Security A			
Loan	Outstanding Mortgage Balance ($)	Weight in Pool (%)	Mortgage Rate (%)	Months Remaining
1	152,000	17.88	5.80	156
2	86,000	10.12	6.32	169
3	92,000	10.82	6.15	150
4	128,000	15.06	6.20	175
5	185,000	21.77	6.00	187
6	101,000	11.88	5.75	162
7	106,000	12.47	6.25	157
Total	850,000	100.00		

42. In the prevailing economic environment, which of the following *best* describes the risk encountered by investors in mortgage passthrough securities?

    A. Extension risk, because prepayments are most likely to increase.

    B. Extension risk, because prepayments are most likely to decrease.

    C. Cycle risk, because prepayments are most likely to increase.

43. The WAC and WAM for Security A are *closest* to:

	WAC	WAM
A.	6.04%	167 months
B.	6.07%	165 months
C.	6.07%	167 months

44. Which of the securities is *most likely* subject to higher interest-rate risk?

    A. Security A, because it has a longer maturity.

    B. Security B, because it has a higher coupon.

    C. Security B, because it has a longer average life.

45. Given 150 PSA, the CPR (conditional prepayment rate) and SMM (single monthly mortality rate) for Security B for month 140 are *closest* to:

	CPR	SMM
A.	6.0%	0.5143%
B.	6.0%	0.7828%
C.	9.0%	0.7828%

46. The monthly mortgage-servicing fee for Security B is *closest* to:

  A. 0.05%.

  B. 0.50%.

  C. 0.60%.

47. Which of the two securities is *most likely* to have the lower credit risk?

  A. Security A because it has the shortest average life.

  B. Security B because it has an "agency" guarantee.

  C. Security B because it has conventional mortgages.

SOLUTIONS FOR READING 51

1. A.

Month	Beginning Mortgage ($)	Mortgage Payment ($)	Interest ($)	Sch. Prin. Repayment ($)	End-of-Month Balance ($)
1	150,000.00	1,023.26	906.25	117.01	149,882.99
2	149,882.99	1,023.26	905.54	117.72	149,765.26
3	149,765.26	1,023.26	904.83	118.43	149,646.83
4	149,646.83	1,023.26	904.12	119.15	149,527.68
5	149,527.68	1,023.26	903.40	119.87	149,407.82
6	149,407.82	1,023.26	902.67	120.59	149,287.22
7	149,287.22	1,023.26	901.94	121.32	149,165.90
8	149,165.90	1,023.26	901.21	122.05	149,043.85
9	149,043.85	1,023.26	900.47	122.79	148,921.06
10	148,921.06	1,023.26	899.73	123.53	148,797.52
11	148,797.52	1,023.26	898.99	124.28	148,673.25
12	148,673.25	1,023.26	898.23	125.03	148,548.21
13	148,548.21	1,023.26	897.48	125.79	148,422.43
14	148,422.43	1,023.26	896.72	126.55	148,295.88

B.

Month	Beginning Mortgage ($)	Mortgage Payment ($)	Interest ($)	Sch. Prin. Repayment ($)	End-of-Month Balance ($)
357	4,031.97	1,023.26	24.36	998.90	3,033.07
358	3,033.07	1,023.26	18.32	1,004.94	2,028.13
359	2,028.13	1,023.26	12.25	1,011.01	1,017.12
360	1,017.12	1,023.26	6.15	1,017.12	0.00

2. A. The monthly servicing fee is found by dividing the servicing fee of 0.005 (50 basis points) by 12. The monthly servicing fee is therefore 0.0004167. Multiplying the monthly servicing fee by the beginning mortgage balance gives the servicing fee for the month.

Month	Beginning Mortgage ($)	Mortgage Payment ($)	Servicing Fee ($)	Net Interest ($)	Sch. Prin. Repayment ($)	End-of-Month Balance ($)
1	150,000.00	1,023.26	62.50	843.75	117.01	149,882.99
2	149,882.99	1,023.26	62.45	843.09	117.72	149,765.26
3	149,765.26	1,023.26	62.40	842.43	118.43	149,646.83
4	149,646.83	1,023.26	62.35	841.76	119.15	149,527.68
5	149,527.68	1,023.26	62.30	841.09	119.87	149,407.82
6	149,407.82	1,023.26	62.25	840.42	120.59	149,287.22

B. The investor's cash flow is the sum of the net interest and the scheduled principal repayment.

Month	Net Interest ($)	Sch. Prin. Repayment ($)	Investor Cash Flow ($)
1	843.75	117.01	960.76
2	843.09	117.72	960.81
3	842.43	118.43	960.86
4	841.76	119.15	960.91
5	841.09	119.87	960.96
6	840.42	120.59	961.01

3. The statement is incorrect. While the guarantee by the U.S. government means that there will not be a loss of principal and that interest payments will be made in full, there is uncertainty about the timing of the principal repayments because the borrower may prepay at any time, in whole or in part.

4. A. and B. The weighted average coupon (WAC) and weighted average maturity (WAM) for the mortgage pool are computed below:

Loan	Outstanding Mortgage Balance ($)	Weight in Pool (%)	Mortgage Rate (%)	Months Remaining	WAC (%)	WAM
1	215,000	26.06	6.75	200	1.7591	52.12
2	185,000	22.42	7.75	185	1.7379	41.48
3	125,000	15.15	7.25	192	1.0985	29.09
4	100,000	12.12	7.00	210	0.8485	25.45
5	200,000	24.24	6.50	180	1.5758	43.64
Total	825,000	100.00			7.02	191.79

WAC = 7.02%   WAM = 192 (rounded)

5. A. The SMM is equal to

$$\frac{\$2,450,000}{\$260,000,000 - \$1,000,000} = 0.009459 = 0.9459\%$$

B. Mr. Jamison should interpret the SMM as follows: 0.9459% of the mortgage pool available to prepay in month 42 prepaid in the month.

C. Given the SMM, the CPR is computed using Equation 2 in the reading:

$$CPR = 1 - (1 - SMM)^{12}$$

Therefore,

$$CPR = 1 - (1 - 0.009459)^{12} = 0.107790 = 10.78\%$$

D. Mr. Jamison should interpret the CPR as follows: ignoring scheduled principal payments, approximately 10.79% of the outstanding mortgage balance at the beginning of the year will be prepaid by the end of the year.

6. The CPR and SMM for each month are shown below:

Month	PSA	CPR	SMM
5	100	0.010	0.000837
15	80	0.024	0.002022
20	175	0.070	0.006029
27	50	0.027	0.002278
88	200	0.120	0.010596
136	75	0.045	0.003829
220	225	0.135	0.012012

7. According to the PSA prepayment benchmark, after month 30 the CPR is constant over the life of the security. Specifically, it is equal to

$$\text{CPR} = 6\% \times (\text{PSA}/100)$$

So, for example, if the assumed PSA is 225, the CPR for the life of the security is

$$\text{CPR} = 6\% \times (225/100) = 13.5\%$$

Thus, the statement is correct that one CPR can be used to describe the PSA 30 months after the origination of the mortgages.

8. The amount of the prepayment for the month is determined as follows:

$$(\text{Beginning mortgage balance} - \text{Scheduled principal payment}) \times \text{SMM}$$

We know that

$$(\$537{,}000{,}000 - \$440{,}000) \times \text{SMM}$$

The CPR for month 140 assuming 175 PSA is

$$\text{CPR} = 6\% \times (175/100) = 10.5\%$$

The SMM is then

$$\text{SMM} = 1 - (1 - 0.105)^{0.08333} = 0.009201$$

Therefore, the prepayment in month 140 is

$$(\$537{,}000{,}000 - \$440{,}000) \times 0.009201 = \$4{,}936{,}889 \text{ (rounded)}$$

(Note: You will get a slightly different answer if you carried the SMM to more decimal places.)

9. The PSA model, or PSA prepayment benchmark, is not a prepayment model in that it does not predict prepayments for a mortgage-backed security. It is a generic benchmark that hypothesizes about what the pattern of prepayments will be over the life of a mortgage-backed security—that there is a prepayment ramp (that increases linearly) for 30 months, after which the CPR is assumed to be constant for the life of the security.

10. A. GNMA refers to passthrough securities issued by the Government National Mortgage Association. "30-YEAR" indicates that the mortgage loans were originated with 30-year terms.

B. This means GNMA 30-year passthrough securities with a coupon rate of 8.5% that were originated in 1994.

C. These are the prepayment rates that are projected for various periods. The prepayment rates are expressed in term of the PSA prepayment benchmark. There is a prepayment rate projection for each of the subsequent three months, a prepayment rate projection for one year, and a long-term prepayment rate.

D. First, the prepayments are only for 7.5% coupon GNMA issues originated in 1993. But there are many 7.5% coupon GNMA issues that were issued in 1993. The prepayments are for a generic issue. This means that when a specific Ginnie Mae 7.5% coupon originated in 1993 is delivered to the buyer, it can realize a prepayment rate quite different from the generic prepayment rate in the report, but on average, 1993 GNMA 7.5%'s are projected to have this prepayment rate.

E. One factor that affects prepayments is the prevailing mortgage rate relative to the rate that borrowers are paying on the underlying mortgages. As noted in the question, the mortgage rate at the time was 8.13%. The higher the coupon rate, the higher the rate that the borrowers in the underlying mortgage pool are paying and the greater the incentive to prepay. So, as the coupon rate increases, prepayments are expected to be greater because of the incentive to prepay.

11. Since the mortgage passthrough being analyzed has been outstanding for more than 15 years, there have been probably several opportunities for borrowers in the underlying mortgage pool to refinance at a lower rate than they are paying. Consequently, the low mortgage rate of 8% relative to 13% may not result in an increase in prepayments and the same is true for a further decline over the year to 7%. This characteristic of prepayments is referred to as "prepayment burnout."

12. An investor in a short-term security is concerned with extension risk. This is the risk that the security's average life will increase.

13. A. For tranche A:

Month	Sch. Principal Repayment/ Prepayments ($)	Beginning Principal ($)	Tranche A Principal Repayment ($)	Interest at 6% ($)	Cash Flow ($)
1	520,000	3,000,000	520,000	15,000	535,000
2	510,000	2,480,000	510,000	12,400	522,400
3	490,000	1,970,000	490,000	9,850	499,850
4	450,000	1,480,000	450,000	7,400	457,400
5	448,000	1,030,000	448,000	5,150	453,150
6	442,000	582,000	442,000	2,910	444,910
7	410,000	140,000	140,000	700	140,700
		Total	3,000,000		

From months 8 through 48, the principal repayment, interest, and cash flow are zero.

B. For tranche B:

Month	Sch. Principal Repayment/ Prepayments ($)	Beginning Principal ($)	Tranche B Principal Repayment ($)	Interest at 7% ($)	Cash Flow ($)
1	520,000	8,000,000	0	46,667	46,667
2	510,000	8,000,000	0	46,667	46,667
3	490,000	8,000,000	0	46,667	46,667
4	450,000	8,000,000	0	46,667	46,667
5	448,000	8,000,000	0	46,667	46,667
6	442,000	8,000,000	0	46,667	46,667
7	410,000	8,000,000	270,000	46,667	316,667
8	405,000	7,730,000	405,000	45,092	450,092
9	400,000	7,325,000	400,000	42,729	442,729
10	396,000	6,925,000	396,000	40,396	436,396
11	395,000	6,529,000	395,000	38,086	433,086
12	390,000	6,134,000	390,000	35,782	425,782
13	388,000	5,744,000	388,000	33,507	421,507
14	385,000	5,356,000	385,000	31,243	416,243
15	380,000	4,971,000	380,000	28,998	408,998
16	377,000	4,591,000	377,000	26,781	403,781
17	375,000	4,214,000	375,000	24,582	399,582
18	370,000	3,839,000	370,000	22,394	392,394
19	369,000	3,469,000	369,000	20,236	389,236
20	366,000	3,100,000	366,000	18,083	384,083
21	300,000	2,734,000	300,000	15,948	315,948
22	298,000	2,434,000	298,000	14,198	312,198
23	292,000	2,136,000	292,000	12,460	304,460
24	290,000	1,844,000	290,000	10,757	300,757
25	287,000	1,554,000	287,000	9,065	296,065
26	285,000	1,267,000	285,000	7,391	292,391
27	283,000	982,000	283,000	5,728	288,728
28	280,000	699,000	280,000	4,078	284,078
29	278,000	419,000	278,000	2,444	280,444
30	275,000	141,000	141,000	823	141,823
		Total	8,000,000		

For months 31 through 48 the principal payment, interest, and cash flow are zero.

C. For tranche C:

Month	Sch. Principal Repayment Prepayments ($)	Beginning Principal ($)	Tranche C Principal Repayment ($)	Interest at 8% ($)	Cash Flow ($)
1	520,000	30,000,000	0	200,000	200,000
2	510,000	30,000,000	0	200,000	200,000
3	490,000	30,000,000	0	200,000	200,000
4	450,000	30,000,000	0	200,000	200,000
5	448,000	30,000,000	0	200,000	200,000
6	442,000	30,000,000	0	200,000	200,000
7	410,000	30,000,000	0	200,000	200,000
8	405,000	30,000,000	0	200,000	200,000
9	400,000	30,000,000	0	200,000	200,000
10	396,000	30,000,000	0	200,000	200,000
11	395,000	30,000,000	0	200,000	200,000
12	390,000	30,000,000	0	200,000	200,000
13	388,000	30,000,000	0	200,000	200,000
14	385,000	30,000,000	0	200,000	200,000
15	380,000	30,000,000	0	200,000	200,000
16	377,000	30,000,000	0	200,000	200,000
17	375,000	30,000,000	0	200,000	200,000
18	370,000	30,000,000	0	200,000	200,000
19	369,000	30,000,000	0	200,000	200,000
20	366,000	30,000,000	0	200,000	200,000
21	300,000	30,000,000	0	200,000	200,000
22	298,000	30,000,000	0	200,000	200,000
23	292,000	30,000,000	0	200,000	200,000
24	290,000	30,000,000	0	200,000	200,000
25	287,000	30,000,000	0	200,000	200,000
26	285,000	30,000,000	0	200,000	200,000
27	283,000	30,000,000	0	200,000	200,000
28	280,000	30,000,000	0	200,000	200,000
29	278,000	30,000,000	0	200,000	200,000
30	275,000	30,000,000	134,000	200,000	334,000
31	271,000	29,866,000	271,000	199,107	470,107
32	270,000	29,595,000	270,000	197,300	467,300

(continued on next page . . .)

(continued)

Month	Sch. Principal Repayment Prepayments ($)	Beginning Principal ($)	Tranche C Principal Repayment ($)	Interest at 8% ($)	Cash Flow ($)
33	265,000	29,325,000	265,000	195,500	460,500
34	260,000	29,060,000	260,000	193,733	453,733
35	255,000	28,800,000	255,000	192,000	447,000
36	252,000	28,545,000	252,000	190,300	442,300
37	250,000	28,293,000	250,000	188,620	438,620
38	245,000	28,043,000	245,000	186,953	431,953
39	240,000	27,798,000	240,000	185,320	425,320
40	210,000	27,558,000	210,000	183,720	393,720
41	200,000	27,348,000	200,000	182,320	382,320
42	195,000	27,148,000	195,000	180,987	375,987
43	190,000	26,953,000	190,000	179,687	369,687
44	185,000	26,763,000	185,000	178,420	363,420
45	175,000	26,578,000	175,000	177,187	352,187
46	170,000	26,403,000	170,000	176,020	346,020
47	166,000	26,233,000	166,000	174,887	340,887
48	164,000	26,067,000	164,000	173,780	337,780

D. The average life for tranche A is computed as follows:

Month	Tranche A Principal Repayment ($)	Month × Principal Repayment ($)
1	520,000	520,000
2	510,000	1,020,000
3	490,000	1,470,000
4	450,000	1,800,000
5	448,000	2,240,000
6	442,000	2,652,000
7	140,000	980,000
Total	3,000,000	10,682,000

$$\text{Average life} = \frac{\$10,682,000}{12\,(\$3,000,000)} = 0.30$$

14. A. The coupon interest that would be paid to tranche C is diverted as principal repayment to tranche A. In the table below, the total principal paid to tranche A is tranche A's principal repayment as in KMF-01 plus the interest diverted from tranche C.

Month	Beginning Principal for Tranche A ($)	Principal Repayment before C int[a] ($)	Interest at 6% ($)	Principal for Tranche C ($)	Tranche C Diverted to Tranche A ($)	Principal Repayment for Tranche A ($)	Cash Flow ($)
1	3,000,000	520,000	15,000	30,000,000	200,000	720,000	735,000
2	2,280,000	510,000	11,400	30,200,000	201,333	711,333	722,733
3	1,568,667	490,000	7,843	30,401,333	202,676	692,676	700,519
4	875,991	450,000	4,380	30,604,009	204,027	654,027	658,407
5	221,964	448,000	1,110	30,808,036	205,387	221,964	223,074
					Total	3,000,000	

[a] This is the amount before the accrued interest from Tranche C is allocated to Tranche A.

B. The principal balance for tranche C is increased each month by the amount of interest diverted from tranche C to tranche A. The principal balance for the first five months is shown in the fifth column of the schedule for part A.

C.

Month	Principal Repayment for Tranche A ($)	Month × Principal ($)
1	720,000	720,000
2	711,333	1,422,667
3	692,676	2,078,027
4	654,027	2,616,107
5	221,964	1,109,822
	3,000,000	7,946,622

$$\text{Average life} = \frac{\$7,946,622}{12(\$3,000,000)} = 0.22$$

The average life is shorter for tranche A in KMF-02 relative to KMF-01 due to the presence of the accrual tranche.

15. There is typically a floor placed on an inverse floater to prevent the coupon rate from being negative. In order to fund this floor, the floater must be capped.

16. The principal payments that would have gone to the tranche used to create the floater and inverse floater are distributed proportionately to the floater and inverse floater based on their percentage of the par value. That is, if the floater's par value is 80% of the tranche from which it is created and the inverse floater 20%, then if $100 is received in principal payment, $80 is distributed to the floater and $20 to the inverse floater. The effect is that the average life for the floater and the inverse floater will be the same as the tranche from which they are created, six years in this example.

17. A CMO redistributes prepayment risk by using rules for the distribution of principal payments and interest payments from the collateral. The collateral for a CMO has prepayment risk and its cash flow consists of interest payments and principal payments (both scheduled principal and prepayments). Prepayment risk consists of contraction risk and extension risk. In a CMO there are different bond classes (tranches) which are exposed to different degrees of prepayment risk. The exposure to different degrees of prepayment risk relative to the prepayment risk for the collateral underlying a CMO is due to rules as to how the principal and the interest are to be redistributed to the CMO tranches—hence, redistributing prepayment risk amongst the tranches in the structure. In the simplest type of CMO structure—a sequential-pay structure—the rules for the distribution of the cash flow are such that some tranches receive some protection against extension risk while other tranches in the CMO have some protection against contraction risk. In a CMO with PAC tranches, the rules for the distribution of the cash flow result in the PAC tranches having protection against both contraction risk and extension risk while the support tranches (non-PAC tranches) have greater prepayment risk than the underlying collateral for the CMO.

18. By creating any mortgage-backed security, prepayment risk cannot ever be eliminated. Rather, the character of prepayment risk can be altered. Specifically, prepayment risk consists of contraction risk and extension risk. A CMO alters but does not eliminate the prepayment risk of the underlying mortgage loans. Therefore, the statement is incorrect.

19. Ms. Morgan should inform the trustee that the statement about the riskiness of the different sectors of the mortgage-backed securities market in terms of prepayment risk is incorrect. There are CMO tranches that expose an investor to less prepayment risk—in terms of extension or contraction risk—than the mortgage passthrough securities from which the CMO was created. There are CMO tranche types such as planned amortization classes that have considerably less prepayment risk than the mortgage passthrough securities from which the CMO was created. However, in order to create CMO tranches such as PACs, it is necessary to create tranches where there is considerable prepayment risk—prepayment risk that is greater than the underlying mortgage passthrough securities. These tranches are called support tranches.

20. A support tranche is included in a structure in which there are PAC tranches. The sole purpose of the support tranche is to provide prepayment protection for the PAC tranches. Consequently, support tranches are exposed to substantial prepayment risk.

21. The manager of an S&L portfolio is concerned with prepayment risk but more specifically extension risk. Moreover, to better match the average life of the investment to that of the S&L's funding cost, the manager will seek a shorter term investment. With the Fannie Mae PAC issue with an average life of 2 years the manager is buying a shorter term security and one with some protection against extension risk. In contrast, the Fannie Mae passthrough is probably a longer term average life security because of its WAM of 310 months, and it will expose the S&L to substantial extension risk. Therefore, the Fannie Mae PAC tranche is probably a better investment from an asset/liability perspective.

22. Since the prepayments are assumed to be at a constant prepayment rate over the PAC tranche's life at 140 PSA, which is within the PSA collar in which the PAC was created, the average life will be equal to five years.

23. A. The PAC tranche will have the least average life variability. This is because the PAC tranche is created to provide protection against extension risk and contraction risk—the support tranches providing the protection.

    B. The support tranche will have the greatest average life variability. This is because it is designed to absorb the prepayment risk to provide protection for the PAC tranche.

24. The PAC structure in KMF-06 will have less prepayment protection than in KMF-05 because the support tranche is smaller ($200 million in KMF-06 versus $350 for KMF-05).

25. A. The PAC II is a support tranche and as a result will have more average life variability than the PAC I tranche. Consequently, PAC I has the less average life variability.

    B. The support tranche without a schedule must provide prepayment protection for both the PAC I and the PAC II. Therefore, the support tranche without a schedule will have greater average life variability than the PAC II.

26. In a PAC tranche structure in which the PAC tranches are paid off in sequence, the support tranches absorb any excess prepayments above the scheduled amount. Once the support tranches are paid off, any prepayments must go to the PAC tranche that is currently receiving principal payments. Thus, the structure effectively becomes a typical (plain vanilla) sequential-pay structure.

27. If the prepayments are well below the initial upper PAC collar, this means that there will be more support tranches available four years after the deal is structured than if prepayments were actually at the initial upper PAC collar. This means that there will be more support tranches to absorb prepayments. Hence, the effective upper collar will increase.

28. The notional amount of an 8% IO tranche is computed below:

Tranche	Par Amount ($)	Coupon Rate (%)	Excess Interest (%)	Excess Dollar Interest ($)	Notional Amount for an 8% Coupon Rate IO ($)
A	400,000,000	6.25	1.75	7,000,000	87,500,000
B	200,000,000	6.75	1.25	2,500,000	31,250,000
C	225,000,000	7.50	0.50	1,125,000	14,062,500
D	175,000,000	7.75	0.25	437,500	5,468,750
				Notional amount for 8% IO	138,281,250

29. A. The coupon rate for tranche G is found as follows:

Coupon interest for tranche F in Structure I = $500,000,000 \times 0.085$

$$= \$42,500,000$$

Coupon interest for tranche F in Structure II = $200,000,000 \times 0.0825$

$$= \$16,500,000$$

Coupon interest available to tranche G in Structure II
$$= \$42,500,000 - \$16,500,000 = \$26,000,000$$

Coupon rate for tranche G $= \dfrac{\$26,000,000}{\$300,000,000} = 0.0867 = 8.67\%$

B. There is no effect on the average life of the PAC tranches because the inclusion of the PAC II only impacts the support tranche in Structure I compared to Structure II.

C. There is greater average life variability for tranche G in Structure II than tranche F in Structure I because tranche G must provide prepayment protection in Structure II for not only the PACs but also tranche F.

30. A broken or busted PAC is a structure where all of the support tranches (the tranches that provide prepayment support for the PAC tranches in a structure) are completely paid off.

31. A. The formula for the cap rate on the inverse floater:

$$\frac{\text{Inverse floater interest when reference rate for floater is zero}}{\text{Principal for inverse floater}}$$

The total interest to be paid to tranche C if it was not split into the floater and the inverse floater is the principal of $96,500,000 times 7.5%, or $7,237,500. The maximum interest for the inverse floater occurs if 1-month LIBOR is zero. In that case, the coupon rate for the floater is

1-month LIBOR + 1% = 1%

Since the floater receives 1% on its principal of $80,416,667, the floater's interest is $804,167. The remainder of the interest of $7,237,500 from tranche C goes to the inverse floater. That is, the inverse floater's interest is $6,433,333 (= $7,237,500 − $804,167). Since the inverse floater's principal is $16,083,333.33, the cap rate for the inverse floater is

$$\frac{\$6,433,333}{\$16,083,333} = 40.0\%$$

B. Assuming a floor of zero for inverse floater, the cap rate is determined as follows:

$$\text{Cap rate for floater} = \frac{\text{Collateral tranche interest}}{\text{Principal for floater}}$$

The collateral tranche interest is $7,237,500. The floater principal is $80,416,667. Therefore,

$$\text{Cap rate for floater} = \frac{\$7,237,500}{\$80,416,667} = 9\%$$

32. A. The PAC collar indicates the prepayment protection afforded the investor in a PAC tranche. Prepayment protection means the ability of the collateral to satisfy the PAC tranche's schedule of principal payments. The initial PAC collar only indicates the protection at issuance. As prepayments occur over time, the amount of the support tranches decline and, as a result, the PAC collars change. In fact, in the extreme case, if the support tranches pay off completely, there is no longer a PAC collar since there is no longer prepayment protection for the PAC tranche.

B. To assess the prepayment protection at any given time for the PAC tranche, the effective PAC collar is computed. This measure is computed by determining the PSA prepayment rate range that given the current amount of the support tranche would be able to meet the remaining PAC schedule.

33. A. For a mortgage loan, the higher the loan-to-value ratio, the greater the credit risk faced by a lender. The reason is that if the property is repossessed and sold, the greater the ratio, the greater the required sale price necessary to recover the loan amount.

B. Studies of residential mortgage loans have found that the loan-to-value ratio is a key determinant of whether a borrower will default and that the higher the ratio, the greater the likelihood of default.

34. A. Mortgage strips are created when the principal (both scheduled principal repayments plus prepayments) and the coupon interest are allocated to different bond classes. The tranche that is allocated the principal payments is called the principal-only mortgage strip, and the tranche that is allocated the coupon interest is called the interest-only mortgage strip.

B. With an interest-only mortgage strip, there is no specific amount that will be received over time since the coupon interest payments depend on how prepayments occur over the security's life. In contrast, for a Treasury strip created from the coupon interest, the amount and the timing of the single cash flow is known with certainty.

C. Because prepayments increase when interest rates decrease and prepayments decrease when interest rates increase, the expected cash flow changes in the same direction as the change in interest rates. Thus, when interest rates increase, prepayments are expected to decrease and there will be an increase in the expected coupon interest payments since more of the underlying mortgages are expected to be outstanding. This will typically increase the value of an interest-only mortgage strip because the increase in the expected cash flow more than offsets the higher discount rates used to discount the cash flow. When interest rates decrease, the opposite occurs. So, an interest-only mortgage strip's value is expected to change in the same direction as the change in interest rates.

35. A. The purchase price per $100 par value is 1.02. Therefore

$$1.02 \times \$10,000,000 \times 0.72 = \$7,344,000$$

The investor pays $7,344,000 plus accrued interest.

B. Because the value and characteristics of a principal-only mortgage strip are highly sensitive to the underlying mortgage pool, an investor would not want the seller to have the option of which specific trust to deliver. If the trade is done on a TBA basis, the seller has the choice of the trust to deliver. To avoid this, a trade is done by the buyer specifying the trust that he or she is purchasing.

36. Ginnie Mae, Fannie Mae, and Freddie Mac have underwriting standards that must be met in order for a mortgage loan to qualify for inclusion in a mortgage pool underlying an agency mortgage-backed security. Mortgage loans that do qualify are called conforming loans. A loan may fail to be conforming because the loan balance exceeds the maximum permitted by the underwriting standard or the loan-to-value ratio is too high, or the payment-to-income ratio is too high. Loans that do not qualify are called nonconforming loans.

37. Since there is no implicit or explicit government guarantee for a non-agency mortgage-backed security, a mechanism is needed to reduce credit risk for bondholders when there are defaults. That is, there is a need to "enhance" the credit of the securities issued. These mechanisms are called credit enhancements, of which there are two types, internal and external.

38. With a residential mortgage loan the lender relies on the ability of the borrower to repay and has recourse to the borrower if the payment terms are not satisfied. In contrast, commercial mortgage loans are nonrecourse loans, which means that the lender can only look to the income-producing property backing the loan for interest and principal repayment. Should a default occur, the lender looks to the proceeds from the sale of the property for repayment and has no recourse to the borrower for any unpaid balance.

39. The figure used for "value" in the loan-to-value ratio is either market value or appraised value. In valuing commercial property, there can be considerable variance in the estimates of the property's market value. Thus, investors tend to be skeptical about estimates of market value and the resulting LTVs reported for properties in a pool of commercial loans. Therefore, the debt-to-service ratio is more objective, and a more reliable measure of risk.

40. A. Call protection at the loan level is provided in one or more of the following forms: 1) prepayment lockout, 2) defeasance, 3) prepayment penalty points, and 4) yield maintenance charges. A prepayment lockout is a contractual agreement that prohibits any prepayments during the lockout period (from 2 to 5 years). After the lockout period, call protection comes in the form of either prepayment penalty points or yield maintenance charges. With defeasance, rather than prepaying a loan, the borrower provides sufficient funds for the servicer to invest in a portfolio of Treasury securities that replicates the cash flows that would exist in the absence of prepayments. Prepayment penalty points are predetermined penalties that must be paid by the borrower if the borrower wishes to refinance. Yield maintenance charge provisions are designed to make the lender whole if prepayments are made.

  B. A CMBS deal can be structured as a sequential-pay structure, thereby providing tranches some form of protection against prepayment risk at the structure level.

41. Typically commercial loans are balloon loans that require substantial principal payment at the end of the term of the loan. Balloon risk is the risk that a borrower will not be able to make the balloon payment because either the borrower cannot arrange for refinancing at the balloon payment date or cannot sell the property to generate sufficient funds to pay off the balloon balance. Since the term of the loan will be extended by the lender during the workout period, balloon risk is also referred to as extension risk.

42. B is correct. Extension risk describes the risk that mortgage prepayments will slow down more than the investor anticipates. Slow prepayments are associated with a rise in interest rates, declining housing turnover, or changing characteristics of underlying residential mortgage loans.

43. A is correct. The WAC is the weighted-average of the coupon rates for each mortgage in the pool, and the WAM is the weighted-average remaining months to maturity for each mortgage in the pool.

WAC = 0.1788 (5.80%) + 0.1012 (6.32%) + 0.1082 (6.15%) + 0.1506 (6.20%) + 0.2177 (6.00%) + 0.1188 (5.75%) + 0.1247 (6.25%) = 6.04%

WAM = 0.1788 (156) + 0.1012 (169) + 0.1082 (150) + 0.1506 (175) + 0.2177 (187) + 0.1188 (162) + 0.1247 (157) = 167.11 ≈ 167 months

44. C is correct. Security B has the longer average life and is considered to have the greater interest rate risk. In the bond market, for a given coupon, the greater the maturity, the greater the interest rate risk. For mortgage-backed securities, the legal maturity (the time until the last scheduled principal payment) does not give investors much information regarding the characteristics of the security as related to interest rate risk. Prepayments must be accounted for as well as scheduled payments. Therefore, for mortgage-backed securities, market participants generally use the weighted-average life (or simply average life) as the convention-based average time to receipt of principal payments or as the appropriate measure of maturity in evaluating interest-rate risk.

45. C is correct. Because the pool is seasoned more than 30 months, we use 6% as the CPR of the 100 PSA prepayment benchmark. The CPR of a mortgage pool is equal to the CPR of the PSA benchmark × (PSA of mortgage pool/100).

CPR of Security B = 6% × (150/100) = 9.0%. This is an annual rate.

The SMM is a monthly rate. SMM = $1 - (1 - 0.09)^{1/12} = 1 - (0.91)^{0.08333}$ = 0.007828 = 0.7828%.

46. A is correct. The monthly mortgage servicing fee is the difference between the mortgage rate and the passthrough rate divided by 12.

Servicing fee = (6.10% − 5.50%)/12 = 0.05%

47. B is correct. Security B has less credit risk since it is guaranteed by Fannie Mae, a corporate instrumentality of the U.S. government. Generally, non-agency securities are considered to be exposed to credit risk. The fact that Security A has non-conforming mortgages does not necessarily mean it has lower credit quality.

ASSET-BACKED SECTOR OF THE BOND MARKET

by Frank J. Fabozzi, CFA

LEARNING OUTCOMES

The candidate should be able to:	Mastery
a. describe the basic structural features of and parties to a securitization transaction;	☐
b. explain and contrast prepayment tranching and credit tranching;	☐
c. distinguish between the payment structure and collateral structure of a securitization backed by amortizing assets and non-amortizing assets;	☐
d. distinguish among various types of external and internal credit enhancements;	☐
e. describe cash flow and prepayment characteristics for securities backed by home equity loans, manufactured housing loans, automobile loans, student loans, SBA loans, and credit card receivables;	☐
f. describe collateralized debt obligations (CDOs), including cash and synthetic CDOs;	☐
g. distinguish among the primary motivations for creating a collateralized debt obligation (arbitrage and balance sheet transactions).	☐

INTRODUCTION  1

As an alternative to the issuance of a bond, a corporation can issue a security backed by loans or receivables. Debt instruments that have as their collateral loans or receivables are referred to as asset-backed securities. The transaction in which asset-backed securities are created is referred to as a **securitization**.

While the major issuers of asset-backed securities are corporations, municipal governments use this form of financing rather than issuing municipal bonds and several European central governments use this form of financing. In the United

States, the first type of asset-backed security (ABS) was the residential mortgage loan. We discussed the resulting securities, referred to as mortgage-backed securities, in the reading on the mortgage-backed sector of the bond market. Securities backed by other types of assets (consumer and business loans and receivables) have been issued throughout the world. The largest sectors of the asset-backed securities market in the United States are securities backed by credit card receivables, auto loans, home equity loans, manufactured housing loans, student loans, Small Business Administration loans, corporate loans, and bonds (corporate, emerging market, and structured financial products). Since home equity loans and manufactured housing loans are backed by real estate property, the securities backed by them are referred to as **real estate-backed asset-backed securities**. Other asset-backed securities include securities backed by home improvement loans, health care receivables, agricultural equipment loans, equipment leases, music royalty receivables, movie royalty receivables, and municipal parking ticket receivables. Collectively, these products are called **credit-sensitive structured products**.

In this reading, we will discuss the securitization process, the basic features of a securitization transaction, and the major asset types that have been securitized. In the last section of this reading, we look at collateralized debt obligations. While this product has traditionally been classified as part of the ABS market, we will see how the structure of this product differs from that of a typical securitization.

There are two topics not covered in this reading. The first is the valuation of an ABS. This topic is covered in the reading on valuing mortgage-backed and asset-backed securities. Second, the factors considered by rating agencies in rating an ABS transaction are not covered here.

2   THE SECURITIZATION PROCESS AND FEATURES OF ABS

The issuance of an asset-backed security is more complicated than the issuance of a corporate bond. In this section, we will describe the securitization process and the parties to a securitization. We will do so using a hypothetical securitization.

A. The Basic Securitization Transaction

Quality Home Theaters Inc. (QHT) manufactures high-end equipment for home theaters. The cost of one of QHT's home theaters ranges from $20,000 to $200,000. Some of its sales are for cash, but the bulk of its sales are by installment sales contracts. Effectively, an installment sales contract is a loan to the buyer of the home theater who agrees to repay QHT over a specified period of time. For simplicity we will assume that the loans are typically four years. The collateral for the loan is the home theater purchased by the borrower. The loan specifies an interest rate that the buyer pays.

The credit department of QHT makes the decision as to whether or not to extend credit to a customer. That is, the credit department will request a credit loan application form be completed by a customer and based on criteria established by QHT will decide on whether to extend a loan. The criteria for extending credit are referred to as underwriting standards. Because QHT is extending the loan, it is referred to as the originator of the loan. Moreover, QHT may have a department that is responsible for servicing the loan. Servicing involves collecting payments from borrowers, notifying borrowers who may be delinquent, and, when necessary, recovering and disposing of the collateral (i.e., home theater equipment in our illustration) if the borrower does not make loan repayments by a specified time. While the servicer of the loans need not be the originator of the loans, in our illustration we are assuming that QHT will be the servicer.

Now let's see how these loans can be used in a securitization. We will assume that QHT has $100 million of installment sales contracts. This amount is shown on QHT's balance sheet as an asset. We will further assume that QHT wants to raise $100 million. Rather than issuing corporate bonds for $100 million, QHT's treasurer decides to raise the funds via a securitization. To do so, QHT will set up a legal entity referred to as a **special purpose vehicle** (SPV). In our discussion of asset-backed securities we described the critical role of this legal entity; its role will become clearer in our illustration. In our illustration, the SPV that is set up is called *Homeview Asset Trust* (HAT). QHT will then sell to HAT $100 million of the loans. QHT will receive from HAT $100 million in cash, the amount it wanted to raise. But where does HAT get $100 million? It obtains those funds by selling securities that are backed by the $100 million of loans. These securities are the asset-backed securities we referred to earlier and we will discuss these further in Section 2.C.

In the prospectus, HAT (the SPV) would be referred to as either the "issuer" or the "trust." QHT, the seller of the collateral to HAT, would be referred to as the "seller." The prospectus might then state: "The securities represent obligations of the issuer only and do not represent obligations of or interests in Quality Home Theaters Inc. or any of its affiliates."

The transaction is diagramed in panel a of Exhibit 1 on the next page. In panel b, the parties to the transaction are summarized.

The payments that are received from the collateral are distributed to pay servicing fees, other administrative fees, and principal and interest to the security holders. The legal documents in a securitization (prospectus or private placement memorandum) will set forth in considerable detail the priority and amount of payments to be made to the servicer, administrators, and the security holders of each bond class. The priority and amount of payments are commonly referred to as the "waterfall" because the flow of payments in a structure is depicted as a waterfall.

B. Parties to a Securitization

Thus far we have discussed three parties to a securitization: the seller of the collateral (also sometimes referred to as the originator), the special purpose vehicle (referred to in a prospectus or private placement memorandum as the issuer or the trust), and the servicer. There are other parties involved in a securitization: attorneys, independent accountants, trustees, underwriters, rating agencies, and guarantors. All of these parties plus the servicer are referred to as "third parties" to the transaction.

There is a good deal of legal documentation involved in a securitization transaction. The attorneys are responsible for preparing the legal documents. The first is the *purchase agreement* between the seller of the assets (QHT in our

EXHIBIT 1	Securitization Illustration for QHT

Panel A: Securitization Process

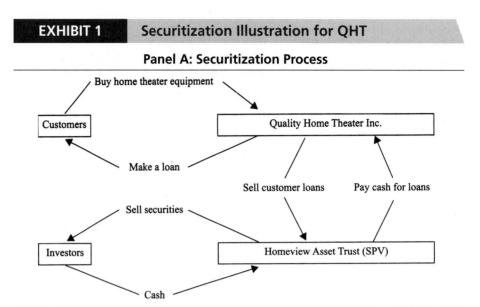

Panel B: Parties to the Securitization

Party	Description	Party in Illustration
Seller	Originates the loans and sells loans to the SPV	Quality Home Theaters Inc.
Issuer/Trust	The SPV that buys the loans from the seller and issues the asset-backed securities	Homeview Asset Trust
Servicer	Services the loans	Quality Home Theaters Inc.

illustration) and the SPV (HAT in our illustration).[1] The purchase agreement sets forth the representations and warranties that the seller is making about the assets. The second is one that sets forth how the cash flows are divided among the bond classes (i.e., the structure's waterfall). Finally, the attorneys create the *servicing agreement* between the entity engaged to service the assets (in our illustration QHT retained the servicing of the loans) and the SPV.

An independent accounting firm will verify the accuracy of all numerical information placed in either the prospectus or private placement memorandum.[2] The result of this task results in a *comfort letter* for a securitization.

The trustee or trustee agent is the entity that safeguards the assets after they have been placed in the trust, receives the payments due to the bond holders,

---

[1] There are concerns that both the creditors to the seller of the collateral (QHT's creditors in our illustration) and the investors in the securities issued by the SPV have about the assets. Specifically, QHT's creditors will be concerned that the assets are being sold to the SPV at less than fair market value, thereby weakening their credit position. The buyers of the asset-backed securities will be concerned that the assets were purchased at less than fair market value, thereby weakening their credit position. Because of this concern, the attorney will issue an opinion that the assets were sold at a fair market value.

[2] The way this is accomplished is that a copy of the transaction's payment structure, underlying collateral, average life, and yield are supplied to the accountants for verification. In turn, the accountants reverse engineer the deal according to the deal's payment rules (i.e., the waterfall). Following the rules and using the same collateral that will actually generate the cash flows for the transaction, the accountants reproduce the yield and average life tables that are put into the prospectus or private placement memorandum.

and provides periodic information to the bond holders. The information is provided in the form of *remittance reports* that may be issued monthly, quarterly or whenever agreed to by the terms of the prospectus or the private placement memorandum.

The underwriters and rating agencies perform the same function in a securitization as they do in a standard corporate bond offering. The rating agencies make an assessment of the collateral and the proposed structure to determine the amount of credit enhancement required to achieve a target credit rating for each bond class.

Finally, a securitization may have an entity that guarantees part of the obligations issued by the SPV. These entities are called guarantors and we will discuss their role in a securitization later.

C. Bonds Issued

Now let's take a closer look at the securities issued, what we refer to as the asset-backed securities.

A simple transaction can involve the sale of just one bond class with a par value of $100 million in our illustration. We will call this Bond Class A. Suppose HAT issues 100,000 certificates for Bond Class A with a par value of $1,000 per certificate. Then, each certificate holder would be entitled to 1/100,000 of the payment from the collateral after payment of fees and expenses. Each payment made by the borrowers (i.e., the buyers of the home theater equipment) consists of principal repayment and interest.

A structure can be more complicated. For example, there can be rules for distribution of principal and interest other than on a pro rata basis to different bond classes. As an example, suppose HAT issues Bond Classes A1, A2, A3, and A4 whose total par value is $100 million as follows:

Bond Class	Par Value ($ in Millions)
A1	40
A2	30
A3	20
A4	10
Total	100

As with a collateralized mortgage obligation (CMO) structure described in the reading on the mortgage-backed sector of the bond market, there are different rules for the distribution of principal and interest to these four bond classes or tranches. A simple structure would be a sequential-pay one. In a basic sequential-pay structure, each bond class receives periodic interest. However, the principal is repaid as follows: all principal received from the collateral is paid first to Bond Class A1 until it is fully paid off its $40 million par value. After Bond Class A1 is paid off, all principal received from the collateral is paid to Bond Class A2 until it is fully paid off. All principal payments from the collateral are then paid to Bond Class A3 until it is fully paid off, and then all principal payments are made to Bond Class A4.

The reason for the creation of the structure just described is to redistribute the prepayment risk among different bond classes. Prepayment risk is the uncertainty about the cash flow due to prepayments. This risk can be decomposed into contraction risk (i.e., the undesired shortening in the average life of a security) or extension risk (i.e., the undesired lengthening in the average life of a security). The creation of these bond classes is referred to as prepayment tranching or time tranching.

Now let's look at a more common structure in a transaction. As will be explained later, there are structures where there is more than one bond class, and the bond classes differ as to how they will share any losses resulting from defaults of the borrowers. In such a structure, the bond classes are classified as senior bond classes and subordinate bond classes. This structure is called a senior-subordinate structure. Losses are realized by the subordinate bond classes before there are any losses realized by the senior bond classes. For example, suppose that HAT issued $90 million par value of Bond Class A, the senior bond class, and $10 million par value of Bond Class B, the subordinate bond class. So the structure is as follows:

Bond Class	Par Value ($ in Millions)
A (senior)	90
B (subordinate)	10
Total	100

In this structure, as long as there are no defaults by the borrower greater than $10 million, then Bond Class A will be repaid fully its $90 million.

The purpose of this structure is to redistribute the credit risk associated with the collateral. This is referred to as credit tranching. As explained later, the senior-subordinate structure is a form of credit enhancement for a transaction.

There is no reason why only one subordinate bond class is created. Suppose that HAT issued the following structure:

Bond Class	Par Value ($ in Millions)
A (senior)	90
B (subordinate)	7
C (subordinate)	3
Total	100

In this structure, Bond Class A is the senior bond class while both Bond Classes B and C are subordinate bond classes from the perspective of Bond Class A. The rules for the distribution of losses would be as follows. All losses on the collateral are absorbed by Bond Class C before any losses are realized by Bond Classes A or B. Consequently, if the losses on the collateral do not exceed $3 million, no losses will be realized by Bond Classes A and B. If the losses exceed $3 million, Bond Class B absorbs the loss up to $7 million (its par value). As an example, if the total loss on the collateral is $8 million, Bond Class C loses its entire par value ($3 million) and Bond Class B realizes a loss of $5 million of its $7 million par value. Bond Class A does not realize any loss in this scenario. It should be clear that Bond Class A only realizes a loss if the loss from the collateral exceeds $10 million. The bond class that must absorb the losses first is referred to as the first loss piece. In our hypothetical structure, Bond Class C is the first loss piece.

PRACTICE QUESTION 1

Suppose that the structure for an asset-backed security structure is as follows:

senior bond class	$380 million
subordinated bond class 1	$40 million
subordinated bond class 2	$20 million

The value of the collateral for the structure is $440 million and subordinated bond class 2 is the first loss piece.

A. What is the amount of the loss for each bond class if losses due to defaults over the life of the structure total $15 million?

B. What is the amount of the loss for each bond class if losses due to defaults over the life of the structure total $50 million?

C. What is the amount of the loss for each bond class if losses due to defaults over the life of the structure total $90 million?

Now we will add just one more twist to the structure. Often in larger transactions, the senior bond class will be carved into different bond classes in order to redistribute the prepayment risk. For example, HAT might issue the following structure:

Bond Class	Par Value ($ in Millions)
A1 (senior)	35
A2 (senior)	28
A3 (senior)	15
A4 (senior)	12
B (subordinate)	7
C (subordinate)	3
Total	100

In this structure there is both prepayment tranching for the senior bond class (creation of Bond Classes A1, A2, A3, and A4) and credit tranching (creation of the senior bond classes and the two subordinate bond classes, Bond Classes B and C).

As explained in the reading on the mortgaged-backed sector of the bond market, a bond class in a securitization is also referred to as a "tranche." Consequently, throughout this reading the terms "bond class" and "tranche" are used interchangeably.

D. General Classification of Collateral and Transaction Structure

Later in this reading, we will describe some of the major assets that have been securitized. In general, the collateral can be classified as either amortizing or non-amortizing assets. Amortizing assets are loans in which the borrower's periodic payment consists of scheduled principal and interest payments over the life of the loan. The schedule for the repayment of the principal is called an amortization schedule. The standard residential mortgage loan falls into this category. Auto loans and certain types of home equity loans (specifically, closed-end home equity loans discussed later in this reading) are amortizing assets. Any excess payment over the scheduled principal payment is called a prepayment. Prepayments can be made to pay off the entire balance or a partial prepayment, called a curtailment.

In contrast to amortizing assets, non-amortizing assets require only minimum periodic payments with no scheduled principal repayment. If that payment is less than the interest on the outstanding loan balance, the shortfall is added to the outstanding loan balance. If the periodic payment is greater than the interest on the outstanding loan balance, then the difference is applied to the reduction of the outstanding loan balance. Since there is no schedule of principal payments (i.e., no amortization schedule) for a non-amortizing asset, the concept of a prepayment does not apply. A credit card receivable is an example of a non-amortizing asset.

The type of collateral—amortizing or non-amortizing—has an impact on the structure of the transaction. Typically, when amortizing assets are securitized, there is no change in the composition of the collateral over the life of the securities except for loans that have been removed due to defaults and full principal repayment due to prepayments or full amortization. For example, if at the time of issuance the collateral for an ABS consists of 3,000 four-year amortizing loans, then the same 3,000 loans will be in the collateral six months from now assuming no defaults and no prepayments. If, however, during the first six months, 200 of the loans prepay and 100 have defaulted, then the collateral at the end of six months will consist of 2,700 loans (3,000 − 200 − 100). Of course, the remaining principal of the 2,700 loans will decline because of scheduled principal repayments and any partial prepayments. All of the principal repayments from the collateral will be distributed to the security holders.

In contrast, for an ABS transaction backed by non-amortizing assets, the composition of the collateral changes. The funds available to pay the security holders are principal repayments and interest. The interest is distributed to the security holders. However, the principal repayments can be either 1) paid out to security holders or 2) reinvested by purchasing additional loans. What will happen to the principal repayments depends on the time since the transaction was originated. For a certain amount of time after issuance, all principal repayments are reinvested in additional loans. The period of time for which principal repayments are reinvested rather than paid out to the security holders is called the lockout period or revolving period. At the end of the lockout period, principal repayments are distributed to the security holders. The period when the principal repayments are not reinvested is called the principal amortization period. Notice that unlike the typical transaction that is backed by amortizing assets, the collateral backed by non-amortizing assets changes over time. A structure in which the principal repayments are reinvested in new loans is called a revolving structure.

While the receivables in a revolving structure may not be prepaid, all the bonds issued by the trust may be retired early if certain events occur. That is, during the lockout period, the trustee is required to use principal repayments to retire the securities rather than reinvest principal in new collateral if certain events occur. The most common trigger is the poor performance of the collateral. This provision that specifies the redirection of the principal repayments during the lockout period to retire the securities is referred to as the early amortization provision or rapid amortization provision.

Not all transactions that are revolving structures are backed by non-amortizing assets. There are some transactions in which the collateral consists of amortizing assets but during a lockout period, the principal repayments are reinvested in additional loans. For example, there are transactions in the European market in which the collateral consists of residential mortgage loans, but during the lockout period principal repayments are used to acquire additional residential mortgage loans.

E. Collateral Cash Flow

For an amortizing asset, projection of the cash flows requires projecting prepayments. One factor that may affect prepayments is the prevailing level of interest rates relative to the interest rate on the loan. In projecting prepayments it is critical to determine the extent to which borrowers take advantage of a decline in interest rates below the loan rate in order to refinance the loan.

As with nonagency mortgage-backed securities, described in the reading on the mortgage-backed sector of the bond market, modeling defaults for the collateral is critical in estimating the cash flows of an asset-backed security. Proceeds that are recovered in the event of a default of a loan prior to the scheduled principal repayment date of an amortizing asset represent a prepayment and are referred to as an involuntary prepayment. Projecting prepayments for amortizing assets requires an assumption about the default rate and the recovery rate. For a non-amortizing asset, while the concept of a prepayment does not exist, a projection of defaults is still necessary to project how much will be recovered and when.

The analysis of prepayments can be performed on a pool level or a loan level. In pool-level analysis it is assumed that all loans comprising the collateral are identical. For an amortizing asset, the amortization schedule is based on the gross weighted average coupon (GWAC) and weighted average maturity (WAM) for that single loan. We explained in the previous reading what the WAC and WAM of a pool of mortgage loans is and illustrated how it is computed. In this reading, we refer to the WAC as gross WAC. Pool-level analysis is appropriate where the underlying loans are homogeneous. Loan-level analysis involves amortizing each loan (or group of homogeneous loans).

The expected final maturity of an asset-backed security is the maturity date based on expected prepayments at the time of pricing of a deal. The legal final maturity can be two or more years after the expected final maturity. The average life, or weighted average life, was explained previously.

Also explained is a tranche's principal window, which refers to the time period over which the principal is expected to be paid to the bondholders. A principal window can be wide or narrow. When there is only one principal payment that is scheduled to be made to a bondholder, the bond is referred to as having a bullet maturity. Due to prepayments, an asset-backed security that is expected to have a bullet maturity may have an actual maturity that differs from that specified in the prospectus. Hence, asset-backed securities bonds that have an expected payment of only one principal are said to have a soft bullet.

F. Credit Enhancements

All asset-backed securities are credit enhanced. That means that support is provided for one or more of the bondholders in the structure. Credit enhancement levels are determined relative to a specific rating desired by the issuer for a security by each rating agency. Specifically, an investor in a triple A rated security expects to have "minimal" (virtually no) chance of losing any principal due to defaults. For example, a rating agency may require credit enhancement equal to four times expected losses to obtain a triple A rating or three times expected losses to obtain a double A rating. The amount of credit enhancement necessary depends on rating agency requirements.

There are two general types of credit enhancement structures: external and internal. We describe each type below.

1. External Credit Enhancements

In an ABS, there are two principal parties: the issuer and the security holder. The issuer in our hypothetical securitization is HAT. If another entity is introduced into the structure to guarantee any payments to the security holders, that entity is referred to as a "third party."

The most common third party in a securitization is a monoline insurance company (also referred to as a monoline insurer). A monoline insurance company is an insurance company whose business is restricted to providing guarantees for financial products such as municipal securities and asset-backed securities.[3] When a securitization has external credit enhancement that is provided by a monoline insurer, the securities are said to be "wrapped." The insurance works as follows. The monoline insurer agrees to make timely payment of interest and principal up to a specified amount should the issuer fail to make the payment. Unlike municipal bond insurance which guarantees the entire principal amount, the guarantee in a securitization is only for a percentage of the par value at origination. For example, a $100 million securitization may have only $5 million guaranteed by the monoline insurer.

Two less common forms of external credit enhancement are a letter of credit from a bank and a guarantee by the seller of the assets (i.e., the entity that sold the assets to the SPV—QHT in our hypothetical illustration).[4] The reason why these two forms of credit enhancement are less commonly used is because of the "weak link approach" employed by rating agencies when they rate securitizations. According to this approach, when rating a proposed structure, the credit quality of a security is only as good as the weakest link in its credit enhancement regardless of the quality of underlying assets. Consequently, if an issuer seeks a triple A rating for one of the bond classes in the structure, it would be unlikely to be awarded such a rating if the external credit enhancer has a rating that is less than triple A. Since few corporations and banks that issue letters of credit have a sufficiently high rating themselves to achieve the rating that may be sought in a securitization, these two forms of external credit enhancement are not as common as insurance.

There is credit risk in a securitization when there is a third-party guarantee because the downgrading of the third party *could* result in the downgrading of the securities in a structure.

2. Internal Credit Enhancements

Internal credit enhancements come in more complicated forms than external credit enhancements. The most common forms of internal credit enhancement are reserve funds, overcollateralization, and senior/subordinate structures.

---

[3] The major monoline insurance companies in the United States are Capital Markets Assurance Corporation (CapMAC), Financial Security Assurance Inc. (FSA), Financial Guaranty Insurance Corporation (FGIC), and Municipal Bond Investors Assurance Corporation (MBIA).

[4] As noted earlier, the seller is not a party to the transaction once the assets are sold to the SPV who then issues the securities. Hence, if the seller provides a guarantee, it is viewed as a third-party guarantee.

Suppose that the collateral for an asset-backed securities structure has a gross weighted average coupon of 9.5%. The servicing fee is 75 basis points. The tranches issued have a weighted average coupon rate of 7.5%. What is the excess spread?

a. Reserve Funds

Reserve funds come in two forms:

▶ cash reserve funds,

▶ excess spread accounts.

Cash reserve funds are straight deposits of cash generated from issuance proceeds. In this case, part of the underwriting profits from the deal are deposited into a fund which typically invests in money market instruments. Cash reserve funds are typically used in conjunction with external credit enhancements.

Excess spread accounts involve the allocation of excess spread or cash into a separate reserve account after paying out the net coupon, servicing fee, and all other expenses on a monthly basis. The excess spread is a design feature of the structure. For example, suppose that:

1. gross weighted average coupon (gross WAC) is 8.00%—this is the interest rate paid by the borrowers

2. servicing and other fees are 0.25%

3. net weighted average coupon (net WAC) is 7.25%—this is the rate that is paid to all the tranches in the structure

So, for this hypothetical deal, 8.00% is available to make payments to the tranches, to cover servicing fees, and to cover other fees. Of that amount, 0.25% is paid for servicing and other fees and 7.25% is paid to the tranches. This means that only 7.50% must be paid out, leaving 0.50% (8.00% − 7.50%). This 0.50% or 50 basis points is called the excess spread. This amount is placed in a reserve account—the excess servicing account—and it will gradually increase and can be used to pay for possible future losses.

b. Overcollateralization

Overcollateralization in a structure refers to a situation in which the value of the collateral exceeds the amount of the par value of the outstanding securities issued by the SPV. For example, if $100 million par value of securities are issued and at issuance the collateral has a market value of $105, there is $5 million in overcollateralization. Over time, the amount of overcollateralization changes due to 1) defaults, 2) amortization, and 3) prepayments. For example, suppose that two years after issuance, the par value of the securities outstanding is $90 million and the value of the collateral at the time is $93 million. As a result, the overcollateralization is $3 million ($93 million − $90 million).

Overcollateralization represents a form of internal credit enhancement because it can be used to absorb losses. For example, if the liability of the structure (i.e., par value of all the bond classes) is $100 million and the collateral's value is $105 million, then the first $5 million of losses will not result in a loss to any of the bond classes in the structure.

c. Senior-Subordinate Structure

Earlier in this section we explained a senior-subordinate structure in describing the bonds that can be issued in a securitization. We explained that there are senior bond classes and subordinate bond classes. The subordinate bond classes are also referred to as junior bond classes or non-senior bond classes.

As explained earlier, the creation of a senior-subordinate structure is done to provide credit tranching. More specifically, the senior-subordinate structure is a form of internal credit enhancement because the subordinate bond classes provide credit support for the senior bond classes. To understand why, the hypothetical HAT structure with one subordinate bond class that was described earlier is reproduced below:

Bond Class	Par Value ($ in Millions)
A (senior)	90
B (subordinate)	10
Total	100

The senior bond class, A, is credit enhanced because the first $10 million in losses is absorbed by the subordinate bond class, B. Consequently, if defaults do not exceed $10 million, then the senior bond will receive the entire par value of $90 million.

Note that one subordinate bond class can provide credit enhancement for another subordinate bond class. To see this, consider the hypothetical HAT structure with two subordinate bond classes presented earlier:

Bond Class	Par Value ($ in Millions)
A (senior)	90
B (subordinate)	7
C (subordinate)	3
Total	100

Bond Class C, the first loss piece, provides credit enhancement for not only the senior bond class, but also the subordinate bond class B.

The basic concern in the senior-subordinate structure is that while the subordinate bond classes provide a certain level of credit protection for the senior bond class at the closing of the deal, the level of protection changes over time due to prepayments. Faster prepayments can remove the desired credit protection. Thus, the objective after the deal closes is to distribute any prepayments such that the credit protection for the senior bond class does not deteriorate over time.

In real-estate related asset-backed securities, as well as nonagency mortgage-backed securities, the solution to the credit protection problem is a well developed mechanism called the shifting interest mechanism. Here is how it works. The percentage of the mortgage balance of the subordinate bond class to that of the mortgage balance for the entire deal is called the level of subordination or the subordinate interest. The higher the percentage, the greater the level of protection for the senior bond classes. The subordinate interest changes after the deal is closed due to prepayments. That is, the subordinate interest shifts (hence the term "shifting interest"). The purpose of a shifting interest mechanism is to allocate prepayments so that the subordinate interest is maintained at an acceptable level to protect the senior bond class. In effect, by paying down the senior bond class more quickly, the amount of subordination is maintained at the desired level.

The prospectus will provide the shifting interest percentage schedule for calculating the senior prepayment percentage (the percentage of prepayments paid to the senior bond class). For mortgage loans, a commonly used shifting interest percentage schedule is as follows:

Year after Issuance	Senior Prepayment (%)
1–5	100
6	70
7	60
8	40
9	20
after year 9	0

So, for example, if prepayments in month 20 are $1 million, the amount paid to the senior bond class is $1 million and no prepayments are made to the subordinated bond classes. If prepayments in month 90 (in the seventh year after issuance) are $1 million, the senior bond class is paid $600,000 (60% × $1 million).

The shifting interest percentage schedule given in the prospectus is the "base" schedule. The set of shifting interest percentages can change over time depending on the performance of the collateral. If the performance is such that the credit protection for the senior bond class has deteriorated because credit losses have reduced the subordinate bond classes, the base shifting interest percentages are overridden and a higher allocation of prepayments is made to the senior bond class.

Performance analysis of the collateral is undertaken by the trustee for determining whether or not to override the base schedule. The performance analysis is in terms of tests, and if the collateral fails any of the tests, this will trigger an override of the base schedule.

It is important to understand that the presence of a shifting interest mechanism results in a trade-off between credit risk and contraction risk for the senior bond class. The shifting interest mechanism reduces the credit risk to the senior bond class. However, because the senior bond class receives a larger share of any prepayments, contraction risk increases.

G. Call Provisions

Corporate, federal agency, and municipal bonds may contain a call provision. This provision gives the issuer the right to retire the bond issue prior to the stated maturity date. The issuer motivation for having the provision is to benefit from a decline in interest rates after the bond is issued. Asset-backed securities typically have call provisions. The motivation is twofold. As with other bonds, the issuer (the SPV) will want to take advantage of a decline in interest rates. In addition, to reduce administrative fees, the trustee may want to call in the issue because the par value of a bond class is small and it is more cost-effective to pay off the one or more bond classes.

Typically, for a corporate, federal agency, and municipal bond the trigger event for a call provision is that a specified amount of time has passed.[5] In the case of asset-backed securities, it is not simply the passage of time whereby the trustee is permitted to exercise any call option. There are trigger events for exercising the call option based on the amount of the issue outstanding.

There are two call provisions where the trigger that grants the trustee to call in the issue is based on a date being reached: 1) call on or after specified date and 2) auction call. A call on or after specified date operates just like a standard call provision for corporate, federal agency, and municipal securities: once a specified date is reached, the trustee has the option to call all the outstanding bonds. In an auction call, at a certain date a call will be exercised if an auction results in the outstanding collateral being sold at a price greater than its par value. The premium over par value received from the auctioned collateral is retained by the trustee and is eventually distributed to the seller of the assets.

Provisions that allow the trustee to call an issue or a tranche based on the par value outstanding are referred to as optional clean-up call provisions. Two examples are 1) percent of collateral call and 2) percent of bond call. In a percent of collateral call, the outstanding bonds can be called at par value if the outstanding *collateral's* balance falls below a predetermined percent of the original collateral's balance. This is the most common type of clean-up call provision for amortizing assets and the predetermined level is typically 10%. For example, suppose that the value for the collateral is $100 million. If there is a percent of collateral call provision with a trigger of 10%, then the trustee can call the entire issue if the value of the call is $10 million or less. In a percent of bond call, the outstanding bonds can be called at par value if the outstanding *bond's* par value relative to the original par value of bonds issued falls below a specified amount.

There is a call option that combines two triggers based on the amount outstanding and date. In a latter of percent or date call, the outstanding bonds can be called if either 1) the collateral's outstanding balance reaches a predetermined level before the specified call date or 2) the call date has been reached even if the collateral outstanding is above the predetermined level.

In addition to the above call provisions which permit the trustee to call the bonds, there may be an insurer call. Such a call permits the insurer to call the bonds if the collateral's cumulative loss history reaches a predetermined level.

---

[5] The calling of a portion of the issue is permitted to satisfy any sinking fund requirement.

HOME EQUITY LOANS   3

A home equity loan (HEL) is a loan backed by residential property. At one time, the loan was typically a second lien on property that was already pledged to secure a first lien. In some cases, the lien was a third lien. In recent years, the character of a home equity loan has changed. Today, a home equity loan is often a first lien on property where the borrower has either an *impaired credit history* and/or the payment-to-income ratio is too high for the loan to qualify as a conforming loan for securitization by Ginnie Mae, Fannie Mae, or Freddie Mac. Typically, the borrower used a home equity loan to consolidate consumer debt using the current home as collateral rather than to obtain funds to purchase a new home.

Home equity loans can be either closed end or open end. A closed-end HEL is structured the same way as a fully amortizing residential mortgage loan. That is, it has a fixed maturity and the payments are structured to fully amortize the loan by the maturity date. With an open-end HEL, the homeowner is given a credit line and can write checks or use a credit card for up to the amount of the credit line. The amount of the credit line depends on the amount of the equity the borrower has in the property. Because home equity loan securitizations are predominately closed-end HELs, our focus in this section is securities backed by them.

There are both fixed-rate and variable-rate closed-end HELs. Typically, variable-rate loans have a reference rate of 6-month LIBOR and have periodic caps and lifetime caps. (A periodic cap limits the change in the mortgage rate from the previous time the mortgage rate was reset; a lifetime cap sets a maximum that the mortgage rate can ever be for the loan.) The cash flow of a pool of closed-end HELs is comprised of interest, regularly scheduled principal repayments, and prepayments, just as with mortgage-backed securities. Thus, it is necessary to have a prepayment model and a default model to forecast cash flows. The prepayment speed is measured in terms of a conditional prepayment rate (CPR).

A. Prepayments

As explained in the reading on the mortgage-backed sector of the bond market, in the agency MBS market the PSA prepayment benchmark is used as the base case prepayment assumption in the prospectus. This benchmark assumes that the conditional prepayment rate (CPR) begins at 0.2% in the first month and increases linearly for 30 months to 6% CPR. From month 30 to the last month that the security is expected to be outstanding, the CPR is assumed to be constant at 6%. At the time that the prepayment speed is assumed to be constant, the security is said to be seasoned. For the PSA benchmark, a security is assumed to be seasoned in month 30. When the prepayment speed is depicted graphically, the linear increase in the CPR from month 1 to the month when the security is assumed to be seasoned is called the prepayment ramp. For the PSA benchmark, the prepayment ramp begins at month 1 and extends to month 30. Speeds that are assumed to be faster or slower than the PSA prepayment benchmark are quoted as a multiple of the base case prepayment speed.

There are differences in the prepayment behavior for home equity loans and agency MBS. Wall Street firms involved in the underwriting and market making of securities backed by HELs have developed prepayment models for these deals. Several firms have found that the key difference between the prepayment behavior of HELs and agency residential mortgages is the important role played by the credit characteristics of the borrower.[6]

Borrower characteristics and the amount of seasoning (i.e., how long the loans have been outstanding) must be kept in mind when trying to assess prepayments for a particular deal. In the prospectus of an HEL, a base case prepayment assumption is made. Rather than use the PSA prepayment benchmark as the base case prepayment speed, issuer's now use a base case prepayment benchmark that is specific to that issuer. The benchmark prepayment speed in the prospectus is called the prospectus prepayment curve or PPC. As with the PSA benchmark, faster or slower prepayments speeds are quoted as a multiple of the PPC. Having an issuer-specific prepayment benchmark is preferred to a generic benchmark such as the PSA benchmark. The drawback for this improved description of the prepayment characteristics of a pool of mortgage loans is that it makes comparing the prepayment characteristics and investment characteristics of the collateral between issuers and issues (newly issued and seasoned issues) difficult.

PRACTICE QUESTION 3

The base case prepayment for the Champion Home Equity Loan Trust 1996-1 is provided for the fixed-rate loans (referred to as Group One in the prospectus) and floating-rate loans (referred to as Group Two in the prospectus). The following is taken from the prospectus for the Group One loans:

> The model used with respect to the fixed rate certificates (the "prepayment ramp") assumes that the home equity loans in loan Group One prepay at a rate of 4% CPR in the first month after origination, and an additional 1.5% each month thereafter until the 14th month. Beginning in the 15th month and each month thereafter, the prepayment ramp assumes a prepayment rate of 25% CPR.

What is the CPR assuming 150% PPC for the fixed-rate collateral for the following months:

Month	CPR	Month	CPR	Month	CPR
1		11		30	
2		12		125	
3		13		150	
4		14		200	
5		15		250	
6		16		275	
7		17		300	
8		18		325	
9		19		350	
10		20		360	

---

[6] Dale Westhoff and Mark Feldman, "Prepayment Modeling and Valuation of Home Equity Loan Securities," Chapter 18 in Frank J. Fabozzi, Chuck Ramsey, and Michael Marz (eds.), *The Handbook of Nonagency Mortgage-Backed Securities: Second Edition* (New Hope, PA: Frank J. Fabozzi Associates, 2000).

Since HEL deals are backed by both fixed-rate and variable-rate loans, a separate PPC is provided for each type of loan. For example, in the prospectus for the Contimortgage Home Equity Loan Trust 1998-2, the base case prepayment assumption for the fixed-rate collateral begins at 4% CPR in month 1 and increases 1.45455% CPR per month until month 12, at which time it is 20% CPR. Thus, the collateral is assumed to be seasoned in 12 months. The prepayment ramp begins in month 1 and ends in month 12. If an investor analyzed the deal based on 200% PPC, this means doubling the CPRs cited and using 12 months for when the collateral seasons. For the variable-rate collateral in the ContiMortgage deal, 100% PPC assumes the collateral is seasoned after 18 months with the CPR in month 1 being 4% and increasing 1.82353% CPR each month. From month 18 on, the CPR is 35%. Thus, the prepayment ramp starts at month 1 and ends at month 18. Notice that for this issuer, the variable-rate collateral is assumed to season slower than the fixed-rate collateral (18 versus 12 months), but has a faster CPR when the pool is seasoned (35% versus 20%).

B. Payment Structure

As with nonagency mortgage-backed securities discussed in the reading on the mortgage-backed sector of the bond market, there are passthrough and paythrough home equity loan-backed structures.

Typically, home equity loan-backed securities are securitized by both closed-end fixed-rate and adjustable-rate (or variable-rate) HELs. The securities backed by the latter are called HEL floaters. The reference rate of the underlying loans typically is 6-month LIBOR. The cash flow of these loans is affected by periodic and lifetime caps on the loan rate.

Institutional investors that seek securities that better match their floating-rate funding costs are attracted to securities that offer a floating-rate coupon. To increase the attractiveness of home equity loan-backed securities to such investors, the securities typically have been created in which the reference rate is 1-month LIBOR. Because of 1) the mismatch between the reference rate on the underlying loans (6-month LIBOR) and that of the HEL floater and 2) the periodic and life caps of the underlying loans, there is a cap on the coupon rate for the HEL floater. Unlike a typical floater, which has a cap that is fixed throughout the security's life, the effective periodic and lifetime cap of an HEL floater is variable. The effective cap, referred to as the available funds cap, will depend on the amount of funds generated by the net coupon on the principal, less any fees.

Let's look at one issue, Advanta Mortgage Loan Trust 1995-2 issued in June 1995. At the offering, this issue had approximately $122 million closed-end HELs. There were 1,192 HELs consisting of 727 fixed-rate loans and 465 variable-rate loans. There were five classes (A-1, A-2, A-3, A-4, and A-5) and a residual. The five classes are summarized below:

Class	Paramount ($)	Passthrough Coupon Rate (%)
A-1	9,229,000	7.30
A-2	30,330,000	6.60
A-3	16,455,000	6.85
A-4	9,081,000	floating rate
A-5	56,917,000	floating rate

The collateral is divided into group I and group II. The 727 fixed-rate loans are included in group I and support Classes A-1, A-2, A-3, and A-4 certificates. The 465 variable-rate loans are in group II and support Class A-5.

Tranches have been structured in home equity loan deals so as to give some senior tranches greater prepayment protection than other senior tranches. The two types of structures that do this are the non-accelerating senior tranche and the planned amortization class tranche.

1. Non-Accelerating Senior Tranches

A non-accelerating senior tranche (NAS tranche) receives principal payments according to a schedule. The schedule is not a dollar amount. Rather, it is a principal schedule that shows for a given month the share of pro rata principal that must be distributed to the NAS tranche. A typical principal schedule for a NAS tranche is as follows:[7]

Months	Share of Pro Rata Principal (%)
1 through 36	0
37 through 60	45
61 through 72	80
73 through 84	100
After month 84	300

The average life for the NAS tranche is stable for a large range of prepayments because for the first three years all prepayments are made to the other senior tranches. This reduces the risk of the NAS tranche contracting (i.e., shortening) due to fast prepayments. After month 84, 300% of its pro rata share is paid to the NAS tranche, thereby reducing its extension risk.

The average life stability over a wide range of prepayments is illustrated in Exhibit 2. The deal analyzed is the ContiMortgage Home Equity Loan Trust 1997-2.[8] Class A-9 is the NAS tranche. The analysis was performed on Bloomberg shortly after the deal was issued using the issue's PPC. As can be seen, the average life is fairly stable between 75% to 200% PPC. In fact, the difference in the average life between 75% PPC and 200% PPC is slightly greater than one year.

In contrast, Exhibit 2 also shows the average life over the same prepayment scenarios for a non-NAS sequential-pay tranche in the same deal—Class A-7. Notice the substantial average life variability. While the average life difference between 75% and 200% PPC for the NAS tranche is just over 1 year, it is more than 9 years for the non-NAS tranche. Of course, the non-NAS in the same deal will be less stable than a regular sequential tranche because the non-NAS gets a greater share of principal than it would otherwise.

[7] Charles Schorin, Steven Weinreich, and Oliver Hsiang, "Home Equity Loan Transaction Structures," Chapter 6 in Frank J. Fabozzi, Chuck Ramsey, and Michael Marz, *Handbook of Nonagency Mortgage-Backed Securities: Second Edition* (New Hope, PA: Frank J. Fabozzi Associates, 2000).

[8] This illustration is from Schorin, Weinreich, and Hsiang, "Home Equity Loan Transaction Structures."

EXHIBIT 2	Average Life for NAS Tranche (Class A-9) and Non-NAS Tranche (Class A-7) for ContiMortgage Home Equity Loan Trust 1997-2 for a Range of Prepayments

	% PPC												Avg. Life Difference
	0	50	75	100	120	150	200	250	300	350	400	500	75% to 200% PPC
Plateau CPR	0	10	15	20	24	30	40	50	60	70	80	100	
Avg. Life													
NAS Bond	11.71	7.81	7.06	6.58	6.30	6.06	5.97	3.98	2.17	1.73	1.38	0.67	1.09
Non-NAS Bond	21.93	14.54	11.94	8.82	6.73	4.71	2.59	1.96	1.55	1.25	1.03	0.58	9.35

Calculation: Bloomberg Financial Markets.

Reported in Charles Schorin, Steven Weinreich, and Oliver Hsiang, "Home Equity Loan Transaction Structures," Chapter 6 in Frank J. Fabozzi, Chuck Ramsey, and Michael Marz, *Handbook of Nonagency Mortgage-Backed Securities: Second Edition* (New Hope, PA: Frank J. Fabozzi Associates, 2000).

2. Planned Amortization Class Tranche

In our discussion of collateralized mortgage obligations issued by the agencies in the reading on the mortgage-backed sector of the bond market, we explained how a planned amortization class tranche can be created. These tranches are also created in HEL structures. Unlike agency CMO PAC tranches that are backed by fixed-rate loans, the collateral for HEL deals is both fixed rate and adjustable rate.

An example of an HEL PAC tranche in an HEL-backed deal is tranche A-6 in ContiMortgage 1998-2. We described the PPC for this deal in Section 3.A.1 above. There is a separate PAC collar for both the fixed-rate and adjustable-rate collateral. For the fixed-rate collateral the PAC collar is 125%–175% PPC; for the adjustable-rate collateral the PAC collar is 95%–130% PPC. The average life for tranche A-6 (a tranche backed by the fixed-rate collateral) is 5.1 years. As explained, the effective collar for shorter tranches can be greater than the upper collar specified in the prospectus. The effective upper collar for tranche A-6 is actually 180% PPC (assuming that the adjustable-rate collateral pays at 100% PPC).[9]

For shorter PACs, the effective upper collar is greater. For example, for tranche A-3 in the same deal, the initial PAC collar is 125% to 175% PPC with an average life of 2.02 years. However, the effective upper collar is 190% PPC (assuming the adjustable-rate collateral pays at 100% PPC).

The effective collar for PAC tranches changes over time based on actual prepayments and therefore based on when the support tranches depart from the initial PAC collar. For example, if for the next 36 months after the issuance of the ContiMortgage 1998-2 actual prepayments are a constant 150% PPC, then the effective collar would be 135% PPC to 210% PPC.[10] That is, the lower and

---

[9] For a more detailed analysis of this tranche, see Schorin, Weinreich, and Hsiang, "Home Equity Loan Transaction Structures."

[10] Schorin, Weinreich, and Hsiang, "Home Equity Loan Transaction Structures."

upper collar will increase. If the actual PPC is 200% PPC for the 10 months after issuance, the support bonds will be fully paid off and there will be no PAC collateral. In this situation the PAC is said to be a broken PAC.

4   MANUFACTURED HOUSING-BACKED SECURITIES

Manufactured housing-backed securities are backed by loans for manufactured homes. In contrast to site-built homes, manufactured homes are built at a factory and then transported to a site. The loan may be either a mortgage loan (for both the land and the home) or a consumer retail installment loan.

Manufactured housing-backed securities are issued by Ginnie Mae and private entities. The former securities are guaranteed by the full faith and credit of the U.S. government. The manufactured home loans that are collateral for the securities issued and guaranteed by Ginnie Mae are loans guaranteed by the Federal Housing Administration (FHA) or Veterans Administration (VA).

Loans not backed by the FHA or VA are called conventional loans. Manufactured housing-backed securities that are backed by such loans are called conventional manufactured housing-backed securities. These securities are issued by private entities.

The typical loan for a manufactured home is 15 to 20 years. The loan repayment is structured to fully amortize the amount borrowed. Therefore, as with residential mortgage loans and HELs, the cash flow consists of net interest, regularly scheduled principal, and prepayments. However, prepayments are more stable for manufactured housing-backed securities because they are not sensitive to refinancing.

There are several reasons for this. First, the loan balances are typically small so that there is no significant dollar savings from refinancing. Second, the rate of depreciation of mobile homes may be such that in the earlier years depreciation is greater than the amount of the loan paid off. This makes it difficult to refinance the loan. Finally, typically borrowers are of lower credit quality and therefore find it difficult to obtain funds to refinance.

As with residential mortgage loans and HELs, prepayments on manufactured housing-backed securities are measured in terms of CPR and each issue contains a PPC.

The payment structure is the same as with nonagency mortgage-backed securities and home equity loan-backed securities.

5   RESIDENTIAL MBS OUTSIDE THE UNITED STATES

Throughout the world where the market for securitized assets has developed, the largest sector is the residential mortgage-backed sector. It is not possible to provide a discussion of the residential mortgage-backed securities market in every country. Instead, to provide a flavor for this market sector and the similarities with the U.S. nonagency mortgage-backed securities market, we will discuss just the market in the United Kingdom and Australia.

A. U.K. Residential Mortgage-Backed Securities

In Europe, the country in which there has been the largest amount of issuance of asset-backed securities is the United Kingdom.[11] The largest component of that market is the residential mortgage-backed security market, which includes "prime" residential mortgage-backed securities and "nonconforming" residential mortgage-backed securities. In the U.S. mortgage market, a nonconforming mortgage loan is one that does not meet the underwriting standards of Ginnie Mae, Fannie Mae, or Freddie Mac. However, this does not mean that the loan has greater credit risk. In contrast, in the U.K. mortgage market, nonconforming mortgage loans are made to borrowers that are viewed as having greater credit risk—those that do not have a credit history and those with a history of failing to meet their obligations.

The standard mortgage loan is a variable rate, fully amortizing loan. Typically, the term of the loan is 25 years. As in the U.S. mortgage market, borrowers seeking a loan with a high loan-to-value ratio are required to obtain mortgage insurance, called a "mortgage indemnity guarantee" (MIG).

The deals are more akin to the nonagency market since there is no guarantee by a federally related agency or a government sponsored enterprise as in the United States. Thus, there is credit enhancement as explained below.

Because the underlying mortgage loans are floating rate, the securities issued are floating rate (typically, LIBOR is the reference rate). The cash flow depends on the timing of the principal payments. The deals are typically set up as a sequential-pay structure. For example, consider the Granite Mortgage 00-2 transaction, a typical structure in the United Kingdom.[12] The mortgage pool consists of prime mortgages. There are four bond classes. The two class A tranches, Class A-1 and Class A-2, are rated AAA. One is a dollar-denominated tranche and the other a pound sterling tranche. Class B is rated single A and tranche C is rated BBB. The sequence of principal payments is as follows: Class A-1 and Class A-2 are paid off on a pro rata basis, then Class B is paid off, and then Class C is paid off.

The issuer has the option to call the outstanding notes under the following circumstances:

▶ a withholding tax is imposed on the interest payments to noteholders;

▶ a clean-up call (if the mortgage pool falls to 10% or less of the original pool amount);

▶ on a specified date (called the "step-up date") or dates in the future.

For example, for the Granite Mortgage 00-02 transaction, the step-up date is September 2007. The issuer is likely to call the issue because the coupon rate on the notes increases at that time. In this deal, as with most, the margin over LIBOR doubles.

---

[11] Information about the U.K. residential mortgage-backed securities market draws from the following sources: Phil Adams, "UK Residential Mortgage-Backed Securities," and "UK Non-Conforming Residential Mortgage-Backed Securities," in *Building Blocks*, Asset-Backed Securities Research, Barclays Capital, January 2001; Christopher Flanagan and Edward Reardon, *European Structured Products: 2001 Review and 2002 Outlook*, Global Structured Finance Research, J.P. Morgan Securities Inc., January 11, 2002; and "UK Mortgages—MBS Products for U.S. Investors," *Mortgage Strategist*, UBS Warburg, February 27, 2001, pp. 15–21.

[12] For a more detailed discussion of this structure, see Adams, "UK Residential Mortgage-Backed Securities," pp. 31–37.

Credit enhancement can consist of excess spread, reserve fund, and subordination. For the Granite Mortgage 00-2, there was subordination: Class B and C tranches for the two Class A tranche and Class C tranche for the Class B tranche. The reserve was fully funded at the time of issuance, and the excess spread was used to build up the reserve fund. In addition, there is a "principal shortfall provision." This provision requires that if the realized losses for a period are such that the excess reserve for that period is not sufficient to cover the losses, as excess spread becomes available in future periods they are used to cover these losses. Also there are performance triggers that under certain conditions will provide further credit protection to the senior bonds by modifying the payment of principal. When the underlying mortgage pool consists of nonconforming mortgage loans, additional protections are provided for investors.

Since prepayments will reduce the average life of the senior notes in a transaction, typical deals have provisions that permit the purchase of substitute mortgages if the prepayment rate exceeds a certain rate. For example, in the Granite Mortgage 00-02 deal, this rate is 20% per annum.

B. Australian Mortgage-Backed Securities

In Australia, lending is dominated by mortgage banks, the larger ones being ANZ, Commonwealth Bank of Australia, National Australia Bank, Westpac, and St. George Bank.[13] Non-mortgage bank competitors who have entered the market have used securitization as a financing vehicle. The majority of the properties are concentrated in New South Wales, particularly the city of Sydney. Rating agencies have found that the risk of default is considerably less than in the U.S. and the U.K.

Loan maturities are typically between 20 and 30 years. As in the United States, there is a wide range of mortgage designs with respect to interest rates. There are fixed-rate, variable-rate (both capped and uncapped), and rates tied to a benchmark.

There is mortgage insurance for loans to protect lenders, called "lenders mortgage insurance" (LMI). Loans typically have LMI covering 20% to 100% of the loan. The companies that provide this insurance are private corporations.[14] When mortgage loans that do not have LMI are securitized, typically the issuer will purchase insurance for those loans.

LMI is important for securitized transactions since it is the first layer of credit enhancement in a deal structure. The rating agencies recognize this in rating the tranches in a structure. The amount that a rating agency will count toward credit enhancement for LMI depends on the rating agency's assessment of the mortgage insurance company.

When securitized, the tranches have a floating rate. There is an initial revolving period—which means that no principal payments are made to the tranche holders but instead reinvested in new collateral. As with the U.K. Granite Mortgage 00-02 deal, the issuer has the right to call the issue if there is

---

[13] Information about the Australian residential mortgage-backed securities market draws from the following sources: Phil Adams, "Australian Residential Mortgage-Backed Securities," in *Building Blocks;* Karen Weaver, Eugene Xu, Nicholas Bakalar, and Trudy Weibel, "Mortgage-Backed Securities in Australia," Chapter 41 in *The Handbook of Mortgage-Backed Securities: Fifth Edition* (New York, NY: McGraw-Hill, 2001); and, "Australian Value Down Under," *Mortgage Strategist,* UBS Warburg, February 6, 2001, pp. 14–22.

[14] The five major ones are Royal and Sun Alliance Lenders Mortgage Insurance Limited, CGU Lenders Mortgage Insurance Corporation Ltd., PMI mortgage insurance limited, GE Mortgage Insurance Property Ltd., and GE Mortgage Insurance Corporation.

an imposition of a withholding tax on note holders' interest payments, after a certain date, or if the balance falls below a certain level (typically, 10%).

Australian mortgage-backed securities have tranches that are U.S. dollar denominated and some that are denominated in euros.[15] These global deals typically have two or three AAA senior tranches and one AA or AA—junior tranche.

For credit enhancement, there is excess spread (which in most deals is typically small), subordination, and, as noted earlier, LMI. To illustrate this, consider the Interstar Millennium Series 2000-3E Trust—a typical Australian MBS transaction. There are two tranches: a senior tranche (Class A) that was rated AAA and a subordinated tranche (Class B) that was AA–. The protection afforded the senior tranche is the subordinated tranche, LMI (all the properties were covered up to 100% and were insured by all five major mortgage insurance companies), and the excess spread.

AUTO LOAN-BACKED SECURITIES ▬▬▬ 6

Auto loan-backed securities represents one of the oldest and most familiar sectors of the asset-backed securities market. Auto loan-backed securities are issued by:

1. the financial subsidiaries of auto manufacturers
2. commercial banks
3. independent finance companies and small financial institutions specializing in auto loans

Historically, auto loan-backed securities have represented between 18% to 25% of the asset-backed securities market. The auto loan market is tiered based on the credit quality of the borrowers. "Prime auto loans" are of fundamentally high credit quality and originated by the financial subsidiaries of major auto manufacturers. The loans are of high credit quality for the following reasons. First, they are a secured form of lending. Second, they begin to repay principal immediately through amortization. Third, they are short-term in nature. Finally, for the most part, major issuers of auto loans have tended to follow reasonably prudent underwriting standards.

Unlike the sub-prime mortgage industry, there is less consistency on what actually constitutes various categories of prime and sub-prime auto loans. Moody's assumes the *prime* market is composed of issuers typically having cumulative losses of less than 3%; *near-prime* issuers have cumulative losses of 3–7%; and sub-prime issuers have losses exceeding 7%.

The auto sector was a small part of the European asset-backed securities market in 2002, about 5% of total securitization. There are two reasons for this. First, there is lower per capita car ownership in Europe. Second, there is considerable variance of tax and regulations dealing with borrower privacy rules in Europe, thereby making securitization difficult.[16] Auto deals have been done in Italy, the U.K., Germany, Portugal, and Belgium.

---

[15] The foreign exchange risk for these deals is typically hedged using various types of swaps (fixed/floating, floating/floating, and currency swaps).

[16] Flanagan and Reardon, *European Structures Products: 2001 Review and 2002 Outlook,* p. 9.

A. Cash Flow and Prepayments

The cash flow for auto loan-backed securities consists of regularly scheduled monthly loan payments (interest and scheduled principal repayments) and any prepayments. For securities backed by auto loans, prepayments result from 1) sales and trade-ins requiring full payoff of the loan, 2) repossession and subsequent resale of the automobile, 3) loss or destruction of the vehicle, 4) payoff of the loan with cash to save on the interest cost, and 5) refinancing of the loan at a lower interest cost.

Prepayments due to repossession and subsequent resale are sensitive to the economic cycle. In recessionary economic periods, prepayments due to this factor increase. While refinancings may be a major reason for prepayments of mortgage loans, they are of minor importance for automobile loans. Moreover, the interest rates for the automobile loans underlying some deals are substantially below market rates since they are offered by manufacturers as part of a sales promotion.

B. Measuring Prepayments

For most asset-backed securities where there are prepayments, prepayments are measured in terms of the conditional prepayment rate, CPR. As explained in the reading on the mortgage-backed sector of the bond market, monthly prepayments are quoted in terms of the single monthly mortality (SMM) rate. The *convention* for calculating and reporting prepayment rates for auto loan-backed securities is different. Prepayments for auto loan-backed securities are measured in terms of the absolute prepayment speed, denoted by ABS.[17] The ABS is the monthly prepayment expressed as a percentage of the original collateral amount. The SMM (monthly CPR) expresses prepayments based on the prior month's balance.

There is a mathematical relationship between the SMM and the ABS measures. Letting M denote the number of months after loan origination, the SMM rate can be calculated from the ABS rate using the following formula:

$$SMM = \frac{ABS}{1 - [ABS \times (M - 1)]}$$

where the ABS and SMM rates are expressed in decimal form.

For example, if the ABS rate is 1.5% (i.e., 0.015) at month 14 after origination, then the SMM rate is 1.86%, as shown below:

$$SMM = \frac{0.015}{1 - [0.015 \times (14 - 1)]} = 0.0186 = 1.86\%$$

---

[17] The only reason for the use of ABS rather than SMM/CPR in this sector is historical. Auto loan-backed securities (which were popularly referred to at one time as CARS (Certificates of Automobile Receivables)) were the first non-mortgage assets to be developed in the market. (The first non-mortgage asset-backed security was actually backed by computer lease receivables.) The major dealer in this market at the time, First Boston (now Credit Suisse First Boston) elected to use ABS for measuring prepayments. You may wonder how one obtains "ABS" from "absolute prepayment rate." Again, it is historical. When the market first started, the ABS measure probably meant "asset-backed security" but over time to avoid confusion evolved to absolute prepayment rate.

PRACTICE QUESTION 4

A. If the ABS for a security is 2% at month 11, what is the corresponding SMM?

B. If the SMM for a security is 1.7% at month 21, what is the corresponding ABS?

The ABS rate can be calculated from the SMM rate using the following formula:

$$ABS = \frac{SMM}{1 + [SMM \times (M - 1)]}$$

For example, if the SMM rate at month 9 after origination is 1.3%, then the ABS rate is:

$$ABS = \frac{0.013}{1 + [0.013 \times (9 - 1)]} = 0.0118 = 1.18\%$$

Historically, when measured in terms of SMM rate, auto loans have experienced SMMs that increase as the loans season.

STUDENT LOAN-BACKED SECURITIES   7

Student loans are made to cover college cost (undergraduate, graduate, and professional programs such as medical and law school) and tuition for a wide range of vocational and trade schools. Securities backed by student loans, popularly referred to as SLABS (student loan asset-backed securities), have similar structural features as the other asset-backed securities we discussed above.

The student loans that have been most commonly securitized are those that are made under the Federal Family Education Loan Program (FFELP). Under this program, the government makes loans to students via private lenders. The decision by private lenders to extend a loan to a student is not based on the applicant's ability to repay the loan. If a default of a loan occurs and the loan has been properly serviced, then the government will guarantee up to 98% of the principal plus accrued interest.[18]

Loans that are not part of a government guarantee program are called alternative loans. These loans are basically consumer loans, and the lender's decision to extend an alternative loan will be based on the ability of the applicant to repay the loan. Alternative loans have been securitized.

A. Issuers

Congress created Fannie Mae and Freddie Mac to provide liquidity in the mortgage market by allowing these government sponsored enterprises to buy mortgage loans in the secondary market. Congress created the Student Loan

---

[18] Actually, depending on the origination date, the guarantee can be up to 100%.

Marketing Association (nicknamed "Sallie Mae") as a government sponsored enterprise to purchase student loans in the secondary market and to securitize pools of student loans. Since its first issuance in 1995, Sallie Mae is now the major issuer of SLABS, and its issues are viewed as the benchmark issues.[19] Other entities that issue SLABS are either traditional corporate entities (e.g., the Money Store and PNC Bank) or non-profit organizations (Michigan Higher Education Loan Authority and the California Educational Facilities Authority). The SLABS of the latter typically are issued as tax-exempt securities and therefore trade in the municipal market. In recent years, several not-for-profit entities have changed their charter and applied for "for profit" treatment.

B. Cash Flow

Let's first look at the cash flow for the student loans themselves. There are different types of student loans under the FFELP including subsidized and unsubsidized Stafford loans, Parental Loans for Undergraduate Students (PLUS), and Supplemental Loans to Students (SLS). These loans involve three periods with respect to the borrower's payments—deferment period, grace period, and loan repayment period. Typically, student loans work as follows. While a student is in school, no payments are made by the student on the loan. This is the deferment period. Upon leaving school, the student is extended a grace period of usually six months when no payments on the loan must be made. After this period, payments are made on the loan by the borrower.

Student loans are floating-rate loans, exclusively indexed to the 3-month Treasury bill rate. As a result, some issuers of SLABs issue securities whose coupon rate is indexed to the 3-month Treasury bill rate. However, a large percentage of SLABS issued are indexed to LIBOR floaters.[20]

Prepayments typically occur due to defaults or loan consolidation. Even if there is no loss of principal faced by the investor when defaults occur, the investor is still exposed to contraction risk. This is the risk that the investor must reinvest the proceeds at a lower spread and in the case of a bond purchased at a premium, the premium will be lost. Studies have shown student loan prepayments are insensitive to the level of interest rates. Consolidations of a loan occur when the student who has loans over several years combines them into a single loan. The proceeds from the consolidation are distributed to the original lender and, in turn, distributed to the bondholders.

8   SBA LOAN-BACKED SECURITIES

The Small Business Administration (SBA) is an agency of the U.S. government empowered to guarantee loans made by approved SBA lenders to qualified borrowers. The loans are backed by the full faith and credit of the government. Most SBA loans are variable-rate loans where the reference rate is the prime rate.

---

[19] In 1997 Sallie Mae began the process of unwinding its status as a GSE; until this multi-year process is completed, all debt issued by Sallie Mae under its GSE status will be "grandfathered" as GSE debt until maturity.

[20] This creates a mismatch between the collateral and the securities. Issuers have dealt with this by hedging with the risk by using derivative instruments such as interest rate swaps (floating-to-floating rate swaps) or interest rate caps.

The rate on the loan is reset monthly on the first of the month or quarterly on the first of January, April, July, and October. SBA regulations specify the maximum coupon allowable in the secondary market. Newly originated loans have maturities between 5 and 25 years.

The Small Business Secondary Market Improvement Act passed in 1984 permitted the pooling of SBA loans. When pooled, the underlying loans must have similar terms and features. The maturities typically used for pooling loans are 7, 10, 15, 20, and 25 years. Loans without caps are not pooled with loans that have caps.

Most variable-rate SBA loans make monthly payments consisting of interest and principal repayment. The amount of the monthly payment for an individual loan is determined as follows. Given the coupon formula of the prime rate plus the loan's quoted margin, the interest rate is determined for each loan. Given the interest rate, a level payment amortization schedule is determined. It is this level payment that is paid for the next month until the coupon rate is reset.

The monthly cash flow that the investor in an SBA-backed security receives consists of:

▶ the coupon interest based on the coupon rate set for the period;

▶ the scheduled principal repayment (i.e., scheduled amortization);

▶ prepayments.

Prepayments for SBA-backed securities are measured in terms of CPR. Voluntary prepayments can be made by the borrower without any penalty. There are several factors contributing to the prepayment speed of a pool of SBA loans. A factor affecting prepayments is the maturity date of the loan. It has been found that the fastest speeds on SBA loans and pools occur for shorter maturities.[21] The purpose of the loan also affects prepayments. There are loans for working capital purposes and loans to finance real estate construction or acquisition. It has been observed that SBA pools with maturities of 10 years or less made for working capital purposes tend to prepay at the fastest speed. In contrast, loans backed by real estate that are long maturities tend to prepay at a slow speed.

CREDIT CARD RECEIVABLE-BACKED SECURITIES

9

When a purchase is made on a credit card, the issuer of the credit card (the lender) extends credit to the cardholder (the borrower). Credit cards are issued by banks (e.g., Visa and MasterCard), retailers (e.g., Sears and Target Corporation), and travel and entertainment companies (e.g., American Express). At the time of purchase, the cardholder is agreeing to repay the amount borrowed (i.e., the cost of the item purchased) plus any applicable finance charges. The amount that the cardholder has agreed to pay the issuer of the credit card is a receivable from the perspective of the issuer of the credit card. Credit card receivables are used as collateral for the issuance of an asset-backed security.

---

[21] Donna Faulk, "SBA Loan-Backed Securities," in *Asset-Backed Securities*.

A. Cash Flow

For a pool of credit card receivables, the cash flow consists of finance charges collected, fees, and principal. Finance charges collected represent the periodic interest the credit card borrower is charged based on the unpaid balance after the grace period. Fees include late payments fees and any annual membership fees.

Interest to security holders is paid periodically (e.g., monthly, quarterly, or semiannually). The interest rate may be fixed or floating—roughly half of the securities are floaters. The floating rate is uncapped.

A credit card receivable-backed security is a nonamortizing security. For a specified period of time, the lockout period or revolving period, the principal payments made by credit card borrowers comprising the pool are retained by the trustee and reinvested in additional receivables to maintain the size of the pool. The lockout period can vary from 18 months to 10 years. So, during the lockout period, the cash flow that is paid out to security holders is based on finance charges collected and fees. After the lockout period, the principal is no longer reinvested but paid to investors. The principal-amortization period and the various types of structures are described next.

B. Payment Structure

There are three different amortization structures that have been used in credit card receivable-backed security deals: 1) passthrough structure, 2) controlled-amortization structure, and 3) bullet-payment structure. The latter two are the more common. One source reports that 80% of the deals are bullet structures and the balance are controlled amortization structures.[22]

In a passthrough structure, the principal cash flows from the credit card accounts are paid to the security holders on a pro rata basis. In a controlled-amortization structure, a scheduled principal amount is established, similar to the principal window for a PAC bond. The scheduled principal amount is sufficiently low so that the obligation can be satisfied even under certain stress scenarios, where cash flow is decreased due to defaults or slower repayment by borrowers. The security holder is paid the lesser of the scheduled principal amount and the pro rata amount. In a bullet-payment structure, the security holder receives the entire amount in one distribution. Since there is no assurance that the entire amount can be paid in one lump sum, the procedure is for the trustee to place principal monthly into an account that generates sufficient interest to make periodic interest payments and accumulate the principal to be repaid. These deposits are made in the months shortly before the scheduled bullet payment. This type of structure is also often called a soft bullet because the maturity is technically not guaranteed, but is almost always satisfied. The time period over which the principal is accumulated is called the accumulation period.

C. Performance of the Portfolio of Receivables

There are several concepts that must be understood in order to assess the performance of the portfolio of receivables and the ability of the issuer to meet its interest obligation and repay principal as scheduled.

We begin with the concept of the gross portfolio yield. This yield includes finance charges collected and fees. Charge-offs represent the accounts charged off as uncollectible. Net portfolio yield is equal to gross portfolio yield minus

---

[22] Thompson, "MBNA Tests the Waters."

charge-offs. The net portfolio yield is important because it is from this yield that the bondholders will be paid. So, for example, if the average yield (WAC) that must be paid to the various tranches in the structure is 5% and the net portfolio yield for the month is only 4.5%, there is the risk that the bondholder obligations will not be satisfied.

Delinquencies are the percentages of receivables that are past due for a specified number of months, usually 30, 60, and 90 days. They are considered an indicator of potential future charge-offs.

The monthly payment rate (MPR) expresses the monthly payment (which includes finance charges, fees, and any principal repayment) of a credit card receivable portfolio as a percentage of credit card debt outstanding in the previous month. For example, suppose a $500 million credit card receivable portfolio in January realized $50 million of payments in February. The MPR would then be 10% ($50 million divided by $500 million).

There are two reasons why the MPR is important. First, if the MPR reaches an extremely low level, there is a chance that there will be extension risk with respect to the principal payments on the bonds. Second, if the MPR is very low, then there is a chance that there will not be sufficient cash flows to pay off principal. This is one of the events that could trigger early amortization of the principal (described below).

At issuance, portfolio yield, charge-offs, delinquency, and MPR information are provided in the prospectus. Information about portfolio performance is then available from Bloomberg, the rating agencies, and dealers.

D. Early Amortization Triggers

There are provisions in credit card receivable-backed securities that require early amortization of the principal if certain events occur. Such provisions, which as mentioned earlier in this reading are referred to as early amortization or rapid amortization provisions, are included to safeguard the credit quality of the issue. The only way that the principal cash flows can be altered is by the triggering of the early amortization provision.

Typically, early amortization allows for the rapid return of principal in the event that the 3-month average excess spread earned on the receivables falls to zero or less. When early amortization occurs, the credit card tranches are retired sequentially (i.e., first the AAA bond, then the AA rated bond, etc.). This is accomplished by paying the principal payments made by the credit card borrowers to the investors instead of using them to purchase more receivables. The length of time until the return of principal is largely a function of the monthly payment rate. For example, suppose that a AAA tranche is 82% of the overall deal. If the monthly payment rate is 11%, then the AAA tranche would return principal over a 7.5-month period (82%/11%). An 18% monthly payment rate would return principal over a 4.5-month period (82%/18%).

COLLATERALIZED DEBT OBLIGATIONS   10

A collateralized debt obligation (CDO) is a security backed by a diversified pool of one or more of the following types of debt obligations:

▶ U.S. domestic high-yield corporate bonds;

▶ structured financial products (i.e., mortgage-backed and asset-backed securities);

- ▶ emerging market bonds;
- ▶ bank loans;
- ▶ special situation loans and distressed debt.

When the underlying pool of debt obligations are bond-type instruments (high-yield corporate, structured financial products, and emerging market bonds), a CDO is referred to as a collateralized bond obligation (CBO). When the underlying pool of debt obligations are bank loans, a CDO is referred to as a collateralized loan obligation (CLO).

A. Structure of a CDO

In a CDO structure, there is an asset manager responsible for managing the portfolio of debt obligations. There are restrictions imposed (i.e., restrictive covenants) as to what the asset manager may do and certain tests that must be satisfied for the tranches in the CDO to maintain the credit rating assigned at the time of issuance and determine how and when tranches are repaid principal.

The funds to purchase the underlying assets (i.e., the bonds and loans) are obtained from the issuance of debt obligations (i.e., tranches) and include one or more senior tranches, one or more mezzanine tranches, and a subordinate/equity tranche. There will be a rating sought for all but the subordinate/equity tranche. For the senior tranches, at least an A rating is typically sought. For the mezzanine tranches, a rating of BBB but no less than B is sought. As explained below, since the subordinate/equity tranche receives the residual cash flow, no rating is sought for this tranche.

The ability of the asset manager to make the interest payments to the tranches and pay off the tranches as they mature depends on the performance of the underlying assets. The proceeds to meet the obligations to the CDO tranches (interest and principal repayment) can come from 1) coupon interest payments of the underlying assets, 2) maturing assets in the underlying pool, and 3) sale of assets in the underlying pool.

In a typical structure, one or more of the tranches is a floating-rate security. With the exception of deals backed by bank loans which pay a floating rate, the asset manager invests in fixed-rate bonds. Now that presents a problem—paying tranche investors a floating rate and investing in assets with a fixed rate. To deal with this problem, the asset manager uses derivative instruments to be able to convert fixed-rate payments from the assets into floating-rate payments. In particular, interest rate swaps are used. This derivative instrument allows a market participant to swap fixed-rate payments for floating-rate payments or vice versa. Because of the mismatch between the nature of the cash flows of the debt obligations in which the asset manager invests and the floating-rate liability of any of the tranches, the asset manager must use an interest rate swap. A rating agency will require the use of swaps to eliminate this mismatch.

B. Family of CDOs

The family of CDOs is shown in Exhibit 3. While each CDO shown in the exhibit will be discussed in more detail below, we will provide an overview here.

The first breakdown in the CDO family is between cash CDOs and synthetic CDOs. A cash CDO is backed by a pool of cash market debt instruments. We described the range of debt obligations earlier. These were the original types of

EXHIBIT 3   **CDO Family Tree**

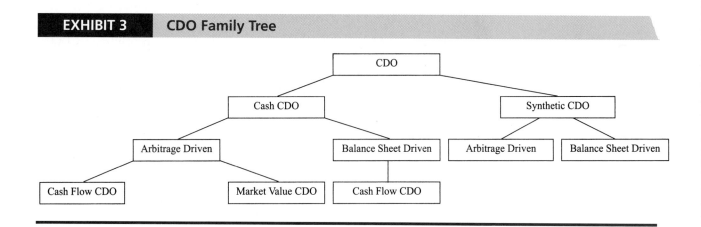

CDOs issued. A synthetic CDO is a CDO where the investor has the economic exposure to a pool of debt instrument, but this exposure is realized via a credit derivative instrument rather than the purchase of the cash market instruments. We will discuss the basic elements of a synthetic CDO later.

Both a cash CDO and a synthetic CDO are further divided based on the motivation of the sponsor. The motivation leads to balance sheet and arbitrage CDOs. As explained below, in a balance sheet CDO, the motivation of the sponsor is to remove assets from its balance sheet. In an arbitrage CDO, the motivation of the sponsor is to capture a spread between the return that it is possible to realize on the collateral backing the CDO and the cost of borrowing funds to purchase the collateral (i.e., the interest rate paid on the obligations issued).

Cash CDOs that are arbitrage transactions are further divided in cash flow and market value CDOs depending on the primary source of the proceeds from the underlying asset used to satisfy the obligation to the tranches. In a cash flow CDO, the primary source is the interest and maturing principal from the underlying assets. In a market value CDO, the proceeds to meet the obligations depend heavily on the total return generated from the portfolio. While cash CDOs that are balance sheet motivated transactions can also be cash flow or market value CDOs, only cash flow CDOs have been issued.

C. Cash CDOs

In this section, we take a closer look at cash CDOs. Before we look at cash flow and market value CDOs, we will look at the type of cash CDO based on the sponsor motivation: arbitrage and balance sheet transactions. As can be seen in Exhibit 3, cash CDOs are categorized based on the motivation of the sponsor of the transaction. In an arbitrage transaction, the motivation of the sponsor is to earn the spread between the yield offered on the debt obligations in the underlying pool and the payments made to the various tranches in the structure. In a balance sheet transaction, the motivation of the sponsor is to remove debt instruments (primarily loans) from its balance sheet. Sponsors of balance sheet transactions are typically financial institutions such as banks seeking to reduce their capital requirements by removing loans due to their higher risk-based capital requirements. Our focus in this section is on arbitrage transactions because such transactions are the largest part of the cash CDO sector.

1. Cash CDO Arbitrage Transactions

The key as to whether or not it is economic to create an arbitrage CDO is whether or not a structure can be created that offers a competitive return for the subordinate/equity tranche.

To understand how the subordinate/equity tranche generates cash flows, consider the following basic $100 million CDO structure with the coupon rate to be offered at the time of issuance as shown below:

Tranche	Par Value ($)	Coupon Rate
Senior	80,000,000	LIBOR + 70 basis points
Mezzanine	10,000,000	10-year Treasury rate plus 200 basis points
Subordinate/Equity	10,000,000	—

Suppose that the collateral consists of bonds that all mature in 10 years and the coupon rate for every bond is the 10-year Treasury rate plus 400 basis points. The asset manager enters into an interest rate swap agreement with another party with a notional amount of $80 million in which it agrees to do the following:

▶ pay a fixed rate each year equal to the 10-year Treasury rate plus 100 basis points;
▶ receive LIBOR.

The interest rate agreement is simply an agreement to periodically exchange interest payments. The payments are benchmarked off of a notional amount. This amount is not exchanged between the two parties. Rather it is used simply to determine the dollar interest payment of each party. This is all we need to know about an interest rate swap in order to understand the economics of an arbitrage transaction. Keep in mind, the goal is to show how the subordinate/equity tranche can be expected to generate a return.

Let's assume that the 10-year Treasury rate at the time the CDO is issued is 7%. Now we can walk through the cash flows for each year. Look first at the collateral. The collateral will pay interest each year (assuming no defaults) equal to the 10-year Treasury rate of 7% plus 400 basis points. So the interest will be:

Interest from collateral: 11% × $100,000,000 = $11,000,000

Now let's determine the interest that must be paid to the senior and mezzanine tranches. For the senior tranche, the interest payment will be:

Interest to senior tranche: $80,000,000 × (LIBOR + 70 bps)

The coupon rate for the mezzanine tranche is 7% plus 200 basis points. So, the coupon rate is 9% and the interest is:

Interest to mezzanine tranche: 9% × $10,000,000 = $900,000

Finally, let's look at the interest rate swap. In this agreement, the asset manager is agreeing to pay some party (we'll call this party the "swap counterparty") each year 7% (the 10-year Treasury rate) plus 100 basis points, or 8%. But 8% of what? As explained above, in an interest rate swap payments are based on a notional amount. In our illustration, the notional amount is $80 million. The reason the asset manager selected the $80 million was because this is the amount of principal for the senior tranche which receives a floating rate. So, the asset manager pays to the swap counterparty:

Interest to swap counterparty: 8% × $80,000,000 = $6,400,000

The interest payment received from the swap counterparty is LIBOR based on a notional amount of $80 million. That is,

Interest from swap counterparty: $80,000,000 × LIBOR

Now we can put this all together. Let's look at the interest coming into the CDO:

Interest from collateral $11,000,000
Interest from swap counterparty . . . . $80,000,000 × LIBOR
Total interest received . . . . $11,000,000 + $80,000,000 × LIBOR

The interest to be paid out to the senior and mezzanine tranches and to the swap counterparty include:

Interest to senior tranche . . . . $80,000,000 × (LIBOR + 70 bps)
Interest to mezzanine tranche $900,000
Interest to swap counterparty $6,400,000
Total interest paid . . . . $7,300,000 + $80,000,000 × (LIBOR + 70 bps)

Netting the interest payments coming in and going out we have:

Total interest received . . . . $11,000,000 + $80,000,000 × LIBOR
Total interest paid . . . . $ 7,300,000 + $80,000,000 × (LIBOR + 70 bps)
Net interest . . . . $ 3,700,000 − $80,000,000 × (70 bps)

Since 70 bps times $80 million is $560,000, the net interest remaining is $3,140,000 (= $3,700,000 − $560,000). From this amount any fees (including the asset management fee) must be paid. The balance is then the amount available to pay the subordinate/equity tranche. Suppose that these fees are $640,000. Then the cash flow available to the subordinate/equity tranche for the year is $2.5 million. Since the tranche has a par value of $10 million and is assumed to be sold at par, this means that the annual return is 25%.

Obviously, some simplifying assumptions have been made. For example, it is assumed that there are no defaults. It is assumed that all of the issues purchased by the asset manager are noncallable and therefore the coupon rate would not decline because issues are called. Moreover, as explained below, after some period the asset manager must begin repaying principal to the senior and mezzanine tranches. Consequently, the interest rate swap must be structured to take this into account since the entire amount of the senior tranche is not outstanding for the life of the collateral. Despite the simplifying assumptions, the illustration does demonstrate the basic economics of an arbitrage transaction, the need for the use of an interest rate swap, and how the subordinate/equity tranche will realize a return.

2. *Cash Flow CDO Structure*

In a cash flow CDO, the objective of the asset manager is to generate cash flow (primarily from interest earned and proceeds from bonds that have matured, have been called, or have amortized) to repay investors in the senior and mezzanine tranches. Because the cash flows from the structure are designed to accomplish the objective for each tranche, restrictions are imposed on the asset managers. The conditions for disposing of issues held are specified and are usually driven by credit risk considerations. Also, in assembling the portfolio, the asset manager must meet certain requirements set forth by the rating agency or agencies that rate the deal.

There are three relevant periods. The first is the *ramp-up period*. This is the period that follows the closing date of the transaction where the manager begins investing the proceeds from the sale of the debt obligations issued. This period is usually less than one year. The *reinvestment period* or *revolving period* is where principal proceeds are reinvested and is usually for five or more years. In the final period, the portfolio assets are sold and the debt holders are paid off as described below.

a. Distribution of Income

Income is derived from interest income from the underlying assets and capital appreciation. The income is then used as follows. Payments are first made to the trustee and administrators and then to the asset manager.[23] Once these fees are paid, then the senior tranches are paid their interest. At this point, before any other payments are made, there are certain tests that must be passed.

These tests are called coverage tests and will be discussed later. If the coverage tests are passed, then interest is paid to the mezzanine tranches. Once the mezzanine tranches are paid, interest is paid to the subordinate/equity tranche.

In contrast, if the coverage tests are not passed, then there are payments that are made so as to protect the senior tranches. The remaining income after paying the fees and senior tranche interest is used to redeem the senior tranches (i.e., pay off principal) until the coverage tests are brought into compliance. If the senior tranches are paid off fully because the coverage tests are not brought into compliance, then any remaining income is used to redeem the mezzanine tranches. Any remaining income is then used to redeem the subordinate/equity tranche.

b. Distribution of Principal Cash Flow

The principal cash flow is distributed as follows after the payment of the fees to the trustees, administrators, and asset manager. If there is a shortfall in interest paid to the senior tranches, principal proceeds are used to make up the shortfall. Assuming that the coverage tests are satisfied, during the reinvestment period the principal is reinvested. After the reinvestment period or if the coverage tests are failed, the principal cash flow is used to pay down the senior tranches until the coverage tests are satisfied. If all the senior tranches are paid down, then the mezzanine tranches are paid off and then the subordinate/equity tranche is paid off.

c. Restrictions on Management

The asset manager in both a cash flow CDO and a market value CDO (discussed next) actively manage the portfolio. The difference is in the degree of active management. In a cash flow CDO, the asset manager initially structures and then

---

[23] There are other management fees that are usually made based on performance. But these payments are made after payments to the mezzanine tranches.

rebalances the portfolio so that interest from the pool of assets plus repaid principal is sufficient to meet the obligations of the tranches. In contrast, the asset manager in a market value CDO seeks to generate trading profits to satisfy a portion of the obligations to the tranches.

The asset manager for both types of CDOs must monitor the collateral to ensure that certain tests imposed by the rating agencies are being met. For cash flow CDOs there are two types of tests: quality tests and coverage tests.

In rating a transaction, the rating agencies are concerned with the diversity of the assets. There are tests that relate to the diversity of the assets. These tests are called quality tests. An asset manager may not undertake a trade that will result in the violation of any of the quality tests. Quality tests include 1) a minimum asset diversity score,[24] 2) a minimum weighted average rating, and 3) maturity restrictions.

There are tests to ensure that the performance of the collateral is sufficient to make payments to the various tranches. These tests are called coverage tests. There are two types of coverage tests: par value tests and interest coverage ratio. Recall that if the coverage tests are violated, then income from the collateral is diverted to pay down the senior tranches.

3. Market Value CDO

As with a cash flow CDO, in a market value CDO there are debt tranches and a subordinate/equity tranche. However, because in a market value CDO the asset manager must sell assets in the underlying pool in order to generate proceeds for interest and repayment of maturing tranches, there is a careful monitoring of the assets and their price volatility. This is done by the frequent marking to market of the assets.

Because a market value CDO relies on the activities of the asset manager to generate capital appreciation and enhanced return to meet the obligations of the tranches in the structure, greater flexibility is granted to the asset manager with respect to some activities compared to a cash flow CDO. For example, while in a cash flow CDO the capital structure is fixed, in a market value CDO the asset manager is permitted to utilize additional leverage after the closing of the transaction.

D. Synthetic CDOs

A synthetic CDO is so named because the CDO does not actually own the underlying assets on which it has risk exposure. That is, in a synthetic CDO the CDO debt holders absorb the economic risks, but not the legal ownership, of a pool of assets.

1. Key Elements of a Synthetic CDO

In a synthetic CDO there is credit risk exposure to a portfolio of assets, called the reference asset. The reference asset serves as the basis for a contingent payment as will be explained later. The reference asset can be a bond market index such as a high-yield bond index or a mortgage index. Or, the reference asset can be a portfolio of corporate loans that is owned by a bank.

The credit risk associated with the reference asset is divided into two sections: 1) senior section and 2) junior section. In a typical synthetic CDO

---

[24] Rating agencies have developed measures that quantify the diversity of a portfolio. These measures are referred to as "diversity scores."

structure, the senior section is about 90% and the junior section is about 10%. (We'll see what we mean by 90% and 10% shortly.) The losses that are realized from the reference are first realized by the junior section up to a notional amount and then after that full loss is realized, the senior section begins realizing losses.

For example, let's suppose that the reference asset is a high-yield corporate bond index. An amount of credit risk exposure in terms of market value must be determined. Suppose that it is $500 million. The $500 million is referred to as the notional amount. Suppose further that the credit risk associated with the $500 million credit exposure is divided into a $450 million senior section and $50 million junior section. The $450 million is the notional amount for the senior section and the $50 million is the notional amount for the junior section. The first $50 million of loss to the reference asset due to a credit event (explained later) is absorbed by the junior section. Only after the junior section absorbs the first $50 million in loss will the senior section realize any loss.

You may wonder why we refer to senior and junior "sections" rather than senior and junior "note holders." The reason is that in a synthetic CDO structure, no debt obligations are issued to fund the senior section. However, for the junior section, debt obligations are issued. In our illustration, $50 million of junior notes are issued. They are issued in the same way as in a cash CDO structure. That is, there are typically several tranches of junior notes issued by the special purpose vehicle (SPV). There will be the most senior tranche of the junior notes and there will be the subordinate/equity tranche.

The proceeds received from the issuance of the junior notes are then invested by the asset manager. However, the investments are restricted to high-quality debt instruments. This includes government securities, federal agency debentures, and corporate, mortgage-backed, and asset-backed securities rated triple A.

Now we introduce the key to a synthetic CDO—a credit derivative instrument. An interest rate derivative is used by an investor to protect against interest rate risk. (We actually illustrated the use of one type of interest rate derivative, an interest rate swap, earlier when we demonstrated the economics of an arbitrage CDO transaction.) A credit derivative, as the name indicates, is used to protect against credit risk. The type of credit derivative used in a synthetic CDO is a credit default swap. Here we discuss the essential elements of a credit default swap, just enough to understand its role in a synthetic CDO.

A credit default swap is conceptually similar to an insurance policy. There is a "protection buyer" who purchases protection against credit risk on the reference asset. In a synthetic CDO, the insurance buyer is the asset manager. The protection buyer (the asset manager in a synthetic CDO) pays a periodic fee (like an insurance premium) and receives, in return, payment from the protection seller in the event of a "credit event" affecting any asset included in the reference asset. Who is the protection seller? It is the SPV on behalf of the junior note holders.

As with an interest rate swap, a credit default swap has a notional amount. The notional amount will be equal to the senior section, $450 million in our example.

Let's clarify this by continuing with our earlier illustration and look at the return to the junior note holder in the structure. The junior note holders are getting payments that come from two sources:

1) the income from the high-quality securities purchased with the funds from the issuance of the junior debt obligations and

2) the insurance premium (premium from the credit default swap) paid by the asset manager to the SPV

Effectively, the junior note holders are receiving the return on a portfolio of high-quality assets subsidized by the insurance premium (i.e., the payment from the credit default swap). However, this ignores the obligation of the junior note holders with respect to the credit default swap. If there is a credit event (discussed below) that requires the junior note holders to make a payment to the protection buyer, then this reduces the return to the junior note holders. As noted earlier, the effect on a particular tranche of the junior section depends on its priority. That is, the subordinate/equity tranche is affected first before the most senior tranche, and the other tranches superior to the subordinate/equity tranche is affected.

So what becomes critical for the junior note holders' return is when it must make a payment. In credit derivatives, a payoff by the protection seller occurs when there is a credit event. Credit events are defined in the credit derivative documentation. On a debt instrument a credit event generally includes bankruptcy, failure to pay when due, cross default/cross acceleration, repudiation, and restructuring. This credit event applies to any of the assets within the reference asset. For example, if a high-yield corporate bond index is the reference asset and Company X is in the index, a credit event with respect to Company X results in a payment to the protection buyer. If a designated portfolio of bank loans to corporations is the reference asset and Corporation Y's loan is included, then a credit event with respect to Corporation Y results in a payment to the protection buyer.

How much must be paid by the protection seller (the junior tranches in our illustration) to the protection buyer (the asset manager)? Should a credit event occur, there is an intent that the protection buyer be made whole: The protection buyer should be paid the difference between par and the "fair value" of the securities. How this is determined is set forth in the credit derivative agreement.

What is the motivation for the creation of synthetic CDOs? There exist two types: synthetic balance sheet CDOs and synthetic arbitrage CDOs. In the case of a synthetic balance sheet CDO, by embedding a credit default swap within a CDO structure, a bank can shed the credit risk of a portfolio of bank loans without having to notify any borrowers that they are selling the loans to another party, a requirement in some countries. No consent is needed from borrowers to transfer the credit risk of the loans, as is effectively done in a credit default swap. This is the reason synthetic balance sheet CDOs were initially set up to accommodate European bank balance sheet deals.

For a synthetic arbitrage CDO, there are several economic advantages of using a synthetic CDO structure rather than a cash CDO structure. First, it is not necessary to obtain funding for the senior section, thus making it easier to do a CDO transaction.[25] Second, the ramp-up period is shorter than for a cash CDO structure since only the high-quality assets need be assembled, not all of the assets contained in the reference asset. Finally, there are opportunities in the market to be able to effectively acquire the assets included in the reference asset via a credit default swap at a cheaper cost than buying the assets directly.[26] It's because of these three advantages that issuance of synthetic CDO structures has increased dramatically since 2001 and is expected to continue to increase relative to cash CDO structures.

---

[25] It is for this reason that a nonsynthetic CDO structure is referred to as a "cash" CDO structure because cash is required to be raised to purchase all the collateral assets.

[26] For a more detailed discussion of these advantages and how it impacts the economics of a CDO, see Laurie S. Goodman and Frank J. Fabozzi, *Collateralized Debt Obligations: Structures and Analysis* (New York, NY: John Wiley & Sons, 2002).

SUMMARY

▶ An entity that wants to raise funds via a securitization will sell assets to a special purpose vehicle and is referred to as the "seller" in the transaction.

▶ The buyer of assets in a securitization is a special purpose vehicle, and this entity, referred to as the issuer or trust, raises funds to buy the assets via the sale of securities (the asset-backed securities).

▶ There will be an entity in a securitization that will be responsible for servicing the loans or receivables.

▶ Third-party entities in the securitization are attorneys, independent accountants, trustee, rating agencies, servicer, and possibly a guarantor.

▶ The waterfall of a transaction describes how the distribution of the cash flow will be distributed to the bond classes after fees are paid.

▶ In a securitization structure, the bond classes issued can consist of a senior bond that is tranched so as to redistribute prepayment risk and one or more subordinate bonds; the creation of the subordinate bonds provides credit tranching for the structure.

▶ The collateral for an asset-backed security can be either amortizing assets (e.g., auto loans and closed-end home equity loans) or nonamortizing assets (e.g., credit card receivables).

▶ For amortizing assets, projection of the cash flow requires projecting prepayments.

▶ For non-amortizing assets, prepayments by an individual borrower do not apply since there is no schedule of principal repayments.

▶ When the collateral is amortizing assets, typically the principal repayments are distributed to the security holders.

▶ When the collateral consists of non-amortizing assets, typically there is a lockout period, a period where principal repayments are reinvested in new assets; after the lockout period, principal repayments are distributed to the security holders.

▶ A structure where there is a lockout for principal repayments is called a revolving structure.

▶ One factor that may affect prepayments is the prevailing level of interest rates relative to the interest rate on the loan.

▶ Since a default is a prepayment (an involuntary prepayment), prepayment modeling for an asset-backed security backed by amortizing assets requires a model for projecting the amount that will be recovered and when it will be recovered.

▶ Cash flow analysis can be performed on a pool level or a loan level.

▶ The expected final maturity of an asset-backed security is the maturity date based on expected prepayments at the time of pricing of a deal; the legal final maturity can be two or more years after the expected final maturity.

▶ Average life is commonly used as a measure for the length of time an asset-backed security will be outstanding.

▶ With an asset-backed security, due to prepayments a bond that is expected to have a bullet maturity may have an actual maturity that differs from that specified in the prospectus and is therefore referred to as a soft bullet.

▶ Asset-backed securities are credit enhanced; that is, there must be support from somewhere to absorb a certain amount of defaults.

▶ Credit enhancement levels are determined relative to a specific rating desired for a security.

▶ There are two general types of credit enhancement structures: external and internal.

▶ External credit enhancements come in the form of third-party guarantees that provide for first loss protection against losses up to a specified level.

▶ External credit enhancement includes insurance by a monoline insurer, a guarantee by the seller of the assets, and a letter of credit.

▶ The most common forms of internal credit enhancements are reserve funds and senior/subordinate structures.

▶ The senior/subordinated structure is the most widely used internal credit support structure with a typical structure having a senior tranche and one or more non-senior tranches.

▶ For mortgage-related asset-backed securities and nonagency mortgage-backed securities there is a concern that prepayments will erode the protection afforded by the non-senior (i.e., subordinated) tranches after the deal closes.

▶ A shifting interest structure is used to protect against a deterioration in the senior tranche's credit protection due to prepayments by redistributing the prepayments disproportionately from the non-senior tranches to the senior tranche according to a specified schedule.

▶ With an asset-backed security, one of the following call provisions may be granted to the trustee: 1) percent of collateral call, 2) percent of bonds, 3) percent of tranche, 4) call on or after specified date, 5) latter of percent or date, or 6) auction call.

▶ The collateral for a home equity loan is typically a first lien on residential property, and the loan fails to satisfy the underwriting standards for inclusion in a loan pool of Ginnie Mae, Fannie Mae, or Freddie Mac because of the borrower's impaired credit history or too high a payment-to-income ratio.

▶ Typically, a home equity loan is used by a borrower to consolidate consumer debt using the current home as collateral rather than to obtain funds to purchase a new home.

▶ Home equity loans can be either closed end (i.e., structured the same way as a fully amortizing residential mortgage loan) or open end (i.e., homeowner given a credit line).

▶ The monthly cash flow for a home equity loan-backed security backed by closed-end HELs consists of 1) net interest, 2) regularly scheduled principal payments, and 3) prepayments.

▶ Several studies by Wall Street firms have found that the key difference between the prepayment behavior of HELs and traditional residential mortgages is the important role played by the credit characteristics of the borrower.

▶ Studies strongly suggest that borrower credit quality is the most important determinant of prepayments, with the sensitivity of refinancing to interest rates being greater the higher the borrower's credit quality.

▶ The prospectus of an HEL offering contains a base case prepayment assumption regarding the initial speed and the amount of time until the collateral is expected to season.

▶ A prospectus prepayment curve is a multiple of the base case prepayments assumed in the prospectus (i.e., base case is equal to 100% PPC).

▶ Typically, home equity loan-backed securities are securitized by both closed-end fixed-rate and adjustable-rate (or variable-rate) HELs.

▶ Unlike a typical floater which has a cap that is fixed throughout the security's life, the available funds cap of a HEL floater is variable and depends on the amount of funds generated by the net coupon on the principal, less any fees.

▶ To provide stability to the average life of a senior tranche, closed-end home equity loan transactions will include either a non-accelerating senior (NAS) tranche or a planned amortization class (PAC) tranche.

▶ A NAS tranche receives principal payments according to a schedule based not on a dollar amount for a given month, but instead on a schedule that specifies for each month the share of pro rata principal that must be distributed to the NAS tranche.

▶ For a PAC tranche a schedule of the dollar amount for each month is specified.

▶ The structure of residential mortgage-backed securities outside the United States is similar to that of the nonagency mortgage market; there are internal and external credit enhancements.

▶ Auto loan-backed securities are issued by the financial subsidiaries of auto manufacturers, commercial banks, and independent finance companies and small financial institutions specializing in auto loans.

▶ The cash flow for auto loan-backed securities consists of regularly scheduled monthly loan payments (interest and scheduled principal repayments), and any prepayments.

▶ Prepayments on auto loans are not sensitive to interest rates.

▶ Prepayments on auto loan-backed securities are measured in terms of the absolute prepayment speed (denoted ABS) which measures monthly prepayments relative to the original collateral amount.

▶ Manufactured housing-backed securities are backed by loans on manufactured homes (i.e., homes built at a factory and then transported to a site).

▶ Manufactured housing-backed securities are issued by Ginnie Mae and private entities, the former being guaranteed by the full faith and credit of the U.S. government.

▶ A manufactured housing loan's cash flow consists of net interest, regularly scheduled principal, and prepayments.

▶ Prepayments are more stable for manufactured housing-backed securities because they are not sensitive to interest rate changes.

▶ SLABS are asset-backed securities backed by student loans.

▶ The student loans most commonly securitized are those that are made under the Federal Family Education Loan Program (FFELP), whereby the government makes loans to students via private lenders and the government guaranteeing up to 98% of the principal plus accrued interest.

▶ Alternative loans are student loans that are not part of a government guarantee program and are basically consumer loans.

▶ In contrast to government guaranteed loans, the lender's decision to extend an alternative loan is based on the ability of the applicant to repay the loan.

▶ Student loans involve three periods with respect to the borrower's payments—deferment period, grace period, and loan repayment period.

▶ Prepayments typically occur due to defaults or a loan consolidation (i.e., a loan to consolidate loans over several years into a single loan).

▶ Issuers of SLABs include the Student Loan Marketing Association (Sallie Mae), traditional corporate entities, and non-profit organizations.

▶ Student loan-backed securities offer a floating rate; for some issues the reference rate is the 3-month Treasury bill rate, but for most issues the reference rate is LIBOR.

▶ Small Business Administration (SBA) loans are backed by the full faith and credit of the U.S. government.

▶ Most SBA loans are variable-rate loans where the reference rate is the prime rate with monthly payments consisting of interest and principal repayment.

▶ Voluntary prepayments can be made by the SBA borrower without any penalty.

▶ Factors contributing to the prepayment speed of a pool of SBA loans are 1) the maturity date of the loan (it has been found that the fastest speeds on SBA loans and pools occur for shorter maturities), 2) the purpose of the loan, and 3) whether or not there is a cap on the loan.

▶ Credit card receivable-backed securities are backed by credit card receivables for credit cards issued by banks, retailers, and travel and entertainment companies.

▶ Credit card deals are structured as a master trust.

▶ For a pool of credit card receivables, the cash flow consists of finance charges collected, fees, and principal.

▶ The principal repayment of a credit card receivable-backed security is not amortized; instead, during the lockout period, the principal payments made by credit card borrowers are retained by the trustee and reinvested in additional receivables, and after the lockout period (the principal-amortization period), the principal received by the trustee is no longer reinvested but paid to investors.

▶ There are provisions in credit card receivable-backed securities that require early amortization of the principal if certain events occur.

▶ Since for credit card receivable-backed securities the concept of prepayments does not apply, participants look at the monthly payment rate (MPR) which expresses the monthly payment (which includes interest, finance charges, and any principal) of a credit card receivable portfolio as a percentage of debt outstanding in the previous month.

▶ The MPR for credit card receivable-backed securities is important because 1) if it reaches an extremely low level, there is a chance that there will be extension risk with respect to the principal payments and 2) if the MPR is very low, there is a chance that there will not be sufficient cash flows to pay off principal (which can trigger early amortization of the principal).

▶ To assess the performance of the portfolio of credit card receivables and the ability of the issuer to meet its interest obligation and repay principal as scheduled, an investor must analyze the gross portfolio yield (which includes finance charges collected and fees), charge-offs (which represents the accounts charged off as uncollectible), the net portfolio yield, gross portfolio yield minus charge-offs, and delinquencies (the percentage of receivable that are past due as specified number of months).

► There are three amortization structures that have been used in credit card receivable-backed security structures: 1) passthrough structure, 2) controlled-amortization structure, and 3) bullet-payment structure.

► A collateralized debt obligation is an asset-backed security backed by a diversified pool of debt obligations (high-yield corporate bonds, structured financial products, emerging market bonds, bank loans, and special situation loans and distressed debt).

► A collateralized bond obligation is a CDO in which the underlying pool of debt obligations consists of bond-type instruments (high-yield corporate and emerging market bonds).

► A collateralized loan obligation is a CDO in which the underlying pool of debt obligations consists of bank loans.

► In a CDO there is an asset manager responsible for managing the portfolio of assets.

► The tranches in a CDO include senior tranches, mezzanine tranches, and subordinate/equity tranches.

► The senior and mezzanine tranches are rated and the subordinate/equity tranche is unrated.

► The proceeds to meet the obligations to the CDO tranches (interest and principal repayment) can come from 1) coupon interest payments of the underlying assets, 2) maturing assets in the underlying pools, and 3) sale of assets in the underlying pool.

► CDOs are categorized based on the motivation of the sponsor of the transaction—arbitrage and balance sheet transactions.

► The motivation in an arbitrage transaction is for the sponsor to earn the spread between the yield offered on the debt obligations in the underlying pool and the payments made to the various tranches in the structure.

► In a balance sheet transaction the motivation of the sponsor is to remove debt instruments (primarily loans) from its balance sheet.

► The key as to whether or not it is economic to create an arbitrage transaction is whether or not a structure can offer a competitive return to the subordinated/equity tranche.

► Arbitrage transactions are classified as either cash flow CDOs or market value CDOs depending on where the primary source of the proceeds from the underlying asset is to come from to satisfy the obligation to the tranches.

► In a cash flow CDO the primary source is the interest and maturing principal from the underlying assets; in a market value CDO the proceeds to meet the obligations depend heavily on the total return generated from the portfolio.

► The three relevant periods in a CDO are the ramp-up period, the reinvestment period or revolving period, and the final period where the portfolio assets are sold and the debt holders are paid off.

► In a CDO transaction, senior tranches are protected against a credit deterioration by coverage tests; a failure of coverage tests results in the paying off of the senior tranches until the coverage tests are satisfied.

► The tests imposed in a cash flow structure are quality tests (e.g., minimum asset diversity score, a minimum weighted average rating, and maturity restrictions) and coverage tests.

▶ Coverage tests are tests to ensure that the performance of the collateral is sufficient to make payments to the various tranches and include par value tests and interest coverage ratio.

▶ In market value structures the focus is on monitoring of the assets and their price volatility by the frequent marking to market of the assets.

▶ In a synthetic CDO a credit derivative instrument is used to allow the CDO issuer to transfer the economic risk, but not the legal ownership of a reference asset.

▶ In a synthetic CDO, the credit derivative used is a credit default swap and this instrument allows the "protection buyer" (the asset manager in a synthetic CDO) to protect against default risk on a reference asset; the protection sellers are the tranches in the junior section of the CDO.

▶ In a synthetic CDO, the return to the junior note holders is based on the return from a portfolio of high-quality debt instruments plus the premium received in the credit default swap, reduced by the payment that must be made as a result of a credit event.

▶ There are synthetic balance sheet CDO transactions and synthetic arbitrage CDO transactions.

PRACTICE PROBLEMS FOR READING 52

1. Caterpillar Financial Asset Trust 1997-A is a special purpose vehicle. The collateral (i.e., assets) for the trust is a pool of fixed-rate retail installment sales contracts that are secured by new and used machinery manufactured primarily by Caterpillar Inc. The retail installment sales contracts were originated by the Caterpillar Financial Funding Corporation, a wholly-owned subsidiary of Caterpillar Financial Services Corporation. Caterpillar Financial Services Corporation is a wholly-owned subsidiary of Caterpillar Inc. The prospectus for the trust states that:

> "THE NOTES REPRESENT OBLIGATIONS OF THE ISSUER ONLY AND DO NOT REPRESENT OBLIGATIONS OF OR INTERESTS IN CATERPILLAR FINANCIAL FUNDING CORPORATION, CATERPIL-LAR FINANCIAL SERVICES CORPORATION, CATERPILLAR INC. OR ANY OF THEIR RESPECTIVE AFFILIATES."

The servicer of the retail installment sales contracts is Caterpillar Financial Services Corporation, a wholly-owned finance subsidiary of Caterpillar Inc. and is referred to as the servicer in the prospectus. For servicing the collateral, Caterpillar Financial Services Corporation receives a servicing fee of 100 basis points of the outstanding loan balance.

The securities were issued on May 19, 1997 and had a par value of $337,970,000. In the prospectus the securities are referred to as "asset-backed notes." There were four rated bond classes:

Bond Class	Par Value ($)
Class A-1	88,000,000
Class A-2	128,000,000
Class A-3	108,100,000
Class B	13,870,000

A. In the prospectus, the term "Seller" is used. Who in this transaction would be the "Seller" and why?

B. In the prospectus, the term "Issuer" is used. Who in this transaction would be the "Issuer" and why?

C. Despite not having the waterfall for this structure, which bond classes do you think are the senior bonds?

D. Despite not having the waterfall for this structure, which bond classes do you think are the subordinate bonds?

E. Despite not having the waterfall for this structure, explain why there appears to be credit and prepayment tranching in this structure?

2. In the securitization process, what is the role played by the a) attorneys and b) independent accountants?

3. How are principal repayments from the collateral used by the trustee in a securitization transaction?

4. Suppose that the collateral for an asset-backed securities structure has a gross weighted average coupon of 8.6%. The servicing fee is 50 basis points. The tranches issued have a weighted average coupon rate of 7.1%. What is the excess servicing spread?

5. Suppose that the structure for an asset-backed security transaction is as follows:

senior tranche	$220 million
subordinate tranche 1	$ 50 million
subordinate tranche 2	$ 30 million

and that the value of the collateral for the structure is $320 million. Subordinate tranche 2 is the first loss tranche.

  A. How much is the overcollateralization in this structure?

  B. What is the amount of the loss for each tranche if losses due to defaults over the life of the structure total $15 million?

  C. What is the amount of the loss for each tranche if losses due to defaults over the life of the structure total $35 million?

  D. What is the amount of the loss for each tranche if losses due to defaults over the life of the structure total $85 million?

  E. What is the amount of the loss for each tranche if losses due to defaults over the life of the structure total $110 million?

6. A. Explain why individual loans that are of a non-amortizing type are not subject to prepayment risk.

  B. Explain why securities backed by collateral consisting of non-amortizing assets may expose an investor to prepayment risk.

7. An asset-backed security has been credit enhanced with a letter of credit from a bank with a single A credit rating. If this is the only form of credit enhancement, explain why this issue is unlikely to receive a triple A credit rating.

8. Why is it critical for monoline insurance companies that provide insurance for asset-backed security transactions to maintain a triple A credit rating?

9. What is the difference between a cash reserve fund and an excess servicing spread account?

10. Why is the assumption about how defaults may occur over the life of an asset-backed security transaction important in assessing the effectiveness of excess servicing spread as a form of internal credit enhancement?

11. A. Explain why a senior-subordinate structure is a form of internal credit enhancement.

  B. Explain the need for a shifting interest mechanism in a senior-subordinate structure when the underlying assets are subject to prepayments.

12. A. What is meant by the "senior prepayment percentage" in a shifting interest mechanism of a senior-subordinate structure?

  B. Why does a shifting interest mechanism affect the cash flow of the senior tranche and increase the senior tranche's exposure to contraction risk?

13. What is a "latter of percent or call date" call provision?

14. A. What is the cash flow of a closed-end home equity loan?

  B. Indicate whether you agree or disagree with the following statement: "Typically, closed-end home equity loans are loans to borrowers of the highest credit quality."

15. The Izzobaf Home Equity Loan Trust 2000-1 is backed by fixed-rate closed-end home equity loans. The base case prepayment for this deal is specified in the prospectus as follows:

> The model used with respect to the loans (the "prepayment ramp") assumes that the home equity loans prepay at a rate of 5% CPR in the first month after origination, and an additional 1.8% each month thereafter until the 12th month. Beginning in the 12th month and each month thereafter, the prepayment ramp assumes a prepayment rate of 24.8% CPR.

What is the CPR assuming 200% PPC for the following months?

Month	CPR	Month	CPR	Month	CPR
1		11		30	
2		12		125	
3		13		150	
4		14		200	
5		15		250	
6		16		275	
7		17		300	
8		18		325	
9		19		350	
10		20		360	

16. James Tellmen is an assistant portfolio manager for a mortgage-backed securities portfolio. Mr. Tellmen's responsibility is to analyze agency mortgage-backed securities. Recently, the portfolio manager has been given authorization to purchase closed-end home equity loan-backed securities. Mr. Tellmen is analyzing his first structure in this sector of the asset-backed securities market. Upon reading the prospectus he finds that the base case prepayment is specified and believes that this prepayment assumption is the benchmark used in all closed-end home equity loan-backed securities. Explain why you agree or disagree with Mr. Tellmen.

17. Why is there an available funds cap in an asset-backed security in which the collateral is adjustable-rate home equity loans?

18. Suppose that the base case shifting interest percentage schedule for a closed-end home equity loan-backed security is as follows:

Years after Issuance	Senior Prepayment Percentage (%)
1–4	100
5	90
6	80
7	50
8	20
after year 8	0

    A. If there are prepayments in month 36 of $100,000, how much of the prepayments is paid to the senior tranche? How much is paid to the subordinate tranches?

    B. If there are prepayments in the 8th year after issuance of $100,000, how much of the prepayments is paid to the senior tranche? How much is paid to the subordinate tranches?

    C. If there are prepayments in the 10th year after issuance of $100,000, how much of the prepayments is paid to the senior tranche? How much is paid to the subordinate tranches?

19. Larry Forest is an analyst reviewing for the first time a closed-end home equity loan-backed structure in order to determine whether or not to purchase the deal's senior tranche. He understands how the shifting interest percentage schedule is structured so as to provide the senior tranches with protection after the deal is closed. However, he is concerned that the schedule in the prospectus will not be adequate if the collateral's performance deteriorates (i.e., there is considerably greater losses for the collateral than expected). Explain to Mr. Forest what provision is included in the prospectus for protecting the senior tranches if the performance of the collateral deteriorates.

20. How is a non-accelerating senior tranche provided protection to reduce contraction risk and extension risk?

21. A. What are the components of the cash flow for a manufactured housing-backed security?

    B. What are the reasons why prepayments due to refinancing are not significant for manufactured housing loans?

22. Why are residential mortgage-backed securities outside the United States structured more like transactions in the nonagency U.S. market than the agency market?

23. A. What are the components of the cash flow for an auto loan-backed security?

    B. How important are prepayments due to refinancing for auto loans?

24. What is the difference between a single monthly mortality rate and an absolute prepayment speed?

25. A. If the ABS for a security is 1.5% at month 21, what is the corresponding SMM?

  B. If the SMM for a security is 1.9% at month 11, what is the corresponding ABS?

26. A trustee for a pension fund is working with a consultant to develop investment guidelines for the fund's bond portfolio. The trustee states that the fund should be able to invest in securities backed by student loans because the loans are fully guaranteed by the U.S. government. How should the consultant respond?

27. For a student loan-backed security, what is the difference between the deferment period and the grace period?

28. A. What are the components of the cash flow for a Small Business Administration-backed security?

  B. What reference rate is used for setting the coupon interest and how often is the coupon rate reset?

29. A. What is the cash flow for a credit card receivable-backed security during the lockout or revolving period?

  B. How is the principal received from credit card borrowers handled during the lockout or revolving period?

  C. Explain why you agree or disagree with the following statement: "After the lockout period, the principal is paid to bondholders in one lump sum amount at the maturity date of the security."

30. A manager of a corporate bond portfolio is considering the purchase of a credit card receivable-backed security. The manager believes that an advantage of such securities is that there is no contraction risk and no extension risk. Explain why you agree or disagree with this view.

31. A. What is meant by the monthly payment rate for a credit card deal?

  B. What is the significance of the monthly payment rate?

  C. How is the net portfolio yield determined for a credit card deal?

32. What is a typical cash CDO structure?

33. Explain why you agree or disagree with the following statement: "The asset manager for a CDO is free to actively manage the portfolio without any constraints."

34. Explain why you agree or disagree with the following statement: "By using an interest rate swap, the asset manager for a CDO increases the risk associated with meeting the obligations that must be paid to the senior tranche."

35. What is the key factor in determining whether or not an arbitrage CDO can be issued?

36. Consider the following CDO transaction:

  1. The CDO is a $200 million structure. That is, the assets purchased will be $200 million.

  2. The collateral consists of bonds that all mature in 8 years, and the coupon rate for every bond is the 8-year Treasury rate plus 600 basis points.

  3. The senior tranche comprises 75% of the structure ($150 million) and pays interest based on the following coupon formula: LIBOR plus 90 basis points.

  4. There is only one junior tranche ($30 million) with a coupon rate that is fixed. The coupon rate is the 8-year Treasury rate plus 300 basis points.

  5. The asset manager enters into an agreement with a counterparty in which it agrees to pay the counterparty a fixed rate each year equal to the 8-year Treasury rate plus 120 basis points and receive LIBOR. The notional amount of the agreement is $150 million.

  A. How much is the equity tranche in this CDO?

  B. Assume that the 8-year Treasury rate at the time the CDO is issued is 6%. Assuming no defaults, what is the cash flow for each year and how is it distributed?

  C. Ignoring the asset management fee, what is the amount available each year for the equity tranche?

37. What are the elements of the return for the junior note holders in a synthetic CDO structure?

38. Why have banks issued synthetic balance sheet CDOs?

The following information relates to Questions 39–44

Krista Boldon is the CFO of Whisper Spa, a company that sells high-quality spa and sauna equipment and accessories to homeowners through direct distribution. Approximately 76% of the company's sales are financed by direct-lending revolving credit card accounts funded internally by Whisper Spa. Boldon has recently proposed that the company raise cash to fund additional credit sales by securitizing Whisper Spa's existing credit card receivables. Boldon's proposal includes the multi-tranche, senior-subordinate structure with multiple internal credit enhancements shown in Exhibit 1. The total value of the collateral for the structure is $68.0 million, the lockout period is two years, and the B2 bond class is the first loss piece.

EXHIBIT 1   Proposed ABS Structure

Bond Class	Par Value ($ Millions)
A1	27
A2	23
A3	8
B1 (subordinate)	6
B2 (subordinate)	4
Total	68

Melvin Haggerty, Whisper Spa's CEO, reviewed Boldon's proposal and responded with the following statement:

> "I am concerned that the debt will not sell well in the market because Whisper Spa's credit rating is marginal."

39. The *primary* motivation for creating the three senior bond classes, represented by Class A in the structure shown in Exhibit 1, is:
- **A.** redistribution of credit risk.
- **B.** redistribution of prepayment risk.
- **C.** redistribution of interest rate risk.

40. The *primary* motivation for creating two different classes of bonds, A and B, in the structure in Exhibit 1 is:
- **A.** redistribution of credit risk.
- **B.** redistribution of prepayment risk.
- **C.** redistribution of interest rate risk.

41. If default losses over the life of the structure total $8.0 million, what is the loss to the class B1 bondholders?
- **A.** $2.0 million.
- **B.** $4.0 million.
- **C.** $6.0 million.

42. Which of the following credit enhancements is *most likely* to be incorporated into Whisper Spa's asset-backed securities?
- **A.** Letter of credit.
- **B.** Insurance "wrapping."
- **C.** Overcollateralization.

43. Haggerty's statement is *most likely*:
- **A.** justified, because the security will include internal credit enhancements.
- **B.** justified, because Whisper Spa has the ultimate responsibility for repaying the bondholders.
- **C.** not justified, because only internal credit enhancements are being used.

44. By the end of the fourteenth month after the securities were issued, the underlying credit card accounts have prepaid $30 million in principal in addition to regularly scheduled principal and interest payments. The amount of this principal prepaid to the holders of the A2 bond class is *closest* to:
- **A.** $0.
- **B.** $12.0 million.
- **C.** $23.0 million.

SOLUTIONS FOR READING 52

1. A. Since Caterpillar Financial Funding Corporation sold the retail installment sales contracts to Caterpillar Financial Asset Trust 1997-A, Caterpillar Financial Funding Corporation would be referred to in the prospectus as the "Seller."

   B. The special purpose vehicle in a securitization issues the securities and therefore is referred to as the "Issuer." In this transaction, Caterpillar Asset Financial Trust 1997-A is the "Issuer."

   C. Without having a full description of the waterfall for this structure, it appears that Bond Classes A-1, A-2, and A-3 are the senior classes.

   D. Without having a full description of the waterfall for this structure, it appears that Bond Class B is the subordinate class.

   E. Credit tranching in this structure was done by creating the senior and subordinate tranches. Prepayment tranching appears to have been done by offering three classes of the senior tranche.

2. A. In the securitization process, the attorneys prepare the legal documentation which includes i) the purchase agreement between the seller of the assets and the special purpose vehicle, ii) how the cash flows are divided among the bond classes, and iii) the servicing agreement between the entity engaged to service the assets and the special purpose vehicle.

   B. The independent accountant verifies the accuracy of all numerical information (e.g., yield and average life) placed in either the prospectus or private placement memorandum and then issues a comfort letter.

3. How the principal repayments from the collateral are used by the trustee in a securitization transaction depends on the waterfall which, in turn, is affected by the character of the collateral (amortizing versus non-amortizing). In a typical structure backed by amortizing assets, the principal repayments are distributed to the bond classes. In a typical structure backed by non-amortizing assets, the principal repayments for a specified period of time (the lockout period) are used to purchase new assets and after that period (assuming no early amortization provision is triggered), the principal repayments are distributed to the bond classes. This structure is referred to as a revolving structure.

4. The excess servicing spread is determined as follows:

Gross weighted average coupon	=	8.60%
− Servicing fee	=	0.50%
Spread available to pay tranches	=	8.10%
− Net weighted average coupon	=	7.10%
Excess servicing spread	=	1.00% = 100 basis points

5. A. The amount of overcollateralization is the difference between the value of the collateral, $320 million, and the par value for all the tranches, $300 million. In this structure it is $20 million.

   B. If the losses total $15 million, then the loss is entirely absorbed by the overcollateralization. No tranche will realize a loss.

C.–E.

	Total Loss ($)	Senior Tranche ($)	Subordinate Tranche 1 ($)	Subordinate Tranche 2 ($)
C.	35 million	zero	zero	15 million
D.	85 million	zero	35 million	30 million
E.	110 million	10 million	50 million	30 million

6. A. For a non-amortizing loan, there is no schedule for repayment of principal. Consequently, for individual loans of this type there can be no prepayments.

    B. While there may be no prepayments for individual loans that are non-amortizing, the securities that are backed by these loans may be prepayable. For example, credit card receivable-backed securities can be prepaid under certain conditions. Such conditions are referred to as "early amortization" or "rapid amortization" events or triggers.

7. The rating agencies take the weak-link approach to credit enhancement. Typically a structure cannot receive a rating higher than the rating on any third party providing an external guarantee. Since the question specifies that the only form of credit enhancement is the letter of credit, then the rating will not exceed the single A rating of the bank providing the letter credit. Thus, a triple A rating is not likely.

8. Since credit agencies take the weak-link approach to credit enhancement, if an insurance company wants to offer bond insurance for an asset-backed security transaction where a triple A credit rating is sought, the insurance company must have a triple A credit rating.

9. Both a cash reserve fund and an excess servicing spread account are forms of internal credit enhancement. A cash reserve fund is provided by a deposit of cash at issuance. Excess servicing spread account is the cash available to absorb losses from the collateral after payment of interest to all the tranches and to the servicer.

10. The excess servicing spread account builds up over time in order to offset future losses. However, if losses occur early in the life of the collateral, there may not be enough time to accumulate the excess servicing spread to adequately cover future losses.

11. A. A senior-subordinate structure is a form of internal credit enhancement because it does not rely on the guarantee of a third party. Instead, the enhancement comes from within the structure by creating senior and subordinate tranches. The subordinate tranches provide credit protection for the senior tranche.

    B. Once a deal is closed, the percentage of the senior tranche and the percentage of the subordinate tranche change when the underlying assets are subject to prepayments. If the subordinate interest in a structure decreases after the deal is closed, the credit protection for the senior tranche decreases. The shifting interest mechanism seeks to prevent the senior tranche's credit protection provided by the subordinate tranche (or tranches) from declining by establishing a schedule that provides for a higher allocation of the prepayments to the senior tranche in the earlier years.

12. A. The senior prepayment percentage is the percentage of prepayments that are allocated to the senior tranche. The senior prepayment percentage is specified in the prospectus.

B. Because the shifting interest mechanism results in a greater amount of the prepayments be paid to the senior tranche in the earlier years than in the absence of such a mechanism, the senior tranches are exposed to greater contraction risk.

13. The outstanding bonds in a structure can be called if either 1) the collateral outstanding reaches a predetermined level before the specified call date or 2) the call date has been reached even if the collateral outstanding is above the predetermined level.

14. A. The cash flow for a closed-end home equity loan is the same as for a standard mortgage loan: interest, regularly scheduled principal repayments (i.e., regular amortization), and prepayments.

B. The statement is incorrect. Typically, a closed-end home equity loan borrower is a credit impaired borrower.

15. For month 1, the CPR for 100% PPC is 5%, so the CPR for 200% PPC is 10% (= 2 × 5%). For month 2, the CPR for 100% PPC is 5% plus 1.8%, which is 6.8%. Therefore, the CPR for 200% PPC for month 2 is 13.6% (2 × 6.8%).

In month 12, the CPR for 100% PPC is

$$5\% + 1.8\% \times 11 = 24.8\%$$

Therefore, the CPR for 200% PPC is 49.6% (2 × 24.8%). For all months after month 12, the CPR for 200% CPR is 49.6%.

Month	CPR (%)	Month	CPR (%)	Month	CPR (%)
1	10.0	11	46.0	30	49.6
2	13.6	12	49.6	125	49.6
3	17.2	13	49.6	150	49.6
4	20.8	14	49.6	200	49.6
5	24.4	15	49.6	250	49.6
6	28.0	16	49.6	275	49.6
7	31.6	17	49.6	300	49.6
8	35.2	18	49.6	325	49.6
9	38.8	19	49.6	350	49.6
10	42.4	20	49.6	360	49.6

16. The base case prepayment specified in the prospectus is called the prospectus prepayment curve (PPC). It is unique to each issuer and should be used instead of the generic PSA prepayment benchmark. However, it is not a generic prepayment benchmark for all closed-end home equity loan-securities as Mr. Tellmen assumes.

17. For adjustable-rate HELs, the reference rate is typically 6-month LIBOR. However, the floating-rate securities that these loans back typically are referenced to 1-month LIBOR in order to make them attractive to investors who fund themselves based on 1-month LIBOR. As a result, there will be a mismatch between the reference rate on the floating-rate HELs used as collateral and the securities backed by that collateral that will prevent the cap from being fixed over the life of the securities. In addition, there are periodic caps and a lifetime cap.

18. A. Since month 36 is in the first five years after issuance, the schedule specifies that all prepayments are allocated to the senior tranche and none to the subordinate tranches. Thus, the prepayments of $100,000 are allocated only to the senior tranche.

B. According to the schedule, if prepayments occur 8 years after issuance, 20% is allocated to the senior tranche and the balance is paid to the subordinate tranches. Since the prepayments are assumed to be $100,000, the senior tranche receives $20,000 and the subordinate tranches $80,000.

C. All prepayments that occur 10 years after issuance are paid to the subordinate tranches. Thus, the $100,000 of prepayments some time in year 10 are paid to the subordinate tranches.

19. The schedule in the prospectus is the base schedule. The schedule can change so as to allocate less to the subordinate tranches if the collateral's performance deteriorates after the deal is closed. Determination of whether or not the base schedule should be overridden is made by the trustee based on tests that are specified in the prospectus.

20. The protection is provided by establishing a schedule for the allocation of principal payments (both regularly scheduled principal payments and prepayments) between the NAS tranche and the non-NAS tranches such that contraction risk and extension risk are reduced. For example, a schedule would specify a lockout period for the principal payments to the NAS tranche. This means that the NAS tranche would not receive any payments until the lockout period ends, and therefore contraction risk is mitigated. Extension risk is provided by allocating a large percentage to the NAS tranche in later years.

21. A. The cash flow is the same as for mortgage-backed securities backed by standard mortgage loans: 1) interest, 2) regularly scheduled principal repayments (amortization), and 3) prepayments.

B. The reasons why the securities backed by manufactured housing loans tend not to be sensitive to refinancing are:

1. the loan balances are typically small so that there is no significant dollar savings from refinancing.

2. the rate of depreciation of manufactured homes may be such that in the earlier years depreciation is greater than the amount of the loan paid off, making it difficult to refinance the loan.

3. typically borrowers are of lower credit quality and therefore find it difficult to obtain funds to refinance.

22. The deals are more akin to the nonagency market since there is no guarantee by a federally related agency or a government sponsored enterprise as in the United States. As such, the deals must be rated and therefore require credit enhancement.

23. A. The cash flow for auto-loan backed securities consists of 1) interest, 2) regularly scheduled principal repayments (amortization), and 3) prepayments.

B. Prepayments due to refinancing on auto loans tend to be of minor importance.

24. A conditional prepayment rate measures prepayments relative to the amount outstanding in the previous year that could prepay. For a monthly CPR, called the single monthly mortality rate, SMM, prepayments are measured relative to the amount available in the previous month that was available to prepay.

The absolute prepayment speed, denoted ABS, is the monthly prepayment expressed as a percentage of the *original* collateral amount.

25. A. $$\text{SMM} = \frac{0.015}{1 - \left[0.015 \times (21 - 1)\right]} = 0.0214 = 2.14\%$$

B. $$\text{ABS} = \frac{0.019}{1 + \left[0.019 \times (11 - 1)\right]} = 0.016 = 1.60\%$$

26. The trustee is wrong. For certain student loans the government will guarantee up to 98% of the principal plus accrued interest (assuming the loans have been properly serviced). Moreover, there are securities backed by alternative student loans that carry no government guarantee.

27. While a student is in school, no payments are made by the student on the loan. This period is the deferment period. Upon leaving school, the student is extended a period of time (typically six months) when no payments on the loan must be made. This is called the grace period.

28. A. The cash flow for an SBA-backed security consists of 1) interest for the period, 2) the scheduled principal repayment, and 3) prepayments.

B. The interest is based on a coupon formula where the prime rate is the reference rate. The rate on the loan is reset monthly on the first of the month or quarterly on the first of January, April, July, and October.

29. A. During the lockout period, only finance charges and fees collected are distributed to the bondholders.

B. During the lockout period, principal paid by borrowers is reinvested in new receivables and not distributed to the bondholders.

C. The statement is incorrect because principal repayment can be made by either 1) a bullet payment structure (as stated in the question), 2) a controlled amortization structure, or 3) a passthrough structure.

30. While there is no schedule of principal repayments for credit card borrowers, there is the potential risk of contraction for the securities. This is because there is a provision for early or rapid amortization if certain triggers are reached.

There is also the potential for extension risk because principal repayment from the credit card borrowers and defaults and delinquencies may be such that the schedule specified for principal repayment of the security during the amortization period may not be adequate to completely pay off bondholders by the stated maturity.

While these are nontrivial risks, neither of these occurs frequently.

31. A. The monthly payment rate (MPR) expresses the monthly payment of a credit card receivable portfolio as a percentage of debt outstanding in the previous month. The monthly payment includes finance charges, fees, and any principal repayment collected.

B. There are two reasons why the MPR is important. First, if the MPR reaches an extremely low level, there is a chance that there will be extension risk with respect to the repayment of principal. The length of time until the return of principal is largely a function of the monthly payment rate. Second, if the MPR is very low, then there is a chance that there will not be sufficient cash flow to pay off principal. This is one of the events that could trigger early amortization of the principal.

C. The net portfolio yield for a credit card receivable portfolio is equal to the gross portfolio yield minus charge-offs. The gross portfolio yield includes finance charges collected and fees. From the gross portfolio yield charge-offs are deducted. Charge-offs represent the accounts charged off as uncollectible.

32. The typical structure of a CDO is as follows. There is 1) a senior tranche (between 70% and 80% of the deal) with a floating rate, 2) different layers of subordinate or junior debt tranches with a fixed rate, and 3) an equity tranche.

33. The statement is incorrect. The asset manager responsible for purchasing the debt obligations for the portfolio will have restrictions that are imposed by the rating agencies that rate the securities in the deal (coverage and quality tests). There will be certain tests that must be satisfied for the tranches in the CBO to maintain its credit rating at the time of issuance.

34. The statement is not correct. In fact, it is because of interest rate swaps that the risk is reduced for the senior tranche. This is because the collateral is typically fixed-rate bonds and the senior tranche must be paid a floating rate. An interest rate swap is used to convert the fixed-rate payments from the collateral into floating-rate payments that can be made to the senior tranche.

35. The key determinant is whether or not the CDO can be issued such that the subordinate/equity tranche can be offered a competitive return.

36. A. Given that the senior tranche is $150 million and the junior tranche is $30 million, the equity tranche is $20 million ($200 million minus $180 million).

B. The collateral will pay interest each year (assuming no defaults) equal to the 8-year Treasury rate of 6% plus 600 basis points. So the interest will be:

Interest from collateral: $12\% \times \$200,000,000 = \$24,000,000$

The interest that must be paid to the senior tranche is:

Interest to senior tranche: $\$150,000,000 \times (\text{LIBOR} + 90 \text{ bps})$

The coupon rate for the junior tranche is 6% plus 300 basis points. So, the coupon rate is 9% and the interest is:

Interest to junior tranche: $9\% \times \$30,000,000 = \$2,700,000$

For the interest rate swap, the asset manager is agreeing to pay the swap counterparty each year 6% (the 8-year Treasury rate) plus 120 basis points, or 7.2%. Since the swap payments are based on a notional amount of $150 million, the asset manager pays to the swap counterparty:

Interest to swap counterparty: $7.2\% \times \$150,000,000 = \$10,800,000$

The interest payment received from the swap counterparty is LIBOR based on a notional amount of $150 million. That is,

Interest from swap counterparty: $150,000,000 × LIBOR
The interest for the CBO is:

Interest from collateral $24,000,000
Interest from swap counterparty ....$150,000,000 × LIBOR

Total interest received ....$24,000,000 + $150,000,000 × LIBOR

The interest to be paid out to the senior and junior tranches and to the swap counterparty include:

Interest to senior tranche..............$150,000,000 × (LIBOR + 90 bps)
Interest to junior tranche.................$2,700,000
Interest to swap counterparty..........$10,800,000

Total interest paid...........................$13,500,000 + $150,000,000
                                                                          × (LIBOR + 90 bps)

Netting the interest payments paid and received:

Total interest received......$24,000,000 + $150,000,000 × LIBOR
− Total interest paid ....$13,500,000 + $150,000,000 × (LIBOR + 90 bps)

Net interest ....$10,500,000 − $150,000,000 × (90 bps)

> Since 90 bps times $150 million is $1,350,000, the net interest remaining is $9,150,000. This is the cash flow ignoring the asset management fee.

C. The amount available for the equity tranche is $9,150,000. This is the cash flow computed in Part B.

37. The return includes:

> the return on a portfolio of high-quality debt instruments
> plus
> the payment from the asset manager as part of the credit default swap
> minus
> the payment that must be made by a junior tranche due to a credit event

38. By issuing a synthetic CDO, a bank can remove the economic risk of bank loans without having to notify any borrowers that they are selling the loans to another party. Thus, no consent would be needed from borrowers to transfer loans, a requirement in some countries.

39. B is correct. The primary motivation for the sequential-pay structure is to redistribute prepayment risk among the holders of different bond classes. This is known as a sequential pay structure.

40. A is correct. The primary motivation for the senior-subordinate structure is to redistribute credit risk (referred to as credit tranching), a form of internal credit enhancement for the senior bond classes.

41. B is correct. Given the sequential pay structure, the B2 bond class is the first-loss piece, and those bondholders would absorb the first $4.0 million in default losses. The remaining $4.0 million of losses would be absorbed by the B1 bond class. As long as the default losses do not exceed $10 million, the senior (A) classes would not suffer any default losses.

42. C is correct. Overcollateralization is a form of internal credit enhancement. Letters of credit and insurance wrapping are external credit enhancements.

43. C is correct. Whisper Spa's credit rating would not be taken into account when assigning a credit rating to the asset-backed securities unless they, as the seller, were to guarantee repayment on the bonds. Because Whisper Spa only plans to use internal credit enhancements, a guarantee would not apply, and Whisper Spa's credit rating would be irrelevant to the rating on the securities.

44. A is correct. Because the securities have a two-year lockout period, all principal prepayments within the first two years will be used to fund new loans. No security tranche will receive principal prepayments until after the 24-month lockout period. Credit card prepayments are usually just rolled into new loans (not repaid to bondholders).

SOLUTIONS FOR READING 52

Solutions are for Practice Questions found in Reading

1. Losses by bond class

	Total Loss ($)	Senior Bond Class ($)	Subordinate Bond Class 1 ($)	Subordinate Bond Class 2 ($)
A.	15 million	zero	zero	15 million
B.	50 million	zero	30 million	20 million
C.	90 million	30 million	40 million	20 million

2. The excess servicing spread is determined as follows:

Gross weighted average coupon	=	9.50%
− Servicing fee	=	0.75%
Spread available to pay tranches	=	8.75%
− Net weighted average coupon	=	7.50%
Excess servicing spread	=	1.25% = 125 basis points

3. For month 1 the CPR is 4% as per the prospectus. Since we are interested in 150% PPC, the CPR in month 1 is 6% ($1.5 \times 4\%$). For month 2, 1.5% is added to 4%, so 100% PPC is 5.5%. Then 150% PPC is a CPR of 8.3% ($= 1.5 \times 5.5\%$). In month 15, the CPR is 25% for 100% PPC and for 150% PPC, the CPR is 37.5% ($1.5 \times 25\%$). For all months after month 15, the CPR is 37.5%.

Month	CPR (%)	Month	CPR (%)	Month	CPR (%)
1	6.0	11	28.5	30	37.5
2	8.3	12	30.8	125	37.5
3	10.5	13	33.0	150	37.5
4	12.8	14	35.3	200	37.5
5	15.0	15	37.5	250	37.5
6	17.3	16	37.5	275	37.5
7	19.5	17	37.5	300	37.5
8	21.8	18	37.5	325	37.5
9	24.0	19	37.5	350	37.5
10	26.3	20	37.5	360	37.5

4. A. $\text{SMM} = \dfrac{0.02}{1 - [0.02 \times (11 - 1)]} = 0.025 = 2.5\%$

B. $\text{ABS} = \dfrac{0.017}{1 + [0.017 \times (21 - 1)]} = 0.0127 = 1.27\%$

$4\frac{5}{8}$ $4\frac{11}{16}$ — $\frac{3}{8}$

$5\frac{1}{2}$ $5\frac{1}{2}$ —

$5\frac{1}{2}$ $21\frac{3}{16}$ — $\frac{1}{16}$

$20\frac{5}{8}$ $21\frac{3}{16}$ + $\frac{7}{8}$

$17\frac{3}{8}$ $18\frac{1}{8}$ +

$13\frac{1}{2}$ $6\frac{1}{2}$ — $\frac{1}{2}$

$6\frac{1}{2}$ $6\frac{1}{2}$ —

$7\frac{1}{4}$ $31\frac{1}{32}$ — $\frac{1}{16}$

$\frac{15}{16}$

$\frac{9}{16}$ $\frac{9}{8}$

$1\frac{9}{32}$

$7\frac{13}{16}$ $7\frac{15}{16}$

$7\frac{15}{16}$ $7\frac{13}{16}$

$2\frac{5}{8}$ $2\frac{11}{32}$ $2\frac{1}{2}$ +

$2\frac{3}{4}$ $2\frac{1}{4}$ $2\frac{1}{4}$

$12\frac{1}{16}$ $11\frac{3}{8}$ $11\frac{3}{4}$ +

$6\frac{1}{5}$ $33\frac{3}{4}$ 33 $33\frac{1}{8}$ —

87

652 $25\frac{5}{8}$ $24\frac{9}{16}$ $25\frac{3}{8}$ +

633 12 $11\frac{5}{8}$ $11\frac{7}{8}$ +

16 $10\frac{1}{2}$ $10\frac{1}{2}$ $10\frac{1}{2}$ —

78 $15\frac{7}{8}$ $15\frac{13}{16}$ $15\frac{3}{8}$ —

4508 $9\frac{1}{16}$ $8\frac{1}{4}$ $8\frac{7}{8}$ +

430 $11\frac{1}{4}$ $10\frac{1}{8}$

VALUING MORTGAGE-BACKED AND ASSET-BACKED SECURITIES

by Frank J. Fabozzi, CFA

LEARNING OUTCOMES

The candidate should be able to: Mastery

a. explain the calculation, use, and limitations of the cash flow yield,   ☐
nominal spread, and zero-volatility spread for a mortgage-backed
security and an asset-backed security;

b. describe the Monte Carlo simulation model for valuing a   ☐
mortgage-backed security;

c. describe path dependency in passthrough securities and the implications   ☐
for valuation models;

d. explain how the option-adjusted spread is calculated using the Monte   ☐
Carlo simulation model and how this spread measure is interpreted;

e. evaluate a mortgage-backed security using option-adjusted spread   ☐
analysis;

f. explain why effective durations reported by various dealers and vendors   ☐
may differ;

g. analyze the interest rate risk of a security, given the security's effective   ☐
duration;

h. explain cash flow, coupon curve, and empirical measures of duration,   ☐
and describe limitations of each in relation to mortgage-backed
securities;

i. determine whether the nominal spread, zero-volatility spread, or   ☐
option-adjusted spread should be used to evaluate a specific fixed
income security.

1   INTRODUCTION

In previous readings, we looked at mortgage-backed and asset-backed securities. Our focus was on understanding the risks associated with investing in these securities, how they are created (i.e., how they are structured), and why the products are created. Specifically, in the case of agency mortgage-backed securities we saw how prepayment risk can be redistributed among different tranches to create securities with a prepayment risk profile that is different from the underlying pool of mortgages. For asset-backed securities and nonagency mortgage-backed security, we saw how to create tranches with different degrees of credit risk.

What we did not discuss in describing these securities is how to value them and how to quantify their exposure to interest rate risk. That is, we know, for example, that a support tranche in a CMO structure has greater prepayment risk than a planned amortization class (PAC) tranche. However, how do we determine whether or not the price at which a support tranche is offered in the market adequately compensates for the greater prepayment risk? In this reading, we will describe and then apply a methodology for valuing mortgage-backed securities and some types of asset-backed securities—Monte Carlo simulation. A byproduct of a valuation model is the option-adjusted spread. We will see how the option-adjusted spread for a mortgage-backed or an asset-backed security is computed and applied. From a valuation model the effective duration and effective convexity of any security can be computed. We will explain how to compute effective duration and effective convexity using the Monte Carlo simulation model. However, in the case of mortgage-backed securities, there have been several alternative measures of duration used by practitioners. These measures will be identified along with their advantages and disadvantages.

Admittedly, the majority of this reading is devoted to the valuation of mortgage-backed securities and by extension to all real estate-related asset-backed securities. They are the most difficult asset-backed products to value and to quantify in terms of interest rate exposure. At the end of this reading, we provide a framework for determining which analytical measures discussed in this reading are appropriate for valuing any asset-backed security. In fact, the principles apply to all fixed income products.

2   CASH FLOW YIELD ANALYSIS

Let's begin with the traditional analysis of mortgage-backed and asset-backed securities—cash flow yield analysis. The yield on any financial instrument is the interest rate that makes the present value of the expected cash flow equal to its market price plus accrued interest. When applied to mortgage-backed and asset-backed securities, this yield is called a cash flow yield. The problem in calculating the cash flow yield of mortgage-backed and asset-backed securities is that the cash flow is unknown because of prepayments. Consequently, to determine a cash flow yield, some assumption about the prepayment rate must be made. And, in the case of all but agency mortgage-backed securities, an assumption about default rates and recovery rates must be made.

The cash flow for mortgage-backed and asset-backed securities is typically monthly. The convention is to compare the yield on mortgage-backed and asset-backed securities to that of a Treasury coupon security by calculating the security's *bond-equivalent yield*. The bond-equivalent yield for a Treasury coupon security is found by doubling the semiannual yield to maturity. However, it is incorrect to do this for a mortgage-backed or an asset-backed security because the investor has the opportunity to generate greater reinvestment income by reinvesting the more frequent (i.e., monthly) cash flows. The market convention is to calculate a yield so as to make it comparable to the yield to maturity on a bond-equivalent basis. The formula for annualizing the monthly cash flow yield for a monthly-pay product is therefore:

$$\text{Bond-equivalent yield} = 2[(1 + i_M)^6 - 1]$$

where i_M is the monthly interest rate that will equate the present value of the projected monthly cash flow equal to the market price (plus accrued interest) of the security.

To illustrate the calculation of the bond-equivalent yield, suppose that the monthly yield is 0.6%. That is, i_M is 0.006. Then

$$\text{Bond-equivalent yield} = 2[(1.006)^6 - 1] = 0.0731 = 7.31\%$$

A. Limitations of Cash Flow Yield Measure

All yield measures suffer from problems that limit their use in assessing a security's potential return. The yield to maturity has two major shortcomings as a measure of a bond's potential return. To realize the stated yield to maturity, the investor must:

1. reinvest the coupon payments at a rate equal to the yield to maturity, and

2. hold the bond to the maturity date.

The reinvestment of the coupon payments is critical and for long-term bonds can be as much as 80% of the bond's return. Reinvestment risk is the risk of having to reinvest the interest payments at less than the computed yield. Interest rate risk is the risk associated with having to sell the security before its maturity date at a price less than the purchase price.

These shortcomings are equally applicable to the cash flow yield measure:

1. the projected cash flows are assumed to be reinvested at the cash flow yield, and

2. the mortgage-backed or asset-backed security is assumed to be held until the final payout based on some prepayment assumption.

The importance of reinvestment risk, the risk that the cash flow will have to be reinvested at a rate less than the cash flow yield, is particularly important for many mortgage-backed and asset-backed securities because payments are monthly and both interest and principal must be reinvested. Moreover, an additional assumption is that the projected cash flow is actually realized. If the prepayment, default, and recovery experience is different from that assumed, the cash flow yield will not be realized.

B. Nominal Spread

Given the computed cash flow yield and the average life for a mortgage-backed or asset-backed security based on some prepayment, default, and recovery assumption, the next step is to compare the yield to the yield for a comparable Treasury security. "Comparable" is typically defined as a Treasury security with the same maturity as the security's average life. The difference between the cash flow yield and the yield on a comparable Treasury security is called the nominal spread.

Unfortunately, it is the nominal spread that some managers will use as a measure of relative value. However, this spread masks the fact that a portion of the nominal spread is compensation for accepting prepayment risk. For example, CMO support tranches have been offered at large nominal spreads. However, the nominal spread embodies the substantial prepayment risk associated with support tranches. The manager who buys solely on the basis of nominal spread fails to determine whether or not that nominal spread offered adequate compensation given the substantial prepayment risk faced by the holder of a support tranche.

Instead of nominal spread, managers need a measure that indicates the potential compensation after adjusting for prepayment risk. This measure is called the option-adjusted spread. We discussed this measure in the reading on valuing bonds with embedded options where we covered the valuation of corporate and agency bonds with embedded options. Before discussing this measure for structured products, we describe another spread measure commonly quoted for structured products called the zero-volatility spread.

3   ZERO-VOLATILITY SPREAD

The proper procedure to compare any security to a U.S. Treasury security is to compare it to a portfolio of Treasury securities that have the same cash flow. The value of the security is then equal to the present value of all of the cash flows. The security's value, assuming the cash flows are default-free, will equal the present value of the replicating portfolio of Treasury securities. In turn, these cash flows are valued at the Treasury spot rates.

The zero-volatility spread is a measure of spread that the investor would realize over the entire Treasury spot rate curve if the mortgage-backed or asset-backed security is held to maturity. It is not a spread off one point on the Treasury yield curve, as is the nominal spread. The zero-volatility spread (also called the Z-spread and the static spread) is the spread that will make the present value of the cash flows from the mortgage-backed or asset-backed security when discounted at the Treasury spot rate plus the spread equal to the price of the security. A trial-and-error procedure (or search algorithm) is required to determine the zero-volatility spread.[1]

In general, the shorter the maturity or average life of a structured product, the less the zero-volatility spread will differ from the nominal spread. The magnitude of the difference between the nominal spread and the zero-volatility spread also depends on the shape of the yield curve. The steeper the yield curve, the greater the difference.

One of the objectives of this reading is to explain when it is appropriate to use the Z-spread instead of the OAS. What will be seen is that if a structured product has an option and the borrower tends to take advantage of that option

---

[1] Most common spreadsheet programs offer this type of algorithm.

when interest rates decline, then the OAS should be used. If the borrower has an option but tends not to take advantage of it when interest rates decline, then the Z-spread should be used.

MONTE CARLO SIMULATION MODEL AND OAS 4

In the reading on valuing bonds with embedded options, we discussed one model that is used to value callable agency debentures and corporate bonds, the binomial model. This valuation model accommodates securities in which the decision to exercise a call option is not dependent on how interest rates evolved over time. That is, the decision of an issuer to call a bond will depend on the level of the rate at which the issue can be refunded relative to the issue's coupon rate, and not the path interest rates took to get to that rate. In contrast, there are fixed-income securities and derivative instruments for which the periodic cash flows are "interest rate path-dependent." This means that the cash flow received in one period is determined not only by the current interest rate level, but also by the path that interest rates took to get to the current level.

For example, in the case of passthrough securities, prepayments are interest rate path-dependent because this month's prepayment rate depends on whether there have been prior opportunities to refinance since the underlying mortgages were originated. This phenomenon is referred to as "prepayment burnout." Pools of passthroughs are used as collateral for the creation of CMOs. Consequently, there are typically two sources of path dependency in a CMO tranche's cash flows. First, the collateral prepayments are path-dependent as discussed above. Second, the cash flows to be received in the current month by a CMO tranche depend on the outstanding balances of the other tranches in the deal. Thus, we need the history of prepayments to calculate these balances.

Conceptually, the valuation of agency passthrough using the Monte Carlo model is simple. In practice, however, it is very complex. The simulation involves generating a set of cash flows based on simulated future mortgage refinancing rates, which in turn imply simulated prepayment rates.

Valuation modeling for agency CMOs is similar to valuation modeling for passthroughs, although the difficulties are amplified because the issuer has distributed both the prepayment risk and the interest rate risk into different tranches. The sensitivity of the passthroughs comprising the collateral to these two risks is not transmitted equally to every tranche. Some of the tranches wind up more sensitive to prepayment risk and interest rate risk than the collateral, while some of them are much less sensitive.

The objective is to figure out how the value of the collateral gets transmitted to the tranches in a deal. More specifically, the objective is to find out where the value goes and where the risk goes so that one can identify the tranches with low risk and high value: the tranches a manager wants to consider for purchase. The good news is that this combination usually exists in every deal. The bad news is that in every deal there are usually tranches with low value and high risk that managers want to avoid purchasing.

A. Simulating Interest Rate Paths and Cash Flows

To generate these random interest rate paths, the typical model used by Wall Street firms and commercial vendors takes as input today's term structure of interest rates and a volatility assumption. (We discussed these topics in the reading on valuing bonds with embedded options.) The term structure of interest rates is the theoretical spot rate (or zero coupon) curve implied by today's Treasury securities. The simulations should be calibrated so that the average simulated price of a zero-coupon Treasury bond equals today's actual price.

On-the-run Treasury issues are often used in the calibration process. Some dealers and vendors of analytical systems use the LIBOR curve instead of the Treasury curve—or give the user a choice to use either the Treasury curve or the LIBOR curve. The reason is that some investors are interested in spreads that they can earn relative to their funding costs, and LIBOR for many investors is a better proxy for that cost than Treasury rates.

As explained in the reading on valuing bonds with embedded options, every dealer and vendor of analytical systems employs an interest rate model. This is a model that assumes how interest rates will change over time. The interest rate models employed by most dealers and vendors of analytical systems are similar. However, one input to all interest rate models is the interest rate volatility assumption. It is that assumption that varies by dealer and vendor. As will be illustrated later in this reading, it is a critical input.

The volatility assumption determines the dispersion of future interest rates in the simulation. Today, many dealers and vendors do not use one volatility number for the yield of all maturities of the yield curve. Instead, they use either a short/long yield volatility or a term structure of yield volatility. A short/long yield volatility means that volatility is specified for maturities up to a certain number of years (short yield volatility) and a different yield volatility for longer maturities (long yield volatility). The short yield volatility is assumed to be greater than the long yield volatility. A term structure of yield volatilities means that a yield volatility is assumed for each maturity.

Based on the interest rate model and the assumed volatility, a series of interest rate paths will be generated. We will see shortly how a security is valued on each interest rate path. However, there is nothing that we have explained thus far that assures us that the values produced by the model will be arbitrage free. Recall from the reading on valuing bonds with embedded options that the binomial interest rate tree by design is constructed to be arbitrage free. That is, if any of the on-the-run issues that were used to construct the binomial interest rate tree are valued using the tree, the model would produce a value for that on-the-run issue equal to its market value. There is nothing we described so far about the Monte Carlo simulation to assure this.

More specifically, in the case of Monte Carlo simulation for valuing mortgage-backed and asset-backed securities, the on-the-run Treasury issues are typically used. What assurance is there that if an on-the-run Treasury issue is valued using the Monte Carlo simulation model it will be arbitrage free? That is, what assurance is there that the value produced by the model will equal the market price? Nothing. That's right, nothing. What the model builder must do is "adjust" the interest rate paths so that the model produces the correct values for the on-the-run Treasury issues. A discussion of this adjustment process is not important to us. In fact, there are very few published sources that describe how this is done. The key point here is that no such adjustment is necessary in a binomial model for valuing corporate and agency bonds with embedded options because the tree is built to be arbitrage free. In the case of the Monte Carlo simulation model, the builder must make an arbitrary adjustment to the interest rate paths to get the model to be arbitrage free.

The simulation works by generating many scenarios of future interest rate paths. As just explained, the "raw" interest rate paths that are simulated must be "adjusted" so as to make the model generate arbitrage-free values for whatever benchmark interest rates are used—typically, the on-the-run Treasury issues. *So, in the remainder of this reading, when we refer to interest rate paths it is understood that it is the "adjusted" interest rate paths where "adjusted" means that each interest rate path is adjusted so that the model will produce arbitrage-free values.*

In each month of the scenario (i.e., path), a monthly interest rate and a mortgage refinancing rate are generated. The monthly interest rates are used to discount the projected cash flows in the scenario. The mortgage refinancing rate is needed to determine the cash flows because it represents the opportunity cost the borrower (i.e., mortgagor) is facing at that time.

If the refinancing rates are high relative to the borrower's original coupon rate (i.e., the rate on the borrower's loan), the borrower will have less incentive to refinance, or even a disincentive (i.e., the homeowner will avoid moving in order to avoid refinancing). If the refinancing rate is low relative to the borrower's original coupon rate, the borrower has an incentive to refinance.

Prepayments are projected by feeding the refinancing rate and loan characteristics into a prepayment model. Given the projected prepayments, the cash flows along an interest rate path can be determined.

To make this more concrete, consider a newly issued mortgage passthrough security with a maturity of 360 months. Exhibit 1 shows N "adjusted" simulated interest rate path scenarios—adjusted to be arbitrage free. Each scenario consists of a path of 360 simulated 1-month future interest rates. (The number of paths generated is based on a well-known principle in simulation which will not be discussed here.) So, our first assumption that we make to get Exhibit 1 is the volatility of interest rates.

Exhibit 2 shows the paths of simulated mortgage refinancing rates corresponding to the scenarios shown in Exhibit 1. In going from Exhibit 1 to Exhibit 2, an assumption must be made about the relationship between the

EXHIBIT 1	"Adjusted" Simulated Paths of Arbitrage-Free 1-Month Future Interest Rates[a]						
	Interest Rate Path Number						
Month	1	2	3	...	n	...	N
1	$f_1(1)$	$f_1(2)$	$f_1(3)$	...	$f_1(n)$	...	$f_1(N)$
2	$f_2(1)$	$f_2(2)$	$f_2(3)$	...	$f_2(n)$	...	$f_2(N)$
3	$f_3(1)$	$f_3(2)$	$f_3(3)$	...	$f_3(n)$	...	$f_3(N)$
...	...	...	...	...	...	...	...
t	$f_t(1)$	$f_t(2)$	$f_t(3)$	...	$f_t(n)$	...	$f_t(N)$
...	...	...	...	...	...	...	...
358	$f_{358}(1)$	$f_{358}(2)$	$f_{358}(3)$	...	$f_{358}(n)$	...	$f_{358}(N)$
359	$f_{359}(1)$	$f_{359}(2)$	$f_{359}(3)$	...	$f_{359}(n)$	...	$f_{359}(N)$
360	$f_{360}(1)$	$f_{360}(2)$	$f_{360}(3)$	...	$f_{360}(n)$	...	$f_{360}(N)$

Notation:

$f_t(n)$ = 1-month future interest rate for month t on path n

N = total number of interest rate paths

[a] As explained in the reading, the "raw" interest rate paths that are simulated must be "adjusted" so as to make the model generate arbitrage-free values for whatever benchmark interest rates are used—typically, the on-the-run Treasury issues. The interest rates shown in the exhibit are the "adjusted" arbitrage-free interest rates.

EXHIBIT 2	Simulated Paths of Mortgage Refinancing Rates						

Interest Rate Path Number

Month	1	2	3	. . .	n	. . .	N
1	$r_1(1)$	$r_1(2)$	$r_1(3)$	. . .	$r_1(n)$	. . .	$r_1(N)$
2	$r_2(1)$	$r_2(2)$	$r_2(3)$	. . .	$r_2(n)$	. . .	$r_2(N)$
3	$r_3(1)$	$r_3(2)$	$r_3(3)$	. . .	$r_3(n)$	. . .	$r_3(N)$
. . .	. . .	. . .	. . .	. . .	. . .	. . .	. . .
t	$r_t(1)$	$r_t(2)$	$r_t(3)$	. . .	$r_t(n)$	. . .	$r_t(N)$
. . .	. . .	. . .	. . .	. . .	. . .	. . .	. . .
358	$r_{358}(1)$	$r_{358}(2)$	$r_{358}(3)$	. . .	$r_{358}(n)$	. . .	$r_{358}(N)$
359	$r_{359}(1)$	$r_{359}(2)$	$r_{359}(3)$	. . .	$r_{359}(n)$	. . .	$r_{359}(N)$
360	$r_{360}(1)$	$r_{360}(2)$	$r_{360}(3)$	. . .	$r_{360}(n)$	. . .	$r_{360}(N)$

Notation:

$r_t(n)$ = mortgage refinancing rate for month t on path n

N = total number of interest rate paths

Treasury rates and refinancing rates. The assumption is that there is a constant spread relationship between the rate that the borrower will use to determine whether or not to refinance (i.e., the refinancing rate) and the 1-month interest rates shown in Exhibit 1. For example, for 30-year mortgage loans, model builders use the 10-year Treasury rate as a proxy for the refinancing rate.

Given the mortgage refinancing rates, the cash flows on each interest rate path can be generated. For agency mortgage-backed securities, this requires a

EXHIBIT 3	Simulated Cash Flows on Each of the Interest Rate Paths						

Interest Rate Path Number

Month	1	2	3	. . .	n	. . .	N
1	$C_1(1)$	$C_1(2)$	$C_1(3)$	. . .	$C_1(n)$	. . .	$C_1(N)$
2	$C_2(1)$	$C_2(2)$	$C_2(3)$	. . .	$C_2(n)$	. . .	$C_2(N)$
3	$C_3(1)$	$C_3(2)$	$C_3(3)$	. . .	$C_3(n)$	. . .	$C_3(N)$
. . .	. . .	. . .	. . .	. . .	. . .	. . .	. . .
t	$C_t(1)$	$C_t(2)$	$C_t(3)$	. . .	$C_t(n)$	. . .	$C_t(N)$
. . .	. . .	. . .	. . .	. . .	. . .	. . .	. . .
358	$C_{358}(1)$	$C_{358}(2)$	$C_{358}(3)$	. . .	$C_{358}(n)$	. . .	$C_{358}(N)$
359	$C_{359}(1)$	$C_{359}(2)$	$C_{359}(3)$	. . .	$C_{359}(n)$	. . .	$C_{359}(N)$
360	$C_{360}(1)$	$C_{360}(2)$	$C_{360}(3)$	. . .	$C_{360}(n)$	. . .	$C_{360}(N)$

Notation:

$C_t(n)$ = cash flow for month t on path n

N = total number of interest rate paths

prepayment model. For asset-backed securities and nonagency mortgage-backed securities, this requires both a prepayment model and a model of defaults and recoveries. So, our next assumption is that the outputs of these models (prepayments, defaults, and recoveries) are correct. The resulting cash flows are depicted in Exhibit 3.

B. Calculating the Present Value for an Interest Rate Path

Given the cash flows on an interest rate path, the path's present value can be calculated. The discount rate for determining the present value is the simulated spot rate for each month on the interest rate path plus an appropriate spread. The spot rate on a path can be determined from the simulated future monthly rates. The relationship that holds between the simulated spot rate for month T on path n and the simulated future 1-month rates is:

$$z_T(n) = \{[1 + f_1(n)][1 + f_2(n)] \cdots [1 + f_T(n)]\}^{1/T} - 1$$

where

$z_T(n)$ = simulated spot rate for month T on path n
$f_T(n)$ = simulated future 1-month rate for month t on path n

We previously explained the relationship between spot rates and forward rates.

Consequently, the interest rate path for the simulated future 1-month rates can be converted to the interest rate path for the simulated monthly spot rates as shown in Exhibit 4. Therefore, the present value of the cash flows for month T on

EXHIBIT 4	"Adjusted" Simulated Paths of Monthly Arbitrage-Free Spot Rates						
	Interest Rate Path Number						
Month	**1**	**2**	**3**	...	**n**	...	**N**
1	$z_1(1)$	$z_1(2)$	$z_1(3)$	...	$z_1(n)$	...	$z_1(N)$
2	$z_2(1)$	$z_2(2)$	$z_2(3)$	...	$z_2(n)$	...	$z_2(N)$
3	$z_3(1)$	$z_3(2)$	$z_3(3)$	...	$z_3(n)$	...	$z_3(N)$
...	...	...	...	...	...	...	...
t	$z_t(1)$	$z_t(2)$	$z_t(3)$	...	$z_t(n)$	...	$z_t(N)$
...	...	...	...	...	...	...	...
358	$z_{358}(1)$	$z_{358}(2)$	$z_{358}(3)$	...	$z_{358}(n)$	...	$z_{358}(N)$
359	$z_{359}(1)$	$z_{359}(2)$	$z_{359}(3)$	...	$z_{359}(n)$	...	$z_{359}(N)$
360	$z_{360}(1)$	$z_{360}(2)$	$z_{360}(3)$	...	$z_{360}(n)$	...	$z_{360}(N)$

Notation:

$z_t(n)$ = spot rate for month t on path n
N = total number of interest rate paths

interest rate path n discounted at the simulated spot rate for month T plus some spread is:

$$\text{PV}\big[C_T(n)\big] = \frac{C_T(n)}{\big[1 + z_T(n) + K\big]^T}$$

where

$\text{PV}[C_T(n)]$ = present value of cash flows for month T on path n
$C_T(n)$ = cash flow for month T on path n
$z_T(n)$ = spot rate for month T on path n
K = spread

The spread, K, reflects the risks that the investor feels are associated with realizing the cash flows.

The present value for path n is the sum of the present value of the cash flows for each month on path n. That is,

$$\text{PV}[\text{Path}(n)] = \text{PV}[C_1(n)] + \text{PV}[C_2(n)] + \ldots + \text{PV}[C_{360}(n)]$$

where $\text{PV}[\text{Path}(n)]$ is the present value of interest rate path n.

C. Determining the Theoretical Value

The present value of a given interest rate path can be thought of as the theoretical value of a passthrough if that path was actually realized. The theoretical value of the passthrough can be determined by calculating the average of the theoretical values of all the interest rate paths. That is, the theoretical value is equal to

$$\text{Theoretical value} = \frac{\text{PV}[\text{Path}(1)] + \text{PV}[\text{Path}(2)] + \ldots + \text{PV}[\text{Path}(N)]}{N}$$

where N is the number of interest rate paths. The theoretical value derived from the above equation is based on some spread, K. It follows the usual practice of discounting cash flows at spot rates plus a spread—in this case the spread is K.

This procedure for valuing a passthrough is also followed for a CMO tranche. The cash flow for each month on each interest rate path is found according to the principal repayment and interest distribution rules of the deal.

D. Selecting the Number of Interest Rate Paths

Let's now address the question of the number of scenario paths, N, needed to value a security. The number of interest rate paths determines how "good" the estimate is, not relative to the truth but relative to the model used. The more paths, the more the average value produced tends to converge. It is simply a statistical sampling problem.

Most models employ some form of variance reduction to cut down on the number of sample paths necessary to get a good statistical sample.[2] Several vendor firms have developed computational procedures that reduce the number

---

[2] The variance reduction technique is described in books on management science and Monte Carlo simulation.

of paths required but still provide the accuracy of a full Monte Carlo analysis. The procedure is to use statistical techniques to reduce the number of interest rate paths to sets of similar paths. These paths are called representative paths. For example, suppose that 2,000 sample paths are generated. Using a certain statistical technique, these 2,000 sample paths can be collapsed to, say, 16 representative paths. The security is then valued on each of these 16 representative paths. The theoretical value of the security is then the *weighted* average of the 16 representative paths. The weight for a path is the percentage of that representative path relative to the total sample paths. Vendors often give the investor or portfolio manager the choice of whether to use the "full Monte Carlo simulation" or to specify a number of representative paths.

E. Option-Adjusted Spread

In the reading on valuing bonds with embedded options, we explained the option-adjusted spread (OAS). Specifically, we explained 1) how to compute the OAS for corporate and agency bonds with embedded options and 2) how to interpret the OAS and apply it in relative analysis. Below we cover the same issues for the OAS computed for mortgage-backed securities.

1. Computing the OAS

In the Monte Carlo model, the OAS is the spread that when added to all the spot rates on all interest rate paths will make the average present value of the paths equal to the observed market price (plus accrued interest). Mathematically, OAS is the value for K (the spread) that will satisfy the following condition:

$$\frac{\mathrm{PV}\left[\mathrm{Path}(1)\right] + \mathrm{PV}\left[\mathrm{Path}(2)\right] + \ldots + \mathrm{PV}\left[\mathrm{Path}(N)\right]}{N} = \text{Market price}$$

where N is the number of interest rate paths. The left-hand side of the above equation looks identical to that of the equation for the theoretical value. The difference is that the objective is to determine what spread, K, will make the model produce a theoretical value equal to the market price.

The procedure for determining the OAS is straightforward and involves the same search algorithm explained for the zero-volatility spread. The next question, then, is how to interpret the OAS. Basically, the OAS is used to reconcile value with market price. On the ***right***-hand side of the previous equation is the market's statement: the price of a structured product. The average present value over all the paths on the ***left***-hand side of the equation is the model's output, which we refer to as the theoretical value.

2. Interpreting the OAS and Relative Value Application

What an investor or a portfolio manager seeks to do is to buy a mortgage-backed security where value is greater than price. By using a valuation model such as the Monte Carlo model, a portfolio manager could estimate the value of a security, which at this point would be sufficient in determining whether to buy a security. That is, the portfolio manager can say that this security is 1 point cheap or 2 points cheap, and so on. The model does not stop here. Instead, it converts the divergence between price and value into some type of spread measure since most market participants find it more convenient to think about spreads than price differences.

The OAS was developed as a measure of the spread that can be used to convert dollar differences between value and price. As we explained in the reading on valuing bonds with embedded options, in the binomial model a spread is measured relative to the benchmark interest rates used to generate the interest rate tree and which is therefore used to make the tree arbitrage free. The same is true in the case of the Monte Carlo simulation model. The spread is measured relative to the benchmark interest rates that were used to generate the interest rate paths and to adjust the interest rate paths to make them arbitrage free. Typically, for a mortgage-backed security the benchmark interest rates are the on-the-run Treasury rates. The OAS is then measuring the average spread over the Treasury spot rate curve, not the Treasury yield as explained in the reading on valuing bonds with embedded options. It is an average spread since the OAS is found by averaging over the interest rate paths for the possible Treasury spot rate curves. Of course, if the LIBOR curve is used, the OAS is the spread over that curve.

This spread measure is superior to the nominal spread, which gives no recognition to the prepayment risk. As explained in the reading on valuing bonds with embedded options, the OAS is "option adjusted" because the cash flows on the interest rate paths are adjusted for the option of the borrowers to prepay. While we may understand the mechanics of how to compute the OAS and why it is appropriate to use the OAS rather than the nominal spread or Z-spread, the question is what does the spread represent? In the reading on valuing bonds with embedded options, a discussion of what compensation the OAS reflects for corporate and agency bonds with embedded options was presented. The compensation is for a combination of credit risk and liquidity risk. The compensation depends on the benchmark interest rates used in the analysis. For example, consider the use of Treasury interest rates and more specifically the Treasury spot rate curve since this is the benchmark typically used in the calculation of an OAS for a mortgage-backed security. If there is an OAS computed using the Treasury benchmark, then what is that OAS compensating?

Consider first Ginnie Mae mortgage passthrough securities. Ginnie Mae is an arm of the U.S. government. The securities it issues are backed by the full faith and credit of the U.S. government. Effectively, a Ginnie Mae mortgage-backed security is a Treasury security with prepayment risk. The OAS removes the prepayment risk (i.e., the option risk). Additionally, if the benchmark is Treasury rates, the OAS should not be compensation for credit risk. That leaves liquidity risk. While Ginnie Mae mortgage passthrough securities may not be as liquid as on-the-run Treasury issues, they are fairly liquid as measured by the bid-ask spread. Nevertheless, part of the OAS should reflect compensation for liquidity risk. There is one more risk that was not the focus of the reading on valuing bonds with embedded options, modeling risk. In our explanation of the Monte Carlo model, there were several critical assumptions and parameters required. If those assumptions prove incorrect or if the parameters are misestimated, the prepayment model will not calculate the true level of risk. Thus, probably a good part of the compensation for a Ginnie Mae mortgage passthrough security reflects payment for this model uncertainty.

If we consider CMOs issued by Ginnie Mae rather than the mortgage passthrough securities, the OAS would reflect the complexity associated with a particular tranche. For example, a planned amortization class (PAC) tranche would be less exposed to modeling risk than a support tranche in the same CMO structure. Hence, compensation for modeling risk would be greater for a support tranche than a PAC tranche in the same structure. Moreover, PAC tranches have greater liquidity than support tranches, so compensation is less for the former relative to the latter.

As we move from Ginnie Mae issued mortgage products to those issued by Freddie Mac and Fannie Mae, we introduce credit risk. Freddie Mac and Fannie Mae are government sponsored enterprises (GSEs). As such, there is no requirement that a GSE be bailed out by the U.S. government. The GSEs are viewed as triple A rated. Consequently, in addition to modeling risk and liquidity risk, a portion of the OAS reflects credit risk relative to Treasury securities.

Moving on to nonagency mortgage-backed securities and real estate backed asset-backed securities, the OAS is compensating for 1) credit risk (which varies depending on the credit rating for the tranche under consideration), 2) liquidity risk (which is greater than for Ginnie Mae, Fannie Mae, and Freddie Mac mortgage products), and 3) modeling risk.

F. Option Cost

The implied cost of the option embedded for a mortgage-backed or asset-backed security can be obtained by calculating the difference between the option-adjusted spread at the assumed volatility of interest rates and the zero-volatility spread. That is,

Option cost = Zero-volatility spread − Option-adjusted spread

The option cost measures the prepayment (or option) risk embedded in the security. Note that the cost of the option is a byproduct of the option-adjusted spread analysis, not valued explicitly with some option pricing model.

G. Illustrations

We will use two deals to show how CMOs can be analyzed using the Monte Carlo model/OAS procedure discussed above—a simple structure and a PAC/support structure.[3]

1. Simple Structure

The simple structure analyzed is Freddie Mac (FHLMC) 1915. It is a simple sequential-pay CMO bond structure. The structure includes eight tranches, A, B, C, D, E, F, G, and S. The focus of our analysis is on tranches A, B, and C. All three tranches were priced at a premium.

The top panel of Exhibit 5 shows the OAS, the option cost, and effective duration[4] for the collateral and the three tranches in the CMO structure. However, tranche A had the smallest effective duration and tranche C had the largest effective duration. The OAS for the collateral is 51 basis points. Since the option cost is 67 basis points, the zero-volatility spread is 118 basis points (51 basis points plus 67 basis points).

At the time this analysis was performed, March 10, 1998, the Treasury yield curve was not steep. When the yield curve is relatively flat, the zero-volatility spread will not differ significantly from the nominal spread. Thus, for the three tranches shown in Exhibit 5, the zero-volatility spread is 83 basis points for A, 115 basis points for B, and 116 basis points for C.

[3] These illustrations are from Frank J. Fabozzi, Scott F. Richard, and David S. Horowitz, "Valuation of CMOs," Chapter 6 in Frank J. Fabozzi (ed.), *Advances in the Valuation and Management of Mortgage-Backed Securities* (New Hope, PA: Frank J. Fabozzi Associates, 1998).

[4] We will explain how to compute the effective duration using the Monte Carlo methodology in Section 5A.

EXHIBIT 5	OAS Analysis of FHLMC 1915 Classes A, B, and C (as of 3/10/98)

All three tranches were trading at a premium as of the date of the analysis.

Base Case (Assumes 13% Interest Rate Volatility)				
	OAS (in Basis Points)	Option Cost (in Basis Points)	Z-Spread (in Basis Points)	Effective Duration (in Years)
Collateral	51	67	118	1.2
Tranche				
A	32	51	83	0.9
B	33	82	115	2.9
C	46	70	116	6.7

Prepayments at 80% and 120% of Prepayment Model (Assumes 13% Interest Rate Volatility)

	New OAS (in Basis Points)		Change in Price per $100 Par (Holding OAS Constant)	
	80%	120%	80%	120%
Collateral	63	40	$0.45	−$0.32
Tranche				
A	40	23	0.17	−0.13
B	43	22	0.54	−0.43
C	58	36	0.97	−0.63

Interest Rate of Volatility of 9% and 17%

	New OAS (in Basis Points)		Change in Price per $100 Par (Holding OAS Constant)	
	9%	17%	9%	17%
Collateral	79	21	$1.03	−$0.94
Tranche				
A	52	10	0.37	−0.37
B	66	−3	1.63	−1.50
C	77	15	2.44	−2.08

Notice that the tranches did not share the OAS equally. The same is true for the option cost. Both the Z-spread and the option cost increase as the effective duration increases. Whether or not any of these tranches were attractive investments requires a comparison to other tranches in the market with the same effective duration. While not presented here, all three tranches offered an OAS similar to other sequential-pay tranches with the same effective duration available in the market. On a relative basis (i.e., relative to the other tranches analyzed in the deal), the only tranche where there appears to be a bit of a bargain is tranche C. A portfolio manager contemplating the purchase of this last cash flow tranche can see that C offers a higher OAS than B and appears to bear less of the risk (i.e., has lower option cost), as measured by the option cost. The problem portfolio managers may face is that they might not be able to go out as long on the yield curve as tranche C because of effective duration, maturity, and average life constraints relative to their liabilities, for example.

Now let's look at modeling risk. Examination of the sensitivity of the tranches to changes in prepayments and interest rate volatility will help us to understand the interaction of the tranches in the structure and who is bearing the risk. How the deal behaves under various scenarios should reinforce and be consistent with the valuation (i.e., a tranche may look "cheap" for a reason).

We begin with prepayments. Specifically, we keep the same interest rate paths as those used to get the OAS in the base case (the top panel of Exhibit 5), but reduce the prepayment rate on each interest rate path to 80% of the projected rate. As can be seen in the second panel of Exhibit 5, slowing down prepayments increases the OAS and price for the collateral. The exhibit reports two results of the sensitivity analysis. First, it indicates the change in the OAS. Second, it indicates the change in the price, holding the OAS constant at the base case.

To see how a portfolio manager can use the information in the second panel, consider tranche A. At 80% of the prepayment speed, the OAS for this tranche increases from 32 basis points to 40 basis points. If the OAS is held constant, the panel indicates that the buyer of tranche A would gain $0.17 per $100 par value.

Notice that for all of the tranches reported in Exhibit 5 there is a gain from a slowdown in prepayments. This is because all of the sequential tranches in this deal are priced over par. (An investor in a tranche priced at a premium benefits from a slowdown in prepayments because the investor receives the higher coupon for a longer period and postpones the capital loss from a prepayment.) Also notice that while the changes in OAS are about the same for the different tranches, the changes in price are quite different. This arises because the shorter tranches have less duration. Therefore, their prices do not move as much from a change in OAS as a longer average life tranche. A portfolio manager who is willing to go to the long end of the yield curve, such as tranche C, would realize the most benefit from the slowdown in prepayments.

Also shown in the second panel of the exhibit is the second part of our experiment to test the sensitivity of prepayments: the prepayment rate is assumed to be 120% of the base case. The collateral loses money in this scenario because it is trading above par. This is reflected in the OAS of the collateral, which declines from 51 basis points to 40 basis points. Now look at the three tranches. They all lost money because the tranches were all at a premium and the speeding of prepayments adversely affects the tranche.

Before looking at the last panel that shows the effect of a change in interest rate volatility on the OAS, let's review the relationship between expected interest rate volatility and the value of a mortgage-backed security. Recall that the investor in a mortgage-backed security has sold an option to homeowners (borrowers). Thus, the investor is short an option. The value of an option depends on expected interest rate volatility. When expected interest rate volatility decreases, the value of the option embedded in a mortgage-backed security decreases and therefore the value of a mortgage-backed security increases. The opposite is true when expected interest rate volatility increases—the value of the embedded option increases and the value of a mortgage-backed security decreases.

Now let's look at the sensitivity to the interest rate volatility assumption, 13% in the base case. Two experiments are performed: reducing the volatility assumption to 9% and increasing it to 17%. These results are reported in the third panel of Exhibit 5.

Reducing the volatility to 9% increases the dollar price of the collateral by $1.03 and increases the OAS from 51 in the base case to 79 basis points. However, this $1.03 increase in the price of the collateral is not equally distributed among the three tranches. Most of the increase in value is realized by the longer tranches. The OAS gain for each of the tranches follows more or less the effective durations of those tranches. This makes sense, because the longer the duration, the greater the risk, and when volatility declines, the reward is greater for the accepted risk. At the higher level of assumed interest rate volatility of 17%, the collateral is severely affected. The longer the duration, the greater the loss. These results for a decrease and an increase in interest rate volatility are consistent with what we explained earlier.

Using the Monte Carlo simulation/OAS analysis, a fair conclusion that can be made about this simple structure is: what you see is what you get. The only surprise in this structure is the lower option cost in tranche C. In general, however, a portfolio manager willing to extend duration gets paid for that risk in this structure.

2. PAC/Support Tranche Structure

Now let's look at how to apply the methodology to a more complicated CMO structure, FHLMC Series 1706. The collateral (i.e., pool of passthroughs) for this structure is Freddie Mac 7s (7% coupon rate). A partial summary of the deal is provided in Exhibit 6. That is, only the tranches we will be discussing in this section are shown in the exhibit.[5]

While this deal looks complicated, it is relatively simple compared to many deals that have been issued. Nonetheless, it brings out all the key points about application of OAS analysis, specifically, the fact that most deals include cheap bonds, expensive bonds, and fairly priced bonds. The OAS analysis helps identify how a tranche should be classified. A more proper analysis would compare the OAS for each tranche to a similar duration tranche available in the market.

All of the tranches in Exhibit 6 were discussed in the reading on mortgage-backed sector of the bond market. At issuance, there were 10 PAC tranches, three scheduled tranches, a floating-rate support tranche, and an inverse floating-rate support. Recall that the "scheduled tranches" are support tranches with a schedule, referred to the reading on mortgage-backed sector of the bond market as "PAC II tranches."

The first two PAC tranches in the deal, tranche A and tranche B, were paid off at the time of the analysis. The other PAC tranches were still available at the time of the analysis. The prepayment protection for the PAC tranches is provided by the support tranches. The support tranches in this deal that are shown in Exhibit 6 are tranches LA, LB, and M. There were other support tranches not shown in Exhibit 6. LA is the shortest average life support tranche (a scheduled (SCH) bond).

The collateral for this deal was trading at a premium. That is, the homeowners (borrowers) were paying a higher mortgage rate than available in the market at the time of the analysis. This meant that the value of the collateral would increase if prepayments slow down but would decrease if prepayments increase. What is important to note, however, is that a tranche could be trading at a discount, par, or

---

[5] This deal was described in the reading on the mortgage-backed sector of the bond market.

EXHIBIT 6	Summary of Federal Home Loan Mortgage Corporation—Multiclass Mortgage Participation Certificates (Guaranteed), Series 1706

Total Issue: $300,000,000   **Issue Date:** 2/18/94

Tranche	Original Balance ($)	Coupon (%)	Stated Maturity	Original Issue Pricing (225% PSA Assumed)	
				Average Life (Yrs)	Expected Maturity
PAC Tranches					
C (PAC Bond)	25,500,000	5.25	4/15/14	3.5	6/15/98
D (PAC Bond)	9,150,000	5.65	8/15/15	4.5	1/15/99
E (PAC Bond)	31,650,000	6.00	1/15/19	5.8	1/15/01
G (PAC Bond)	30,750,000	6.25	8/15/21	7.9	5/15/03
H (PAC Bond)	27,450,000	6.50	6/15/23	10.9	10/15/07
J (PAC Bond)	5,220,000	6.50	10/15/23	14.4	9/15/09
K (PAC Bond)	7,612,000	7.00	3/15/24	18.8	5/15/19
Support Tranches					
LA (SCH Bond)	26,673,000	7.00	11/15/21	3.5	3/15/02
LB (SCH Bond)	36,087,000	7.00	6/15/23	3.5	9/15/02
M (SCH Bond)	18,738,000	7.00	3/15/24	11.2	10/15/08

premium even though the collateral is priced at a premium. For example, PAC C had a low coupon rate at the time of the analysis and therefore was trading at a discount. Thus, while the collateral (which was selling at a premium) loses value from an increase in prepayments, a discount tranche such as tranche C would increase in value if prepayments increase. (Recall that in the simple structure analyzed earlier, the collateral and all the tranches were trading at a premium.)

The top panel of Exhibit 7 shows the base case OAS, the option cost, and the effective duration for the collateral and tranches in Exhibit 7. The collateral OAS is 60 basis points, and the option cost is 44 basis points. The Z-spread of the collateral to the Treasury spot curve is 104 basis points.

The 60 basis points of OAS did not get equally distributed among the tranches—as was the case with the simple structure analyzed earlier. Tranche LB, the scheduled support, did not realize a good OAS allocation, only 29 basis points, and had an extremely high option cost. Given the prepayment uncertainty associated with this tranche, its OAS would be expected to be higher. The reason for the low OAS is that this tranche was priced so that its cash flow yield is high. Using the Z-spread as a proxy for the nominal spread (i.e., spread over the Treasury yield curve), the 103 basis point spread for tranche LB is high given that this appears to be a short average life tranche. Consequently, "yield buyers" (i.e., investors with a preference for high nominal yield, who may not be attentive to compensation for prepayment risk) probably bid aggressively for this tranche and thereby drove down its OAS, trading off "yield" for OAS. From a total return perspective, however, tranche LB should be avoided. It is a rich, or expensive, tranche. The other support tranche analyzed, tranche M, had an OAS of 72 basis points and at the time of this analysis was similar to that offered on comparable duration tranches available in the market.

EXHIBIT 7	OAS Analysis of FHLMC 1706 (as of 3/10/98)

Base Case (Assumes 13% Interest Rate Volatility)

	OAS (in Basis Points)	Option Cost (in Basis Points)	Z-Spread (in Basis Points)	Effective Duration (in Years)
Collateral	**60**	**44**	**104**	**2.6**
PAC Tranches				
C (PAC)	15	0	15	0.2
D (PAC)	16	4	20	0.6
E (PAC)	26	4	30	1.7
G (PAC)	42	8	50	3.3
H (PAC)	50	12	62	4.9
J (PAC)	56	14	70	6.8
K (PAC)	57	11	68	8.6
Support Tranches				
LA (SCH)	39	12	51	1.4
LB (SCH)	29	74	103	1.2
M (SCH)	72	53	125	4.9

Prepayments at 80% and 120% of Prepayment Model (Assumes 13% Interest Rate Volatility)

	Base Case OAS	New OAS (in Basis Points)		Change in Price per $100 Par (Holding OAS Constant)	
		80%	120%	80%	120%
Collateral	**60**	**63**	**57**	**$0.17**	**−$0.11**
PAC Tranches					
C (PAC)	15	15	15	0.00	0.00
D (PAC)	16	16	16	0.00	0.00
E (PAC)	26	27	26	0.01	−0.01
G (PAC)	42	44	40	0.08	−0.08
H (PAC)	50	55	44	0.29	−0.27
J (PAC)	56	63	50	0.50	−0.47
K (PAC)	57	65	49	0.77	−0.76
Support Tranches					
LA (SCH)	39	31	39	−0.12	0.00
LB (SCH)	29	39	18	0.38	−0.19
M (SCH)	72	71	76	−0.07	0.18

(Exhibit continued on next page . . .)

EXHIBIT 7	(continued)

Interest Rate Volatility of 9% and 17%

	Base Case OAS	New OAS (in Basis Points)		Change in Price per $100 Par (Holding OAS Constant)	
		9%	17%	9%	17%
Collateral	**60**	**81**	**35**	**$0.96**	**−$0.94**
PAC Tranches					
C (PAC)	15	15	15	0.00	0.00
D (PAC)	16	16	16	0.00	0.00
E (PAC)	26	27	24	0.02	−0.04
G (PAC)	42	48	34	0.21	−0.27
H (PAC)	50	58	35	0.48	−0.72
J (PAC)	56	66	41	0.70	−1.05
K (PAC)	57	66	44	0.82	−1.19
Support Tranches					
LA (SCH)	39	47	24	0.09	−0.18
LB (SCH)	29	58	−4	0.80	−0.82
M (SCH)	72	100	41	1.80	−1.72

The analysis reported in the top panel of Exhibit 7 helps us identify where the cheap tranches are in the deal. The long average life and effective duration tranches in the deal are the PAC tranches G, H, J, and K. These tranches have high OAS relative to the other tranches and low option cost. They appear to be the cheap tranches in the deal. These PAC tranches had well-protected cash flows and exhibited positive convexity (i.e., these tranches lose less in an adverse scenario than they gain in a positive scenario).

The next two panels in Exhibit 7 show the sensitivity of the OAS and the price (holding OAS constant at the base case) to changes in the prepayment speed (80% and 120% of the base case) and to changes in volatility (9% and 17%). This analysis shows that the change in the prepayment speed does not affect the collateral significantly, while the change in the OAS (holding the price constant) and price (holding OAS constant) for each tranche can be significant.

Tranches C and D at the time of the analysis were priced at a discount with short average lives. The OAS and price of these two tranches were not affected by a slowing down or a speeding up of the prepayment model. Tranche H was a premium tranche with a medium-term average life at the time of the analysis. Because tranche H was trading at a premium, it benefits from a slowing in prepayments, as the bondholder will receive the coupon for a longer time. Faster prepayments represent an adverse scenario. The PAC tranches are quite well-protected. The longer average life PACs will actually benefit from a reduced prepayment rate because they will be earning the higher coupon interest longer. So, on an OAS basis, the earlier conclusion that the long PACs were allocated a good part of the deal's value holds up under our first stress test (i.e., changing prepayments).

The sensitivity of the collateral and the tranches to changes in volatility are shown in the third panel of Exhibit 7. A lower volatility increases the value of the collateral, while a higher volatility reduces its value (This is consistent with our option cost equation in Section 4.E.) The long average life PACs continue to be fairly well protected, whether the volatility is lower or higher. In the two volatility scenarios they continue to get a good OAS on a relative value basis, although not as much as in the base case if volatility is higher (but the OAS still looks like a reasonable value in this scenario). This reinforces the earlier conclusion concerning the investment merit of the long PACs in this deal. Note, however, that PAC tranches H, J, and K are more sensitive to the volatility assumption than tranches C, D, E, and G and therefore the investor is accepting greater volatility risk (i.e., the risk that volatility will change) with tranches H, J, and K relative to tranches C, D, E, and G.

5   MEASURING INTEREST RATE RISK

Duration and convexity can be used to estimate the interest rate exposure to parallel shifts in the yield curve (i.e., a measure of level risk). In this section we will discuss duration measures for mortgage-backed securities. There are several duration measures that are used in practice. Two researchers who have done extensive work in measuring duration, Lakhbir Hayre and Hubert Chang, conclude that "No single duration measure will consistently work well for mortgage securities."[6] To that conclusion should be added that there are some measures that do not work at all.

A. Duration Measures

Duration is a measure of the price sensitivity to changes in interest rates. We have seen how to compute the duration of a security by shocking rates up and down and determining how the price of the security changes. Duration is then computed as follows:

$$\text{Duration} = \frac{V_- - V_+}{2V_0(\Delta y)}$$

where

Δy = change in rate used to calculate new values (i.e., the interest rate shock)
V_+ = estimated value if yield is increased by Δy
V_- = estimated value if yield is decreased by Δy
V_0 = initial price (per $100 of par value)

For bonds with embedded options such as mortgage-backed securities, the appropriate measure is effective duration, and to capture the negative convexity of a bond with an embedded option, effective convexity should be computed. We will see how to calculate the effective duration for a mortgage-backed security using the Monte Carlo simulation model. Then we will see how the assumptions of the model impact the duration estimate. Dealers and vendors use other measures of duration that will be described later.

---

[6] Lakhbir Hayre and Hubert Chang, "Effective and Empirical Duration of Mortgage Securities," *The Journal of Fixed Income* (March 1997), pp. 17–33.

1. *Effective Duration*

To calculate effective duration, the value of the security must be estimated when rates are shocked up and down a given number of basis points. In terms of the Monte Carlo model, the yield curve used (either the Treasury yield curve or LIBOR curve) is shocked up and down, and the new curve is used to generate the values to be used in the effective duration and effective convexity formulas. This is analogous to the process we used to compute effective duration and effective convexity using the binomial model in the reading on valuing bonds with embedded options.

In generating the prices when rates are shocked up and down, there is an assumption that the relationships assumed in generating the initial price do not change when rates are shocked up and down. Specifically, the yield volatility is assumed to be unchanged to derive the new interest rate paths for a given shock (i.e., the new Exhibit 1), the spread between the mortgage rate and the 10-year Treasury rate is assumed to be unchanged in constructing the new Exhibit 2 from the newly constructed Exhibit 1, and the OAS is assumed to be constant. The constancy of the OAS comes into play because when discounting the new cash flows (i.e., the cash flows in the new Exhibit 3), the current OAS that was computed is assumed to be the same and is added to the new rates in the new Exhibit 1.

We'll use an illustration by Lakhbir Hayre and Hubert Chang to explain the calculation of effective duration for a mortgage-backed security, a FNMA 7.5% TBA passthrough on May 1, 1996.[7] On that day, the base mortgage rate was 7.64%. The price of the issue at the time was 98.781 (i.e., 98-25). The OAS was 65 basis points. Based on a shock of 25 basis points, the estimated prices holding the OAS constant at 65 basis points were as follows:

V_- = 99.949 for a decrease in the yield curve of 25 basis points
V_+ = 97.542 for an increase in the yield curve of 25 basis points

The effective duration based on a Δy of 0.0025 is then

$$\frac{99.949 - 97.542}{2 \times 98.781 \times 0.0025} = 4.87$$

There are differences in the effective durations for a given mortgage-backed security reported by dealers and vendors of analytical systems. Several practitioners have explained and illustrated why there are differences in effective duration estimates reported by dealers and vendors. The differences result from, among others:[8]

1. differences in the amount of the rate shock used
2. differences in prepayment models
3. differences in option-adjusted spread
4. differences in the relationship between short-term interest rates and refinancing rates

We previously discussed the first reason. As explained, the rate shock is the amount interest rates are increased and decreased to obtain the two values that

---

[7] Hayre and Chang, "Effective and Empirical Duration of Mortgage Securities."

[8] Sam Choi, "Effective Durations for Mortgage-Backed Securities: Recipes for Improvement," *The Journal of Fixed Income* (March 1996), pp. 24–30; and, Hayre and Chang, "Effective and Empirical Duration of Mortgage Securities."

are inserted into the effective duration formula. If the change is too large, there is the problem with picking up the effect of convexity.

Prepayment models differ across dealers and vendors. Some dealer models consistently forecast slower prepayments relative to other dealer models and others the reverse.

The effective duration is dependent on the OAS computed. Recall that the calculation of the OAS is a byproduct of the Monte Carlo model. Therefore, the computed value for the OAS depends on all of the assumptions in the Monte Carlo model. Specifically, it depends on the yield volatility assumed and the prepayment model employed. Dealers and vendors make different assumptions regarding yield volatility and use proprietary prepayment models. These can result in differences in OAS. Since the OAS is added to the new simulated short-term rates to compute the new values for V_- and V_+, a different OAS will result in different effective durations.

Finally, recall that in explaining the Monte Carlo simulation model that we stated that in moving from Exhibit 1 (the simulated short-term rates) to Exhibit 2 (the refinancing rates), an assumption must be made about the relationship between short-term rates and the 10-year Treasury rate (i.e., the rate used as a proxy for refinancing). Differences in models about how large the spread between these rates will be affect the value of a mortgage-backed security and therefore the values used in the duration equation when rates are shocked.

2. Other Duration Measures

There have been other measures proposed for estimating the duration of a mortgage-backed security. These measures include cash flow duration, coupon curve duration, and empirical duration. The first two duration measures are forms of effective duration in that they do recognize that the values that should be used in the duration formula should take into account how the cash flows may change due to changes in prepayments when interest rates change. In contrast, empirical duration is a duration that is computed statistically using observed market prices. Below we describe how each of these duration measures is calculated, as well as the advantages and limitations of each.

a. Cash Flow Duration

Recall from the general duration formula that there are two values that must be substituted into the numerator of the formula—the value if rates are decreased (V_-) and the value if rates are increased (V_+). With effective duration, these two values consider how changes in interest rates change the cash flow due to prepayments. This is done through the Monte Carlo simulation by allowing for the cash flows to change on the interest rate paths.

For cash flow duration, there is recognition that the cash flow can change but the analysis to obtain the cash flow is done following a static methodology. Specifically, the cash flow duration is calculated as follows:

Step 1: Calculate the cash flow based on some prepayment assumption.

Step 2: From the cash flow in Step 1 and the market price (V_0), compute the cash flow yield.

Step 3: Increase the cash flow yield by Δy and from a prepayment model determine the new prepayment rate at that higher cash flow yield. Typically, the prepayment rate will be lower than in Step 1 because of the higher yield level.

Step 4: Using the lower prepayment rate in Step 3 determine the cash flow and then value the cash flow using the higher cash flow yield as the discount rate. This gives the value (V_+).

Step 5: Decrease the cash flow yield by Δy and from a prepayment model determine the new prepayment rate at that lower cash flow yield. Typically, the prepayment rate will be higher than in Step 1 because of the lower yield level.

Step 6: Using the higher prepayment rate in Step 5 determine the cash flow and then value the cash flow using the lower cash flow yield as the discount rate. This gives the value (V_-).

From the change in basis points (Δy), the values for V_+ and V_- found in Steps 4 and 6, and the initial value V_0, the duration can be computed.

We can use the hypothetical CMO structure to illustrate how to calculate cash flow duration. Specifically, in FJF-2, there were four tranches, A, B, C, and Z. Let's focus on tranche C. Suppose that the price for this tranche is 100.2813. Then the cash flow duration is computed as follows:

Step 1: Suppose that the assumed prepayment rate for this tranche is 165 PSA.

Step 2: Based on the assumed prepayment rate of 165 PSA and the price of 100.2813, it can be demonstrated that the cash flow yield is 7%.

Step 3: Suppose that the cash flow yield is increased (i.e., shocked) by 25 basis points (from 7% to 7.25%) and suppose that some prepayment model projects a prepayment rate of 150 PSA. (Note that this is a slower prepayment rate than at 7%.)

Step 4: Based on 150 PSA, a new cash flow can be generated. The cash flow is then discounted at 7.25% (the new cash flow yield). It can be demonstrated that the value of this tranche based on these assumptions would be 98.3438. This is the value V_+.

Step 5: Suppose that the cash flow yield is decreased (i.e., shocked) by 25 basis points (from 7% to 6.75%) and suppose that some prepayment model projects a prepayment rate of 200 PSA. (Note that this is a faster prepayment rate than at 7%.)

Step 6: Based on 200 PSA, the new cash flow can be generated. The cash flow is then discounted at 6.75% (the new cash flow yield). It can be demonstrated that the value of this tranche based on these assumptions would be 101.9063. This is the value V_-.

Now we have the following information:

$$V_0 = 100.2813$$
$$V_+ = 98.3438$$
$$V_- = 101.9063$$
$$\Delta y = 0.0025$$

Then using the general form of duration, we obtain:

$$\text{Duration} = \frac{101.9063 - 98.3438}{2(100.2813)(0.0025)} = 7.11$$

What type of duration measure is the cash flow duration—effective duration or modified duration? Technically, it is a form of effective duration because notice that in Steps 3 and 5 when the rate is changed, the cash flow is allowed to change. However, as has been stressed throughout, the valuation model that is used to get the new values to substitute into the duration formula is critical. The valuation model in the case of the cash flow duration is based on the naive assumption that there is a single prepayment rate over the life of the mortgage-backed security for any given interest rate shock. This is in contrast to the values produced by the Monte Carlo simulation model that does more sophisticated analyses of how the cash flow can change when interest rates change.

Why bother discussing the cash flow duration if it is an inferior form of effective duration? The reason is that it is a commonly cited duration measure and practitioners should be aware of how it is computed. Likewise, we did discuss in detail yield calculations despite their limitations.

An interesting question is how does this form of duration compare to modified duration? Recall that modified duration does not assume that cash flows will change when rates are shocked. That is, in the steps discussed above to obtain cash flow duration, in Steps 3 and 5 it is assumed that the prepayment rate is the same as in Step 1.

To illustrate this, we'll once again use tranche C in FJF-2. In Step 3, the prepayment rate assumed is still 165 PSA despite the fact that rates are assumed to increase. That is, the cash flow is not assumed to change. Based on a cash flow yield of 7.25% and a prepayment rate of 165 PSA, the value of this tranche would decline to 98.4063. When the cash flow yield is assumed to decline to 6.75%, the prepayment rate is still assumed to be 165 PSA and the value of this tranche would be 102.1875. Then to calculate the modified duration we know:

$$V_0 = 100.2813$$
$$V_+ = 98.4063$$
$$V_- = 102.1875$$
$$\Delta y = 0.0025$$

The modified duration is then:

$$\text{Duration} = \frac{102.1875 - 98.4063}{2(100.2813)(0.0025)} = 7.54$$

Thus, the modified duration is greater than the cash flow duration for this tranche.

It is important to reiterate that the modified duration is inferior to the cash flow duration because the former gives absolutely no recognition to how repayments may change when interest rates change. While cash flow duration is commonly cited in practice, it is a form of effective duration that does give some recognition that prepayments and therefore cash flow may change when interest rates change, but it is based on a naive assumption about how prepayments may change. The effective duration as computed using Monte Carlo simulation is superior to cash flow duration.

b. Coupon Curve Duration

The coupon curve duration uses market prices to estimate the duration of a mortgage-backed security. This approach, first suggested by Douglas Breeden,[9]

---

[9] Douglas Breeden, "Risk, Return, and Hedging of Fixed-Rate Mortgages," *The Journal of Fixed Income* (September 1991), pp. 85–107.

starts with the coupon curve of prices for similar mortgage-backed securities. The coupon curve represents generic passthrough securities of a particular issuer with different coupon rates. By rolling up and down the coupon curve of prices, the duration can be obtained. Because of the way it is estimated, this approach to duration estimation was referred to by Breeden as the "roll-up, roll-down approach." The prices obtained from rolling up and rolling down the coupon curve of prices are substituted into the duration formula.

To illustrate this approach, suppose that the coupon curve of prices for a passthrough security for some month is as follows:

Coupon (%)	Price ($)
6	85.19
7	92.06
8	98.38
9	103.34
10	107.28
11	111.19

Suppose that the coupon curve duration for the 8% coupon passthrough is sought. If the yield declines by 100 basis points, the assumption is that the price of the 8% coupon passthrough will increase to the price of the current 9% coupon passthrough. Thus, the price will increase from 98.38 to 103.34. Similarly, if the yield increases by 100 basis points, the assumption is that the price of the 8% coupon passthrough will decline to the price of the 7% coupon passthrough (92.06). Using the duration formula, the corresponding values are:

$$V_0 = 98.38$$
$$V_+ = 92.06$$
$$V_- = 103.34$$
$$\Delta y = 0.01$$

The estimated duration based on the coupon curve is then:

$$\text{Duration} = \frac{103.34 - 92.06}{2(98.38)(0.01)} = 5.73$$

Breeden tested the coupon curve durations and found them to be relatively accurate in estimating the interest rate risk of generic passthrough securities.[10] Bennett Golub reports a similar finding.[11]

While the advantages of the coupon curve duration are the simplicity of its calculation and the fact that current prices embody market expectations, there are disadvantages. The approach is limited to generic mortgage-backed securities and difficult to use for mortgage derivatives such as CMOs.

---

[10] Breeden, "Risk, Return, and Hedging of Fixed-Rate Mortgages."

[11] See Bennett W. Golub, "Towards a New Approach to Measuring Mortgage Duration," Chapter 32 in Frank J. Fabozzi (ed.), *The Handbook of Mortgage-Backed Securities* (Chicago: Probus Publishing, 1995), p. 673.

c. Empirical Duration

When computing effective duration and cash flow duration, the values to be substituted into the duration formula are those based on some valuation model. For coupon curve duration, the observed market prices are used in the duration formula. In contrast, empirical duration is estimated statistically using historical market prices and market yields.[12] Regression analysis is used to estimate the relationship. Some firms such as PaineWebber use empirical duration, also called implied duration, as their primary measure of the duration of an MBS.

There are three advantages to the empirical duration approach.[13] First, the duration estimate does not rely on any theoretical formulas or analytical assumptions. Second, the estimation of the required parameters is easy to compute using regression analysis. Finally, the only inputs that are needed are a reliable price series and Treasury yield series.

There are disadvantages.[14] First, a reliable price series for the mortgage security may not be available. For example, there may be no price series available for a thinly traded mortgage or the prices may be matrix priced (i.e., priced by a pricing service based on issues with similar characteristics) or model priced rather than actual transaction prices. Second, an empirical relationship does not impose a structure for the options embedded in a mortgage-backed security and this can distort the empirical duration. This may occur after a sharp and sustained shock to interest rates has been realized. Finally, the volatility of the spread to Treasury yields can distort how the price of a mortgage-backed security reacts to yield changes.

6   VALUING ASSET-BACKED SECURITIES

From the description of the Monte Carlo model, it can be seen that the valuation process is complex. Rather than build their own valuation model, portfolio managers typically use a model of a third-party vendor of analytical systems or a model of a dealer firm to value mortgage-backed securities. But mortgage-backed securities are only one type of structured product. Asset-backed securities are also structured products. Is it necessary to use the Monte Carlo model for all asset-backed securities? Below we will explain the circumstances as to when the Monte Carlo model must be used and when it is sufficient to use the Z-spread.

---

[12] This approach was first suggested in 1986 in Scott M. Pinkus and Marie A. Chandoha, "The Relative Price Volatility of Mortgage Securities," *Journal of Portfolio Management* (Summer 1986), pp. 9–22 and then in 1990 by Paul DeRossa, Laurie Goodman, and Mike Zazzarino, "Duration Estimates on Mortgage-Backed Securities," *Journal of Portfolio Management* (Winter 1993), pp. 32–37, and more recently in Laurie S. Goodman and Jeffrey Ho, "Mortgage Hedge Ratios: Which One Works Best?" *The Journal of Fixed Income* (December 1997), pp. 23–33, and Laurie S. Goodman and and Jeffrey Ho, "An Integrated Approach to Hedging and Relative Value Analysis," Chapter 15 in Frank J. Fabozzi (ed.), *Advances in the Valuation and Management of Mortgage-Backed Securities* (New Hope, PA: Frank J. Fabozzi Associates, 1999).

[13] Golub, "Towards a New Approach to Measuring Mortgage Duration," p. 672.

[14] Golub, "Towards a New Approach to Measuring Mortgage Duration."

The model that should be used for valuing an asset-backed security (ABS) depends on the characteristic of the loans or receivables backing the deal. An ABS can have one of the following three characteristics:

Characteristic 1: The ABS does not have a prepayment option.

Characteristic 2: The ABS has a prepayment option but borrowers do not exhibit a tendency to prepay when refinancing rates fall below the loan rate.

Characteristic 3: The ABS has a prepayment option and borrowers do exhibit a tendency to prepay when refinancing rates fall below the loan rate.

An example of a Characteristic 1 type ABS is a security backed by credit card receivables. An example of a Characteristic 2 type ABS is a security backed by automobile loans. A security backed by closed-end home equity loans where the borrowers are high quality borrowers (i.e., prime borrowers) is an example of a Characteristic 3 type ABS. There are some real-estate backed ABS that we discussed in the reading on the asset-backed sector of the bond market, where the verdict is still out as to the degree to which borrowers take advantage of refinancing opportunities. Specifically, these include securities backed by manufactured housing loans and securities backed by closed-end home equity loans to borrowers classified as low-quality borrowers.

There are two possible approaches to valuing an ABS. They are the

1. zero-volatility spread (Z-spread) approach
2. option-adjusted spread (OAS) approach

For the Z-spread approach the interest rates used to discount the cash flows are the spot rates plus the zero-volatility spread. The value of an ABS is then the present value of the cash flows based on these discount rates. The Z-spread approach does not consider the prepayment option. Consequently, the Z-spread approach should be used to value Characteristic 1 type ABS. (In terms of the relationship between the Z-spread, OAS, and option cost discussed earlier in this reading, this means that the value of the option is zero and therefore the Z-spread is equal to the OAS.) Since the Z-spread is equal to the OAS, the Z-spread approach to valuation can be used.

The Z-spread approach can also be used to value Characteristic 2 type ABS because while the borrowers do have a prepayment option, the option is not typically exercised. Thus, as with Characteristic 1 type ABS, the Z-spread is equal to the OAS.

The OAS approach—which is considerably more computationally extensive than the Z-spread approach—is used to value securities where there is an embedded option and there is an expectation that the option is expected to be exercised if it makes economic sense for the borrower to do so. Consequently, the OAS approach is used to value Characteristic 3 type ABS. The choice is then whether to use the binomial model (or a comparable model) or the Monte Carlo simulation model. Since typically the cash flow for an ABS with a prepayment option is interest rate path dependent—as with a mortgage-backed security—the Monte Carlo simulation model is used.

VALUING ANY SECURITY $\qquad$ 7

We conclude this reading with a summary of the approaches to valuing any fixed income security using the two approaches that we discussed in the previous section—the Z-spread approach and the OAS approach.

Below we match the valuation approach with the type of security.

1. For an *option-free bond* the correct approach is the Z-spread approach.

2. For a *bond with an embedded option where the cash flow is not interest rate path dependent* (such as a callable corporate or agency debenture bond or a putable bond) the correct approach is the OAS approach. Since the backward induction method can be used for such bonds, the binomial model or its equivalent should be used.

3. For a bond with an embedded option where the cash flow is interest rate path dependent (such as a mortgage-backed security or certain real estate-backed ABS) the correct approach is the OAS approach. However, because of the interest rate path dependency of the cash flow, the Monte Carlo simulation model should be used.

SUMMARY

▶ The cash flow yield is the interest rate that makes the present value of the projected cash flow for a mortgage-backed or asset-backed security equal to its market price plus accrued interest.

▶ The convention is to compare the yield on mortgage-backed and asset-backed securities to that of a Treasury coupon security by calculating the security's bond-equivalent yield. This measure is found by computing an effective semiannual rate and doubling it.

▶ The cash flow yield is based on three assumptions that thereby limit its use as a measure of relative value: 1) a prepayment assumption and default/recovery assumption, 2) an assumption that the cash flows will be reinvested at the computed cash flow yield, and 3) an assumption that the investor will hold the security until the last loan in the pool is paid off.

▶ The nominal spread is commonly computed as the difference between the cash flow yield and the yield on a Treasury security with the same maturity as the mortgage-backed or asset-backed security's average life.

▶ The nominal spread masks the fact that a portion of the spread is compensation for accepting prepayment risk.

▶ An investor or portfolio manager who buys solely on the basis of nominal spread fails to determine whether or not that nominal spread offers an adequate compensation for prepayment risk.

▶ An investor or portfolio manager needs a measure that indicates the potential compensation after adjusting for prepayment risk, and this measure is the option-adjusted spread.

▶ The zero-volatility spread is a measure of the spread that the investor would realize over the entire Treasury spot rate curve if the mortgage-backed or asset-backed security is held to maturity.

▶ The zero-volatility spread is not a spread off one point on the Treasury yield curve, as is the nominal spread, but a spread that will make the present value of the cash flows from the mortgage-backed or asset-backed security when discounted at the Treasury spot rate plus the spread equal to the market price of the security plus accrued interest.

▶ The binomial model and other similar models that use the backward induction method can be used to value securities where the decision to exercise a call option is not dependent on how interest rates evolved over time—that is, the decision of an issuer to call a bond will depend on the level of the rate at which the issue can be refunded relative to the issue's coupon rate, and not the path interest rates took to get to that rate.

▶ Mortgage-backed securities and some types of asset-backed securities are products where the periodic cash flows are "interest rate path-dependent"—meaning that the cash flow received in one period is determined not only by the current interest rate level, but also by the path that interest rates took to get to the current level.

▶ The Monte Carlo simulation model for valuing mortgage-backed securities involves generating a set of cash flows based on simulated future mortgage refinancing rates, which in turn imply simulated prepayment rates.

▶ In the Monte Carlo simulation model there is nothing to assure that the simulated interest rates will generate arbitrage-free values of the benchmark securities used in the valuation process; consequently, the simulated interest rates must be adjusted so as to produce arbitrage-free values.

▶ The present value of a given interest rate path can be thought of as the theoretical value of a security if that path was actually realized.

▶ The theoretical value of a mortgage-backed security can be determined by calculating the average of the theoretical values of all the interest rate paths.

▶ In the Monte Carlo simulation model, the option-adjusted spread is the spread that when added to all the spot rates on all interest rate paths will make the average present value of the paths equal to the observed market price (plus accrued interest).

▶ The OAS is measured relative to the benchmark interest rates that were used to generate the interest rate paths and to adjust the interest rate paths to make them arbitrage free.

▶ Since typically for a mortgage-backed security the benchmark interest rates are the on-the-run Treasury rates, the OAS measures the average spread over the Treasury spot rate curve, not the Treasury yield curve.

▶ Depending on the mortgage product being valued, the OAS reflects credit risk, liquidity risk, and modeling risk.

▶ The OAS is superior to the nominal spread which gives no recognition to the prepayment risk.

▶ The implied cost of the option embedded in a mortgage-backed or an asset-backed security can be obtained by calculating the difference between the option-adjusted spread at the assumed interest rate volatility and the zero-volatility spread.

▶ The option cost measures the prepayment (or option) risk embedded in the security and is a byproduct of the option-adjusted spread analysis, not valued explicitly with some option pricing model.

▶ In valuation modeling of collateralized mortgage obligations, the objective is to figure out how the value and risks of the collateral get transmitted to the tranches in a deal.

▶ There are several duration measures for mortgage-backed securities that are used in practice—effective duration, cash flow duration, coupon curve duration, and empirical duration.

▶ For bonds with embedded options such as mortgage-backed securities, the appropriate measure is effective duration, and to capture negative convexity, effective convexity should be computed.

▶ Effective duration is computed using Monte Carlo simulation by shocking the short-term interest rates for each interest rate path generated up and down and obtaining the new value for the security; the new values determined when rates are shocked up and down are used in the duration formula.

▶ There are differences in the effective duration reported for a given mortgage-backed security by dealers and vendors of analytical systems primarily due to differences in 1) the amount of the rate shock used, 2) the prepayment model used, 3) the option-adjusted spread computed, and 4) the relationship between short-term interest rates and refinancing rates assumed.

▶ Cash flow duration and coupon curve duration measures are forms of effective duration in that they do recognize that the values that should be used in the duration formula should take into account how the cash flows may change due to changes in prepayments when interest rates change.

▶ Cash flow duration is based on an initial cash flow yield and initial prepayment rate and computes the new values when rates are shocked (i.e., when the cash flow yield is shocked) allowing the cash flow to change based on a new prepayment rate as determined by a prepayment model.

▶ Cash flow duration is superior to modified duration (which assumes that cash flows do not change when rates are shocked) but inferior to effective duration as computed using the Monte Carlo simulation model.

▶ The coupon curve duration begins with the coupon curve of prices for similar mortgage-backed securities and uses values in the duration formula found by rolling up and down the coupon curve of prices.

▶ Empirical duration is a duration measure that is computed statistically using regression analysis based on observed market prices and yields.

▶ Empirical duration imposes no structure on the embedded option.

▶ A limitation of empirical duration and coupon curve duration is that they are difficult to apply to CMOs because of a lack of valid market price data.

▶ The zero-volatility spread added to the spot rates can be used to value an asset-backed security if either 1) the security does not have a prepayment option or 2) the borrower has the right to prepay but it has been observed that the borrower does not tend to exercise that option if interest rates decline below the loan rate.

▶ The option-adjusted spread approach to valuation using the Monte Carlo simulation model is used for an asset-backed security if the borrower does have the right to prepay and it has been observed that the borrower does tend to refinance when interest rates decline below the loan rate.

▶ For any fixed income security, the valuation approaches that can be employed are the zero-volatility spread approach and the option-adjusted spread approach.

▶ For option-free bonds, the zero-volatility spread approach should be used.

▶ The choice of whether to use the binomial model (or a similar "nomial" model that uses the backward induction method) or the Monte Carlo simulation model for a security with an embedded option depends on the characteristics of the security.

▶ For corporate and agency debentures with an embedded option the binomial model or its equivalent should be used for valuation.

▶ For securities such as mortgage-backed and asset-backed securities (those where it is observed that borrowers do exercise the prepayment option) the Monte Carlo simulation model should be used since the cash flows are typically interest rate path dependent.

PRACTICE PROBLEMS FOR READING 53

1. Suppose that based on a prepayment assumption of 200 PSA the cash flow yield for a spccific agency passthrough security is 7.5% and the stated maturity is 15 years. Suppose further that the average life of this security is 8 years. Assume the following yield curve for Treasuries:

Maturity	Yield (%)
6-year	6.2
8-year	6.3
10-year	6.4
15-year	6.6

   A. What is the nominal spread for this agency passthrough security?

   B. What must occur over the life of this agency passthrough security for the cash flow yield of 7.5% to be realized?

2. Suppose that the monthly cash flow yield is 0.74%. What is the cash flow yield on a bond-equivalent basis?

3. Jane Howard is a corporate bond analyst. Recently she has been asked to extend her responsibilities to mortgage-backed securities. In researching the methodology for valuing mortgage-backed securities she read that these securities are valued using the Monte Carlo simulation model. She was unfamiliar with this approach to valuation because in valuing callable corporate bonds she used the binomial model. Explain to Ms. Howard why the Monte Carlo simulation method is used to value mortgage-backed securities rather than the binomial method.

4. The following questions have to do with the Monte Carlo simulation model.

   A. What assumption must be made in generating the path of short-term interest rates?

   B. Why must the paths of short-term interest rates be adjusted?

   C. In determining the path of refinancing rates, what assumption must be made?

5. Nat Hawthorne, a portfolio manager, discussed the valuation of a particular mortgage-backed security with his broker, Steven Ruthledge. Mr. Hawthorne is considering the purchase of the security and asked what valuation model the brokerage firm used. Mr. Ruthledge responded that the Monte Carlo simulation model was used. Mr. Hawthorne then asked about what prepayment assumption is used in the Monte Carlo simulation model. Mr. Ruthledge responded that for the particular security Mr. Hawthorne is considering, 175 PSA was assumed. Mr. Hawthorne was confused by the response because he did not believe that a particular PSA assumption was made in the Monte Carlo simulation model. Is Mr. Hawthorne correct? Explain your answer.

6. What interest rates are used to value a mortgage-backed security on each interest rate path when using the Monte Carlo simulation model?

7. Juan Rodriguez is the manager of a portfolio containing mortgage passthrough securities. He is reviewing output of his firm's analytical system for several passthrough securities that are in the portfolio. Below is a portion of the report for three passthrough securities:

Passthrough	Price Based on an Assumed Interest Rate Volatility of			
	11%	13%	15%	16%
Security 1	100	98	95	93
Security 2	92	90	88	87
Security 3	102	104	106	107

Mr. Rodriguez believes that there is an error in the analytical system. Why does he suspect that there is an error?

8. Suppose that the pool of passthroughs used as collateral for a collateralized mortgage obligation is selling at a premium. Also suppose that one tranche in the deal, Tranche X, is selling at a discount and another tranche, Tranche Y, is selling at a premium.

A. Explain why a slowdown in prepayments will tend to increase the value of the collateral.

B. Explain why a slowdown in prepayments will not affect the value of Tranches X and Y in the same way.

9. Assume for simplicity that only ten interest rate paths are used in the Monte Carlo simulation model to a value Tranche W of a CMO deal. Suppose further that based on a spread of 70 basis points, the present value of the interest rate paths is as follows:

Interest rate path	1	2	3	4	5	6	7	8	9	10
PV for path	80	90	84	88	94	92	86	91	99	87

Based on the Monte Carlo simulation model and assuming a spread required by the market of 70 basis points, what is the theoretical value of Tranche W?

10. Jane Hubert is using an analytical system purchased by her firm to analyze mortgage-backed securities. The analytical system uses the Monte Carlo simulation model for valuation. She is given a choice when using the system to use either the "full Monte Carlo analysis" or "16 representative interest rate paths."

A. What is meant by "16 representative interest rate paths"?

B. How is the theoretical value of a mortgage-backed security determined when representative paths are used?

C. What is the trade-off when using representative interest rate paths versus using the full Monte Carlo analysis?

11. A portfolio manager is using an analytical system to value Tranche K of a CMO deal. The Monte Carlo simulation model uses eight representative interest rate paths. The present value of each of the representative interest rate paths and the weight of each path are shown below:

Representative path	1	2	3	4	5	6	7	8
Weight of representative path	20%	18%	16%	12%	12%	12%	6%	4%
PV of representative path	70	82	79	68	74	86	91	93

What is the theoretical value of Tranche K?

12. Mr. Wacker is a bond analyst whose primary responsibility has been to manage the corporate bond portfolio. Recently, his firm's analyst responsible for the mortgage-backed securities portfolio left. Mr. Wacker was asked to monitor the mortgage-backed securities portfolio until a new analyst is hired. The portfolio contains only Ginnie Mae mortgage products. In reviewing the Ginnie Mae portfolio and the option-adjusted spread (OAS) for each security, he was troubled by the values he observed. He was told that the benchmark interest rates used in the calculation of the OAS are Treasury rates. Below are two questions raised by Mr. Wacker. Respond to each one.

A. "I don't understand why the Ginnie Mae securities in my portfolio have a positive OAS. These securities are backed by the full faith and credit of the U.S. government, so there is no credit risk. Why is there a positive OAS?"

B. "There are different types of Ginnie Mae mortgage products in the portfolio. There are passthroughs, sequential-pay CMO tranches, planned amortization class CMO tranches, and support CMO tranches. Why do they have different OASs?"

13. Suppose that 10 representative paths are used in the Monte Carlo simulation model and that each path has a weight of 10%. The present value for each representative path is based on discounting the cash flows on an interest rate path by the short-term interest rates on that path plus a spread. For the different spreads used, the present value of each representative path is shown below for Tranche L in a CMO deal:

Representative Path	Present Value If the Spread Used Is			
	70 bps	75 bps	80 bps	85 bps
1	77	72	70	68
2	82	80	77	72
3	86	84	81	78
4	89	86	83	81
5	74	70	68	65
6	88	86	82	80
7	96	92	88	86
8	92	90	86	84
9	74	71	67	65
10	68	64	61	59

A. Suppose that the market price of Tranche L is 79.5. What is the option-adjusted spread?

B. Suppose instead of a market price for Tranche L of 79.5 the market price is 73.8. What is the option-adjusted spread?

14. Below are the results of a Monte Carlo simulation analysis using eight representative paths for two tranches of a CMO deal, Tranches M and N:

Representative Path	1	2	3	4	5	6	7	8
PV of path for:								
Tranche M	60	55	90	105	110	50	48	70
Tranche N	86	85	89	91	84	92	87	86

One of the tranches is a PAC tranche and the other is a support tranche. Which tranche is probably the PAC tranche and which is probably the support tranche?

15. An analysis of an agency CMO structure using the Monte Carlo simulation model based on 12% volatility found the following:

	OAS (Basis Points)	Z-Spread (Basis Points)	Effective Duration
Collateral	90	130	8.0
Tranche			
PAC I A	50	60	1.5
PAC I B	70	80	3.0
PAC I C	30	120	5.0
PAC I D	30	150	9.0
PAC II A	80	150	4.0
PAC II B	20	280	6.0
Support S1	35	165	11.0
Support S2	50	190	14.0

A. What is the option cost for PAC I A, PAC II A, and Support S1?

B. Which of the PAC tranches appears to be expensive in the deal on a relative value basis?

C. PAC II tranches are support tranches with schedules. The four support tranches in the deal are therefore PAC II A, PAC II B, Support S1, and Support S2. Which of the support tranches appears to be expensive on a relative value basis?

D. Despite its low OAS of 20 basis points, why might a yield buyer be induced to purchase PAC II B?

16. How is the effective duration and effective convexity of a mortgage-backed security computed using the Monte Carlo simulation model? Be sure to explain what assumption is made regarding the option-adjusted spread when computing the effective duration and effective convexity.

17. Joel Winters is a junior portfolio manager of a corporate bond portfolio. A decision has been made to include mortgage-backed securities in the portfolio. Mr. Winters is considering the purchase of a CMO tranche called a support bond. Before he buys this tranche, he wants to know its effective duration. Because he does not have the use of an analytical system to compute effective duration, Mr. Winters contacts three dealers and inquires as to the effective duration for this tranche. He is given the following effective duration from the three dealer firms:

Dealer	1	2	3
Effective duration	8.1	4.6	11.6

Mr. Winters is puzzled by the significant variation in the effective durations, especially since all the dealers indicated that the Monte Carlo simulation model was used. In his experience with corporate bonds with embedded options he has never observed such a significant variation in the effective duration from dealer firm to dealer firm.

Explain to Mr. Winters why there is such a significant variation in the effective durations. Be sure to clearly identify the reasons for the variation in the effective durations.

18. Explain why you agree or disagree with the following statement: "If the collateral for a CMO deal has negative convexity, then all the tranches in the deal must have negative convexity. The only difference is the degree of negative convexity from one tranche to another."

19. A. What is the cash flow duration of a mortgage-backed security?

B. What are the limitations of cash flow duration as a measure of the price sensitivity of a mortgage-backed security to changes in interest rates?

20. Suppose that the coupon curve of prices for a passthrough security for some month is as follows:

Coupon (%)	Price ($)
7	94.00
8	97.06
9	99.50
10	102.60
11	105.25
12	106.19

What is the coupon curve duration for the 9% coupon passthrough?

21. Karen Brown is considering alternative measures for estimating the duration of some complex CMO tranches. One measure she is considering is empirical duration. Explain to Ms. Brown the difficulties of using empirical duration for complex CMO tranches.

22. Thomas Larken is a portfolio manager who is considering investing in the asset-backed securities market. In particular, Mr. Larken is considering investing in either credit card receivables, auto loan-backed securities, or prime home equity loan-backed securities. Examination of the nominal spreads in these three sectors of the market indicates that the largest nominal spread for AAA and AA issues is home equity loan-backed securities. Based on this analysis, Mr. Larken believes that the best sector in which to invest is in home equity loan-backed securities because it offers the greatest relative value as measured by the nominal spread. Explain whether or not you agree with Mr. Larken's assessment of the relative attractiveness of home equity loan-backed securities.

23. An investment banker has created an asset-backed security in which the collateral is the future royalties of a songwriter. Which valuation approach do you think should be used to value this security, the zero-volatility spread or the option-adjusted spread?

24. Suppose that empirical evidence on prepayments for manufactured housing loans suggests that borrowers do not take advantage of refinancing when interest rates decline. Explain whether the zero-volatility spread approach or OAS approach is appropriate for valuing securities backed by manufacturing housing loans.

25. Evidence by Wall Street firms on home equity loans strongly suggests that high-quality borrowers do take advantage of a decline in interest rates to refinance a loan. In contrast, low-quality borrowers tend not to take advantage of a decline in interest rates to refinance.

    A. What is the appropriate valuation approach (option-adjusted spread approach or zero-volatility spread approach) to value home equity loan-backed securities where the underlying pool of loans are those of high-quality borrowers? Explain why.

    B. What is the appropriate valuation approach (option-adjusted spread approach or zero-volatility spread approach) to value home equity loan-backed securities where the underlying pool of loans are those of low-quality borrowers? Explain why.

The following information relates to Questions 26–31 and is based on "Mortgage-Backed Sector of the Bond Market" and this reading

Atul Gupta is a mortgage-backed securities analyst at a macro hedge fund. Although mortgage rates have been fairly constant in recent years, Gupta expects interest rates to be higher in the coming months. His analysis of mortgage-backed securities leads him to the following conclusions:

1. Contraction risk occurs when interest rates increase. Therefore, mortgage securities will prepay faster than expected.

2. A sequential-pay collateralized mortgage obligation (CMO) with an accrual tranche lowers the prepayment risk and shortens the average life of the sequential-pay tranches relative to a sequential-pay CMO without an accrual tranche.

3. A planned amortization class (PAC) bond with a very narrow PAC window resembles a corporate bond with a bullet payment.

4. In general, principal-only strips (POs) should underperform interest-only strips (IOs) if interest rates increase.

Gupta receives the dealer quotes on mortgage-backed securities given in Exhibit 1:

	EXHIBIT 1	**Dealer Quotes**		
Tranche	**Option-Adjusted Spread (bps)**	**Zero-Volatility Spread (bps)**	**Nominal Spread (bps)**	**Effective Duration (Years)**
PAC 1	50	60	68	1.50
PAC 2	70	80	85	3.00
PAC 3	30	120	128	5.00
PAC II A	80	150	156	4.00
Support 1	35	165	178	11.00

Note: bps = basis points

26. Is Gupta's first conclusion correct?
    A. Yes.
    B. No, because contraction risk occurs when interest rates fall.
    C. No, because contraction risk occurs when principal payments are received later than expected.

27. Is Gupta's second conclusion correct?
    A. Yes.
    B. No, because an accrual tranche increases prepayment risk.
    C. No, because an accrual tranche has an indeterminable effect on prepayment risk.

28. Is Gupta's third conclusion correct?
    A. Yes.
    B. No, because the PAC bond is an accrual tranche.
    C. No, because the PAC bond is a scheduled tranche.

29. Is Gupta's fourth conclusion correct?
    A. Yes.
    B. No, IOs should underperform POs.
    C. No, both POs and IOs should increase in value.

30. Given the data in Exhibit 1, the cost of the embedded option for the PAC 1 tranche, in basis points, is *closest* to:
    A. 8.
    B. 10.
    C. 18.

31. Given the data in Exhibit 1, which PAC tranche is likely to be the *most* expensive in terms of option cost?
    A. PAC 1.
    B. PAC 2.
    C. PAC 3.

SOLUTIONS FOR READING 53

1. A. The convention is to determine the nominal spread relative to the spread on a Treasury security with the same maturity as the average life of the mortgage-backed security. Since the average life is 8 years, the benchmark Treasury issue is the 8-year issue. The nominal spread is then 7.5% minus the 6.3% of the 8-year Treasury issue. So, the nominal spread is 120 basis points.

B. For the 7.5% cash flow yield to be realized the following must occur:

▶ actual prepayments must be 200 PSA over the life of the security;

▶ the monthly cash flow (interest plus principal repayment) must be reinvested at a rate of 7.5%;

▶ the security must be held until the last mortgage pays off.

2. The monthly cash flow yield, i_M, is 0.0074. Therefore,

Bond-equivalent yield $= 2[(1.0074)^6 - 1] = 0.0905 = 9.05\%$

3. The binomial model used to value a corporate bond with an embedded option can handle securities in which the decision to exercise a call option is not dependent on how interest rates evolved over time. That is, the decision of a corporate issuer to call a bond will depend on the level of the rate at which the issue can be refunded relative to the issue's coupon rate. The decision to call does not depend on the path interest rates took to get to that rate. Ms. Howard must understand that this is not a characteristic of mortgage-backed securities. These securities are "interest rate path-dependent," meaning that the cash flow received in one period is determined not only by the interest rate level at that period, but also by the path that interest rates took to get to that rate.

For example, in the case of passthrough securities, prepayments are interest rate path-dependent because this month's prepayment rate depends on whether there have been prior opportunities to refinance since the underlying mortgages were originated. For CMOs there are typically two sources of path dependency in a CMO tranche's cash flows. First, the collateral prepayments are path-dependent as just described. Second, the cash flows to be received in the current month by a CMO tranche depend on the outstanding balances of the other tranches in the deal. Thus, we need the history of prepayments to calculate these balances.

4. A. To generate the path of short-term interest rates, an assumption about the volatility of short-term interest rates must be made.

B. If the short-term interest rates on each path are used without an adjustment, there is no assurance that the Monte Carlo simulation model will correctly value the on-the-run Treasury issues. An adjustment to the short-term interest rates is required in order to have the model properly price on-the-run Treasury issues so that the model will provide arbitrage-free values.

C. In moving from the short-term interest rates to the refinancing rates, it is necessary to make an assumption about the spread between these rates.

5. In the Monte Carlo simulation model, a prepayment *model* is used. The prepayment model provides a prepayment rate for each month on each interest rate path. Thus, no specific PSA prepayment assumption is made. Consequently, the statement by Mr. Ruthledge that a 175 PSA was made is inconsistent with the Monte Carlo simulation model. Therefore, Mr. Hawthorne should have been confused by Mr. Ruthledge's response.

6. On an interest rate path, the short-term interest rates are the forward rates. It is the forward rates plus an appropriate spread that is used to value a mortgage-backed security on an interest rate path.

7. The investor in a passthrough security has effectively sold a call option to borrowers (homeowners). The higher the assumed interest rate volatility the greater the value of this embedded call option and therefore the lower the price of a passthrough security. Securities 1 and 2 have the correct relationship between price and assumed interest rate volatility. Security 3 has the opposite relationship. Therefore, the error that Mr. Rodriguez discovered is with the relationship between assumed interest rate volatility and price for Security 3.

8. A. Since the collateral is trading at a premium, a slowdown in prepayments will allow the investor to receive the higher coupon for a longer period of time. This will increase the value of the collateral.

   B. Because Tranche Y is selling at a premium, its value will increase with a slowdown in prepayments. In contrast, because Tranche X is selling at a discount, a slowdown in prepayments will decrease its value. This is because for Tranche X, there will be less principal returned to be reinvested at the new, higher rates. Also, assuming that X was purchased when it was trading at a discount, there will be less of a capital gain realized (since principal is returned at par).

9. The theoretical value based on the ten interest rate paths is the average of the present value of the interest rate paths. The average value is 89.1.

10. A. Rather than sampling a large number of interest rate paths, some vendors of mortgage analytical systems have developed computational procedures that reduce the number of paths required. The procedure involves using statistical techniques to reduce the number of interest rate paths to sets of similar paths. These paths are called representative paths. The security is then valued on each of the representative interest rate paths—16 in the question.

   B. The theoretical value of a security when the representative interest rate paths are used is the weighted average of the 16 representative paths. The weight for a path is the percentage of that representative path relative to the total paths in a full Monte Carlo analysis.

   C. The trade-off between the full Monte Carlo analysis and the 16 representative paths is one of speed versus accuracy. The full Monte Carlo analysis provides the true value of the security—*true only based on all the assumptions of the model.* Using 16 representative samples is less accurate but requires less computational time.

11. The theoretical value is the weighted average of the present value of the representative interest rate paths. The weighted average of the present value of the representative interest rate paths is 77.94 as shown below:

Weight	PV	Weight × PV
0.20	70	14.00
0.18	82	14.76
0.16	79	12.64
0.12	68	8.16
0.12	74	8.88
0.12	86	10.32
0.06	91	5.46
0.04	93	3.72
Theoretical value		77.94

12. A. While there is no credit risk for a Ginnie Mae mortgage product, there is liquidity risk (relative to on-the-run Treasury issues) and modeling risk. The latter risk is due to the assumptions that must be made in valuing a mortgage-backed security. If those assumptions prove incorrect or if the parameters used as inputs are wrong, the valuation model will not calculate the true level of risk. A major portion of the compensation for a Ginnie Mae mortgage product reflects payment for this model uncertainty.

  B. The OAS should differ by the type of Ginnie Mae mortgage product. The more complex the security to model and value, the greater the OAS should be to reflect the associated modeling risk. Moreover, the more complex the security, the less liquid the security tends to be. Consequently, the OAS will also differ because of liquidity risk.

13. Using the representative interest rate paths, the theoretical value of a mortgage-backed security is the weighted average of the present value of the paths. Since it is assumed in the question that each path has the same weight, the theoretical value is the simple average of the present values of the interest rate paths. For the four spreads, the average PV is given below:

Representative Path	Present Value if the Spread Used Is			
	70 bps	75 bps	80 bps	85 bps
Average PV	82.6	79.5	76.3	73.8

  A. The option-adjusted spread is the spread that will make the theoretical value equal to the market price. Since the question assumes that Tranche L has a market price of 79.5, then a spread of 75 basis points will produce a theoretical value equal to the market price of 79.5. Therefore, the OAS is 75 basis points.

B. If the price is 73.8 instead of 79.5, then the OAS is the spread that will make the theoretical value equal to 73.8. From the table above it can be seen that a spread of 85 basis points will produce a theoretical value equal to 73.8. Therefore, the OAS is 85 basis points.

14. Tranche M has a substantial variation in the present value for the paths. This is a characteristic of a support tranche since a support tranche is exposed to substantial prepayment risk. Tranche N has little variation in the present value for the paths and this is a characteristic of a PAC tranche. Therefore, Tranche M is probably the support tranche and Tranche N is probably the PAC tranche.

15. **A.** The option cost is the difference between the Z-spread and the OAS. Therefore,

PAC I A:	$60 - 50 = 10$ basis points
PAC II A:	$150 - 80 = 70$ basis points
Support S1:	$165 - 35 = 130$ basis points

B. Typically, the OAS increases with effective duration. The two longer PAC tranches, PAC I C and PAC I D, have lower OAS than the two shorter duration PACs. Therefore, the two longer duration PACs appear to be expensive.

C. On a relative value basis, all but PAC II A appear to be expensive. PAC II B has a lower OAS than PAC II A even though it has a higher effective duration. The other two support tranches without a schedule have a low OAS relative to their effective durations.

D. Investors who do not appreciate the significance of the option risk associated with a tranche can be induced to buy PAC II B because they look exclusively at the nominal spread. While the nominal spread is not provided as part of the information in the question, it can be estimated from the Z-spread. A Z-spread of 280 basis points is extremely appealing to investors for a security with no credit risk (since the deal is an agency CMO deal). Also, investors who do not realize that a PAC II is a support bond will believe that they have purchased a PAC tranche with a high "spread" to Treasuries.

16. The effective duration and effective convexity require the calculation of V_- and V_+. To calculate V_-, each path of short-term interest rates is decreased by a small number of basis points, say 25 basis points. Then, the cash flows are generated for each interest rate path. When the new cash flows are valued using the short-term interest rates plus a spread, the spread used is the original OAS. That is, it is assumed that the OAS does not change when interest rates are decreased. The same procedure is followed to compute V_+, but each path of short-term rates is increased by the same small number of basis points as was used to compute V_-. Again, it is assumed that the OAS does not change, so the new short-term interest rates plus the original OAS are used to discount the new cash flows on the interest rate paths.

17. First it is important to note that the CMO tranche is a support tranche and therefore has considerable prepayment risk. Despite Mr. Winters having been told that all the dealer firms used the Monte Carlo simulation model to compute the effective duration, there are assumptions in the model that can vary from dealer to dealer. This is the reason for the variation in the

effective duration. These different assumptions in computing the value of a mortgage-backed security include:

1. differences in the amount of the rate shock used

2. differences in prepayment models

3. differences in option-adjusted spread (recall that the OAS is held constant when rates are shocked)

4. differences in the relationship between short-term interest rates and refinancing rates

18. This statement is incorrect. From a collateral with negative convexity, tranches with both positive and negative convexity can be created. For example, a PAC bond that is well protected will have little prepayment risk and therefore positive convexity—effectively the convexity of an option-free bond. However, one or more of the other tranches in the deal would have to have more negative convexity than the collateral itself, since the tranching of the collateral can only reallocate prepayment risk; it cannot eliminate it entirely.

19. A. Cash flow duration is computed assuming that if interest rates are changed, the prepayment rate will change when computing the new value.

B. The problem is that this duration measure is based on one initial prepayment speed, and when rates are changed, it is assumed the prepayment speed will change to another prepayment speed. It is a static approach because it considers only one prepayment speed if rates change. It does not consider the dynamics that interest rates can change in the future and therefore there is not just one potential cash flow or prepayment rate that must be considered in valuing a mortgage-backed security.

20. To compute the coupon curve duration the assumption is that if the yield declines by 100 basis points, the price of the 9% coupon passthrough will increase to the price of the current 10% coupon passthrough. Thus, the price will increase from 99.50 to 102.60. Similarly, if the yield increases by 100 basis points, the assumption is that the price of the 9% coupon passthrough will decline to the price of the 8% coupon passthrough (97.06). Using the duration formula, the corresponding values are:

$$
\begin{aligned}
V_0 &= 99.50 \\
V_+ &= 97.06 \\
V_- &= 102.60 \\
\Delta y &= 0.01
\end{aligned}
$$

The estimated duration based on the coupon curve is then:

$$
\frac{102.60 - 97.06}{2(99.50)(0.01)} = 2.78
$$

21. Empirical duration is computed using statistical analysis. It requires good price data for the tranche whose empirical duration is to be computed. A major problem with applying empirical duration to complex CMO tranches is that a reliable series of price data is often not available for a thinly traded mortgage product or the prices may be matrix priced or model priced rather than actual transaction prices. The second problem is that an empirical relationship does not impose a structure for the options embedded in a mortgage-backed security, and this can distort the empirical duration. Finally, the volatility of the spread to Treasury yields can distort how the price of a mortgage-backed security reacts to yield changes.

22. The nominal spread of an asset-backed security hides the associated option or prepayment risk. For auto loan-backed securities, refinancing is not an important factor and therefore prepayment risk is not significant. For credit card receivables, there is prepayment risk only at the security level— that is, a credit card borrower cannot prepay because there is no schedule of payments, but a security can be prepaid if certain rapid or early amortization triggers are realized. However, prepayment risk is not significant. In contrast, for home equity loan-backed securities prepayment risk is significant and the nominal spread reflects that risk. Consequently, assessing relative value for these three types of asset-backed securities based on the nominal spread is incorrect because the spread is not adjusted for the prepayment risk. Home equity loan-backed securities offer a higher nominal spread because of the prepayment risk.

23. The appropriate valuation approach depends on whether or not the borrower has an option to prepay. Furthermore, even if the borrower has the right to prepay, it depends on whether or not the borrower will take advantage of this option to prepay when interest rates decline. Since the security involves future royalties, there is no prepayment option. Consequently, there is no option value and the appropriate valuation approach is the zero-volatility spread.

24. While there is an option to prepay, if the empirical evidence is correct that borrowers do not prepay when rates decline, then the option value is zero. Consequently, the zero-volatility spread approach is the appropriate approach since the OAS is equal to the zero-volatility spread.

25. **A.** Since high-quality borrowers are observed to take advantage of refinancing opportunities, there is a value to the prepayment option. Consequently, the option-adjusted spread approach is appropriate when the underlying pool of home equity loans are those of high-quality borrowers.

    B. Since low-quality borrowers may prepay but have been observed not to take advantage of refinancing opportunities, there is very little value to the prepayment option. Since the option cost has a value of zero, the zero-volatility spread is equal to the option-adjusted spread. Consequently, the zero-volatility spread approach can be used to value securities backed by a pool of home equity loans of low-quality borrowers.

    However, there is a caveat here regarding the behavior of low-quality borrowers. The answer ignores the adverse selection impact of borrowers who upgrade their credit profile and refinance out, leaving a potentially longer average life, and worse credit, pool.

26. B is correct. Gupta's first conclusion is incorrect. When interest rates fall, prepayments rise due to refinancing and contraction risk occurs. When interest rates increase, prepayments fall and mortgage securities extend rather than contract.

27. C is correct. Gupta's second conclusion is incorrect. An accrual tranche (Z tranche) is paid only after all other tranches have been paid in full. The payments that would otherwise have been paid to the accrual tranche are used to pay off the principal balance of earlier tranches. This increases the contraction risk and decreases the extension risk of the earlier

tranches. The effect on prepayment risk (contraction and extension) is thus not determinable.

28. A is correct. A planned amortization class (PAC) bond is a mortgage-backed security wherein the investor has greater assurance of the timing of the repayment of principal. The window of the PAC describes the width of the period of time for the repayment of principal. A very narrow window, in effect, provides a single repayment date (maturity date). Thus, such a PAC bond resembles a corporate bond.

29. A is correct. If interest rates increase, prepayments slow and mortgage securities extend. IO strips benefit from the extension in the number of interest payments. Further, the interest received can be reinvested at the new higher rates. PO strips must wait longer to receive repayment of principal as prepayments decrease. Further, the principal repayments are discounted at higher rates and worth less even without the extended time. The time extension and the higher discount rate together make PO strips very poor investments should interest rates increase.

30. B is correct. The zero-volatility spread (also called the static spread or the Z-spread) indicates the increased yield on a MBS above the Treasury spot rate curve. It incorporates credit risk, liquidity risk, and any option risk. The option-adjusted spread (OAS) takes prepayment into account and removes (adjusts for) the option risk. The OAS reflects credit risk and liquidity risk. The difference between the two spreads reflects the cost of the option. In this problem the cost of the embedded option is $60 - 50 = 10$ basis points.

31. C is correct. To answer this question, trade off OAS versus effective duration. The lower the OAS, the lower the return offered by the security. A lower return might be acceptable if effective duration (risk) is less. Of the three selected tranches, PAC3 has the lowest OAS (lowest return), yet its risk (effective duration) is higher than either PAC1 or PAC2. Furthermore, the option cost of PAC3 is 90, which exceeds the option cost for the other choices.

$4\frac{5}{8}$ $4\frac{11}{16}$ $-\frac{3}{8}$

$5\frac{1}{2}$ $5\frac{1}{2}$ $-\frac{3}{8}$

$20\frac{5}{8}$ $21\frac{3}{16}$ $-\frac{1}{16}$

$17\frac{3}{8}$ $18\frac{1}{8}$ $+\frac{7}{8}$

$6\frac{1}{2}$ $6\frac{1}{2}$ $-\frac{1}{2}$

$7\frac{1}{4}$ $31\frac{1}{32}$ $-\frac{1}{16}$

$15\frac{1}{16}$ $\frac{9}{16}$

$9\frac{1}{16}$

$\frac{9}{32}$ $7\frac{13}{16}$ $7\frac{15}{16}$

$7\frac{15}{16}$ $2\frac{11}{32}$ $2\frac{1}{2}$ $+$

$2\frac{5}{8}$ $2\frac{1}{4}$ $2\frac{1}{4}$

27 $2\frac{3}{4}$ $11\frac{3}{8}$ $11\frac{1}{4}$ $+$

$6\frac{1}{6}$ $12\frac{1}{16}$ $11\frac{3}{8}$ $11\frac{1}{4}$ $+$

67 $33\frac{3}{4}$ 33 $33\frac{1}{8}$ $-$

602 $25\frac{5}{8}$ $24\frac{9}{16}$ $25\frac{3}{8}$ $+$

633 12 $11\frac{5}{8}$ $11\frac{7}{8}$ $+$

16 $10\frac{1}{2}$ $10\frac{1}{2}$ $10\frac{1}{2}$ $-$

78 $15\frac{7}{8}$ $15\frac{13}{16}$ $15\frac{7}{8}$ $-$

4538 $9\frac{1}{16}$ $8\frac{1}{4}$ $8\frac{1}{4}$ $+$

430 $11\frac{1}{4}$ $10\frac{1}{8}$

A priori probability   A probability based on logical analysis rather than on observation or personal judgment.

Abandonment option   The ability to terminate a project at some future time if the financial results are disappointing.

Abnormal earnings   See *Residual income.*

Absolute dispersion   The amount of variability present without comparison to any reference point or benchmark.

Absolute frequency   The number of observations in a given interval (for grouped data).

Absolute valuation model   A model that specifies an asset's intrinsic value.

Accelerated methods of depreciation   Depreciation methods that allocate a relatively large proportion of the cost of an asset to the early years of the asset's useful life.

Account   With the accounting systems, a formal record of increases and decreases in a specific asset, liability, component of owners' equity, revenue, or expense.

Account format   A method of presentation of accounting transactions in which effects on assets appear at the left and effects on liabilities and equity appear at the right of a central dividing line; also known as T-account format.

Accounting estimates   Estimates of items such as the useful lives of assets, warranty costs, and the amount of uncollectible receivables.

Accounting profit (income before taxes or **pretax income)**   Income as reported on the income statement, in accordance with prevailing accounting standards, before the provisions for income tax expense.

Accounting risk   The risk associated with accounting standards that vary from country to country or with any uncertainty about how certain transactions should be recorded.

Accounts payable   Amounts that a business owes to its vendors for goods and services that were purchased from them but which have not yet been paid.

Accounts receivable turnover   Ratio of sales on credit to the average balance in accounts receivable.

Accrual basis   Method of accounting in which the effect of transactions on financial condition and income are recorded when they occur, not when they are settled in cash.

Accrued expenses (accrued liabilities)   Liabilities related to expenses that have been incurred but not yet paid as of the end of an accounting period—an example of an accrued expense is rent that has been incurred but not yet paid, resulting in a liability "rent payable."

Accrued interest   Interest earned but not yet paid.

Accumulated benefit obligation   Under U.S. GAAP, a measure used in estimating a defined-benefit pension plan's liabilities, defined as "the actuarial present value of benefits (whether vested or non-vested) attributed by the pension benefit formula to employee service rendered before a specified date and based on employee service and compensation (if applicable) prior to that date."

Accumulated depreciation   An offset to property, plant, and equipment (PPE) reflecting the amount of the cost of PPE that has been allocated to current and previous accounting periods.

Acquiring company, or **acquirer**   The company in a merger or acquisition that is acquiring the target.

Acquisition   The purchase of some portion of one company by another; the purchase may be for assets, a definable segment of another entity, or the purchase of an entire company.

Acquisition method   A method of accounting for a business combination where the acquirer is required to measure each identifiable asset and liability at fair value. This method was the result of a joint project of the IASB and FASB aiming at convergence in standards for the accounting of business combinations.

Active factor risk   The contribution to active risk squared resulting from the portfolio's different-than-benchmark exposures relative to factors specified in the risk model.

Active investment managers   Managers who hold portfolios that differ from their benchmark portfolio in an attempt to produce positive risk-adjusted returns.

Active portfolio   In the context of the Treynor-Black model, the portfolio formed by mixing analyzed stocks of perceived nonzero alpha values. This portfolio is ultimately mixed with the passive market index portfolio.

Active return   The return on a portfolio minus the return on the portfolio's benchmark.

Active risk   The standard deviation of active returns.

Active risk squared   The variance of active returns; active risk raised to the second power.

Active specific risk or **asset selection risk**   The contribution to active risk squared resulting from the portfolio's active weights on individual assets as those weights interact with assets' residual risk.

Active strategy   In reference to short-term cash management, an investment strategy characterized by monitoring and attempting to capitalize on market conditions to optimize the risk and return relationship of short-term investments.

Activity ratios (asset utilization or **operating efficiency ratios)**   Ratios that measure how efficiently a company performs day-to-day tasks, such as the collection of receivables and management of inventory.

Addition rule for probabilities   A principle stating that the probability that A or B occurs (both occur) equals the probability that A occurs, plus the probability that B occurs, minus the probability that both A and B occur.

Add-on interest   A procedure for determining the interest on a bond or loan in which the interest is added onto the face value of a contract.

Adjusted beta   Historical beta adjusted to reflect the tendency of beta to be mean reverting.

Adjusted present value (APV)   As an approach to valuing a company, the sum of the value of the company, assuming no use of debt, and the net present value of any effects of debt on company value.

Adjusted R^2   A measure of goodness-of-fit of a regression that is adjusted for degrees of freedom and hence does not automatically increase when another independent variable is added to a regression.

After-tax cash flow (ATCF)   Net operating income less debt service and less taxes payable on income from operations.

After-tax equity reversion (ATER)   Sales price less disposition costs, amortized mortgage loan balance, and capital gains taxes.

Agency costs   Costs associated with the conflict of interest present when a company is managed by non-owners. Agency costs result from the inherent conflicts of interest between managers and equity owners.

Agency costs of equity The smaller the stake that managers have in the company, the less is their share in bearing the cost of excessive perquisite consumption or not giving their best efforts in running the company.

Agency problem, or **principal-agent problem** A conflict of interest that arises when the agent in an agency relationship has goals and incentives that differ from the principal to whom the agent owes a fiduciary duty.

Agency relationships An arrangement whereby someone, an agent, acts on behalf of another person, the principal.

Aging schedule A breakdown of accounts into categories of days outstanding.

Allowance for bad debts An offset to accounts receivable for the amount of accounts receivable that are estimated to be uncollectible.

Alpha (or **abnormal return**) The return on an asset in excess of the asset's required rate of return; the risk-adjusted return.

Alternative hypothesis The hypothesis accepted when the null hypothesis is rejected.

American Depositary Receipt A negotiable certificate issued by a depositary bank that represents ownership in a non-U.S. company's deposited equity (i.e., equity held in custody by the depositary bank in the company's home market).

American option An option that can be exercised at any time until its expiration date.

Amortization The process of allocating the cost of intangible long-term assets having a finite useful life to accounting periods; the allocation of the amount of a bond premium or discount to the periods remaining until bond maturity.

Amortizing and accreting swaps A swap in which the notional principal changes according to a formula related to changes in the underlying.

Analysis of variance (ANOVA) The analysis of the total variability of a dataset (such as observations on the dependent variable in a regression) into components representing different sources of variation; with reference to regression, ANOVA provides the inputs for an F-test of the significance of the regression as a whole.

Annual percentage rate The cost of borrowing expressed as a yearly rate.

Annuity A finite set of level sequential cash flows.

Annuity due An annuity having a first cash flow that is paid immediately.

Anticipation stock Excess inventory that is held in anticipation of increased demand, often because of seasonal patterns of demand.

Antidilutive With reference to a transaction or a security, one that would increase earnings per share (EPS) or result in EPS higher than the company's basic EPS—antidilutive securities are not included in the calculation of diluted EPS.

Arbitrage 1) The simultaneous purchase of an undervalued asset or portfolio and sale of an overvalued but equivalent asset or portfolio, in order to obtain a riskless profit on the price differential. Taking advantage of a market inefficiency in a risk-free manner. 2) The condition in a financial market in which equivalent assets or combinations of assets sell for two different prices, creating an opportunity to profit at no risk with no commitment of money. In a well-functioning financial market, few arbitrage opportunities are possible. 3) A risk-free operation that earns an expected positive net profit but requires no net investment of money.

Arbitrage opportunity An opportunity to conduct an arbitrage; an opportunity to earn an expected positive net profit without risk and with no net investment of money.

Arbitrage portfolio The portfolio that exploits an arbitrage opportunity.

Arithmetic mean The sum of the observations divided by the number of observations.

Arrears swap A type of interest rate swap in which the floating payment is set at the end of the period and the interest is paid at that same time.

Asian call option A European-style option with a value at maturity equal to the difference between the stock price at maturity and the average stock price during the life of the option, or $0, whichever is greater.

Asset beta The unlevered beta; reflects the business risk of the assets; the asset's systematic risk.

Asset purchase An acquisition in which the acquirer purchases the target company's assets and payment is made directly to the target company.

Asset retirement obligations (AROs) The fair value of the estimated costs to be incurred at the end of a tangible asset's service life. The fair value of the liability is determined on the basis of discounted cash flows.

Assets Resources controlled by an enterprise as a result of past events and from which future economic benefits to the enterprise are expected to flow.

Asset-based approach Approach that values a private company based on the values of the underlying assets of the entity less the value of any related liabilities.

Asset-based loan A loan that is secured with company assets.

Asset-based valuation An approach to valuing natural resource companies that estimates company value on the basis of the market value of the natural resources the company controls.

Assignment of accounts receivable The use of accounts receivable as collateral for a loan.

Asymmetric information The differential of information between corporate insiders and outsiders regarding the company's performance and prospects. Managers typically have more information about the company's performance and prospects than owners and creditors.

At the money An option in which the underlying value equals the exercise price.

Autocorrelation The correlation of a time series with its own past values.

Automated Clearing House An electronic payment network available to businesses, individuals, and financial institutions in the United States, U.S. Territories, and Canada.

Autoregressive (AR) model A time series regressed on its own past values, in which the independent variable is a lagged value of the dependent variable.

Available-for-sale investments Debt and equity securities not classified as either held-to-maturity or held-for-trading securities. The investor is willing to sell but not actively planning to sell. In general, available-for-sale securities are reported at fair value on the balance sheet.

Backtesting With reference to portfolio strategies, the application of a strategy's portfolio selection rules to historical data to assess what would have been the strategy's historical performance.

Backward integration A merger involving the purchase of a target ahead of the acquirer in the value or production chain; for example, to acquire a supplier.

Backwardation A condition in the futures markets in which the benefits of holding an asset exceed the costs, leaving the futures price less than the spot price.

Balance of payments accounts A country's record of international trading, borrowing, and lending.

Balance sheet (statement of financial position or **statement of financial condition)**   The financial statement that presents an entity's current financial position by disclosing resources the entity controls (its assets) and the claims on those resources (its liabilities and equity claims), as of a particular point in time (the date of the balance sheet).

Balance sheet ratios   Financial ratios involving balance sheet items only.

Balance-sheet-based accruals ratio   The difference between net operating assets at the end and the beginning of the period compared to the average net operating assets over the period.

Balance-sheet-based aggregate accruals   The difference between net operating assets at the end and the beginning of the period.

Band-of-investment method   A widely used approach to estimate an overall capitalization rate. It is based on the premise that debt and equity financing is typically involved in a real estate transaction.

Bank discount basis   A quoting convention that annualizes, on a 360-day year, the discount as a percentage of face value.

Bargain purchase   When a company is acquired and the purchase price is less than the fair value of the net assets. The current treatment of the excess of fair value over the purchase price is different under IFRS and U.S. GAAP. The excess is never accounted for as negative goodwill.

Basic earnings per share (EPS)   Net earnings available to common shareholders (i.e., net income minus preferred dividends) divided by the weighted average number of common shares outstanding during the period.

Basis point value (BPV)   Also called *present value of a basis point* or *price value of a basis point* (PVBP), the change in the bond price for a 1 basis point change in yield.

Basis swap   1) An interest rate swap involving two floating rates. 2) A swap in which both parties pay a floating rate.

Bayes' formula   A method for updating probabilities based on new information.

Bear hug   A tactic used by acquirers to circumvent target management's objections to a proposed merger by submitting the proposal directly to the target company's board of directors.

Bear spread   An option strategy that involves selling a put with a lower exercise price and buying a put with a higher exercise price. It can also be executed with calls.

Before-tax cash flow   A measure of the expected annual cash flow from the operation of a real estate investment after all expenses but before taxes.

Benchmark   A comparison portfolio; a point of reference or comparison.

Benchmark value of the multiple   In using the method of comparables, the value of a price multiple for the comparison asset; when we have comparison assets (a group), the mean or median value of the multiple for the group of assets.

Bernoulli random variable   A random variable having the outcomes 0 and 1.

Bernoulli trial   An experiment that can produce one of two outcomes.

Bill-and-hold basis   Sales on a bill-and-hold basis involve selling products but not delivering those products until a later date.

Binomial model   A model for pricing options in which the underlying price can move to only one of two possible new prices.

Binomial random variable   The number of successes in n Bernoulli trials for which the probability of success is constant for all trials and the trials are independent.

Binomial tree   The graphical representation of a model of asset price dynamics in which, at each period, the asset moves up with probability p or down with probability $(1 - p)$.

Block   Orders to buy or sell that are too large for the liquidity ordinarily available in dealer networks or stock exchanges.

Blockage factor   An illiquidity discount that occurs when an investor sells a large amount of stock relative to its trading volume (assuming it is not large enough to constitute a controlling ownership).

Bond equivalent yield   A calculation of yield that is annualized using the ratio of 365 to the number of days to maturity. Bond equivalent yield allows for the restatement and comparison of securities with different compounding periods.

Bond indenture   A legal contract specifying the terms of a bond issue.

Bond option   An option in which the underlying is a bond; primarily traded in over-the-counter markets.

Bond yield plus risk premium approach   An estimate of the cost of common equity that is produced by summing the before-tax cost of debt and a risk premium that captures the additional yield on a company's stock relative to its bonds. The additional yield is often estimated using historical spreads between bond yields and stock yields.

Bond-equivalent basis   A basis for stating an annual yield that annualizes a semiannual yield by doubling it.

Bond-equivalent yield   The yield to maturity on a basis that ignores compounding.

Bonding costs   Costs borne by management to assure owners that they are working in the owners' best interest (e.g., implicit cost of non-compete agreements).

Book value equity per share   The amount of book value (also called carrying value) of common equity per share of common stock, calculated by dividing the book value of shareholders' equity by the number of shares of common stock outstanding.

Book value of equity (or book value)   Shareholders' equity (total assets minus total liabilities) minus the value of preferred stock; common shareholders' equity.

Bootstrapping earnings   An increase in a company's earnings that results as a consequence of the idiosyncrasies of a merger transaction itself rather than because of resulting economic benefits of the combination.

Bottom-up analysis   With reference to investment selection processes, an approach that involves selection from all securities within a specified investment universe, i.e., without prior narrowing of the universe on the basis of macroeconomic or overall market considerations.

Bottom-up forecasting approach   A forecasting approach that involves aggregating the individual company forecasts of analysts into industry forecasts, and finally into macroeconomic forecasts.

Bottom-up investing   An approach to investing that focuses on the individual characteristics of securities rather than on macroeconomic or overall market forecasts.

Box spread   An option strategy that combines a bull spread and a bear spread having two different exercise prices, which produces a risk-free payoff of the difference in the exercise prices.

Break point   In the context of the weighted average cost of capital (WACC), a break point is the amount of capital at which the cost of one or more of the sources of capital changes, leading to a change in the WACC.

Breakeven point   The number of units produced and sold at which the company's net income is zero (revenues = total costs).

Breakup value or **private market value**   The value derived using a sum-of-the-parts valuation.

Breusch–Pagan test A test for conditional heteroskedasticity in the error term of a regression.

Broker 1) An agent who executes orders to buy or sell securities on behalf of a client in exchange for a commission. 2) *See* Futures commission merchants.

Brokerage The business of acting as agents for buyers or sellers, usually in return for commissions.

Build-up method A method for determining the required rate of return on equity as the sum of risk premiums, in which one or more of the risk premiums is typically subjective rather than grounded in a formal equilibrium model.

Built-up method A method of identifying the basic elements of the overall capitalization rate.

Bull spread An option strategy that involves buying a call with a lower exercise price and selling a call with a higher exercise price. It can also be executed with puts.

Bundling Offering two or more products for sale as a set.

Business risk The risk associated with operating earnings. Operating earnings are uncertain because total revenues and many of the expenditures contributed to produce those revenues are uncertain.

Butterfly spread An option strategy that combines two bull or bear spreads and has three exercise prices.

Buy-side analysts Analysts who work for investment management firms, trusts, and bank trust departments, and similar institutions.

Call An option that gives the holder the right to buy an underlying asset from another party at a fixed price over a specific period of time.

Cannibalization Cannibalization occurs when an investment takes customers and sales away from another part of the company.

Cap 1) A contract on an interest rate, whereby at periodic payment dates, the writer of the cap pays the difference between the market interest rate and a specified cap rate if, and only if, this difference is positive. This is equivalent to a stream of call options on the interest rate. 2) A combination of interest rate call options designed to hedge a borrower against rate increases on a floating-rate loan.

Capital account A record of foreign investment in a country minus its investment abroad.

Capital allocation line (CAL) A graph line that describes the combinations of expected return and standard deviation of return available to an investor from combining the optimal portfolio of risky assets with the risk-free asset.

Capital asset pricing model (CAPM) An equation describing the expected return on any asset (or portfolio) as a linear function of its beta relative to the market portfolio.

Capital budgeting The allocation of funds to relatively long-range projects or investments.

Capital charge The company's total cost of capital in money terms.

Capital market line (CML) The line with an intercept point equal to the risk-free rate that is tangent to the efficient frontier of risky assets; represents the efficient frontier when a risk-free asset is available for investment.

Capital rationing A capital rationing environment assumes that the company has a fixed amount of funds to invest.

Capital structure The mix of debt and equity that a company uses to finance its business; a company's specific mixture of long-term financing.

Capitalization rate The divisor in the expression for the value of a perpetuity.

Capitalized cash flow model (method) In the context of private company valuation, valuation model based on an assumption of a constant growth rate of free cash flow to the firm or a constant growth rate of free cash flow to equity.

Capitalized inventory costs Costs of inventories including costs of purchase, costs of conversion, other costs to bring the inventories to their present location and condition, and the allocated portion of fixed production overhead costs.

Caplet Each component call option in a cap.

Capped swap A swap in which the floating payments have an upper limit.

Captive finance subsidiary A wholly-owned subsidiary of a company that is established to provide financing of the sales of the parent company.

Capture hypothesis A theory of regulatory behavior that predicts that regulators will eventually be captured by special interests of the industry being regulated.

Carried interest A share of any profits that is paid to the general partner (manager) of an investment partnership, such as a private equity or hedge fund, as a form of compensation designed to be an incentive to the manager to maximize performance of the investment fund.

Carrying amount (book value) The amount at which an asset or liability is valued according to accounting principles.

Cash In accounting contexts, cash on hand (e.g., petty cash and cash not yet deposited to the bank) and demand deposits held in banks and similar accounts that can be used in payment of obligations.

Cash basis Accounting method in which the only relevant transactions for the financial statements are those that involve cash.

Cash conversion cycle (net operating cycle) A financial metric that measures the length of time required for a company to convert cash invested in its operations to cash received as a result of its operations; equal to days of inventory on hand + days of sales outstanding − number of days of payables.

Cash equivalents Very liquid short-term investments, usually maturing in 90 days or less.

Cash flow additivity principle The principle that dollar amounts indexed at the same point in time are additive.

Cash flow at risk (CFAR) A variation of VAR that reflects the risk of a company's cash flow instead of its market value.

Cash flow from operations (cash flow from operating activities or **operating cash flow)** The net amount of cash provided from operating activities.

Cash flow statement (statement of cash flows) A financial statement that reconciles beginning-of-period and end-of-period balance sheet values of cash; consists of three parts: cash flows from operating activities, cash flows from investing activities, and cash flows from financing activities.

Cash offering A merger or acquisition that is to be paid for with cash; the cash for the merger might come from the acquiring company's existing assets or from a debt issue.

Cash price or **spot price** The price for immediate purchase of the underlying asset.

Cash ratio A liquidity ratio calculated as (cash + short-term marketable investments) divided by current liabilities; measures a company's ability to meet its current obligations with just the cash and cash equivalents on hand.

Cash settlement A procedure used in certain derivative transactions that specifies that the long and short parties engage in the equivalent cash value of a delivery transaction.

Cash-flow-statement-based accruals ratio The difference between reported net income on an accrual basis and the cash flows from operating and investing activities compared to the average net operating assets over the period.

Cash-flow-statement-based aggregate accruals The difference between reported net income on an accrual basis and the cash flows from operating and investing activities.

Cash-generating unit The smallest identifiable group of assets that generates cash inflows that are largely independent of the cash inflows of other assets or groups of assets.

Catalyst An event or piece of information that causes the marketplace to re-evaluate the prospects of a company.

Central limit theorem A result in statistics that states that the sample mean computed from large samples of size n from a population with finite variance will follow an approximate normal distribution with a mean equal to the population mean and a variance equal to the population variance divided by n.

Centralized risk management or **companywide risk management** When a company has a single risk management group that monitors and controls all of the risk-taking activities of the organization. Centralization permits economies of scale and allows a company to use some of its risks to offset other risks. (See also *enterprise risk management*.)

Chain rule of forecasting A forecasting process in which the next period's value as predicted by the forecasting equation is substituted into the right-hand side of the equation to give a predicted value two periods ahead.

Chart of accounts A list of accounts used in an entity's accounting system.

Cheapest to deliver A bond in which the amount received for delivering the bond is largest compared with the amount paid in the market for the bond.

Cherry-picking When a bankrupt company is allowed to enforce contracts that are favorable to it while walking away from contracts that are unfavorable to it.

Classical growth theory A theory of economic growth based on the view that the growth of real GDP per person is temporary and that when it rises above subsistence level, a population explosion eventually brings it back to subsistence level.

Classified balance sheet A balance sheet organized so as to group together the various assets and liabilities into subcategories (e.g., current and noncurrent).

Clean surplus accounting Accounting that satisfies the condition that all changes in the book value of equity other than transactions with owners are reflected in income. The bottom-line income reflects all changes in shareholders' equity arising from other than owner transactions. In the absence of owner transactions, the change in shareholders' equity should equal net income. No adjustments such as translation adjustments bypass the income statement and go directly to shareholders equity.

Clean surplus relation The relationship between earnings, dividends, and book value in which ending book value is equal to the beginning book value plus earnings less dividends, apart from ownership transactions.

Clearinghouse An entity associated with a futures market that acts as middleman between the contracting parties and guarantees to each party the performance of the other.

Clientele effect The preference some investors have for shares that exhibit certain characteristics.

Closeout netting Netting the market values of *all* derivative contracts between two parties to determine one overall value owed by one party to another in the event of bankruptcy.

Coefficient of variation (CV) The ratio of a set of observations' standard deviation to the observations' mean value.

Cointegrated Describes two time series that have a long-term financial or economic relationship such that they do not diverge from each other without bound in the long run.

Collar An option strategy involving the purchase of a put and sale of a call in which the holder of an asset gains protection below a certain level, the exercise price of the put, and pays for it by giving up gains above a certain level, the exercise price of the call. Collars also can be used to provide protection against rising interest rates on a floating-rate loan by giving up gains from lower interest rates.

Combination A listing in which the order of the listed items does not matter.

Commercial paper Unsecured short-term corporate debt that is characterized by a single payment at maturity.

Committed lines of credit A bank commitment to extend credit up to a pre-specified amount; the commitment is considered a short-term liability and is usually in effect for 364 days (one day short of a full year).

Commodity forward A contract in which the underlying asset is oil, a precious metal, or some other commodity.

Commodity futures Futures contracts in which the underlying is a traditional agricultural, metal, or petroleum product.

Commodity option An option in which the asset underlying the futures is a commodity, such as oil, gold, wheat, or soybeans.

Commodity swap A swap in which the underlying is a commodity such as oil, gold, or an agricultural product.

Common size statements Financial statements in which all elements (accounts) are stated as a percentage of a key figure such as revenue for an income statement or total assets for a balance sheet.

Common-size analysis The restatement of financial statement items using a common denominator or reference item that allows one to identify trends and major differences; an example is an income statement in which all items are expressed as a percent of revenue.

Company fundamental factors Factors related to the company's internal performance, such as factors relating to earnings growth, earnings variability, earnings momentum, and financial leverage.

Company share-related factors Valuation measures and other factors related to share price or the trading characteristics of the shares, such as earnings yield, dividend yield, and book-to-market value.

Comparable company A company that has similar business risk; usually in the same industry and preferably with a single line of business.

Comparables (comps, guideline assets, guideline companies) Assets used as benchmarks when applying the method of comparables to value an asset.

Comparative advantage A person or country has a comparative advantage in an activity if that person or country can perform the activity at a lower opportunity cost than anyone else or any other country.

Compiled financial statements Financial statements that are not accompanied by an auditor's opinion letter.

Complement In probability, with reference to an event S, the event that S does not occur; in economics, a good that is used in conjunction with another good.

Completed contract A method of revenue recognition in which the company does not recognize any revenue until the contract is completed; used particularly in long-term construction contracts.

Component cost of capital The rate of return required by suppliers of capital for an individual source of a company's funding, such as debt or equity.

Compounding The process of accumulating interest on interest.

Comprehensive income All changes in equity other than contributions by, and distributions to, owners; income under clean surplus accounting; includes all changes in equity during a period except those resulting from investments by owners and distributions to owners; comprehensive income equals net income plus other comprehensive income.

Conditional expected value The expected value of a stated event given that another event has occurred.

Conditional heteroskedasticity Heteroskedasticity in the error variance that is correlated with the values of the independent variable(s) in the regression.

Conditional probability The probability of an event given (conditioned on) another event.

Conditional variances The variance of one variable, given the outcome of another.

Confidence interval A range that has a given probability that it will contain the population parameter it is intended to estimate.

Conglomerate discount The discount possibly applied by the market to the stock of a company operating in multiple, unrelated businesses.

Conglomerate merger A merger involving companies that are in unrelated businesses.

Consistent With reference to estimators, describes an estimator for which the probability of estimates close to the value of the population parameter increases as sample size increases.

Consolidation The combining of the results of operations of subsidiaries with the parent company to present financial statements as if they were a single economic unit. The assets, liabilities, revenues and expenses of the subsidiaries are combined with those of the parent company, eliminating intercompany transactions.

Constant dividend payout ratio policy A policy in which a constant percentage of net income is paid out in dividends.

Constant maturity swap or CMT swap A swap in which the floating rate is the rate on a security known as a constant maturity treasury or CMT security.

Constant maturity treasury or CMT A hypothetical U.S. Treasury note with a constant maturity. A CMT exists for various years in the range of 2 to 10.

Contango A situation in a futures market where the current futures price is greater than the current spot price for the underlying asset.

Contingent claims Derivatives in which the payoffs occur if a specific event occurs; generally referred to as options.

Contingent consideration Potential future payments to the seller that are contingent on the achievement of certain agreed on occurrences.

Continuing residual income Residual income after the forecast horizon.

Continuous random variable A random variable for which the range of possible outcomes is the real line (all real numbers between ($-\infty$ and $+\infty$) or some subset of the real line.

Continuous time Time thought of as advancing in extremely small increments.

Continuously compounded return The natural logarithm of 1 plus the holding period return, or equivalently, the natural logarithm of the ending price over the beginning price.

Contra account An account that offsets another account.

Contribution margin The amount available for fixed costs and profit after paying variable costs; revenue minus variable costs.

Control premium An increment or premium to value associated with a controlling ownership interest in a company.

Controlling interest An investment where the investor exerts control over the investee, typically by having a greater than 50 percent ownership in the investee.

Convenience yield The nonmonetary return offered by an asset when the asset is in short supply, often associated with assets with seasonal production processes.

Conventional cash flow A conventional cash flow pattern is one with an initial outflow followed by a series of inflows.

Conversion factor An adjustment used to facilitate delivery on bond futures contracts in which any of a number of bonds with different characteristics are eligible for delivery.

Convertible debt Debt with the added feature that the bondholder has the option to exchange the debt for equity at prespecified terms.

Corporate governance The system of principles, policies, procedures, and clearly defined responsibilities and accountabilities used by stakeholders to overcome the conflicts of interest inherent in the corporate form.

Corporate raider A person or organization seeking to profit by acquiring a company and reselling it, or seeking to profit from the takeover attempt itself (e.g., greenmail).

Corporation A legal entity with rights similar to those of a person. The chief officers, executives, or top managers act as agents for the firm and are legally entitled to authorize corporate activities and to enter into contracts on behalf of the business.

Correlation A number between -1 and $+1$ that measures the co-movement (linear association) between two random variables.

Correlation analysis The analysis of the strength of the linear relationship between two data series.

Cost approach to value A method of valuing property based on site value plus current construction costs less accrued depreciation.

Cost averaging The periodic investment of a fixed amount of money.

Cost leadership The competitive strategy of being the lowest cost producer while offering products comparable to those of other firms, so that products can be priced at or near the industry average.

Cost of capital The rate of return that suppliers of capital require as compensation for their contribution of capital.

Cost of carry The cost associated with holding some asset, including financing, storage, and insurance costs. Any yield received on the asset is treated as a negative carrying cost.

Cost of carry model A model for pricing futures contracts in which the futures price is determined by adding the cost of carry to the spot price.

Cost of debt The cost of debt financing to a company, such as when it issues a bond or takes out a bank loan.

Cost of equity The required rate of return on common stock.

Cost of goods sold For a given period, equal to beginning inventory minus ending inventory plus the cost of goods acquired or produced during the period.

Cost of preferred stock The cost to a company of issuing preferred stock; the dividend yield that a company must commit to pay preferred stockholders.

Cost recovery method A method of revenue recognition in which the seller does not report any profit until the cash amounts paid by the buyer—including principal and interest on any financing from the seller—are greater than all the seller's costs for the merchandise sold.

Cost structure The mix of a company's variable costs and fixed costs.

Cost-of-service regulation Regulation that allows prices to reflect only the actual average cost of production and no monopoly profits.

Covariance   A measure of the co-movement (linear association) between two random variables.

Covariance matrix   A matrix or square array whose entries are covariances; also known as a variance–covariance matrix.

Covariance stationary   Describes a time series when its expected value and variance are constant and finite in all periods and when its covariance with itself for a fixed number of periods in the past or future is constant and finite in all periods.

Covered call   An option strategy involving the holding of an asset and sale of a call on the asset.

Covered interest arbitrage   A transaction executed in the foreign exchange market in which a currency is purchased (sold) and a forward contract is sold (purchased) to lock in the exchange rate for future delivery of the currency. This transaction should earn the risk-free rate of the investor's home country.

Crawling peg   A policy regime is one that selects a target path for the exchange rate with intervention in the foreign exchange market to achieve that path.

Creative response   Behavior on the part of a firm that allows it to comply with the letter of the law but violate the spirit, significantly lessening the law's effects.

Credit   With respect to double-entry accounting, a credit records increases in liability, owners' equity, and revenue accounts or decreases in asset accounts; with respect to borrowing, the willingness and ability of the borrower to make promised payments on the borrowing.

Credit analysis   The evaluation of credit risk; the evaluation of the creditworthiness of a borrower or counterparty.

Credit derivatives   A contract in which one party has the right to claim a payment from another party in the event that a specific credit event occurs over the life of the contract.

Credit risk or **default risk**   The risk of loss caused by a counterparty's or debtor's failure to make a promised payment.

Credit scoring model   A statistical model used to classify borrowers according to creditworthiness.

Credit spread option   An option on the yield spread on a bond.

Credit swap   A type of swap transaction used as a credit derivative in which one party makes periodic payments to the other and receives the promise of a payoff if a third party defaults.

Credit VAR, **default VAR**, or **credit at risk**   A variation of VAR that reflects credit risk.

Credit-linked notes   Fixed-income securities in which the holder of the security has the right to withhold payment of the full amount due at maturity if a credit event occurs.

Creditor nation   A country that during its entire history has invested more in the rest of the world than other countries have invested in it.

Creditworthiness   The perceived ability of the borrower to pay what is owed on the borrowing in a timely manner; it represents the ability of a company to withstand adverse impacts on its cash flows.

Cross-product netting   Netting the market values of all contracts, not just derivatives, between parties.

Cross-sectional analysis   Analysis that involves comparisons across individuals in a group over a given time period or at a given point in time.

Cross-sectional data   Observations over individual units at a point in time, as opposed to time-series data.

Cumulative distribution function   A function giving the probability that a random variable is less than or equal to a specified value.

Cumulative relative frequency   For data grouped into intervals, the fraction of total observations that are less than the value of the upper limit of a stated interval.

Currency forward   A forward contract in which the underlying is a foreign currency.

Currency option   An option that allows the holder to buy (if a call) or sell (if a put) an underlying currency at a fixed exercise rate, expressed as an exchange rate.

Currency swap   A swap in which each party makes interest payments to the other in different currencies.

Current account   A record of receipts from exports of goods and services, payments for imports of goods and services, net income and net transfers received from the rest of the world.

Current assets, or **liquid assets**   Assets that are expected to be consumed or converted into cash in the near future, typically one year or less.

Current cost   With reference to assets, the amount of cash or cash equivalents that would have to be paid to buy the same or an equivalent asset today; with reference to liabilities, the undiscounted amount of cash or cash equivalents that would be required to settle the obligation today.

Current credit risk   The risk associated with the possibility that a payment currently due will not be made.

Current exchange rate   For accounting purposes, the spot exchange rate on the balance sheet date.

Current liabilities   Short-term obligations, such as accounts payable, wages payable, or accrued liabilities, that are expected to be settled in the near future, typically one year or less.

Current rate method   Approach to translating foreign currency financial statements for consolidation in which all assets and liabilities are translated at the current exchange rate. The current rate method is the prevalent method of translation.

Current ratio   A liquidity ratio calculated as current assets divided by current liabilities.

Current taxes payable   Tax expenses that have been recognized and recorded on a company's income statement but which have not yet been paid.

Cyclical businesses   Businesses with high sensitivity to business- or industry-cycle influences.

Daily settlement   See *Marking to market.*

Data mining   The practice of determining a model by extensive searching through a dataset for statistically significant patterns.

Day trader   A trader holding a position open somewhat longer than a scalper but closing all positions at the end of the day.

Days of inventory on hand (DOH)   An activity ratio equal to the number of days in the period divided by inventory turnover over the period.

Days of sales outstanding (DSO)   An activity ratio equal to the number of days in period divided by receivables turnover.

Dead-hand provision   A poison pill provision that allows for the redemption or cancellation of a poison pill provision only by a vote of continuing directors (generally directors who were on the target company's board prior to the takeover attempt).

Dealing securities   Securities held by banks or other financial intermediaries for trading purposes.

Debit   With respect to double-entry accounting, a debit records increases of asset and expense accounts or decreases in liability and owners' equity accounts.

Debt covenants   Agreements between the company as borrower and its creditors.

Debt incurrence test   A financial covenant made in conjunction with existing debt that restricts a company's ability to incur additional debt at the same seniority based on one or more financial tests or conditions.

Debt rating approach A method for estimating a company's before-tax cost of debt based upon the yield on comparably rated bonds for maturities that closely match that of the company's existing debt.

Debt ratings An objective measure of the quality and safety of a company's debt based upon an analysis of the company's ability to pay the promised cash flows, as well as an analysis of any indentures.

Debt with warrants Debt issued with warrants that give the bondholder the right to purchase equity at prespecified terms.

Debtor nation A country that during its entire history has borrowed more in the rest of the world than other countries have lent in it.

Debt-to-assets ratio A solvency ratio calculated as total debt divided by total assets.

Debt-to-capital ratio A solvency ratio calculated as total debt divided by total debt plus total shareholders' equity.

Debt-to-equity ratio A solvency ratio calculated as total debt divided by total shareholders' equity.

Decentralized risk management A system that allows individual units within an organization to manage risk. Decentralization results in duplication of effort but has the advantage of having people closer to the risk be more directly involved in its management.

Deciles Quantiles that divide a distribution into 10 equal parts.

Decision rule With respect to hypothesis testing, the rule according to which the null hypothesis will be rejected or not rejected; involves the comparison of the test statistic to rejection point(s).

Declaration date The day that the corporation issues a statement declaring a specific dividend.

Deductible temporary differences Temporary differences that result in a reduction of or deduction from taxable income in a future period when the balance sheet item is recovered or settled.

Deep in the money Options that are far in-the-money.

Deep out of the money Options that are far out-of-the-money.

Default risk premium An extra return that compensates investors for the possibility that the borrower will fail to make a promised payment at the contracted time and in the contracted amount.

Defensive interval ratio A liquidity ratio that estimates the number of days that an entity could meet cash needs from liquid assets; calculated as (cash + short-term marketable investments + receivables) divided by daily cash expenditures.

Deferred tax assets A balance sheet asset that arises when an excess amount is paid for income taxes relative to accounting profit. The taxable income is higher than accounting profit and income tax payable exceeds tax expense. The company expects to recover the difference during the course of future operations when tax expense exceeds income tax payable.

Deferred tax liabilities A balance sheet liability that arises when a deficit amount is paid for income taxes relative to accounting profit. The taxable income is less than the accounting profit and income tax payable is less than tax expense. The company expects to eliminate the liability over the course of future operations when income tax payable exceeds tax expense.

Defined benefit obligation Under IFRS, the liability of a defined benefit pension.

Defined-benefit pension plans Plan in which the company promises to pay a certain annual amount (defined benefit) to the employee after retirement. The company bears the investment risk of the plan assets.

Defined-contribution pension plans Individual accounts to which an employee and typically the employer makes contributions, generally on a tax-advantaged basis. The amounts of contributions are defined at the outset, but the future value of the benefit is unknown. The employee bears the investment risk of the plan assets.

Definition of value (or **standard of value**) A specification of how "value" is to be understood in the context of a specific valuation.

Definitive merger agreement A contract signed by both parties to a merger that clarifies the details of the transaction, including the terms, warranties, conditions, termination details, and the rights of all parties.

Degree of confidence The probability that a confidence interval includes the unknown population parameter.

Degree of financial leverage (DFL) The ratio of the percentage change in net income to the percentage change in operating income; the sensitivity of the cash flows available to owners when operating income changes.

Degree of operating leverage (DOL) The ratio of the percentage change in operating income to the percentage change in units sold; the sensitivity of operating income to changes in units sold.

Degree of total leverage The ratio of the percentage change in net income to the percentage change in units sold; the sensitivity of the cash flows to owners to changes in the number of units produced and sold.

Degrees of freedom (df) The number of independent observations used.

Delivery A process used in a deliverable forward contract in which the long pays the agreed-upon price to the short, which in turn delivers the underlying asset to the long.

Delivery option The feature of a futures contract giving the short the right to make decisions about what, when, and where to deliver.

Delta The relationship between the option price and the underlying price, which reflects the sensitivity of the price of the option to changes in the price of the underlying.

Delta hedge An option strategy in which a position in an asset is converted to a risk-free position with a position in a specific number of options. The number of options per unit of the underlying changes through time, and the position must be revised to maintain the hedge.

Delta-normal method A measure of VAR equivalent to the analytical method but that refers to the use of delta to estimate the option's price sensitivity.

Dependent With reference to events, the property that the probability of one event occurring depends on (is related to) the occurrence of another event.

Dependent variable The variable whose variation about its mean is to be explained by the regression; the left-hand-side variable in a regression equation.

Depreciation The process of systematically allocating the cost of long-lived (tangible) assets to the periods during which the assets are expected to provide economic benefits.

Deregulation The elimination or phasing out of regulations on economic activity.

Derivative A financial instrument whose value depends on the value of some underlying asset or factor (e.g., a stock price, an interest rate, or exchange rate).

Derivatives dealers Commercial and investment banks that make markets in derivatives.

Descriptive statistics The study of how data can be summarized effectively.

Designated fair value instruments Financial instruments that an entity chooses to measure at fair value per IAS 39 or SFAS 159. Generally, the election to use the fair value option is irrevocable.

Diff swaps A swap in which the payments are based on the difference between interest rates in two countries but payments are made in only a single currency.

Differential expectations Expectations that differ from consensus expectations.

Differentiation The competitive strategy of offering unique products or services along some dimensions that are widely valued by buyers so that the firm can command premium prices.

Diffuse prior The assumption of equal prior probabilities.

Diluted earnings per share (diluted EPS) Net income, minus preferred dividends, divided by the number of common shares outstanding considering all dilutive securities (e.g., convertible debt and options); the EPS that would result if all dilutive securities were converted into common shares.

Diluted shares The number of shares that would be outstanding if all potentially dilutive claims on common shares (e.g., convertible debt, convertible preferred stock, and employee stock options) were exercised.

Dilution A reduction in proportional ownership interest as a result of the issuance of new shares.

Diminishing balance method An accelerated depreciation method, i.e., one that allocates a relatively large proportion of the cost of an asset to the early years of the asset's useful life.

Direct debit program An arrangement whereby a customer authorizes a debit to a demand account; typically used by companies to collect routine payments for services.

Direct financing lease A type of finance lease, from a lessor perspective, where the present value of the lease payments (lease receivable) equals the carrying value of the leased asset. The revenues earned by the lessor are financing in nature.

Direct format (direct method) With reference to the cash flow statement, a format for the presentation of the statement in which cash flow from operating activities is shown as operating cash receipts less operating cash disbursements.

Direct income capitalization approach Division of net operating income by an overall capitalization rate to arrive at market value.

Direct sales-comparison approach Method of valuing property based on recent sales prices of similar properties.

Direct write-off method An approach to recognizing credit losses on customer receivables in which the company waits until such time as a customer has defaulted and only then recognizes the loss.

Dirty surplus accounting Accounting in which some income items are reported as part of stockholders' equity rather than as gains and losses on the income statement; certain items of comprehensive income bypass the income statement and appear as direct adjustments to shareholders' equity.

Dirty surplus items Items that affect comprehensive income but which bypass the income statement.

Disbursement float The amount of time between check issuance and a check's clearing back against the company's account.

Discount To reduce the value of a future payment in allowance for how far away it is in time; to calculate the present value of some future amount. Also, the amount by which an instrument is priced below its face value.

Discount for lack of control An amount or percentage deducted from the pro rata share of 100 percent of the value of an equity interest in a business to reflect the absence of some or all of the powers of control.

Discount for lack of marketability An amount or percentage deducted from the value of an ownership interest to reflect the relative absence of marketability.

Discount interest A procedure for determining the interest on a loan or bond in which the interest is deducted from the face value in advance.

Discount rate Any rate used in finding the present value of a future cash flow.

Discounted cash flow analysis In the context of merger analysis, it is an estimate of a target company's value found by discounting the company's expected future free cash flows to the present.

Discrete random variable A random variable that can take on at most a countable number of possible values.

Discrete time Time thought of as advancing in distinct finite increments.

Discriminant analysis A multivariate classification technique used to discriminate between groups, such as companies that either will or will not become bankrupt during some time frame.

Dispersion The variability around the central tendency.

Divestiture The sale, liquidation, or spin-off of a division or subsidiary.

Dividend coverage ratio The ratio of net income to dividends.

Dividend discount model (DDM) A present value model of stock value that views the intrinsic value of a stock as present value of the stock's expected future dividends.

Dividend discount model based approach An approach for estimating a country's equity risk premium. The market rate of return is estimated as the sum of the dividend yield and the growth rate in dividends for a market index. Subtracting the risk-free rate of return from the estimated market return produces an estimate for the equity risk premium.

Dividend displacement of earnings The concept that dividends paid now displace earnings in all future periods.

Dividend imputation tax system A taxation system which effectively assures that corporate profits distributed as dividends are taxed just once, at the shareholder's tax rate.

Dividend policy The strategy a company follows with regard to the amount and timing of dividend payments.

Dividend payout ratio The ratio of cash dividends paid to earnings for a period.

Dividend rate The most recent quarterly dividend multiplied by four.

Dividends per share The dollar amount of cash dividends paid during a period per share of common stock.

Double declining balance depreciation An accelerated depreciation method that involves depreciating the asset at double the straight-line rate. This rate is multiplied by the book value of the asset at the beginning of the period (a declining balance) to calculate depreciation expense.

Double taxation system Corporate earnings are taxed twice when paid out as dividends. First, corporate earnings are taxed regardless of whether they will be distributed as dividends or retained at the G-13 corporate level, and second, dividends are taxed again at the individual shareholder level.

Double-entry accounting The accounting system of recording transactions in which every recorded transaction affects at least two accounts so as to keep the basic accounting equation (assets = liabilities + owners' equity) in balance.

Down transition probability The probability that an asset's value moves down in a model of asset price dynamics.

Downstream A transaction between two affiliates, an investor company and an associate company such that the investor company records a profit on its income statement. An example is a sale of inventory by the investor company to the associate.

Drag on liquidity   When receipts lag, creating pressure from the decreased available funds.

Due diligence   Investigation and analysis in support of a recommendation; the failure to exercise due diligence may sometimes result in liability according to various securities laws.

Dummy variable   A type of qualitative variable that takes on a value of 1 if a particular condition is true and 0 if that condition is false.

Dumping   The sale by a foreign firm of exports at a lower price than the cost of production.

DuPont analysis   An approach to decomposing return on investment, e.g., return on equity, as the product of other financial ratios.

Duration   A measure of an option-free bond's average maturity. Specifically, the weighted average maturity of all future cash flows paid by a security, in which the weights are the present value of these cash flows as a fraction of the bond's price. A measure of a bond's price sensitivity to interest rate movements.

Dutch Book theorem   A result in probability theory stating that inconsistent probabilities create profit opportunities.

Dynamic hedging   A strategy in which a position is hedged by making frequent adjustments to the quantity of the instrument used for hedging in relation to the instrument being hedged.

Earnings at risk (EAR)   A variation of VAR that reflects the risk of a company's earnings instead of its market value.

Earnings expectation management   Attempts by management to encourage analysts to forecast a slightly lower number for expected earnings than the analysts would otherwise forecast.

Earnings game   Management's focus on reporting earnings that meet consensus estimates.

Earnings management activity   Deliberate activity aimed at influencing reporting earnings numbers, often with the goal of placing management in a favorable light; the opportunistic use of accruals to manage earnings.

Earnings per share   The amount of income earned during a period per share of common stock.

Earnings yield   Earnings per share divided by price; the reciprocal of the P/E ratio.

Economic exposure   The risk associated with changes in the relative attractiveness of products and services offered for sale, arising out of the competitive effects of changes in exchange rates.

Economic growth   The expansion of production possibilities that results from capital accumulation and technological change.

Economic growth rate   The annual percentage change in real GDP.

Economic order quantity–reorder point   An approach to managing inventory based on expected demand and the predictability of demand; the ordering point for new inventory is determined based on the costs of ordering and carrying inventory, such that the total cost associated with inventory is minimized.

Economic profit   See *Residual income*.

Economic sectors   Large industry groupings.

Economic value added (EVA®)   A commercial implementation of the residual income concept; the computation of EVA® is the net operating profit after taxes minus the cost of capital, where these inputs are adjusted for a number of items.

Economies of scale   In reference to mergers, it is the savings achieved through the consolidation of operations and elimination of duplicate resources.

Effective annual rate   The amount by which a unit of currency will grow in a year with interest on interest included.

Effective annual yield (EAY)   An annualized return that accounts for the effect of interest on interest; EAY is computed by compounding 1 plus the holding period yield forward to one year, then subtracting 1.

Efficiency   In statistics, a desirable property of estimators; an efficient estimator is the unbiased estimator with the smallest variance among unbiased estimators of the same parameter.

Efficient frontier   The portion of the minimum-variance frontier beginning with the global minimum-variance portfolio and continuing above it; the graph of the set of portfolios offering the maximum expected return for their level of variance of return.

Efficient portfolio   A portfolio offering the highest expected return for a given level of risk as measured by variance or standard deviation of return.

Elasticity   A measure of sensitivity; the incremental change in one variable with respect to an incremental change in another variable.

Electronic funds transfer   The use of computer networks to conduct financial transactions electronically.

Empirical probability   The probability of an event estimated as a relative frequency of occurrence.

Enhanced derivatives products companies (EDPC)   A type of subsidiary engaged in derivatives transactions that is separated from the parent company in order to have a higher credit rating than the parent company.

Enterprise risk management   A form of *centralized risk management* that typically encompasses the management of a broad variety of risks, including insurance risk.

Enterprise value (EV)   Total company value (the market value of debt, common equity, and preferred equity) minus the value of cash and investments.

Enterprise value multiple   A valuation multiple that relates the total market value of all sources of a company's capital (net of cash) to a measure of fundamental value for the entire company (such as a pre-interest earnings measure).

Entry price   The price paid to buy an asset.

Equilibrium   The condition in which supply equals demand.

Equitizing cash   A strategy used to replicate an index. It is also used to take a given amount of cash and turn it into an equity position while maintaining the liquidity provided by the cash.

Equity   Assets less liabilities; the residual interest in the assets after subtracting the liabilities.

Equity carve-out   A form of restructuring that involves the creation of a new legal entity and the sale of equity in it to outsiders.

Equity charge   The estimated cost of equity capital in money terms.

Equity dividend rate   Income rate that reflects the relationship between equity income and equity capital.

Equity forward   A contract calling for the purchase of an individual stock, a stock portfolio, or a stock index at a later date at an agreed-upon price.

Equity method   A basis for reporting investment income in which the investing entity recognizes a share of income as earned rather than as dividends when received. These transactions are typically reflected in Investments in Associates or Equity Method Investments.

Equity options   Options on individual stocks; also known as stock options.

Equity risk premium   The expected return on equities minus the risk-free rate; the premium that investors demand for investing in equities.

Equity swap   A swap transaction in which at least one cash flow is tied to the return to an equity portfolio position, often an equity index.

Error autocorrelation   The autocorrelation of the error term.

Error term   The portion of the dependent variable that is not explained by the independent variable(s) in the regression.

Estimate   The particular value calculated from sample observations using an estimator.

Estimated (or **fitted**) **parameters**   With reference to regression analysis, the estimated values of the population intercept and population slope coefficient(s) in a regression.

Estimation   With reference to statistical inference, the subdivision dealing with estimating the value of a population parameter.

Estimator   An estimation formula; the formula used to compute the sample mean and other sample statistics are examples of estimators.

Eurodollar   A dollar deposited outside the United States.

European option   An option that can only be exercised on its expiration date.

Event   Any outcome or specified set of outcomes of a random variable.

Excess kurtosis   Degree of peakedness (fatness of tails) in excess of the peakedness of the normal distribution.

Exchange for physicals (EFP)   A permissible delivery procedure used by futures market participants, in which the long and short arrange a delivery procedure other than the normal procedures stipulated by the futures exchange.

Exchange rate   The value of the U.S. dollar in terms of other currencies in the foreign exchange market.

Exchange ratio   The number of shares that target stockholders are to receive in exchange for each of their shares in the target company.

Ex-dividend   Trading ex-dividend refers to shares that no longer carry the right to the next dividend payment.

Ex-dividend date   The first date that a share trades without (i.e., "ex") the dividend.

Ex-dividend price   The price at which a share first trades without (i.e., "ex") the right to receive an upcoming dividend.

Exercise or **exercising the option**   The process of using an option to buy or sell the underlying.

Exercise date   The day that employees actually exercise the options and convert them to stock.

Exercise price (strike price, striking price, or **strike)**   The fixed price at which an option holder can buy or sell the underlying.

Exercise rate or **strike rate**   The fixed rate at which the holder of an interest rate option can buy or sell the underlying.

Exhaustive   Covering or containing all possible outcomes.

Exit price   The price received to sell an asset or transfer a liability.

Expanded CAPM   An adaptation of the CAPM that adds to the CAPM a premium for small size and company-specific risk.

Expectational arbitrage   Investing on the basis of differential expectations.

Expected holding-period return   The expected total return on an asset over a stated holding period; for stocks, the sum of the expected dividend yield and the expected price appreciation over the holding period.

Expected value   The probability-weighted average of the possible outcomes of a random variable.

Expensed   Taken as a deduction in arriving at net income.

Expenses   Outflows of economic resources or increases in liabilities that result in decreases in equity (other than decreases because of distributions to owners); reductions in net assets associated with the creation of revenues.

Expiration date   The date on which a derivative contract expires.

Exports   The goods and services that we sell to people in other countries.

Exposure to foreign exchange risk   The risk of a change in value of an asset or liability denominated in a foreign currency due to a change in exchange rates.

External growth   Company growth in output or sales that is achieved by buying the necessary resources externally (i.e., achieved through mergers and acquisitions).

Externality   The effect of an investment on other things besides the investment itself.

Face value (also **principal, par value, stated value,** or **maturity value**)   The amount of cash payable by a company to the bondholders when the bonds mature; the promised payment at maturity separate from any coupon payment.

Factor   A common or underlying element with which several variables are correlated.

Factor risk premium (or **factor price**)   The expected return in excess of the risk-free rate for a portfolio with a sensitivity of 1 to one factor and a sensitivity of 0 to all other factors.

Factor sensitivity (also **factor betas** or **factor loadings**)   An asset's sensitivity to a particular factor; a measure of the response of return to each unit of increase in a factor, holding all other factors constant.

Fair market value   The market price of an asset or liability that trades regularly.

Fair value   The amount at which an asset (or liability) could be bought (or incurred) or sold (or settled) in a current transaction between willing parties, that is, other than in a forced or liquidation sale; the price that would be received to sell an asset or paid to transfer a liability in an orderly transaction between market participants at the measurement date.

Fiduciary call   A combination of a European call and a risk-free bond that matures on the option expiration day and has a face value equal to the exercise price of the call.

Finance lease (capital lease)   Essentially, the purchase of some asset by the buyer (lessee) that is directly financed by the seller (lessor).

Financial analysis   The process of selecting, evaluating, and interpreting financial data in order to formulate an assessment of a company's present and future financial condition and performance.

Financial distress   Heightened uncertainty regarding a company's ability to meet its various obligations because of lower or negative earnings.

Financial flexibility   The ability to react and adapt to financial adversities and opportunities.

Financial futures   Futures contracts in which the underlying is a stock, bond, or currency.

Financial leverage   The extent to which a company can effect, through the use of debt, a proportional change in the return on common equity that is greater than a given proportional change in operating income; also, short for the financial leverage ratio.

Financial leverage ratio   A measure of financial leverage calculated as average total assets divided by average total equity.

Financial reporting quality   The accuracy with which a company's reported financials reflect its operating performance and their usefulness for forecasting future cash flows.

Financial risk   The risk that environmental, social, or governance risk factors will result in significant costs or other losses to a company and its shareholders; the risk arising from a company's obligation to meet required payments under its financing agreements.

Financial transaction A purchase involving a buyer having essentially no material synergies with the target (e.g., the purchase of a private company by a company in an unrelated industry or by a private equity firm would typically be a financial transaction).

Financing activities Activities related to obtaining or repaying capital to be used in the business (e.g., equity and long-term debt).

First-differencing A transformation that subtracts the value of the time series in period $t - 1$ from its value in period t.

First-in, first-out (FIFO) The first in, first out, method of accounting for inventory, which matches sales against the costs of items of inventory in the order in which they were placed in inventory.

First-order serial correlation Correlation between adjacent observations in a time series.

Fixed asset turnover An activity ratio calculated as total revenue divided by average net fixed assets.

Fixed charge coverage A solvency ratio measuring the number of times interest and lease payments are covered by operating income, calculated as (EBIT + lease payments) divided by (interest payments + lease payments).

Fixed costs Costs that remain at the same level regardless of a company's level of production and sales.

Fixed exchange rate An exchange rate pegged at a value decided by the government or central bank and that blocks the unregulated forces of demand and supply by direct intervention in the foreign exchange market.

Fixed-income forward A forward contract in which the underlying is a bond.

Fixed-rate perpetual preferred stock Nonconvertible, noncallable preferred stock with a specified dividend rate that has a claim on earnings senior to the claim of common stock, and no maturity date.

Flexible exchange rate An exchange rate is determined by demand and supply with no direct intervention in the foreign exchange market by the central bank.

Flip-in pill A poison pill takeover defense that dilutes an acquirer's ownership in a target by giving other existing target company shareholders the right to buy additional target company shares at a discount.

Flip-over pill A poison pill takeover defense that gives target company shareholders the right to purchase shares of the acquirer at a significant discount to the market price, which has the effect of causing dilution to all existing acquiring company shareholders.

Float In the context of customer receipts, the amount of money that is in transit between payments made by customers and the funds that are usable by the company.

Float factor An estimate of the average number of days it takes deposited checks to clear; average daily float divided by average daily deposit.

Floating-rate loan A loan in which the interest rate is reset at least once after the starting date.

Floor A combination of interest rate put options designed to hedge a lender against lower rates on a floating-rate loan.

Floor traders or **locals** Market makers that buy and sell by quoting a bid and an ask price. They are the primary providers of liquidity to the market.

Floored swap A swap in which the floating payments have a lower limit.

Floorlet Each component put option in a floor.

Flotation cost Fees charged to companies by investment bankers and other costs associated with raising new capital.

Focus The competitive strategy of seeking a competitive advantage within a target segment or segments of the industry, either on the basis of cost leadership (**cost focus**) or differentiation (**differentiation focus**).

Foreign currency The money of other countries regardless of whether that money is in the form of notes, coins, or bank deposits.

Foreign currency transactions Transactions that are denominated in a currency other than a company's functional currency.

Foreign exchange market The market in which the currency of one country is exchanged for the currency of another.

Forward contract An agreement between two parties in which one party, the buyer, agrees to buy from the other party, the seller, an underlying asset at a later date for a price established at the start of the contract.

Forward dividend yield A dividend yield based on the anticipated dividend during the next 12 months.

Forward integration A merger involving the purchase of a target that is farther along the value or production chain; for example, to acquire a distributor.

Forward P/E (also **leading P/E** or **prospective P/E**) A P/E calculated on the basis of a forecast of EPS; a stock's current price divided by next year's expected earnings.

Forward price or **forward rate** The fixed price or rate at which the transaction scheduled to occur at the expiration of a forward contract will take place. This price is agreed on at the initiation date of the contract.

Forward rate agreement (FRA) A forward contract calling for one party to make a fixed interest payment and the other to make an interest payment at a rate to be determined at the contract expiration.

Forward swap A forward contract to enter into a swap.

Franking credit A tax credit received by shareholders for the taxes that a corporation paid on its distributed earnings.

Free cash flow The actual cash that would be available to the company's investors after making all investments necessary to maintain the company as an ongoing enterprise (also referred to as free cash flow to the firm); the internally generated funds that can be distributed to the company's investors (e.g., shareholders and bondholders) without impairing the value of the company.

Free cash flow hypothesis The hypothesis that higher debt levels discipline managers by forcing them to make fixed debt service payments and by reducing the company's free cash flow.

Free cash flow method Income approach that values an asset based on estimates of future cash flows discounted to present value by using a discount rate reflective of the risks associated with the cash flows.

Free cash flow to equity The cash flow available to a company's common shareholders after all operating expenses, interest, and principal payments have been made, and necessary investments in working and fixed capital have been made.

Free cash flow to equity model A model of stock valuation that views a stock's intrinsic value as the present value of expected future free cash flows to equity.

Free cash flow to the firm The cash flow available to the company's suppliers of capital after all operating expenses (including taxes) have been paid and necessary investments in working and fixed capital have been made.

Free cash flow to the firm model A model of stock valuation that views the value of a firm as the present value of expected future free cash flows to the firm.

Frequency distribution A tabular display of data summarized into a relatively small number of intervals.

Frequency polygon A graph of a frequency distribution obtained by drawing straight lines joining successive points representing the class frequencies.

Friendly transaction A potential business combination that is endorsed by the managers of both companies.

Full price   The price of a security with accrued interest.

Functional currency   The currency of the primary economic environment in which an entity operates.

Fundamental beta   A beta that is based at least in part on fundamental data for a company.

Fundamental factor models   A multifactor model in which the factors are attributes of stocks or companies that are important in explaining cross-sectional differences in stock prices.

Fundamentals   Economic characteristics of a business such as profitability, financial strength, and risk.

Future value (FV)   The amount to which a payment or series of payments will grow by a stated future date.

Futures commission merchants (FCMs)   Individuals or companies that execute futures transactions for other parties off the exchange.

Futures contract   A variation of a forward contract that has essentially the same basic definition but with some additional features, such as a clearinghouse guarantee against credit losses, a daily settlement of gains and losses, and an organized electronic or floor trading facility.

Futures exchange   A legal corporate entity whose shareholders are its members. The members of the exchange have the privilege of executing transactions directly on the exchange.

Gains   Asset inflows not directly related to the ordinary activities of the business.

Gamma   A numerical measure of how sensitive an option's delta is to a change in the underlying.

General Agreement on Tariffs and Trade   An international agreement signed in 1947 to reduce tariffs on international trade.

Generalized least squares   A regression estimation technique that addresses heteroskedasticity of the error term.

Geometric mean   A measure of central tendency computed by taking the nth root of the product of n non-negative values.

Giro system   An electronic payment system used widely in Europe and Japan.

Going-concern assumption   The assumption that the business will maintain its business activities into the foreseeable future.

Going-concern value   A business's value under a going-concern assumption.

Goodwill   An intangible asset that represents the excess of the purchase price of an acquired company over the value of the net assets acquired.

Government sector surplus or **deficit**   An amount equal to net taxes minus government expenditure on goods and services.

Grant date   The day that options are granted to employees; usually the date that compensation expense is measured if both the number of shares and option price are known.

Greenmail   The purchase of the accumulated shares of a hostile investor by a company that is targeted for takeover by that investor, usually at a substantial premium over market price.

Gross domestic product   A money measure of the goods and services produced within a country's borders over a stated time period.

Gross income multiplier (GIM)   A ratio derived from the market; sales price divided by annual gross income equals GIM.

Gross profit (gross margin)   Sales minus the cost of sales (i.e., the cost of goods sold for a manufacturing company).

Gross profit margin   The ratio of gross profit to revenues.

Grouping by function   With reference to the presentation of expenses in an income statement, the grouping together of expenses serving the same function, e.g., all items that are costs of good sold.

Grouping by nature   With reference to the presentation of expenses in an income statement, the grouping together of expenses by similar nature, e.g., all depreciation expenses.

Growth accounting   A tool that calculates the contribution to real GDP growth of each of its sources.

Growth investors   With reference to equity investors, investors who seek to invest in high-earnings-growth companies.

Growth option or **expansion option**   The ability to make additional investments in a project at some future time if the financial results are strong.

Growth phase   A stage of growth in which a company typically enjoys rapidly expanding markets, high profit margins, and an abnormally high growth rate in earnings per share.

Guideline public companies   Public-company comparables for the company being valued.

Guideline public company method   A variation of the market approach; establishes a value estimate based on the observed multiples from trading activity in the shares of public companies viewed as reasonably comparable to the subject private company.

Guideline transactions method   A variation of the market approach; establishes a value estimate based on pricing multiples derived from the acquisition of control of entire public or private companies that were acquired.

Harmonic mean   A type of weighted mean computed by averaging the reciprocals of the observations, then taking the reciprocal of that average.

Hedge ratio   The relationship of the quantity of an asset being hedged to the quantity of the derivative used for hedging.

Hedging   A general strategy usually thought of as reducing, if not eliminating, risk.

Held-for-trading securities (trading securities)   Debt or equity financial assets bought with the intention to sell them in the near term, usually less than three months; securities that a company intends to trade.

Held-to-maturity investments   Debt (fixed-income) securities that a company intends to hold to maturity; these are presented at their original cost, updated for any amortization of discounts or premiums.

Herfindahl–Hirschman Index   A measure of market concentration that is calculated by summing the squared market shares for competing companies in an industry; high HHI readings or mergers that would result in large HHI increases are more likely to result in regulatory challenges.

Heteroskedastic   With reference to the error term of a regression, having a variance that differs across observations.

Heteroskedasticity   The property of having a nonconstant variance; refers to an error term with the property that its variance differs across observations.

Heteroskedasticity-consistent standard errors   Standard errors of the estimated parameters of a regression that correct for the presence of heteroskedasticity in the regression's error term.

Histogram   A bar chart of data that have been grouped into a frequency distribution.

Historical cost   In reference to assets, the amount paid to purchase an asset, including any costs of acquisition and/or preparation; with reference to liabilities, the amount of proceeds received in exchange in issuing the liability.

Historical equity risk premium approach   An estimate of a country's equity risk premium that is based upon the historical averages of the risk-free rate and the rate of return on the market portfolio.

Historical exchange rates   For accounting purposes, the exchange rates that existed when the assets and liabilities were initially recorded.

Historical method   A method of estimating VAR that uses data from the returns of the portfolio over a recent past period and compiles this data in the form of a histogram.

Historical simulation (or **back simulation**) Another term for the historical method of estimating VAR. This term is somewhat misleading in that the method involves not a *simulation* of the past but rather what *actually happened* in the past, sometimes adjusted to reflect the fact that a different portfolio may have existed in the past than is planned for the future.

Holder-of-record date The date that a shareholder listed on the corporation's books will be deemed to have ownership of the shares for purposes of receiving an upcoming dividend; two business days after the ex-dividend date.

Holding period return The return that an investor earns during a specified holding period; a synonym for total return.

Holding period yield (HPY) The return that an investor earns during a specified holding period; holding period return with reference to a fixed-income instrument.

Homogenization Creating a contract with standard and generally accepted terms, which makes it more acceptable to a broader group of participants.

Homoskedasticity The property of having a constant variance; refers to an error term that is constant across observations.

Horizontal analysis Common-size analysis that involves comparing a specific financial statement with that statement in prior or future time periods; also, cross-sectional analysis of one company with another.

Horizontal common-size analysis A form of common-size analysis in which the accounts in a given period are used as the benchmark or base period, and every account is restated in subsequent periods as a percentage of the base period's same account.

Horizontal merger A merger involving companies in the same line of business, usually as competitors.

Hostile transaction An attempt to acquire a company against the wishes of the target's managers.

Human capital The value of skills and knowledge possessed by the workforce.

Hurdle rate The rate of return that must be met for a project to be accepted.

Hypothesis With reference to statistical inference, a statement about one or more populations.

Hypothesis testing With reference to statistical inference, the subdivision dealing with the testing of hypotheses about one or more populations.

Identifiable intangible An intangible that can be acquired singly and is typically linked to specific rights or privileges having finite benefit periods (e.g., a patent or trademark).

If-converted method A method for accounting for the effect of convertible securities on earnings per share (EPS) that specifies what EPS would have been if the convertible securities had been converted at the beginning of the period, taking account of the effects of conversion on net income and the weighted average number of shares outstanding.

Illiquidity discount See *Liquidity discount.*

Impairment Diminishment in value as a result of carrying (book) value exceeding fair value and/or recoverable value.

Impairment of capital rule A legal restriction that dividends cannot exceed retained earnings.

Implied repo rate The rate of return from a cash-and-carry transaction implied by the futures price relative to the spot price.

Implied volatility The volatility that option traders use to price an option, implied by the price of the option and a particular option-pricing model.

Implied yield A measure of the yield on the underlying bond of a futures contract implied by pricing it as though the underlying will be delivered at the futures expiration.

Imports The goods and services that we buy from people in other countries.

Imputation In reference to corporate taxes, a system that imputes, or attributes, taxes at only one level of taxation. For countries using an imputation tax system, taxes on dividends are effectively levied only at the shareholder rate. Taxes are paid at the corporate level but they are *attributed* to the shareholder. Shareholders deduct from their tax bill their portion of taxes paid by the company.

Income Increases in economic benefits in the form of inflows or enhancements of assets, or decreases of liabilities that result in an increase in equity (other than increases resulting from contributions by owners).

Income approach Valuation approach that values an asset as the present discounted value of the income expected from it.

Income statement (statement of operations or **profit and loss statement)** A financial statement that provides information about a company's profitability over a stated period of time.

Income tax paid The actual amount paid for income taxes in the period; not a provision, but the actual cash outflow.

Income tax payable The income tax owed by the company on the basis of taxable income.

Income tax recoverable The income tax expected to be recovered, from the taxing authority, on the basis of taxable income. It is a recovery of previously remitted taxes or future taxes owed by the company.

Incremental cash flow The cash flow that is realized because of a decision; the changes or increments to cash flows resulting from a decision or action.

Indenture A written contract between a lender and borrower that specifies the terms of the loan, such as interest rate, interest payment schedule, maturity, etc.

Independent With reference to events, the property that the occurrence of one event does not affect the probability of another event occurring.

Independent and identically distributed (IID) With respect to random variables, the property of random variables that are independent of each other but follow the identical probability distribution.

Independent projects Independent projects are projects whose cash flows are independent of each other.

Independent variable A variable used to explain the dependent variable in a regression; a right-hand-side variable in a regression equation.

Index amortizing swap An interest rate swap in which the notional principal is indexed to the level of interest rates and declines with the level of interest rates according to a predefined schedule. This type of swap is frequently used to hedge securities that are prepaid as interest rates decline, such as mortgage-backed securities.

Index option An option in which the underlying is a stock index.

Indexing An investment strategy in which an investor constructs a portfolio to mirror the performance of a specified index.

Indirect format (indirect method) With reference to cash flow statements, a format for the presentation of the statement which, in the operating cash flow section, begins with net income then shows additions and subtractions to arrive at operating cash flow.

Industry structure An industry's underlying economic and technical characteristics.

Infant-industry argument The argument that it is necessary to protect a new industry to enable it to grow into a mature industry that can compete in world markets.

Inflation premium An extra return that compensates investors for expected inflation.

Information ratio (IR) Mean active return divided by active risk; or alpha divided by the standard deviation of diversifiable risk.

Initial margin requirement The margin requirement on the first day of a transaction as well as on any day in which additional margin funds must be deposited.

Initial public offering (IPO) The initial issuance of common stock registered for public trading by a formerly private corporation.

In-process research and development Research and development costs relating to projects that are not yet completed, such as have been incurred by a company that is being acquired.

In-sample forecast errors The residuals from a fitted time-series model within the sample period used to fit the model.

Instability in the minimum-variance frontier The characteristic of minimum-variance frontiers that they are sensitive to small changes in inputs.

Installment Said of a sale in which proceeds are to be paid in installments over an extended period of time.

Installment method (installment-sales method) With respect to revenue recognition, a method that specifies that the portion of the total profit of the sale that is recognized in each period is determined by the percentage of the total sales price for which the seller has received cash.

Intangible assets Assets lacking physical substance, such as patents and trademarks.

Interest coverage A solvency ratio calculated as EBIT divided by interest payments.

Interest rate A rate of return that reflects the relationship between differently dated cash flows; a discount rate.

Interest rate call An option in which the holder has the right to make a known interest payment and receive an unknown interest payment.

Interest rate cap or **cap** A series of call options on an interest rate, with each option expiring at the date on which the floating loan rate will be reset, and with each option having the same exercise rate. A cap in general can have an underlying other than an interest rate.

Interest rate collar A combination of a long cap and a short floor, or a short cap and a long floor. A collar in general can have an underlying other than an interest rate.

Interest rate floor or **floor** A series of put options on an interest rate, with each option expiring at the date on which the floating loan rate will be reset, and with each option having the same exercise rate. A floor in general can have an underlying other than the interest rate.

Interest rate forward See *Forward rate agreement.*

Interest rate option An option in which the underlying is an interest rate.

Interest rate parity A formula that expresses the equivalence or parity of spot and forward rates, after adjusting for differences in the interest rates.

Interest rate put An option in which the holder has the right to make an unknown interest payment and receive a known interest payment.

Interest rate swap A swap in which the underlying is an interest rate. Can be viewed as a currency swap in which both currencies are the same and can be created as a combination of currency swaps.

Intergenerational data mining A form of data mining that applies information developed by previous researchers using a dataset to guide current research using the same or a related dataset.

Internal rate of return (IRR) Rate of return that discounts future cash flows from an investment to the exact amount of the investment; the discount rate that makes the present value of an investment's costs (outflows) equal to the present value of the investment's benefits (inflows).

Interquartile range The difference between the third and first quartiles of a dataset.

Interval With reference to grouped data, a set of values within which an observation falls.

Interval scale A measurement scale that not only ranks data but also gives assurance that the differences between scale values are equal.

In-the-money Options that, if exercised, would result in the value received being worth more than the payment required to exercise.

Intrinsic value or **exercise value** The value of an asset given a hypothetically complete understanding of the asset's investment characteristics; the value obtained if an option is exercised based on current conditions.

Inventory The unsold units of product on hand.

Inventory blanket lien The use of inventory as collateral for a loan. Though the lender has claim to some or all of the company's inventory, the company may still sell or use the inventory in the ordinary course of business.

Inventory turnover An activity ratio calculated as cost of goods sold divided by average inventory.

Inverse floater A floating-rate note or bond in which the coupon is adjusted to move opposite to a benchmark interest rate.

Inverse price ratio The reciprocal of a price multiple, e.g., in the case of a P/E ratio, the "earnings yield" E/P (where P is share price and E is earnings per share).

Investing activities Activities which are associated with the acquisition and disposal of property, plant, and equipment; intangible assets; other long-term assets; and both long-term and short-term investments in the equity and debt (bonds and loans) issued by other companies.

Investment constraints Internal or external limitations on investments.

Investment objectives Desired investment outcomes; includes risk objectives and return objectives.

Investment opportunity schedule A graphical depiction of a company's investment opportunities ordered from highest to lowest expected return. A company's optimal capital budget is found where the investment opportunity schedule intersects with the company's marginal cost of capital.

Investment strategy An approach to investment analysis and security selection.

Investment value The value to a specific buyer, taking account of potential synergies based on the investor's requirements and expectations.

IRR rule An investment decision rule that accepts projects or investments for which the IRR is greater than the opportunity cost of capital.

Joint probability The probability of the joint occurrence of stated events.

Joint probability function A function giving the probability of joint occurrences of values of stated random variables.

Joint venture An entity (partnership, corporation, or other legal form) where control is shared by two or more entities called venturers.

Justified (fundamental) P/E The price-to-earnings ratio that is fair, warranted, or justified on the basis of forecasted fundamentals.

Justified price multiple (or warranted price multiple or intrinsic price multiple) The estimated fair value of the price multiple, usually based on forecasted fundamentals or comparables.

Just-in-time method   Method of managing inventory that minimizes in-process inventory stocks.

***k*th order autocorrelation**   The correlation between observations in a time series separated by *k* periods.

Kurtosis   The statistical measure that indicates the peakedness of a distribution.

Labor productivity   The quantity of real GDP produced by an hour of labor.

Lack of marketability discount   An extra return to investors to compensate for lack of a public market or lack of marketability.

Laddering strategy   A form of active strategy which entails scheduling maturities on a systematic basis within the investment portfolio such that investments are spread out equally over the term of the ladder.

Last-in, first-out (LIFO)   The last in, first out, method of accounting for inventory, which matches sales against the costs of items of inventory in the reverse order the items were placed in inventory (i.e., inventory produced or acquired last are assumed to be sold first).

Law of one price   The condition in a financial market in which two equivalent financial instruments or combinations of financial instruments can sell for only one price. Equivalent to the principle that no arbitrage opportunities are possible.

Leading dividend yield   Forecasted dividends per share over the next year divided by current stock price.

Leading P/E (or forward P/E or prospective P/E)   A stock's current price divided by the next year's expected earnings.

Legal risk   The risk that failures by company managers to effectively manage a company's environmental, social, and governance risk exposures will lead to lawsuits and other judicial remedies, resulting in potentially catastrophic losses for the company; the risk that the legal system will not enforce a contract in case of dispute or fraud.

Legislative and regulatory risk   The risk that governmental laws and regulations directly or indirectly affecting a company's operations will change with potentially severe adverse effects on the company's continued profitability and even its long-term sustainability.

Lemons problem   The potential for asymmetric information to bring about a general decline in product quality in an industry.

Leptokurtic   Describes a distribution that is more peaked than a normal distribution.

Lessee   The party obtaining the use of an asset through a lease.

Lessor   The owner of an asset that grants the right to use the asset to another party.

Level of significance   The probability of a Type I error in testing a hypothesis.

Leverage   In the context of corporate finance, leverage refers to the use of fixed costs within a company's cost structure. Fixed costs that are operating costs (such as depreciation or rent) create operating leverage. Fixed costs that are financial costs (such as interest expense) create financial leverage.

Leveraged buyout (LBO)   A transaction whereby the target company management team converts the target to a privately held company by using heavy borrowing to finance the purchase of the target company's outstanding shares.

Leveraged floating-rate note or **leveraged floater**   A floating-rate note or bond in which the coupon is adjusted at a multiple of a benchmark interest rate.

Leveraged recapitalization   A post-offer takeover defense mechanism that involves the assumption of a large amount of debt that is then used to finance share repurchases; the effect is to dramatically change the company's capital structure while

attempting to deliver a value to target shareholders in excess of a hostile bid.

Liabilities   Present obligations of an enterprise arising from past events, the settlement of which is expected to result in an outflow of resources embodying economic benefits; creditors' claims on the resources of a company.

LIFO layer liquidation (LIFO liquidation)   With respect to the application of the LIFO inventory method, the liquidation of old, relatively low-priced inventory; happens when the volume of sales rises above the volume of recent purchases so that some sales are made from relatively old, low-priced inventory.

LIFO reserve   The difference between inventory reported as FIFO and inventory reported as LIFO (FIFO inventory value less LIFO inventory value).

Likelihood   The probability of an observation, given a particular set of conditions.

Limit down   A limit move in the futures market in which the price at which a transaction would be made is at or below the lower limit.

Limit move   A condition in the futures markets in which the price at which a transaction would be made is at or beyond the price limits.

Limit up   A limit move in the futures market in which the price at which a transaction would be made is at or above the upper limit.

Linear association   A straight-line relationship, as opposed to a relationship that cannot be graphed as a straight line.

Linear interpolation   The estimation of an unknown value on the basis of two known values that bracket it, using a straight line between the two known values.

Linear regression   Regression that models the straight-line relationship between the dependent and independent variable(s).

Linear trend   A trend in which the dependent variable changes at a constant rate with time.

Liquidation   To sell the assets of a company, division, or subsidiary piecemeal, typically because of bankruptcy; the form of bankruptcy that allows for the orderly satisfaction of creditors' claims after which the company ceases to exist.

Liquidation value   The value of a company if the company were dissolved and its assets sold individually.

Liquidity   A company's ability to satisfy its short-term obligations using assets that are most readily converted into cash; the ability to trade a futures contract, either selling a previously purchased contract or purchasing a previously sold contract.

Liquidity discount   A reduction or discount to value that reflects the lack of depth of trading or liquidity in that asset's market.

Liquidity premium   An extra return that compensates investors for the risk of loss relative to an investment's fair value if the investment needs to be converted to cash quickly.

Liquidity ratios   Financial ratios measuring the company's ability to meet its short-term obligations.

Liquidity risk   The risk that a financial instrument cannot be purchased or sold without a significant concession in price due to the size of the market.

Local currency   The currency of the country where a company is located.

Lockbox system   A payment system in which customer payments are mailed to a post office box and the banking institution retrieves and deposits these payments several times a day, enabling the company to have use of the fund sooner than in a centralized system in which customer payments are sent to the company.

Locked limit   A condition in the futures markets in which a transaction cannot take place because the price would be beyond the limits.

Logit model A qualitative-dependent-variable multiple regression model based on the logistic probability distribution.

Log-linear model With reference to time-series models, a model in which the growth rate of the time series as a function of time is constant.

Log-log regression model A regression that expresses the dependent and independent variables as natural logarithms.

London Interbank Offer Rate (LIBOR) The Eurodollar rate at which London banks lend dollars to other London banks; considered to be the best representative rate on a dollar borrowed by a private, high-quality borrower.

Long The buyer of a derivative contract. Also refers to the position of owning a derivative.

Longitudinal data Observations on characteristic(s) of the same observational unit through time.

Long-lived assets (or **long-term assets**) Assets that are expected to provide economic benefits over a future period of time, typically greater than one year.

Long-term contract A contract that spans a number of accounting periods.

Long-term debt-to-assets ratio The proportion of a company's assets that is financed with long-term debt.

Long-term equity anticipatory securities (LEAPS) Options originally created with expirations of several years.

Long-term liability An obligation that is expected to be settled, with the outflow of resources embodying economic benefits, over a future period generally greater than one year.

Look-ahead bias A bias caused by using information that was not available on the test date.

Losses Asset outflows not directly related to the ordinary activities of the business.

Lower bound The lowest possible value of an option.

Macaulay duration The duration without dividing by 1 plus the bond's yield to maturity. The term, named for one of the economists who first derived it, is used to distinguish the calculation from modified duration. (See also *modified duration*.)

Macroeconomic factor A factor related to the economy, such as the inflation rate, industrial production, or economic sector membership.

Macroeconomic factor model A multifactor model in which the factors are surprises in macroeconomic variables that significantly explain equity returns.

Maintenance margin requirement The margin requirement on any day other than the first day of a transaction.

Management buyout (MBO) A corporate transaction in which management repurchases all outstanding common stock, usually using the proceeds of debt issuance.

Managerialism theories Theories that posit that corporate executives are motivated to engage in mergers to maximize the size of their company rather than shareholder value.

Manufacturing resource planning (MRP) The incorporation of production planning into inventory management. A MRP analysis provides both a materials acquisition schedule and a production schedule.

Margin The amount of money that a trader deposits in a margin account. The term is derived from the stock market practice in which an investor borrows a portion of the money required to purchase a certain amount of stock. In futures markets, there is no borrowing so the margin is more of a down payment or performance bond.

Marginal investor An investor in a given share who is very likely to be part of the next trade in the share and who is therefore important in setting price.

Market approach Valuation approach that values an asset based on pricing multiples from sales of assets viewed as similar to the subject asset.

Market efficiency A finance perspective on capital markets that deals with the relationship of price to intrinsic value. The **traditional efficient markets formulation** asserts that an asset's price is the best available estimate of its intrinsic value. The **rational efficient markets formulation** asserts that investors should expect to be rewarded for the costs of information gathering and analysis by higher gross returns.

Market-extraction method Method used to estimate the overall capitalization rate by dividing the sale price of a comparable income property into the net operating income.

Market price of risk The slope of the capital market line, indicating the market risk premium for each unit of market risk.

Market rate The rate demanded by purchasers of bonds, given the risks associated with future cash payment obligations of the particular bond issue.

Market risk The risk associated with interest rates, exchange rates, and equity prices.

Market risk premium The expected excess return on the market over the risk-free rate.

Market share test The percentage of a market that a particular firm supplies; used as the primary measure of monopoly power.

Market timing Asset allocation in which the investment in the market is increased if one forecasts that the market will outperform T-bills.

Market value of invested capital The market value of debt and equity.

Marketability discount A reduction or discount to value for shares that are not publicly traded.

Market-oriented investors With reference to equity investors, investors whose investment disciplines cannot be clearly categorized as value or growth.

Marking to market A procedure used primarily in futures markets in which the parties to a contract settle the amount owed daily. Also known as the *daily settlement*.

Markowitz decision rule A decision rule for choosing between two investments based on their means and variances.

Mark-to-market The revaluation of a financial asset or liability to its current market value or fair value.

Matching principle The accounting principle that expenses should be recognized when the associated revenue is recognized.

Matching strategy An active investment strategy that includes intentional matching of the timing of cash outflows with investment maturities.

Materiality The condition of being of sufficient importance so that omission or misstatement of the item in a financial report could make a difference to users' decisions.

Matrix pricing In the fixed income markets, to price a security on the basis of valuation-relevant characteristics (e.g., debt-rating approach).

Mature growth rate The earnings growth rate in a company's mature phase; an earnings growth rate that can be sustained long term.

Mature phase A stage of growth in which the company reaches an equilibrium in which investment opportunities on average just earn their opportunity cost of capital.

Maturity premium An extra return that compensates investors for the increased sensitivity of the market value of debt to a change in market interest rates as maturity is extended.

Mean The sum of all values in a distribution or dataset, divided by the number of values summed; a synonym of arithmetic mean.

Mean absolute deviation With reference to a sample, the mean of the absolute values of deviations from the sample mean.

Mean excess return The average rate of return in excess of the risk-free rate.

Mean reversion   The tendency of a time series to fall when its level is above its mean and rise when its level is below its mean; a mean-reverting time series tends to return to its long-term mean.

Mean–variance analysis   An approach to portfolio analysis using expected means, variances, and covariances of asset returns.

Measure of central tendency   A quantitative measure that specifies where data are centered.

Measure of location   A quantitative measure that describes the location or distribution of data; includes not only measures of central tendency but also other measures such as percentiles.

Measurement scales   A scheme of measuring differences. The four types of measurement scales are nominal, ordinal, interval, and ratio.

Median   The value of the middle item of a set of items that has been sorted into ascending or descending order; the 50th percentile.

Merger   The absorption of one company by another; two companies become one entity and one or both of the pre-merger companies ceases to exist as a separate entity.

Mesokurtic   Describes a distribution with kurtosis identical to that of the normal distribution.

Method based on forecasted fundamentals   An approach to using price multiples that relates a price multiple to forecasts of fundamentals through a discounted cash flow model.

Method of comparables   An approach to valuation that involves using a price multiple to evaluate whether an asset is relatively fairly valued, relatively undervalued, or relatively overvalued when compared to a benchmark value of the multiple.

Minimum-variance frontier   The graph of the set of portfolios that have minimum variance for their level of expected return.

Minimum-variance portfolio   The portfolio with the minimum variance for each given level of expected return.

Minority active investments   Investments in which investors exert significant influence, but not control, over the investee. Typically, the investor has 20 to 50% ownership in the investee.

Minority interest (noncontrolling interest)   The proportion of the ownership of a subsidiary not held by the parent (controlling) company.

Minority passive investments (passive investments)   Investments in which the investor has no significant influence or control over the operations of the investee.

Mismatching strategy   An active investment strategy whereby the timing of cash outflows is not matched with investment maturities.

Mispricing   Any departure of the market price of an asset from the asset's estimated intrinsic value.

Mixed factor models   Factor models that combine features of more than one type of factor model.

Mixed offering   A merger or acquisition that is to be paid for with cash, securities, or some combination of the two.

Modal interval   With reference to grouped data, the most frequently occurring interval.

Mode   The most frequently occurring value in a set of observations.

Model risk   The use of an inaccurate pricing model for a particular investment, or the improper use of the right model.

Model specification   With reference to regression, the set of variables included in the regression and the regression equation's functional form.

Modified duration   A measure of a bond's price sensitivity to interest rate movements. Equal to the Macaulay duration of a bond divided by one plus its yield to maturity.

Molodovsky effect   The observation that P/Es tend to be high on depressed EPS at the bottom of a business cycle, and tend to be low on unusually high EPS at the top of a business cycle.

Momentum indicators   Valuation indicators that relate either price or a fundamental (such as earnings) to the time series of their own past values (or in some cases to their expected value).

Monetary assets and liabilities   Assets and liabilities with value equal to the amount of currency contracted for, a fixed amount of currency. Examples are cash, accounts receivable, mortgages receivable, accounts payable, bonds payable, and mortgages payable. Inventory is not a monetary asset. Most liabilities are monetary.

Monetary/nonmonetary method   Approach to translating foreign currency financial statements for consolidation in which monetary assets and liabilities are translated at the current exchange rate. Nonmonetary assets and liabilities are translated at historical exchange rates (the exchange rates that existed when the assets and liabilities were acquired).

Money market   The market for short-term debt instruments (one-year maturity or less).

Money market yield (or CD equivalent yield)   A yield on a basis comparable to the quoted yield on an interest-bearing money market instrument that pays interest on a 360-day basis; the annualized holding period yield, assuming a 360-day year.

Moneyness   The relationship between the price of the underlying and an option's exercise price.

Money-weighted rate of return   The internal rate of return on a portfolio, taking account of all cash flows.

Monitoring costs   Costs borne by owners to monitor the management of the company (e.g., board of director expenses).

Monopolization   The possession of monopoly power in the relevant market and the willful acquisition or maintenance of that power, as distinguished from growth or development as a consequence of a superior product, business acumen, or historical accident.

Monte Carlo simulation method   An approach to estimating a probability distribution of outcomes to examine what might happen if particular risks are faced. This method is widely used in the sciences as well as in business to study a variety of problems.

Multicollinearity   A regression assumption violation that occurs when two or more independent variables (or combinations of independent variables) are highly but not perfectly correlated with each other.

Multiple linear regression   Linear regression involving two or more independent variables.

Multiple linear regression model   A linear regression model with two or more independent variables.

Multiple R   The correlation between the actual and forecasted values of the dependent variable in a regression.

Multiplication rule for probabilities   The rule that the joint probability of events A and B equals the probability of A given B times the probability of B.

Multi-step format   With respect to the format of the income statement, a format that presents a subtotal for gross profit (revenue minus cost of goods sold).

Multivariate distribution   A probability distribution that specifies the probabilities for a group of related random variables.

Multivariate normal distribution   A probability distribution for a group of random variables that is completely defined by the means and variances of the variables plus all the correlations between pairs of the variables.

Mutually exclusive events   Events such that only one can occur at a time.

Mutually exclusive projects Mutually exclusive projects compete directly with each other. For example, if Projects A and B are mutually exclusive, you can choose A or B, but you cannot choose both.

n Factorial For a positive integer n, the product of the first n positive integers; 0 factorial equals 1 by definition. n factorial is written as $n!$.

Negative serial correlation Serial correlation in which a positive error for one observation increases the chance of a negative error for another observation, and vice versa.

Neoclassical growth theory A theory of economic growth that proposes that real GDP per person grows because technological change induces a level of saving and investment that makes capital per hour of labor grow.

Net asset balance sheet exposure When assets translated at the current exchange rate are greater in amount than liabilities translated at the current exchange rate. Assets exposed to translation gains or losses exceed the exposed liabilities.

Net book value The remaining (undepreciated) balance of an asset's purchase cost. For liabilities, the face value of a bond minus any unamortized discount, or plus any unamortized premium.

Net borrower A country that is borrowing more from the rest of the world than it is lending to it.

Net exports The value of exports of goods and services minus the value of imports of goods and services.

Net income (loss) The difference between revenue and expenses; what remains after subtracting all expenses (including depreciation, interest, and taxes) from revenue.

Net lender A country that is lending more to the rest of the world than it is borrowing from it.

Net liability balance sheet exposure When liabilities translated at the current exchange rate are greater than assets translated at the current exchange rate. Liabilities exposed to translation gains or losses exceed the exposed assets.

Net operating assets The difference between operating assets (total assets less cash) and operating liabilities (total liabilities less total debt).

Net operating cycle An estimate of the average time that elapses between paying suppliers for materials and collecting cash from the subsequent sale of goods produced.

Net operating profit less adjusted taxes, or NOPLAT A company's operating profit with adjustments to normalize the effects of capital structure.

Net present value (NPV) The present value of an investment's cash inflows (benefits) minus the present value of its cash outflows (costs).

Net profit margin (profit margin or return on sales) An indicator of profitability, calculated as net income divided by revenue; indicates how much of each dollar of revenues is left after all costs and expenses.

Net realisable value Estimated selling price in the ordinary course of business less the estimated costs necessary to make the sale.

Net revenue Revenue after adjustments (e.g., for estimated returns or for amounts unlikely to be collected).

Netting When parties agree to exchange only the net amount owed from one party to the other.

New growth theory A theory of economic growth based on the idea that real GDP per person grows because of the choices that people make in the pursuit of profit and that growth can persist indefinitely.

Node Each value on a binomial tree from which successive moves or outcomes branch.

No-growth company A company without positive expected net present value projects.

No-growth value per share The value per share of a no-growth company, equal to the expected level amount of earnings divided by the stock's required rate of return.

Nominal exchange rate The value of the U.S. dollar expressed in units of foreign currency per U.S. dollar.

Nominal rate A rate of interest based on the security's face value.

Nominal risk-free interest rate The sum of the real risk-free interest rate and the inflation premium.

Nominal scale A measurement scale that categorizes data but does not rank them.

Nonconventional cash flow In a nonconventional cash flow pattern, the initial outflow is not followed by inflows only, but the cash flows can flip from positive (inflows) to negative (outflows) again (or even change signs several times).

Noncurrent Not due to be consumed, converted into cash, or settled within one year after the balance sheet date.

Noncurrent assets Assets that are expected to benefit the company over an extended period of time (usually more than one year).

Nondeliverable forwards (NDFs) Cash-settled forward contracts, used predominately with respect to foreign exchange forwards.

Nonearning assets Cash and investments (specifically cash, cash equivalents, and short-term investments).

Nonlinear relation An association or relationship between variables that cannot be graphed as a straight line.

Nonmonetary assets and liabilities Assets and liabilities that are not monetary assets and liabilities. Nonmonetary assets include inventory, fixed assets, and intangibles, and nonmonetary liabilities include deferred revenue.

Nonparametric test A test that is not concerned with a parameter, or that makes minimal assumptions about the population from which a sample comes.

Nonstationarity With reference to a random variable, the property of having characteristics such as mean and variance that are not constant through time.

Nontariff barrier Any action other than a tariff that restricts international trade.

Normal backwardation The condition in futures markets in which futures prices are lower than expected spot prices.

Normal contango The condition in futures markets in which futures prices are higher than expected spot prices.

Normal distribution A continuous, symmetric probability distribution that is completely described by its mean and its variance.

Normalized earnings Earnings adjusted for nonrecurring, noneconomic, or other unusual items to eliminate anomalies and/or facilitate comparisons.

Normalized earnings per share (or normal earnings per share) The earnings per share that a business could achieve currently under mid-cyclical conditions.

Normalized P/E P/Es based on normalized EPS data.

North American Free Trade Agreement An agreement, which became effective on January 1, 1994, to eliminate all barriers to international trade between the United States, Canada, and Mexico after a 15-year phasing-in period.

Notes payable Amounts owed by a business to creditors as a result of borrowings that are evidenced by (short-term) loan agreements.

n-Period moving average The average of the current and immediately prior $n - 1$ values of a time series.

NPV rule An investment decision rule that states that an investment should be undertaken if its NPV is positive but not undertaken if its NPV is negative.

NTM P/E   Next twelve months P/E: current market price divided by an estimated next twelve months EPS.

Null hypothesis   The hypothesis to be tested.

Number of days of inventory   An activity ratio equal to the number of days in a period divided by the inventory ratio for the period; an indication of the number of days a company ties up funds in inventory.

Number of days of payables   An activity ratio equal to the number of days in a period divided by the payables turnover ratio for the period; an estimate of the average number of days it takes a company to pay its suppliers.

Number of days of receivables   Estimate of the average number of days it takes to collect on credit accounts.

Objective probabilities   Probabilities that generally do not vary from person to person; includes a priori and objective probabilities.

Off-balance sheet financing   Arrangements that do not result in additional liabilities on the balance sheet but nonetheless create economic obligations.

Official settlements account   A record of the change in official reserves, which are the government's holdings of foreign currency.

Off-market FRA   A contract in which the initial value is intentionally set at a value other than zero and therefore requires a cash payment at the start from one party to the other.

Offsetting   A transaction in exchange-listed derivative markets in which a party re-enters the market to close out a position.

One third rule   The rule that, on the average, with no change in technology, a 1 percent increase in capital per hour of labor brings a 1/3 percent increase in labor productivity.

One-sided hypothesis test (or **one-tailed hypothesis test**)   A test in which the null hypothesis is rejected only if the evidence indicates that the population parameter is greater than (smaller than) θ_0. The alternative hypothesis also has one side.

Operating activities   Activities that are part of the day-to-day business functioning of an entity, such as selling inventory and providing services.

Operating breakeven   The number of units produced and sold at which the company's operating profit is zero (revenues = operating costs).

Operating cycle   A measure of the time needed to convert raw materials into cash from a sale; it consists of the number of days of inventory and the number of days of receivables.

Operating lease   An agreement allowing the lessee to use some asset for a period of time; essentially a rental.

Operating leverage   The use of fixed costs in operations.

Operating profit (operating income)   A company's profits on its usual business activities before deducting taxes.

Operating profit margin (operating margin)   A profitability ratio calculated as operating income (i.e., income before interest and taxes) divided by revenue.

Operating return on assets (operating ROA)   A profitability ratio calculated as operating income divided by average total assets.

Operating risk   The risk attributed to the operating cost structure, in particular the use of fixed costs in operations; the risk arising from the mix of fixed and variable costs; the risk that a company's operations may be severely affected by environmental, social, and governance risk factors.

Operations risk or **operational risk**   The risk of loss from failures in a company's systems and procedures (for example, due to computer failures or human failures) or events completely outside of the control of organizations (which would include "acts of God" and terrorist actions).

Opportunity cost   The value that investors forgo by choosing a particular course of action; the value of something in its best alternative use.

Opportunity set   The set of assets available for investment.

Optimal capital structure   The capital structure at which the value of the company is maximized.

Optimizer   A specialized computer program or a spreadsheet that solves for the portfolio weights that will result in the lowest risk for a specified level of expected return.

Option   A financial instrument that gives one party the right, but not the obligation, to buy or sell an underlying asset from or to another party at a fixed price over a specific period of time. Also referred to as contingent claims.

Option price, option premium, or **premium**   The amount of money a buyer pays and seller receives to engage in an option transaction.

Orderly liquidation value   The estimated gross amount of money that could be realized from the liquidation sale of an asset or assets, given a reasonable amount of time to find a purchaser or purchasers.

Ordinal scale   A measurement scale that sorts data into categories that are ordered (ranked) with respect to some characteristic.

Ordinary annuity   An annuity with a first cash flow that is paid one period from the present.

Ordinary least squares (OLS)   An estimation method based on the criterion of minimizing the sum of the squared residuals of a regression.

Ordinary shares (common stock or **common shares)**   Equity shares that are subordinate to all other types of equity (e.g., preferred equity).

Organic growth   Company growth in output or sales that is achieved by making investments internally (i.e., excludes growth achieved through mergers and acquisitions).

Orthogonal   Uncorrelated; at a right angle.

Other comprehensive income   Changes to equity that bypass (are not reported in) the income statement; the difference between comprehensive income and net income.

Other post-employment benefits   Promises by the company to pay benefits in the future, other than pension benefits, such as life insurance premiums and all or part of health care insurance for its retirees.

Other receivables   Amounts owed to the company from parties other than customers.

Outcome   A possible value of a random variable.

Outliers   Small numbers of observations at either extreme (small or large) of a sample.

Out-of-sample forecast errors   The differences between actual and predicted value of time series outside the sample period used to fit the model.

Out-of-sample test   A test of a strategy or model using a sample outside the time period on which the strategy or model was developed.

Out-of-the-money   Options that, if exercised, would require the payment of more money than the value received and therefore would not be currently exercised.

Overall capitalization rate   A ratio in property valuation; net operating income divided by sale price. Also known as the going-in rate.

Overnight index swap (OIS)   A swap in which the floating rate is the cumulative value of a single unit of currency invested at an overnight rate during the settlement period.

Owners' equity   The excess of assets over liabilities; the residual interest of shareholders in the assets of an entity after deducting the entity's liabilities.

Paired comparisons test   A statistical test for differences based on paired observations drawn from samples that are dependent on each other.

Paired observations   Observations that are dependent on each other.

Pairs arbitrage   A trade in two closely related stocks that involves buying the relatively undervalued stock and selling short the relatively overvalued stock.

Pairs arbitrage trade   A trade in two closely related stocks involving the short sale of one and the purchase of the other.

Pairs trading   An approach to trading that uses pairs of closely related stocks, buying the relatively undervalued stock and selling short the relatively overvalued stock.

Panel data   Observations through time on a single characteristic of multiple observational units.

Parameter   A descriptive measure computed from or used to describe a population of data, conventionally represented by Greek letters.

Parameter instability   The problem or issue of population regression parameters that have changed over time.

Parametric test   Any test (or procedure) concerned with parameters or whose validity depends on assumptions concerning the population generating the sample.

Partial regression coefficients or **partial slope coefficients**   The slope coefficients in a multiple regression.

Partnership   A business owned and operated by more than one individual.

Passive portfolio   A market index portfolio.

Passive strategy   In reference to short-term cash management, it is an investment strategy characterized by simple decision rules for making daily investments.

Payables turnover   An activity ratio calculated as purchases divided by average trade payables.

Payer swaption   A swaption that allows the holder to enter into a swap as the fixed-rate payer and floating-rate receiver.

Payment date   The day that the company actually mails out (or electronically transfers) a dividend payment.

Payment netting   A means of settling payments in which the amount owed by the first party to the second is netted with the amount owed by the second party to the first; only the net difference is paid.

Payoff   The value of an option at expiration.

Payout policy   The principles by which a company distributes cash to common shareholders by means of cash dividends and/or share repurchases.

Payout ratio   The percentage of total earnings paid out in dividends in any given year (in per-share terms, DPS/EPS).

Pecking order theory   The theory that managers take into account how their actions might be interpreted by outsiders and thus order their preferences for various forms of corporate financing. Forms of financing that are least visible to outsiders (e.g., internally generated funds) are most preferable to managers and those that are most visible (e.g., equity) are least preferable.

PEG   The P/E-to-growth ratio, calculated as the stock's P/E divided by the expected earnings growth rate.

PEG ratio   The ratio of P/E-to-growth, calculated as the stock's P/E divided by the expected earnings growth rate in percent.

Pension obligation   The present value of future benefits earned by employees for service provided to date. Under IFRS it is defined as "the present value, without deducting any plan assets, of expected future payments required to settle the obligation arising from employee service in the current and prior periods."

Per unit contribution margin   The amount that each unit sold contributes to covering fixed costs—that is, the difference between the price per unit and the variable cost per unit.

Percentage-of-completion   A method of revenue recognition in which, in each accounting period, the company estimates what percentage of the contract is complete and then reports that percentage of the total contract revenue in its income statement.

Percentiles   Quantiles that divide a distribution into 100 equal parts.

Perfect capital markets   Markets in which, by assumption, there are no taxes, transactions costs, or bankruptcy costs, and in which all investors have equal ("symmetric") information.

Perfect collinearity   The existence of an exact linear relation between two or more independent variables or combinations of independent variables.

Performance appraisal   The evaluation of risk-adjusted performance; the evaluation of investment skill.

Performance guarantee   A guarantee from the clearinghouse that if one party makes money on a transaction, the clearinghouse ensures it will be paid.

Performance measurement   The calculation of returns in a logical and consistent manner.

Period costs   Costs (e.g., executives' salaries) that cannot be directly matched with the timing of revenues and which are thus expensed immediately.

Periodic inventory system   An inventory accounting system in which inventory values and costs of sales are determined at the end of the accounting period.

Periodic rate   The quoted interest rate per period; the stated annual interest rate divided by the number of compounding periods per year.

Permanent differences   Differences between tax and financial reporting of revenue (expenses) that will not be reversed at some future date. These result in a difference between the company's effective tax rate and statutory tax rate and do not result in a deferred tax item.

Permutation   An ordered listing.

Perpetual inventory system   An inventory accounting system in which inventory values and costs of sales are continuously updated to reflect purchases and sales.

Perpetuity   A perpetual annuity, or a set of never-ending level sequential cash flows, with the first cash flow occurring one period from now.

Pet projects   Projects in which influential managers want the corporation to invest. Often, unfortunately, pet projects are selected without undergoing normal capital budgeting analysis.

Plain vanilla swap   An interest rate swap in which one party pays a fixed rate and the other pays a floating rate, with both sets of payments in the same currency.

Platykurtic   Describes a distribution that is less peaked than the normal distribution.

Point estimate   A single numerical estimate of an unknown quantity, such as a population parameter.

Point of sale   Systems that capture transaction data at the physical location in which the sale is made.

Poison pill   A pre-offer takeover defense mechanism that makes it prohibitively costly for an acquirer to take control of a target without the prior approval of the target's board of directors.

Poison puts   A pre-offer takeover defense mechanism that gives target company bondholders the right to sell their bonds back to the target at a pre-specified redemption price, typically at or above par value; this defense increases the need for cash and raises the cost of the acquisition.

Pooled estimate   An estimate of a parameter that involves combining (pooling) observations from two or more samples.

Pooling of interests accounting method   A method of accounting in which combined companies were portrayed as if they had always operated as a single economic entity. Called pooling of interests under U.S. GAAP and uniting of interests under IFRS. (No longer allowed under U.S. GAAP or IFRS.)

Population   All members of a specified group.

Population mean   The arithmetic mean value of a population; the arithmetic mean of all the observations or values in the population.

Population standard deviation   A measure of dispersion relating to a population in the same unit of measurement as the observations, calculated as the positive square root of the population variance.

Population variance   A measure of dispersion relating to a population, calculated as the mean of the squared deviations around the population mean.

Portfolio implementation problem   The part of the execution step of the portfolio management process that involves the implementation of portfolio decisions by trading desks.

Portfolio performance attribution   The analysis of portfolio performance in terms of the contributions from various sources of risk.

Portfolio possibilities curve   A graphical representation of the expected return and risk of all portfolios that can be formed using two assets.

Portfolio selection/composition problem   The part of the execution step of the portfolio management process in which investment strategies are integrated with expectations to select a portfolio of assets.

Position trader   A trader who typically holds positions open overnight.

Positive serial correlation   Serial correlation in which a positive error for one observation increases the chance of a positive error for another observation, and a negative error for one observation increases the chance of a negative error for another observation.

Posterior probability   An updated probability that reflects or comes after new information.

Potential credit risk   The risk associated with the possibility that a payment due at a later date will not be made.

Power of a test   The probability of correctly rejecting the null—that is, rejecting the null hypothesis when it is false.

Precautionary stocks   A level of inventory beyond anticipated needs that provides a cushion in the event that it takes longer to replenish inventory than expected or in the case of greater than expected demand.

Pre-investing   The strategy of using futures contracts to enter the market without an immediate outlay of cash.

Premise of value   The status of a company in the sense of whether it is assumed to be a going concern or not.

Prepaid expense   A normal operating expense that has been paid in advance of when it is due.

Present value (PV)   The present discounted value of future cash flows: For assets, the present discounted value of the future net cash inflows that the asset is expected to generate; for liabilities, the present discounted value of the future net cash outflows that are expected to be required to settle the liabilities.

Present (price) value of a basis point (PVBP)   The change in the bond price for a 1 basis point change in yield. Also called *basis point value* (BPV).

Present value of growth opportunities (or **value of growth**)   The difference between the actual value per share and the no-growth value per share.

Present value model or **discounted cash flow model**   A model of intrinsic value that views the value of an asset as the present value of the asset's expected future cash flows.

Presentation currency   The currency in which financial statement amounts are presented.

Pretax margin   A profitability ratio calculated as earnings before taxes divided by revenue.

Price discovery   A feature of futures markets in which futures prices provide valuable information about the price of the underlying asset.

Price limits   Limits imposed by a futures exchange on the price change that can occur from one day to the next.

Price momentum   A valuation indicator based on past price movement.

Price multiple   The ratio of a stock's market price to some measure of value per share.

Price relative   A ratio of an ending price over a beginning price; it is equal to 1 plus the holding period return on the asset.

Price to book value   A valuation ratio calculated as price per share divided by book value per share.

Price to cash flow   A valuation ratio calculated as price per share divided by cash flow per share.

Price to sales   A valuation ratio calculated as price per share divided by sales per share.

Priced risk   Risk for which investors demand compensation for bearing (e.g., equity risk, company-specific factors, macroeconomic factors).

Price-setting option   The operational flexibility to adjust prices when demand varies from forecast. For example, when demand exceeds capacity, the company could benefit from the excess demand by increasing prices.

Principal   The amount of funds originally invested in a project or instrument; the face value to be paid at maturity.

Prior probabilities   Probabilities reflecting beliefs prior to the arrival of new information.

Prior transaction method   A variation of the market approach; considers actual transactions in the stock of the subject private company.

Private sector surplus or **deficit**   An amount equal to saving minus investment.

Probability   A number between 0 and 1 describing the chance that a stated event will occur.

Probability density function   A function with non-negative values such that probability can be described by areas under the curve graphing the function.

Probability distribution   A distribution that specifies the probabilities of a random variable's possible outcomes.

Probability function   A function that specifies the probability that the random variable takes on a specific value.

Probit model   A qualitative-dependent-variable multiple regression model based on the normal distribution.

Production-flexibility   The operational flexibility to alter production when demand varies from forecast. For example, if demand is strong, a company may profit from employees working overtime or from adding additional shifts.

Profitability ratios   Ratios that measure a company's ability to generate profitable sales from its resources (assets).

Project sequencing   To defer the decision to invest in a future project until the outcome of some or all of a current project is known. Projects are sequenced through time, so that investing in a project creates the option to invest in future projects.

Proportionate consolidation   A method of accounting for joint ventures where the venturer's share of the assets, liabilities, income and expenses of the joint venture are combined on a line-by-line basis with similar items on the venturer's financial statements.

Protective put   An option strategy in which a long position in an asset is combined with a long position in a put.

Provision   In accounting, a liability of uncertain timing or amount.

Proxy fight   An attempt to take control of a company through a shareholder vote.

Proxy statement   A public document that provides the material facts concerning matters on which shareholders will vote.

Pseudo-random numbers   Numbers produced by random number generators.

Pull on liquidity   When disbursements are paid too quickly or trade credit availability is limited, requiring companies to expend funds before they receive funds from sales that could cover the liability.

Purchase method   A method of accounting for a business combination where the acquiring company allocates the purchase price to each asset acquired and liability assumed at fair value. If the purchase price exceeds the allocation, the excess is recorded as goodwill.

Purchased in-process research and development costs   Costs of research and development in progress at an acquired company; often, part of the purchase price of an acquired company is allocated to such costs.

Purchasing power gain   A gain in value caused by changes in price levels. Monetary liabilities experience purchasing power gains during periods of inflation.

Purchasing power loss   A loss in value caused by changes in price levels. Monetary assets experience purchasing power losses during periods of inflation.

Purchasing power parity   The equal value of different monies.

Pure discount instruments   Instruments that pay interest as the difference between the amount borrowed and the amount paid back.

Pure factor portfolio   A portfolio with sensitivity of 1 to the factor in question and a sensitivity of 0 to all other factors.

Pure-play method   A method for estimating the beta for a company or project; it requires using a comparable company's beta and adjusting it for financial leverage differences.

Put   An option that gives the holder the right to sell an underlying asset to another party at a fixed price over a specific period of time.

Put–call parity   An equation expressing the equivalence (parity) of a portfolio of a call and a bond with a portfolio of a put and the underlying, which leads to the relationship between put and call prices.

Put–call–forward parity   The relationship among puts, calls, and forward contracts.

p-Value   The smallest level of significance at which the null hypothesis can be rejected; also called the marginal significance level.

Pyramiding   Controlling additional property through reinvestment, refinancing, and exchanging.

Qualifying special purpose entities   Under U.S. GAAP, a special purpose entity structured to avoid consolidation that must meet qualification criteria.

Qualitative dependent variables   Dummy variables used as dependent variables rather than as independent variables.

Quality of earnings analysis   The investigation of issues relating to the accuracy of reported accounting results as reflections of economic performance; quality of earnings analysis is broadly understood to include not only earnings management, but also balance sheet management.

Quantile (or **fractile**)   A value at or below which a stated fraction of the data lies.

Quartiles   Quantiles that divide a distribution into four equal parts.

Quick assets   Assets that can be most readily converted to cash (e.g., cash, short-term marketable investments, receivables).

Quick ratio, or **acid test ratio**   A stringent measure of liquidity that indicates a company's ability to satisfy current liabilities with its most liquid assets, calculated as (cash + short-term marketable investments + receivables) divided by current liabilities.

Quintiles   Quantiles that divide a distribution into five equal parts.

Quota   A quantitative restriction on the import of a particular good, which specifies the maximum amount that can be imported in a given time period.

Random number   An observation drawn from a uniform distribution.

Random number generator   An algorithm that produces uniformly distributed random numbers between 0 and 1.

Random variable   A quantity whose future outcomes are uncertain.

Random walk   A time series in which the value of the series in one period is the value of the series in the previous period plus an unpredictable random error.

Range   The difference between the maximum and minimum values in a dataset.

Rate of return   The proportional annual benefit that results from making an investment.

Rate-of-return regulation   Regulation that seeks to keep the rate of return in the industry at a competitive level by not allowing excessive prices to be charged.

Ratio scales   A measurement scale that has all the characteristics of interval measurement scales as well as a true zero point as the origin.

Ratio spread   An option strategy in which a long position in a certain number of options is offset by a short position in a certain number of other options on the same underlying, resulting in a risk-free position.

Rational efficient markets formulation   See *Market efficiency*.

Real exchange rate   The relative price of foreign-made goods and services to U.S.-made goods and services.

Real GDP per person   Real GDP divided by the population.

Real options   Options that relate to investment decisions such as the option to time the start of a project, the option to adjust its scale, or the option to abandon a project that has begun.

Real risk-free interest rate   The single-period interest rate for a completely risk-free security if no inflation were expected.

Realizable value (settlement value)   With reference to assets, the amount of cash or cash equivalents that could currently be obtained by selling the asset in an orderly disposal; with reference to liabilities, the undiscounted amount of cash or cash equivalents expected to be paid to satisfy the liabilities in the normal course of business.

Recapture premium   Provision for a return of investment, net of value appreciation.

Receivables turnover   An activity ratio equal to revenue divided by average receivables.

Receiver swaption   A swaption that allows the holder to enter into a swap as the fixed-rate receiver and floating-rate payer.

Reconciliation   Resolving differences in indications of value when estimating market value.

Regime   With reference to a time series, the underlying model generating the times series.

Regression coefficients   The intercept and slope coefficient(s) of a regression.

Regulatory risk   The risk associated with the uncertainty of how derivative transactions will be regulated or with changes in regulations.

Rejection point (or **critical value**)   A value against which a computed test statistic is compared to decide whether to reject or not reject the null hypothesis.

Relative dispersion   The amount of dispersion relative to a reference value or benchmark.

Relative frequency With reference to an interval of grouped data, the number of observations in the interval divided by the total number of observations in the sample.

Relative strength (RSTR) indicators Valuation indicators that compare a stock's performance during a period either to its own past performance or to the performance of some group of stocks.

Relative valuation models A model that specifies an asset's value relative to the value of another asset.

Rent seeking The pursuit of wealth by capturing economic rent—consumer surplus, producer surplus, or economic profit.

Reorganization Agreements made by a company in bankruptcy under which a company's capital structure is altered and/or alternative arrangements are made for debt repayment; U.S. Chapter 11 bankruptcy. The company emerges from bankruptcy as a going concern.

Replacement value The market value of a swap.

Report format With respect to the format of a balance sheet, a format in which assets, liabilities, and equity are listed in a single column.

Reporting unit An operating segment or one level below an operating segment (referred to as a component).

Reputational risk The risk that a company will suffer an extended diminution in market value relative to other companies in the same industry due to a demonstrated lack of concern for environmental, social, and governance risk factors.

Required rate of return The minimum rate of return required by an investor to invest in an asset, given the asset's riskiness.

Residual autocorrelations The sample autocorrelations of the residuals.

Residual claim The owners' remaining claim on the company's assets after the liabilities are deducted.

Residual dividend approach A dividend payout policy under which earnings in excess of the funds necessary to finance the equity portion of company's capital budget are paid out in dividends.

Residual dividend policy A policy in which dividends are paid from any internally generated funds remaining after such funds are used to finance positive NPV projects.

Residual income (or **economic profit** or **abnormal earnings**) Earnings for a given time period, minus a deduction for common shareholders' opportunity cost in generating the earnings.

Residual income method (or **excess earnings method**) Income approach that estimates the value of all intangible assets of the business by capitalizing future earnings in excess of the estimated return requirements associated with working capital and fixed assets.

Residual income model (RIM) (also **discounted abnormal earnings model** or **Edwards-Bell-Ohlson model**) A model of stock valuation that views intrinsic value of stock as the sum of book value per share plus the present value of the stock's expected future residual income per share.

Residual loss Agency costs that are incurred despite adequate monitoring and bonding of management.

Retail method An inventory accounting method in which the sales value of an item is reduced by the gross margin to calculate the item's cost.

Return on assets (ROA) A profitability ratio calculated as net income divided by average total assets; indicates a company's net profit generated per dollar invested in total assets.

Return on common equity (ROCE) A profitability ratio calculated as (net income − preferred dividends) divided by average common equity; equal to the return on equity ratio when no preferred equity is outstanding.

Return on equity (ROE) A profitability ratio calculated as net income divided by average shareholders' equity.

Return on invested capital (ROIC) The after-tax net operating profits as a percent of total assets or capital.

Return on total capital A profitability ratio calculated as EBIT divided by the sum of short- and long-term debt and equity.

Revaluation The process of valuing long-lived assets at fair value, rather than at cost less accumulated depreciation. Any resulting profit or loss is either reported on the income statement and/or through equity under revaluation surplus.

Revenue The amount charged for the delivery of goods or services in the ordinary activities of a business over a stated period; the inflows of economic resources to a company over a stated period.

Reverse stock split A reduction in the number of shares outstanding with a corresponding increase in share price, but no change to the company's underlying fundamentals.

Reviewed financial statements A type of non-audited financial statements; typically provide an opinion letter with representations and assurances by the reviewing accountant that are less than those in audited financial statements.

Revolving credit agreements The strongest form of short-term bank borrowing facilities; they are in effect for multiple years (e.g., 3–5 years) and may have optional medium-term loan features.

Rho The sensitivity of the option price to the risk-free rate.

Risk budgeting The establishment of objectives for individuals, groups, or divisions of an organization that takes into account the allocation of an acceptable level of risk.

Risk governance The setting of overall policies and standards in risk management.

Risk management The process of identifying the level of risk an entity wants, measuring the level of risk the entity currently has, taking actions that bring the actual level of risk to the desired level of risk, and monitoring the new actual level of risk so that it continues to be aligned with the desired level of risk.

Risk premium The expected return on an investment minus the risk-free rate.

Risk-neutral probabilities Weights that are used to compute a binomial option price. They are the probabilities that would apply if a risk-neutral investor valued an option.

Risk-neutral valuation The process by which options and other derivatives are priced by treating investors as though they were risk neutral.

Robust The quality of being relatively unaffected by a violation of assumptions.

Robust standard errors Standard errors of the estimated parameters of a regression that correct for the presence of heteroskedasticity in the regression's error term.

Root mean squared error (RMSE) The square root of the average squared forecast error; used to compare the out-of-sample forecasting performance of forecasting models.

Roy's safety first criterion A criterion asserting that the optimal portfolio is the one that minimizes the probability that portfolio return falls below a threshold level.

Rule of 70 A rule that states that the number of years it takes for the level of a variable to double is approximately 70 divided by the annual percentage growth rate of the variable.

Rule of 72 The principle that the approximate number of years necessary for an investment to double is 72 divided by the stated interest rate.

Safety stock A level of inventory beyond anticipated needs that provides a cushion in the event that it takes longer to replenish inventory than expected or in the case of greater than expected demand.

Safety-first rules Rules for portfolio selection that focus on the risk that portfolio value will fall below some minimum acceptable level over some time horizon.

Sales Generally, a synonym for revenue; "sales" is generally understood to refer to the sale of goods, whereas "revenue" is understood to include the sale of goods or services.

Sales returns and allowances An offset to revenue reflecting any cash refunds, credits on account, and discounts from sales prices given to customers who purchased defective or unsatisfactory items.

Sales risk Uncertainty with respect to the quantity of goods and services that a company is able to sell and the price it is able to achieve; the risk related to the uncertainty of revenues.

Sales-type lease A type of finance lease, from a lessor perspective, where the present value of the lease payments (lease receivable) exceeds the carrying value of the leased asset. The revenues earned by the lessor are operating (the profit on the sale) and financing (interest) in nature.

Salvage value The amount the company estimates that it can sell the asset for at the end of its useful life.

Sample A subset of a population.

Sample excess kurtosis A sample measure of the degree of a distribution's peakedness in excess of the normal distribution's peakedness.

Sample kurtosis A sample measure of the degree of a distribution's peakedness.

Sample mean The sum of the sample observations, divided by the sample size.

Sample selection bias Bias introduced by systematically excluding some members of the population according to a particular attribute—for example, the bias introduced when data availability leads to certain observations being excluded from the analysis.

Sample skewness A sample measure of degree of asymmetry of a distribution.

Sample standard deviation The positive square root of the sample variance.

Sample statistic or **statistic** A quantity computed from or used to describe a sample.

Sample variance A sample measure of the degree of dispersion of a distribution, calculated by dividing the sum of the squared deviations from the sample mean by the sample size minus 1.

Sampling The process of obtaining a sample.

Sampling distribution The distribution of all distinct possible values that a statistic can assume when computed from samples of the same size randomly drawn from the same population.

Sampling error The difference between the observed value of a statistic and the quantity it is intended to estimate.

Sampling plan The set of rules used to select a sample.

Sandwich spread An option strategy that is equivalent to a short butterfly spread.

Sarbanes–Oxley Act An act passed by the U.S. Congress in 2002 that created the Public Company Accounting Oversight Board (PCAOB) to oversee auditors.

Scaled earnings surprise Unexpected earnings divided by the standard deviation of analysts' earnings forecasts.

Scalper A trader who offers to buy or sell futures contracts, holding the position for only a brief period of time. Scalpers attempt to profit by buying at the bid price and selling at the higher ask price.

Scatter plot A two-dimensional plot of pairs of observations on two data series.

Scenario analysis Analysis that shows the changes in key financial quantities that result from given (economic) events, such as the loss of customers, the loss of a supply source, or a catastrophic event; a risk management technique involving examination of the performance of a portfolio under specified situations. Closely related to stress testing.

Screening The application of a set of criteria to reduce a set of potential investments to a smaller set having certain desired characteristics.

Seats Memberships in a derivatives exchange.

Sector neutral Said of a portfolio for which economic sectors are represented in the same proportions as in the benchmark, using market-value weights.

Sector neutralizing Measure of financial reporting quality by subtracting the mean or median ratio for a given sector group from a given company's ratio.

Sector rotation strategy A type of top-down investing approach that involves emphasizing different economic sectors based on considerations such as macroeconomic forecasts.

Securities Act of 1933 An act passed by the U.S. Congress in 1933 that specifies the financial and other significant information that investors must receive when securities are sold, prohibits misrepresentations, and requires initial registration of all public issuances of securities.

Securities Exchange Act of 1934 An act passed by the U.S. Congress in 1934 that created the Securities and Exchange Commission (SEC), gave the SEC authority over all aspects of the securities industry, and empowered the SEC to require periodic reporting by companies with publicly traded securities.

Securities offering A merger or acquisition in which target shareholders are to receive shares of the acquirer's common stock as compensation.

Security market line (SML) The graph of the capital asset pricing model.

Segment debt ratio Segment liabilities divided by segment assets.

Segment margin Segment profit (loss) divided by segment revenue.

Segment ROA Segment profit (loss) divided by segment assets.

Segment turnover Segment revenue divided by segment assets.

Sell-side analysts Analysts who work at brokerages.

Semideviation The positive square root of semivariance (sometimes called semistandard deviation).

Semilogarithmic Describes a scale constructed so that equal intervals on the vertical scale represent equal rates of change, and equal intervals on the horizontal scale represent equal amounts of change.

Semivariance The average squared deviation below the mean.

Sensitivity analysis Analysis that shows the range of possible outcomes as specific assumptions are changed.

Serially correlated With reference to regression errors, errors that are correlated across observations.

Service period The period benefited by the employee's service, usually the period between the grant date and the vesting date.

Settlement date or **payment date** The date on which the parties to a swap make payments.

Settlement period The time between settlement dates.

Settlement price The official price, designated by the clearinghouse, from which daily gains and losses will be determined and marked to market.

Settlement risk When settling a contract, the risk that one party could be in the process of paying the counterparty while the counterparty is declaring bankruptcy.

Share repurchase   A transaction in which a company buys back its own shares. Unlike stock dividends and stock splits, share repurchases use corporate cash.

Shareholders' equity   Total assets minus total liabilities.

Share-the-gains, share-the-pains theory   A theory of regulatory behavior that holds that regulators must take account of the demands of three groups: legislators, who established and oversee the regulatory agency; firms in the regulated industry; and consumers of the regulated industry's products.

Shark repellents   A pre-offer takeover defense mechanism involving the corporate charter (e.g., staggered boards of directors and supermajority provisions).

Sharpe ratio   The average return in excess of the risk-free rate divided by the standard deviation of return; a measure of the average excess return earned per unit of standard deviation of return.

Sharpe's measure   Reward-to-volatility ratio; ratio of portfolio excess return to standard deviation.

Short   The seller of a derivative contract. Also refers to the position of being short a derivative.

Shortfall risk   The risk that portfolio value will fall below some minimum acceptable level over some time horizon.

Simple interest   The interest earned each period on the original investment; interest calculated on the principal only.

Simple random sample   A subset of a larger population created in such a way that each element of the population has an equal probability of being selected to the subset.

Simple random sampling   The procedure of drawing a sample to satisfy the definition of a simple random sample.

Simulation   Computer-generated sensitivity or scenario analysis that is based on probability models for the factors that drive outcomes.

Simulation trial   A complete pass through the steps of a simulation.

Single-payment loan   A loan in which the borrower receives a sum of money at the start and pays back the entire amount with interest in a single payment at maturity.

Single-step format   With respect to the format of the income statement, a format that does not subtotal for gross profit (revenue minus cost of goods sold).

Sinking fund factor   Amount that must be set aside each period to have $1 at some future point in time.

Skewed   Not symmetrical.

Skewness   A quantitative measure of skew (lack of symmetry); a synonym of skew.

Sole proprietorship   A business owned and operated by a single person.

Solvency   With respect to financial statement analysis, the ability of a company to fulfill its long-term obligations.

Solvency ratios   Ratios that measure a company's ability to meet its long-term obligations.

Sovereign yield spread   An estimate of the country spread (country equity premium) for a developing nation that is based on a comparison of bonds yields in country being analyzed and a developed country. The sovereign yield spread is the difference between a government bond yield in the country being analyzed, denominated in the currency of the developed country, and the Treasury bond yield on a similar maturity bond in the developed country.

Spearman rank correlation coefficient   A measure of correlation applied to ranked data.

Special purpose entity (special purpose vehicle or variable interest entity)   A non-operating entity created to carry out a specified purpose, such as leasing assets or securitizing receivables; can be a corporation, partnership, trust, limited liability, or partnership formed to facilitate a specific type of business activity.

Specific identification method   An inventory accounting method that identifies which specific inventory items were sold and which remained in inventory to be carried over to later periods.

Spin-off   A form of restructuring in which shareholders of a parent company receive a proportional number of shares in a new, separate entity; shareholders end up owning stock in two different companies where there used to be one.

Split-off   A form of restructuring in which shareholders of the parent company are given shares in a newly created entity in exchange for their shares of the parent company.

Split-rate tax system   In reference to corporate taxes, a split-rate system taxes earnings to be distributed as dividends at a different rate than earnings to be retained. Corporate profits distributed as dividends are taxed at a lower rate than those retained in the business.

Spread   An option strategy involving the purchase of one option and sale of another option that is identical to the first in all respects except either exercise price or expiration.

Spreadsheet modeling   As used in this book, the use of a spreadsheet in executing a dividend discount model valuation, or other present value model valuation.

Spurious correlation   A correlation that misleadingly points towards associations between variables.

Stable dividend policy   A policy in which regular dividends are paid that reflect long-run expected earnings. In contrast to a constant dividend payout ratio policy, a stable dividend policy does not reflect short-term volatility in earnings.

Standard cost   With respect to inventory accounting, the planned or target unit cost of inventory items or services.

Standard deviation   The positive square root of the variance; a measure of dispersion in the same units as the original data.

Standard normal distribution (or unit normal distribution)   The normal density with mean equal to 0 and standard deviation (σ) equal to 1.

Standardized beta   With reference to fundamental factor models, the value of the attribute for an asset minus the average value of the attribute across all stocks, divided by the standard deviation of the attribute across all stocks.

Standardized unexpected earnings (SUE)   Unexpected earnings per share divided by the standard deviation of unexpected earnings per share over a specified prior time period.

Standardizing   A transformation that involves subtracting the mean and dividing the result by the standard deviation.

Stated annual interest rate or **quoted interest rate**   A quoted interest rate that does not account for compounding within the year.

Stated rate (nominal rate or **coupon rate)**   The rate at which periodic interest payments are calculated.

Statement of cash flows (cash flow statement)   A financial statement that reconciles beginning-of-period and end-of-period balance sheet values of cash; provides information about an entity's cash inflows and cash outflows as they pertain to operating, investing, and financing activities.

Statement of changes in shareholders' equity (statement of owners' equity)   A financial statement that reconciles the beginning-of-period and end-of-period balance sheet values of shareholders' equity; provides information about all factors affecting shareholders' equity.

Statement of retained earnings   A financial statement that reconciles beginning-of-period and end-of-period balance sheet values of retained income; shows the linkage between the balance sheet and income statement.

Static trade-off theory of capital structure A theory pertaining to a company's optimal capital structure; the optimal level of debt is found at the point where additional debt would cause the costs of financial distress to increase by a greater amount than the benefit of the additional tax shield.

Statistic A quantity computed from or used to describe a sample of data.

Statistical factor models A multifactor model in which statistical methods are applied to a set of historical returns to determine portfolios that best explain either historical return covariances or variances.

Statistical inference Making forecasts, estimates, or judgments about a larger group from a smaller group actually observed; using a sample statistic to infer the value of an unknown population parameter.

Statistically significant A result indicating that the null hypothesis can be rejected; with reference to an estimated regression coefficient, frequently understood to mean a result indicating that the corresponding population regression coefficient is different from 0.

Statistics The science of describing, analyzing, and drawing conclusions from data; also, a collection of numerical data.

Statutory merger A merger in which one company ceases to exist as an identifiable entity and all its assets and liabilities become part of a purchasing company.

Stock grants The granting of stock to employees as a form of compensation.

Stock options (stock option grants) The granting of stock options to employees as a form of compensation.

Stock purchase An acquisition in which the acquirer gives the target company's shareholders some combination of cash and securities in exchange for shares of the target company's stock.

Stock-out losses Profits lost from not having sufficient inventory on hand to satisfy demand.

Storage costs or **carrying costs** The costs of holding an asset, generally a function of the physical characteristics of the underlying asset.

Straddle An option strategy involving the purchase of a put and a call with the same exercise price. A straddle is based on the expectation of high volatility of the underlying.

Straight-line method A depreciation method that allocates evenly the cost of a long-lived asset less its estimated residual value over the estimated useful life of the asset.

Strangle A variation of a straddle in which the put and call have different exercise prices.

Strap An option strategy involving the purchase of two calls and one put.

Strategic transaction A purchase involving a buyer that would benefit from certain synergies associated with owning the target firm.

Stratified random sampling A procedure by which a population is divided into subpopulations (strata) based on one or more classification criteria. Simple random samples are then drawn from each stratum in sizes proportional to the relative size of each stratum in the population. These samples are then pooled.

Stress testing A set of techniques for estimating losses in extremely unfavorable combinations of events or scenarios.

Strip An option strategy involving the purchase of two puts and one call.

Structured note A variation of a floating-rate note that has some type of unusual characteristic such as a leverage factor or in which the rate moves opposite to interest rates.

Subjective probability A probability drawing on personal or subjective judgment.

Subsidiary merger A merger in which the company being purchased becomes a subsidiary of the purchaser.

Subsistence real wage rate The minimum real wage rate needed to maintain life.

Sum-of-the-parts valuation A valuation that sums the estimated values of each of a company's businesses as if each business were an independent going concern.

Sunk cost A cost that has already been incurred.

Supernormal growth Above average or abnormally high growth rate in earnings per share.

Surprise The actual value of a variable minus its predicted (or expected) value.

Survey approach An estimate of the equity risk premium that is based upon estimates provided by a panel of finance experts.

Survivorship bias Bias that may result when failed or defunct companies are excluded from membership in a group.

Sustainable growth rate The rate of dividend (and earnings) growth that can be sustained over time for a given level of return on equity, keeping the capital structure constant and without issuing additional common stock.

Swap An agreement between two parties to exchange a series of future cash flows.

Swap spread The difference between the fixed rate on an interest rate swap and the rate on a Treasury note with equivalent maturity; it reflects the general level of credit risk in the market.

Swaption An option to enter into a swap.

Synthetic call The combination of puts, the underlying, and risk-free bonds that replicates a call option.

Synthetic forward contract The combination of the underlying, puts, calls, and risk-free bonds that replicates a forward contract.

Synthetic index fund An index fund position created by combining risk-free bonds and futures on the desired index.

Synthetic lease A lease that is structured to provide a company with the tax benefits of ownership while not requiring the asset to be reflected on the company's financial statements.

Synthetic put The combination of calls, the underlying, and risk-free bonds that replicates a put option.

Systematic factors Factors that affect the average returns of a large number of different assets.

Systematic sampling A procedure of selecting every kth member until reaching a sample of the desired size. The sample that results from this procedure should be approximately random.

Takeover A merger; the term may be applied to any transaction, but is often used in reference to hostile transactions.

Takeover premium The amount by which the takeover price for each share of stock must exceed the current stock price in order to entice shareholders to relinquish control of the company to an acquirer.

Tangible assets Long-term assets with physical substance that are used in company operations, such as land (property), plant, and equipment.

Tangible book value per share Common shareholders' equity minus intangible assets from the balance sheet, divided by the number of shares outstanding.

Target balance A minimum level of cash to be held available—estimated in advance and adjusted for known funds transfers, seasonality, or other factors.

Target capital structure A company's chosen proportions of debt and equity.

Target company, or target The company in a merger or acquisition that is being acquired.

Target payout ratio A strategic corporate goal representing the long-term proportion of earnings that the company intends to distribute to shareholders as dividends.

Target semideviation The positive square root of target semivariance.

Target semivariance The average squared deviation below a target value.

Tariff A tax that is imposed by the importing country when an imported good crosses its international boundary.

Tax base (tax basis) The amount at which an asset or liability is valued for tax purposes.

Tax expense An aggregate of an entity's income tax payable (or recoverable in the case of a tax benefit) and any changes in deferred tax assets and liabilities. It is essentially the income tax payable or recoverable if these had been determined based on accounting profit rather than taxable income.

Tax loss carry forward A taxable loss in the current period that may be used to reduce future taxable income.

Tax risk The uncertainty associated with tax laws.

Taxable income The portion of an entity's income that is subject to income taxes under the tax laws of its jurisdiction.

Taxable temporary differences Temporary differences that result in a taxable amount in a future period when determining the taxable profit as the balance sheet item is recovered or settled.

t-Distribution A symmetrical distribution defined by a single parameter, degrees of freedom, that is largely used to make inferences concerning the mean of a normal distribution whose variance is unknown.

Technical indicators Momentum indicators based on price.

Temporal method A variation of the monetary/nonmonetary translation method that requires not only monetary assets and liabilities, but also nonmonetary assets and liabilities that are measured at their current value on the balance sheet date to be translated at the current exchange rate. Assets and liabilities are translated at rates consistent with the timing of their measurement value. This method is typically used when the functional currency is other than the local currency.

Tender offer A public offer whereby the acquirer invites target shareholders to submit ("tender") their shares in return for the proposed payment.

Tenor The original time to maturity on a swap.

Terminal price multiple The price multiple for a stock assumed to hold at a stated future time.

Terminal share price The share price at a particular point in the future.

Terminal value of the stock (or **continuing value of the stock**) The analyst's estimate of a stock's value at a particular point in the future.

Termination date The date of the final payment on a swap; also, the swap's expiration date.

Terms of trade The quantity of goods and services that a country exports to pay for its imports of goods and services.

Test statistic A quantity, calculated based on a sample, whose value is the basis for deciding whether or not to reject the null hypothesis.

Theory of contestable markets A hypothesis concerning pricing behavior that holds that even though there are only a few firms in an industry, they are forced to price their products more or less competitively because of the ease of entry by outsiders. The key aspect of a contestable market is relatively costless entry into and exit from the industry.

Theta The rate at which an option's time value decays.

Tie-in sales Purchases of one product that are permitted by the seller only if the consumer buys another good or service from the same firm.

Time series A set of observations on a variable's outcomes in different time periods.

Time to expiration The time remaining in the life of a derivative, typically expressed in years.

Time value decay The loss in the value of an option resulting from movement of the option price toward its payoff value as the expiration day approaches.

Time value of money The principles governing equivalence relationships between cash flows with different dates.

Time value or **speculative value** The difference between the market price of the option and its intrinsic value, determined by the uncertainty of the underlying over the remaining life of the option.

Time-period bias The possibility that when we use a time-series sample, our statistical conclusion may be sensitive to the starting and ending dates of the sample.

Time-series data Observations of a variable over time.

Time-weighted rate of return The compound rate of growth of one unit of currency invested in a portfolio during a stated measurement period; a measure of investment performance that is not sensitive to the timing and amount of withdrawals or additions to the portfolio.

Tobin's q The ratio of the market value of debt and equity to the replacement cost of total assets.

Top-down analysis With reference to investment selection processes, an approach that starts with macro selection (i.e., identifying attractive geographic segments and/or industry segments) and then addresses selection of the most attractive investments within those segments.

Top-down forecasting approach A forecasting approach that involves moving from international and national macroeconomic forecasts to industry forecasts and then to individual company and asset forecasts.

Top-down investing An approach to investing that typically begins with macroeconomic forecasts.

Total asset turnover An activity ratio calculated as revenue divided by average total assets.

Total invested capital The sum of market value of common equity, book value of preferred equity, and face value of debt.

Total probability rule A rule explaining the unconditional probability of an event in terms of probabilities of the event conditional on mutually exclusive and exhaustive scenarios.

Total probability rule for expected value A rule explaining the expected value of a random variable in terms of expected values of the random variable conditional on mutually exclusive and exhaustive scenarios.

Total return swap A swap in which one party agrees to pay the total return on a security. Often used as a credit derivative, in which the underlying is a bond.

Tracking portfolio A portfolio having factor sensitivities that are matched to those of a benchmark or other portfolio.

Tracking risk (tracking error) The standard deviation of the differences between a portfolio's returns and its benchmark's returns; a synonym of active risk.

Trade credit A spontaneous form of credit in which a purchaser of the goods or service is financing its purchase by delaying the date on which payment is made.

Trade receivables (commercial receivables or **accounts receivable)** Amounts customers owe the company for products that have been sold as well as amounts that may be due from suppliers (such as for returns of merchandise).

Trade-weighted index The average exchange rate, with individual currencies weighted by their importance in U.S. international trade.

Trading securities (held-for-trading securities)   Securities held by a company with the intent to trade them.

Traditional efficient markets formulation   See *Market efficiency.*

Trailing dividend yield   Current market price divided by the most recent quarterly per-share dividend multiplied by four.

Trailing P/E (or **current P/E**)   A stock's current market price divided by the most recent four quarters of earnings per share.

Transaction exposure   The risk of a change in value between the transaction date and the settlement date of an asset or liability denominated in a foreign currency.

Transactions motive   In the context of inventory management, the need for inventory as part of the routine production–sales cycle.

Transition phase   The stage of growth between the growth phase and the mature phase of a company in which earnings growth typically slows.

Translation exposure   The risk associated with the conversion of foreign financial statements into domestic currency.

Treasury shares   Shares that were issued and subsequently repurchased by the company.

Treasury stock method   A method for accounting for the effect of options (and warrants) on earnings per share (EPS) that specifies what EPS would have been if the options and warrants had been exercised and the company had used the proceeds to repurchase common stock.

Tree diagram   A diagram with branches emanating from nodes representing either mutually exclusive chance events or mutually exclusive decisions.

Trend   A long-term pattern of movement in a particular direction.

Trimmed mean   A mean computed after excluding a stated small percentage of the lowest and highest observations.

Trust receipt arrangement   The use of inventory as collateral for a loan. The inventory is segregated and held in trust, and the proceeds of any sale must be remitted to the lender immediately.

***t*-Test**   A hypothesis test using a statistic (*t*-statistic) that follows a *t*-distribution.

Two-sided hypothesis test (or **two-tailed hypothesis test**)   A test in which the null hypothesis is rejected in favor of the alternative hypothesis if the evidence indicates that the population parameter is either smaller or larger than a hypothesized value.

Type I error   The error of rejecting a true null hypothesis.

Type II error   The error of not rejecting a false null hypothesis.

U.S. interest rate differential   The U.S. interest rate minus the foreign interest rate.

U.S. official reserves   The government's holding of foreign currency.

Unbiasedness   Lack of bias. A desirable property of estimators, an unbiased estimator is one whose expected value (the mean of its sampling distribution) equals the parameter it is intended to estimate.

Unbilled revenue (accrued revenue)   Revenue that has been earned but not yet billed to customers as of the end of an accounting period.

Unclassified balance sheet   A balance sheet that does not show subtotals for current assets and current liabilities.

Unconditional heteroskedasticity   Heteroskedasticity of the error term that is not correlated with the values of the independent variable(s) in the regression.

Unconditional probability (or **marginal probability**)   The probability of an event *not* conditioned on another event.

Underlying   An asset that trades in a market in which buyers and sellers meet, decide on a price, and the seller then delivers the asset to the buyer and receives payment. The underlying is the asset or other derivative on which a particular derivative is based. The market for the underlying is also referred to as the spot market.

Underlying earnings (or **persistent earnings**, **continuing earnings**, or **core earnings**)   Earnings excluding nonrecurring components.

Unearned fees   Unearned fees are recognized when a company receives cash payment for fees prior to earning them.

Unearned revenue (deferred revenue)   A liability account for money that has been collected for goods or services that have not yet been delivered; payment received in advance of providing a good or service.

Unexpected earnings (also **earnings surprise**)   The difference between reported earnings per share and expected earnings per share.

Unidentifiable intangible   An intangible that cannot be acquired singly and that typically possesses an indefinite benefit period; an example is accounting goodwill.

Unit root   A time series that is not covariance stationary is said to have a unit root.

Uniting of interests method   A method of accounting in which combined companies were portrayed as if they had always operated as a single economic entity. Called pooling of interests under U.S. GAAP and uniting of interests under IFRS. (No longer allowed under U.S. GAAP or IFRS.)

Units-of-production method   A depreciation method that allocates the cost of a long-lived asset based on actual usage during the period.

Univariate distribution   A distribution that specifies the probabilities for a single random variable.

Unlimited funds   An unlimited funds environment assumes that the company can raise the funds it wants for all profitable projects simply by paying the required rate of return.

Up transition probability   The probability that an asset's value moves up.

Upstream   A transaction between two affiliates, an investor company and an associate company such that the associate company records a profit on its income statement. An example is a sale of inventory by the associate to the investor company.

Valuation   The process of determining the value of an asset or service on the basis of variables perceived to be related to future investment returns, or on the basis of comparisons with closely similar assets.

Valuation allowance   A reserve created against deferred tax assets, based on the likelihood of realizing the deferred tax assets in future accounting periods.

Valuation ratios   Ratios that measure the quantity of an asset or flow (e.g., earnings) in relation to the price associated with a specified claim (e.g., a share or ownership of the enterprise).

Value   The amount for which one can sell something, or the amount one must pay to acquire something.

Value at risk (VAR)   A money measure of the minimum value of losses expected during a specified time period at a given level of probability.

Value investors   With reference to equity investors, investors who are focused on paying a relatively low share price in relation to earnings or assets per share.

Variable costs   Costs that fluctuate with the level of production and sales.

Variance   The expected value (the probability-weighted average) of squared deviations from a random variable's expected value.

Variation margin   Additional margin that must be deposited in an amount sufficient to bring the balance up to the initial margin requirement.

Vega   The relationship between option price and volatility.

Venture capital investors   Private equity investors in development-stage companies.

Venturers   The owners of a joint venture. Each is active in the management and shares control of the joint venture.

Vertical analysis   Common-size analysis using only one reporting period or one base financial statement; for example, an income statement in which all items are stated as percentages of sales.

Vertical common-size analysis   The most common type of common-size analysis, in which the accounts in a given period are compared to a benchmark item in that same year.

Vertical merger   A merger involving companies at different positions of the same production chain; for example, a supplier or a distributor.

Versioning   Selling a product in slightly altered forms to different groups of consumers.

Vested benefit obligation   Under U.S. GAAP, a measure used in estimating a defined-benefit pension plan's liabilities, defined as the "actuarial present value of vested benefits."

Vested benefits   Future benefits promised to the employee regardless of continuing service. Benefits typically vest after a specified period of service or a specified period of service combined with age.

Vesting date   The date that employees can first exercise stock options; vesting can be immediate or over a future period.

Visibility   The extent to which a company's operations are predictable with substantial confidence.

Volatility   As used in option pricing, the standard deviation of the continuously compounded returns on the underlying asset.

Voluntary export restraint   An agreement between two governments in which the government of the exporting country agrees to restrain the volume of its own exports.

Warehouse receipt arrangement   The use of inventory as collateral for a loan; similar to a trust receipt arrangement except there is a third party (i.e., a warehouse company) that supervises the inventory.

Weighted average cost   An inventory accounting method that averages the total cost of available inventory items over the total units available for sale.

Weighted harmonic mean   See *Harmonic mean*.

Weighted mean   An average in which each observation is weighted by an index of its relative importance.

Weighted-average cost of capital (WACC)   A weighted average of the after-tax required rates of return on a company's common stock, preferred stock, and long-term debt, where the weights are the fraction of each source of financing in the company's target capital structure.

White knight   A third party that is sought out by the target company's board to purchase the target in lieu of a hostile bidder.

White squire   A third party that is sought out by the target company's board to purchase a substantial minority stake in the target—enough to block a hostile takeover without selling the entire company.

White-corrected standard errors   A synonym for robust standard errors.

Winner's curse   The tendency for the winner in certain competitive bidding situations to overpay, whether because of overestimation of intrinsic value, emotion, or information asymmetries.

Winsorized mean   A mean computed after assigning a stated percent of the lowest values equal to one specified low value, and a stated percent of the highest values equal to one specified high value.

Working capital   The difference between current assets and current liabilities.

Working capital management   The management of a company's short-term assets (such as inventory) and short-term liabilities (such as money owed to suppliers).

Working capital turnover   A comparison of revenues with working capital to produce a measure that shows how efficiently working capital is employed.

World Trade Organization   An international organization that places greater obligations on its member countries to observe the GATT rules.

Write-down   A reduction in the value of an asset as stated in the balance sheet.

Yield   The actual return on a debt security if it is held to maturity.

Yield beta   A measure of the sensitivity of a bond's yield to a general measure of bond yields in the market that is used to refine the hedge ratio.

Yield spread   The difference between the yield on a bond and the yield on a default-free security, usually a government note, of the same maturity. The yield spread is primarily determined by the market's perception of the credit risk on the bond.

Yield to maturity   The annual return that an investor earns on a bond if the investor purchases the bond today and holds it until maturity.

Zero-cost collar   A transaction in which a position in the underlying is protected by buying a put and selling a call with the premium from the sale of the call offsetting the premium from the purchase of the put. It can also be used to protect a floating-rate borrower against interest rate increases with the premium on a long cap offsetting the premium on a short floor.

INDEX